AN AMERICAN
PROFESSION OF ARMS

MODERN WAR STUDIES

Theodore A. Wilson
General Editor

Raymond A. Callahan
J. Garry Clifford
Jacob W. Kipp
Jay Luvaas
Allan R. Millett
Series Editors

AN AMERICAN PROFESSION OF ARMS
THE ARMY OFFICER CORPS, 1784-1861

WILLIAM B. SKELTON

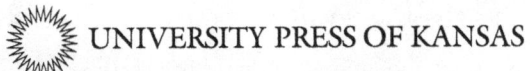
UNIVERSITY PRESS OF KANSAS

© 1992 by the University Press of Kansas
All rights reserved

Published by the University Press of Kansas (Lawrence, Kansas 66049), which was organized by the Kansas Board of Regents and is operated and funded by Emporia State University, Fort Hays State University, Kansas State University, Pittsburg State University, the University of Kansas, and Wichita State University

Library of Congress Cataloging-in-Publication Data

Skelton, William B., 1939–
  An American profession of arms : the army officer corps. 1784–1861 / William B. Skelton.
    p. cm. — (Modern war studies)
  Includes bibliographical references and index.
  ISBN 0-7006-0560-6 (hardcover)
  1. United States. Army—Officers—History—19th century.
  2. United States. Army—Officers—History—18th century.
  I. Title. II. Series.
  UB413.S54 1992
  355.3'3'097309033—dc20   92-10089

British Library Cataloguing in Publication Data is available.

Printed in the United States of America
10 9 8 7 6 5 4 3 2 1

Produced digitally by Lightning Source Inc.

For Gail and Beckie

CONTENTS

List of Figures, Tables, and Illustrations	ix
Preface	xiii
Part One—Roots of the American Military Profession, 1784–1815	1
1 Army Organization in the Early National Period	3
2 Recruiting an Officer Corps, 1784–1815	12
3 Military Careers in the Early Republic	34
4 A Frontier Constabulary: Civil-Military Relations, 1784–1815	68
5 Seeds of Military Professionalism	87
Part Two—Emergence of the American Military Profession, 1815–1861	107
6 The Era of Army Reform, 1815–1821	109
7 The Organizational Setting, 1821–1861	131
8 The Stabilization of Officer Recruitment	137
9 Social Origins and Career Motivations	154
10 The West Point Experience	167
11 Military Careers in the Antebellum Era	181
12 The Emergence of the General Staff Officer	221
13 Professional Thought and Institutions	238
14 Officers and Enlisted Men	260
15 Officers, Politicians, and Citizens	282

16 Officers and Indians	305
17 Officers, Foreign Affairs, and War	326
18 The Officer Corps in the Sectional Crisis	348
Conclusion	359
Notes	363
Selected Bibliography	447
Index	469

FIGURES, TABLES, AND ILLUSTRATIONS

Figures

1.1	Authorized Strength of U.S. Army Officer Corps, 1784–1815	10
7.1	Strength of U.S. Army Officer Corps, 1821–1860	136
11.1	Annual Resignation Rate for Officers, 1823–1860	216

Tables

2.1	Geographical Origins of Officers on Army List of 1797	19
2.2	Fathers' Occupations of Officers on Army List of 1797	21
2.3	Estimated Occupational Distribution of Free Population, 1805	21
3.1	Postservice Occupations of Officers on 1786 and 1797 Army Lists	64
9.1	Geographical Distribution of Officers on Army Registers of 1830 and 1860	155
9.2	Distribution of Officers' Appointments by Branch, 1830	156
9.3	Distribution of Officers' Appointments by Branch, 1860	157
9.4	Fathers' Occupations of Army Officers, 1830 and 1860, and of West Point Graduates, 1844–1860	159
9.5	Occupational Distribution of Free Male Population, 1850	160

x   Figures, Tables, and Illustrations

9.6	Officers' Religious Preferences, 1830 and 1860	162
11.1	Officers' Career Lengths, 1797, 1830, 1860	182
11.2	Career Length of Men Appointed to Lowest Commissioned Ranks in Selected Years	183
11.3	Promotion Rates to Company Grades and Major, Selected West Point Classes	194
11.4	Attrition among Officers on Army Register of 1830	213
11.5	Principal Postservice Occupations of Officers on 1830 Army Register	218
12.1	Permanent General Staff Officers, 1830 and 1860	222
18.1	Officers Leaving the U.S. Army to Join the Confederacy, by Rank	356
18.2	Officers Staying in the U.S. Army or Joining the Confederacy, by Region of Birth	356

Illustrations

Brigadier General Wade Hampton	28
Fort Washington, 1790	40
Brigadier General James Wilkinson	52
Colonel Jacob Kingsbury	75
Major General Anthony Wayne	91
Colonel Jonathan Williams	100
Brigadier General Edmund P. Gaines	112
Brigadier General Winfield Scott	113
Superintendent Sylvanus Thayer	124
View of Hudson River from West Point	176
Fort Winnebago in 1831	185
Second Lieutenant Ulysses S. Grant	191
Fort Snelling	208
Colonel Roger Jones	224
Colorado River expedition, 1857–1858	230
Title page of Delafield's report on Crimean War mission	242

Fort Sumter before 1861	245
Jefferson Barracks, Missouri, 1841	251
Illustration from heavy-artillery manual	256
Major John Macrae Washington	301
Colonel Albert Sidney Johnston	303
"Dakota Encampment"	312
"Medicine Dance of the Winnebagoes"	313
Fort Deynaud, Florida, 1855	323
Bombardment of Vera Cruz	342
"Heights of Monterey"	344

PREFACE

Between the Revolution and the Civil War, a military profession emerged for the first time in America. Although tiny by twentieth-century standards, the officer corps of the United States Army eventually acquired a regular system of recruitment and professional education, a well-defined area of responsibility, a considerable degree of continuity in its membership, and permanent institutions to maintain internal cohesion and military expertise. Through a common process of socialization and a lengthening of career commitments, officers came to share a complex of ideas concerning their collective role, civil-military relations, foreign and Indian affairs, and other matters—in effect, they came to share a distinctive "military mind." A military subculture took shape, rooted in tightly knit garrison communities on the frontier and along the seaboards, and army life assumed a pace and a tone that would persist well into the twentieth century. Of particular significance, officers worked out a relationship with the political sphere. Although they resorted to political channels in seeking support for professional goals, most regulars avoided involvement in civilian controversies, viewed political parties and partisanship as divisive and potentially dangerous, and saw the army as a neutral instrument of the government. The Civil War temporarily eroded the division between civil and military life, but the process of professional consolidation resumed in the late nineteenth century and went far toward shaping the permanent place of the army in American society.

Historians have devoted surprisingly little attention to the profession of arms during its formative years. An extensive literature exists on the army's role in connection with foreign wars, Indian relations, frontier expansion, and internal transportation, and biographers have traced the careers of a large number of individual officers, especially those who later achieved fame in the Civil War. However, only a few studies have focused on the internal history of the officer corps, its relationship to the civilian world, and the process of professionalization. One of the earliest and most influential of these works was Samuel P. Huntington's classic, *The Soldier and the State: The Theory and Politics of Civil-Military Relations* (1957), which analyzed the general problem of civil-military relations. Although Huntington thought that a true military profession did not emerge until after the Civil War, he found its roots in a southern "military enlightenment" during the 1830s and 1840s, the product of the unique military interests of the conservative planter class. In *Soldiers & Civilians: The Martial Spirit in America, 1775-1865* (1968), Marcus Cunliffe challenged Huntington's thesis, arguing that southerners did not dominate the leadership of the antebellum army. Although Cunliffe's book was more descriptive than analytical, it seemed to find the source of the military profession in an enthusiasm for military things that pervaded nineteenth-century American culture. Americans both distrusted a professional army and encouraged its rise as an expression of a popular "martial spirit." Edward M. Coffman, in *The Old Army: A Portrait of the American Army in Peacetime, 1784-1898* (1986), has described with great sensitivity the peacetime military community—including enlisted men, women, and children—from the formation of the regular army to the end of the nineteenth century. Coffman has offered a wealth of insights on the careers of the antebellum officers and has projected the flavor of life in the old army, but he has generally followed Huntington in thinking that the key steps toward professional consolidation occurred in the closing decades of the nineteenth century. Other scholars dealing with the early military profession, mainly general historians of the army and historians of West Point, have focused primarily on the United States Military Academy, which they perceive as virtually synonymous with military professionalism.

In this book I maintain that the early national and antebellum eras were crucial to the rise of the American profession of arms, and the argument is pursued along two interconnected paths. First, I develop a collective biography of the officers themselves by examining their geographical and social origins, career motivations and channels of entry into the army, career patterns within the service, methods of attrition from the army, and postservice lives. Not all the officers could be studied in detail, so special attention has been given to the men whose names appear on four army registers from four of the first eight decades of the peacetime army—those of 1786, 1797, 1830, and 1860. The intention is to ground the study as firmly as possible in the actual experience of the officers, not only the highest leaders or those men destined for wartime fame, but also the great majority of commissioned regulars who served out their careers in relative obscurity. Because of the extent of the records kept by the War Department, especially after the War of 1812, it is possible to compile a fairly thorough portrait of the emerging military profession.

The second path of analysis concentrates on the culture of the officer corps: officers' training and socialization; their values, attitudes, and identities; their perceptions of their collective role, including the conduct of warfare; and the internal dynamics of the officer corps and its relationships with the groups most central to its public mission—enlisted men, Indians, politicians, and civilians in general. Inevitably, this aspect of the study must rely on less quantifiable "literary" sources, particularly officers' memoirs, journals, published professional writings, and official and unofficial correspondence. As with any attempt to reconstruct the *mentalité* of a large group, generalizations on the nineteenth-century military mind must be based on the minority of members whose views were recorded and have survived for the historian to use. The available writings of antebellum regulars are extensive, however, and represent all ranks and branches of the army. I am confident—at least as confident as it is possible to be given the circumstances—that the mental world described in this study represents that of the majority of the officer corps.

The book is organized topically within two chronological periods. During the first period, extending from the formation of the regular army in 1784 to the end of the War of 1812 (chapters 1–5), the nation came to accept a small regular army as a permanent feature of the emerging federal system. Nevertheless, the social and political environment obstructed the professional consolidation of the officer corps. The army fluctuated in size and organization because of popular distrust of military power and the generally unsettled nature of national administration. Relatively few officers made a long-term commitment to military service, and military leaders failed to develop effective procedures to instill group values, build internal cohesion, or develop and transmit professional knowledge. Thus, the dominant characteristics of the officer corps were administrative instability, dissension, and a high rate of turnover. The line between the military and the civilian spheres remained vague, as expansions of the army brought civilian leaders directly into high command positions and officers of all ranks engaged in a range of political and quasi-political activities. Although reformers sporadically attempted to rationalize military procedures and develop professional standards of conduct, their efforts made little impact on the bulk of the officers.

The emergence of a stable profession of arms occurred between the War of 1812 and the Civil War (chapters 6–18). The disastrous events of the War of 1812 discredited the prewar army and permitted a generation of young officers to rise to high command positions. Because of their wartime experiences and career ambitions, these men defined the army's principal role as continual preparation for a war with a major European power. Organized as a cadre, it was now believed that the officer corps should emphasize long-term service, administrative efficiency, and formal military training in order to facilitate future mobilization. This conception of the army's mission received tacit government approval in the reduction and reorganization of the army in 1821. More basically, it meshed with general conditions in the antebellum social environment, especially the spread of communication and trends toward occupational specialization and impersonal, bureaucratic institutional forms.

As a result, there was a gradual but basic transformation of the officer corps. Military administrators introduced formal regulations and rational patterns of procedure; through West Point and a variety of other institutions, regulars developed fairly successful methods of educating aspiring professionals and enforcing group norms. Military careers grew dramatically longer. Although the practical demands of westward expansion continued to absorb the attention of most commanders, a large number cultivated an intellectual approach to military problems, expressed through an ongoing interest in European developments, professional publications, and a variety of military boards set up to consider professional questions. With the formation of permanent staff departments, the definition of military leadership broadened to incorporate managerial and technical abilities as well as combat-related skills. Ironically, the widespread criticism of the regular army in antebellum America strengthened the officers' sense of group identity and encouraged a feeling of alienation from civilian society. Frontier service, especially the inglorious and morally disturbing suppression of the Indians, led regulars to perceive themselves as a faithful and long-suffering instrument of the national will, performing unpleasant but essential tasks for an uncaring and somewhat degenerate public.

This work contains a great many quotations from primary sources, especially from the writings of the officers themselves. I have chosen to keep the original spelling and punctuation in order to be as true as possible to the tone of the documents. I have also decided to forgo altogether the use of *sic*. To include it would detract from the readability of many of the quotations from the eighteenth and early nineteenth centuries, in which spelling and punctuation aberrations are frequent and obvious. However, readers may be jarred to find occasional minor errors in otherwise correctly written documents, particularly from the later part of the period under study.

This book has been many years in gestation, and I have contracted debts sufficient to place me in permanent academic peonage. My greatest debt is to Richard W. Leopold of Northwestern University, who supervised the dissertation from which this study evolved. As a mentor and as a model for careful, thorough, and judicious scholarship, he sustained me through every phase of the research and writing. At an early stage, the late Morris Janowitz of the

University of Chicago, one of the founders of modern military sociology, supplied encouragement and knowledge about methodology and conceptualization. Over the years, Christopher McKee of Grinnell College and Edward M. Coffman of the University of Wisconsin–Madison frequently provided leads and constructive criticism and generously shared material from their parallel research on the naval profession and the peacetime army community. Professors Coffman and John Shy of the University of Michigan carefully reviewed the entire manuscript for the University Press of Kansas and made many suggestions for improvement.

A number of other scholars read and commented on sections of the study, including Edward Hagerman of York University (Toronto), Peter Karsten of the University of Pittsburgh, William Woolley of Ripon College, and Robert Zieger of the University of Florida. Although decidedly not a military historian, my colleague at the University of Wisconsin–Stevens Point, Jon H. Roberts, spurred me on to complete the project through his scholarly example, encouragement, and infectious intellectual enthusiasm. Several other colleagues read portions of the study and otherwise offered helpful advice: Charles H. Rumsey, Robert Wolensky, Lawrence Weiser, and the members of the Friday-afternoon writing group. Several grants from the University Personnel Development Committee of the UW–Stevens Point and one from the Inter-University Seminar on Armed Forces and Society funded essential research trips. Support from the American Council of Learned Societies and the Institute for Research in the Humanities at the University of Wisconsin–Madison made possible two year-long sabbaticals in 1979–1980 and 1989–1990, during the latter of which I was resident in Madison and enjoyed the benefits of the excellent library of the State Historical Society of Wisconsin.

Of the many librarians and archivists who aided me over the years, I owe a special debt to Arthur Fish, former head of the superb Government Documents Division of the UW–Stevens Point library, who collected and preserved a remarkably extensive run of the Congressional Serial Set and procured a vast amount of National Archives microfilm, without which this study could not have been completed. Antonette Dul, program assistant in the UW–Stevens Point History Department, shepherded me through the computer revolution and went far beyond her regular responsibilities to help with a myriad of problems relating to the completion of the manuscript. Finally, I am especially grateful to my wife, Gail, and daughter, Rebecca, for their intellectual and emotional support and their cheerful tolerance of the long summer research trips and the countless evenings and weekends that I spent holed up in my basement office.

PART ONE

ROOTS OF THE AMERICAN MILITARY PROFESSION, 1784–1815

1
ARMY ORGANIZATION IN THE EARLY NATIONAL PERIOD

Although shaped in part by the universals of military organization, modern armies take much of their character from the particular societies that produce them. Thus, the structure of the United States Army in the thirty years after the Revolution reflected the suspicion of centralized power and the institutional experimentation that characterized American life generally during the early national period, when the United States was a loosely knit agrarian republic. The primitive condition of internal communication, traditional ethnic and religious differences, and the carryover of intercolonial rivalries perpetuated a pattern of regional and local autonomy that the common struggle for independence had failed to dissolve. Under the Articles of Confederation, the states controlled taxation and held the initiative in political matters. Although the Constitution greatly expanded the potential power of the federal government, the continuing tension between state and federal authority, compounded by the rise of political parties and the bitter ideological divisions of the 1790s, long kept national administration in an unsettled condition. Only gradually did the new federal system achieve an aura of permanence and legitimacy.

The army was a particularly sensitive issue during this formative period. The English had a heritage of distrust for standing armies, heightened by the controversies surrounding the political role of the army during the English upheavals of the seventeenth century. Although this attitude carried over to the colonies, it remained diffuse until the British government decided to station a permanent force of regulars in North America after the French and Indian War. By the outbreak of the Revolution, many Americans had come to see this force as a foreign army of occupation that threatened political liberty and served as a source of moral corruption. Originally a stopgap measure to meet the demands of the colonial frontier, the militia assumed new stature as the safest bulwark of a free people.¹ The exigencies of the Revolution led the Continental Congress to incorporate into the Continental Army the basic features of eighteenth-century military administration: relatively long-term enlistments; a rigid distinction between officers and enlisted men; a strict regimen of discipline and punishment; and specialized staff departments to handle supply and support functions. Many Americans were uncomfortable with that army, however, especially when officers' unrest over postservice pay and the formation of the Society of the Cincinnati raised the specter of military intervention into politics. Congress moved quickly to disband the army after the Peace of Paris in 1783. The debate over the future character of the military system ran through the political struggles of the early republic, closely intertwined with the larger issue of the limits of federal authority. No consensus existed on the size, organization, or functions of a permanent army—or, until the mid-1790s, on the very need for such a force.²

On 3 June 1784, one day after ordering the disbandment of the last units of the Continental Army, the Confederation Congress approved a resolution that called for a force of 700 men, intended to push federal authority into the trans-Appalachian Northwest.³ Although the resolution marks the beginning of a permanent military establishment in the United States, it was a compromise measure, passed after heated debate on the dangers of standing armies and an overly powerful central government. The states appointed the officers and recruited the enlisted men, and service was limited to one year. In 1785, Congress authorized three-year enlistments, but the force remained on shaky ground to the close of the Confederation era, balanced uneasily between federal and state authority.⁴ Many leaders saw it at best as a temporary expedient, at worst as a potential menace to liberty.

As originally organized, the Confederation force consisted of a single regiment of seven infantry and two artillery companies, commanded by a lieutenant colonel and staffed by 37 commissioned officers. On 20 October 1786, Congress tripled the authorized strength of the army, ostensibly to prevent Indian war in the Northwest but actually to crush the uprising of debtor farmers in western Massachusetts led by Daniel Shays.⁵ The creation of this additional force marked a major extension of the army's functions to include the suppression of domestic disorders. In view of contemporary attitudes toward military authority, it was an extraordinary step, explicable only as a response to exaggerated conservative fears of social revolution. The states were slow to appropriate funds, however, and recruiting lagged. Moreover, the Massachusetts militia put down the rebellion, thereby undercutting Congress's rationale for expansion. During the spring of 1787, the government disbanded most of the newly organized units, retaining only two companies of artillery that were later incorporated into the original force.[6] In 1789, at the end of the Confederation period, the army consisted of only 46 officers and fewer than 700 enlisted men, mainly dispersed in small garrisons along the Ohio River frontier.

The army's central bureaucracy was minimal. Congress had established a small Department of War late in the Revolution, headed by a civilian secretary at war, and this institution survived through the 1780s. Henry Knox, formerly chief of artillery in the Continental Army, assumed the post in 1785, but his range of authority was ill defined—a common feature of eighteenth-century bureaucracy, in which the character of the officeholder rather than precise regulations shaped the office. In practice, Knox performed a variety of functions: advising Congress on military matters, supervising Indian affairs, coordinating the army's logistical services, and issuing military orders to the principal officers. In the absence of a uniformed staff, Knox relied on a tiny group of clerks for administrative support.[7]

Beginning in 1789, several events prompted a series of major changes in the size and organization of the army. Most important, the adoption of the Constitution ended the system of divided control. The federal government received the power to levy taxes and the clear authority to raise and support armies and navies. The executive branch appointed officers, subject to Senate approval, and officers took oaths of allegiance to uphold the Constitution and obey the president. For the first time, the army was unquestionably a federal institution. In addition, after years of uneasy peace on the northwestern frontier, the army suffered two humiliating defeats at the hands of the Indians. Late in 1790, an alliance of Ohio tribes turned back a joint regular-militia expedition led by Brevet Brigadier General Josiah Harmar, killing 183 soldiers. An even greater blow fell a year later, when the Indians routed a poorly organized army of 1,400 regulars, six-month federal levies, and militiamen commanded by Major General Arthur St. Clair, leaving about 600 whites dead in the Ohio forests.[8]

Although military issues continued to arouse intense controversy, these defeats brought about a significant expansion of the army. Congress added a second infantry regiment in 1791 and, after St. Clair's disaster, increased the army to five infantry regiments, a battalion of artillery, and a squadron of light dragoons—an authorized strength of about 5,424 officers and men.[9] The government later arranged this force into the "American Legion," replacing the regimental organization with four sublegions, consisting of a mixture of infantry, artillery, riflemen, and dragoons. Presumably, the sublegions would operate independently as miniature field armies, allowing greater flexibility in frontier warfare. Commanded by a stern revolutionary veteran, Major General Anthony Wayne, the Legion defeated the Indian alliance at the Battle of Fallen

Timbers in August 1794, thereby extending federal control over much of the vast area north of the Ohio River.[10] A further addition came in 1794, when fear of war with Great Britain over interference with American trade and the continued British occupation of military posts in the Northwest led Congress to authorize coastal fortifications and establish a corps of artillerists and engineers to construct and man them.[11]

The military buildup of the 1790s engendered a moderate increase in the army's central bureaucracy. The War Department continued under the Constitution as one of the executive departments, and Knox remained at its head, now with the title of secretary *of* war. By 1794, the secretary's office staff had grown to include a chief clerk—the rough equivalent of a departmental undersecretary—seven clerks, and a messenger. Several civil offices were established to handle the procurement and distribution of military supplies, an administrative area in which the War and Treasury departments shared jurisdiction. In the field, the legislation of the 1790s provided the major general commanding the army with a rudimentary staff: an adjutant who also served as inspector; a quartermaster general, assisted by a small group of agents; and a paymaster of the army. As with the powers of the secretary of war, however, the respective functions of these offices were ill defined, shaped largely by the personality and energy of the incumbents. Generally, military administration remained in flux throughout the 1790s, characterized by overlapping jurisdictions, confused lines of responsibility, and bureaucratic infighting, especially between the Treasury and War departments over control of army supply.[12]

The army did not continue long at its expanded level. With the end of the Indian war and the ratification of the Jay Treaty in 1795, which temporarily improved British-American relations, the emerging Democratic Republican party called for a drastic reduction of the Legion. As advocates of limited government, the Republicans opposed a standing army that might require high taxes and threaten to intervene in politics. Since the Federalists favored a strong military establishment, Congress settled on a compromise measure in May 1796 that made moderate cuts in the army's authorized strength and abolished the legionary structure. The army was to consist of four understrength regiments of infantry, the Corps of Artillerists and Engineers, and two troops of light dragoons—a total of 3,359 officers and men.[13] In the course of the debates on this measure, the Washington administration developed for the first time a rationale for maintaining a permanent army: It was necessary in order to man the coastal fortifications and posts along the Canadian and Spanish frontiers, preserve peace between whites and Indians, prevent unlawful settlement on the public lands, and serve as a "model and school for an army" in case of a major war.[14] Perhaps the most important effect of the reduction of 1796 was to end the army's dependence on specific crises for its institutional survival. The size and functions of the military establishment would remain controversial, but few political leaders would henceforth question seriously the need for some type of permanent force.

In 1798, the Quasi-war with France prompted yet another sharp change in army structure. The first of America's undeclared foreign wars, this conflict was a sidelight to the great war in Europe and resulted from French privateering against American trade, the efforts of French agents to influence American politics, and alleged insults to American diplomatic commissioners in Paris. The danger of French invasion was remote, and the fighting was limited to privateering and small-scale naval engagements. Nevertheless, Federalist leaders hoped to demonstrate the strength and resolve of the government, both to awe the French and to check the Republican opposition at home. There was a surge of military legislation—establishing a second regiment of artillerists and engineers, expanding the navy and founding the marine corps, approving plans for a provisional army of 10,000 men to be raised in case of invasion, and creating twelve new regiments of infantry and six companies of light dragoons as well as increasing the size of the existing regiments.[15] In only a few months, the authorized personnel of the regular army had swelled from 3,359 officers and men to over 14,000. The new regiments, usually termed the "new" or "additional" army, were more than a paper force, as officers were appointed, regiments were organized, and recruiting went forward. In the spring of 1799, Congress authorized an extensive military staff, resembling that of the Continental Army. Conservative Federalists—including Alexander Hamilton, the inspector general and dominant figure in the army of the Quasi-war period—hoped to make this enlarged army permanent and thus provide the United States with the equivalent of a European standing army. As such, it would strengthen the federal government and prevent the administration's domestic opponents from destroying the constitutional system, as many Federalists feared possible.[16]

The aspirations of conservative Federalists notwithstanding, the fate of the additional army paralleled on a larger scale that of the federal force raised at the time of Shays's Rebellion. The diplomatic settlement with France in 1800 deprived it of a specific function, and it became entangled in a struggle between Hamilton and John Adams for control of the Federalist party. With Adams's support, Congress abolished the additional army in May 1800, leaving only the pre-1798 establishment and the Second Regiment of Artillerists and Engineers.[17] The election of Thomas Jefferson cleared the way for a further reduction. Always suspicious of a peacetime army, the Jeffersonians preferred a strong and well-organized militia as the military system best suited to a republic, a conviction reinforced by the political manipulation of the army during the Quasi-war. On 16 March 1802, Congress fixed the army at two regiments of infantry, one regiment of artillery, and a small corps of engineers, commanded by a single brigadier general—a total of 3,287 officers and men. In response to proposals circulating since the Revolution, the same act stated that the Corps of Engineers would be stationed at West Point, New York, and that site would constitute a "military academy" for the instruction of cadets.[18]

The reductions of 1800 and 1802 also diminished the army's central bureaucracy, leaving only a paymaster and an adjutant and inspector. Both were headquartered at the new federal capital, and the adjutant and inspector served as a military assistant to the secretary of war, issuing orders in the secretary's name, keeping army personnel records, and generally helping with the paperwork at the army's center. Although the administration did not intend it, this was a modest step toward the accumulation of staff officers in Washington, D.C., where they developed into the army's administrative hub. At the same time, the abolition of the Quartermaster Department in 1802 left supply mainly in the hands of civilian officials of the War and Treasury departments.[19]

The tiny force of the Jeffersonian period performed a wide range of tasks. As before, it regulated Indian-white relations on the frontiers, and the Louisiana Purchase also gave regulars their first sustained experience with civil administration. As the principal representatives of the federal government in the West, regulars occupied the new territory and exercised extensive civil as well as military powers. In an ambivalent way, the army was involved in Aaron Burr's western conspiracy, as some officers were drawn into the expansionist and secessionist schemes associated with Burr, while the main body of the army cooperated with the administration in suppressing them. Beginning in 1808, the army attempted to enforce the Embargo Act, by which the administration hoped to pressure the British and French into concessions on American neutral trade, and became embroiled in acrimonious civil-military controversies in the coastal towns and along the Canadian border. Finally, regulars conducted sensitive diplomatic relations on the troubled Spanish frontiers and supervised the construction of seacoast fortifications, designed for defense against a European foe.[20]

As the spreading war in Europe heightened tensions with Great Britain and France, Democratic Republicans began to qualify their customary opposition to a peacetime army. A major war would require the defense of thousands of miles of seacoast and northern frontier; New Orleans and the thinly populated western territories appeared especially vulnerable. Moreover, the expansionist ambition to acquire Canada would demand extensive land operations for which the existing army and the decaying militia system seemed inadequate.

In April 1808, in response to the humiliating attack in 1807 by the British warship *Leopard* on the American frigate *Chesapeake*, Congress added to the army five infantry regiments and one regiment each of riflemen, light artillery, and light dragoons, thereby tripling the authorized strength to 9,921 officers and men. Since many Republicans were uneasy about this reversal of their party's traditional military policy, the new regiments were specifically designated an "additional military force," and service was limited to five years unless the troops were disbanded sooner. The congressional debates made clear that most Jeffersonians still hoped to avoid the type of large and permanent standing army sought by the conservative Federalists during the Quasi-war.[21]

As with its predecessors of 1786–1787 and 1798–1800, the additional force established in 1808 had a rocky history. Recruiting lagged, and the regiments did not approach their mandated strength. The sudden expansion brought hundreds of inexperienced men into the officer corps, generating administrative confusion and bitter personal dissension. The miniscule staff of the Jeffersonian army proved totally inadequate to handle the logistical burdens imposed by the new regiments. One of the greatest disasters in the history of the peacetime army occurred in 1809, when between 500 and 1,000 men of a force of about 2,500 died from disease and bad supplies on the lower Mississippi River.[22] Meanwhile the dispute with the European belligerents continued, and early in 1812, a Congress increasingly dominated by war-minded Republicans added thirteen more regiments to the army. According to Henry Adams, this rejection by the party of Jefferson and Madison of its antimilitarist heritage "passed the bounds of inconsistency and proclaimed a revolution."[23] Nevertheless, the government moved further along this path after the declaration of war on Great Britain in June 1812, as the deficiency of the militia for mounting offensive operations and the refusal of the New England states to support the war left the Madison administration little choice but to expand the regular forces. By 1814, the army had reached an authorized level of 62,000 officers and men, though actual troop strength fell far short of this total.[24]

The wartime mobilization brought a rapid growth in the army's command and staff apparatus. By 1813, Congress had provided an array of support departments, largely modeled on those of the Revolution: adjutant and inspector general, quartermaster, ordnance, pay, purchasing, and hospital. Most of these branches were headed by high-ranking chiefs, and permanent staff officers composed roughly one-fifth of the total officer corps.[25] As with the general increase of the army, however, the expansion of the staff was an uncoordinated and haphazard affair, a response to an immediate crisis rather than the result of careful planning. Because of the vast area of military operations and

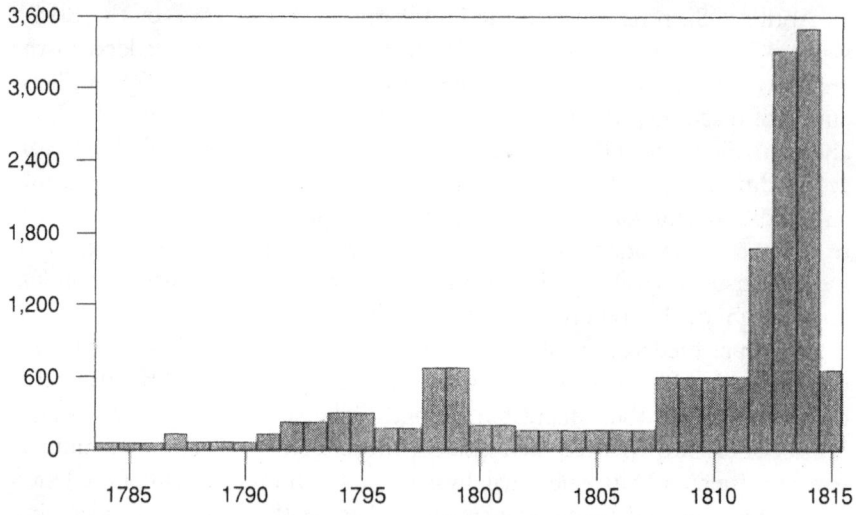

Figure 1.1. Authorized Strength of U.S. Army Officer Corps, 1784–1815. *Source*: Francis B. Heitman, comp., *Historical Register and Dictionary of the United States Army* (Washington, D.C.: Government Printing Office, 1903).

the primitive condition of internal transportation, the War Department found it virtually impossible to give central direction to the logistical services. The bureaucratic tradition inherited from the eighteenth century, with its emphasis on the character of the officeholder, retarded the development of uniform, impersonal codes of administrative procedures. The wartime staff was a motley collection of decentralized, overlapping, and shifting fiefdoms, unable to provide a steady level of support to the field armies.[26]

In March 1815, after the Peace of Ghent, Congress once again reduced the army, leaving a peace establishment of 12,383 officers and men. As later chapters will demonstrate, the years that followed were among the most important in the institutional history of the United States Army, bringing an unprecedented degree of permanence and order to military administration. Yet during the first thirty years of the army's existence its central feature was the instability of its size and organization, a condition that profoundly influenced the officer corps (see Figure 1.1). At times of expansion—1786, 1791–1794, 1798, 1808, 1812–1814—large numbers of citizens flooded the officer corps and frequently superseded more experienced regulars in positions of command. During the subsequent contractions—1787, 1796, 1800, 1802, 1815—officers faced the gloomy prospect of discharge or demotion. A small core of regular units did remain in service: the first two infantry regiments and a corps of artillerists and engineers or its equivalent. However, the overall instability of army structure combined with other conditions of military life—the uncertainty of pay, the isolation and hardships of frontier duty, the lack of institutions of professional education and socialization—to retard the formation of a cohesive group of professional officers committed to military service as a career-long endeavor.

2
RECRUITING AN OFFICER CORPS, 1784–1815

Crucial to the development of any military force is the recruitment of its leadership. The social composition, education, and career motivations of the officer corps strongly influence both the army itself and the relationship of the army to the larger civilian society. Despite national variations and the major exception of the French revolutionary army, the military elites of European states in the late eighteenth century generally derived from the landed aristocracy, the class that dominated political life and enjoyed a privileged social and economic position.[1] Because the enlisted men were recruited from the lower classes—peasants, laborers, and the urban poor—there was rigid stratification within the army, with an immense gap separating most officers from the rank and file. On the other hand, the ascriptive status of the aristocratic officers and their class and kinship ties to the civilian leadership gave the officer corps a stake in the existing order, ensuring that its members were unlikely to become an alienated elite seeking to impose their will through coup or revolution.

North America lacked a strong feudal legacy, but a similar interpenetration of civilian and military leaderships had characterized the militias of the colonial era. During the early decades of settlement, the New England colonies had permitted the election of militia officers at the local and colonywide levels, a manifestation of Puritan covenant theology that emphasized community participation in all activities of church and state. This method of selection soon faded, and by the late seventeenth century nearly all the colonies had placed the power to make military appointments in the hands of the governor, who usually acted on the recommendations of local elites. Not surprisingly, high- and middle-ranking officers in the militia establishments were generally solid members of the "better sort" of society: lawyers, merchants, planters, and prosperous farmers who also held leadership positions in government and the church.[2]

In practice, however, military leadership seems to have been considerably less exclusive than the official militia lists would indicate. During the later colonial wars in particular, provincial governments relied on volunteer units for operations outside their borders, which were raised independently of the militia. To command such expeditions, some colonies developed pools of "semiprofessional" officers—men who, because of military ambition or economic need, were willing to serve whenever forces were raised and who achieved a considerable degree of practical skill in the recruitment and command of troops. Frequently, such leaders were not militia officers and were drawn from the middle levels of the social order; many had served in the ranks before acquiring their commissions.[3]

The Revolution endorsed the colonial experience. The leaders of the Continental Congress and the states agreed with George Washington that social status should reinforce military rank and that "Gentlemen of Fortune and reputable Families generally make the most useful Officers."[4] Despite this opinion, the conflict did provide an opportunity for many young men from relatively humble backgrounds to advance themselves through military service, if only because of the attrition caused by eight years of warfare and the division of the prewar elites into loyalists and revolutionaries. As Charles Royster has noted, "The revolutionaries did not have enough gentlemen to go around," at least not enough to fill the thousands of openings in the wartime officer corps, and the likelihood of advancement grew even greater during the middle stages of the war when the revolutionary fervor declined.[5] Although there has been no comprehensive study of the social composition of the revolutionary army, it is probable that former enlisted men, artisans, and farmers from poor or middling backgrounds composed a significant minority of the officer corps by the closing years of the conflict.

AMERICA'S FIRST REGULARS

Whatever its functions as a social escalator, the Continental Army was a temporary institution and its disbandment left no lasting pattern of officer recruitment. The states had controlled most military appointments during the Revolution, and this procedure continued when Congress established the first force of regular troops in 1784. The Articles of Confederation specified that Congress was to requisition troops for the common defense on a quota basis and that the states raising the troops were to select all officers below the rank of general.[6] Since no generals were in service after the Revolution, the four states called upon to supply troops for the First American Regiment—Pennsylvania, Connecticut, New Jersey, and New York—regulated entry into the original officer corps. Pennsylvania had the largest quota and selected the lieutenant colonel commanding the regiment; New York and Connecticut each chose a major, and the company officers were distributed in proportion to each state's contribution. Congress followed the same procedure in raising the additional force at the time of Shays's Rebellion. State control of appointments meant that the officer corps of the Confederation army was a regional rather than a truly national institution. As late as 1789, all forty-six officers in the army were supplied by the four states that contributed to the original First Regiment plus Massachusetts, the source of the two additional artillery companies retained in 1787; about one-third of the officers came from Pennsylvania alone.[7]

An examination of the thirty-seven officers in service in 1786 may establish a baseline for tracing the subsequent development of the officer corps as a social institution.[8] As might be expected, Confederation officers were veterans; at least thirty-five had seen military service during the Revolution, mainly as junior officers in the Continental Army. Moreover, they tended to represent the nucleus of the Continental Army—the minority of officers and soldiers who had remained in the army for several years and furnished the backbone of the military effort. The median length of their revolutionary service was an extraordinary seven years, and three-quarters of the group had five or more years of wartime service. Most of them were members of the Society of the Cincinnati. Although no Confederation officer appears to have received a formal military education, their wartime experiences provided a web of shared habits, loyalties, and memories nurtured in the camps of the Continental Army—in effect, a common socialization into military life. Probably because of this bond, they did not engage in the bitter personal feuds that would disrupt the officer corps in later years.

Confederation officers were relatively young men. The twenty-one officers whose birth dates could be determined averaged thirty-one years of age in 1786, and eighteen had been born after 1750. Most had entered the revolutionary army in their teens or early twenties, too young to have left behind established civilian careers. A significant minority—at least fourteen of thirty-seven (38.8 percent)—had served in the ranks of the Continental Army or the state forces before obtaining their commissions; one may have been a common soldier in a foreign army. Indeed, the proportion of rankers may have been higher in the 1780s than at any subsequent time in the history of the peacetime army. On the other hand, at least three officers were college graduates and a fourth had a year of college training, meaning that 10.8 percent of the officer corps had received higher education at a time when only a tiny fraction of the population—surely less than 1 percent of the adult white male citizens—had such schooling.

Few of the Confederation officers appear to have been members of wealthy or socially prominent families. The father of Major John P. Wyllys was for many years the secretary of the colony and then state of Connecticut. Lieutenant Mahlon Ford belonged to an influential landholding family of Morris County, New Jersey, that pioneered in iron mining and forging. Although he was an apprentice when the Revolution began and rose from the ranks, Lieutenant Erkuries Beatty was the grandson of a colonial governor of New Jersey, the brother of a delegate to the Continental Congress, and the son of a clergyman of intercolonial reputation. The father of Surgeon's Mate Joshua Sumner had risen to lieutenant colonel in the Continental Army.[9] The majority, however, appear to have come from middling backgrounds. Of the twenty-two fathers of officers whose occupations are known, nine were farmers, three were merchants or storekeepers, two were clergymen, two were magistrates, and there was one in each of the following occupations: army officer, physician, surveyor, jeweler, innkeeper, and barber. As far as can be determined, the father of no officer except Wyllys and Sumner served in Congress, held high rank in the Continental Army, or occupied a key office in a colonial or state government.

This profile suggests that many Confederation officers did not have solid ties to the local elites, who, bound to one another by kinship and marriage and commanding respect through traditional patterns of deference, continued to dominate society and politics in postrevolutionary America. Left rootless by the disbandment of the Continental Army, lacking the skills or the social connections to merge easily into civilian life, and perhaps recalling with nostalgia the excitement and camaraderie of the Revolution, they looked to military service under Congress as a source of status and security.

Such was certainly the case with David Ziegler, a native of Heidelberg in the German Palatinate. By 1784, he had spent at least thirteen of his thirty-six years in military service, first as a soldier or junior officer in the Russian army and later as an officer in the Revolution. At the last review of the Continental Army, he had burst into tears, explaining his emotions as follows: "I cannot but remember that I am left alone on the busy scene of life, a wanderer, without friends, and without employment; and that a soldier from infancy, I am now compelled to seek a precarious subsistence in some new channel, where ignorance and inability may mar my fortune, and condemn me to perpetual obscurity." Not surprisingly, Ziegler was later willing to give up his grocery store in Carlisle, Pennsylvania, for a captaincy in the First American Regiment. Jonathan Heart was a Yale graduate who had failed as a merchant before the Revolution and had been forced to appeal to the Connecticut legislature for relief from imprisonment for debt. He had joined the first volunteers called out for the Lexington alarm in 1775 and had served through the war, rising to major in the Continental Army. His postwar business prospects were bleak, and he was learning the surveyor's trade when appointed captain in the First Regiment. After giving nine years of continuous duty, Major John Doughty feared that Congress would dissolve the army in 1785, and throw him "upon the wide world without a profession, or a Capital to create one." Because of the irregularity of army pay, he had spent his limited savings to support himself and buy professional books. In case of discharge, he solicited the secretary at war for another government appointment "that may place me in a respectable station in Life, & afford me the means of supporting it."[10]

THE FEDERALISTS

With the adoption of the Constitution, the authority to make military appointments passed from the states to the executive branch of the federal government. Early in his administration, George Washington set a precedent followed by most of his successors when he delegated this power to his secretary of war, Henry Knox, though he reviewed Knox's decisions and undoubtedly conferred with him on important selections.[11] Knox continued the earlier practice of raising new units from specific states and regions, which reflected the prevailing localism of the American social order. Officers' appointments, especially at the company level, were linked to this recruitment pattern on the apparent assumption that the personal reputation and social standing of the officers would attract prospective soldiers to the colors. Thus the administration issued commissions in the Second Infantry Regiment on the basis of the distribution of its companies, six of which were raised in Massachusetts, two in Connecticut, and one each in South Carolina, Delaware, Rhode Island, and New Hampshire. Knox followed the same procedure in selecting officers for the Legion in 1792 and the Corps of Artillerists and Engineers in 1794. However, he seems to have filled the occasional or "accidental" vacancies in established units with less regard for the candidate's place of origin, so that the state and regional identities of units tended to fade over time.[12]

The Washington administration continued to draw on the pool of discharged revolutionary officers, and Knox in particular maintained a network of contacts with former comrades in arms and considered their views on appointments. Understandably, high-ranking veterans hesitated to leave the comforts of civil life for the hardship and dubious prestige of frontier service; four men in succession rejected the command of the Second Infantry Regiment, leaving it to conduct the disastrous campaign of 1791 without a commanding officer.¹³ The legislation creating the Legion in 1792, however, authorized several generals, and the prospect of high rank lured experienced leaders again into uniform. Generals Anthony Wayne, James Wilkinson, Rufus Putnam, Thomas Posey, and John Brooks, all appointed in the early 1790s, had been generals, regimental commanders, or senior staff officers in the Revolution.

Many lower-ranking veterans who had no roots in local communities or were restless in civil life also sought to return to the army. After serving in the Continental Army and the Massachusetts regiment raised at the time of Shays's Rebellion, Samuel Newman and Patrick Phelon found themselves down on their luck in Boston. Phelon was unable even to pay his landlord for his washing and sewing, and his former commander implored Knox to find him a government post: "As to wages he will ask for none, only to give him a shirt & a pair of shoes—& the Rations of a soldier—only place him where he can be kept *a live* until his country may want his services." Both men received appointments in the Second Infantry Regiment, and both perished in St. Clair's defeat.¹⁴ One of eleven children who had "no expectations earthly" from his father, John Heth of Virginia depended for subsistence solely on his land warrants and pay certificates after his discharge from the Continental Army. He too entered the federal force raised in 1786 in the mistaken hope that it would be permanent. Later appointed an officer on a state revenue boat, he faced discharge for a third time in 1789, and his older brother feared that the "poor *soldier of fortune* will once more be thrown upon the world." Heth obtained an ensign's commission in the Second Infantry, survived the 1791 campaign, and rose to captain before his final release in the reduction of 1802.¹⁵

By the early 1790s, revolutionary veterans were too old to fill the most junior positions in the expanding army, and the administration tapped other sources, including at times the ranks of enlisted men. Concerned about the shortage of competent officers in the Legion, Anthony Wayne and other commanders occasionally recommended noncommissioned officers for promotion. Knox hoped that the commissioning of soldiers would encourage them to make military service a career, and the patrician Washington reluctantly agreed to the practice, though he advised caution "as there have been some impositions already in people of this class."¹⁶

Most junior appointments, however, went to young men without significant military experience. No formal requirements defined eligibility, though Washington later wrote that, with one exception, he had knowingly appointed no one under the age of twenty-one. Certainly service ties continued to influence nominations during Knox's tenure in the War Department, and many junior officers, themselves too young to have fought for independence, were closely related to veterans of the Revolution.[17] More difficult to gauge is the role political considerations played. As early as Washington's term, the Federalists made extensive use of civil service appointments to build a party organization, and the army could hardly have escaped this stratagem. Such officers as Horatio R. Dayton, George Izard, and Donald G. Mitchell were close relatives of Federalist congressmen or senators.[18] Until the Quasi-war, however, the administration probably made no systematic attempt to bar Republicans from the officer corps.

One can only speculate about the motivations that led young men to seek commissions in the early peacetime army. In 1800, a fire in the War Department destroyed most of the official army records of the 1790s, including letters of application for army appointments—by far the best source for this type of information. Like the revolutionary veterans, some aspirants sought the economic security of a commission. At the time of his appointment in 1791, Lieutenant Winslow Warren was deeply in debt in Massachusetts; he requested leave in order to serve a forty-day prison term for nonpayment, then "swear out" and return to duty. Joseph G. Andrews applied to the secretary of war for a medical appointment in 1792: "The Profession of Physic is at this time so amazingly crowded, that any person must be divested of every spark of ambition & every aspiring motive, who can wait with patience the arrival of his tour of business, which is generally protracted till the decease of those, whose age & experience will ever command the preference."[19]

Perhaps a more compelling incentive than economic pressures was the positive attraction of military service. The Revolution was a very recent event in the 1790s, and the sacrifices and triumphs of the war, already enshrined in myth, pervaded the imaginations of the American people. Although the suppression of Indians and the extension of federal control into the West lacked the emotional appeal of the struggle for independence, dreams of martial glory and the desire to follow in the footsteps of revolutionary heroes exerted a powerful influence on young men who came of age after 1783, especially if relatives or friends had served in the Revolution. In 1794, Meriwether Lewis grew bored with managing the plantation that he had inherited from his father, a Continental Army officer who had died in 1779, and he joined the Virginia militia sent to suppress the Whiskey Rebellion. Delighted with the excitement of military life, he obtained a regular army commission the following year. William Preston enjoyed economic circumstances that were "not only comfortable but easy," yet he sought a military appointment in 1792: "I have from my infancy felt a fondness for a military life, in which I have some little experience in the Indian mode of warfare living on the Frontiers." The son of

TABLE 2.1. Geographical Origins of Officers on Army List of 1797

Region	N	%	% Free Population (1790)
New England	41	23.2	33.7
Middle Atlantic States (N.Y., Pa., N.J.)	67	37.8	30.9
South	62	35.0	35.4
Northwest Territory	1	0.6	
Foreign	6	3.4	
Total known	177		
Total officer corps	189		

Source: Army list of 1797; U.S. Census of 1790; Francis B. Heitman, comp., *Historical Register and Dictionary of the United States Army, from Its Organization, September 29, 1789, to March 2, 1903* (Washington, D.C.: Government Printing Office, 1903).

a militia colonel who had been wounded at Guilford Courthouse, Preston regretted that he had been too young to serve in the Revolution. As a boy, William Clark had been inspired by tales of the Revolution, especially the exploits of his older brothers, Lieutenant Colonel Jonathan Clark of the Continental Army and militia Brigadier General George Rogers Clark, the conqueror of the Northwest. Young Clark served in several militia campaigns against the Ohio Indians before his appointment as a lieutenant in the Legion.[20]

An analysis of the 189 men who survived the 1796 cutback of the army and whose names appear on the army list of 1797 reveals the contours of the military profession as it stabilized temporarily at the end of the eighteenth century.[21] In contrast to the Confederation force, the army had become a truly national institution. Undoubtedly, Washington, Knox, and Knox's successors as secretary of war—Timothy Pickering (1795) and James McHenry (1795–1800)—had purposely sought geographical balance, both to insure the survival of the army in the face of popular suspicions of military power and to make it a pillar of the still-fragile federal system. Table 2.1 indicates the place of origin of the 177 officers for whom information is available and compares the totals to the distribution of the free population according to the 1790 census. Although New England was somewhat underrepresented in the officer corps as a whole, Yankees predominated in the upper ranks, claiming nine of the twenty officers at or above the rank of major. At the unit level, geographical concentrations are more evident. While the old First Infantry Regiment and the Corps of Artillerists and Engineers were relatively well-balanced, 48 percent of the officers of the Second Infantry whose origins are known came from New

England, 52 percent of those of the Third Infantry from the South, and 50 percent of those of the Fourth Infantry from the Middle Atlantic States. Compared with the Revolution, however, when most regiments had carried state designations, state and regional identities appear to have been weak.

The influence of the revolutionary generation remained strong in the officer corps of 1797, but it was waning. Veterans of the Continental Army continued to dominate the upper ranks: Of seventy-two officers at or above the grade of captain, forty-two (58.3 percent) had served as officers in the Revolution and three others (4.2 percent) as enlisted men. On the other hand, young men coming of age since the Revolution now filled the lower grades. Only one of the ninety-four ensigns, cornets, and lieutenants on the 1797 list had held an officer's commission in the Continental Army, and only one of the medical officers seems to have been a revolutionary veteran. The shared memories of revolutionary service, widespread in the Confederation army, had disappeared as a cohesive force in the lower ranks of the officer corps.

Although biographical information is missing for many of the officers of 1797, the army appears to have become more socially restrictive, less a channel of upward social mobility than it had been a decade earlier. First, the proportion of officers known to have begun their careers as enlisted men had declined from 38.8 percent of the total in 1786 to 13.5 percent, and only 6 officers on the 1797 list had been promoted from the ranks since the Revolution. Moreover, prominent families were increasingly represented in the officer corps, especially at the junior grades. Table 2.2 describes the occupations of the fathers of 72 men on the 1797 register for whom information is available. For purposes of comparison, Table 2.3 gives estimates of the occupational distribution of the free population as a whole. Agriculturists composed the largest broad occupational group among the officers' fathers (51.4 percent), and it is likely they would have been even more strongly represented if the backgrounds of all officers had been known. Yeoman farmers predominated within this group, as they did in the general population. However, 13 of the fathers (18.1 percent) appear to have been southern planters, and 2 of those listed as farmers (2.7 percent) were prominent Hudson Valley landlords.

Perhaps the most striking feature of the distribution of fathers' occupations is the comparatively large number in the nonagricultural categories. Men employed in commerce, industry, and the professions made up only about 15 percent of the total labor force, but they constituted about one-third of the officers' fathers who were tallied. Government employment, mainly at the federal level, occupied 16.7 percent of the fathers, though such service certainly engaged less than 1 percent of the work force as a whole. Of course, the nonagricultural categories included some men of modest means: artisans,

TABLE 2.2. Fathers' Occupations of Officers on Army List of 1797

Occupation	Number	Percent
Agricultural	37	51.4
Farmer	24	33.3
Planter	13	18.1
Commercial/Industrial	16	22.2
Merchant/Sea captain	10	13.9
Manufacturer/Founder	3	4.2
Artisan	3	4.2
Professional	7	9.7
Lawyer/Judge	2	2.7
Physician	3	4.2
Clergyman	1	1.4
Teacher	1	1.4
Government service	12	16.6
Congressman/Senator	1	1.4
Federal civil servant	1	1.4
Army officer	6	8.3
Enlisted man	1	1.4
Local magistrate	3	4.2
Total known	72	
Total officer corps	189	

Source: Army list of 1797; miscellaneous biographical and genealogical sources.

shopkeepers, small-town magistrates, and one enlisted soldier (that is, a man described as dying in British service during the French and Indian War). A significant number, however, held occupations that indicated elite status. The father of Captain Donald G. Mitchell, for example, was a federal judge and a former United States senator from Connecticut, and Lieutenant John M. Lovell's father was a former delegate to Congress and a high-ranking customs official at Boston. Ensign George Salmon, Jr., was the son of a Baltimore mer-

TABLE 2.3. Estimated Occupational Distribution of Free Population, 1805

Occupation	Percent
Farmers and planters	82
Artisans	7
Seamen/Fishermen	8
Professional and others	3

Source: Based on the estimates of Samuel Blodgett, an early American economist, and adapted from table in Manning J. Dauer, *The Adams Federalists* (Baltimore, Md.: Johns Hopkins University Press, 1953), p. 4.

chant, bank president, and judge who served as business agent for Secretary of War James McHenry.[22] As far as can be determined, no seaman, tenant farmer, or unskilled laborer sent a son into the army officer corps.

Other indicators support the generalization that many officers on the 1797 list derived from relatively prestigious social backgrounds. Although the percentage of college-educated officers had declined since 1786, it remained well above the proportion found in the population as a whole. At least eight and possibly ten officers in 1797 were college graduates, and at least two others had attended college. Thus, no less than 5.3 percent of the officer corps had been exposed to higher education when such an experience was still a rare phenomenon. In addition, at least three officers and possibly several others had studied at European military schools.[23]

Moreover, many officers were tied by blood or marriage to families with records of public service. Close relatives of at least twenty-two regulars occupied or had previously occupied such high civil offices as delegate to the Continental Congress, United States senator or representative, federal judge, governor or other high state official, or member of the upper house of a state legislature. At least thirty-two officers were near relations of men who held or had held field-grade commissions (major or higher) in the Continental or regular armies or in the militia during the Revolution. If the two groups are combined to avoid duplication, then forty-three men on the 1797 list had one or more relatives in high military or civil office—22.7 percent of the total and one-half of the men for whom significant information is available.

It would be easy, however, to exaggerate the identification between the military profession and the "better sort" of the population in the 1790s. Most of the officers whose backgrounds are known came from middling circumstances, and the very obscurity of the remainder implies that the proportion of such men was considerably larger in the officer corps as a whole. Some of the regulars whose family connections indicate fairly high status seem to have entered the service out of economic need. Andrew and John McClary, for example, were younger sons of a prosperous farmer, tavern keeper, and potash manufacturer of Epsom, New Hampshire, who was also a town selectman, representative in the assembly, and militia major—clearly a local leader in that region of yeoman farmers and small property holders. Yet the father was killed at Bunker Hill, and an older brother inherited most of the family business, causing Andrew and John to embark on military careers in 1792.[24] In fact, the fathers of twenty of the fifty-nine officers for whom information is available (33.9 percent) had died before their sons' first military appointments, implying that economic pressures had at least contributed to their career choices. At any rate, the rapid turnover of personnel in the lower commissioned grades, discussed in the next chapter, prevented the officer corps from coalescing into a rigid caste and provided the opportunity for at least some young men to use military service as a means of upward mobility.

Politics had influenced military appointments in the early 1790s, but its importance boomed during the Quasi-war with France, one of the most bitterly partisan periods in American history. The size and role of the military establishment were central issues in the political debates of these years. Viewing the Democratic Republican opposition as illegitimate, even treasonous, the conservative High Federalists, led by Alexander Hamilton, hoped to use the crisis to build a "classic, European standing army," capable of repelling foreign invasion and, in conjunction with the Alien and Sedition Acts, suppressing internal dissension.[25] The expansion of the army in 1798, notably the addition of a second regiment of artillerists and engineers and twelve infantry regiments, nearly tripled the authorized size of the officer corps and added a lieutenant general, three major generals, and three brigadiers to the army's command structure. To Federalist leaders, the appointment of men of "sound" politics to these new positions seemed crucial if the army was to provide a reliable check on internal disorder.

President Adams appointed George Washington to the office of lieutenant general and, following Washington's recommendation, nominated high-ranking revolutionary veterans and staunch Federalists to be the major generals: Alexander Hamilton, Charles Cotesworth Pinckney, and Henry Knox. The Senate approved these men, but a controversy ensued over their relative standing. Washington, Secretary of War McHenry, and other supporters of Hamilton favored ranking him as the senior major general and inspector general, the key office in the army since Washington intended to assume active command only in case of invasion or a declaration of war. Hamilton had stood lower in the Continental Army than the other appointees, however, and Adams wished to place Knox and Pinckney above him, a procedure that he thought conformed to military usage. He also resented interference in the president's appointment powers. After months of intrigue orchestrated by Hamilton, Adams succumbed to pressure and reluctantly accepted the arrangement of Hamilton as second in command to Washington. Refusing to "consent to his own degradation," Knox rejected the appointment and Henry Lee, formerly the Federalist governor of Virginia, replaced him. The appointments controversy of 1798 widened the gap between the Adams and Hamilton factions and contributed to Adams's disillusionment with the ambitious military program of the High Federalists.[26]

The quest for political orthodoxy penetrated far below the top command level. Of the two brigadiers who saw actual service, William North had been inspector of the Confederation army and a Federalist senator from New York, and William Washington, a lieutenant colonel in the Continental Army, was a South Carolina legislator and kinsman of the commanding general. Following past precedent, the administration distributed the new infantry regiments among the states on the basis of population and relied on George Washington and the major generals to recommend officers. Washington proposed giving the first priority to active revolutionary veterans and the second to "young Gentlemen of good families, liberal education, and high sense of honour"; in no case should the president appoint "any who are known enemies to their own government: for they will as certainly attempt to create disturbances in the Military, as they have done in the Civil administration of their Country."[27]

In making their selections, Washington, Hamilton, and Pinckney solicited advice from prominent Federalists and compiled rosters of the applicants from the various states; they then summarized the candidates' qualifications, added their own comments, and listed separately those they considered worthy of appointment. No single factor determined their choices; college education, wealth, and gentlemanly standing were all correlated strongly with a positive recommendation. However, identification as a Federalist certainly worked in favor of a candidate, and Democratic Republicans were far more likely than others to be rejected.[28] When Adams reviewed the generals' lists and dropped several more applicants suspected of Republicanism, even Hamilton thought that the president had gone too far in his quest for a Federalist officer corps. Although the generals had been "very attentive to the importance of appointing friends of the Governt.," they had properly relaxed this rule in the case of a few candidates for junior rank. "It does not seem adviseable to exclude all hope & give to appointments too absolute a party feature. Military situations, on young minds particularly, are of all others best calculated to inspire a zeal for the service and the cause in which the Incumbants are employed."[29]

The settlement with France thwarted High Federalist hopes for a European-style standing army. Never enthusiastic about the military program of 1798 and resentful of Hamilton's challenge to his leadership, Adams took no action to prevent Congress from dissolving the additional army in 1800. At the very end of his administration, however, the president made a final attempt to influence the political coloration of the army. On 4 February 1801, in a military version of his midnight judicial appointments, he nominated eighty-seven men to fill vacancies in the six regiments of the permanent military establishment.[30] These openings had accumulated during the closing stages of the Quasi-war, when the fate of the army had been uncertain, and they amounted to nearly a third of the authorized strength of the officer corps. Although there is no direct evidence about the political loyalties of most of Adams's nominees, forty-four were former officers of the additional army, and fourteen of the fifteen men whose allegiances are known were Federalists. The Senate seems to have debated these nominations but ultimately approved them, guaranteeing that the army would remain predominantly Federalist for years to come.

THE REPUBLICANS

By politicizing military appointments, the Federalists might have set a precedent of great importance for the future of civil-military relations in the United States. Such a development did not noticeably occur. Although the Jefferson administration was concerned about the Federalist orientation of the army, the reduction of 1802 cut the officer corps to 191 men—only slightly larger than the membership of the two houses of Congress. Consequently, until the expansion of the army in 1808, the administration had few appointments to make, and those consisted of filling occasional vacancies at the lowest grades. Thus the selection of officers was a routine matter, and Thomas Jefferson left it to his secretary of war, Henry Dearborn. Dearborn required only that aspiring officers procure "good recommendations, from gentlemen of known character."[31] Although applicants enlisted political sponsors and letters of reference frequently mentioned the candidates' Republicanism, Dearborn apparently did not make political affiliation the pivotal criterion for selection, nor did he systematically use junior officers' appointments to "Republicanize" the officer corps.[32] As before, an occasional enlisted man received a commission, but such appointments seem to have been less common than under the Federalists, and not all reflected a commitment to democracy. Philip Ostrander, for example, was the son of a former sheriff of Albany County, New York, who, "owing to some youthful imprudence, without the knowledge of his family & friends," had enlisted as a private. He was immediately made a sergeant and, on the appeal of an influential friend, promoted to ensign three years later.[33]

During Jefferson's administration, the appointment of cadets became for the first time an important element of the officer selection process. The term *cadet*, used interchangeably with *volunteer*, appears in the military correspondence of the late 1780s and early 1790s. The War Department, probably following the tradition of European armies, permitted some youths to serve unofficial military apprenticeships as a way to eventually acquire commissions. Congress officially introduced the rank into the American service in 1794, when it authorized two cadets in each of the sixteen companies of the Corps of Artillerists and Engineers; the military legislation of the Quasi-war greatly expanded this number.[34] The Federalists seem to have filled few of these openings, however, and the status of the cadets remained unclear.

On 16 March 1802, the act reducing the army established a separate corps of engineers that was to function in part as a military academy; it also authorized the appointment of forty cadets in the Regiment of Artillerists and ten in the engineers'.[35] The cadets then in service gathered at West Point for instruction, and the government selected others in the years that followed, though the number fell far short of the allowable total. Though no law or regulation guaranteed cadets permanent officers' appointments, young men trained at West Point gradually filtered into the lower rungs of the officer corps, especially in the artillery and engineers.

Before the War of 1812, cadet appointments followed no uniform pattern. The military academy was isolated and obscure during its early years, lacking the prestige it would later acquire, and few citizens applied, probably because few knew that it existed. According to Dearborn in 1805, candidates should have reached the age of thirteen or fourteen and should qualify "as tolerable English scholars, with some knowledge of writing and arithmetic."[36] A survey of the early cadets suggests that family traditions of military service and residential proximity to West Point were the most consistent factors influencing appointments. The first cadets to receive systematic training, selected by the Adams administration in 1801, were four sergeants, four sons of regular army officers, and a son of an officer of the Revolution.[37] Although the Jeffersonians inexplicably stopped naming enlisted men as cadets, they continued to favor applicants with military connections: Of the eighty-nine graduates between 1802 and 1812, at least twenty-five (28.1 percent) were related closely to revolutionary or regular army officers.

More surprisingly, in light of the War Department's concern for geographical balance, cadets were overwhelmingly residents of the Northeast. Sixty-five of the pre–War of 1812 graduates (73 percent) had been appointed from the New England states or New York, twenty-three (25.8 percent) from Vermont alone. In contrast, the states south of Pennsylvania produced only ten of the early graduates (11.2 percent).[38] The reason for this sectional bias is unclear. It may have reflected the superior educational backgrounds of northeastern applicants or favoritism toward fellow Yankees by the secretaries of war during this period, Dearborn and William Eustis. More likely, northeasterners were simply in a better position to know of the tiny school's existence and to seek admission. However, this pattern did not distort the overall geographical distribution of the officer corps, as the Republicans strongly preferred westerners and southerners for direct appointments into the infantry regiments.[39]

Beginning with the *Chesapeake* affair of 1807, the crisis with Great Britain caused an immense expansion of the regular army. From a low of 191 during most of Jefferson's administration, the authorized strength of the officer corps rose to 574 in 1808, 1,657 in 1812, and 3,495 in the last year of the war. Unlike the High Federalists in 1798, Republican leaders considered these increases as temporary measures, made necessary by the emergency and by the unreliability of the militia. Nevertheless, thousands of new officers were selected between 1808 and 1814, many of whom remained in the service after the war and dominated the middle and higher grades of the army for decades to come. The Jefferson and Madison administrations thus played a major, though unintentional, role in shaping the postwar military profession.

As during the Quasi-war, the buildup brought an infusion of partisanship into the officer selection process. The Burr conspiracy and the possibility of using the army to enforce the controversial embargo had sensitized Jefferson and Madison to the political identity of the officer corps. Republicans were no more prepared than Federalists to accept the opposition party as a legitimate and permanent rival; rather, their ideal was a political culture based on consensus. To many Jeffersonians, Federalist resistance to the administration's foreign policy smacked of "Toryism" or treason. Since most of the field officers in the regular army were suspected Federalists, Jefferson and Madison chose Republican political leaders with only limited military experience—and that mainly in the Revolution over a generation ago—to fill the new generals' positions.

The two brigadiers appointed in 1809, for example, were Wade Hampton, a militia colonel serving late in the Revolution and formerly a Republican congressman from South Carolina, and Peter Gansevoort, another revolutionary veteran, military supply agent of the army's Northern Department, and a member of a prominent Republican family in Albany, New York.[40] Among the new generals of 1812, all revolutionary veterans and Republicans, were Henry Dearborn, former congressman from Massachusetts and secretary of war; Morgan Lewis, former governor of New York; John Chandler, former congressman from Massachusetts; and John Armstrong, former senator from New York and minister to France. Altogether, of the thirty-five men who served as generals between 1808 and 1815, eight had been Republican congressmen or senators, four others had been Republican state or territorial governors, and at least five more had been Republican state legislators.[41] Only nine wartime generals would qualify as professional soldiers (using that term loosely), and five of these men did not attain their rank until the final year of the conflict.[42]

The Republican administrations faced a formidable task in filling the thousands of lesser vacancies in the new regiments. For the most part, they abdicated responsibility to Congress, converting the military appointment process

Brigadier General Wade Hampton. A revolutionary war veteran and former congressman from South Carolina, Hampton served in the regular army from 1808 to 1814 and was typical of the politician-generals of the War of 1812 era. (Photo by Wearn & Hix, Columbia, S.C.; reproduced courtesy of the State Historical Society of Wisconsin)

into a type of local patronage. On 14 April 1808, Dearborn sent lists of candidates to Republican congressmen of all the states except Connecticut. Consulting with "such other members of Congress" as they wished, they were to select nominees from the lists or recommend other qualified men from their states. Apparently unable to locate a Republican in the delegation of staunchly Federalist Connecticut, Dearborn wrote separately to an administration supporter in that state: "As we have quite a sufficient number of our opponents political now in the Army, it may be advisable to pay some attention to the political feelings of the Candidates."[43] The secretary of war seems to have used his power of selection only in the case of his native Massachusetts, and then only because the congressional delegation claimed that it lacked the necessary information to decide. Dearborn carefully checked the political loyalties of his state's applicants in an effort to bar Federalists altogether: "After the outragious conduct of that party within the last few months, no individual among them can pretend to any claims on the government."[44]

Each state followed its own procedures in choosing nominees. The North Carolina delegation, for example, allowed each member to nominate two company officers, while the Kentucky representatives favored "the sons of antient settlers, who had distinguish'd themselves in the Defence of the Country" or suffered during the early days of settlement.[45] President Madison and Secretary of War Eustis followed similar procedures during the expansion of 1812, and congressmen came to see military appointments as a matter of right. In February, Senator William H. Crawford complained that the higher officers of the new regiments were to be named by the more populous states, discriminating against Georgia: "Any state would rather have the appointment of a Colo[nel] than a dozen Ensigns." The War Department appears to have exercised partial control over field officers' appointments in the regiments added in 1813 and 1814, sometimes selecting men who had been successful militia commanders in the early stages of the war. In the case of some regiments, however, the administration further decentralized the selection process by allowing the field officers to choose their own company officers.[46]

At the end of his long career, Lieutenant General Winfield Scott described the officers who had entered the army with him in 1808, adding that his characterization applied equally to the 1812 and 1813 nominees.

> It may . . . be safely said that many of the appointments were positively bad, and a majority of the remainder indifferent. Party spirit of that day knew no bounds, and, of course, was blind to policy. Federalists were almost entirely excluded from selection, though great numbers were eager for the field, and in the New England and some other States, there were

but very few educated Republicans. Hence the selections from those communities consisted mostly of coarse and ignorant men. In the other States, where there was no lack of educated men in the dominant party, the appointments consisted, generally, of swaggerers, dependents, decayed gentlemen, and others—"fit for nothing else," which always turned out *utterly unfit for any military purpose whatever*.[47]

Scott's evaluation was no doubt colored by memories of the army's poor showing in the War of 1812 and by his longtime advocacy of formal military education. Although the wartime officer corps had its share of incompetents, it reflected fairly well the distribution of power in the localized, community-centered social order of the early republic. The conflict was unpopular in many areas, but patriotism, hatred of the British, and dreams of martial glory exerted a powerful pull, making military commissions far more attractive than during peacetime. The senior regimental officers who entered the army between 1808 and 1814 were typically lawyers, merchants, substantial farmers and planters, holders of local and state offices, and Republican activists—men of prominence in their communities. As such, they were in the best position to know the congressmen who determined most appointments; moreover, their social standing would likely make them successful recruiters, a vital component of military leadership in the new nation. At least seven officers below the rank of general were former congressmen, and scores of new field officers and company commanders had served as state legislators, local officeholders, or high-ranking militia officers. Especially striking was the overlap between the legal profession and the upper rungs of the wartime officer corps. Of 123 field-grade regimental officers whose preservice occupations are known, 44 (35.8 percent) had been lawyers, judges, court clerks, or law students.[48]

The individual careers of many new appointees provide further evidence of the integration of political and military leadership in the early republic. In requesting an appointment for Joseph Constant, the governor of New York described him as an affluent and "liberally educated" lawyer, secretary of the state constitutional convention, for several years sheriff of New York City, a member of the state assembly, a former militia officer, and Republican in his politics. The qualifications of Simon Larned, a western Massachusetts merchant appointed to command a new regiment in 1812, included eight years as an officer in the Continental Army, at least one term in the state legislature, twenty years as county treasurer, a brief stint in Congress, and the rank of colonel and deputy adjutant general of the state militia. Major George Tod had been an Ohio state senator and a judge on the state supreme court, while Colonel William Drayton, the son of a federal judge, had been a prosperous lawyer, South Carolina legislator, and officer of volunteer militia. Before his appointment as colonel in 1813, Robert Bogardus had enjoyed prestige in New York City as an eminent lawyer, a substantial taxpayer and propertyholder, member of the city council, state legislator, and brigadier general of militia.[49]

No comprehensive analysis has been attempted of the thousands of young men who entered the lower rungs of the officer corps between 1808 and 1814, most of whose military careers were limited to the war years. The relatively extensive evidence that is available, however, suggests that socially prominent and politically active families were strongly represented at those ranks as well. At least twenty-five sons of members of the Continental or United States congresses are known to have served as company officers—a number that is certainly far short of the actual total—and hundreds of other captains, lieutenants, and ensigns were close relatives of federal, state, and local officeholders. For example, John G. and William A. Blount, commissioned as company officers in 1812, were the sons of one of the largest landowners in North Carolina; an uncle had been a delegate to the Constitutional Convention, another had served in Congress, and a third was governor of Tennessee during the War of 1812. Captain Robert Desha, Lieutenant George W. Jackson, and Captain George H. Grosvenor each had a brother in Congress before or at the time of his appointment to the army. The father of lieutenants Benjamin K. and John S. Pierce was a leading citizen of Hillsborough, New Hampshire—a state representative, councilor, sheriff, and militia general. Lieutenant James J. Bowie was the son of the governor of Maryland.[50]

Despite the linkage between the upper echelons of the political and military spheres in the War of 1812 period, the officer corps did not develop into a closed elite. One reason was that American political leadership was relatively broad-based. The son of a Vermont farmer and state representative would have had little in common with the son of a Virginia planter-lawyer or a New York merchant other than a family tradition of leadership in local affairs and perhaps military service. In other words, the officer corps mirrored, albeit imperfectly, the diversity of the larger society. Moreover, the greatly expanded size of the officer corps and its fairly balanced geographical distribution gave many young men without wealth, formal education, or social standing the opportunity to advance themselves, especially as martial enthusiasm waned in 1813 and 1814. Although few enlisted men received commissions when new regiments were formed, the high attrition rate in the junior grades of existing units, caused by deaths and resignations, made promotions from the ranks increasingly frequent as the war progressed. It is impossible to calculate exactly the number of rankers in the officer corps because registers of commissioned officers do not always mention previous enlisted service. However, the War

Department encouraged commanders to recommend noncommissioned officers for advancement. On two lists of original appointments submitted to the Senate on 17 February 1814, 66 of 365 nominees to the line regiments (18.1 percent) were described as "sergeants promoted," and such designations appeared on other appointment rolls as well.[51]

The Republican administrations—or perhaps more accurately the congressmen and regimental field officers who made most selections—also commissioned citizens from humble circumstances directly into the officer corps, though rarely to high rank. At the age of fifteen, Thomas Ramsey had fought as a common soldier in St. Clair's Indian campaign; before his appointment as a second lieutenant in 1809, he had worked as a carpenter, and his letters indicate a very rudimentary education. Bennet Riley was a foreman in a shoe shop and then a sailor on a privateer until an appointment as ensign in 1813 launched him on a long and distinguished military career. Before he received his military commission, John G. Munn had worked five years as a guard at the Connecticut state prison.[52] In larger towns and cities, prewar membership in volunteer militia companies helped some artisans gain access to the officer corps. Indeed, the many officers who claimed economic hardship in order to stay in the army at the end of the war suggests that men with such backgrounds constituted a substantial minority of the wartime officer corps. Even some high-ranking commanders entered the army at least partly for economic reasons. James Miller, a lawyer and farmer from Greenfield, New Hampshire, explained his motives for accepting a major's commission in 1808.

> I am willing for a while to leave home and friends in order if possible to place myself and little family in a less state of dependance: if we have war, I have the first appointment in the state of New Hampshire; which no one ought to be ashamed of: my pay will be in the whole about ninety dollars a month, if I should get killed in the service (a thing that I won't calculat[e] to take place) I shall be under half pay which will be a handsome support for my family; if I live I am sure of a genteel living: therefore I think it the best for me in the end.[53]

During the early national period, American political leaders worked gradually toward a consistent pattern of officer recruitment. Most important, they emphasized a broad geographical distribution in an effort to make the army a truly national institution. Only in the selection of West Point cadets did they stray from this pattern, probably because they considered such positions to be of little consequence. During tranquil periods, entry into the officer corps was usually confined to the most junior levels: ensigns of infantry, lieutenants of artillery and engineers, cornets of dragoons, and surgeon's mates. The secretaries of war controlled these appointments, and they favored young men from "respectable" families with traditions of military and political leadership. Partisanship no doubt influenced selection, but it does not seem to have been a dominant factor. While never completely abandoned, the commissioning of enlisted men became a relatively rare occurrence during peacetime. When the army experienced major expansions—1791–1792, 1798–1799, 1808, 1812–1814—the administration made use of lateral appointments, bringing prominent citizens directly into the high and middle ranks. Partisanship then played a more central role, as the administration inevitably favored its supporters. In the War of 1812 period, there was a trend toward localizing the selection process, as the Republican administrations relied heavily on congressmen and other political leaders to make the actual choices. In general, the result was an officer corps that reflected the distribution of political influence in the diffuse social order of the early republic, but one that also offered at least limited opportunity, especially in wartime, to ambitious but poorly connected young men.

3
MILITARY CAREERS IN THE EARLY REPUBLIC

"In broadest terms," wrote Morris Janowitz in his classic study of the modern military profession, "the professional soldier can be defined as a person who has made the military establishment the locus of his career."[1] Certainly, a long-term commitment to the practice of a specialized occupation is central to any definition of professionalism. Yet for the thirty years following the Revolution, the most important characteristic of the army officer corps was the instability of its membership. The officer corps consisted of a mass of individuals from different backgrounds, whose generally brief military careers were simply interruptions of their civilian lives. In fact, it is more accurate to speak of not one but a succession of officer corps in this period, each largely distinct from the others. This situation arose of course from the shifting and uncertain place of the regular army in the emerging federal system. Without institutions to educate officers and enforce consistent standards of behavior, the rapid turnover in the commissioned ranks undermined all efforts to develop cohesion in the military establishment before 1815.

High attrition characterized the officer corps throughout the early national period. Compared to the men who entered the army during the 1790s and afterwards, the officers of the tiny Confederation army were a relatively homogeneous group; primarily natives of the Middle Atlantic states and southern New England, they shared recent memories of revolutionary service, and many of them hoped to remain in the army permanently. The disastrous Indian campaigns of 1790 and 1791, however, demoralized the officer corps and resulted in a major change in personnel. Several Confederation veterans died in combat, and the new commanders of the Legion pressured others out of the service, allegedly because of their incompetence and moral shortcomings. In the opinion of Brigadier General James Wilkinson, the officers of the old First Regiment, "with a few exceptions, had contracted Ideas of speculation incompatible with the principles of [a] Soldier of Honor, some were pedlars, some drunkards, almost all fools." Whatever the truth of this statement—and Wilkinson, the early republic's most notorious intriguer, is hardly a reliable judge of character—the officer corps of the mid–1790s was mostly a new group, appointed after St. Clair's defeat. Of the forty-six officers in 1789, twenty-eight (60.9 percent) had left the service by 1795, including thirteen of the sixteen officers at or above the rank of captain.[2]

The personnel of the officer corps continued to fluctuate through the following decades. During 1791 and 1792, the building years of the Legion, a total of 165 men received original commissions in the regular army. Sixty (36.4 percent) of these men remained in service by 1800, and only 20 (12.1 percent) wore the uniform in 1803. The trend was similar among the 149 officers who entered the army between 1803 and 1807, the period of relative stability between the reduction of 1802 and the military buildup in 1808. Of these men, 70 (47 percent) were still in the army in 1812, and the names of only 27 (18.1 percent) appeared on the army register of 1816.[3] At least in terms of membership, the officer corps of the Jeffersonian army was related only tenuously to the force that had conducted the Indian campaigns a decade earlier or to the military establishment of the post–War of 1812 period.

As might be expected, turnover was greatest at the lower rungs of the officer corps. The median career length of all the company-grade officers on the army list of 1797 was nine years; at the grade of ensign, the basic rank in the infantry regiments, it was only six years. If one assumes twenty years of service to be the minimal definition of a "lifetime" career commitment, only 11 percent of the company officers in 1797 qualified as careerists, and a mere 2 percent spent three decades or longer in uniform. Turnover was likewise high among the medical officers, whose median commitment was six years. On the other hand, the median career length, including revolutionary service, of the field and general officers on the 1797 list was eighteen years, and 30 percent served twenty years or longer. A fairly stable group of revolutionary veterans had come to dominate the field grades in the handful of permanent regiments. Indeed, the careers of such men as Jacob Kingsbury, Daniel Bissell, Moses Porter, Henry Burbeck, Constant Freeman, and Thomas H. Cushing ran almost continuously from the Revolution through the War of 1812. They were isolated figures, however, surrounded by a constantly shifting mass of subordinates, most of whose careers were short and who did not identify fully with military life. Moreover, their influence was recurrently diluted by expansions of the army, which brought waves of citizen-soldiers directly into the upper ranks.

ARMY LIFE

High attrition interacted with other conditions to keep the officer corps of the early army in a state of flux. One such factor was the army's failure to develop effective procedures to train newly appointed officers, inculcate group values and identities, or even define the content of military leadership—a situation not unique to the United States. Samuel P. Huntington has emphasized the central place of "natural genius" in the eighteenth-century conception of command: the view of military leadership as an art to be grasped intuitively by men born to command rather than a logical and fixed set of principles mastered through formal study.[4] This idea meshed with the class interests of the European aristocracies and their attempt to justify their hereditary domination of the officer corps. Before the nineteenth century, European military schools were rudimentary and had limited influence. Some served as finishing schools for young aristocrats destined for the public service; others provided specialized training to the officers of the artillery and engineers, branches frequently shunned by the nobility as pedestrian. Rather than creating formal institutions to socialize aspiring officers, European military elites relied on the shared values of an aristocratic ethos.

Few American officers described military leadership strictly in terms of individual genius; indeed, few appear to have reflected on the subject at all. The journals, orders, and official and unofficial correspondence examined for this study have not yielded a single extended statement by an officer on active duty in the early national period that specified the criteria of successful command. Implicit in the writings of officers, however, was a conception of officership as a blend of character and learned skills. The first element resembled European standards and included such qualities as a commanding appearance, physical energy and courage, social respectability, and a keen sense of personal honor—traits presumably inborn or instilled during the officer's early life. Reflecting American experience, especially the two centuries of frontier warfare against the eastern woodland Indians, commanders often mentioned physical stamina and individual enterprise among the attributes desirable in an officer. The second part of the concept embraced such practical skills as handling the administrative routine of a company or regiment, enforcing discipline, and conducting troops through a series of structured tactical formations. Linking the two elements was the desirability of a "liberal education," an imprecise term that presumed a degree of formal schooling. Education was a functional necessity, of course, if the officer was to complete administrative returns and write reports, but it was also a sign of social status—the ornament of a gentleman to whom deference was due.

Officers' letters recommending subordinates for promotion or retention may not have been reliable as honest assessments of their subjects, but they do reveal the characteristics considered most important in a military leader. Brigadier General Edmund P. Gaines came close to depicting the ideal infantry officer in a letter for Major Francis W. Armstrong in 1815: "He is young, remarkably healthy, athletic and active—his mind is strong and promising—He is brave hardy and enterprising. We have few officers better acquainted with the discipline of Infantry, or better qualified for the command of a company or Battalion—And for the heavy duties of a wilderness campaign he is surpassed by none." While under Gaines's command, Armstrong had "transformed a mass of awkward recruits into one of the finest companies I have ever seen formed in so short a period." In 1800, Major General Charles Cotesworth Pinckney described Major William D. Beall as "brave, modest, active, intelligent, industrious, rigid in his notions of honour, an excellent disciplinarian, a good tactician." In recommending Josiah Dunham to be the senior captain of his regiment in 1799, Lieutenant Colonel Rufus Graves portrayed him as "a man of liberal Education, of splendid genius, a finished penman and componist, and possessed of very commanding talents." He was over six feet tall, "strait & well made," and had a reputation as "an excellent Disciplinarian." According to Colonel Alexander Smyth in 1812, Captain William King's "dauntless Bravery, refined mind, high sence of honor, & ambition to distinguish himself" qualified him for promotion, "and he is perhaps the best disciplinarian in the army."[5]

The formation of the Corps of Artillerists and Engineers in 1794 and especially the establishment of the United States Military Academy in 1802 suggested a different view of officership, centering on the need for prolonged, specialized professional training. However, the prevailing opinion in the army through the War of 1812, was that the rather simple skills of command could be acquired by actual service with the troops. A similar belief shaped procedures in law and medicine during the early national period, when professional schools were few and small and most aspirants trained by apprenticing in the offices of established practitioners. On receiving his commission, an officer reported straight to his company or, if assigned to a new unit, went on recruiting duty, frequently in his home district. In the latter case, he remained several months or longer out of direct contact with military organization, living virtually as a civilian until he had enlisted the nucleus of his command. Many older officers appointed to the middle and higher ranks during expansions of the army had previous experience in the revolutionary army, militia, or volunteers, which eased their transition to the regular service. The few noncommissioned officers promoted to the junior grades had gained a basic knowledge of tactics and military routine. But most new officers began at the lowest grades, and most had no significant military experience.

Regrettably, little is known about the process by which newly appointed subalterns in the early national period acquired the skills and knowledge needed for command. During the early 1800s, the United States Navy developed an informal but highly effective system for the education and professional socialization of midshipmen that laid the foundations for that service's impressive performance in the War of 1812. It centered on practical shipboard training in seamanship, navigation, and command, but it also imbued midshipmen with the collective norms, traditions, and identity of the naval officer corps. Midshipmen were evaluated by their commanding officers, and favorable ratings were essential before they received their permanent commissions.[6]

With the exception of the small minority who entered as cadets, fledgling army officers moved directly from civil life into the commissioned ranks. Thus, they obtained their professional skills and modes of behavior haphazardly, by reading military manuals and following the examples of their peers and superiors. Although officers used a variety of manuals before 1815, the most significant by far were Baron von Steuben's *Regulations for the Order and Discipline of the Troops of the United States*, usually called the "Blue Book" or "the Baron," and the Rules and Articles of War. Written during the Revolution, Steuben's small volume remained for decades the army's standard guide for both infantry tactics and basic military administration.[7] Designed for the amateur soldiers of the Continental Army, it simplified the highly structured movements typical of eighteenth-century warfare and also included rules for the conduct of marches, the organization of camps, the posting of guards and sentinels, and other aspects of military routine. The final section described the fundamental duties of each military rank, from regimental commander down to private.

The Rules and Articles of War, adapted from the British service and occasionally revised, established the basic system of military justice.[8] Although covering a wide range of topics, from the granting of furloughs and the handling of complaints to the organization and conduct of courts-martial, the articles contained provisions that functioned for the officer corps as a rough code of professional ethics. Among other things, officers were forbidden to use profanity, express disrespect for their commanding officer or high federal or state officials, be drunk on duty or absent without leave, or in any way participate in duels. Moreover, they were subject to dismissal if convicted of "behaving in a scandalous and infamous manner, such as is unbecoming an officer and a gentleman."[9] General orders supplemented these rules. An order of 11 November 1800, for example, elaborated at length on the submission of army returns and other administrative details. A set of regulations appearing first in 1797 and again in 1808 expounded on army procedures, defined aspects of the officers' relationship to enlisted men to prevent the exploitation of the latter, and published additional ethical standards for the officer corps: prohibiting the use of cards or dice in army camps or garrisons, denouncing the feigning of illness to avoid duty, and forbidding officers to keep mistresses, a habit "repugnant to the rules of society— . . . burthensome to the service—ever pregnant with discord—often afflictive to the meritorious soldier—always disgraceful and frequently destructive to men of merit."[10]

Taken together, the articles and the regulations derived from general orders went far toward clarifying the content of military leadership as it applied to junior and middle-ranking officers in the late eighteenth century. The rules appeared erratically, however, and the War Department failed to codify them, fix clearly their authority, or make them generally available to the officer corps. Some of the provisions, notably the proscription against dueling, were nullified by established practice in the army. The clause prohibiting conduct "unbecoming an officer and a gentleman" may have had meaning in the British service, with its commonly accepted aristocratic values, but it was too vague to serve as a normative guide for a body of men as heterogeneous as the American officer corps. Although not without influence, the mere existence of regulations and manuals could not produce uniformity and cohesion.

More important than official regulations in the socialization of young officers were the informal pressures of garrison life. On rare occasions during the early national period, large segments of the army served together, encouraging esprit de corps and exposing young officers to a stimulating environment. Such was the case between 1792 and 1794, when Major General Anthony Wayne built the Legion into a miniature replica of the Continental Army, and in the spring and summer of 1814, when Major General Jacob Brown and Brigadier General Winfield Scott instilled discipline and élan into the army on the Niagara frontier. Under ordinary circumstances, however, the army's role as a frontier constabulary caused it to disperse into small, isolated garrisons. In 1803, the major concentrations of officers and men were at New Orleans (276), Fort Wilkinson in Georgia (228), and Detroit (199). The rest of the army—nearly three-quarters of the actual strength—was scattered at thirty-one garrisons ranging in size from 11 to 132 officers and men; at twenty-seven posts the total personnel was less than 100.[11] In this situation, the influence of the army's central bureaucracy was minimal. Generals and regimental commanders rarely conducted tours of inspection, and the few officers designated as inspectors served principally as stationary staff assistants to the commanding general or secretary of war. The primitive state of communication, especially

Fort Washington, at the present site of Cincinnati, the largest post in the Northwest during the Indian war of the 1790s. Drawn by Captain Jonathan Heart in 1790, the year before he was killed at St. Clair's defeat. (Courtesy of the State Historical Society of Wisconsin)

west of the Appalachian Mountains, kept small garrisons isolated from army and regimental headquarters—an archipelago of tiny islets strung along thousands of miles of remote frontier.

Even though government policy might demand it, experienced regulars agreed that dispersion undermined the army's military character. In the fall of 1799, Lieutenant Colonel John F. Hamtramck inspected the posts on the northwestern frontier and reported a sorry picture. The commands suffered from lack of pay, clothing, and military manuals; some were so depleted that they had barely enough men for guard and fatigue duty, leaving few or none for military training. The principal cause of the army's disorganized state was the "Scattered, mutilated and mixed situation of the Regiments—Companies at an immense distance from their own doing duty with other Regiments, others Cut up and distributed to Different Posts, and officers for years together doing Duty with Regiments they do not belong to." Hamtramck had "frequently gone in to a Garrison Composed of a small Detachment where an uninterrupted Silence reigned, giving it the resemblance more of a Convent (where two or three foot paths Seen thro' the grass were the only indications of its being inhabited) than a place of Arms."[12] Although the effects of dispersion were greatest in the West, similar conditions existed at artillery garrisons near the coastal cities. Lieutenant Colonel William Duane complained in 1809 that the veteran artillery commander of Fort Mifflin had requested to be excused from attending a Fourth of July celebration in Philadelphia, as "there was not a man in his garrison who knew how to handle a [cannon] sponge."[13]

Garrison life varied with the location of the post, the size of the command, the number of women present, and the personality and standards of the commanding officer. No doubt typical of many small garrisons, however, was Fort Defiance, a post established in northwestern Ohio after Wayne's victory at Fallen Timbers. A Harvard-educated medical officer, Surgeon's Mate Joseph G. Andrews, served there during 1795 and kept a journal that captures the flavor of life in the early peacetime army.[14] According to Andrews's monthly tabulations, the number of residents ranged between 68 and 166, including 5 to 8 commissioned officers and 55 to 149 enlisted men. Among the other relatively permanent inhabitants were several women—soldiers' wives and laundresses or the mistresses of officers or enlisted men, as no officers' wives are mentioned—one child, two contractors' agents, an interpreter, and one or two other citizens. In addition, the fort received many visitors: delegations of Indians, traders, deserters from the British service, and whites redeemed from Indian captivity.

Perhaps because Andrews was absorbed with his medical duties, his journal does not elaborate on the military routine of the garrison. Fort Defiance was not far from posts still held by the British, and Indian-white violence continued to flare in the surrounding forests. As a result, concern for military readiness was probably greater than at posts in more tranquil areas. Andrews's journal mentions evening parades and the punishment of enlisted men for various derelictions of duty; one court-martial found two soldiers guilty of putting their muskets aside and sitting down while on guard and sentenced each to receive one hundred lashes.[15] Desertion was a problem at Fort Defiance as it was at nearly every garrison, but the isolation of the post in the midst of Indian country seems to have checked the temptation to flee. When a private deserted in November 1795, the officers offered two Shawnees a reward of ten dollars for capturing him alive and twenty dollars for his scalp. One of the warriors returned the following day with the soldier's scalp and collected the reward, as well as "many compliments from the officers."[16]

In general, Andrews's journal describes an informal social mingling of officers, civilians, Indians, and, to a lesser extent, enlisted men. Andrews and the other officers spent their leisure time gardening, fishing, and walking near the post; in the spring, they formed a "copartnership" to produce maple sugar, though it did not become profitable. Andrews took an interest in the Indians of the area, visiting nearby camps and beginning a vocabulary of the Shawnee language with the help of a trader. On one occasion, he and another officer "raised & joined in a dance with the Tawney Ladies & Gentlemen."[17] The officers' social life revolved around the evening meal, and Andrews recorded the surprisingly diverse fare: corned beef, pork, chicken, fish, and wild game, as well as corn and other vegetables from the officers' gardens. Andrews shared a mess with the post commander, Major Thomas Hunt, and a lieutenant, but they frequently dined with other officers, traders, and Indians. On 8 May, for example, they invited the chiefs of a visiting band of Delawares, and on the following day, the "Delaware females of note."[18]

Allusions to heavy drinking and wenching suggest that the officers cultivated a flamboyant style of life. Andrews apparently quarreled with Major Thomas H. Cushing over a woman, and he mentions the departure in October of Cushing and "Madam pro tem."[19] Sexual contacts between officers and Indian women appear to have been common. On 30 December, a Delaware chief informed Lieutenant Piercy S. Pope that his "Lady had that morning introduced to the world a young artillerist." When the other officers applied for the "usual fee" on such occasions—a gallon of wine—Pope ungallantly denied paternity, "his first connection being in May last; & notwithstanding all that could be said on the subject, would not be persuaded that it was possible for a child to be born in less than 9 [months] from the conception."[20] Andrews speculated with some relish on the discomfiture of Ensign Peter Frothingham, a devout Methodist and teetotaler compelled to share a mess with "the two wild Virginians," Pope and Ensign George Strother. Sickly and morose, Frothingham declined steadily in health. He sought medical advice from an Indian woman, much to Andrews's professional chagrin, and died in December. After giving him a military burial, the officers retired to their quarters, "drank a glass of wine, [ate] a little bread & cheese, smoked a pipe & wished well to the soul of the deceased."[21]

The military experience of most officers consisted of small-unit drill, seldom involving more than two or three companies, and occasional expeditions arising from the army's constabulary role. These circumstances suggest that another quality of officership in the early republic was its lack of differentiation. Although units carried specialized designations—infantry, artillery, and dragoons—the diffusion and intermingling of regiments and even companies and the unavailability of military manuals prevented officers from achieving a specialized competence. The great majority of regulars served as infantry, absorbing at most the basic drill described in Steuben's regulations. The distinction between staff and line, basic to the organization of eighteenth-century European armies, played only a minor part in the American service. Except for medical officers and, after 1802, the handful of officers of the Corps of Engineers, few regulars held permanent staff positions; administrative and logistical tasks were performed mainly by civilian employees of the War Department or by line officers on temporary staff detail. Moreover, there was remarkably little differentiation in function according to rank, at least under peacetime conditions. Because of the isolation of the garrisons, regimental commanders and other field officers seldom had effective control of more than three or four companies, while lieutenants and even ensigns frequently exercised independent command.

The economics of army life offered few inducements for officers to make a permanent or exclusive commitment to a military career. During the Confederation era, annual compensation (basic pay supplemented by allowances for subsistence and forage for horses) ranged from $1,584 for the lieutenant colonel commanding the army down to $408 for lieutenants and $336 for ensigns.[22] Pay rose only slightly in subsequent decades. In 1802, Brigadier General James Wilkinson, the army's highest-ranking officer, had a total annual compensation of $2,053. Lieutenant colonels commanding regiments received $1,350 in salary and allowances, captains $633, and second lieutenants of infantry $402.[23] Some officers were able to increase their income through extra allowances. Junior officers serving in such staff capacities as regimental adjutants, paymasters, and quartermasters (after 1802, known as assistant military agents) were entitled to additional compensation, and a law of 1797 provided a double-ration allowance for commanders of separate posts, apparently because they had special entertainment responsibilities.[24] Officers on recruiting duty received a premium of two dollars for every enlistee.[25] While not calculated as part of their official pay, regulars had other benefits. Each officer was allowed at least one soldier from the line as a personal servant, for example, and officers in garrisons could take advantage of free medical care, publicly owned quarters, and group messing arrangements.[26]

It is difficult to compare the economic situation of army officers with those of other occupational groups because there is so little reliable data on income in the early national period. Certainly officers' compensation was well above enlisted men's: In 1802, the highest-paid noncommissioned officer, a sergeant major, earned $120 annually, less than a third of the pay of the most junior subaltern. The status of regulars was far less advantageous when compared with civil employees of the federal government. According to the federal list of 1802, six officials of the Treasury Department in Washington received higher compensation than any army officer, and the pay of regimental commanders was well below that of several senior clerks in the executive departments. All twenty-seven clerks of the War and Navy departments were paid more than army captains, and the compensation of office messengers and the assistant doorkeepers of the houses of Congress exceeded that of second lieutenants.[27] William Duane stated in 1809 that he paid higher salaries to two clerks in his newspaper office than he received as lieutenant colonel of a regiment of riflemen.[28] Officers were required to buy their uniforms with their limited compensation, and most were stationed in cities and in the West, where the cost of living was high. In 1805, regulars at St. Louis petitioned Congress for a raise, arguing that the army pay scale had not changed since 1792 even though prices had doubled generally and tripled in the western territories. Captain Walker K. Armistead requested double rations in 1807 while supervising the construction of fortifications at New Orleans. Without such an allowance, *"I am a ruined man. And shall not be able to support that dignity which is expected from the Engineer of the Louisiana Territory."*[29]

If they were dependent solely on their salaries, the economic position of most regulars was not secure, and lower-ranking and married officers in particular had only a precarious grip on middle-class respectability. Not surprisingly, officers tried to supplement their income by engaging in business outside the army. The prevailing concept of office holding in the early republic reinforced this tendency. Seldom was public service seen as an exclusive, self-contained career, highly specialized and demanding the undivided attention of the officeholder. Planter-statesmen such as Washington and Jefferson, who apportioned their time among agriculture, intellectual interests, and civic duties, were only the most obvious examples of the amateurism of American leadership. Until 1816, congressmen and senators received a per diem allowance rather than a salary and had to have an independent means of support. Although there were exceptions, federal employees outside the capital—customs officials at the smaller ports, land agents, postmasters, district attorneys, federal marshals, consuls, and others—could rarely live on their government pay alone, and for many of them public office merely augmented more lucrative endeavors in commerce, agriculture, land speculation, and law. Although the conditions of military life, especially its susceptibility to changes in location, somewhat restricted officers' outside interests, neither regulations nor tradition channeled their energy exclusively into their military duties.

Senior commanders set an example of dilettantism for their subordinates. Few of the prominent citizens appointed directly to high rank during expansions of the army regarded their service as permanent or were willing to abandon completely their former occupations. As inspector general and de facto commander of the army during the Quasi-war, Alexander Hamilton seldom left his residence in New York City and continued his legal practice. He admitted that it was "impossible to serve two masters" but claimed that without additional compensation he could not give up the law.[30] After his appointment to the army in 1808, William Duane wrote the president that his financial obligations in Philadelphia required him to continue publishing his Republican newspaper, the *Aurora*. Except in case of actual war, "I could not accept of any remote station that would take me farther than two days journey from this place." While serving as a lieutenant colonel from 1808 to 1810 and an adjutant general from 1813 to 1815, Duane apparently never left Philadelphia on military assignment or interrupted his editorship of the *Aurora*.[31] Arthur St. Clair, Winthrop Sargent, and Rufus Putnam saw no reason to resign their respective civil posts as governor, secretary, and judge of the Northwest Territory when appointed to high military rank in the early 1790s. Between 1808 and 1812, Robert Brent served simultaneously as paymaster of the army, mayor of Washington, D.C., justice of the peace, judge of the orphan's court, and member of the school board.[32]

At the scattered garrisons, officers of all ranks pursued a variety of economic activities that often absorbed more of their attention than did their military tasks. Land speculation was an especially tempting enterprise. During the 1780s and 1790s, regulars invested in the Ohio Company and other ventures and took advantage of their location in the West to speculate in the bounty land warrants issued to revolutionary veterans. Major John Armstrong, for example, carried on an extensive correspondence with eastern investors, serving as their agent and partner in large land purchases.[33] The interests of Lieutenant Colonel John F. Hamtramck included distilleries in Detroit, a farm near Fort Wayne, Indiana, lots in Pittsburgh, and shares in the Ohio Company. While stationed at remote Michilimackinac, Surgeon's Mate Francis LeBarron plunged into various enterprises, founding a distillery and a mill and serving as agent of a fur trading company, though he complained that he lost heavily in these projects.[34] In 1797, Brigadier General Wilkinson prohibited officers from farming and raising livestock: "The national bounty is expended not to improve the agricultural arts, but to instruct men in the use of arms: the hoe and the plough must be laid aside, and every moment from professional duty, devoted to form[,] instruct and to train them in the glorious science of war." Wilkinson's order was not rigidly enforced, however, and officers continued to use soldier labor to cultivate crops at frontier garrisons.[35] Medical officers serving in the West supplemented their income by engaging in private practice. In 1810, Hospital Surgeon John M. Daniel, the army's ranking medical officer, circulated a printed handbill offering his services to citizens in the vicinity of Cantonment Washington, Mississippi Territory.[36]

Inevitably, the isolation of the garrisons, the vagueness of professional standards of conduct, and the lack of effective inspection procedures opened the way for some officers to boost their income through fraud or exploitation of enlisted men. During the Confederation period, the irregularity of army pay caused many soldiers to buy essential items on credit at inflated prices, going so deeply into debt that their pay passed directly to local merchants. Hearing reports that officers were involved in "this dishonorable traffic," Lieutenant Colonel Josiah Harmar repeatedly denounced the practice and also warned commanders not to use soldiers as labor for their private profit.[37] Although the improvement of the pay service in the 1790s bettered the economic position of the enlisted men, rumors of exploitation by officers continued to circulate, occasionally resulting in court-martial charges. General Wilkinson thought it necessary to remind officers in 1797 that the "soldier by voluntary compact, becomes the servant of the state, but not the slave of an individual," and to require a wage of a third of a dollar a day for labor performed by soldiers outside their military duties.[38] Another area of potential abuse arose from the post commander's authority to appoint the sutler, a licensed merchant assigned to each permanent garrison. Responding to reports that commanders were using this prerogative to profiteer, Secretary of War Dearborn prohibited officers from engaging directly or indirectly in sutling. In his opinion, the privilege of appointing sutlers had converted some commanders "into Traders, & Speculators on the Soldiers, whose Guardians they ought to be, and for whose comfort and accommodation, the power was placed in the hands of their Officers."[39]

Economic activities combined with prolonged tenure at small posts to encourage a local orientation in the early officer corps—a tendency to identify with a particular community or region more strongly than with the army as a national institution. Faced with orders to distant or undesirable locations, officers frequently resigned or threatened to do so rather than break their local ties. Thus, Lieutenant Henry Hopkins left the army in 1805 rather than go to Detroit; he had become involved in the affairs of the Orleans Territory, where he had held the quasi-political office of civil commandant, and he thought the transfer would defeat his "present hopes of prosperity." Lieutenant Heman A. Fay submitted his resignation on the eve of the War of 1812 rather than leave Baltimore for the unhealthy climate of New Orleans. He assured the War Department, however, that if there was need of someone "who stands ready to fight at any place between the 36th & the 50th degrees of Latitude, I am the man."[40] Irritated by this type of parochialism, Secretary Dearborn pressured a major out of the army in 1803 and refused to accept the resignation of a lieutenant until he had completed his assigned duty. According to Dearborn, too many officers considered "a military commission as a convenience, and that when military duty in any degree interferes with private concerns, the service is no longer an object worthy of attention."[41]

PROMOTION

An important feature of any military organization—indeed, of any bureaucracy—is its system of rank and promotion, since it affects directly the morale, cohesion, and efficiency of the institution as a whole. The promotion issue had the potential to be more significant in the American service than in the armies of contemporary Europe, as American officers lacked the ascribed status of aristocratic birth and, in most cases, the independence conferred by inherited wealth. Compared with other periods of the army's history, however, questions of rank and promotion do not appear to have caused sustained friction during the early national era. This is not to say that American officers were a humble or self-effacing lot; personal grievances constantly racked the service and will be discussed later in this chapter. But relatively little of this conflict stemmed from disputes over rank and promotion.

One explanation for this situation is the prevailing amateurism of military leadership. The brevity of most military careers and the absorption of regulars in economic and political affairs outside the service diluted somewhat their preoccupation with promotion. Second, the high attrition rate in the junior grades made promotion to captain relatively rapid, at least for those officers who managed to survive the periodic reductions of the army. Young men who were appointed to the lowest grades in the years 1791 and 1792 and who served long enough to achieve the rank of captain reached that goal in an average of 4.4 years; those appointed between 1803 and 1807 attained their captaincies in an average of 6.3 years. In comparison, West Point graduates in the classes of 1821–1824 served an average of 13.2 years before becoming captains.[42] Advancement beyond captain was much less rapid, as long-lived revolutionary veterans dominated the field grades of the permanent regiments until the War of 1812. Nevertheless, a company commander was a significant figure in the army of the early republic; he frequently commanded separate posts and detachments and conducted sensitive political and diplomatic missions. The success of many young officers in reaching that grade by their mid or late twenties probably defused frustration with the system as a whole. However, the most important reason for the relative harmony on questions of rank was the emergence of a regular system of promotion—a system that the officer corps accepted as legitimate and that the executive branch enforced fairly consistently, at least before the War of 1812.

During the Revolution, matters of rank and promotion had caused constant discord within the Continental Army. The states had claimed jurisdiction in these matters and had struggled to protect their prerogatives from encroachments by Congress or high military commanders. Although seniority had been recognized as the basic criterion for promotion, each state had controlled appointments and promotions to its "line"—the term given the state contingents of the Continental Army—and had selected generals in rough proportion to its contribution to the army as a whole.[43] The states retained the appointment power under the Articles of Confederation, but the First Regiment was staffed by officers of several states and the articles did not specify how vacancies would be filled. If a high-ranking officer left the service, could his state appoint another man, either a junior officer or a civilian, directly to his place? Secretary at War Knox, a veteran commander ever sensitive to officers' interests, opposed such a procedure as harmful to morale; instead, he proposed that such "accidental" vacancies be filled by promotion based on seniority without regard to state of origin and that all new appointees enter at the lowest grades.[44] Congress seems to have agreed to this proposal since the War Department followed it during the last years of the Confederation.

The expansion of the army in the early 1790s produced a host of problems concerning rank and precedence. Especially troublesome was the status of the many revolutionary veterans reentering the service. Washington and Knox eventually adopted an arrangement that decided preference for officers appointed to the same rank according to the dates of the acts under which they received their commissions, beginning with the one that established the First Regiment on a permanent footing on 7 April 1785. Although this plan placed some men ahead of officers who had commanded them in the Continental Army, Knox considered it essential "to give each officer confidence in his rank, otherwise he would be always liable to be superseded in his grade by the introduction of the officers of the late war." Revolutionary veterans without postwar service were arranged according to their relative rank at the end of the war, and a lottery system determined the standing of appointees of identical rank and service.[45] Once a new unit had been organized, promotion through the grade of captain was determined by seniority within each regiment; promotion to the field grades (major, lieutenant colonel, and colonel, after the reintroduction of the last grade in 1802) followed seniority in each branch, such as infantry and artillerists and engineers.[46] Only the selection of general officers remained clearly at the discretion of the administration, though provision was made for exceptions to the seniority rule in extraordinary cases. During the Quasi-war, the War Department revised the system slightly, making promotion regimental through the rank of major. However, the Jefferson administration restored the earlier procedures in 1801; Congress confirmed them by law in 1812, and they continued without substantial change through the nineteenth century.[47] Only rarely before the War of 1812 did the executive branch attempt to violate the seniority rule, and on several such occasions the

Senate upheld the principle by rejecting or delaying presidential nominations.[48]

So began the controversial seniority system of the old army. As time passed, critics in and out of the army would denounce it as stifling to men of talent—indeed, as the principal cause of the intellectual stagnation that supposedly permeated the nineteenth-century military establishment. Nevertheless, the officer corps of the early republic overwhelmingly accepted this system as the best way to handle the potentially disruptive problem of promotion. Its most important virtues were its clarity and objectivity, as it restricted the play of personal connections and political influence—a major achievement in a strongly partisan age. While officers' opportunities were by no means equal, the inequities arose mainly by chance—from the varying rates of attrition in the regiments and branches—rather than from differences in wealth, status, or family clout. Given conditions in the early army, especially the dearth of clear and generally accepted standards of military leadership, the alternative to the seniority rule was not a rational system of promotion by merit but an arrangement more closely resembling the contemporary British system, in which the purchase of commissions and personal influence were the key criteria for advancement.

The worst strains on the seniority system resulted from expansions of the army. Generally, the executive branch officered new regiments by direct appointments from civil life rather than by promotion from existing units. One reason was to facilitate recruitment, which depended heavily on the local prestige of the regimental officers; another was to avoid discriminating among officers' applications, since not all could be selected. Unless the administration adhered to uniform standards in such cases, wrote Washington, who was one of the strongest supporters of the seniority rule, "discontents [would] be endless, and disorder great."[49] Regulars themselves were ambivalent on this issue, realizing that promotion into a new regiment might be a transitory advantage, that would end in their discharge if the army was reduced. In a letter to Hamilton during the Quasi-war, Lieutenant Colonel John F. Hamtramck expressed misgivings about a possible promotion. "To be promoted for a few Days, and be discharged would be a fatal Stroke to me. . . . [L]et me entreat you to guard against an appointment which might be the means of throwing me out of Service; *that is* if it Can be done with honor to my Self."[50] Nevertheless, regulars recurrently faced the disheartening prospect of being outranked by citizens appointed directly to high positions in new units.

Until the War of 1812, the executive branch usually upheld the seniority rule and kept new regiments separate from the older establishment. The massive wartime increases, however, eroded traditional practices, producing a tangle of quarrels over rank and precedence that resembled the controversies in the Continental Army a generation earlier. The most serious source of tension was an act of 20 January 1813 authorizing a second major in each regiment and an officer with the new grade of third lieutenant in each company, the latter ranking just above ensign.[51] The administration treated these positions as original vacancies and appointed citizens and junior officers from other regiments to many of the slots. Veterans thought that the openings should be filled by seniority, and the result was an explosion of discontent. Officers bombarded the War Department with petitions and letters of complaint, and there were threats of mass resignations.[52] Although the administration compromised by withdrawing some of the objectionable nominations, the war brought a general decline in the seniority principle, as junior officers of talent or political influence were promoted over the heads of their seniors.[53]

For the institutional history of the officer corps, the most important effect of the wartime erosion of the seniority rule was the infusion of political patronage into the army's personnel system. The Jefferson and Madison administrations had inadvertently encouraged this trend by relying on congressmen to make original military appointments. Once in the army and competing for advancement, officers continued to solicit aid from their congressmen and other influential friends and relatives. In January 1812, for example, Lieutenant Thomas S. Jesup informed an Ohio politician that he had convinced "the western members" of Congress to block the appointment of citizens to vacancies in his regiment. Requesting support for his own promotion, he urged his correspondent to write a congressman rather than the secretary of war: "Letters in this way receive more attention."[54] Most officers shared Jesup's opinion that patronage strongly affected promotion. Lieutenant Colonel Josiah Snelling attributed his failure to obtain a regimental command to his residence in Federalist Massachusetts, which deprived him of political support. According to Lieutenant Patrick McDonogh, the promotion of Thomas Mann Randolph, Jr., over his head had been due to the influence of Randolph's "very powerful friends"—presumably his father, a colonel and former congressman, and his grandfather Thomas Jefferson. McDonogh, on the other hand, had no other chance "than what may fall to my lot in the field—a few balls might make some vacancies." As Captain William A. Blount wrote in 1814, "In the Army as at court every thing is done by favours, . . . the President and Secretary of War hold out to the army one principle of promotion and act upon another."[55] After the war, officers petitioned the Senate for a return to the seniority rule, and the administration eventually restored the prewar system.[56] The conflict had produced a generation of officers accustomed to the use of patronage, however, and political intervention in the army's personnel system became a familiar feature of nineteenth-century army life.

THE PROBLEM OF DISSENSION

The absence of significant ruptures over rank and promotion, at least before the War of 1812, did not reflect a spirit of harmony in the military profession of the early republic. On the contrary, one of the dominant characteristics of the officer corps was internal dissension; indeed, seldom has an army been led by a more refractory and contentious group of men. That officer was a rarity whose career was not punctuated by acts of indiscipline and acrimonious controversies with his comrades-in-arms, many of which led to courts-martial or duels. Controlling factionalism in the officer corps was one of the most serious problems facing military administrators during the early national period.

Although few disputes occurred in the Confederation period, quarrels erupted with a vengeance during the expansion of the army in the early 1790s. The central figure was James Wilkinson, a charming, cosmopolitan, perhaps charismatic officer, but a fiercely ambitious man who was utterly devoid of scruples. After his promotion to brigadier general in 1792, Wilkinson attempted to purge the officer corps of holdovers from the old First Regiment, ostensibly because of their incompetence and unethical behavior but probably because they were not amenable to his influence. Superseded as senior officer in the army by Anthony Wayne, Wilkinson built up a faction within the officer corps in opposition to Wayne, exploiting widespread dissatisfaction with the strict discipline imposed by the new commander and turning the Legion into a hotbed of intrigue and recrimination. Wilkinson openly challenged Wayne for command of the army in 1794, after the Battle of Fallen Timbers; he publicly criticized the conduct of the campaign, disparaging the significance of the victory and blaming his commander for dissension in the officer corps. He called for an official investigation of Wayne's behavior and intrigued to have his rank of major general dropped in the cutback of 1796. In turn, Wayne denounced the "Malignant and groveling charges" brought by "that worst of all bad men, to whom I feel myself as much superior in every Virtue—as Heaven is to Hell."[57] Although Wilkinson failed to drive his rival from the service, Wayne's death late in 1796 left him again the senior officer in the army. Even so, Wilkinson remained a focal point of officers' infighting for the next two decades: In 1809, a newly appointed major informed his wife that "there is a great division among the officers of the army concerning him. Some are his warm advocates, whilst others are his deadly enemies."[58]

Brigadier General James Wilkinson. (Courtesy of the State Historical Society of Wisconsin)

The conflicts surrounding Wilkinson were only the most visible examples of officers' contentiousness. Virtually every military command had its share of friction, and the threat of violence simmered constantly near the surface. The Legion in particular was riddled with quarrels, only some of which stemmed from the Wilkinson-Wayne dispute. During 1795 and 1796, the resentment of the officers of the Corps of Artillerists and Engineers toward their French-born commander, Lieutenant Colonel Stephen Rochefontaine, kept that branch in a state of near chaos and brought about the collapse of the army's first experiment with formal military education. Officers' dissension continued through the early nineteenth century and reached new heights in the years before the War of 1812. Regulars pilloried their rivals in the press and appealed to political friends for redress; at times personal enmity threatened to destabilize entire sections of the army. Captain Benjamin Forsyth's description of Fort Norfolk in 1811 would fit many garrisons: "Quarrelling slandering, Arresting & threatening of Arrests is common, & probably more on account of individual animosity than public good."⁵⁹

The unruly nature of the officer corps arose from a complex of attitudes and conditions, deeply imbedded in the general character of eighteenth-century military life and the peculiar circumstances of the American army. The principal model for American officers was the officer corps of European armies, which were characterized by contentious individualism and an aristocratic ethic centered on honor.⁶⁰ An imprecise and often contradictory concept, honor could require an officer to carry out the orders of his superiors, deal openly and honestly with his fellow officers, refuse to shun combat, and take a paternalistic interest in the welfare of the enlisted men. It could also compel him to disobey "dishonorable" orders, resent suspected insults to himself, his regiment, or his profession, jealously guard the prerogatives of rank, and maintain an ostentatious style of life suitable to his station. Central to military honor was an obsession with reputation—an officer's image in the eyes of his comrades in arms. For European officers, honor was a vaguely defined higher law that encouraged individual autonomy and frequently clashed with formal regulations and other bureaucratic restraints. Its most dramatic manifestation was the nearly universal practice of dueling to settle personal disputes.

American regulars patterned their behavior after their European counterparts, or perhaps more accurately, after a generalized idea of what constituted appropriate conduct for an army officer. The principal source of this emulation had been the attempt by Washington and other conservative leaders to model the Continental Army on a European standing army. Officers were to be gentlemen whose social standing would reinforce their military rank.⁶¹ Given the immense authority of Washington and the prevailing images of officership in the early national period, an alternative image, representing a "republican officer," was slow to develop. Moreover, the aristocratic ideal drew support from the patrician values of the southern planter class and the mercantile and landed elites of the Middle Atlantic states. It seems to have influenced officers of all ranks, however, and its validity was seldom called into question. Indeed, officers insecure in their social status may have paid special attention to matters of honor as a means to establish their claims to gentility. In 1814, a former officer probably captured the sentiments of the officer corps as a whole when he defended the actions of his stepson, one of the very few regulars to be dismissed for dueling. To have been publicly insulted—denounced as not a gentleman in the presence of other officers—and not to have sought redress would have made the youth "the scoff and ridicule, and what is worse the contempt of his brothers in arms."⁶²

If the dominant military ethic legitimatized refractory conduct, the particular circumstances of the American service reinforced the tendency. One factor was the constant turnover of commissioned personnel. The high attrition rate and the sudden expansions and contractions of the army retarded the growth of informal ties—the friendships, shared memories, and institutional loyalties essential to the harmonious functioning of any large organization. Although an ever-present part of army life, personal quarrels tended to multiply during periods of expansion, when masses of new officers flooded the service: in Wayne's Legion during the early 1790s, in the Corps of Artillerists and Engineers after its establishment in 1794, and in the new forces raised in 1808 and the War of 1812. According to Captain Lewis Howard, "a small degree of Fermentation" should be expected in new units "to carry off the useless or injurious parts, that it is always impossible to prevent the admission of in the first formation." The problem in the American service was that such periods of turbulence occurred frequently.[63]

A closely related source of trouble was the heterogeneity of the officer corps, compounded by the absence of effective methods of socialization. The officer corps was one of the few places in the early republic in which Americans from a variety of regional, religious, ethnic, educational, and social-class backgrounds mingled, and many conflicts stemmed at least partially from such differences. In requesting a transfer, Surgeon Fenn Deming attributed his difficulties with his fellow officers to "a difference in sentiments & manners, which prevents me from being considered a social and *Jolly* companion—to which is added a prejudice against me on account of my not being originally from New Jersey." Among the charges brought against a regimental commander in 1809 were "disseminating among his officers, on frequent occasions, the principles of infidelity, denying the doctrine of future existence, treating with contempt and ridicule the holy scriptures, & all forms of religion," discouraging his officers from attending church, and using obscene language. Anti-Semitism was a factor in at least some of the numerous disputes involving Captain Abraham Massias, one of a handful of Jewish officers in the early army. During an altercation in 1811, Captain John McClelland called him "a little jew, who is almost too contemptible for me to be offended at" and "a dam'd Isrealite," and threatened to take "the ballance of the prepuce off if he was not well circumcized." In 1814, officers of the Ninth Infantry petitioned for the removal of two lieutenants who fell short of gentlemanly standards. "Their general character is such as precludes the possibility of associating with them, disgraces the Regt. while in Camp, and the army while in Public, and yet eludes any specific charge."[64]

Finally, friction among junior officers may have reflected somewhat the general spirit of adolescent rebellion that pervaded the early national period and that was revealed most dramatically in the wave of riots and disorders at colleges between 1798 and 1815. A number of conditions probably contributed to this unrest: emotional stresses arising from urbanization and the resulting expansion of career choices available to middle- and upper-class youths; the erosion of the patriarchal family and other traditional restraints on youthful behavior; the spread of egalitarian political values; and the desire of the postrevolutionary generation to imitate the revolutionary spirit of its elders.[65] In a recent study of the naval officer corps of the early republic, Christopher McKee has suggested a link between this phenomenon and the large number of "wild youths" appointed as midshipmen—young men who plagued their superiors with heavy drinking and carousing and outbursts of disruptive, violent conduct. He believes that families may have seen the navy as a place of last resort for the disciplining of their problem sons.[66] The navy's system of professional socialization suppressed most aberrant conduct at the midshipman stage; young men either conformed to the norms or left the service before receiving their commissions. Having no such system during the early national period, the army had to deal with its "wild youths" as junior commissioned officers, a situation that surely spiced the brew of discord.

The officer corps handled the problem of dissension by formal and informal methods. One of the most common expedients was the practice of dueling, which was of course a central feature of the aristocratic code of honor. In European armies it served an important social function, maintaining the officer corps's barriers against the encroachment of the bourgeoisie. Dueling was a badge of manhood, a rite of initiation into the military fraternity, and the prerogative of a gentleman. Although it was less firmly rooted in the American social order, military authorities long condoned and tacitly encouraged dueling to settle quickly the myriad personal conflicts of the officer corps.

The Rules and Articles of War, a part of the federal code of law, banned dueling in no uncertain terms and prescribed dismissal for any officer who issued or accepted a challenge, served as a second, permitted a duel to take place if in charge of a guard, or even upbraided a fellow officer for refusing a challenge. Moreover, the articles officially cleared officers of "any disgrace, or opinion of disadvantage, which might arise from their having refused to accept of challenges, as they will only have acted in accordance with the laws, and done their duty as good soldiers, who subject themselves to discipline."[67] In practice, neither the War Department nor high commanders made the slightest effort to enforce these regulations before the War of 1812. As commander of the Legion, Major General Anthony Wayne repeatedly urged officers to find "some other mode of settling their private disputes" than by troubling the army with courts-martial. He permitted officers killed in duels to be buried with partial military honors; when the brother of an unsuccessful duelist demanded the opponent's arrest for murder, Wayne assured the War Department that the encounter had been conducted fairly.[68] Although Brigadier General James Wilkinson expressed his own dislike for "private combat," he stated that "when gentlemen will differ & hold out obstinately, the shortest I have always found the best mode of adjustment, and after much experience I have determined never to interfere except in extraordinary cases." Indeed, Wilkinson set an example for his subordinates by challenging his political critics.[69] The army's civilian leaders were no more willing than military commanders to suppress dueling. Secretary of War William Eustis actually accepted a challenge from Brigadier General Wade Hampton in 1812, though in this case the dispute was settled peacefully.[70]

Whatever the views of high authorities, dueling was certainly an accepted component of military life. One or both of the participants have been identified in forty-three duels involving army officers between 1792 and 1815, and both adversaries were regulars in at least twenty-five of these affairs—a figure certainly far short of the actual total.[71] In February 1794, Major John H. Buell described an encounter in which two subalterns died as "the fifteenth duel which has been fought within one year and all by young officers."[72] Even with the dispensation offered by the Articles of War, refusal to duel could bring disgrace. In 1799 or 1800, a court-martial acquitted Major Adam Hoops with honor in a case involving an assault on Captain Frederick Frye. The court did not deny that Hoops had struck Frye with a cane but considered the blow too light to constitute a breach of order. It then issued a discourse on honor—"the *Vital principle*, of every *military Establishment*" that should be "an article in the *Religion* of every *true Soldier*"—and chastised Frye for failing to demand satisfaction. On another occasion, an officer tried to bring charges of cowardice and conduct unbecoming an officer and a gentleman against a rival because he had tolerated insults rather than calling "for such satisfaction, or explanation as every gentleman and officer is bound to require."[73]

Only during the War of 1812 did the administration act to restrain dueling, probably because the custom threatened the army's combat efficiency. A number of officers were arrested for dueling, and a few were dismissed; in May 1814, the War Department underscored the proscription against dueling by issuing it as a general order.[74] The military leadership enforced the regulation erratically, however, and officers continued to resort to the field of honor. In 1815, thirty-seven officers stationed at Plattsburgh, New York, published a broadside announcing that Captain George H. Richards had "disgraced himself as to be guilty of conduct unbecoming an officer and a gentleman, in attempting, by low, base, and cowardly means, to evade meeting Doct. [William] Beaumont, Surgeon's Mate of the 6th reg. U. S. Infantry, after having traduced, and attempted to injure his character."[75] Government policy notwithstanding, dueling remained a common occurrence in the postwar army.

The army's court system offered a second, more formal method of resolving the internal tensions of the officer corps. The American system of military justice evolved without substantial change from the practices of the eighteenth-century British army and retained strongly conservative elements.[76] The Rules and Articles of War authorized military tribunals of several types. First, regimental and garrison commanders could convene courts-martial with three officers to try enlisted men for relatively minor infractions. More important were general courts-martial, consisting after 1786 of between five and thirteen officers, that tried enlisted men for such serious offenses as mutiny and desertion and officers for violations of the Articles of War. The commanding general of the army or the commander of a separate military department convened these courts, reviewed their proceedings, and authorized the execution of sentences. However, the president exercised review power in "capital" cases—those involving sentences of death (nearly always issued to enlisted men) or the dismissal of commissioned officers. A final type of tribunal was a court of inquiry. Usually called at the request of an officer whose conduct was in question, this court heard testimony and reported its findings, but it had no power to establish guilt or pass sentence.[77]

Military courts served several functions for the early officer corps. One was to control the rank and file and preserve the rigid social class barrier separating officers from enlisted men (a topic that will be explored in chapter 14). Another function was to restrict aberrant conduct within the officer corps. Although Brigadier General Wilkinson no doubt exaggerated when he described the army in 1797 as an "Augean stable of anarchy and confusion," garrison life in the early national period certainly provided ample fuel for legal action: heavy drinking, casual disregard of regulations, insubordination, fraudulent use of public property, civil-military friction, and chronic mistreatment of enlisted men.[78] Because of the weakness of bureaucratic restraints and informal methods of socialization, military courts were often a commander's only means to enforce minimal standards of conduct or to rid the army of incompetents. As with officers' quarrels, courts-martial tended to proliferate during expansions of the army, and the majority of officers brought before such tribunals were junior officers or ones with limited military experience.

Military courts issued three types of sentence in officers' cases: reprimands in general orders, suspensions from rank and pay ranging from a month to two years, and dismissals from the service. Compared with the draconian corporal punishments regularly imposed on enlisted men, the treatment of officers was rather lenient, perhaps reflecting the hazy leadership standards of the early army. For example, seventy-four officers' courts-martial are recorded in the surviving orderly books of generals Wayne and Wilkinson, covering the main portion of the army at intervals between 1792 and 1808. Twenty-five of these trials (33.8 percent) resulted in acquittals, twenty (27 percent) in reprimands, and eleven (14.9 percent) in suspensions, in all but three cases for three months or less. One man was convicted but not sentenced. Of the seventeen men sentenced to dismissal (23 percent of the total), the reviewing officer or the president allowed one to resign and remitted the sentence of three others as overly harsh. Thus only thirteen of the officers (17.5 percent) were actually ejected from the service, and the great majority suffered no more than a few months' loss of income and seniority.[79]

As with any legal system, however, the indirect influence of military courts was probably as effective in enforcing compliance as was the formal sentencing power of courts-martial. In a surprisingly large number of cases, the threat of court-martial induced errant regulars to resign rather than risk a conviction and the disgrace of dismissal. Because the charges and decisions of general courts-martial appeared in general orders and frequently in the civilian press as well, even lesser sentences and acquittals could prove embarrassing. In 1792, for example, Secretary of War Knox informed Washington that Lieutenant Dirck Schuyler, "accused of a long course of intoxication," had been ordered to take his trial or resign. Schuyler chose the latter alternative, as did Captain William McCurdy in 1791, Captain Mark McPherson in 1792, and others in similar circumstances.[80] Captain James House brought charges against Lieutenant Joseph Kimball in 1809, accusing him of public drunkenness and disorderly conduct, "chasing Women through the Streets," and "indecent, insulting and injurious language" toward a citizen and his wife. House had no objection to Kimball's forestallment by resignation, as his main purpose was to rid the army of an unsuitable character.[81] It is impossible to calculate exactly the number of such cases, as most officers' letters of resignation gave no explanation or referred blandly to ill health or "private concerns," but forced resignations surely terminated more military careers than did formal sentences of dismissal.

Military courts also served as a forum to air officers' private conflicts—in essence, as an alternative to dueling. Although officers necessarily framed charges as violations of military law, personal animosity lay behind many tribunals. By far the most common charge was the general article prohibiting conduct "unbecoming an officer and a gentleman," an elastic clause that could be stretched to incorporate a broad range of human behavior: personal slights or insults to fellow officers; off-duty inebriation; associating with enlisted men, prostitutes, and other "low company"; gambling; disrespectful treatment of civilians; fistfighting; and even actions such as "declaring on honour that he was married and afterwards denying the Same."[82] In contrast to duels, courts tended to perpetuate rather than resolve personal disputes; officers under arrest often brought countercharges against their accusers, resulting in complex webs of litigation that tied up entire commands. A commander complained in 1810 that twice within a year most of the garrison of Fort Claiborne, Alabama Territory—a total of about fifty people—had journeyed several hundred miles to attend courts-martial at Fort Adams on the Mississippi River. Altogether, the travel and court sessions had consumed five months' time.[83] Courts and reviewing officers continually denounced frivolous charges arising from pique, but to no avail. Hoping to subdue the army's "Litigious spirit," Secretary of War Eustis favored amending the Articles of War to require an officer bringing suit against another to pay the court costs in case of acquittal.[84] Certainly, the desire of military leaders to avoid the expense and inconvenience of frequent courts-martial lay behind their toleration of dueling.

ATTRITION AND POSTSERVICE CAREERS

For most regular army officers, military service was but an interval in early manhood before they returned to civil life. Only a small minority were able or willing to make the military the center of their adult lives. Because the early army lacked a retirement system and because administrative tradition restrained the president from arbitrarily discharging military officers, nearly all regulars left the army by one of four routes: death, resignation, dismissal (usually by sentence of court-martial), or discharge during reductions of the army. Although the numbers coinciding with each of these methods of attrition fluctuated, the experience of the men on the 1797 army list was probably typical of the more permanent establishment. Of 181 officers for whom information is available, 43 (23.8 percent) died while in the service, 69 (38.1 percent) resigned, 62 (34.3 percent) were released in cutbacks of the army, and 7 (3.9 percent) were dismissed by sentence of court-martial or dropped from the rolls of the army by executive order for misconduct.[85]

Little is known of the specific circumstances under which most regulars died. However, frontier posts, especially those in the Ohio and Mississippi valleys, were notoriously unhealthy places, which may explain why a large number of officers died while still in their prime. Three-quarters of the officers on the 1797 list who died in service did so before their promotion to field rank, and the median age at death of the seventeen for whom information is available was forty-seven. Like the enlisted men who served with them, the majority probably succumbed to the infectious diseases rampant in the West, such as malaria, yellow fever, and typhus, or to chronic dysentery and other intestinal disorders.[86] Combat had a very uneven effect on attrition during the early national period. Of the forty-six officers in service at the end of the Confederation period, seven (15.2 percent) were killed in action or died of battle wounds in the bloody northwestern Indian war of the early 1790s—a casualty rate that almost certainly exceeds that of any comparable group in the army's history. In contrast, no officer on the 1797 register died as a result of combat. Altogether, combat claimed the lives of ninety-eight officers in the first thirty years of the regular army—seventy-six in the War of 1812, twenty-one in the northwestern Indian war of the 1790s, and one in the Battle of Tippecanoe in 1811.[87]

Although it is clear that many officers surrendered their commissions under pressure, usually to avoid facing courts-martial, most resignations seem to have been voluntary. The prevalence of that method of departure demonstrates the instability of the early military profession and the reluctance of officers to make a firm or a permanent commitment to a military career. Many men appointed during crisis periods viewed their service as temporary and left the army when the emergency passed. Although their regiments remained in existence, colonels Edward Pasteur and Alexander Parker, captains Isaac A. Coles and Jacob J. Faust, and others commissioned during the buildup of 1808 resigned when relations with Britain improved in the aftermath of the *Chesapeake* crisis. According to Coles, the government's efforts to preserve peace had removed "a sufficient object for the sacrifice of private interest."[88] Throughout the early national period, officers most frequently attributed their resignations to poor health and the inability to perform arduous duty, though such excuses sometimes masked more sensitive motives. Other factors included outside economic interests, family responsibilities, and dissatisfaction with the pay and living conditions of the frontier army. "I feel perfectly weary and sick of the noise and bustle of a military life, and long for a change for a domestic situation," wrote Captain Ebenezer Denny shortly before his resignation in 1792. Another stimulus to resignations was the erosion of the seniority principle during the War of 1812, which angered officers passed over for promotion.[89]

Except in rare cases, the administration accepted officers' resignations without question, requiring only that they settle their accounts. In sharp contrast to their efforts to stanch desertion among the enlisted men, military authorities seem to have considered it the prerogative of an officer and a gentleman to terminate his service whenever he wished, and resignation carried surprisingly little stigma. The War Department even accepted resignations during the War of 1812, including that of a lieutenant who, in the midst of his nation's greatest crisis since the Revolution, claimed that "private prospects and *matrimonial ties,* have overruled my military ardor—and compelled me to abandon a service which I was from infancy attached to."[90]

More controversial than resignation as a cause of attrition were the periodic reductions of the army. On the five occasions during the early national period—1787, 1796, 1800, 1802, and 1815—when Congress made significant cuts in military strength, the executive branch followed no single procedure in reducing the officer corps to conform to these acts. The cutbacks of 1787 and 1800 were confined mainly to the additional forces raised for Shays's Rebellion and the Quasi-war, although a few officers of the permanent establishment were released on the latter occasion. The reduction of 1796 fell relatively lightly on the officer corps, as Wayne's Legion had not reached its authorized strength; the War Department found places for most officers who wished to stay on, discharging three majors and a small number of company officers on the basis of seniority. In cutting the officer corps by one-fourth in 1802, the Jefferson administration seems to have consulted a copy of the army register of 1801 in which an unidentified person had rated the officers on the basis of both political affiliation and merit. Although historians disagree as to the criteria used in selecting which officers would be retained, Noble Cunningham, Jr., is probably correct in his belief that merit counted more heavily than politics: Only seven of the forty-four officers described as "Unworthy of the commissions they bear" (15.9 percent) survived the cutback, compared with thirty-seven of the fifty-one officers (72.5 percent) designated as opposed in varying degrees to the administration. In contrast to previous reductions, the blow affected many veteran regulars: Thirty of the officers released in 1802 had spent ten years or longer in service.[91]

The most significant reduction followed the Peace of Ghent, when Congress cut the authorized strength of the officer corps from a wartime peak of 3,495 to 656. Much to the resentment of veterans of the prewar establishment, the Madison administration did not adhere to the seniority rule or confine its discharges to the additional forces raised between 1808 and 1814. Instead, the War Department consolidated regiments and appointed a board of generals, headed by Major General Jacob Brown, to recommend men for retention. Regimental and other high-ranking commanders were instructed to submit confidential reports on the relative merit of the officers of their commands—probably the earliest "efficiency reports" in the army's history. Most commanders merely divided the officers desiring to continue their service into the three categories suggested by the secretary of war: officers of "highest merit," "good" officers, and officers of "moderate" ability. Others included remarks on the character and talents of their subordinates. Colonel Nicholas Long, for example, rated officers of the Forty-third Infantry in such terms as "Active, intelligent, & qualified for command," "weak, & addicted to intoxication," and "Sensible & intelligent, but indolent." Of the fifteen officers of the Tenth Infantry whom Lieutenant Colonel William S. Hamilton knew well enough to evaluate, he considered one to be physically unfit for duty and ten others to be unworthy. "Incapacity, or drunkenness, will apply to each one of them, & some of them (in addition) are not strictly honorable."[92] As in 1802, the reduction of 1815 ended the careers of many senior commanders, including nearly all the remaining veterans of the Revolution, the Confederation army, and the Legion. Indeed, the army register of 1816 contained the names of only nineteen officers who had received their first commissions in the eighteenth century (2.9 percent of the total), and the majority of those retained had seen no regular service before 1812.[93]

Most officers appear to have accepted their discharges in 1815 without protest. As noted in the preceding chapter, the men who entered the army during 1808–1814, particularly the high-ranking commanders, tended to be socially prominent and economically settled members of their communities who never considered military service as a long-term career. Nevertheless, a substantial number of officers had hoped to remain in the peacetime army. By 1815, the appointees of 1808 had worn the uniform longer than had most Continental Army officers a generation earlier, and many of the men commissioned since 1812 had likewise developed strong service ties. Some officers did not relish the prospect of "the dull monotony of civil life" after the action and camaraderie of wartime; others had come to view their commissions as a source of status and economic security.[94] In any case, news of the reduction produced anger and dismay in army camps from Plattsburgh, New York, to New Orleans. Disappointed officers resented the administration's emphasis on merit—an exceedingly slippery standard in the absence of clear criteria for evaluating military leadership—and accused their commanders and the board of generals of favoritism. They formed an association to push their interests, complained to Congress, and aired their grievances in the press; a rumor even circulated of a plot to assassinate the secretary of war and the adjutant and inspector general.[95] Disbandment came as an especially cruel blow to veteran regulars such as Jacob Kingsbury, Thomas H. Cushing, Constant Freeman, Henry Burbeck, Robert Purdy, and John Bowyer, who had spent the greater part of their lives in the army and now faced old age without a livelihood. Cushing, who feared that he could not support his family for more than three months outside the army, expressed his despair to a friend in the administration.

> The Die is cast—my occupation is gone—and unless it should please the President of the United States, to reward me for long and faithful services by a civil office, I shall be left, on the verge of sixty years of age, after devoting almost forty years to the military service of my country, with no other prospect before me but that of spending the remnant of my days in poverty and wretchedness.[96]

However officers left the army, postservice economic benefits were meager. Officers lobbied for a retirement system before the War of 1812 but were unsuccessful—although Congress did authorize small amounts of severance pay for disbanded officers in the reductions of 1796, 1800, 1802, and 1815. An act of 1790, reaffirmed on several later occasions, established a list of officers and enlisted men wounded or disabled in the line of duty. Invalid officers received allowances fixed by the president, not exceeding half pay for men with the most severe disabilities. Few regulars appear to have qualified for such pensions before the War of 1812, and the War Department tried to compensate by permitting an occasional debilitated officer to remain on the army rolls, drawing his pay but performing no military duty.[97] Finally, Congress provided survivor benefits to families of officers who died from combat wounds: half the victim's pay at the time of his death, continued for a period of five years. This allowance ceased if the widow remarried or, if there was no surviving widow, when the children reached the age of sixteen. As the army saw no combat between the Indian campaign of 1794 and the Battle of Tippecanoe in 1811, few officers' families could have benefited from this provision during the early national period.[98]

Most former officers relied on their own resources to make their way in the civilian world, and their occupational pursuits were shaped by such factors as age, economic circumstances, family influence, and personal talents. Although evidence is uneven and probably weighted toward the more successful, an analysis of officers' later careers indicates that a large proportion adjusted remarkably well to civil life. Indeed, military service provided many veterans with a means of upward social mobility. In the first place, the status attached to a military commission often carried over into civilian life. Despite strong currents of antimilitarism in the political culture of the early republic, former officers, especially those with wartime service, were usually respected members of their communities; their experience in command made them prime candidates for leadership roles in local government and militia affairs. Second, the

TABLE 3.1. Postservice Occupations of Officers on 1786 and 1797 Army Lists

Occupation	1786		1797	
	N	%	N	%
Farmer/Planter	7	38.9	8	20.0
Merchant	5	27.8	3	7.5
Lawyer/Judge	1	5.6	2	5.0
Medical doctor	3	16.7	6*	15.0
Editor			1	2.5
Federal employee	2	11.1	19	47.5
Foreign official			1	2.5
Totals	18		40	
No information	10		106	

Source: Army lists of 1786 and 1797; miscellaneous War Department records; biographical sources, local histories, city directories, and registers of government employees.

*Includes five medical officers, U.S. Navy.

government frequently appointed former regulars to civil offices, at least partly as a way to compensate them for the inadequacy of veterans' benefits. Finally, frontier service allowed opportunities for officers to speculate in land and engage in other economic ventures in the West. On leaving the army, many found it easy to merge into the civilian society of the areas in which they had been stationed.

A look at the later careers of officers on the 1786 and 1797 army registers illustrates these patterns. Table 3.1 lists the postservice occupations of eighteen regulars on the 1786 roster for whom information is extant; they represent just under two-thirds of the total, exclusive of those who died in service. Virtually all of these men assumed positions of leadership in their communities. After resigning as inspector of the army, William North served as speaker of the New York assembly and United States senator before returning briefly to the military as a brigadier general during the Quasi-war. Ebenezer Denny became a leading citizen of Pittsburgh: manufacturer, army contractor, bank director, county treasurer, and the first mayor when Pittsburgh became a city in 1816. Several veterans settled in Cincinnati, where they had been stationed during the 1790s. John Armstrong became a prominent land speculator and treasurer of the Northwest Territory, Cornelius R. Sedam a prosperous farmer and high-ranking militia officer, and David Ziegler a well-to-do shopkeeper and real estate owner, president of the city council, adjutant general of the Ohio militia, and United States marshal for Ohio. At least three other Confederation veterans held seats in their state legislatures as well as other offices, and an additional two occupied the important post of adjutant general of their state militia organizations.⁹⁹ Altogether, it would be difficult to find a more generally successful group of men than the officer-veterans of the tiny Confederation army.

The available information is more spotty for the officers on the 1797 register, most of whom were obscure men whose military careers were brief. The postservice occupations of only forty could be determined with any certainty—just over one-fourth of the total, excluding those who died in the army—although scattered data were found on the later careers of several others. As indicated on Table 3.1, federal employees constituted the largest category, followed by farmers and planters. Though not as uniformly successful as their Confederation counterparts, many officers on the 1797 list achieved relatively high status, at least partially because of their army service. For example, three former officers became territorial governors. A member of a wealthy and influential Virginia family, William Henry Harrison established strong ties in the Northwest while stationed there as a junior officer during the 1790s, speculating in land and marrying into one of the region's leading families. Before resigning in 1798, he solicited the prestigious office of secretary of the Northwest Territory; he later served as territorial delegate to Congress before his appointment as governor of Indiana Territory in 1800 launched him on the path that would lead to the presidency. Jefferson's selection of Meriwether Lewis to govern the Upper Louisiana Territory in 1806 was a reward for that officer's exploits as an army explorer. George Izard, the son of a wealthy planter, diplomat, and United States senator, resigned in 1803 but reentered the army in 1812 and rose to major general. Although there were other considerations, his military record certainly contributed to his appointment as governor of Arkansas Territory in 1825.¹⁰⁰

The later careers of other veterans reveal similar patterns of leadership. Resigning in 1806 after thirteen years in the army, Howell Cobb returned to Georgia and was elected to Congress the following year. An eight-year veteran, Major Solomon Van Rensselaer left the service in the reduction of 1800 but was immediately appointed adjutant general of the New York militia and later served in Congress—though in his case membership in a prominent New York family eased his adjustment to civil life. Griffith J. McRee resigned in 1798 to accept a lucrative customs appointment in North Carolina, while former captain William Eaton won a place in history as the daring American consul in Tunis during the Barbary Wars.¹⁰¹ Like their Confederation counterparts, many former officers settled in the West during the early nineteenth century. Released in the reduction of 1802, Bartholomew Shaumburgh worked as an army contractor or supply agent in Orleans Territory and also held the offices of justice of the peace and militia colonel; he reluctantly reentered the army as a quartermaster officer in the War of 1812. The Mississippi territorial delegate complained in 1808 that discharged officers formed the core of the Federalist party in that territory. He alleged that Isaac Guion had used his influence as brigade inspector and adjutant general of the militia to push the Federalist cause, and he pointed to three other regular army veterans who served as aides-de-camp to the governor. The delegate neglected to mention that yet another discharged officer, Andrew Marschalk, edited a Republican newspaper in Natchez and was the leading journalist of the Southwest, or that former captain Ferdinand L. Claiborne was a Republican delegate to the territorial legislature and a colonel of militia.[102]

The large percentage of officeholders in the 1797 group reflects distortions in the available data; it is easy to spot the names of former officers on lists of federal employees but far more difficult to trace the later careers of veterans who took up agriculture, commerce, or other private occupations. Nevertheless, many former regulars did seek government employment, a trend that suggests another aspect of their postservice careers. Despite the unsettled nature of military administration during the early national period, army officers were members of a large bureaucracy when such institutions were extremely rare in American society. Individualistic and refractory though they often were, officers functioned in a hierarchical setting that, in theory at least, emphasized order and discipline and operated by fixed regulations. Indeed, they were in some respects America's earliest organization men. Not surprisingly, many officers found it difficult to adjust to the relative complexity and insecurity of civil life, especially if they had spent long periods in military service, were not financially independent, or did not have roots in local communities. Becoming a civilian in 1815, after eight years in both the army and the navy, William C. Beard expressed the frustrations of scores of disbanded regulars.

> When I entered the army I abandoned every other pursuit and determined to make it my profession for life; I am now sir, out of employment. [F]rom the misfortunes of a parent I am poor. I never did one moments work except with my pen. I found it easy to quit a business, but I find it hard to be reinstated. Merchants think a millitary life unfits us for any other business, which I fear is too often the case.[103]

To men of this sort, government employment offered a secure berth, protected from the vicissitudes of an increasingly unstructured, expansive economy. The administration tried to find places for many of them, especially the long-term veterans discharged against their will in reductions of the army. One position frequently occupied by former regulars was that of military storekeeper, a quasi-civilian agent of the War Department charged with the preservation of military supplies and certain financial responsibilities at military installations.[104] Other veterans found similar niches in the War Department bureaucracy, working as sutlers, supply agents, contractors, agents for fortifications, clerks, and Indian agents. While less common than War Department appointments, veterans also obtained assignments in the customs service, land office, and other branches of the federal establishment. Especially fortunate were Thomas H. Cushing and Constant Freeman, long-term regulars discharged in 1815, who received the lucrative posts respectively of customs collector at New London, Connecticut, and accountant of the Navy Department.[105]

The ambition of many former officers, unsuccessful or dissatisfied in the civilian sphere, was reinstatement in the army. The result was a phenomenon common to the early officer corps: the broken career pattern. Officers who had resigned or been demobilized frequently reentered the service on a later occasion, and many did so repeatedly. When Congress disbanded the additional force raised at the time of Shays's Rebellion, for example, twenty-six infantry officers of the Massachusetts regiment lost their commissions; thirteen of these men, most of whom were revolutionary veterans, resumed their military careers in the early 1790s, when the army expanded for the northwestern Indian war.[106] Although his record is not entirely clear, Thomas J. Van Dyke seems to have done two stints in the army as a surgeon's mate and two as a line officer; he also served as a surgeon of volunteers in the War of 1812. The career of Robert Gray demonstrates similar tenacity; originally commissioned in 1799, he was discharged in the reduction of 1800, reappointed in 1801, discharged in 1802, reappointed in 1812, discharged in 1815, reinstated later in the same year, and finally released in the reduction of the army in 1821.[107] A surprisingly large number of officers had experience in the navy or marine corps as well as in the army—according to one count, at least one hundred, mainly in the War of 1812 period.[108] While such career patterns suggest a persistent orientation to military service, primarily as a source of economic security, this inclination did not offset the instability and amateurism of military leadership in the early republic.

4
A FRONTIER CONSTABULARY: CIVIL-MILITARY RELATIONS, 1784–1815

Throughout the early national period, no clear line separated the army officer corps from the civilian world. Neither civilian leaders nor regulars consistently defined military leadership as a specialized and exclusive realm of endeavor, distinct from the political forum. Instead, civil-military relations formed in many respects a continuum, with officers carrying out political and diplomatic functions and political considerations influencing the internal operations of the army. In part, this situation revealed the amateurism of the early officer corps, as evidenced by its high attrition rate, the appointment of political leaders directly to high rank, and the lack of institutions of professional socialization. It was also a reflection of the formative state of the federal administration, which had yet to develop consistent procedures for handling civil-military relations. The most important source of the interpenetration of the civilian and military worlds, however, was the army's constabulary mission. From its establishment in 1784 to the eve of the War of 1812, the army functioned almost exclusively as an instrument of internal control. Its principal duties were the maintenance of order on the Indian and international frontiers, the extension of federal authority into newly acquired territories, the suppression of internal disorders, and the enforcement of controversial federal laws. Inevitably, these functions blurred the civil-military distinction.

THE CONFEDERATION ARMY

The first officer corps of the peacetime army, the long-term revolutionary veterans who commanded the Confederation force, remained fairly aloof from the political arena. More than the officers who followed them, these men identified strongly with the army and had developed through their wartime service a quasi-professional perspective on their relationship with civilians. As Charles Royster has shown, the Continental Army had become estranged from civilian society during the course of the Revolution. Officers had come to see the army as the savior of the nation and the embodiment of revolutionary virtue and had begun to resent the seeming indifference of the civilian population to the army's suffering and sacrifice. The acrimonious debates over pensions had sharpened these attitudes during the final years of the war.[1] On the other hand, the negative public reaction to the "Newburgh conspiracy" of 1783, in which a faction of the officer corps had attempted to pressure Congress into concessions on pay, and to the formation of the Society of the Cincinnati discouraged revolutionary veterans from openly pursuing their interests through united political action.

Confederation officers seem to have shared the sense of martyrdom and the belief in the superior virtue of the army that characterized their former comrades in arms. The financial straits of Congress left the army without pay for long periods during the 1780s. The evasiveness of the Board of the Treasury made Lieutenant Erkuries Beatty "wish the Devil had them all, & sincerely curse the day that ever induced me again to enter in such a rascally service, when cringing Sycophants in the midst of plenty, kick the poor worn out soldier out of door, because he does not debase his feelings with the most rascally servility to upstarts of the day." Major John Doughty feared in 1787 that the inability of Congress to pay the troops would cause the disbandment of the army: "God only knows, when we shall be able to procure another; & without one, I can not see how any government worth living under can be kept up in this country, such is the spirit of Licentiousness, & so little constraint have the Laws."[2] Not surprisingly, officers favored the movement to strengthen the central government. Deeply disturbed by Shays's Rebellion and committed to national service, they looked to the Constitution to save the nation from disorder and themselves from unemployment. Without a stronger government, Lieutenant Colonel Josiah Harmar predicted, "the country must soon become a scene of anarchy & confusion." He also hoped that adoption of the Constitution would result in a uniform system of rank and promotion for the army and a more aggressive policy toward the northwestern Indians. A conversation with the governor of Connecticut encouraged Lieutenant John Pratt to believe that ratification would triumph: "If so happy for the 1st U. S. Regiment."[3]

Despite the strong service ties of most Confederation officers, the circumstances of army life eroded the customary barrier separating the officer corps from the civilian world. For instance, the uncertain status of the army required regulars to lobby on service issues in both Congress and the state capitals. Lieutenant Beatty, the paymaster of the First Regiment, and other officers spent much time in New York and Philadelphia striving to obtain pay and settle other army questions. State control of rank and promotion induced officers to cultivate political sponsors. When Lieutenant Colonel Harmar heard rumors that he would be superseded as commander of the army, he contacted the speaker of the Pennsylvania assembly and told him that he wished to be informed if "the intrigues of our Eastern friends" showed signs of success, so that he could "*face to the right about.*" Because of Congress's failure to support the additional force raised at the time of Shays's Rebellion, the commander of the Massachusetts regiment negotiated directly with the state legislature, hoping to have the state fund the regiment.[4]

Even more than the pursuit of service interests, it was the army's constabulary role that drew officers into complex and controversial civil matters. The reliance on armed force for social control and administration was an old tradition in colonial America. The English imperial plan developed during the seventeenth century emphasized the extension to overseas colonies of "garrison government," which had been utilized first in the British Isles before and during the English Civil War. Governors-general, in most cases veteran army officers who were supported by small garrisons of regular troops, exercised broad administrative and military powers and sought to centralize control of the empire in the Crown. Reaching a peak after the Glorious Revolution of 1688, garrison government declined during the second quarter of the eighteenth century, losing ground to the "anti-imperial forces of acquisitive capitalism, individual liberty, provincial autonomy, and Anglo-American oligarchy" as expressed through the colonial assemblies.[5] It revived during the French and Indian War, when the British poured thousands of regular troops into the struggle for mastery of North America, and continued after 1763 as part of the broader effort to tighten and rationalize the empire. Usually acting under the authority of royal governors, British garrisons on the frontier and in the coastal towns attempted to patrol the Proclamation Line that restricted settlement west of the Appalachians, enforce the controversial tax laws, and quell domestic disorders. The resultant civil-military friction reached a peak after the Boston Massacre of 1770 and profoundly influenced American attitudes toward military power, accentuating the vague suspicions of standing armies inherited from seventeenth-century England. In the years that followed, the political and moral dangers of military influence became a central theme of revolutionary ideology.[6]

In light of this experience, it is surprising that Congress resorted to an army as an instrument of internal control so soon after the Revolution. The principal reason was expediency: Armed force was the only means available to exercise federal authority in the loosely knit social order of the early republic. Popular pressures to open the vast northwestern territory to settlement led to the formation of the First Regiment in 1784. Although Congress disguised the temporary expansion of the army in 1786 as a measure of frontier defense, it was intended to suppress the farmers' revolt in western Massachusetts. Even before the adoption of the Constitution, regulars were involved in a variety of quasi-political functions: the expulsion of unauthorized settlers from Indian and public lands, the conduct of negotiations with Indian tribes, the surveillance of dissident political groups, and the administration of remote frontier settlements. While social control was the *raison d'être* of the early army, no body of law, regulations, or precedent clearly defined the parameters of military authority. To further complicate matters, regulars functioned within a society that was extremely suspicious of centralized military power.

The end result was a confused relationship between officers and civilians that swung from cooperation to antagonism. In operations reminiscent of British efforts to enforce the Proclamation Line, regular troops swept the west bank of the Ohio River in 1785 and 1786, expelling squatters from federal lands and destroying their cabins and crops.[7] At the French-speaking settlement of Vincennes, deep in the northwestern wilderness, Major John F. Hamtramck assumed civil as well as military authority. When residents complained of injustices done by the local court, Hamtramck dissolved it, ordered the election of new magistrates, and issued a set of "regulations" that defined their powers and fees. "My code of laws will no doubt make you laugh," he wrote his commanding officer, "but I hope you will consider that I am nither a lawyer or legislator."[8] Regulars closely followed political events south of the Ohio River, where dissatisfaction with the Confederation spawned talk of secession. Reporting that he had ordered the arrest of a dissident leader, Lieutenant Colonel Harmar warned the secretary at war early in 1788 that westerners might force the issue of navigation of the Mississippi by attacking Spanish Natchez or New Orleans. On Harmar's instructions, Ensign John Armstrong made a confidential trip through the unauthorized state of Franklin (Tennessee), where he tried to discover evidence of separatist plotting and foreign influence. Major John P. Wyllys reported on disaffection in Kentucky in 1789.[9]

Indian relations presented the Confederation army with especially difficult problems. Throughout the 1780s, regulars sought to maintain peace along the Ohio River frontier while federal and state commissioners negotiated with the northwestern tribes for land cessions. Most officers had little sympathy for the Indians, whom they referred to routinely as "savages" and "villains."

According to Captain Walter Finney (who was more moderate than some of his colleagues), "Millitary force only can make a perminant peace with Indians, & Circumscribe their Bounds, [and] the Treasure expended on Treatty's might be much more advantageously apply'd to Equipping Troops for that purpos[e]."[10] In practice, however, the task of suppressing Indian-white violence, especially the brutal and indiscriminate raids by Kentucky irregulars into the Northwest Territory, generated constant friction between the army and civilians—partly because regulars lacked the clear jurisdiction to intervene in such affairs.

In March 1787, Lieutenant Colonel Harmar arrested a citizen at Fort Pitt for murdering a peaceful Indian but was obliged to move him to another post to prevent his rescue. As he informed the secretary at war, "It is the prevailing opinion of the people in general upon the frontiers, that it is no harm to kill an Indian."[11] During the following year, Major Hamtramck found his tiny command at Vincennes unable to turn back an expedition of Kentucky Indian hunters. The Kentuckians admitted to killing peaceful Indians and defied Hamtramck's demand that they return horses taken from local residents. After a similar incident in 1789, Hamtramck complained that it was "mortifying . . . to see the authority of the United States so much sneered at and not having sufficient power to chastise the aggressors."[12] When regulars crossed the Ohio during the same year to arrest a citizen accused of maiming an Indian, Kentuckians denounced the action as an abuse of military authority and called for the arrest of the commanding officer.[13]

A PARTISAN OFFICER CORPS

The experience of the Confederation army set the basic pattern for civil-military relations in the decades that followed. In some respects, the officer corps itself became more closely linked to the political forum. Several of the revolutionary veterans appointed to high rank in the expanded army of the 1790s had held political office since the war, and many junior officers belonged to politically active families. These men did not have the strong service ties that had characterized the Confederation officers, nor the inclination to remain aloof from civilian political issues. With the emergence of political parties and the intense ideological conflicts of the mid and late 1790s, the officer corps took on a distinctly Federalist coloration. This bias arose in part from the administration's appointment policies, especially during the Quasi-war with France. Moreover, officers were attracted to Federalist doctrine, with its emphasis on authority, hierarchy, and national power, and those who were revolutionary veterans continued to be loyal to Washington, their former commander-in-chief. Democratic Republicans, in contrast, opposed a strong central government and consistently strove to reduce the army. To many regulars, they were a disruptive influence, the "De*mon*cratic" or "disorganizing" party.[14]

In any case, the officer corps of the 1790s and early 1800s was widely considered a bastion of Federalism. Joseph G. Swift recalled that the officers who served with him in 1800 never discussed politics at the mess table, although they "held decided opinions, and were generally Federalists."[15] The person who noted the political allegiances of the officers on the 1801 army register, presumably for the use of the Jefferson administration in the reduction of 1802, found 12 to be Republicans and 51 to be opposed in varying degrees to the administration. According to a compilation by Secretary of War Dearborn, probably in 1803, Federalists outnumbered Republicans in the army by a majority of 140 to 38.[16] As late as 1807, Major James Bruff attributed his intention to resign in part to "a jealousy I have observed among old officers on account of my political opinions being on the side of government and the persecution it has occasion'd."[17]

During the 1790s, the interaction between politics and the army was considerable. Not all officers became involved; much depended on the individual's family, social standing, and station. Even though the Articles of War prohibited regulars from speaking disrespectfully of high federal and state officials, many officers used their political contacts to pursue their own interests both inside and outside the army. The most obvious example was the elaborate intrigue by which James Wilkinson and his clique tried to wrest the command of the army from Anthony Wayne. This trend reached a peak during the Quasi-war, when prominent Federalist political leaders came to dominate the upper ranks of the army. Jefferson's victory in 1800 had a sobering effect on the officer corps, since it raised the prospect of drastic cuts in military strength. The result was a partial and temporary dissociation of the army from the political arena, as regulars of the Federalist persuasion tried to assure the government of their reliability. No officer was more sensitive to changes in the political climate than Wilkinson, who immediately began to switch his ties to the Republicans. In 1801, he issued instructions to a Federalist subordinate about to embark on an expedition down the Ohio River: "Silence your music in passing & while at all villages—This is not a day for parade & we must conform our Conduct—for your own amusement puff every Cheek at your will—let the Hills resound & the vallies sing—but give no occasion for those who listen with invidious pleasure, to fasten upon us the *foul* imputation of Aristocratic Pomp & parade, at the public expence."[18]

Fearing discharge in 1801, Captain Amos Stoddard admitted that he had made himself "rather conspicuous in political contests, both before and after I entered the army." Under the new administration, he had resolved to be silent on politics for two reasons: "As a soldier I have no apparent right to meddle with any concerns out of the line of my profession—and as an officer of the government, I deem it proper to acquiesce in its measures, so long as I remain in service."[19] As the next chapter will demonstrate, Federalist officers were not completely muzzled, as they continued to lobby for service-related measures under the Jeffersonians, especially for the reform and expansion of the military academy and Corps of Engineers.

The expansions of the army in 1808 and 1812 brought a material shift in the political composition of the officer corps, as the Jefferson and Madison administrations filled the upper grades of the new forces with Republican officeholders and activists. Federalist veterans of the older establishment, now a small and increasingly isolated minority, remained quietly skeptical of Republican foreign policy and the drift toward war. They tended to sympathize with the British in the struggle against Napoleon and were convinced that years of Republican rule had left the United States unprepared for a major conflict. Captain Ebenezer Beebe, who preferred to fight France rather than Great Britain, predicted that "the Poverty of our Treasury will be a formidable objection to war." "War seems to be the determination of the administration," wrote Lieutenant Colonel Alexander Macomb early in 1812, "and they are astonished when I tell them that the people in New York & Jersey do not believe as they do." Dismayed by the lack of energy in the War Department, he could not see "how we can get over fighting without disgracing the national character." Colonel Jacob Kingsbury favored peace with Britain as he thought "the whole world ought to unite against the usurper Bonaparte." Despite their reluctance to fight the British, these Federalist commanders were attached to the army by years of service, and they loyally carried out administration policy. In a letter to Kingsbury in 1812, Colonel Daniel Bissell expressed his "chagrin" that their native New England opposed the war: "That will not do in times like these, the citizens to a man after the declaration of war, ought to subscribe the soldiers creed, viz, not to ask why or wherefore they are to fight,—it is the will of Government, and I think absolutely necessary. It is true I would have liked to have the declaration been against the French also, but whatever is, is right with our Government."[20]

In contrast to the Federalist veterans of the "old army," most of the officers appointed in 1808 and the War of 1812 were not committed to permanent military careers and saw no compelling reason to abjure political opinions or activities in the name of professional neutrality. Overwhelmingly Republican,

Colonel Jacob Kingsbury, one of the long-term Federalist commanders who served almost continually from the early stages of the Revolution through the War of 1812. (From Frederick J. Kingsbury, *The Genealogy of the Descendants of Henry Kingsbury, of Ipswich and Haverhill, Mass.* [Hartford, 1905]; photo courtesy of the State Historical Society of Wisconsin)

they favored the use of armed force to defend national honor and interests and considered Federalist opposition to the war to border on treason. High-ranking commanders in particular, most of them former officeholders, followed political events closely and maintained local bases of support. When Major John Fuller, a former Vermont legislator, clashed with a superior in 1811, he made it clear that "I have as many friends in my Native state as any other man" and threatened to give the matter "extensive publication in the Newspapers." As an officer before and during the war, William Duane corresponded personally with presidents Jefferson and Madison, advising them on political matters. In 1815, Republican editors urged the War Department to retain Hospital Surgeon Benjamin Waterhouse in Boston; all the Republican papers in the area were indebted to Waterhouse for his political writings, and his removal "would very much weaken the cause of Republicanism."[21] Inevitably, political factors influenced the assignment of commanders and, indirectly at least, the conduct of operations.[22] Moreover, the administration's reliance on congressional recommendations in making military appointments, combined with the erosion of the seniority rule for promotions, encouraged even junior officers to seek out political sponsors.

ADMINISTRATORS, POLICEMEN, AND CONSPIRATORS

As in the Confederation era, the most difficult problems of civil-military relations arose from the army's constabulary functions. At the small posts along the inland and seacoast frontiers, regulars faced a variety of complex and ambiguous situations that enmeshed them deeply in civil affairs. Although the government attempted at times to clarify the limits of military authority, the isolation of most garrisons, the unprecedented nature of the problems, and the high rate of turnover in the officer corps prevented the development of a uniform pattern of civil-military interaction. Throughout the early national period, the American version of garrison government remained hazy and troublesome, shaped by immediate circumstances and the personalities of the individuals concerned.

Beginning in the 1790s, the acquisition of new territories greatly extended officers' involvement in civil administration. During 1797, the government assigned regular officers the sensitive task of occupying the southwestern region obtained from Spain by the Pinckney Treaty of 1795. The reluctance of the Spanish to evacuate their posts complicated the situation and might easily have sparked fighting. Captain Isaac Guion, who commanded the regular troops in the region, corresponded with the Spanish governor-general at New

Orleans and other officials in an effort to establish American control without provoking a war; he also tried to reassure the Indians about the implications of United States rule.[23] After the Spanish withdrew from Natchez in March 1798, Guion assumed both military and civil authority. "I am constantly perplexed with all kinds of business," he informed his commanding officer; "complaints for abuse, slander, arrest for debts, thefts, and the whole Catalogue of vexations, and happy am I to find that a government for this country has been formed by the General Government."[24] Not until August, however, did the newly appointed territorial officials take charge.

Despite their distrust of standing armies, the Republicans liberally used the army to govern the vast Louisiana Purchase. The Jefferson administration appointed Brigadier General Wilkinson and Governor William C. C. Claiborne of Mississippi Territory as joint commissioners to supervise the transfer of New Orleans and the southern portion of the Louisiana region. Supported by a small force of regulars, they took official possession of New Orleans in December 1803, but the Spanish troops that had continued to occupy the city during the interim of French control were slow to leave, and the situation remained tense well into 1804. The restlessness of the city's diverse population led Wilkinson to favor a "Military executive Magistrate" to govern the territory.[25]

With the organization of Orleans Territory, Claiborne assumed the governorship, and Wilkinson left the region in April 1804. The secretary of war urged Wilkinson's successor as military commander, Lieutenant Colonel Constant Freeman, to cultivate harmonious relations with the governor and the local population: "You will at all times recollect that those people are gradually to be taught the real principles of our government and that we are not to govern them by mere force."[26] Nevertheless, the administration's failure to delineate the boundary separating the civil and military realms caused recurrent friction, especially over control of public buildings in New Orleans and the stationing of the troops.[27] Meanwhile, lower-ranking officers established American control at outlying territorial settlements and exercised civil authority until the organization of local governments. Several regulars held the post of civil commandant—a local office adopted from the Spanish colonial system that combined military, magisterial, and judicial powers.[28]

The role of the army was most extensive in the administration of the northern portion of the Louisiana Purchase. Because the French government had not occupied Upper Louisiana when the territory as a whole had reverted to French rule in 1802, Captain Amos Stoddard of the Regiment of Artillerists served as the diplomatic agent of both France and the United States in the transfer of the region from Spanish control. As civil commandant with headquarters at St. Louis, he carried out "all the *Functions both civil and military*" previously performed by the Spanish authorities.[29] In effect, he was interim governor of the region until the fall of 1804, when the governor of Indiana Territory assumed temporary jurisdiction. A former lawyer and Massachusetts state legislator, Stoddard proved to be an able administrator; he worked to ease the apprehensions of the French inhabitants, preserve peace with the Indians, and sort out the maze of conflicting land claims inherited from the former regime. In contrast to other officer-administrators, he largely avoided civil-military controversies during his seven months in Upper Louisiana.[30]

Quite a different course was followed by Brigadier General Wilkinson, appointed by Jefferson early in 1805 to be the first official governor of the Upper Louisiana Territory. The president's motives in selecting the infamous schemer are uncertain; he claimed that Wilkinson's military experience was suited to the special needs of the remote territory, but the appointment may have been prompted by Wilkinson's political friends, among whom was Vice-president Aaron Burr.[31] For over a year, Wilkinson served simultaneously as territorial governor and highest-ranking officer of the army. He plunged into local political quarrels, arising mainly from disputed land claims, and territorial politics soon polarized into pro-Wilkinson and anti-Wilkinson factions. The governor refused to cooperate with the territorial judges in legislating for the territory, and they in turn resisted his appointments and other measures.[32] In a letter to the secretary of war, Wilkinson complained that he spent much of his time protecting the poor residents "from the fangs of a Gang of needy, greedy, unfeeling Pettifoggers who compose the Majority of my few Enemies." According to Judge John B. C. Lucas, however, Wilkinson and his officers threatened, challenged, arrested, and assaulted their opponents, and Lucas himself feared assassination. Under pressure from the administration, Wilkinson cautioned his officers against "mingling in the political conflicts of the Territory, as they regard their Honor or that of their General."[33] Even so, tensions did not subside until Wilkinson left for the lower Mississippi in the summer of 1806.

A more routine aspect of the army's administrative function was the practice by which regulars held minor civil offices in the localities where they were stationed. Apparently condoned by the government because of the scarcity of qualified civilians in remote frontier districts, officers sometimes solicited such appointments as a way to supplement their income. Captain Daniel Bissell, for example, was customs collector at Fort Massac near the mouth of the Ohio River in 1803 and 1804, and he later became a justice of the peace in the Upper Louisiana Territory. Captain Josiah Dunham and Garrison Surgeon Francis LeBarron served as civil judges at Michilimackinac. While commanding Fort

Stoddert, Mississippi Territory, Captain Edmund P. Gaines held the offices of postmaster and customs collector and on several occasions inspected the records of the local land office. Surgeon John F. Carmichael was postmaster at Fort Adams and register of the land office at Natchez during the early 1800s.[34] Regulars also acted as temporary Indian agents and, after 1809, as agents of fortifications—a civil position charged with the disbursement of funds for the construction of seacoast fortifications. Civil officeholding meshed with economic interest to strengthen officers' local ties.

Civil administration was only one part of the army's multifaceted constabulary role. As under the Confederation, the regulation of Indian-white relations frequently demanded commanders' attention. Beginning in the 1790s, Congress passed a series of Indian trade and intercourse laws, intended to control contact between the races and prevent unauthorized encroachment by whites into Indian lands. The army was empowered to expel intruders and arrest violators of the laws, turning them over to civil magistrates for prosecution. Military authorities emphasized, however, that officers were to act as auxiliaries of the Indian Department; Indian superintendents and agents were to conduct negotiations, supervise trade, and direct the issues of goods to the tribes, calling for military support only if the situation required it.[35]

By defining the army's powers, the government potentially strengthened the authority of commanders to police the turbulent Indian frontiers. No longer was their legal right to intervene in question. Nevertheless, civil-military tensions persisted, as harried detachments of regulars attempted to shield Native Americans from white pressure. In 1798, Lieutenant Thomas Swaine described military efforts to drive "refractory frontier men" from Indian lands in Tennessee; in response, angry white citizens had wounded an enlisted man, stolen and killed officers' horses, and brought lawsuits against several regulars. An infantry officer reported in 1811 that his three-man command was unable to prevent the persistent violation of the trade and intercourse laws in the vicinity of Fort Pickering, Tennessee. According to Lieutenant Colonel John Bowyer, the "abominable conduct" of frontier whites threatened to provoke war with the Creeks in 1812; he had "begged" influential men in southern Alabama Territory to put a stop to white aggression but had not succeeded.[36] While favoring the use of force to awe recalcitrant tribes into submission, many officers assumed a sympathetic or paternalistic attitude toward the Indians, especially after Wayne's victory at Fallen Timbers temporarily ended large-scale frontier warfare. Almost invariably, they blamed conflict on the whites—on the conniving of British or Spanish agents or the greed of settlers, traders, and land speculators who subjected the Indians to intolerable harrassment.

As during the 1780s, the government relied on the army to counteract dissident political movements, still a controversial assignment. Throughout the Federalist era, officers reported on the continuing disaffection in the trans-Appalachian West.[37] Rumors of subversion and possible insurrection increased with the Quasi-war, the Alien and Sedition Acts, and the bitter party battles of the late 1790s. Writing from the West in 1799, Lieutenant Colonel John F. Hamtramck described the hostility of the people in Kentucky and Tennessee toward the federal government. He was constantly insulted, Congress condemned, and the president damned. "I had twice to command my sword to do its duty, but was at last obliged to give it up, for the occasions were too frequent; and too many at one time against me."[38] When eastern Pennsylvania farmers resisted the federal land tax in Fries's Rebellion of 1799, the administration ordered regular companies to aid the militia in stifling the unrest. Major General Hamilton, who took care to ascertain that the commander of the regular contingent was a Federalist, urged the War Department to use a powerful force at the outset: "Whenever the Government appears in arms it ought to appear like a *Hercules,* and inspire respect by a display of strength." Although a brief and bloodless affair, this incident marked the first actual use of regular troops to subdue a domestic insurrection.[39]

The most complex crisis in civil-military relations during the early national period—and an event that reveals much about the general character of the officer corps—was the web of intrigue known as the Burr conspiracy. John Randolph probably exaggerated when he informed the House of Representatives that "the agency of the Army was the whole pivot on which that plot turned," but there can be little doubt that a significant minority of the officer corps participated to some degree.[40] Aaron Burr apparently hatched this murky and shifting scheme in collaboration with General Wilkinson, the ranking officer of the army. They appear to have contemplated private military expansion into Mexico and West Florida and perhaps even the separation from the Union of a portion of the trans-Appalachian West, although the latter is less certain. Apparently the conspirators hoped that a war with Spain over the disputed southwestern border of the Louisiana Purchase, which was a definite possibility in the early 1800s, would serve as a catalyst for the realization of their plans.[41] The support or at least the neutralization of the army garrisons on the western river system would of course be crucial to their success.

Even before Burr began his journey to the lower Mississippi in 1806, a number of officers at New Orleans and other southern posts were drawn into a related plot: An organization known as the "Mexican Association" intended to invade Spanish territory, perhaps financing its expedition by seizing the banks and shipping at New Orleans. Although the evidence is somewhat contradictory, Captain William L. Cooper, Lieutenant Josiah Taylor, and

Ensign William C. Mead appear to have recruited fellow officers for the enterprise, and more than a dozen regulars stationed in the area may have been involved.[42] As he descended the Ohio and Mississippi rivers, Burr met with other officers at posts along the way, some of whom almost certainly supported his plan. At Fort Massac, he consulted privately with Captain Daniel Bissell, who thereupon detailed a messenger to deliver letters for Burr and granted a furlough to a sergeant to accompany the expedition. Another garrison commander agreed to resign his commission and raise a company to serve under Burr.[43] It is probable that Lieutenant Zebulon M. Pike's controversial expedition into the Spanish southwest, ordered by Wilkinson, was partly a reconnaissance of an invasion route to Santa Fe, though there is no evidence linking Pike directly to the plot.[44]

After he was ordered to command the American forces on the troubled southwestern frontier, Wilkinson seems to have grown pessimistic about the plot's chances of success and decided to betray his fellow conspirator, hoping to emerge as the savior of the nation. On 21 October 1806, he wrote Jefferson of "a numerous & powerful association, extending from New York through the Western States, to Territories bordering on the Mississippi," that intended to attack Vera Cruz and subjugate the Mexican people to a new tyranny.[45] After reaching a temporary settlement of the boundary dispute with the Spanish commander on the Sabine River, Wilkinson hurried to New Orleans to prepare the city's defenses for the arrival of Burr. When territorial officials refused to declare martial law, he instituted it on his own authority, arresting leaders suspected of complicity in the scheme. In general orders, the wily brigadier expressed his shock at reports that army officers were involved. He allowed some "to purge themselves of disloyalty by an oath" and recommended the dismissal of others.[46] Combined with a presidential proclamation denouncing the conspiracy, Wilkinson's actions quashed whatever chance Burr had for success. In February 1807, the former vice-president was arrested by Lieutenant Edmund P. Gaines near Fort Stoddert, Mississippi Territory, where he had fled apparently in the desperate hope of organizing an attack on West Florida.[47]

Wilkinson and other officers testified at Burr's treason trial, held in Richmond, Virginia, in September and October 1807. With some difficulty, the general managed to keep his role in the conspiracy from coming to light; he also survived a subsequent court of inquiry and congressional investigation into his long-standing connection with Spain, and he continued for years as the senior officer in the army.[48] The lower-ranking regulars implicated in the plot likewise escaped punishment. Several swore that they had rejected overtures to join the conspirators or had participated only in the belief that the plan to attack Spanish territory had had the tacit approval of the government. Asked to explain his contact with Burr at Fort Massac, Captain Bissell claimed that he had merely pretended friendship to discover Burr's plans.[49] Probably some officers had been drawn into the plot because they had supposed Wilkinson, their commanding officer, to be involved. Unable to distinguish relative degrees of impropriety and thinking it "at least doubtful" that officers had intentionally engaged in an illegal project, the secretary of war ordered the release of those still under arrest in March 1807.[50] In any case, the Burr crisis demonstrated the chronic instability of the early officer corps—the interpenetration of military and political affairs, the tendency of regulars to form local ties, and the lack of a clearly established code of professional ethics.

Whatever doubts the Burr affair raised about the reliability of the officer corps, it brought no reappraisal of the army's constabulary role. Indeed, the British attack on the American frigate *Chesapeake* in 1807 and the Republican policy of economic coercion that followed expanded the administration's use of military force as an instrument of social control. Although regulars stationed along the eastern seaboard had occasionally enforced federal laws and suppressed disorders, these actions appear to have been exceptional and of questionable legality before the passage of the Embargo Act on 22 December 1807.[51] In a circular dated 1 January 1808, the War Department instructed commanders of the coastal garrisons to come to the aid of revenue collectors charged with enforcing the embargo.[52] Since the greatest resistance occurred along the Canadian border, the army soon extended its constabulary operations to northern Vermont and New York, acting in support of state militia. An act of 7 January 1809 specifically authorized the president to use the army and navy, as well as the militia, to prevent the departure of ships, seize cargoes, and suppress "any armed or riotous assemblage of persons" resisting the customs officials.[53]

Enforcement of the embargo embroiled regulars in virulent civil-military controversy. Captain Moses Swett reported in July 1808 that the people of Eastport, Maine, were "nearly in a state of rebellion." They defied the embargo and used liquor and money to encourage his soldiers to desert. After regulars at Plattsburgh, New York, seized potash intended for trade with Canada, irate Vermonters threatened to kill the guard and retake the potash by mob force. Lieutenant Colonel John Whiting, the commander on the Vermont frontier, complained that local authorities arrested and prosecuted his officers for attempting to enforce the embargo. During one such "mock trial," citizens made off with three sleighs full of produce that had been confiscated by the army.[54] While stationed at Oswego and Sackets Harbor, New York, on the Lake Ontario shoreline, Lieutenant Joseph Cross's command suffered repeated harassment, mob attacks, and sabotage. When Cross tried to impress a ship into federal service at Sackets Harbor, he was grabbed by angry citizens, beaten, nearly strangled, and hauled before a magistrate, though the suit against him was dropped when he agreed to release the ship. Since that time, "the timber which has been cut for my barracks has been repeatedly burnt my boats cut adrift in the night and the sails and rigging cut to pieces my centinels stoned in the night . . . ; myself and detachment repeatedly insulted, every mean act put in practice to annoy and harass me, and one daring attempt made to assassinate me subsequent to the *strangling affair*."[55] Although most of the regular troops had left the northern frontier by the summer of 1809, the army remained for years a focal point of grievances in Federalist areas of the eastern states.

Nearly as troublesome were officers' efforts to implement government policy in the vast and thinly populated Spanish borderlands. There, a volatile mix of harried Spanish officials, refractory traders and settlers, and filibusters posing as revolutionaries periodically threatened to provoke a war. Government policy in those areas was ambiguous at best, as the Jefferson and Madison administrations sometimes insisted on a neutral posture and other times gave tacit support to the expansionists. Caught between contending forces, often without clear instructions, commanders relied on their own judgment to make decisions of great importance. During the boundary crisis with Spain in the early nineteenth century, officers on the southwestern frontier might easily have involved the nation in a war. Brigadier General Wilkinson, who took command in September 1806, at first hoped for armed conflict and the conquest of Mexico, perhaps in connection with the Burr conspiracy. Only Spanish caution and his own decision to oppose Burr led the general to arrange a temporary settlement with the Spanish commander, by which the band of disputed territory east of the Sabine River was declared a neutral zone.[56] Although the threat of war faded after 1806, the Sabine frontier remained a source of sporadic tension. Lieutenant Augustus W. Magee, a West Point graduate and commander of the border post at Natchitoches, Louisiana, resigned in 1812 to lead an expedition of Mexican revolutionaries and Anglo-American filibusters against the Spanish royalists in Texas.[57]

Officers were deeply enmeshed in the tissue of plots, negotiations, and military operations aimed at bringing the Spanish Floridas under the American flag. Most regulars favored annexation, and many longed for a war of conquest. They were torn between their sympathy for the revolutionary movements and their obligation to preserve a modicum of order on the troubled frontier. In the years before the War of 1812, officers at the isolated post of Fort Stoddert negotiated with Spanish officials in Mobile for the right of passage on the rivers flowing into the Gulf of Mexico and even for the transfer of West Florida to the United States. When the Spanish governor complained in 1810 of a filibustering threat to Mobile, Lieutenant Colonel Richard Sparks prepared to assist in squelching the troublemakers, attributing their actions in part to "the arts of cunning, and designing demagogues, ready at all times to foment popular discontent, and fan the embers of sedition." A few months later, however, when the Madison administration annexed the Baton Rouge area and announced United States title to West Florida as far east as the Perdido River, Sparks mustered the same filibusters into the territorial militia and advanced on Mobile. Although the administration did not press its claim to the Mobile region on this occasion, regulars continued their constabulary and quasi-diplomatic activities on the West Florida frontier until the final American occupation of the territory.[58] Similarly, regulars supported an attempt by filibustering "patriots" to spark a revolution in East Florida during 1812, intended to pave the way for American annexation.[59]

The army's constabulary role was the principal but by no means the only source of civil-military tensions. At virtually every garrison, the routine of army life brought interaction between citizens and military personnel and consequent friction. Many civilians viewed the army with suspicion, and, given the erratic behavior of many regulars, such concerns were not without foundation. Several incidents raised the specter of military interference in elections. Captain William Preston requested a leave in 1793 to answer charges that he had permitted recruits to riot at a polling place in Virginia, contributing to his brother's election to Congress. During North Carolina elections in 1810, Major Joseph G. Swift sent his soldiers on a fishing excursion "to prevent any question of interference at the polls, in reference to which, as an abuse of the franchise, much had been said," though Swift himself had never witnessed such intervention.[60] The harsh and often arbitrary character of military punishments, seemingly so contrary to republican values, occasionally aroused civilian reaction.[61]

The recruiting service was a constant provocation. Judges regularly issued writs of habeas corpus for the release of underage or otherwise ineligible recruits, and recruiting officers often faced lawsuits in civilian courts. Although the American tradition of civil liberties inevitably made the recruiting service a controversial operation, officers thought that their troubles were exacerbated in time of crisis by political opponents of the administration. In the opinion of a regimental commander in 1799, a judge's call for the release of a recruit was "a democratic project, calculated to damp the recruiting business." Similarly, a captain complained in 1808 that a New Jersey judge had discharged a soldier who had not obtained his father's permission to enlist, though the father had left the family thirteen years earlier and his whereabouts were unknown. "The enemies to our government in this quarter, exert themselves in throwing every impediment in the way of the recruiting business." Recruiting problems multiplied during the War of 1812, especially in Federalist areas of the Northeast.[62]

The overlap of civil and military jurisdiction in frontier communities also generated many conflicts, some of which arose from the independent and unpredictable conduct of regular officers and the lack of an accepted standard of professional ethics. In 1794, Major General Anthony Wayne permitted civil authorities in Hamilton County, Northwest Territory, to prosecute Captain Isaac Guion, who had allegedly prevented "the free operation of civil law and justice, by rescuing and causing to be rescued, by *force of arms*, a certain Catherine Beverlee," apparently his mistress, when deputy sheriffs had attempted to arrest her. According to the deposition of one of the deputies, the veteran officer had paraded thirty to forty of his men before Beverlee's house and ordered them, if challenged by the militia or a posse, "to blow them to hell"; he had then marched the woman off in the midst of his command.[63] Other incidents reflected institutional strains, especially from the government's failure to define the limits of military law. After the American occupation of Detroit in 1797, regular commanders imposed martial law within the town's fortifications as a way to check foreign influence, prevent desertion, and reduce the disorder caused by the sale of liquor to the soldiers. By 1799, civilian resentment of military rule had brought the town to the brink of insurrection, and Major General Hamilton intervened to suspend martial law. He urged the post commander to make "every effort to bring about an amicable concert with the Civil authority. Collision with it can produce no good and must be attended with much evil."[64]

Perhaps the most serious clash over military authority occurred in New Orleans during the early months of 1815.[65] In December 1814, facing imminent British attack, Major General Andrew Jackson acted on his own authority to proclaim martial law in the city. Although his victory on 8 January ended the immediate threat to New Orleans, he continued to enforce martial law and refused to discharge the Louisiana militia called out for the emergency. Even unofficial reports of peace did not convince Old Hickory to suspend military rule, and the citizens increasingly viewed their savior as a tyrant. In February, the French consul requested the discharge of Creole militiamen on the argument that they were French nationals, whereupon Jackson ordered all Frenchmen to leave the city. When a member of the legislature published an anonymous article calling for a return to civil government, Jackson arrested him and had him court-martialed as a spy; he subsequently arrested the federal district judge, Dominick A. Hall, and the United States district attorney for trying to serve him with a writ of habeas corpus. Only after the arrival of an official report of the Treaty of Ghent did the commander consent to the repeal of martial law. Jackson was later called before Judge Hall and fined heavily when he refused to answer questions concerning his disregard of habeas corpus. According to his most recent biographer, Old Hickory established a "police state" in New Orleans and "clearly overreached himself"; his "lunatic militarism" is explicable only in light of his exaggerated sense of duty.[66] Rather than an aberration, however, Jackson's conduct was merely an extension of the main characteristics of civil-military relations in this period: the ill-defined scope of military authority and the tradition of independent conduct by officers in remote frontier regions.

Although it is difficult to draw broad conclusions from the tangle of civil-military relations in the early republic, one generalization seems certain: The image of the officer corps as a specialized elite, standing apart from the mainstream of civilian life, is certainly inaccurate. Military leadership was quasi-political in nature, and military and political life interpenetrated at every level. Just as civilian leaders moved directly into high command positions, officers spent much of their careers in essentially civilian functions: administering new territories, enforcing federal laws, counteracting political dissension, and conducting diplomatic missions. Moreover, no firmly established law, regulation, or code of professional ethics defined the acceptable limits of officers' political actions. Many regulars aligned openly with parties and factions or plunged into the political affairs of the regions where they were stationed. Only a few officers, principally senior-ranking veterans who felt isolated from the Republican administrations of the early nineteenth century, demonstrated a commitment to apolitical service. Under these circumstances, the army's relationship to the civilian sphere remained unsettled.

5
SEEDS OF MILITARY PROFESSIONALISM

Had they known of the internal character of the officer corps—its heterogeneity, organizational instability, and high rate of attrition—most citizens would not have demanded reformation. During the early national period, military affairs were exceptionally controversial, more volatile perhaps than at any other time in American history. Until the *Chesapeake* affair of 1807 raised the prospect of war, Democratic Republican fears of military power—by no means imaginary, given the experience with the British army and the ambitions of the High Federalists—caused that party to view even the small frontier army with suspicion and to stress the militia as the appropriate defense of a free people. However, to other leaders, mainly but not exclusively Federalists, the condition of the army was disturbing. Concerned about the survival of an agrarian republic in a world dominated by great powers and apprehensive lest internal divisions undo the accomplishments of the Revolution and the Constitution, these men hoped to expand and improve the peacetime army. A strong regular force would enhance American security, establish and maintain national borders, and become one of a core of national institutions that would be able to resist the centrifugal forces endangering the American experiment.

During the early national period, leaders of the latter persuasion, both inside and outside the officer corps, attempted on several occasions to build the army into a more effective instrument of national power. These men seldom used the term *profession* and certainly did not grasp all of its modern connotations, but their efforts at reform pointed toward the development of professional characteristics within the amorphous officer corps.

Although it would be inappropriate to rigidly impose a late twentieth-century social science model upon an eighteenth- and early nineteenth-century group, a definition of professionalism, if employed flexibly, may be useful in understanding the direction in which the officer corps would evolve. Allan R. Millett has summarized the basic attributes currently associated with a professional orientation.

> (1) The occupation is a full-time and stable job, serving continuing societal needs; (2) the occupation is regarded as a lifelong calling by the practitioners, who identify themselves personally with their job subculture; (3) the occupation is organized to control performance standards and recruitment; (4) the occupation requires formal, theoretical education; (5) the occupation has a service orientation in which loyalty to standards of competence and loyalty to clients' needs are paramount; and (6) the occupation is granted a great deal of collective autonomy by the society it serves, presumably because the practitioners have proven their high ethical standards and trustworthiness.[1]

An intellectual component is central to a professional orientation: a claim to the exclusive control of a body of specialized knowledge essential to the fulfillment of an important social need. Moreover, a professional culture is in a sense democratic, emphasizing merit—the mastery of the profession's esoteric skills, as defined and certified by one's colleagues—rather than wealth, family, or social class as the primary determinant of status.

Judged by these standards, military leadership in the eighteenth century was at most quasi-professional.[2] For the aristocrats who dominated the officer corps of European armies, military service was an avocation rather than a self-contained and exclusive career, an extension of the status that came with noble birth. Although many officers pursued military study as individuals, formal educational institutions were few and of limited influence. Most commanders acquired their skills through practical experience in the camp and on campaign. Politics merged with military life, as aristocratic officers used court and family connections to promote both service and nonservice interests. Intuitive genius and breeding, traits presumably monopolized by the aristocracy, remained the central components of the concept of officership.

There were exceptions. During the long rebellion against Spain in the sixteenth and early seventeenth centuries, the Dutch army developed distinctly professional characteristics: a permanent, salaried officer corps; the separation of the army from the civil branches of the government, and the officer corps from a generalized aristocratic milieu; and a conception of military leadership as the mastery of a body of rational, systematically organized principles. During the seventeenth and eighteenth centuries, officers in the technical branches of certain European armies, the artillery and engineers, emphasized the scientific nature of their specialties and the need for formal education. In the French army under Louis XIV, and to a lesser extent in other armies, military bureaucracy became increasingly centralized and assumed an impressive degree of internal specialization and efficiency. However, none of these exceptions disproved the rule. The Dutch reforms resulted from unique circumstances, especially the ascendancy of the urban merchant class with its aversion to military service and its relative immunity from aristocratic pretensions. The technical services, staffed in large part by bourgeois officers, remained separate from the more socially prestigious branches of European armies—the infantry and cavalry. Despite the rationalization of logistics and support, the aristocratic ethos pervaded the combat arms of most military elites in the late eighteenth century, at least before the outbreak of the French Revolution.

The United States, of course, did not have a strong feudal legacy or an entrenched aristocracy. While hardly a microcosm of the larger society, the leadership of the early army was recruited from a relatively broad social spectrum. Moreover, many leaders accepted in general key aspects of a professional orientation: the desirability of long-term, exclusive service; the need for specialized, if not necessarily formal, study; and the importance of cultivating a service ethic and enforcing internal standards of competence.

In the United States, the principal barrier to military professionalism was not the composition of the officer corps or the persistence of an aristocratic ethos but the general social and political environment. The decentralized, overwhelmingly rural social order of the colonial and revolutionary periods, which was bound together by tenuous lines of communication, did not support a high degree of occupational specialization. Even vocations such as law and medicine, which in Europe had incorporated many features of modern professionalism, remained virtually unorganized in America until the late eighteenth century, left in the hands of part-time practitioners or men who had learned their trade through apprenticeship. Although professional schools and associations began to appear in the early national period, they remained minimally influential and oriented toward elite clienteles in the coastal cities. When professional men looked beyond their communities, established lines of communication tied them to their transatlantic intellectual peers rather than to the majority of isolated, unorganized practitioners in the hinterland.[3] Although military bureaucracy gave the profession of arms a potential cohesion missing in civilian callings, officers and political leaders interested in military reform faced the special difficulties presented by the prestige of the militia and the widespread suspicion of centralized military institutions.

THE AMERICAN LEGION

The first significant step toward transforming the regular army occurred during the early 1790s with the establishment of the Legion. The humiliating defeats of 1790 and 1791 had left the officer corps shocked and demoralized. The recently formed Second Infantry Regiment, rushed into action before it had been fully organized or given a modicum of training, had been shattered in the 1791 campaign, with seven of its officers dying in combat. Although official investigations cleared them of blame, the army's two highest commanders, Major General Arthur St. Clair and Brevet Brigadier General Josiah Harmar, resigned their commissions under criticism in 1792.[4] Regulars attributed the failures to the indiscipline of the militia and the short-term levies raised in 1791 and to the inadequacy of the supply system, but they began to doubt their own competence. Writing from the frontier late in 1792, a newly commissioned major reported that "the word is here among the regular Troops, that they must be beat on all occasions, & under this impression poor creatures I wish them to keep garrison."[5]

To recoup the prestige of the government and to rescue its western policy, Washington and Knox pushed through Congress a major expansion of the army and searched for a commander capable of reshaping the fragmented frontier units into an effective combat force. With some reluctance, they selected Anthony Wayne, the son of a prosperous farmer and a local leader of southern Pennsylvania. Wayne had won a reputation for pugnacity and dash as a revolutionary officer, especially for his audacious storming of Stony Point, a British stronghold on the Hudson River, in 1779, but he had not prospered after the Revolution. He had gone so deeply into debt that he could not return to Pennsylvania for fear of arrest; then a stint as a Georgia congressman had been cut short by irregularities in his election.[6] In the opinion of some leaders, he was hot-headed, vain, and lacking in sound judgment. However, Washington and Knox knew him to be an aggressive commander and a strict disciplinarian—important qualities in light of the army's recent failures. Moreover, there were equally serious objections to the other candidates. "Chosen as the least of the possible evils," one historian has written, "Wayne turned out to be among the most brilliant appointments in the Federalist era."[7]

Taking command of the bulk of the army on the Ohio River frontier in the early summer of 1792, Wayne set out to build the Legion into a small replica of the Continental Army. His orders continually emphasized discipline and rigid adherence to the details of military administration as established in the Articles of War and Baron von Steuben's regulations. He instituted a rigorous training program, implicitly oriented toward frontier combat. On numerous

Major General Anthony Wayne. (Engraving from *The National Portrait Gallery of Distinguished Americans* [n.p., 1834]; photo courtesy of the State Historical Society of Wisconsin)

occasions, the Legion engaged in elaborate maneuvers that combined the operations of infantry, riflemen, artillery, and dragoons. The goal was to blend the various arms into a self-sustaining field army capable of conducting an arduous wilderness campaign. By demanding constant attention to appearance, by encouraging emulation among the units, and by referring proudly in orders to the "American Legion," Wayne tried to build morale and esprit de corps, while dispelling the legacy of defeat.[8]

The new commander was unimpressed with the officer corps that he inherited, most of whom had scant military knowledge, in his judgment; the veterans in particular were "rathar *rusty* tho' conceited & refractory." Indeed, Wayne considered several senior officers to be incapacitated for command by drunkenness or ignorance. Resolving to reform such men or drive them out of the army, he answered complaints about hard duty with "an Assurance that it will not be lessen'd but rathar increased."[9] He directed regulars to study their profession, quoting the opinion of the Chevalier Folard that war " '*is a trade for the ignorant, and a science for men of genius.*' "[10] Above all, Wayne demanded subordination, attention to military detail, and an undivided commitment to duty. Staunchly Federalist in his politics, he denounced the encroachment of the "rights of man" into military administration and suppressed the traditional individualism of the frontier army, including the tendency for officers to come and go as they pleased and resign when they considered themselves inconvenienced by orders.[11] Although Wayne's stern and abrasive manner earned him the epithet of martinet, even tyrant, he managed to mold the Legion into a reliable combat force that defeated the northwestern Indian confederation in the summer of 1794 and extended federal control over most of the present state of Ohio.

In the end, Wayne's exertions were overwhelmed by the conditions of life in the early army. His goal was to instill the qualities of the Continental Army at its most effective stage—its discipline, spirit, and tactical proficiency. His idea of military leadership did not extend much further than the practical skills and basic standards of conduct prescribed in "the Baron" and the Articles of War. He made no attempt to develop systematic procedures for the education or professional socialization of junior officers, relying as before on the informal pressures of garrison society. In other words, he failed to institutionalize the standards that he tried to establish. Thus, the Legion's cohesion was tenuous at best, dependent on Wayne's personal charisma to overcome the underlying heterogeneity and independence of the officer corps. Bitter personal friction appeared long before the 1794 campaign and intensified after Fallen Timbers, when Brigadier General Wilkinson openly challenged Wayne for the high command. With the end of the Indian war, the army dispersed again into small, semiautonomous garrisons, in which the hold of central military authority was weak. The reduction of 1796 that ended the legionary structure, the death of Wayne late in the same year, and the continuing high attrition rate in the officer corps dissolved what remained of Wayne's influence and left the army once more an amorphous frontier constabulary.

THE ARTILLERISTS AND ENGINEERS

The decline of the Legion did not end Federalist efforts to reform the army. A second attempt of the 1790s, the establishment of the Corps of Artillerists and Engineers, was motivated in part by a broadened conception of military leadership. By the late eighteenth century, European military thinkers had developed a sizable body of knowledge relating to artillery and fortification. Closely tied to Enlightenment rationalism, this thought overlapped with general fields of science and technology: mathematics, civil engineering, architecture, chemistry, and natural philosophy. In contrast to infantry and cavalry tactics, which were relatively simple and essentially manual, mastery of this doctrine required intensive and prolonged study. Beginning in the late seventeenth century, European governments had set up schools for the instruction of officers destined for the technical branches. France, with its vulnerable frontiers and its strong mathematical and scientific tradition, led the way. By the closing years of the Old Regime, the French government had founded a system of technical institutions that produced the best-qualified artillery and engineering officers in Europe: four battalion schools for artillerists and a school for engineers, the École du Genie, located at Mézières. Although the Revolution temporarily disrupted this system, formal military education revived under the Directory and Empire, as France mobilized for continual warfare. The École Polytechnique, founded at Paris in 1795, served as the gateway, because it provided basic theoretical instruction in mathematics and science to young men seeking careers in the technical branches of the army or the civilian Corps of Roads and Bridges. Advanced "schools of practice," most notably the school for artillerists and engineers located at Metz after 1802, offered more specialized training to graduates of the basic school.[12]

Since few Americans of that era had received technical training, the artillery and engineers of the Continental Army had relied heavily on foreign expertise. In 1782, only one of fourteen officers of the Corps of Engineers was an American, and most were graduates of Mézières or other French schools.[13] To remedy this situation, high-ranking officers recommended the establishment of a military academy with a curriculum emphasizing mathematics, military engineering, and artillery. Such proposals were far too ambitious for the Confederation Congress or the tiny peacetime army of the 1780s. Discussions of a national university, however, were common in the postrevolutionary years and frequently mentioned military subjects as part of the proposed course of study. Even Jefferson advocated such a program, though he wished to finance the institution by private contributions rather than by government revenues.[14] The idea that specialized education should be a prerequisite for military leaders, at least for artillerists and engineers, seems to have been widespread in the high circles of the early republic.

In March 1794, Congress responded to the spreading warfare in Europe and to tension with Great Britain over commerce and the northwestern posts by authorizing the construction of fortifications at the major seaports. Again, the administration had to rely on European experts, in this case civilians, to plan and supervise these projects.[15] Federalist leaders were unhappy with this dependence, however, and the act of 9 May 1794, which created the Corps of Artillerists and Engineers, also authorized the purchase of books and equipment, presumably for the technical instruction of the corps.[16] Washington and his second secretary of war, Timothy Pickering, appointed foreigners to high positions in the new organization, intending that they would impart their knowledge to the native-born officers in the middle and lower grades. Lieutenant Colonel Stephen Rochefontaine, commander of the corps, and Major Lewis Tousard were both graduates of French military schools; both had served as volunteers in the Continental Army, fought with the French forces during the slave revolution in Santo Domingo, and emigrated to the United States to escape the French Revolution. Another major, Swiss-born John J. U. Rivardi, was a veteran of the Russian army, and at least two junior officers had experience in the French service.[17] Recognizing the need for "long attention, study, and practice" to develop qualified artillerists and engineers, Pickering tried to concentrate the corps as much as possible at the isolated post of West Point, New York, where the officers would pursue their studies under their foreign commanders.[18]

The Federalist effort to establish a school for artillerists and engineers marked the emergence of an American view of military leadership as a science, to be grasped at least partially through formal study. As with the Legion, however, the experiment fell victim to the prevailing individualism and indiscipline of the officer corps. Cadets and officers at West Point were required to study von Steuben's regulations, work with the available artillery pieces, and, beginning in February 1796, attend lectures twice daily on the theory of fortification, delivered mainly by the foreign officers.[19] Personal disputes, the bane of the early officer corps, erupted almost immediately. Rochefontaine attributed unrest to the intrigues of Tousard, who supposedly coveted his position, to dissatisfaction with his efforts to control staff officers, and to the reluctance of native-born officers to serve under a foreign commander. Rivardi considered Rochefontaine's personality to be a factor, especially his coolness toward the other officers and his inability to enforce consistent discipline.[20] Perhaps a more basic reason was the heterogeneity of the "students," who varied widely in age, rank, experience, and educational background. According to one disillusioned captain, his colleagues were "in many cases the burthensome dependents of their friends, . . . turned into the Army, rather as an asylum than as an academy for improvement or a station of honor."[21]

Whatever the sources, dissension rapidly undermined the school's operations. Officers and cadets refused to attend classes regularly, and discipline deteriorated. In April 1796, a fire, perhaps the result of arson, destroyed the barracks where classes were held, and Rochefontaine fought a bloodless duel with one of his captains. Soon afterwards, a court of inquiry investigated charges against Rochefontaine brought by another captain, Decius Wadsworth. When the administration took no action to remove the Frenchman, Wadsworth unsuccessfully challenged him to a duel, then resigned his commission and debated the code of honor with Rochefontaine in the press.[22] By that time, instruction had come to a standstill, and the War Department eventually dispersed most of the artillerists and engineers to the coastal fortifications. While teaching seems to have continued sporadically at West Point during the late 1790s, President Adams was suspicious of the foreign officers and gave the project little support. In 1798, after another court of inquiry, the administration dismissed Rochefontaine for financial irregularities.[23] Writing to Henry Knox in August of that year, former secretary of war Timothy Pickering lamented that the Corps of Artillerists and Engineers had made little progress in artillery skills and none at all in engineering during its three years of organized existence: "We have been totally disappointed in our expectations of finding *instructors* in the foreign officers appointed to command the regiment and battalions with that special view."[24]

ALEXANDER HAMILTON AND THE ARMY

A third and far more ambitious attempt at military reform occurred during the Quasi-war with France. Although Congress expanded the army in 1798 mainly as a response to foreign crisis, High Federalist leaders hoped that the increase would be permanent and that a full-fledged standing army would emerge, capable of defending American interests on the international stage and counteracting internal dissent. Washington, appointed lieutenant general in July 1798, nominally commanded the army until his death in December of the following year, and he did participate in organizing the new regiments. He rarely left Mount Vernon, however, and intended to assume active control only in case of an invasion or a formal declaration of war. The administration divided the actual command between major generals Alexander Hamilton and Charles Cotesworth Pinckney, and Hamilton, as inspector general of the army, quickly emerged as the dominant figure. Since his days in the Continental Army, the New Yorker had longed for martial fame. He had at times dreamed of American expansion into the ramshackle Spanish empire to the south. He may also have seen in the command of the army a source of patronage and a secure personal base free from the uncertainties of elective politics.[25] Whatever his motives, Hamilton took his military role seriously and labored to build the army into a permanent, European-style regular force.

Hamilton set up his headquarters at his residence in New York City. A man of immense intellectual energy, he continued to practice law while handling an enormous volume of military correspondence. He kept in daily contact with Adams's secretary of war, James McHenry, a political supporter whom he effectively controlled until Adams dismissed McHenry for disloyalty in the spring of 1800. He also corresponded frequently with generals Washington, Wilkinson, and Pinckney, with Federalist political leaders, and with regimental commanders and other officers of both the basic establishment and the additional army. His interests ranged across the spectrum of military affairs: officers' appointments and promotions, recruiting, pay and supply matters, the organization of regiments and staff departments, military education, discipline and military justice, uniforms, tactics, the location of posts, and the distribution of the army. No figure of the early national period tried to revamp the army as thoroughly as did Hamilton between 1798 and 1800.[26]

The central theme of Hamilton's administrative policies was the rationalization of military bureaucracy. In contrast to Wayne, he saw the need to institutionalize standards through formal regulations and an efficient staff organization. He was especially dissatisfied with the supply services, in which the War and Treasury departments shared jurisdiction and a variety of civil and military offices overlapped in function. Early in 1799, Hamilton drafted a bill relating to army organization that McHenry submitted to Congress; it became law on 3 March. Besides establishing a uniform structure for regiments and defining the army pay scale, clothing allowance, and ration, this act created an elaborate staff apparatus. In place of the existing quartermaster general, who had held no military rank, the bill authorized a quartermaster general with the rank of major general—an officer supposedly assigned to the largest field command—

and a number of deputy quartermasters general and brigade quartermasters attached to lesser commands. The pay service was expanded. Most important, the act set up a network of inspection officers who would be appointed by Hamilton: deputy inspectors general, division inspectors, and brigade inspectors. The adjutant general, Brigadier General William North, was to function under Hamilton as an *ex officio* assistant inspector general, and the bill authorized a separate inspector of fortifications to complement the office of inspector of artillery approved the previous year.[27] A second act of March 1799, drafted in part by Hamilton, organized an elaborate medical department to replace the haphazard medical service of the frontier army, to be headed by a physician general.[28]

Hamilton's staff reforms reflect in part his private ambition to build and command a powerful standing army. For the institutional history of the army, however, they have a broader significance, as they represent the first concerted effort to bring symmetry and uniformity to the army's central command structure. The additional inspection officers certainly increased Hamilton's personal influence, but they were also a potential instrument for enforcing standards of leadership and professional conduct within the heterogeneous officer corps. Moreover, Hamilton attempted to define those standards. In circulars and general orders, he issued clear procedures for important areas of military routine: the recruiting service, channels of official correspondence, and pay and supply returns.[29] He carefully described the duties of staff officers and enjoined regimental, battalion, and company commanders to supervise personally the tactical training of their units.[30] Late in 1799, Hamilton embarked on his most extensive project—the compilation of "a good system for the Tactics and police of the different portions of the Army" to replace von Steuben's brief manual. He divided the task among experienced officers, assigning the cavalry system to Major General Pinckney, the artillery system to Major Lewis Tousard, and the regulations for camp and garrison duty to Brigadier General North and Lieutenant Colonel Aaron Ogden. Devoting himself to the infantry tactics, Hamilton consulted European military works and directed officers in the field to conduct experiments concerning the length of the infantryman's pace.[31] Long an advocate of structured military education, Hamilton also pushed for the formation of a military academy. In November 1799, he submitted to McHenry an elaborate proposal for such an institution, modeled on the French system of military schools, and later drafted his ideas into a bill.[32]

If successful, Hamilton's reforms would have converted the officer corps from a disorganized collection of individuals into a cohesive and professionally trained cadre of regulars. They proved too ambitious, however, for either the political climate or the realities of military management at the end of the eighteenth century. One obstacle was Hamilton's own reputation for intrigue; many leaders despised him and opposed any measure associated with his name. Indeed, Republicans distrusted with good reason the entire Federalist military program of the Quasi-war, and even Adams, resentful of Hamilton's challenge to his leadership, eventually withdrew his support.[33] Moreover, Hamilton was too much of a military dilettante to follow through on his own measures. He remained almost continually in New York City, out of direct contact with any sizable body of troops, firing off directives but in no position personally to enforce compliance. Under these circumstances, an efficient staff was essential, but the elaborate staff system that he promoted and Congress authorized never fully came to be. A physician general was appointed, but he apparently saw no active duty. Many other key positions, including the high-ranking quartermaster general and most of the subordinate inspection offices, remained unfilled. Despite a host of proposals and constant pressure on McHenry, Hamilton never rationalized the army's labyrinthine supply service.[34] His bill for a military academy died in Congress, and he failed to complete his overhaul of the army regulations.[35] On 14 May 1800, Congress abolished the additional army, including Hamilton's office of inspector general, ending Federalist hopes of building a European-style standing army.

AN AMERICAN "CORPS DU GENIE"

A less comprehensive but ultimately more successful effort to instill professional standards into the peacetime army occurred during Jefferson's administration: the formation of a separate corps of engineers and the revival of the experiment with formal military education. At the very end of his term in office, when his rivalry with Hamilton was no longer an obstacle, Adams tried to revitalize the tiny school for artillerists and engineers, appointing a civilian mathematics instructor to assist the officers at West Point in teaching the handful of cadets stationed there. Jefferson and his secretary of war, Henry Dearborn, continued this modest program through 1801, though the old disciplinary problems reappeared.[36] The prime catalyst was the passage of the act reducing the army on 16 March 1802, a provision of which converted the former regiments of artillerists and engineers into a regiment of artillerists and a corps of engineers. This act also fixed the headquarters of the corps at West Point, where it was to "constitute a military academy" under the supervision of the highest-ranking engineer officer.[37]

Jefferson's support for this measure has never been adequately explained and on the face appears to contradict his proverbial antimilitarism. In fact, he had expressed opposition to a military school as recently as 1800. Theodore J. Crackel has argued that the reinstatement of military training at West Point was part of a "chaste reformation" of the military establishment—an attempt to weaken the Federalist hold on the officer corps and instill republican values. In his view, the administration favored members of Republican families in cadet appointments and saw West Point as a means to open higher education to all classes, thus breaking the traditional domination of public office by the "better sort."[38] Appealing as it sounds, this interpretation must rest on speculation, since Jefferson seems to have made little mention of the military school in his public or private correspondence. Indeed, the failure of the administration to seek geographical balance in cadet appointments—three-quarters of the pre–War of 1812 graduates had been appointed from New York or New England—implies strongly that the Republicans considered the school to be of little special consequence. To the extent that Jefferson thought at all about West Point, he probably viewed it in the context of his military policy of passive defense—a means to train engineering and artillery officers to build and man the coastal fortifications. He had long favored military instruction as part of a general university curriculum; almost certainly, his earlier resistance to a military academy had stemmed less from an ideological rejection of formal military education than from the proposed school's association with Hamilton and the hated Federalist military program of the Quasi-war.[39]

Whatever the motives that led to its formation, the direction of the school fell mainly to the officers of the Corps of Engineers, nearly all of whom were Federalists. In 1802, the administration selected Major Jonathan Williams, the inspector of fortifications, to head the corps. In many respects, Williams's career epitomizes the amateurism of military leadership in the early national period. He was forty-nine years old when first appointed to the regular army in 1801. The son of a well-to-do Boston merchant and grandnephew of Benjamin Franklin, he had spent his adulthood in a variety of pursuits: assistant to Franklin and American purchasing agent in France during the Revolution, Philadelphia merchant, gentleman farmer, judge, and War Department supply agent during the Quasi-war. The most consistent theme of Williams's career was an absorbing interest in science and technology, stimulated by his connection with Franklin and his contacts with French scientists during the revolutionary war. He served for a time as secretary of the American Philosophical Society. Although he had seen some active duty as a militia officer in the suppression of the Whiskey Rebellion, his military interests developed mainly from his scientific activities—especially from a fascination with the theories on fortification of the controversial French engineer, Marc René de Montalem-

Colonel Jonathan Williams, chief engineer and first superintendent of the United States Military Academy. (Courtesy of the State Historical Society of Wisconsin)

bert. During the Quasi-war, Williams had translated French works on fortification and artillery for the use of the War Department.[40]

Military historians have usually associated Williams with the early history of West Point, and he certainly promoted the interests of the little school throughout his ten-year military career. To Williams, however, the military academy was not a primary objective but a means to an end—the development of a cadre of scientific officers for the Corps of Engineers. While in France, he had been deeply impressed by the French military engineers, the Corps du Genie, and he hoped to model the American engineering service on that organization. As an officer, his first and strongest loyalty was always to the Corps of Engineers, and from the start he sought to establish its elite status. As early as May 1802, when his second in command visited the War Department to discuss the future of the military academy, Williams described his vision.

In all your conversations with the Secretary, you will, I am sure, never loose sight of our leading *Star,* which is not a little Mathematical School, but a great National Establishment to turn out Characters which in the course of time shall equal any in Europe. To be merely an Engineer, an inventor, a maker or director of Engineers is one thing, but to be an Officer *du Genie* is another. . . . We must always have it in view that our Officers are to be men of Science, and such as will by their acquirements be entitled to the notice of learned Societies. Could we arrive at such a state before the present peace is disturbed, we may defy foreign Invaders of all nations.[41]

Williams's defense of engineer prerogatives entangled him in perpetual disputes with the line regiments and the War Department. The principal locus of controversy was West Point, where an artillery garrison usually shared the post facilities with the engineers. The artillery commander, often a junior officer, refused to obey the orders of higher-ranking engineers, arguing that the garrison and the school constituted separate commands and that engineers, as staff officers, had no authority outside their branch. Williams and his fellow engineers, on their part, strove mightily to win War Department recognition of their right to command line troops. When Secretary of War Dearborn rejected the engineers' claims in 1803, Williams resigned his commission in protest. He reentered the army two years later on the understanding that the Corps of Engineers would be autonomous within the army.[42] When Congress revised the Articles of War in 1806, Williams used his influence to have a clause inserted that defined the elite position of the corps. "The functions of the engineers being generally confined to the most elevated branch of military science," they were not to engage in duties outside their sphere except by special order of the president. Otherwise, they were to enjoy all the respect due their rank and might be transferred by the president into other branches of the army.[43]

Unwilling to surrender completely his hopes of command, Williams clutched now at the straw of presidential discretion. After the declaration of war in 1812, he convinced the administration to place him in charge of the fortifications in New York harbor. Artillery and infantry officers protested that this arrangement damaged their own chances of promotion, and the War Department quickly suspended Williams's assignment. The chief engineer thereupon resigned for a second time, on this occasion permanently.[44] Inspired by Williams's example, engineer officers continued to press for command powers and additional privileges, and friction between the corps and other branches of the army became a fixture of the nineteenth-century army.[45]

Through the Jefferson and Madison administrations, Williams and other engineers tried to build the tiny military school into the bulwark of an American Corps du Genie. Their model was the French system of military education, especially the École Polytechnique. Instruction focused on mathematics, natural philosophy, engineering, and other subjects closely related to the construction and defense of permanent fortifications. A small but competent faculty developed, including both officers and civilians. Because the cadets varied widely in age and educational background and because they arrived at irregular intervals, West Point authorities were unable to establish a single curriculum or divide the cadets into classes. Consequently, Williams emphasized annual examinations as a way to determine cadets' qualifications for permanent commissions.[46]

Engineers' ambitions for their branch spurred them to political action. After his reappointment in 1805, and perhaps encouraged by renewed public interest in a national university, Williams aggressively pushed legislation that would have expanded the military academy and moved it to Washington or New York City, increased the commissioned personnel of the Corps of Engineers, and added a force of engineering troops—sappers and miners. Isolated at West Point, the school was "like a foundling, barely existing among the mountains, and nurtured at a distance out of sight, and almost unknown to its legitimate parents." His plans, apparently based on Hamilton's proposal of 1800, called for a large institution under the engineers' supervision, training both army and navy cadets as well as civilians who would return to private life and improve the militia.[47] Despite intensive lobbying by Williams and a group of protégés, administration indifference and the opposition of congressional Republicans stalled legislation for years, and Williams eventually gave up his hope of moving the school from West Point.[48] During 1810 and 1811, the need for engineers to work on fortification projects and the academy's uncertain status nearly caused its demise; the War Department appointed few cadets and only a handful remained at West Point.[49] Late in 1811, however, Williams and other high-ranking engineers drafted a revised version of their bill, and on 29 April 1812, buoyed by talk of war, it became law. Besides adding six officers and a company of "bombardiers, sappers, and miners" to the Corps of Engineers, the act more than doubled the size of the West Point faculty and authorized the appointment of up to 250 cadets.[50] From that point on, the military academy and the conception of formal, specialized study as a prerequisite of military leadership were indelible features of the United States Army.

One of Williams's most interesting projects was an outgrowth of his aspirations for the military academy and the Corps of Engineers—the United States Military Philosophical Society.[51] Founded at a meeting of officers and cadets at

West Point on 12 November 1802, Williams patterned this organization on the American Philosophical Society and other associations of amateur scientists. Its official purpose was to promote military science, but the engineers also intended it to publicize their branch and push its interests in Congress. In other words, it was an early prototype of such twentieth-century service support organizations as the Navy League of the United States and the Association of the United States Army. Engineer officers and cadets were members by right; all other candidates, civilian and military, gained admission by election, though Williams seems to have controlled entry personally.[52] Both Jefferson and Madison served as the society's "patron" during their presidencies. The organization acquired a substantial membership and a considerable amount of prestige. A membership list of 1810 contained 215 names, including the president and both surviving former presidents, the vice-president, 3 cabinet members, the chief justice and an associate justice of the United States Supreme Court, 6 state and territorial governors, and 33 current and former congressmen and senators, as well as ambassadors, other federal officials, high-ranking naval and militia officers, and such scientific notables as Robert Fulton and Eli Whitney.[53] All but a few of the meetings occurred at West Point, however, so that most of the active participants were officers of the Corps of Engineers. Despite the impressive credentials of the membership, Williams's efforts to have the society lobby for preferential bills bore little fruit.[54]

The functions of the United States Military Philosophical Society were not entirely political. Its sessions considered a variety of subjects within the vaguely defined area of military science: the design of breech-loading firearms, the effects of cannon fire on infantry, the construction of artillery caissons, and floating batteries for harbor defense. The society sponsored several publications, including Williams's translations of European military works and an adaptation of a British manual on court-martial procedure by Major Alexander Macomb that became the army's standard work on the subject. Captain Zebulon M. Pike dedicated his account of his western explorations to the society.[55] A portion of Williams's collection of technical works became the nucleus of the society's library, which also served the military academy.

The principal intellectual focus of the society was military engineering, especially seacoast fortification. Such an orientation was natural, given the special interests of the Corps of Engineers and the centrality of fortification in contemporary military thought. Williams was by far the organization's most active member, and, through his many reports to the society and the War Department, he emerged as the leading military thinker of the young republic. In particular, he promoted Montalembert's theories of fortress architecture, which emphasized rounded, multiple-tiered masonry works designed to trade broadsides with attacking ships, in place of the low-profile, open-topped bastions of the orthodox Vauban system. Despite some skepticism in the administration, Williams built several fortresses according to Montalembert's principles, and variations of this style came to prevail in the United States after the War of 1812.[56] More broadly, Williams advocated "preparedness." Although a Federalist, he realized that a large standing army was incompatible with the current political climate, so he stressed the vital importance of coastal fortifications and a professionally trained core of regular army officers capable of organizing and commanding militia armies in case of war. While some might object to the expense of this program, it was "a greater economy to have a scientific skeleton of an army always existing which might on short notice be filled up & rendered effective with a celerity that would seem like magic."[57] Needless to say, the Corps of Engineers and the military academy were essential for the development of such a body of men. Although he did not formulate it systematically, Williams's image of the regular army as a cadre for a future mobilization anticipated a major element of nineteenth-century military thought.

It is tempting to find in the Corps of Engineers and its auxiliary institutions the nucleus of a professional culture in the pre–War of 1812 officer corps, but such an imputation would be an exaggeration. As with the stabs at military reform during the Federalist period, the corps drew its focus and energy from a single exceptional individual, in this case Jonathan Williams. The military philosophical society in particular never achieved institutional momentum; it virtually disappeared when Williams left the army in 1803, prospered when he returned, then collapsed altogether after his final resignation in 1812. It held its last meeting in December 1813, with Williams as usual in the chair, admitting new members but agreeing to suspend future sessions.[58] Although the military academy survived, it too relied on Williams's prestige and force of personality to maintain discipline within the student body and to give direction to the faculty. In urging his former chief to reenter the service in 1804, an engineer lieutenant described conditions at West Point: "Everything is going to ruin—morals & knowledge thrive little & courts-martial & flogging prevail. The military academy instead of being the seat of knowledge & the place of application is fast turning into that of ignorance & idleness."[59] Williams revived the academy after his reappointment, but the near collapse of West Point in 1810 and 1811 resulted in part from his long absence on fortification duty. In 1812, it was his tenacious lobbying that achieved the passage of the bill revitalizing the institution.

Another condition limited the impact of Williams's reforms: the elitism of the Corps of Engineers. Chief Engineer Williams was largely responsible for this development, since his primary loyalty was always to the engineers—his cherished Corps du Genie—rather than to the army as a whole. From the start, Williams was determined to guarantee its autonomy and special standing, and his two resignations in support of branch prerogatives made him a martyr in the eyes of his subordinates. Through his personal papers, which consist mainly of correspondence with other military engineers, there runs the constant theme of branch pride. In 1809, Major Alexander Macomb wrote to his chief:

> It is but just now that I begin to perseive the lofty attitude and consequence of the Corps you have the honour to command—The present moment affording me an opportunity of contrasting it with the new Levies [the regiments authorized in 1808]—its science with their ignorance—its regularity with their Bustle and confusion—and above all its harmony and *esprit de corps* with their discontents, their murmurings & their bickerings—and I feel, independently, of what I have always stated, much pride in being associated with a body of men emphatically termed *Le corps du genie*.[60]

Three years later, when Macomb accepted the post of acting adjutant general of the army—a key position in organizing the military establishment for war—Williams criticized him for dishonoring his corps.[61] Not surprisingly, the relationship between the Corps of Engineers and the rest of the army was more often antagonistic than harmonious, a situation that would persist to the end of the century. Even so, the engineers represented a tiny pocket of nascent professionalism, isolated from the scattered and amorphous line branches.

PART TWO

EMERGENCE OF THE AMERICAN MILITARY PROFESSION, 1815–1861

6
THE ERA OF ARMY REFORM, 1815–1821

In March 1824, Hezekiah Niles, the editor of the influential *Niles' Weekly Register*, commented on the performance of John C. Calhoun, who was in his seventh year as James Monroe's secretary of war. He noted that the army appropriation bill, then before Congress, was a model of simplicity and frugality. "Judging by the various reports that all of us have seen from the war department, the order and harmony, regularity and promptitude, punctuality and responsibility, introduced by Mr. *Calhoun* in every branch of the service, has never been rivalled, and perhaps, cannot be excelled—and, it must be recollected, that he brought this system out of chaos." Niles attributed Calhoun's success to a "judicious division of labor" among the various War Department branches, each with a chief and able assistants. The result was an amazingly efficient system of record keeping that allowed the department's business to go on "like clockwork."[1]

Niles focused on the internal administration of the War Department and probably exaggerated Calhoun's personal impact. Nevertheless, he captured the essence of a remarkable series of reforms in the United States military establishment during the post–War of 1812 years. Earlier, the principal characteristics of army life—the high rate of attrition, nonexistent training for young officers, and bitter personal conflicts—had frustrated efforts to instill uniform, professional standards of conduct into the army's leadership, but the postwar years brought managerial reform and consolidation. By the 1820s, the officer corps had achieved an orderly system of recruitment, a well-defined concept of its collective role, effective procedures for the education and professional socialization of young officers, and a high degree of regularity in its internal operations. In fact, both the officer corps and the army as a whole assumed during this period the basic form they would retain into the early twentieth century.

SOURCES OF REFORM

Several conditions, both inside and outside the army, coincided to create a favorable climate for reform. The most tangible was the emergence during the later stages of the War of 1812 of a generation of young officers who identified strongly with military service and who sought to place the army on a more secure and respectable footing. At the start of the conflict, the top ranks of the army had been occupied by older men, in most cases veterans of the Revolution. The average age of the army's general officers at the end of 1812 was fifty-five, and only one general was under forty.[2] Eleven of the fourteen men in this group had fought for American independence, but only two of them—James Wilkinson and Thomas H. Cushing—had served in the regular army between the end of the Revolution and the expansion of 1808. Most of the generals were prominent Republican political figures who had been appointed directly to high rank and who saw military service as merely a temporary extension of their broader leadership in state and national affairs.

Repeated military failures opened the way for the rise of new leaders. By 1814, a number of younger men had managed, through a combination of ability and political influence, to push their way into high command positions. While several of these officers left the service or accepted reduced rank in the postwar cutback, the seven generals on the army register of 1816 represented a complete turnover from the 1812 group. They averaged only thirty-seven years of age, and none had served in the Revolution. Four of the generals were transitional figures—wartime appointees whose careers suggest the amateurism of the early officer corps. Andrew Jackson, a former congressman and senator from Tennessee, and Jacob Brown, a local leader in northern New York, had earned reputations as aggressive militia commanders during the middle stages of the war, which had won them direct appointments as generals in the regular army. Eleazar W. Ripley, a Dartmouth graduate, lawyer, and Republican state legislator from the district of Maine, had entered the army as a lieutenant colonel in one of the new regiments of 1812 and had risen to brigadier general on the basis of his military record. The adjutant and inspector general, Brigadier General Daniel Parker, was an administrator rather than a field commander; also a Dartmouth graduate, he had served as chief clerk of the War Department before his direct appointment to general's rank in 1814.[3]

The most significant development in the army's top leadership was the rise of the other three generals: Alexander Macomb, Edmund P. Gaines, and Winfield Scott. Each was an ambitious professional soldier who had spent his young adulthood in the army and harbored strong ties to military service. Among them they would dominate the army's top command structure through most of the antebellum era. Macomb had been born in Detroit in 1782 but had moved to New York City as a boy.[4] His father, a fur trader and land speculator on a grand scale, had gone bankrupt in the 1790s and spent time in prison for debt. At least partly because of his family's financial troubles, Macomb had entered the army in 1799 as a cornet of light dragoons. Transferring to the Corps of Engineers in 1802, he had become a protégé of Jonathan Williams and a central figure in the organization of the military academy and the construction of the early system of seacoast fortifications. A charming, sociable officer with cosmopolitan tastes, Macomb rose rapidly: to lieutenant colonel and second-ranking engineer officer in 1810; to acting adjutant general of the army in the months before the declaration of war; and to command of an artillery regiment in July 1812. Promoted to brigadier general early in 1814, he commanded the forces on the Lake Champlain frontier that, together with the navy's lake flotilla, checked the British advance from Canada during the following summer of crisis. Few regular officers had more varied experience in both staff and line, and none was more fully committed to a military career. "Having been bread up in the Army & attached to the service from experience as I am," he wrote on one occasion, "I should feel myself like a fish out of the water was I to leave it."[5] He was also the patriarch of the most extensive military family in the United States.

The career of Gaines loosely paralleled that of Macomb.[6] One of thirteen children of a prosperous farmer and local officeholder in eastern Tennessee, Gaines had entered the army as an ensign of infantry during the Quasi-war. Serving mainly at isolated posts on the southwestern frontiers, he had moved gradually up the seniority ladder during the early nineteenth century. His most notable achievement was arresting Aaron Burr and testifying at Burr's treason trial. The War of 1812 opened the way for rapid advancement. In common with Macomb, Gaines served as an adjutant general and a regimental commander before his promotion to brigadier general in 1814. As a combat leader, he became known for his tenacity and aggressiveness, especially for his defense of Fort Erie, on the Niagara frontier, against a superior British force in August 1814. Irascible, jealous of his rights, frequently impetuous and insubordinate in his relations with his superiors, Gaines was also an outspoken proponent of a strong defense system. Throughout his long career, he expressed the conviction that *"we are in service mainly for the purpose of acquiring knowledge & habits of service requisite in a state of war."*[7]

Born in 1786, Scott was the youngest of the generals of 1816.[8] His father, a small planter in Virginia and officer of the Continental Army, had died when he was a child, and he had been raised by his mother in comfortable but not affluent circumstances. He was studying law at the time of the *Chesapeake* affair

Brigadier General Edmund P. Gaines. (Courtesy of the State Historical Society of Wisconsin)

and, excited by talk of war, he solicited a captaincy in one of the regiments raised in 1808. From the start, Scott demonstrated the pomposity and disputatiousness that would characterize the rest of his career, but he also proved to be an effective disciplinarian and a serious student of military subjects. Captured in the disastrous American attack on Queenstown, Upper Canada, in 1812, Scott was exchanged early the following year and performed competently as adjutant general of the northern army during the 1813 campaign.

Brigadier General Winfield Scott. (Courtesy of the State Historical Society of Wisconsin)

Promoted to brigadier general in the spring of 1814, he organized a camp of instruction for the forces on the Niagara frontier, molding them into the most cohesive and disciplined element of the generally disordered wartime army. He commanded a brigade in the Niagara campaign of 1814 and emerged a national hero, though a wound suffered at Lundy's Lane left him inactive for the rest of the war. In contrast to Macomb and Gaines, Scott nurtured strong political ambitions. He matched the other young generals, however, in owing his personal status to military service, and he continually advocated a strong regular army.

Scattered through the middle rungs of the postwar officer corps were scores of eager young officers whose careers resembled those of Scott, Macomb, and Gaines. Some had experience in the tiny constabulary of the Jeffersonian period; more had entered the army in the expansions of 1808 and the War of 1812. Although a small but significant group were graduates of West Point, the great majority had received no formal military education, having learned their trade on the drill field and battleground. As junior officers early in the war, they had experienced the incompetent generalship, logistical breakdowns, and administrative confusion that had repeatedly brought disaster. On the other hand, they recalled with exaggerated pride the army's performance later in the conflict, especially the campaigns in the northern theater in the summer of 1814. To many of these regulars, the supreme moments of the war had been the battles at Chippewa, Lundy's Lane, Fort Erie, and Plattsburgh, in which the army seemed to have proven itself the equal of British regulars. Captain William Jenkins Worth was unique only in the intensity of his elation when he described Lundy's Lane as "the fittest subject for the pen and pencil of the poet and artist that has occurred since the coming of Christ. The roar of twenty pieces of artillery and seven thousand small arms hushed the thundering Niagara to a murmuring rill, which only seemed to moarn the fallen brave, the heroes who had the noble daring to chastise an insolent and mercenary foe."[9]

For these veterans, the campaigns of 1814 had been the defining experience of their young lives. They developed a legend of victory, in which a disciplined core of regulars had reclaimed success from humiliating defeat, rescuing national honor and saving the republic from possible dismemberment. Significantly, the other major achievements of the land war—the reconquest of the Northwest in 1813, the Creek campaign, and Jackson's victory at New Orleans—played little part in this legend; these victories had been largely won by volunteers and militia, and most regulars had nothing but contempt for such troops. Through the war, they had complained of the expense, inefficiency, and indiscipline of citizen-soldiers, blaming them for military failure. In an 1813 report on militia reform, Gaines had expressed the emerging consensus: "*Obedience—implicit obedience* must be learned before men can be said to possess discipline, or be prepared for war. This cannot be learned in the sweet social walks of domestic life. The ordinary opperation of civil affairs, in our beloved country, is as deadly hostile to every principle of military discipline, as a complete military government would be to a democracy."[10] Standing in sharp contrast to earlier operations, the northern campaigns of 1814 had a special meaning for regular officers, reinforcing their conviction that the nation could not afford to rely again on the spontaneous mobilization of its citizenry. Only a relatively large, disciplined regular army, led by experienced officers and possessing well-organized staff services, could prevent a repetition of the confusion and near collapse of 1812 and 1813.

Although less central to their consciousness than their wartime experiences, developments in Europe whetted the professional interests of certain veterans. Most reflective officers were aware that the quarter-century of conflict that climaxed at Waterloo had transformed the conduct of warfare. As early as 1807, Macomb had applied for an assignment to tour the "seat of war," where he hoped to find "every thing appertaining to war in the highest degree of perfection and on a scale which never perhaps again will be exhibited."[11] The Republican policy of economic coercion and the war itself had prevented military men from indulging their professional curiosity before 1815. After the Peace of Ghent, however, over a score of officers toured Europe, either on special assignment or leave, where they mingled with foreign officers, surveyed the allied occupation forces in France, and collected military information. Brigadier General Scott, the highest-ranking officer to make the tour, "saturated himself in military lore," consulting with allied and former French commanders and filling notebooks with his observations.[12] Two army engineers, Major William McRee and Captain Sylvanus Thayer, visited French military schools and purchased books, models, and other materials for use at West Point.[13] As before, officers were ambivalent about this reliance on foreign expertise. Some resented the implication of American inferiority, especially when the government recruited Napoleonic veterans to serve in advisory and instructional positions. For many regulars, however, exposure to the rich military culture across the Atlantic strengthened professional identities, and the incorporation of European practices into the American service was a central goal of military reform after 1815.

Finally, personal circumstances deepened the commitment of many postwar officers to a strong military establishment. Most of the commanders with settled civilian careers had left the army voluntarily in the reduction of 1815. Those officers who sought retention tended to see the service as the most advantageous career available to them—a place where they might achieve status and economic security. Although impossible to measure precisely, a few examples illustrate this pattern. Colonel John E. Wool, the son of a shoemaker, was only six years old when his father died. Before his appointment as captain in 1812, Wool had failed as a storekeeper and had run unsuccessfully for local office in Troy, New York. The war rescued him from obscurity, and he won a reputation for gallantry during the Plattsburgh campaign. Not surprisingly, he chose to stay in the army and eventually rose to major general.[14] Thomas S. Jesup was eight when the death of his father, a landless farmer on the Kentucky frontier, left his family in poverty. He worked as a store clerk before an influential friend obtained for him a second lieutenant's commission in 1808. As a twenty-five-year-old major, he commanded a regiment in the Niagara campaign, and he later served as the administration's confidential agent sent to observe the Hartford Convention. Jesup remained in the postwar army and was appointed to the key staff position of quartermaster general in 1818, an office he held until his death forty-two years later.[15] The youngest of eleven children of a farmer and revolutionary colonel, Josiah H. Vose had applied for a military appointment in 1811, stating that his business in Augusta, Maine, had "not prospered to my mind." Although he rose to major and fought in the Niagara campaign, his financial situation had not improved by 1815: "I am destitute of property, have a young family dependent entirely on me for support, and my prospects (if obliged to retire from service) [are] very gloomy indeed." He accepted a loss of rank to stay in the service and was a regimental commander at the time of his death in 1845.[16]

Thus the War of 1812 produced a significant number of young officers who, because of their wartime experiences, their contacts with Europe, and their personal circumstances, identified strongly with military life. These men did not constitute a unified professional cadre: They feuded among themselves, dabbled as before in politics and business, and had for the most part no formal military education. Nevertheless, they carried out of the conflict a pride in their wartime accomplishments and an enthusiasm for military concerns. Although they rarely developed their ideas systematically, they shared a basic conviction that the nation should have a respectable, well-organized regular army, dedicated to preparing for a future contest with a European power. In the years that followed, this War of 1812 generation would provide the driving force behind both army reform and the incorporation of professional standards into the officer corps.

If the original impetus for military reform was internal, it coincided with favorable conditions in the larger society. A major cultural theme of the postwar years was nationalism—an ebullient pride in American accomplishments shored up by an illusion of national unity. Indeed, the political system more nearly approached consensus during this period than at any other time in the nation's history. The Federalist party, long in decline, added the taint of disloyalty to its other liabilities by its opposition to the War of 1812; it faded from organized existence after the election of 1816, leaving the Republicans as the only party on the national level. In this "warm, beneficent climate, eminently suited to the shedding of inconvenient creeds," Republican leaders pushed further along the course begun with the embargo and the military buildup of 1808—away from their traditional doctrine of states' rights and strict constructionism toward neo-Federalist policies of active government. In 1816, Congress reestablished the national bank and approved the republic's first protective tariff. Only Madison's veto on constitutional grounds thwarted a bill the following year to establish a federal fund for internal improvements.[17]

The surge of postwar nationalism benefited the army. The Madison administration favored a military much larger than the tiny Jeffersonian force. On 22 February 1815, Acting Secretary of War James Monroe submitted to Congress a proposal for a peacetime regular army. In his opinion, the war had given the United States "a Character and a rank among other nations which we did not enjoy before.... We cannot go back. The spirit of the nation forbids it." To preserve America's new status and to deal with continuing grievances with Great Britain and Spain, an army of 20,000 officers and men was necessary. Significantly, Monroe did not mention the army's constabulary role, stressing instead preparation for a conflict with a major power. The peacetime force should build and occupy permanent fortifications and retain elements of all the combat arms; in that way, "the knowledge which has been acquired in the science of war may be preserved and improved."[18] Less convinced than the administration of the dangers of foreign war, Congress reduced the army in March 1815 to an authorized level of 12,383 officers and men.[19] This force was nearly four times the size of the pre-1808 army, however, and the act represented a key reorientation of military policy because it implied that the regular army rather than the militia must be the nation's first line of defense.

The army continued to enjoy a relatively high level of support through the early years of Monroe's administration. Monroe reiterated the points of his 1815 report in his first inaugural address.[20] In October 1817, he appointed John C. Calhoun to be his secretary of war. Later the nation's leading exponent of states' rights, Calhoun had been a War Hawk in 1812 and was a strong nationalist at this stage of his career. Intensely ambitious, he saw the War Department as a stepping-stone to the presidency. Calhoun, who remained in Monroe's cabinet until 1825, proved to be one of the most influential secretaries of war of the nineteenth century; his impact on the military establishment was similar to Hamilton's on the Treasury Department a generation earlier. Calhoun's views on military policy and organization paralleled those of the army's War of 1812 generation, and he served as a conduit for the emerging professionalism of the officer corps. As might be expected, he was popular within the army, and many regulars endorsed his political career.[21]

Postwar nationalism was a temporary phenomenon and was fading by

1819. A final condition conducive to military reform was more subtle but in the long run was probably more significant. A great economic boom gained momentum after 1815 and continued, with minor setbacks, through the century. The central dynamic of American history in the antebellum period, economic growth took a number of interrelated forms: the construction of a network of internal transportation routes; the massive movement of population into the trans-Appalachian West; the acceleration of immigration from Europe; the rise of commercial cities throughout the country; and the early stages of industrialization.[22] The economic boom fundamentally undermined the relatively stable social order inherited from the late colonial and early national periods, in which power had resided in tightly knit local elites united by informal ties of kinship and personal friendship and exercising control through habits of deference. Population mobility and expanding economic opportunities disrupted traditional relationships and encouraged a powerful tendency toward "democracy," principally defined as the removal of artificial barriers to the fulfillment of individual aspirations. By the 1820s, and in some cases earlier, institutions as divergent as the Masonic Order, the Bank of the United States, the caucus system for nominating political candidates, chartered transportation companies, and formal licensing associations in law and medicine were coming under attack as aristocratic monopolies that denied the common man his chance to rise. This egalitarian wave was more rhetorical than substantive; commercial and industrial development concentrated wealth in the entrepreneurial class, greatly expanded the population of propertyless wage earners, and generally widened the gap between rich and poor, especially in the cities. Nevertheless, the dominant characteristics of the decades after 1815 were mobility and institutional flux.[23]

In its extreme form, egalitarian rhetoric made little distinction among institutions, denouncing organizational restraints in general and urging the total liberation of the individual. In practice, however, the era spawned a profusion of institutional forms, created either to perform new functions arising from economic growth and political democratization or to preserve older values of community and order threatened by the same disruptive forces. Political historians have traced the rise during the 1820s and 1830s of the modern, mass-based political party, with its emphasis on rational organization and direct appeals to the voters. Other emerging institutions included the business corporation, the factory, the urban public school system, the secular reform group, and the asylum, which handled poverty, deviance, and mental illness. An equally important development was the increasing size and complexity of such federal agencies as the Post Office Department and the Public Land Office in response to population growth and westward expansion.[24] Although established for widely varying purposes, these institutions differed from the personalized, localistic patterns of eighteenth-century American society. They were specialized in function and organized, in theory at least, along impersonal, bureaucratic lines. They aspired to the ideal of efficiency and operated according to fixed rules and procedures.

The effect of these social and economic forces on the professions was two-sided. The broad democratic sentiment combined with the impulse of individual aspiration within the professions themselves to produce attacks on the monopolistic practices of state professional associations. After 1830 in particular, most states eliminated formal licensing requirements in law and medicine, and beleaguered professional men complained bitterly of a decline in standards. On the other hand, the spread of internal communication gradually eroded the pervasive localism of the earlier social order and encouraged occupational specialization within the society as a whole. Formerly isolated in their communities or compelled to look to Europe for inspiration, physicians, lawyers, and other professional men began to identify with national professional cultures. In most professions after 1815, journals, schools, and voluntary societies spread; by the 1840s, several professions were taking the first tentative steps toward national organization.[25]

Thus, the War of 1812 generation of officers found a social climate potentially conducive to military reform and institutional consolidation. In the short run, the postwar spirit of nationalism and the neo-Federalist orientation of the Republican party provided temporary political support for certain programs. Although not evident until the 1820s and 1830s, the currents of economic and social change in nineteenth-century America encouraged occupational specialization, group consciousness, and impersonal, bureaucratic institutional forms. As both a bureaucracy and a nascent profession, the army officer corps was bound to be affected by these trends.

A NEW MODELED ARMY

There were several threads to postwar army reform, one of which was organizational: the development of a permanent staff system. During the war, the army's logistical and support branches had been an uncoordinated jumble of offices, overlapping in jurisdiction and lacking clear procedures. Staff departments had varied widely in structure: Some had headquarters in Washington, some had chiefs stationed at other locations or with field commands, and some had no central headquarters at all. According to Chief Engineer Joseph G. Swift, who tried unsuccessfully to establish his headquarters at the capital, the Madison administration had "an impression that having a military staff at Washington would be placing a personal influence there not congenial with our institutions."[26] The act reducing the army in 1815 made no specific provision for any staff departments other than the Corps of Engineers.[27] Staff functions were to be performed by officers attached to the brigades or regiments, in many cases on temporary assignment from the line. The administration allowed several staff departments to continue through 1815 by executive arrangement; then an act of 24 April 1816 revived most of the wartime staff organization.[28] The problems of decentralization persisted, however, and such important branches as the quartermaster and medical services lacked departmental headquarters.

From the start of his tenure as secretary of war, Calhoun sought to rationalize the army's central bureaucracy. Drawing on the advice of experienced officers, he began to concentrate all staff operations in Washington, under the direct supervision of the War Department. In 1817, only three high-ranking staff officers were residing at the capital: the adjutant and inspector general, the paymaster general, and the chief of ordnance. Calhoun now fixed the headquarters of the Corps of Engineers in Washington and placed the army's six topographical engineers under the chief engineer. An act of 14 April 1818, sponsored by the War Department, added three more positions to this nucleus of officers: a quartermaster general with the rank of brigadier general, a surgeon general, and a commissary general of subsistence, the last heading a new department charged with procuring army rations.[29] To these and other staff offices, Calhoun appointed young and energetic veterans of the War of 1812, and he had them compile formal codes of regulations for their departments. Most branches developed relatively permanent cadres of officers who spent the greater part of their careers in administrative and technical duties. The result was the bureau system, or nineteenth-century General Staff: a collection of small bureaucracies—ordnance, medical, pay, quartermaster, engineering, subsistence, adjutant and inspector general (after 1821, adjutant general)—headquartered at Washington and responsible for the army's logistical and personnel administration. This arrangement, largely complete by 1820, survived without major change until the early years of the twentieth century and brought an unprecedented symmetry to the traditional labyrinth of army administration.

In all areas of the military establishment, the postwar years witnessed quiet trends toward uniform, depersonalized procedures. As adjutant and inspector general, Daniel Parker labored to bring order to the chaotic personnel records left from the rapid wartime buildup. Constantly stressing the need for system, he required commanders to submit prompt and complete returns of the troops and property under their control. "The want of regular paper during the War," he wrote a subordinate, "makes me a little tenacious of having the officers drilled at the bureau as well as in the field."[30] Similarly, artillery and ordnance officers called for uniformity in the design of cannon and other types of materiel. Before and during the war, this equipment had followed a hodgepodge of British, French, and American styles, largely determined by officers' personal inclinations. According to Colonel Decius Wadsworth, the chief of ordnance, the result was "a much greater Number of Calibers than is necessary, with an endless Variety of Patterns in Guns of the same Caliber."[31] At his request, Calhoun established a board of officers in 1818 to consider the problem; they recommended adoption of a French system for the design of field guns and carriages. Although Wadsworth preferred a system of his own adapted from the British artillery, Calhoun approved the board's report, and the Ordnance Department gradually brought a degree of conformity to the army's heavy weaponry.[32] At the same time, ordnance officers embarked on a long-term effort to standardize the production of small arms at the national armories, a project that made them pioneers of industrial technology in the United States.[33]

An especially important feature of the drive for uniform procedures was the compilation of military manuals. Before the War of 1812, Baron von Steuben's "Blue Book" had been the only official guide for both infantry tactics and military administration. Since it was based on practices in the army of Frederick the Great, officers claimed that military developments during the Napoleonic wars had rendered it obsolete as a tactical handbook.[34] During the Quasi-war, Hamilton had begun to draft a new system but had not completed it. The buildup of the army before the War of 1812 renewed interest in the problem. In March 1812, the War Department adopted a manual on infantry tactics by Colonel Alexander Smyth, which was a condensation and adaptation of the French regulations of 1791, the basic infantry system of the Napoleonic armies.[35] A year later, the administration replaced Smyth's work with another version of the same French system by Colonel William Duane, the Philadelphia soldier-journalist.[36] Neither Smyth nor Duane had a high reputation within the army, however, and many field commanders resisted using their manuals. Some officers continued to rely on von Steuben, some dutifully followed Smyth or Duane, and some devised their own tactical precepts.[37] In a belated move to end the confusion, the War Department established a board of experienced officers in December 1814, headed by Winfield Scott, to modify yet another translation of the French infantry tactics for the American service. Completed early in 1815 and revised under Scott's direction in 1824 and 1835, this manual remained the army's basic infantry system into the 1850s, providing officers with a uniform guide for conducting drill and maneuvers.[38]

Even more confusing than the infantry tactics was the state of the army's general regulations. Besides the brief treatment of military administration in von Steuben's work, general orders had elaborated on such matters since the 1790s, but the War Department had not organized these orders into a coherent framework or made them readily available to the officer corps. Responding to a call from Congress, Secretary of War John Armstrong approved a set of regulations in 1813, which mainly described the rank and pay structures, the functions of different staff departments, recruiting procedures, and the uniforms of the various branches. These were published together with the Articles of War and some congressional statutes on army organization in 1814, and subsequent editions appeared during the postwar years.[39]

A stopgap measure, this guide left many subjects uncovered. In September 1818, Brigadier General Scott offered to compile a more complete and integrated version based on his study of the British and French systems.[40] Calhoun assigned him the task, and Congress approved the completed work in 1820. Scott's regulations treated all details of discipline and administration: rank and command, military honors, dress, returns and reports, the organization and administration of geographical commands and posts, and the functioning of an army in camp and on campaign. The regulations of the staff departments, assembled by their chiefs, were included in the manual, as were the Articles of War.[41] For the first time, officers could readily find the correct procedure for each form of duty. Because of a controversy over a provision concerning officers' transfers, Congress revoked its approval of the regulations in 1822.[42] However, the Monroe administration continued them by executive order, and, occasionally revised and expanded, they became a fixture of the nineteenth-century army.

Another significant aspect of postwar reform was the improvement of military education. Although the act of 29 April 1812 had insured the survival of the military academy, quarreling and administrative confusion had continued to plague the school into the postwar years. The War Department did not enforce the provision of the 1812 law that limited admission to youths between the ages of fourteen and twenty-one, and cadets continued to range widely in age and educational preparation. Since there was no uniform curriculum or academic calendar, cadets arrived at the academy at irregular intervals and graduated haphazardly, some after a few months training, others after five years or more at West Point. Most seriously, the faculty clashed with Captain Alden Partridge, the engineer officer who headed the academy in the absence of the chief engineer and who became the permanent superintendent in 1815. In part, tension arose from Partridge's dogmatic, overbearing manner, but it also reflected different ideas about the role of West Point: Partridge viewed it as a strictly military institution, while several of the civilian professors hoped to make it into a national scientific university. Dissension kept the academy in continual turmoil. Faculty charges led to a court of inquiry into Partridge's conduct in 1816, and Partridge later placed the entire academic staff under military arrest.[43]

After a visit by President Monroe to West Point in the summer of 1817, the administration replaced Partridge with Captain Sylvanus Thayer and gave the new superintendent broad authority to reform the academy's procedures and curriculum. The son of a farmer and artisan of Braintree, Massachusetts, Thayer had developed military interests as a student at Dartmouth College. Graduating in 1807, he attended West Point for a year, then entered the Corps of Engineers. He served on fortification projects before and during the War of 1812 and saw combat on the northern frontier in 1813. He also absorbed the quasi-professional ethos instilled into the corps by Jonathan Williams—that is, the conception of military expertise as a science to be acquired through systematic study. During a two-year mission to France after the war, Thayer studied the French system of military education, especially the organization and curriculum of the prestigious École Polytechnique. A rigid, aloof, rather ascetic bachelor, Thayer devoted his energies almost exclusively to West Point during his sixteen years as superintendent. In contrast to Williams's earlier experience, he had the consistent support of the War Department, especially while Calhoun was secretary. As a result, he was able to transform the military academy, investing it with the basic character that it retains to the present day.[44]

As with other projects undertaken by the War of 1812 generation, Thayer sought to introduce uniform, rationalized procedures. In 1818, the War Department approved a new set of regulations for the academy, largely compiled by Thayer, that were the most comprehensive yet to appear. The superintendent was to be the commander of the academy, responsible directly to the secretary of war; all faculty members, officers assigned to the school, and cadets were subject to his orders. New cadets were to report for their entrance examination at the same time each year and commence their studies as a unified class in the fall. None was to receive an officer's commission before completing the full course of instruction, fixed for the first time at four years in length. The regulations specified a set curriculum, centering on mathematics and engineering, and prescribed two general examinations a year to determine cadets' qualifications for advancement. They also established inspection procedures, which designated the chief engineer as inspector of the academy and autho-

Superintendent Sylvanus Thayer as portrayed by Robert W. Weir, professor of drawing at the United States Military Academy. (Portrait in the West Point Museum, United States Military Academy, West Point; photo courtesy of the State Historical Society of Wisconsin)

rized an annual board of visitors, composed of gentlemen "versed in military and other science," to attend the examinations and report generally on the school's operations.[45] During Thayer's administration, the War Department began to enforce the age qualifications for new cadets. Moreover, the superintendent used his broad command powers to exert control over every aspect of cadet life, readily dismissing cadets who failed to meet his academic and disciplinary standards.⁴⁶ Controversial though they were, Thayer's reforms made the military academy into a model of discipline and order.

The postwar years brought important changes in military policy as well as in administration and education. Although the government had supported the construction of coastal fortifications since 1794, the program had proceeded sporadically. Congress's designation of the sites to be fortified had reflected local pressures, and funding had fluctuated with the level of international tension. The experience of the War of 1812, especially the shocking Chesapeake campaign of 1814, increased public concern about the security of the coastal cities. In November 1816, the administration established a board of engineers to examine the coastline systematically and report the best locations for permanent works.⁴⁷ As part of the postwar effort to incorporate European standards, the War Department recruited a former Napoleonic military engineer, Simon Bernard, to serve on the board, granting him the rank and pay of a brigadier general. His appointment rankled the pride of the American engineers, who considered it a poor reflection on both their branch and the military academy. When Calhoun supported the Frenchman, two senior engineer officers, Colonel Joseph G. Swift and Lieutenant Colonel William McRee, followed the earlier example of Jonathan Williams by resigning in protest.⁴⁸

The Board of Engineers made extensive surveys of the nation's harbors. Early in 1821, it summarized its preliminary work and described for the first time an integrated, systematic plan for defense against seaborne attack. An adequate defense should consist of four interdependent features: a navy, coastal fortifications, a network of internal transportation routes, and a regular army supplemented by a well-organized militia. The report earmarked several harbors as naval bases and "rendezvous" for the American fleet and recommended an extensive program of permanent fortifications in order to defend these locations and the major port cities, deprive the enemy of bases on the coastline, and provide havens for the American merchant marine. In wartime, these works would be manned by militia with a stiffening of regulars. Once fortifications had secured the coastline, the government could concentrate on expanding the navy, and future wars would be fought primarily on the seas.⁴⁹ In 1826, the board submitted a longer version of this report, which included provisions for the defense of the recently acquired Floridas.⁵⁰ Although these documents marked no dramatic break with the past, they represented the first systematic analysis of the general problem of national defense undertaken by a professional institution in the nation's history. The government gradually implemented the board's program, and, periodically revised and extended, it remained the basis of defense planning into the late nineteenth century. For certain branches of the army, particularly the Corps of Engineers and Ordnance

Department, the fortification program supplied a clearly defined mission and an incentive to professional development.

Ironically, postwar military reform culminated in 1821, when Congress approved a major reduction of the army. The House had considered a cutback as early as 1818, but a report by Calhoun, arguing that the existing force was necessary to garrison the extended frontiers, had prevented action at that time.[51] By 1819 and 1820, however, antimilitarism was on the rise in Congress. The pending acquisition of the Spanish Floridas seemed to remove any immediate prospect of foreign war. The depression of 1819 and the acrimonious controversy over the admission of Missouri as a slave state eroded the aura of national unity that had prevailed during the initial postwar years. Political rivalry between Calhoun and Secretary of the Treasury William H. Crawford, both hoping to succeed Monroe in 1824, undermined the army's political support. To deflect attention from the Treasury and to embarrass Calhoun, Crawford's congressional supporters sponsored a series of investigations into the War Department and called for cuts in military expenditures. In May 1820, the House directed Calhoun to report a plan for reducing the army's enlisted strength from its authorized postwar level of 11,709 to 6,000.[52]

Calhoun thereupon requested the advice of his generals and their responses plainly expressed the views of the War of 1812 generation on the purpose and organization of the regular army. The generals were virtually unanimous in opposing a cutback.[53] The numerous coastal fortifications, the long and vaguely defined land frontiers, and the "centrifugal" character of the American population convinced Winfield Scott that no reduction could be made without endangering national security. Jacob Brown feared intervention in the Western Hemisphere by the reactionary Holy Alliance. Recalling the early years of the War of 1812, he and other commanders argued that the army's principal function should be preparation for a future war. "Military experience," wrote Brown, "is too laborious & tedious of acquisition to be sacrificed without urgent necessity when once attained." In the opinion of Edmund P. Gaines, "Everything . . . connected with the organization of the army should be strictly applicable to a state of War,—and whatever is found to be otherwise, should be rejected." Quartermaster General Thomas S. Jesup warned that popular antimilitarism—"the miserable cant of more miserable demagogues"—might leave the nation unprepared for a future emergency, courting a repetition of past disasters.

If a reduction proved inevitable, the commanders sought a plan that would allow the army to expand quickly and efficiently to a wartime level. Although several suggested cuts in particular staff departments, most considered a proportionately large general staff to be essential, given the logistical problems posed by the vast size of the United States and the need to direct a wartime mobilization. In any case, a reduction would have to come mainly at the expense of the line. The generals' solution was a cadre arrangement, more commonly known as the "skeleton" or "expansible" army plan. This concept was not entirely new to American military thought; Washington had offered a version of it as early as 1783, and Hamilton, Jonathan Williams, and other leaders had revived it periodically in later years.[54] The unanimity with which the generals proposed this idea in 1820, however, suggests that it had been widely discussed within the officer corps. In essence, the plan would reduce the enlisted strength of the infantry and artillery companies but maintain the officer corps at or near its present level and preserve the general organization of the existing establishment. In a crisis, the army could expand rapidly by fleshing out its skeletonized units with recruits. "Enfeebled in numbers, it may still hold the principles of efficiency & strength."[55] Needless to say, the generals' recommendation was in part self-serving; a cadre arrangement would ease the career anxieties of many officers—their fears that an across-the-board cutback would deprive them of their livelihood.

Calhoun incorporated the generals' ideas into his report to the House of Representatives, one of the most famous policy documents in United States military history.[56] He grounded his argument on the principle that the army had a dual function. First, it must perform its traditional constabulary role, garrisoning the coastal fortifications and keeping order on the Indian frontiers. Far more important, however, was its second mission: preparation for a war with a European power. Although the militia might play an auxiliary part in such a conflict—defending fixed fortifications or serving as light troops—it could never stand up to disciplined European armies in the field. "War is an art, to attain perfection in which, much time and experience, particularly for the officers, are necessary." Since only regulars could achieve such expertise, the regular army must replace the militia as the basis of the land defense system.

> The great and leading objects, then, of a military establishment in peace, ought to be to create and perpetuate military skill and experience; so that, at all times, the country may have at its command a body of officers, sufficiently numerous, and well instructed in every branch of duty, both of the line and staff; and the organization of the army ought to be such as to enable the Government, at the commencement of hostilities, to obtain a regular force, adequate to the emergencies of the country, properly organized and prepared for actual service.

In common with the generals, Calhoun proposed that the army have the framework of a much larger force. The two major generals and four brigadiers then on duty would remain, and the staff departments would undergo only slight reductions. Since 1814, the artillery had been organized into a single corps, with the light or horse artillery a separate regiment. Calhoun now wished to merge the light artillery and the Ordnance Department with the Corps of Artillery, retaining most of the officers but reducing the rank and file. Similarly, the eight regiments of infantry and one regiment of riflemen would keep their basic structure, but the enlisted strength of each company would be cut from 76 to 37. By filling these understrength companies with recruits, the government could swell the army in time of crisis from 6,935 officers and men to 11,805—or even to 16,000 if the regimental structure was slightly altered. In contrast to the buildups of 1808 and 1812–1814, there would be no chaotic reorganization and no need to entrust new regiments to inexperienced officers.

The cadre plan encountered strong opposition in the House of Representatives. Supporters of Crawford and other critics of the army warned of the danger to American liberties posed by an army overburdened with officers. As approved on 23 January 1821, the House bill authorized a force of 6,000 men, commanded by a single brigadier general, "with a due proportion of field and company officers, according to the present organization of companies," and a greatly weakened general staff.[57] The Senate responded more favorably to Calhoun's proposal. Early in February, the Committee on Military Affairs reported a substitute for the entire House bill that incorporated a diluted version of the expansible army plan. Despite claims by opponents that it created "an army of officers," an amended version of this bill became law on 2 March 1821.[58] Although the act cut the authorized enlisted strength of the army by over one-half (from 11,709 to 5,586), it reduced the officer corps by only one-fifth (from 680 to 540) and the number of artillery and infantry companies by less than one-third (from 148 to 106). It allowed for a major general, three brigadiers, and a general staff that, though diminished somewhat in size, conformed to the basic structure introduced after 1815. Although the act did not endorse the cadre principle explicitly, it clearly implied that in a future crisis the government would expand the understrength units by adding recruits and rely on the staff departments to conduct the mobilization, as recommended by the generals and Calhoun.

The unofficial adoption of the cadre principle in 1821 completed the revision of American military policy begun with the reduction of 1815. From that point forward, the executive branch and important congressional leaders tended to view the army as both a frontier police force and the nucleus of a large wartime establishment. The cadre concept became a staple topic in discussions of military policy, and on several occasions—1838, 1846, 1850, 1861—the army expanded partly on that basis. President Andrew Jackson expressed the prevailing opinion in his annual message of 1835, when he stated that the army "contains within itself the power of extension to any useful limit, while at the same time it preserves that knowledge, both theoretical and practical, which education and experience alone can give, and which, if not acquired and preserved in time of peace, must be sought under great disadvantage in time of war."[59] Despite continuing praise for the citizen-soldier as the safest defender of a free people, the regular army effectively replaced the militia at the center of the land defense system.

The officer corps was slow to recognize the implications of the act of 1821. As in 1815, the reduction brought an outburst of resentment toward political leaders and a surge of bickering, as military men struggled to retain their commissions. In the years that followed, the typical line commander remained absorbed in the routine tasks of a frontier constabulary: garrison duty, road building, exploration, and Indian relations. For many perceptive officers, however, the cadre principle became a focal point for their developing professionalism. First, it charged the army with an explicit and permanent mission—defense of the nation from outside threat. Second, it suggested an approach to military subjects that was essentially intellectual. At least in its "preparedness" functions, the officer corps had to be an educational institution as well as a force in being—a storehouse of military expertise for use in a future mobilization. Combined with the technical demands of the expanding fortification system, the cadre plan reinforced the conception of formal military education and ongoing professional study as prerequisites of effective military leadership.

Uniformity, order, system—these were the principal themes of military reform after 1815, as they would be in other areas of institutional development during the antebellum era. By the early 1820s, the officer corps had acquired a clear sense of mission, a permanent organizational structure, a means to educate and socialize aspiring professionals, and a high degree of regularity in its routine operations. Leaders such as Wayne, Hamilton, and Williams had tried to implement some of these changes before the War of 1812, but they had failed to overcome the heterogeneity and organizational instability of the army—characteristics rooted in turn in the sprawling, localized social order of the early republic. The postwar transformation succeeded for two reasons. In contrast to earlier efforts, it had the support of many high- and middle-ranking officers whose wartime experiences and career ambitions committed them to military improvements. Moreover, army reform coincided with favorable conditions in the larger society, notably the postwar surge of nationalism, the stimulus of economic development, and the broader trend toward occupational specialization and bureaucratic institutional forms.

7
THE ORGANIZATIONAL SETTING, 1821–1861

The reduction of 1821 was the last important cutback and reorganization of the peacetime army in the nineteenth century. Indeed, the army's basic structure remained remarkably constant for eighty years, until the next major period of military reform following the Spanish-American War. The reduction left the army with an authorized strength of 540 commissioned officers and 5,586 enlisted men. The four artillery and seven infantry regiments garrisoned forty-five posts along the seacoast and inland frontiers, thirty-one of which contained fewer than 100 officers and men.[1] For purposes of administration, the War Department divided the nation into two geographical departments, separated by a line running roughly from the tip of Florida to the western extremity of Lake Superior. A brigadier general commanded each of these departments and reported to the single major general who resided in Washington, D.C., and was designated the commanding general or general-in-chief. The latter office was new in 1821; no general had formally exercised overall command of the army since Washington's nominal service during the Quasi-war. It had originated with the Senate's compromise between the House of Representatives and the Monroe administration on the size of the army. Although the commanding general remained a fixture of nineteeth-century military administration until replaced by the army chief of staff in 1901, his powers and duties and his relationship with the other branches of the military establishment were not clearly defined. During the antebellum era, he served mainly as an adviser to the secretary of war and the president and occasionally as a field commander.[2]

Despite reductions and reorganizations in the General Staff departments, the act of 1821 made no fundamental changes in the bureaucratic structure set up under Calhoun. The central staff consisted of two inspectors general and six support bureaus attached to the War Department: the Adjutant General's

Office, the Quartermaster Department, the Corps of Engineers, the Subsistence Department, the Medical Department, and the Pay Department. Although the Ordnance Department nominally merged with the artillery regiments in 1821, it too had a central office in Washington and functioned in most respects as a seventh staff bureau. A final support branch, the Purchasing Department, was headed by a civilian official—the commissary general of purchases—and was headquartered at Philadelphia, where it procured army clothing and light equipment. The adjutant general and the inspectors general were at least partially answerable to the commanding general, but the other staff departments reported directly to the secretary of war and were virtually autonomous within the army. Line commanders resented this independence, and the result was persistent intraservice friction, a distinct characteristic of nineteenth-century army administration.

The army stayed at this level through the 1820s. Except for brief Indian campaigns in 1823 and 1827, these were years of unaccustomed peace, both domestically and internationally. Because of continued infighting over the presidential succession and the unpopularity of John Quincy Adams's administration, Congress remained indifferent, even hostile, to military programs. Congressional investigations were frequent, and the House considered further reductions of the army in 1822 and 1830, intending to abolish the cadre organization.³ As before, most of the army spent the decade in routine garrison duties. Within the officer corps, however, the new preparedness mission was providing incentive for professional development. The fortification program moved gradually ahead, and the War Department experimented with advanced "schools of practice" for the artillery and infantry, patterned on the French system of military education. Under Monroe and Adams, the army participated increasingly in civil transportation projects. West Point–trained officers surveyed routes for roads and canals and carried out harbor and river improvements.⁴

In sharp contrast to the tranquil 1820s, the next decade was a time of crisis for the small regular army. Most important, the Jackson and Van Buren administrations employed military force to carry out their controversial policy of Indian removal. In the Black Hawk War of 1832, the Creek War of 1836, and the seemingly interminable Second Seminole War of 1835–1842, regulars conducted tedious, frustrating guerrilla campaigns that offered few chances for martial glory and raised disturbing moral questions about their professional role. The army also prepared for possible action against the South Carolina nullification movement in 1832–1833, handled difficult crises on the Canadian and Mexican borders, and continued the military occupation of the Great Plains. Moreover, tensions with France over debts owed Americans from the Napoleonic Wars and with Great Britain over the disputed Maine–New Brunswick boundary renewed interest in the general problem of national defense, especially the state of the coastal fortifications.[5]

Despite egalitarian criticism of the army as a danger to democracy and a seedbed of elitism, the crises of the 1830s brought a significant expansion of the peacetime establishment. The most notable development was the reintroduction of mounted troops, a branch of the service discontinued for reasons of economy in 1815. During the 1820s and early 1830s, regular officers recommended the addition of mounted units, which could serve as the nucleus of a larger wartime force as well as provide mobility in operations against the Plains Indians. Western political leaders also favored such troops, but they preferred a volunteer force to regulars, arguing that it would be less expensive and better suited for frontier warfare. In 1832, the year of the Black Hawk War, Congress established a battalion of mounted rangers, composed of 600 one-year volunteers drawn largely from the West. The War Department held to its preference for regulars, however, and an act of the following year replaced the rangers with a regiment of regular dragoons, thereby installing the mounted service as a permanent feature of the United States Army.[6] The demand for troops rose greatly after 1835 with the outbreak of the Second Seminole War and threats on the northern and southwestern borders. Congress authorized a second regiment of dragoons in 1836. An act of 5 July 1838 established an eighth infantry regiment and expanded the army for the first time according to the cadre plan, adding one company to each artillery regiment and increasing the enlisted strength of an artillery company from fifty-five to seventy-one and an infantry company from fifty-one to ninety.[7]

Paralleling the expansion of the line was a sizable increase in the General Staff. The primary cause was the multiplicity of duties assigned to the bureaus: support for the army's widely dispersed constabulary operations; supervision of ordnance production, coastal fortification, and other preparedness programs; and such quasi-civilian tasks as transportation projects and exploration. For years, military administrators had recommended a separate status for the topographical engineers, a branch growing in importance because of the army's involvement in civil works. When Congress took no action, the Jackson administration removed the ten topographical engineers from the Corps of Engineers in 1831 and organized them into an independent bureau. During the following year, Congress expanded the Medical Department and reestablished the Ordnance Department as a separate branch, consisting of 14 officers and nearly 300 enlisted men, the latter mainly artisans and storekeepers.[8] The general buildup of 1838 brought the greatest increase. By the act of 5 July, the commissioned personnel of the bureaus rose from 150 to 225, or to about one-third of the total officer corps. The Corps of Engineers and the Ordnance Department doubled in size, while the Corps of Topographical Engineers nearly quadrupled. By the last years of Martin Van Buren's administration, the authorized strength of the army stood at 12,539 officers and men, twice the level set in 1821 and the largest authorized peacetime total since the Quasi-war.[9]

The expansion of the army during the 1830s stemmed mainly from its role in enforcing Democratic policies, especially Indian removal. By the early 1840s, this justification was fading. The end of the Second Seminole War in 1842 and the temporary easing of tensions with Great Britain after the negotiation of the Webster-Ashburton Treaty weakened the rationale for a large peacetime army. The prolonged economic depression that began in 1837 led to congressional retrenchment and pressures to cut military expenditures, the biggest segment of the federal budget.[10] Antimilitarism—a key theme of egalitarian political ideology during the Age of Jackson—peaked in the early 1840s, as editors, state legislators, congressmen, and militia leaders denounced the regular army as useless and undemocratic. On several occasions, Congress considered the abolition of West Point. Aside from demoralization within the officer corps, however, the actual impact of these developments was slight. In August 1842, Congress cut the enlisted strength of the line companies to the pre-1838 levels, disbanded the Purchasing Department, and ordered the conversion of the Second Regiment of Dragoons into a less-expensive regiment of foot riflemen.[11] Even so, the dragoons regained their horses in 1844, and Congress added a regiment of mounted riflemen in May 1846 as a way to protect travelers on the Oregon Trail.[12] Whatever the emotional appeal of antimilitary rhetoric, the army performed functions considered important by large segments of the population in an era of militant national expansion—a circumstance that shielded it from the extreme fluctuations of the early national period.

The Mexican War presented the army with its most serious crisis since the War of 1812. As in the expansion of 1838, the government's first response was to increase the army by the cadre system and to supplement this force with volunteers. On 13 May 1846, Congress authorized the president to double the enlisted strength of artillery, infantry, and dragoon companies and called for up to 50,000 twelve-month volunteers. It later added a major general and two brigadiers to the army's command structure. These steps, combined with the formation of the Regiment of Mounted Riflemen, raised the authorized strength of the regular army to 17,812 officers and men—about its practical limit under the cadre plan.[13] Despite a series of victories by Zachary Taylor's forces in Texas and northern Mexico, the Mexican government continued the war, and the Polk administration faced the need to muster more troops for the campaign of 1847. In February, Congress added ten regiments to the regular army—eight of infantry, one of dragoons, and one of voltigeurs (light infantry and riflemen), a force comparable to the additional armies of 1798, 1808, and 1812. The command structure expanded to four major generals and nine brigadiers, and the artillery regiments each acquired two additional companies.[14] The augmented regular force provided the bulk of Winfield Scott's army during his dramatic march to Mexico City in the summer of 1847. Neither Congress nor the administration intended the new regiments to be permanent, however, and in August 1848, after the Treaty of Guadalupe Hidalgo, they were completely disbanded. Congress also reduced the enlisted personnel of the basic establishment and set the number of generals at the prewar level.[15]

The gradual expansion of the army resumed during the 1850s. The occupation of the Mexican Cession and the Oregon Territory meant the further dispersion of the army into small, isolated garrisons. Besides their normal peacetime functions, regulars conducted nearly continual operations against Indian tribes from Puget Sound to the Everglades. Moreover, the army combated filibustering on the Mexican border and in California, attempted to suppress sectional violence in Kansas, and mounted a large-scale expedition in 1857 to strengthen federal jurisdiction over the Mormon settlements of Utah.[16] To meet the demands of frontier service, Congress again implemented the cadre plan in 1850, permitting the president to expand the enlisted strength of companies serving at frontier posts and "remote and distant stations," a description that fit the great majority of companies in the army. A further increase took place in 1855, when Congress added two regiments of cavalry and two of infantry and authorized the appointment of another brigadier general.[17] On the eve of the Civil War, the army had reached the actual strength of 1,108 officers and 15,259 enlisted men. Its ten infantry, four artillery, and five mounted regiments were spread thinly across the trans-Mississippi West and in a chain of small artillery garrisons along the Atlantic Coast. In place of the two geographical departments set up in 1821, the nation was divided into seven departments, headed by brigadier generals or colonels who reported to the Headquarters of the Army. Although no structural changes had occurred in the staff departments since the 1830s, several had grown modestly, and their permanent personnel constituted about a third of the officer corps.[18]

Thus the officer corps of the regular army doubled in size during the forty years after the reduction of 1821. Despite antimilitarist rhetoric, a consensus had evolved in the government concerning the general size and functions of the peacetime establishment. In contrast to the pre–War of 1812 army, the in-

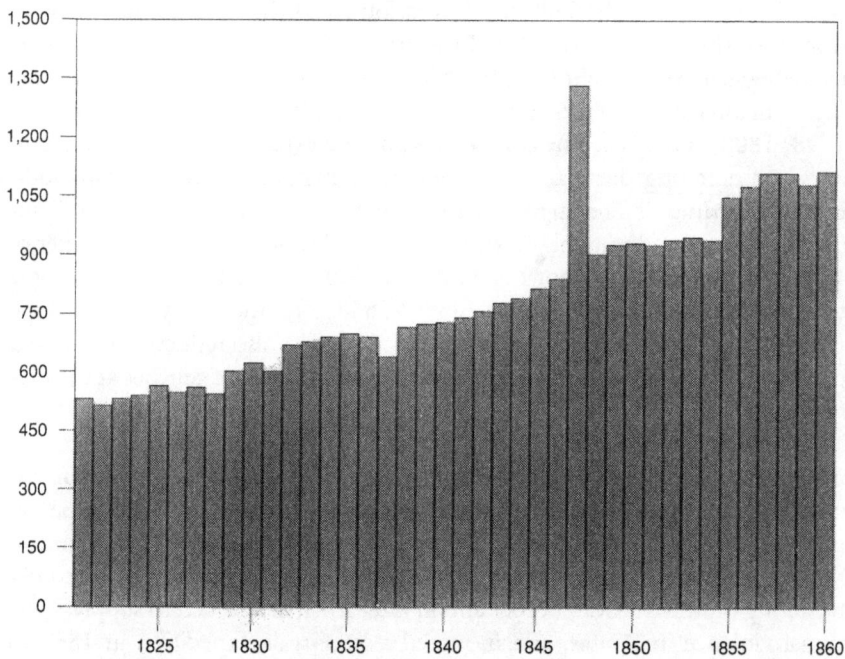

Figure 7.1. Strength of U.S. Army Officer Corps, 1821–1860. *Source*: Francis B. Heitman, comp., *Historical Register and Dictionary of the United States Army* (Washington, D.C.: Government Printing Office, 1903).

crease came gradually and generated no major disruptions of the organization established in 1821 and no massive turnovers of personnel (see Figure 7.1). These conditions provided a stable setting for the most important internal development in the nineteenth-century army—the professional consolidation of the officer corps.

8
THE STABILIZATION OF OFFICER RECRUITMENT

One of the most important administrative developments in the army after 1821 was the regularization of officers' appointments. Before and during the War of 1812, officers had entered the service by a variety of routes and at a variety of levels, and the administration had made little systematic effort to enforce measures of competence. At times, especially during the Quasi-war and the buildup of the army after 1808, political influence had pervaded the selection process. The trend after the War of 1812, however, was toward stricter standards, with access to the corps at least partially controlled by officers themselves. By the late 1830s, few individuals received permanent commissions without first passing some form of competency examination, and the great majority had undergone extended professional training. In this respect, the officer corps differed from the civilian professions during the Age of Jackson, when an egalitarian impulse temporarily eroded licensing procedures.

THE WEST POINT PREDOMINANCE

During the initial postwar years, the Madison and Monroe administrations filled vacancies in the officer corps with a mixture of West Point graduates, citizens, and, to a lesser extent, enlisted men. The War Department favored West Pointers, offering commissions to all graduates of the military academy.[1] The relatively large size of the postwar officer corps, however, and a continuing high turnover rate in the lower grades created far more openings than could be filled by cadets alone. Of the 352 men nominated for lieutenants' commissions between 1817 and 1820, 95 (27 percent) were West Point graduates, 15 (4.2 percent) were enlisted men, and 242 (68.7 percent) were citizens. West Pointers continued to concentrate in the artillery, engineers, and ordnance, making up over one-half of the lieutenants appointed to those branches. Vacancies in the infantry and rifle regiments were handled primarily through direct appointments.[2]

Aside from an effort to maintain geographical balance, the executive branch set no clear standards for appointments from civil life. For several years, the administration drew heavily from the sizable pool of War of 1812 veterans discharged against their will in 1815. Former officers filled most of the positions in 1815 and 1816 and nearly half of those of 1817; after that year, the number of such appointments fell rapidly. Although the War Department occasionally granted commissions to former cadets who had left before graduation, Secretary of War Calhoun tried to enforce the West Point regulation that postponed such appointments until after the graduation of the former cadet's class or, in the case of those dismissed for "idleness, neglect of study, or any species of bad conduct," until five years after that graduation.[3] Candidates continued to seek the support of congressmen and other political sponsors, and many appointees from civil life were members of influential families.

The reduction of the army in 1821 brought a major change in the officer selection process, establishing the military academy as by far the most important gateway to the military profession. On one hand, the contraction of the officer corps, combined in succeeding years with a declining attrition rate in the junior grades, resulted in fewer vacancies each year. On the other hand, the reform of West Point under Sylvanus Thayer increased and then stabilized the size of graduating classes. The average number of graduates each year between 1813 and 1821 was twenty-one; in contrast, the classes of 1822 to 1830 averaged thirty-eight members, and none totaled less than thirty.[4] As a result, graduating cadets could easily fill the available openings in the reduced military establishment. Moreover, the commitment of Calhoun and high-ranking army officers to the new military ideology, with its emphasis on formal professional training as a prerequisite of effective military leadership, led them to favor West Pointers and to reject alternate modes of recruitment.

There resulted a temporary West Point monopoly of military commissions. Throughout the 1820s, the War Department repeatedly stated that all vacancies were reserved for graduating cadets. With the exception of the Pay and Medical departments, only seven nongraduates were given appointments between 1821 and 1831; three of them were former cadets whose classes had graduated, and the others were former officers.[5] Although egalitarian criticism of the military academy and the expansion of the army eroded this monopoly during the 1830s, West Pointers continued to receive most commissions, and their representation in the officer corps rose dramatically: from 14.8 percent in 1817, to 63.8 percent in 1830, to 75.8 percent in 1860 (not including pay and medical officers).[6] By the 1850s, the officer corps of the United States Army was surely one of the world's best-educated military elites and, in terms of training at least, the most homogeneous professional group in American society.

Another development during this period was the emergence of a uniform system of selecting cadets. Before the War of 1812, the secretary of war and high-ranking engineer officers had controlled admissions to the military academy. In the absence of an impartial policy for distributing cadetships, they had favored northeasterners and the relatives of revolutionary and regular army officers, with personal connections weighing heavily. Beginning about 1812, however, the administration broadened the academy's geographical base. Although only 11.2 percent of the graduates between 1802 and 1812 had been southerners, 40.3 percent of the classes of 1815–1821 derived from slaveholding states, and an additional 6.2 percent came from the District of Columbia. Meanwhile, the New England representation fell from 55 percent of the early classes to 17.4 percent of the postwar graduates.[7] Although Calhoun seems to have personally controlled appointments, he relied increasingly on congressional recommendations. His successor as secretary of war, James Barbour, carried the process further, distributing the cadetships among the states on the basis of congressional representation.[8]

By the mid-1830s, the executive branch had transferred control of most cadet appointments to Congress. Secretary of War Joel R. Poinsett explained the system to an applicant's father in 1838. Each congressional district was entitled to one position at the academy, and the appointment "is invariably conferred upon whomever is nominated for it by the representative of that district, whether either or both the representative or the nominee be friend or foe of the administration." If a representative made no choice, the right of appointment passed to the senators of his state. The executive branch controlled only the "general fund"—vacancies over the congressional allotment and any state openings left unfilled by both representatives and senators. These slots usually went to residents of the territories or the District of Columbia or to the sons of army and navy personnel.[9] In 1843, Congress ratified this policy, setting the academy's enrollment at the total number of representatives and territorial delegates with an additional position reserved for the District of Columbia and ten others to be occupied by appointments at large. For the first time, cadets were required to be residents of the districts from which they were nominated.[10] A final rule, introduced by the War Department but occasionally violated, prohibited the appointment of more than one member of a family to West Point.[11]

The cadet appointment policy introduced at this time has survived to the present day, and it influenced the antebellum army in several important ways. Most directly, congressional control of West Point nominations gave Congress a stake in the military academy and helped deflect widespread criticism of the school during the 1830s and 1840s. The appointment system also confirmed the informal trend begun by the Federalists to develop a broad geographical base for the officer corps. The West Point contingent formed a "portrait of Congress," and no section or region dominated its membership.[12] Similarly, the system tended to weaken and divide the political attachments of the officer corps. Earlier, the executive branch had preferred supporters of the party in power, so that the political coloration of the officer corps had reflected that party—or rather, the party dominant in the preceding era, as the effects of the appointments were delayed. Under the new system, cadet appointments continued to be a source of patronage, but it was mainly congressional rather than executive patronage. As a result, the political allegiances that West Point graduates brought to the army resembled the party composition of Congress and presumably of the nation as a whole. This condition contributed to the gradual dissociation of the officer corps from civilian politics.

Finally, the West Point appointment policy strengthened the traditional linkage between the officer corps and local elites. Congressmen of course followed no uniform pattern in selecting cadets. West Point applications frequently mentioned economic hardship and parental death, suggesting that many prospective cadets sought admission for reasons of financial need. Nevertheless, reliance on congressional nominations virtually guaranteed that most of the positions at the military school would be filled by members of "respectable" and politically influential, if not necessarily affluent, families, known personally to the representatives of their districts. This trend accelerated as the rising prestige of West Point transformed cadetships into extremely desirable plums. Competitive admissions procedures were almost unknown before the Civil War. In 1854, Free Soil Representative Gerrit Smith of New York appointed a committee of prominent men from his district to screen applicants, but this was apparently an isolated experiment.[13] Indeed, it was not uncommon for a congressman to nominate his own son or another close relative.

Military authorities were naturally sensitive to charges that the academy was an aristocratic institution, favoring the powerful and wellborn. To counter such criticism, Chief Engineer Joseph G. Totten directed the superintendent in 1842 to collect information "in a quiet & unofficial way" on cadets' family backgrounds. As a result, the academy began keeping a register of the social and economic circumstances of cadets.[14] Newly arrived classes were marched to the office of the post adjutant, informed of the purpose of the register, and questioned about their social origins: their fathers' occupations; their economic situation (i.e., "affluent," "moderate," or "indigent"); whether their parents were living or dead; and whether they were residents of a city, a town, or the country.[15] Not surprisingly, most claimed to be in moderate circumstances, and the War Department used this information to demonstrate the democratic character of the military school. In 1844, for example, the House Committee on Military Affairs reported a table based on the West Point register and urged any remaining skeptics to visit the academy in June, when the new class arrived. "The home-spun clothes, the sun-burnt countenance, the provincial dialect, the hardened hand, and the brawny arm of the new recruit, will attest, beyond the possibility of cavil, that he has been a stranger to the elegancies of the 'drawing room,' and that his paternity is of that great and important 'middle class,' which constitutes the mass, as it does also the pride, the excellence, and the safety of the nation." Despite the committee's claim, the table revealed that 92 (51.7 percent) of the 178 cadets in 1843 whose fathers' occupations had been recorded were the sons of merchants, professional men, army and navy officers, or civil officeholders of the federal or state governments. Only 12 cadets (6.7 percent) were the sons of mechanics.[16]

The executive branch retained direct control of only the "general fund"—the small number of West Point nominations made at large. Officers considered the appointment of their sons to these positions to be a corporate privilege, especially after the act of 1843 made separate allotments for the territories and the District of Columbia. In the opinion of Major General Winfield Scott, such openings "were expressly *designed* for the sons of the Army, Navy & Marine Corps, who could not otherwise receive any of the benefits which the Military Academy is intended to spread throughout the country."[17] Not all administrations accepted the officers' interpretation. In particular, presidents John Tyler and James K. Polk used at-large appointments for patronage purposes, nominating the relatives of prominent political figures; Polk also named two of his nephews to the academy.[18] Scott doggedly pressured the War Department on the subject, however, each year submitting a list of officers' relatives for consideration. His campaign eventually succeeded, as the majority of at-large vacancies during the 1850s went to members of military families.[19] Officers' sons entered the army by other routes as well, and the result was a degree of inbreeding in the officer corps. Even so, nepotism was probably less extensive in the American officer corps than in contemporary European armies, and too limited to produce a self-perpetuating military caste.

Nomination to West Point did not guarantee admission, as the academy tried to maintain at least minimal entrance standards. Before the War of 1812, criteria for admission had been vague, specifying only a rudimentary grasp of writing and arithmetic. Since not even these requirements had been rigidly enforced, new cadets had differed widely in their educational preparation. Because of political pressure, especially from western congressmen who argued that high entrance standards discriminated against their section, formal admission prerequisites did not become significantly more demanding under Thayer. According to the regulations of 1818, new cadets merely had "to read distinctly and pronounce correctly, to write a fair legible hand, and to perform with facility and accuracy the grand rules of arithmetic, both simple and compound, of the rules of reduction, of simple and compound proportion, and also of vulgar and decimal fractions."[20] For the first time, however, the faculty systematically examined new arrivals to determine their readiness for the academy's curriculum. A new cadet, Edward L. Hartz, described the ordeal in 1851. About twenty appointees were brought before the academic board, "the most rigid, cold and merciless looking group of men I ever before beheld." Hartz was especially disheartened when the youth ahead of him failed, but he "spunked up" and passed the test, which consisted of a few simple questions on decimals and a blackboard exercise in parsing a sentence. On the following day, the cadets took a physical examination.[21] Although hardly an awesome barrier, the entrance examination did insure a basic level of competence in the entering classes and probably encouraged congressmen to give some thought to the educational attainments of their nominees.[22]

CITIZENS AND RANKERS

Second in importance to West Point as a method for recruiting officers was the appointment of citizens directly to the army. The revival of this practice in the 1830s arose partly from egalitarian criticism of West Point but mainly from the increased availability of openings when the army expanded. Throughout the "Age of the Common Man," congressmen, state legislators, editors, and militia leaders called for the abolition or the radical reform of the military academy. It was "a school only for the great and the wealthy, where none but the sons or favorites of men possessing power or popularity can be entered."[23] Moreover, it was far too expensive, produced more officers than the army needed, was tyrannical in its governance, and unjustly monopolized military commissions. Western leaders, suspecting that their section was underrepresented in the officer corps, argued that West Pointers were poorly suited for frontier service, especially in the mounted regiments. According to a Kentucky representative in 1836, "a corps of women would be as serviceable against Indians as a corps of West Point graduates."²⁴ The Democratic administrations were themselves ambivalent about the role of the military academy. Although Andrew Jackson and Martin Van Buren praised the effects of the school on the quality of the army, Democratic party ideology rejected formal higher education as a condition for public office, opposed monopolies of any sort, and sought equality of opportunity, unrestricted by birth, wealth, or family influence.²⁵

Nevertheless, the military school managed to retain a good deal of support in Congress and the executive branch. As noted previously, the congressional appointment policy for cadets established strong ties between the academy and political elites throughout the nation. Many congressmen and business leaders saw advantages in a professionally educated officer corps, especially as West Point emerged as the republic's chief source of trained engineers. One historian has suggested that the extent of opposition to the school may be exaggerated and that it stemmed largely from the personal efforts of Alden Partridge, who conducted a lifelong vendetta against West Point after his removal as superintendent in 1817.²⁶ At any rate, the administration generally viewed direct appointments as supplementary to West Point and restricted them to periods of army expansion: the formation of mounted units in 1832–1833, the military buildup of 1836–1839, the Mexican War, and the addition of the four new regiments in 1855. In other words, it was less ideology than the existence of openings that determined the rate of direct appointments to the officer corps.

As in the post–War of 1812 years, the executive branch followed no single pattern in making appointments from civil life. The decision to appoint citizens to the Battalion of Mounted Rangers in 1832 resulted from the irregular character of that unit, which was authorized for only one year, and from the army's lack of experience with the mounted service. To command the new force, Jackson selected Henry Dodge of the Wisconsin region—frontier entrepreneur, Democratic politician, and militia officer in the Black Hawk War. Except for five West Point graduates appointed to the lowest rank, nearly all the positions went to westerners: Seventeen of the total twenty-three came from Missouri, Indiana, and Illinois. When Congress replaced the mounted rangers with a regular regiment of dragoons in 1833, the administration appointed Dodge to be its colonel and divided the subordinate positions between regulars and former rangers.²⁷ Needless to say, promotion-hungry regulars grumbled about the favoritism shown to citizen-soldiers and the West. According to one disgruntled West Pointer, the rangers' claim to dragoon commissions was "a most preposterous presumption—altogether a new & ridiculous species of local internal improvement."²⁸ Nevertheless, the Jackson administration followed a similar procedure in organizing the Second Regiment of Dragoons in 1836, a unit intended for service in Florida. Although a veteran infantry officer, David E. Twiggs, commanded the regiment, thirty of the thirty-four original vacancies were filled by citizens, mainly southerners and westerners.[29]

Martin Van Buren and his influential secretary of war, Joel R. Poinsett, appointed only a handful of citizens to the Eighth Infantry Regiment, established in 1838.[30] Nevertheless, the general buildup of the army in the late 1830s and an exceptionally high officers' resignation rate in 1836 and 1837 temporarily opened more slots than West Point could fill, and the administration renewed the practice of nominating citizens routinely to the existing branches. In 1838, fifteen civilians received commissions in the expanded Corps of Topographical Engineers, though most of these were former officers or cadets who had been employed as civil engineers in the topographical branch.[31] The War Department also named a sizable number of citizens as subalterns in the line regiments.

Although the Van Buren administration undoubtedly paid some attention to the party loyalties of applicants, it made no blatant use of military appointments for patronage purposes. In fact, Secretary of War Poinsett took an important step toward rationalizing the selection process by establishing an examination system for civilian candidates. Applicants certified by the War Department appeared before a board of officers who inquired into their "physical ability, moral character, attainments and general fitness for the service." Specifically, the examination covered basic mathematics, geography, United States history, and the Constitution. Candidates were also required to submit a sample of their handwriting. They were ranked on a point system in which college graduates were awarded extra points; successful candidates received commissions when vacancies occurred. The examination did not test the professional accomplishments of applicants but merely their bearing and general intellectual background—their "capacity to acquire readily a knowledge of the military profession."[32] In connection with the reform of West Point admissions, however, this procedure weakened the direct influence of patronage and gave regulars at least partial control over access to their profession. Excluding the Pay and Medical departments, 102 citizens received military commissions during 1837–1839, 43.4 percent of the total.[33]

The Whig administrations of the early 1840s temporarily suspended the practice of direct appointments. Although Secretary of War John Bell stated his intention in 1841 to take a portion of the officer corps regularly from civil life, the decline in the officer resignation rate after 1837 and the slight contraction of the army in 1842 resulted again in a surplus of West Point graduates.[34]

Under President James K. Polk, however, the commissioning of citizens resumed. One reason was that Polk was no admirer of West Point or the regular army, and he considered many high-ranking officers to be his political opponents. Moreover, the military buildup of 1846–1848—combined with the combat deaths of about 7 percent of the prewar officer corps—again created an exceptional demand for officers. The result was another influx of citizen-soldiers and a politicization of the officer selection process reminiscent of the War of 1812.

Although the Regiment of Mounted Riflemen was a permanent unit intended for duty on the Oregon Trail, Congress approved it in May 1846 in the midst of excitement over the outbreak of war with Mexico. Viewing the legislation as a patronage scheme to reward western Democrats, congressional Whigs tried unsuccessfully to amend it to require the selection of officers from the regular army.[35] According to Polk, the stampede of congressmen seeking appointments for their friends and constituents surpassed "anything of the kind which I have witnessed since I have been President." Although more than one hundred regulars had applied for promotion into the new regiment, the president decided to staff it almost entirely from civil life. Among the motives recorded in his diary were a reluctance to discriminate among officers of equal rank and service, a desire to appoint a majority of westerners to a regiment designed for frontier duty, and the public expectation that the officers "should be selected from citizens."[36] Only two of the original nominees were regulars, though several had been cadets. The bulk of the positions went to Democrats from states west of the Appalachians. As a nod to bipartisanship, Polk did allow Whig senators to select the regiment's major and "three or four lieutenants," and the son of Senator John J. Crittenden, a powerful Kentucky Whig, received a captaincy.[37] Possibly because of the pressure to mobilize for war, the administration did not revive the examination policy for candidates from civil life.

If party loyalties influenced appointments in the mounted riflemen, they permeated the staffing of the temporary "regular" force added in 1847. Polk was convinced by that time that high-ranking Whigs in the army were obstructing the war effort.[38] Moreover, the opposition of congressional Whigs to the war and to territorial annexations led him to discard even the pretense of bipartisanship. Although the president failed in a controversial move to place Senator Thomas Hart Benton in command of the army over the heads of such Whig generals as Winfield Scott and Zachary Taylor, the majority of generalships and field-grade positions in the new force went to Democratic officeholders and party activists. Franklin Pierce, previously a Democratic senator from New Hampshire, was appointed brigadier general, and four former

Democratic congressmen held high regimental rank. Several senior officers had served as Democratic state legislators, and other high commissions went to such men as Lewis Cass, Jr., son of a Democratic senator; Trueman B. Ransom, an unsuccessful Democratic congressional candidate; John H. Savage, a Polk elector in 1844; and Gideon J. Pillow, Polk's former law partner who had helped secure his presidential nomination.[39] Certainly many of the appointees had militia experience, and there were former regulars and cadets scattered through the additional regiments, but only five active-duty army officers received promotions into the new force. The government abolished the ten Mexican War regiments soon after the Treaty of Guadalupe Hidalgo, but about sixty citizens obtained permanent regular commissions in 1847 and 1848, either through direct appointments or transfers from the temporary regiments.[40]

The last influx of citizens before the Civil War occurred in the mid-1850s, when Congress added two regiments of cavalry and two of infantry. President Franklin Pierce and his secretary of war, Jefferson Davis, each had strong connections to the army—Pierce as a Mexican War general and relative of several regulars and Davis as a West Point graduate and former officer. Probably for this reason, they proved more sympathetic than earlier administrations to the aspirations for promotion of regulars who had eagerly awaited the expansion for years. Regulars garnered all sixteen field-grade appointments in the new regiments and a majority of the positions at and below the rank of captain. However, the administration did appoint fifty citizens to the new units in 1855 and nominated others to fill junior vacancies in the older regiments, opened by the accelerated promotion rate among the regulars.[41] Many of the direct appointees were Mexican War veterans, having served in the volunteers or temporary regular forces. As earlier, political influence played a role. Of thirty-nine citizens appointed between 1855 and 1857 whose political allegiances are known, thirty-two (82 percent) were either Democrats themselves or members of Democratic families. Although an active Whig, John Drysdale of St. Augustine, Florida, had the support of local Democrats in his successful quest for a commission, since they believed they could double their majority in the county "if he was out of the way."[42] During this phase, the administration resurrected the use of examining boards to screen prospective officers before issuing permanent commissions.[43]

The sporadic waves of direct appointments prevented the officer corps from becoming a closed corporation of West Point graduates. Excluding the pay and medical officers, approximately one-fifth of the men on the 1860 army register had entered the army directly from civil life. It would be erroneous, however, to view such appointments as a democratizing force that made the officer corps more representative of the larger society. Judging from candidates' application files, political influence was nearly as important in the selection of citizen appointees as it was in the nomination of West Point cadets. Successful candidates tended to be members of socially and politically influential families; in particular, army officers solicited direct appointments for sons denied admission to West Point. In contrast to the bipartisanship intrinsic to cadet appointments, Democratic administrations controlled virtually all direct appointments and tended to favor their own supporters. Thus the contingent of citizen appointees was strongly Democratic in their loyalties. Although the executive branch made an effort to preserve geographical balance, especially in 1837–1839 and 1855–1857, certain new units had a distinct regional character. Such was particularly the case with the dragoon regiments and the mounted riflemen, both staffed disproportionately from the West and South. In other words, the selection of officers from civil life reinforced the social asymmetries of the officer corps in comparison with the general population and introduced political and geographical imbalances not found among West Point graduates because of the congressional appointment system.

The third and by far the least significant method of officer recruitment was the promotion of enlisted men into the officer corps. Although it had rarely accounted for more than a small percentage of officers' appointments, this practice had been fairly common in the early army, especially during the buildup of the 1790s and the closing stages of the War of 1812. During the postwar years, the Madison and Monroe administrations continued to reward an occasional soldier; fifteen enlisted men, mostly sergeants, received commissions between 1816 and 1820.[44] After the reduction of 1821, however, the West Point monopoly entailed a complete suspension of promotions from the ranks. For seventeen years, not a single soldier made the leap from the noncommissioned grades to the officer corps, a phenomenon almost certainly unique among contemporary armies.

Interest in the appointment of enlisted men stirred again during the 1830s and persisted through the following decades. A policy of promoting common soldiers meshed perfectly with the ideology of the Democratic party, which emphasized equality of opportunity for white male citizens. Congressmen, military administrators, and certain officers also favored such appointments to combat a high desertion rate. In their view, the chance for advancement would raise the quality of recruits and lessen the army's dependence on supposedly unreliable immigrants.[45] Finally, enlisted men themselves demanded access to the officer corps. In a petition to Congress in 1837, eighteen current and former noncommissioned officers requested the opportunity to obtain commissions, describing the West Point hegemony as *"contrary to the true spirit* of the constitution of the country, and in opposition to all our republican institutions."⁴⁶

The practical outcome of these proposals was slim. During the expansion of the army in the late 1830s, Secretary of War Poinsett appointed seven sergeants as second lieutenants. When officers complained of this step, the secretary reprimanded them indignantly: "It is foreign to the military character and institution, to exclude from honorable advancement, a gallant soldier, who has earned his promotion by long service, and uniform good conduct."⁴⁷ Poinsett's action was an isolated gesture, however, as there were no more appointments of this type between 1838 and 1847. Moreover, the Mexican War barely cracked the door. On 3 March 1847, Congress authorized the promotion of meritorious noncommissioned officers to the supernumerary rank of brevet second lieutenant, the lowest commissioned grade. Only twenty-nine noncommissioned officers were promoted under this law, and only eleven of these men had been members of the fourteen "old army" regiments in existence before the war.⁴⁸ Sergeant Samuel H. Starr no doubt spoke for many ambitious soldiers when he wrote his wife in 1847: "I have given up the idea of winning that *sword* as I deem it impossible for although I should, unaided and alone *surround* the whole Mexican Army and take them all prisoners of war, Santa Anna included, it would not be deemed a deed worthy of remark, being done as it would be, by a man not a graduate of West-Point."⁴⁹

The most systematic attempt to open the officer corps to enlisted men occurred in 1854. As a way to spur recruiting, Congress restated its earlier support for the promotion of noncommissioned officers to the rank of brevet second lieutenant. In general orders of 4 October 1854, the War Department set up an elaborate system to implement this act. Company commanders were to recommend to their colonels such noncommissioned officers "as, in their opinion, by education, conduct, and service, seem to merit advancement." After a preliminary screening before four-officer regimental boards, qualified candidates would be called before another board, meeting each September in Washington, to be examined in grammar, basic mathematics, geography, United States history, the Constitution, and the "general principles which regulate international intercourse." As with the examination boards that considered direct appointees, this board would rank candidates by a point system, with college graduates receiving a bonus. According to the War Department order, "As a general rule one fourth of the vacancies occurring annually in the Army, will be filled from the noncommissioned grades."⁵⁰ Although this step seemed to institutionalize promotion from the ranks, it had no greater success than earlier efforts to achieve that end. Despite the substantial expansion of the army in 1855, only ten noncommissioned officers and one private received direct appointments into the officer corps during the six years before the Civil War.[51]

It is difficult to explain the reluctance of the government to grant commissions to enlisted men. In this respect, the aristocratic armies of Europe provided more opportunity for advancement than did the army of the world's leading republic, in an age allegedly suffused with egalitarian sentiments.[52] There was little open resistance to the promotion of enlisted men; civilian and military leaders usually professed support for rewarding worthy soldiers. One factor inhibiting promotions from the ranks may have been the unwillingness of company officers to part with their best enlisted men, but probably a more formidable barrier was the prestige of the military academy and its domination of military appointments. High commanders, committed to formal professional education as a prerequisite of military leadership, resisted measures that would dilute the favored position enjoyed by West Point graduates. In May 1847, acting in accordance with the law authorizing the promotion of noncommissioned officers, President Polk decided to grant commissions to a number of soldiers who had distinguished themselves in battle. However, Colonel Roger Jones, the adjutant general of the army, repeatedly refused to submit a list of the vacancies in the officer corps, apparently hoping to stall the appointments until the graduation of the next class of cadets. Only when Polk issued a direct order to Jones, reminding him that he was "by the Constitution commander in chief of the Army," did the veteran officer produce the list.[53] Under ordinary circumstances, therefore, enlisted men had to compete with civilian candidates for the relatively few openings available to nongraduates. Usually poor and lacking formal education or political influence, enlisted men were at a disadvantage in this contest.

Nativism and class prejudice posed other, more subtle obstacles to the appointment of enlisted men. As discussed in chapter 14, a social chasm separated officers from enlisted men in the United States Army, and most officers viewed the rank and file with condescension or even contempt. Sensitive to charges of elitism, officers rarely expressed these opinions publicly, but they resisted accepting rankers on equal terms as "officers and gentlemen." Rodney Glisan, a medical officer during the 1850s and a perceptive observer of army life, described the situation.

> The black sheep in military society are the officers and their families who have been promoted from the ranks. Their generally unrefined, uncultivated and uncongenial manners, make them unwelcome members of the army circle. If they are sensibly disposed, however, these little incongruities gradually wear away. On the other hand, should the new comers, in-

stead of trying to adapt themselves to their new sphere in society, become churlish, they are treated by the other members of the garrison as intruders. Army society is essentially aristocratic.[54]

As a cadet in 1842, George B. McClellan encountered a dashing dragoon sergeant at West Point. This man had reportedly rejected offers of a commission, "saying that other officers who had a better education than his, would never consider him on a par with them & that they would 'but[t] him.' "[55] Officers did not control appointments, of course, but their recommendations were crucial to soldiers seeking advancement. Although the evidence is not conclusive, the reluctance of commanders to push their noncommissioned officers probably thwarted the government's attempt to reform the appointment process during the 1850s.

A closer look at the men who did rise from the ranks suggests that they were not representative of the enlisted personnel as a whole. The army register of 1860 contains the names of thirty-two former soldiers who had received direct appointments from the ranks of the regular army into the officer corps. Twenty-eight of these men have been located on the army's registers of enlistment, which log recruits' preservice employment. While the vast majority of recruits had engaged in manual occupations before entering the army (laborers, artisans, and semiskilled workers), eleven of the future officers (39.2 percent) had been clerks, and two others (7.1 percent) had followed the nonmanual trades of teacher and apothecary.[56] In other words, nearly half of the rankers for whom information is available had pursued occupations that implied the need for some degree of formal education. Personal and political connections influenced the appointments of several men. George L. Willard was a merchant's son who had served as private secretary to Brigadier General Franklin Pierce before his promotion. Caleb Smith, the nephew of the governor of Virginia, and Alexander N. Shipley, a "most respectably connected" citizen of Pennsylvania who had enlisted "in an hour of intoxication while laboring under the influence of the temporary madness therewith," bolstered their applications for promotion with long petitions from their respective state legislatures. Warren L. Lothrop, whose qualifications for promotion included having as a sergeant "kept aloof from the men," was the son of a prosperous farmer, railroad entrepreneur, and Maine state senator.[57] To be sure, there were rankers who had risen on their merits from obscure and humble circumstances. As with appointments from civil life, however, the commissioning of an occasional enlisted man did little to open up the military appointment process.

PAY AND MEDICAL APPOINTMENTS

Two types of military appointment lay outside the normal channels of officer recruitment: the selection of paymasters and medical officers. Although these officers wore uniforms and were subject to military law, they performed highly specialized functions that more closely resembled civilian occupations than traditional military duties, and they were not completely integrated into the chain of command. Before 1821, most pay officers had been regimental officers assigned temporarily to staff duty. The reduction act created a pay department consisting of a paymaster general and fourteen permanent paymasters; by 1860, this bureau had doubled in size. During most of the antebellum period, the executive branch filled openings by a combination of promotions from other branches of the army and direct appointments of civilians. For army officers, such assignments were a mixed blessing. On one hand, paymasters enjoyed the rank and pay of a major—a strong attraction given the usually slow promotion rates in line regiments—and a considerable amount of freedom from unpleasant frontier duty. On the other hand, the government required paymasters to post a sizable bond and limited their tenure to four-year terms, though most were reappointed. Moreover, a pay appointment amounted to a final promotion. Nevertheless, paymasterships were coveted prizes, eagerly sought by both officers and citizens. On 9 January 1849, news arrived in Washington of a paymaster's death, and President Polk had an application for his place within an hour; the following day, a "crowd of applicants" and their supporters descended on his office, including one state's entire congressional delegation.[58] During the 1850s, the executive branch reserved most vacancies for army officers, and the result was a gradual militarization of the Pay Department. By 1860, seventeen of the twenty-eight pay officers (60.7 percent) had prior experience in other branches of the army.[59]

In contrast to pay appointments, political influence was of minor importance in the selection of medical officers. Indeed, during the antebellum period, the army's Medical Department developed an appointment system that served as a model of rationality for other branches of the federal government. Before the War of 1812, the medical service had no central structure, consisting instead of a collection of individual officers attached to separate regiments and garrisons. The War Department had handled medical appointments in the same ad hoc manner as it had handled military appointments in general. Several of the early secretaries of war—James McHenry, Henry Dearborn, and William Eustis—had been physicians and had undoubtedly endeavored to judge the professional attainments of applicants. According to Eustis in 1809, the War Department generally required a candidate to "produce a certificate of the Colledge of Physicians in the State where he resides, or of some other respectable medical Board, that he has passed a competent examination."[60] Few applications included such documents, however, and most medical officers seem to have acquired their training through the apprenticeship method. In 1812, the War Department allowed at least one hospital surgeon to select personally the surgeon's mates who served under him.[61]

Among civilian medical men, however, the trend of the early nineteenth century was toward professional consolidation, represented by the spread of formal medical education and the rise of state professional associations that claimed the right to license practitioners. This growing emphasis on standards of competence influenced the army as well. In 1813, Congress established a hospital department, headed by a physician and surgeon general and giving the medical service a measure of central direction. The War Department also directed some candidates for medical appointment to appear before examining boards, which were composed primarily of senior medical officers at the capital, but this practice lapsed after the reduction of 1815.[62] Departmental regulations of 1825 stipulated that no man was to be appointed an assistant surgeon unless first examined by a medical board, yet this clause too remained for several years a dead letter.[63]

In a general order of 7 July 1832, apparently inspired by reports of incompetence among army medical personnel, the War Department reestablished the examination system. Thereafter, no person was to be appointed or promoted in the medical staff until he had been tested and found qualified by a board of three medical officers. Congress turned this regulation into law in 1834, and it became a permanent feature of the military appointment system.[64] The War Department selected candidates with an eye to geographical balance; these men appeared before a medical board, which met at least once each year at various locations around the country. The examinations lasted two or three days and covered such technical areas as anatomy, surgery, the practice of medicine, pharmacy, medical jurisprudence, and even obstetrics.[65] Viewing medicine as "a *liberal profession,* requiring for its thorough mastery a *liberal general education,*" the medical board also stressed the "classical attainments" of the candidates.[66] Successful applicants were ranked according to merit and commissioned as vacancies opened. The examination was no mere formality: The medical board approved only eight of twenty candidates at Washington in 1834, five of twenty-two at New York City in 1839, eight of nineteen at the same city in 1846, and two of twenty-seven at Richmond in 1858. An officer stated in 1835 that the Medical Department was no longer pestered by requests for appointment "from the dread entertained for this examination."[67] Apparently, the department resisted political pressure to reverse the decisions of the board or to order the reexamination of rejected candidates.[68]

The professional qualifications of medical officers rose in the decades before the Civil War, in part because of the examination system and in part because of the general spread of formal medical education. Although the personnel files of early medical officers do not always describe their schooling, the army register of 1830 contained the names of many who had learned their trade informally, by studying in the offices of established practitioners. By 1860, however, at least 85 of the army's 116 medical officers (73.3 percent) had obtained regular degrees from medical schools, and the actual percentage of educated officers was certainly higher.[69] In the army medical service perhaps more than in any other branch of the federal government, professional credentials had come to replace patronage as the principal criterion for appointment. Ironically, the army succeeded in rationalizing the medical appointment process during the 1830s and 1840s, at the very time that civilian physicians were losing their control of licensing and struggling to preserve the structure of their profession against such unorthodox practices as Thomsonianism and homeopathy.[70]

During the antebellum period, the army developed a relatively permanent system of officer recruitment, which arose from the ongoing trend toward regularity and system in military administration and the army's growing commitment to formal professional education. In the line and in most staff departments, West Point graduates received the vast majority of appointments, with citizens and enlisted men relegated to surplus vacancies that usually occurred during expansions of the army. Similarly, medical commissions went mainly to young men with medical school training. Although political patronage by no means disappeared, several conditions now muted its impact. First, the emphasis on West Point instruction pushed patronage one step away from the commissioning process. Although political influence was essential for most academy appointments, cadets were required to complete the four-year program, rigidly organized to reward "merit," before receiving their second lieutenants' bars. Moreover, the congressional control of cadet appointments guaranteed a broad geographical and political, if not social class, representation in the officer corps. Finally, the increasing use of examinations—for cadets, medical candidates, enlisted men seeking commissions, and, sporadically, applicants from civil life—gave military men at least partial control over entry to their profession.

9
SOCIAL ORIGINS AND CAREER MOTIVATIONS

The standardization of officer recruitment after the War of 1812 stabilized the social composition of the officer corps. Regular army officers did not become a totally homogeneous group, of course, but young men increasingly entered the service from similar backgrounds and with similar expectations. In contrast to the diversity of the early army, the profession of arms now assumed the basic social character that it would retain through the rest of the nineteenth century.

SOCIAL ORIGINS

An analysis of the army registers of 1830 and 1860 reveals the emerging patterns.[1] Contrary to the popular image of the army as a bastion of the southern planter class, the antebellum officer corps was clearly a national institution. Table 9.1 compares the geographical distribution of officers' appointments with the distribution of the white population according to the 1830 and 1860 censuses. Since military appointments came to be linked to congressional representation, the table also lists the regional distribution of the House of Representatives in 1820 and 1848 (the median years of appointment for officers on the two registers). In 1830, the percentages of officers appointed from North and South paralleled almost exactly the sectional distribution of the white population as a whole. Although New England and the old southern states were somewhat overrepresented at the expense of the Northwest and Southwest, the imbalance surely reflected the rapid movement of population westward after the War of 1812. The three-fifths clause of the Constitution allowed the southern states to count a portion of their slaves for purposes of congressional representation, and that gave the South a potential advantage in

TABLE 9.1. Geographical Distribution of Officers on Army Registers of 1830 and 1860

Region	Officers 1830* N	Officers 1830* %	White Population 1830 %	House of Reps. 1820 %	Officers 1860* N	Officers 1860* %	White Population 1860 %	House of Reps. 1848 %
North	380	64.0	65.2	56.7	608	56.0	69.4	60.9
New England	167	28.1	18.3	22.4	171	15.7	11.7	12.9
Mid-Atlantic (N.Y., Pa., N.J.)	186	31.3	33.0	29.9	295	27.2	27.6	27.2
Northwest	27	4.5	13.8	4.3	142	13.1	30.0	20.7
South	212	35.7	34.8	43.3	469	43.2	30.6	39.1
South Atlantic (Del., Md., Va., N.C., S.C., Ga.)	148	24.9	19.7	33.2	273	25.1	12.0	19.8
Southwest	43	7.2	14.8	10.2	152	14.0	18.4	19.4
D.C.	21	3.5	0.2		44	4.1	0.2	
Foreign	2	0.3			9	0.8		
Totals	594				1,086			

Source: Army registers of 1830, 1860; Francis B. Heitman, comp., *Historical Register and Dictionary of the United States Army, from Its Organization, September 29, 1789, to March 2, 1903* (Washington, D.C.: Government Printing Office, 1903).

*Officers whose places of appointment are unknown have been grouped by place of birth.

the distribution of cadet appointments. That this advantage was not yet reflected in the officer corps was probably due to the fact that the congressional appointment policy had only been in effect for a few years. Indeed, the representation of the North in the army of 1830 surpassed its lead in the House of Representatives by a considerable margin.

Northerners continued to outnumber southerners on the army list of 1860, but the South had significantly increased its representation relative to the general population: 43.2 percent of the officers in that year had been appointed from the slave states and the District of Columbia, although those areas held only 30.6 percent of the white population. The sectional distribution of the officer corps more nearly resembled that of the House of Representatives in 1848, however, and the match would be virtually exact if the District of Columbia contingent—a special category that included many sons of government employees—were omitted. In other words, the South's proportional advantage in the officer corps on the eve of the Civil War probably stemmed far more from the effect of the three-fifths clause of the Constitution on the dis-

TABLE 9.2. Distribution of Officers' Appointments by Branch, 1830 (in percent)

Region	Artillery	Infantry	Medical	Pay	Other Staff*
North	61.7	65.7	62.3	73.3	60.9
New England	28.6	28.1	32.1	20.0	21.7
Mid-Atlantic	30.1	32.5	24.5	40.0	37.0
Northwest	2.9	5.1	5.7	13.3	2.2
South	38.3	34.3	37.7	26.6	34.8
South Atlantic	27.2	25.9	22.6	13.3	19.6
Southwest	7.3	7.3	5.7		10.9
D. C.	3.9	1.1	9.4	13.3	4.3
Foreign					4.3

Source: Army register of 1830; Francis B. Heitman, comp., *Historical Register and Dictionary of the United States Army, from Its Organization, September 29, 1789, to March 2, 1903* (Washington, D.C.: Government Printing Office, 1903).

*General officers, adjutant general, inspectors general, Quartermaster Department, Subsistence Department, Corps of Engineers.

tribution of military appointments than from a special predilection of southerners for military service. The western sections had expanded their influence in the officer corps by 1860, but their numbers still lagged behind their contribution to the general population. This discrepancy was especially striking in the case of the Northwest, the most rapidly growing part of the nation. By 1860, it contained 30 percent of the nation's white population but contributed only 13.1 percent of the regular army officers.

A look at the distribution of officers by branch and rank confirms the relatively broad geographical base of the antebellum military profession. As Table 9.2 indicates, the sectional representation in the principal branches in 1830 resembled that in the officer corps as a whole. Northerners dominated each branch, their majorities ranging from 73.3 percent in the Pay Department to 61.7 percent in the artillery regiments. Indeed, southerners held a majority over northerners in only two regiments, and then by very narrow margins: twenty to nineteen in the First Infantry and twenty-eight to twenty-six in the Third Artillery. The geographical origins of senior commanders lend some support to the idea of southern influence. Of fifty-two field-grade officers on the 1830 register, excluding paymasters, twenty-five (48.1 percent) had been appointed from slave states or the District of Columbia, ten from Virginia alone. Although a New Yorker—Major General Alexander Macomb—was the commanding general of the army, the two brigadier generals in charge of the geographical departments, the adjutant general, and seven of eleven regimen-

TABLE 9.3. Distribution of Officers' Appointments by Branch, 1860 (in percent)

Region	Artillery	Infantry	Mounted	Medical	Pay	Other Staff*
North	65.9	58.1	37.7	47.4	51.7	63.3
New England	21.5	16.5	6.3	8.6	17.2	20.1
Mid-Atlantic	29.9	24.9	21.7	31.9	17.2	32.2
Northwest	14.5	16.8	9.7	6.9	17.2	11.1
South	33.2	41.3	60.0	52.6	48.3	36.7
South Atlantic	19.6	22.8	28.6	41.4	24.1	23.1
Southwest	8.9	14.7	26.9	6.9	20.7	10.1
D.C.	4.7	3.8	4.6	4.3	3.4	3.5
Foreign	0.9	0.6	2.3			

Source: Army register of 1860; Francis B. Heitman, comp., *Historical Register and Dictionary of the United States Army, from Its Organization, September 29, 1789, to March 2, 1903* (Washington, D.C.: Government Printing Office, 1903).

*General officers, inspectors general, chief signal officer, judge advocate general, Adjutant General's Department, Quartermaster Department, Subsistence Department, Ordnance Department, Corps of Engineers, Corps of Topographical Engineers.

tal commanders were southerners. Overall, however, there were still more northerners than southerners in this top echelon.

Patterns in the branches were more evident in the officer corps of 1860, as revealed in Table 9.3. Southerners dominated the mounted regiments by a substantial margin, and those units also had a western flavor. Undoubtedly, this trend resulted in part from self-selection; cadets and junior officers imbued with the cavalier culture of the plantation South were more likely than their northern counterparts to seek entry into the mounted service, with its aristocratic associations. The southern edge was greatest in the First and Second Cavalry regiments, which were established in 1855, suggesting favoritism in appointments by Secretary of War Jefferson Davis. Surprisingly, southerners held a majority in two staff branches: the Medical Department (52.6 percent) and the Ordnance Department (53.8 percent). In the first instance, southern influence arose in part from the apparent preference of the army medical board for candidates trained at medical schools in the mid-Atlantic states. Three schools—the University of Pennsylvania, the University of Maryland, and Jefferson Medical School in Philadelphia—had educated 56 percent of the medical officers whose alma maters are known, and 60.3 percent of the army's medical personnel had been appointed from New York, Pennsylvania, Maryland, and Virginia.[2] The North's majority was greatest in the artillery regiments, where it approached the free states' contribution to the general population, and in several staff departments, notably the Corps of Engineers (72.3 percent) and the Corps of Topographical Engineers (73.8 percent). While a Yankee predilection for technical matters may help to explain this pattern, it mainly reflected northern attainment of the top positions in West Point graduating classes, from which vacancies in the prestigious engineering branches were filled.

In 1860 as in 1830, southerners were overrepresented among senior ranking officers, but not by a margin substantially greater than in the officer corps as a whole. Of 131 field-grade officers on the 1860 list, excluding paymasters, 58 (44.3 percent) had been residents of the slave states or the District of Columbia at the time of their original military appointments. Four of the 6 generals were southerners, including Major General Winfield Scott, the commanding general, and so were 9 of the 19 regimental commanders.[3] Northern men dominated the top positions in the staff departments, however; 6 of the 8 bureau chiefs and both of the army's inspectors general were from the North. On the whole, the South had a proportional advantage in the antebellum officer corps, but one too small to detract from the army's national character.

By the antebellum era, the officer corps was firmly in the hands of "respectable" middle- and upper-middle-class families with traditions of public service. Such had been the trend as early as the 1790s, but the rise of West Point and the reform of officer recruitment after the War of 1812 made it permanent. Table 9.4 lists the fathers' occupations of 318 officers on the 1830 army register and 799 officers on the 1860 army register for whom information has been found.[4] It also states the occupations of the fathers of 657 West Point graduates in the classes of 1844–1860, drawn from the register recording the circumstances of cadets' parents. As a means of comparison, Table 9.5 includes a rough occupational profile of the free male population of the United States based on the census of 1850, the first to include occupational data. Significantly, the distribution of fathers' occupations remained relatively consistent between 1830 and 1860, illustrating the stabilization of military appointments.

Although the available evidence probably understates the percentage of officers from agricultural backgrounds, especially in the 1830 group, the majority of regulars clearly derived from families engaged in commerce, the professions, and government service. Not surprisingly, federal officeholders, both civil and military, were the most overrepresented category in relation to the general population; although surely less than 1 percent of the free male work force, such men composed about one-fifth of the known fathers of officers on the 1830 and 1860 registers and 14 percent of the fathers of the West Point graduates. Professional men, 2.5 percent of the work force in 1850, made up ap-

TABLE 9.4. Fathers' Occupations of Army Officers, 1830 and 1860, and of West Point Graduates, 1844–1860

	1830		1860		1844–1860	
	N	%	N	%	N	%
Agricultural	70	22.0	180	22.5	187	28.5
Farmer	47	14.8	143	17.9	161	24.5
Planter	23	7.2	37	4.6	26	4.0
Commercial/Manufacturing	111	34.9	227	28.4	206	31.4
Merchant/Shopkeeper	55	17.3	103	12.9	97	14.8
Banker	3	0.9	5	1.9	12	1.8
Manufacturer/Founder	6	1.9	15	1.9	14	2.1
Company employee/Agent			5	0.6	8	1.2
Editor/Publisher	5	1.6	16	2.0	10	1.5
Sea captain/Pilot	4	1.3	5	0.6	3	0.5
Inn/Tavern/Boardinghouse keeper	16	5.0	10	1.3	9	1.4
Contractor			4	0.5	1	0.2
Civil engineer/Surveyor	5	1.6	7	0.9	5	0.8
Artisan/Machinist	16	5.0	45	5.6	44	6.7
Laborer/Seaman	1	0.3	2	0.3	3	0.5
Professional	73	23.0	209	26.2	150	22.8
Lawyer/Judge	35	11.0	100	12.5	86	13.1
Medical doctor	23	7.2	65	8.1	41	6.2
Clergyman	9	2.8	23	2.9	14	2.1
College professor	1	0.3	5	0.6	3	0.5
Teacher	3	0.9	11	1.4	5	0.8
Other	2	0.6	5	0.6	1	0.2
Government Service	64	20.1	173	21.7	94	14.3
Congressman/Senator	9	2.8	11	1.4	2	0.3
Federal civil servant	18	5.6	36	4.5	19	2.9
Army officer	26	8.2	87	10.9	44	6.7
Navy/Marine officer	2	0.6	24	3.0	16	2.4
State/Local official	8	2.5	13	1.6	12	1.8
Enlisted soldier			2	0.3	1	0.2
Foreign official	1	0.3				
None			10	1.3	20	3.0
Total known	318		799		657	
Total officers	594		1086		682	

Source: Army registers of 1830 and 1860; "Circumstances of Parents of Cadets, 1842–1879," U.S. Military Academy Library; Officers' appointment applications; miscellaneous biographical, genealogical, and local history sources.

TABLE 9.5. Occupational Distribution of Free Male Population, 1850

Occupation	Percentage
Agriculture	45.2
Commerce/Banking/etc.	5.9
Professional	2.5
Manufacturer/Artisan	22.1
Mariner/Fisherman	2.2
Servant/Semiskilled worker	3.7
Laborer (nonagricultural)	16.9
Government service	0.5
Miscellaneous	0.9

Source: U.S. census of 1850.

Note: The categories are necessarily imprecise, as the census does not clearly differentiate among categories of men employed in a particular field (e.g., among industrialists, artisans, and semiskilled workers in many industries), nor does it account for men employed in more than one occupation.

proximately one-fourth of the fathers on all three lists, and merchants, tavern and innkeepers, and other members of the commercial middle class were likewise strongly represented. On the other hand, only a small percentage of officers' fathers—5.3 percent in 1830, 6.1 percent in 1860, and 7.3 percent on the West Point register—pursued nonagricultural manual occupations: artisan, semiskilled worker, laborer, and enlisted soldier. Whatever the role of a military commission as a means of intergenerational social mobility during the early national period, it had largely ceased to perform that function by the antebellum era.

An interesting aspect of officers' social origins was the relatively small proportion of men whose fathers had engaged in agriculture. Although the census of 1850 counts agriculturalists as about 45 percent of the free male work force, farmers and planters composed less than a quarter of the known fathers of officers on the 1830 and 1860 registers and just over a quarter of the fathers of the pre–Civil War West Point graduates, the last a fairly complete group. Thus there would seem to be no positive correlation between a rural upbringing and a military career; indeed, the reverse would appear to be more accurate. Probably the most important reason for the preponderance of officeholders, merchants, and professional men among the fathers of regulars was that such men were in a better position to provide their sons with a formal education and the political influence necessary to procure a military appointment.

Another indicator of the narrowing social base of the officer corps has been discussed in the preceding chapter: the decline in the proportion of regulars who had begun their careers as common soldiers. As far as can be determined, only twenty of the officers on the 1830 army register (3.4 percent) had served as enlisted men in the regular army, the volunteers, or active militia before receiving their commissions—a drop from 38.8 percent in 1786 and 13.5 percent in 1797. Moreover, only fourteen of these men (2.4 percent of the officer corps) had been commissioned directly from the ranks of the regular army. Because of the sporadic efforts to democratize military appointments during and after the Mexican War, the contingent of regulars with enlisted experience had increased to fifty-four by 1860, 5 percent of the total. However, only thirty-two of these rankers (3 percent) had been promoted directly into the officer corps from the regular service. Obviously, enlisted service offered little prospect of advancement for ambitious but poorly connected soldiers.

As might be expected, a sizable number of regulars belonged to families with records of leadership in state and national affairs. The officer corps of 1830 illustrates this pattern well. Although full biographical information is missing for most men, at least 112 regulars (18.9 percent) were related closely to men who occupied or had previously occupied high civil office—including member of Congress, high executive officeholder in the federal government, federal judge, and state or territorial governor, legislator, or other prominent official. Indeed, twenty-two of these men had fathers, uncles, or brothers serving in Congress or other high federal office at the time of their first military appointments. Similarly, no fewer than seventy-eight of the officers in 1830 (13.1 percent) had near relatives who held or had formerly held field or high staff rank in the Continental or regular armies, marine corps, or active militia, or the grade of commander or above in the navy. If the civil and military groups are combined to avoid duplication, at least 26.6 percent of the regulars on the 1830 register had one or more close relations in high office. Moreover, the kin of other officers were prominent in local affairs or held lesser rank in the armed forces, and many regulars were tied by marriage to influential families.

If the families of officers were politically influential, they do not appear to have represented the nation's economic elite—the wealthy merchants, industrialists, cotton barons, and transportation entrepreneurs riding the crest of the antebellum boom. Only 4.4 percent of the pre-1860 West Point graduates whose economic circumstances are recorded on the cadet register claimed to be "affluent," while 84 percent listed their situation as "moderate" and 11.6 percent, as either "reduced" or "indigent." These figures should be viewed with skepticism, of course; cadets surely knew that the main purpose of the register was to deflect criticism of the military academy as a haven for blue

TABLE 9.6. Officers' Religious Preferences, 1830 and 1860

Denomination	1830 N	1830 %	1860 N	1860 %	Congregations (1850)* %
Episcopalian	25	37.3	32	41.0	3.9
Presbyterian	13	19.4	13	16.7	13.0
Congregational	7	10.4	6	7.7	4.6
Reformed					1.8
Methodist	1	1.5	5	6.4	35.7
Baptist	6	9.0	8	10.3	25.2
Lutheran	1	1.5	1	1.3	3.3
Unitarian/Universalist	1	1.5	3	3.8	2.1
Disciples of Christ					5.1
Quaker	1	1.5			2.0
Catholic	9	13.4	8	10.3	3.3
Jewish	3	4.5	2	2.6	0.1
Total	67		78		

Source: Army registers of 1830, 1860; Edwin S. Gaustad, *Historical Atlas of Religion in America* (New York: Harper and Row, 1962); officers' personal papers; miscellaneous biographical sources.

*The percentage of congregations is a very imprecise measure of denominational strength.

bloods. And there was a scattering of regulars who had in fact been raised in wealth and privilege. John R. Fenwick, a career officer who rose to the command of an artillery regiment, was the scion of a prominent South Carolina family and had inherited property in Charleston, a 2,300-acre plantation, and about one hundred slaves. The father of Richard Delafield, later the army's chief engineer, was a merchant prince and one of the wealthiest men of New York City, though his temporary loss of fortune during the War of 1812 may have influenced his son's choice of career.[5] Nevertheless, the majority of officers' biographies, memoirs, and applications for appointment suggest financially comfortable but not affluent backgrounds, and a large number mention economic decline or deprivation. Generally, the economic position of officers' families appears to have been below their occupational and social status.

Evidence about the religious composition of the officer corps is sketchy. Neither the War Department nor the military academy recorded the religion of cadets or officers, and biographies are often silent on the subject. Indeed, the correspondence and journals of many regulars suggest the absence of denominational ties and even an indifference to organized religion. Table 9.6

states the religious preferences of the sixty-seven men on the 1830 army register and the seventy-eight men on the 1860 army register for whom positive information has been found and compares them with estimates for the general population. The apparent overrepresentation of Catholics and Jews is misleading; historical sources tend to assume Protestantism to be the norm in nineteenth-century America and are thus more likely to note the exceptional cases. Not surprisingly, adherents of the oldest and most established Protestant denominations—Episcopalians, Presbyterians, and Congregationalists—formed a substantial majority of the officers whose religions are known, approximately two-thirds of the men on both lists. These were the churches favored by the leadership of the early republic, the families that dominated political affairs during the revolutionary and early national periods and from which a disproportionate number of officers derived. The exceptionally large number of Episcopalians may also suggest a correlation between a hierarchical, ritualistic religious tradition and a predilection for military service.

CAREER MOTIVATIONS

Professional, commercial, and agricultural families with strong records of public service, high in respectability and political influence but in moderate or even straitened economic circumstances—this was the type of background from which most antebellum regulars came. Why did such men embark on military careers? Certainly some were drawn to the army because of what Marcus Cunliffe has described as the "martial spirit" that permeated American culture in the first half of the nineteenth century: the romantic glorification of war and military heroes that flourished in the very shadow of political antimilitarism. Sometimes viewed as a uniquely southern phenomenon, the infatuation with martial life was national in scope and was reflected in the multitude of volunteer militia companies with their splendid uniforms and complex drill, in the proliferation of private and state military academies, and in the immense popularity of military themes in literature, art, and music.[6]

Many youths surely saw a military career as a chance to live out adolescent dreams of martial glory. So it appeared to James S. Thompson, who successfully applied for a cadetship in 1821. "[S]ince first I turned the pages of history," he informed the secretary of war, "and read the achievements of an Alexander, a Scipio & a Washington, I have never ceased to be filled with an emulous admiration of their greatness, & to look forward to the period when my age would permit me to become a soldier." A youthful infatuation with Napoleon led Pierre G. T. Beauregard to choose a military career, despite the misgivings of his Louisiana Creole family about his exposure to Anglo-American culture. A member of a wealthy family with a staunch martial tradition, Philip Kearny was likewise fascinated by military life; as a boy, he drew pictures of military subjects, named his horses after famous generals, and conducted elaborate campaigns involving thousands of toy soldiers. After the death of his grandfather, who had opposed his military ambitions, he procured a direct commission in the regiment of his uncle, Colonel Stephen W. Kearny.[7] In requesting a direct appointment for his son—a former cadet undone by plebe-year mathematics—the Episcopal bishop of California mentioned the youth's independent fortune and his own concern that failure to obtain a commission would make the boy a "lounger." A military career was his "*one absorbing passion*, & I fear, it is this or nothing."[8]

Undoubtedly the romantic appeal of military life influenced most prospective regulars, at least to some extent. Given its pervasiveness in the general culture, it could hardly have done otherwise. Surprisingly few biographical sources, however, mention it as the decisive factor in an officer's choice of career. A related and perhaps more important incentive was a family tradition of military service. As early as the 1790s but especially after the War of 1812, distinct military families emerged in the United States and supplied the armed forces with successive generations of sons—and of daughters, whose military marriages continued the linkage. For clans such as the Macombs, Whitings, Bealls, Taylors, Whistlers, Hunts, Lees, Kirbys, and Smiths, military service was a compelling magnet, the natural, even the assumed career option. "Having been brought up in the Army," wrote Thomas L. Casey, the eldest son of a career regular and the great-grandson of a Continental Army officer, "it has been my desire from earliest youth to enter that branch of the service." Casey married the daughter of the West Point drawing professor and eventually rose to brigadier general and chief engineer. A brother and a son followed him into the army, another brother entered the navy, and two of his three sisters married army officers.[9] When Edmund Kirby Smith entered West Point in 1841, three of his uncles, a brother, and a brother-in-law were on active duty in the army officer corps; moreover, his grandfather had been a Continental Army officer, and his father had reached the rank of colonel before leaving the regular service in the reduction of 1821. Years later, when ordered on frontier duty, Smith reminded his anxious mother that "I have chosen the army, or rather the army has been selected for me as a profession, and I see no prospect of its ever being changed."[10]

Although military families flourished throughout the antebellum period, the restrictions imposed by the West Point appointment policy prevented them from contributing more than a minority of the officer corps. However powerful the stimulus of family military tradition, the career motivation most frequently mentioned in applications for military appointments is economic hardship. Reading these files, one is constantly reminded that the vaunted social mobility of the nineteenth century was not entirely upward and that the fluctuations of an expanding but unstable economy or the death of a key relative could throw middle- and upper-class families into decline or even poverty. When John F. Lee applied for a cadetship in 1829, his mother was dead and his father had gone insane. The family's Virginia estate—seven hundred acres and ten slaves—was too small to support the five children and pay the expense of the father's hospitalization. Although Richard C. Gatlin belonged to a prominent North Carolina family, his father's financial losses forced Richard to drop out of civilian college and seek a free West Point education. The mothers of Frank S. Armistead and Henry B. Clitz, both army widows, operated boarding houses to support their children. Dunbar R. Ransom, James J. Dana, and John R. Cooke all joined the army during the recession year of 1855, after the railroads that had employed them as civil engineers ceased construction. Before entering West Point, George T. Balch provided for his hard-pressed family by making furniture and working as a clerk at a dollar a day; his father had failed as a merchant and died shortly before Balch received notice of his appointment.[11] Running as a leitmotif through officers' application files are such phrases as "a deserving & destitute family"; "high in the estimation of society—but poor"; "suddenly . . . reduced from affluence to want"; "a small estate & that much involved"; and "destitute of the means of procuring an education."[12]

It is impossible to calculate with any precision the actual number of officers who selected their careers for economic reasons. Approximately one-fifth of the applications examined for officers on the 1830 army register refer to economic hardship. Although some candidates probably exaggerated their plight to attract the sympathy of their congressmen or the secretary of war, economic need is by far the most common explanation of career choice given, mentioned nearly four times as frequently as the positive attractions of army life. Possibly more revealing is the large percentage of officers whose fathers had died before their original appointments: 31.1 percent of those on the 1830 register and 29.3 percent of those on the 1860 register for whom information is available. Although paternal death did not inevitably bring poverty, it certainly increased the financial pressures on all but the wealthiest families and reduced the chances that the sons would receive higher education. This was especially true of the families of professional men and government employees, heavily represented in the officer corps, since they depended on the fees or salary of the household head rather than on a farm or independent business that might be continued after his death. In any case, it is likely that a significant portion of the antebellum regulars—perhaps more than a third of the total—entered the army mainly because it offered a free education and a modicum of economic security.

Although difficult to categorize, a variety of other factors influenced the career decisions of antebellum regulars. Some had prior military connections that drew them to the army; Edward Dillon, for example, had been a sutler's clerk at a frontier post before receiving a commission, and several officers had earlier worked as civilian engineers on army exploratory expeditions or other War Department projects.[13] Some young men took up the sword reluctantly, under pressure from their families. Cornelius A. Ogden originally rejected a cadetship, but he later accepted it when his father, an infantry captain in the War of 1812, returned from the northern frontier and advised him to do so. Robert M. McLane, whose father was Andrew Jackson's secretary of the Treasury, despised West Point and twice tried to resign; he consented to stay to please Jackson, who had granted him the appointment.[14]

A few regulars appear to have fallen into their careers by chance. Although John M. Schofield did not intend to be an officer and did not apply for an appointment, his congressman convinced him that a West Point education would be good preparation for the study of law. Schofield graduated in 1853, gave up his plans for a legal career, and reached the position of commanding general of the army before his retirement forty-two years later. "How completely have I in my person, proven that 'man is creature of circumstances,'" wrote Lieutenant Abraham R. Johnston after six years on active duty. "Had my father not placed me at West Point I never would have been a soldier." His family had wanted him to be a preacher, but he showed an aversion to it "and so little inclination for learning that I was changed to a soldier."[15] No doubt many young men drifted into the army as the line of least resistance, viewing military service as a respectable, reasonably stable occupation and perhaps a more appealing prospect than a tame rural or small-town life.

10
THE WEST POINT EXPERIENCE

Although officers' social backgrounds reveal much about the place of the military profession in the larger social order, they were of decreasing significance in shaping the internal service world. More important than social status or initial career incentive was the emergence of West Point as a powerful institution of professional socialization. Before the War of 1812, only a small minority of the officer corps had attended the military academy. Beginning in 1817, however, Sylvanus Thayer brought to the academy a permanent organization, a fixed curriculum, and a set of rational, depersonalized regulations. Moreover, the favored position of West Pointers in the military selection process increased the proportion of graduates in the officer corps to three-quarters of the total in 1860, exclusive of pay and medical officers. Thus most junior and middle-ranking officers had undergone four years of remarkably uniform professional training before receiving their commissions. West Point did not produce an isolated, homogeneous military caste, but it did supply a cohesive force lacking in the early national period. It inspired institutional loyalties and common modes of behavior, and it contributed to the development of a distinctive military subculture before the Civil War.

A TECHNICAL CURRICULUM

The basic curriculum established under Thayer remained virtually the same until the 1850s, and it confirmed the strong technical emphasis introduced by Jonathan Williams before the War of 1812.[1] The academic program of the cadet's first two years (the fourth and third classes) concentrated on mathematics and the French language. The most heavily weighted subject taught at the academy, mathematics was considered an essential foundation for the more advanced parts of the technical curriculum; since French was, in the opinion of Thayer, "the sole repository of military science," a knowledge of the lan-

167

guage was thought necessary to enable cadets and officers to read the literature of their profession.[2] Natural philosophy and chemistry dominated the third year (second class) program, and the fourth year (first class) continued the scientific studies with mineralogy and geology. The central feature of the first class curriculum, however, was a course entitled "Military and Civil Engineering and the Science of War," taught after 1832 by Dennis Hart Mahan, one of the most influential members of the West Point faculty. Considered the capstone of the cadet's academic career, this course was likewise technical in orientation, stressing civil engineering and fortification with only a few days spent on such topics as the composition and organization of armies and the principles of strategy.

Cadets studied drawing during their second and third years, but that subject was also tied to the technical curriculum, intended to prepare them for drafting engineering plans, maps, and topographical sketches. Cadets' principal exposure to the liberal arts was a catchall course during their final year, taught by the academy's chaplain, that supposedly embraced ethics, geography, history, rhetoric, grammar, and national and international law. After 1839, underclassmen also received some training in these subjects. Until the mid-1850s, however, cadets devoted well over twice as much classroom time to mathematics, physical science, and engineering as to all other subjects combined.[3]

In part, the technical bent of the curriculum reflected the persistent emphasis in European military education on artillery and fortification. This tendency was particularly strong in the French military school system, the primary model followed by both Jonathan Williams and Sylvanus Thayer in organizing the academy. Only in the Prussian army—and there at the postgraduate level—did military education expand during this period to include the systematic study of international relations, strategy, logistics, and the "philosophy of war," and the significance of these additions would not be evident until the Prussian victories of 1866 and 1871. Probably the most important source of West Point's technical orientation, however, was the continuing control of the school by the Corps of Engineers. According to West Point regulations, the chief engineer was inspector of the academy, responsible directly to the secretary of war, and only an engineer officer could serve as superintendent. Former engineers also occupied key faculty positions, usually dominating the academic board. Imbued with a strong sense of group mission and intensely suspicious of their colleagues of the line, engineers identified military science with their own area of specialization and directed the curriculum toward the training of engineers. Thayer personally sought to mold West Point into a school of engineering and showed little interest in either liberal arts or strictly military subjects. In addition, the army's growing participation in civil transportation and the status of West Point as the nation's chief source of trained engineers gave the technical program solid support outside the army.

The specialized curriculum did not go unchallenged. As early as 1819, Inspector General John E. Wool recommended more attention to history, geography, and languages, especially in the preparation of infantry officers. The great victories of history "were not achieved by the 'rule and compass' or the 'measurement of angles.' They were the product of enlarged minds, highly cultivated and improved by a constant survey of human events." Three years later, Secretary of War Calhoun reminded Thayer through the chief engineer "that the character of the institution is Military and not Philosophical [i.e. scientific], and while the several branches of the sciences, which are taught at the Academy are deemed highly important and essential in forming Scientific Officers, the main object of the institution is to predominate over all others."[4] Criticism of this kind continued through the antebellum era, and line officers in particular favored expanding the liberal arts and military segments of the curriculum, at least for cadets destined for the infantry and mounted service. A graduate and veteran of frontier service expressed a common opinion in 1857:

> The Professors at West Point, are intent only about magnifying themselves thro' a show of science; they do not care, or do not reflect that a little algebra, a little chemistry, a little mathematics, a little astronomy, in the head of a young man who has *little* aptitude for either, only addle his brains; & when crammed into him at the expense of manly military exercises, & the practical field duty of an officer are fatal to his usefulness; & the infusion of such young men into the army is fatal to the instruction, energy & soldierly effectiveness[,] feeling & tone of the army.[5]

To counter such arguments, academy officials devised an additional rationale for the concentration on mathematics and engineering. Reworking an established pedagogical theory that defended the study of classical languages as a tool to develop "mental discipline," they maintained that the technical curriculum would enhance the reasoning powers of all cadets, instilling orderly, efficient modes of thought. In the opinion of Chief Engineer Joseph G. Totten, mathematics tended "to exercise and discipline the reasoning facilities, and to introduce a system and habit of thought which would prove of the highest value to the pursuit of any profession"; thus it benefited the army as a whole. Even officers who had no immediate use for the content of these courses "must, nevertheless, be always greatly the better for their long continued exercises in a course of investigation and reasoning that excludes, absolutely, all specious and sophistical conclusions."⁶ Presumably, the emphasis on mathematics and engineering would produce tough-minded officers, capable of cutting through ambiguity and making coldly logical decisions under pressure. This argument was of secondary importance during the antebellum period, as academy officials could defend the curriculum more convincingly by referring to the need of both the army and the nation for trained engineers. Later in the century, however, as West Point slipped from its position as a leading school of engineering, the concept of mental discipline reemerged as the academy's basic defense of a prescribed technical curriculum.⁷

During the 1850s, persistent criticism of West Point's engineering orientation led to one of the very few curricular experiments in the history of the military school. To allow more instruction in the liberal arts and military subjects, the academic board recommended extending the cadet's term from four to five years. The War Department adopted this plan in 1854, dividing that year's entering class by age and assigning the younger cadets to the five-year program. The technical courses remained at their previous load, but the time allotted to the humanities and military topics increased considerably. Among other innovations, the academy added military law and Spanish to the curriculum, the latter course intended to prepare cadets for dealing with the subject population of the territory acquired from Mexico. Needless to say, the cadets resented the extra year of schooling, and the faculty complained that the liberal arts lessons were too elementary to be of much value and that the greater focus on military training threatened the scientific character of the school. The War Department dropped the plan at the outbreak of the Civil War. Even during the brief existence of the five-year program, technical subjects continued to outweigh the other academic courses, albeit by a narrower margin than before, and they regained their former predominance when the experiment lapsed.⁸

Whatever the justification, cadets received only limited exposure to ethics, history, government, and international law. Yet these were the academic subjects potentially most useful to men who would spend the bulk of their careers on the Indian and international frontiers, where they would exercise quasi-political authority, conduct morally ambiguous counterinsurgency warfare, and deal with complex diplomatic and civil-military problems. From 1820 to 1843, the ethics textbook used in the fourth year omnibus course was *The Principles of Moral and Political Philosophy* by William Paley, an English theologian; in 1844, the War Department replaced Paley's work with *Elements of Moral Science* by Francis Wayland, professor of ethics at Brown University.⁹ Both were standard textbooks widely used at contemporary civilian colleges.

Interestingly, Wayland's book embraced aspects of the antebellum reform spirit; he criticized slavery, asserted that war was contrary to God's will, and denounced the "military spirit" as a corrupting influence in society. The chief engineer expunged the chapters on slavery from the West Point version of Wayland's work so that "this exciting & dangerous subject shall not be placed under the eyes of the Cadets thereby leading to discussions amongst themselves."[10]

The overall tone of both textbooks, however, was conservative. They praised private property as the foundation of a sound and moral society, encouraged religious observance, and emphasized the citizen's obligation to submit to duly constituted authority. Wayland included a discussion of the duties of "simple" executive officeholders—a category clearly intended to cover military officers—that stressed unconditional service to the government and implicitly encouraged military subordination to civil authority.

> Here the officer has no right to question the *goodness* or *wisdom* of the law; since for these he is not responsible. His only duty is to execute it so long as he retains the office. If he believe the action required of him to be morally wrong or at variance with the constitution, he should resign. He has no right to hold office and refuse to perform the duties which others have been enpowered to require of him.[11]

The academy's treatment of other nontechnical subjects was cursory. Although nominally in the curriculum, history appears to have been rarely taught before the introduction of the five-year program. Cadets spent only a few weeks on geography, and English instruction dealt almost exclusively with rhetoric and the mechanics of style. First classmen did receive some training in international and national law. For several years during the 1820s, the textbook used was Emmerich de Vattel's *The Law of Nations*, a classic eighteenth-century summary of international law that elaborated on the customary rules of war, including protection of the lives and property of noncombatants, humane treatment of prisoners of war, and the need to limit the unnecessary destructiveness of combat.[12] The academy dropped this work in 1825, and from 1826 to 1866, the basic law textbook was the first volume of James Kent's massive *Commentaries on American Law*. Although this work discussed at length the constitutional system and covered such topics of international law as commercial rights, the rights of neutrals, blockades, prizes, and contraband, it touched only lightly on the law of land warfare.[13] Not surprisingly, cadets held their liberal arts courses in low esteem. A recent graduate informed an investigatory commission in 1860 that the study of ethics was "ridiculed by the cadets. . . . A man compelled to go through the present course, would never open a book on moral science again."[14]

The West Point curriculum gave an even lower priority to strictly military subjects than to the humanities. Academic instruction in this area was limited to the fourth year, when cadets took the course in civil and military engineering and the science of war. Despite Dennis Hart Mahan's deserved reputation as a military thinker, his classroom approach was technical, focusing on civil engineering and fortification with the "science of war" confined to a nine-hour block late in the year. Although this segment was popular and no doubt inspired some cadets to pursue the study of strategic theory, it was obviously too brief to deeply affect the thinking of the majority of future officers. Even during the five-year program, when the science of war expanded to thirty-three hours, it was still only slightly ahead of the requirements for the course in veterinary science. Mahan barely touched on the conduct of Indian warfare, the type of combat most relevant to cadets headed for frontier service, and he apparently never mentioned logistics.[15] In addition to Mahan's course, cadets studied the technical aspects of artillery and ordnance; they also received instruction in infantry, artillery, and, after 1853, cavalry tactics at the summer encampments and at drill sessions during the academic year. Although tactical training prepared cadets for the duties of company officers, critics claimed that it was conducted in a dogmatic manner, restricted mostly to the absorption of standard tactical manuals.[16]

In contrast to the humanities, instruction in mathematics, science, and engineering was of high quality. Throughout the antebellum period, West Point was the nation's premier school of engineering, and its faculty included a number of distinguished scholars. The technical curriculum provided excellent professional training for the minority of cadets who entered the engineers, topographical engineers, and ordnance—about 12 percent of the graduating classes—and furnished scores of other graduates with employment when they returned to civil life.[17] Many West Pointers developed from their course work a taste for scientific inquiry that continued through their lives. Nevertheless, most cadets found their formal education of limited value for the duties that would occupy the greater part of their careers, whether as frontier commanders, bureau officers in Washington, or combat leaders in the Mexican and Civil wars.

PROFESSIONAL SOCIALIZATION

Far more important than formal course work in the shaping of future officers was the general milieu of the military academy. As reformed under Thayer, its character was rigidly authoritarian, quintessentially military. On arriving in June, cadets entered a spartan, tightly structured world, almost totally isolated from civilian influences. During the first summer, they lived in tents on the Plain, the academy's drill field, where they were subjected to a mixture of strenuous drill, exaggerated discipline, and hazing administered by the upperclassmen. In September, they moved into permanent barracks and began their academic work, but the regimentation continued. To facilitate control and provide upperclassmen with command experience, the cadets were organized as a battalion of infantry under the immediate authority of the commandant of cadets, the line officer charged with their discipline and tactical instruction. Every cadet carried a rank determined by his soldierly deportment, ranging from the cadet captain down to the privates who constituted the bulk of the student body. Each day followed a uniform pattern, punctuated by roll calls, parades, and inspections. Cadets marched to and from classes and meals and spent approximately three hours a day in military exercises.[18]

A strict code of regulations governed every aspect of cadet life. Cadets were forbidden, among other things, to drink, fight, play cards or other games, leave the limits of the post, possess money, wear any clothing but the assigned uniform, or subscribe to a newspaper or other periodical without the special permission of the superintendent. Cadets ate their meals as squads, each supervised by a "first and a second carver," and unnecessary talking was prohibited at the table. To discourage frivolous reading, cadets were limited to the use of one library book at a time, and that had to be for course work only.[19] Regimentation even extended into the classroom: Cadets were seated on the basis of their academic standing and recited according to a rigidly prescribed system.[20] Needless to say, both rules and tradition demanded strict attention to the hierarchy of rank, and fraternization between cadets and commissioned officers was virtually unknown.[21]

Regimentation was the dominant characteristic of cadet life, but competitive pressure was also very important. A central component of the Thayer system was the merit roll. Cadets were continually graded by an elaborate system of points and demerits that covered academic work, tactics, and general conduct. Their cumulative standing determined both their class rank and branch of the service after graduation. Predictably, mathematics, science, and engineering carried by far the greatest weight in the overall order of merit (55 percent), followed by other academic subjects (17 percent), tactics (14 percent), and conduct (14 percent).[22] Cadets were evaluated daily in the classroom and on the drill field and tested at semiannual general examinations in January and June. The June examination was a particularly trying ordeal, as it was attended by the board of visitors and other distinguished guests and established the cadet's final academic standing for the year. The conduct grade was based on the number of demerits accumulated for violating any of the multitude of regulations that minutely governed West Point life. A cadet receiving more than two hundred demerits in one year faced expulsion, though such cases were rare.[23]

For many cadets, the most powerful source of pressure was not the merit roll but the dread of failure. Although admissions standards were low, the technical curriculum was demanding, especially for youths who did not have a solid academic background or an aptitude for mathematics. A historian of the academy has calculated that one-fourth of the cadets who entered between 1833 and 1854 failed at least one of their subjects and were thus recommended for discharge.[24] Many others resigned as a result of academic obstacles. Because of the status and public character of the school, failure could bring humiliation to the cadet and his family, more so than deficiency at a civilian college. Cadet Edward L. Hartz stated that his brother should not envy his situation: "Let him think how critical is my position and how secure is his—A single false step could drive me from here in disgrace. The burden of disappointed hopes of anxious friends, the contumely of the jealous, the sneers of those who were disappointed in getting here, my own mortification and the deep seated regrets of my family, all would be heaped upon me and drive me from you an outcast."[25]

Reinforcing the Thayer system was the uniquely inbred character of the military academy. Military men and West Point graduates occupied virtually all the significant positions of authority.[26] The superintendent was invariably a senior officer of engineers and a graduate of the school. Although several nongraduates held the post of commandant of cadets before 1838, West Pointers monopolized that key office after that date. Junior officers, nearly all of them recent graduates, served temporary tours of duty as instructors of tactics and assistant professors in the academic departments. Although nominally composed of civilians, the senior faculty became gradually militarized. Early in his administration, Thayer adopted the practice of selecting assistant professors to fill vacancies in the senior faculty. By 1828, West Pointers and former officers had taken permanent possession of the four most important faculty positions: the professorships of mathematics, engineering, natural philosophy, and chemistry, mineralogy, and geology. Only the chaplain and the teachers of drawing, French, and, after 1854, Spanish were recruited outside the circle of alumni, and these were considered lesser positions. From the perspective of West Point administrators, this recruitment policy made sense; graduates understood the system and were better qualified than outsiders to teach the technical curriculum. Nevertheless, inbreeding strengthened the conservative, authoritarian character of the military school and heightened its isolation from civilian society. Within the academy at least, the program introduced by Thayer went unchallenged.

In an intriguing study of the modern military academy, Joseph Ellis and Robert Moore have described the Thayer system, basically unaltered since the antebellum period, as a powerful mechanism for the indoctrination and professional socialization of cadets. Supposedly, the engineering curriculum, strict regimentation, and carefully programmed stress interact to shape the personalities of cadets according to a predetermined pattern. The result is an officer capable of logically dissecting clear-cut problems, making quick decisions under pressure, and performing assigned tasks efficiently—but one who also tends to be intellectually shallow and relatively ineffective in unstructured situations that require independent, creative thought.[27]

Whatever the validity of this generalization for the modern officer corps, there is no precise way to test its applicability to the nineteenth-century army. Evidence suggests that many cadets resisted the homogenizing pressures of the school. Cadet letters and journals abound with complaints about West Point regimentation and descriptions of efforts to beat the system. "I believe that if there were any good reason to justify it, there would be a mutiny," wrote Cadet George D. Bayard of the discipline imposed by the commandant of cadets. "We may hereafter when in active service possibly realize the benefits of all this tyrannical rigor."[28] The memoirs of such West Pointers as Ulysses S. Grant, John M. Schofield, and Henry Heth indicate that they spent a minimum of time on their studies and were not obsessed with improving their positions on the merit roll. Heth admitted that his academic efforts were "measured by the amount of time necessary to be given to prevent failure at the annual examinations."[29] The cadet subculture legitimized infractions of the regulations, even cheating, and it was considered a dishonorable act to report a fellow cadet. In explaining to his father his refusal to testify against his roommates for keeping liquor in their room, Cadet John C. Pemberton expressed the common attitude: "You say I gave my honor to comply with the laws of the place when I entered it. I should suppose you must know that it is a mere form, one which no one expects—and which no one is expected to keep—consequently in which no expectation is disappointed—and which promise Paley [the ethics textbook] says is not obligating."[30]

If the West Point environment did not produce military automatons, it did exert a potent influence on cadets. Except for a furlough after their second year and occasional social contacts with visitors, cadets spent four years of impressionable adolescence in near seclusion from civilian society, immersed in a closed, rigidly hierarchical institution where the principal authority figures were professional soldiers. Of special importance was the mystique that came

View of the Hudson River from West Point, New York, as painted by Seth Eastman, the army's most prominent officer-artist. The spectacular Hudson Valley scenery was an important ingredient of the academy's mystique. (Painting in the United States Capitol Art Collection; photo by Architect of the Capitol)

to surround the academy—a blend of breathtaking scenery, heroic traditions, and the pomp and ceremony of military life. Present as early as the 1820s, this aura grew more compelling after the Mexican War assured West Point of a secure place in the nation's mythology of martial glory. Romantically inclined West Pointers testified to its emotional impact. A graduate recalled his first arrival at the academy during a dress parade: "The place, the season, the fragrant breath of evening, the enlivening presence of hundreds of eager spectators, the stirring music,—and then the dead silence, broken at length by the voice of the officer in charge, as by seeming magic he put in motion the gray clockwork of the manual of arms, made up a scene as I never before, nor since, have witnessed." A first-year cadet described to his mother the rugged beauty of the academy's setting: "In some places you can read at the distance of a quarter of a mile the names of 'Palo Alto,' 'Buena Vista' and 'Monterey,' where they have been carved in gigantic letters in the solid rock. Here too the ruins of Fort Putnam look down upon us, with its Revolutionary memories, reminding us of the gallant men who fought and perished,—as we may fight and perish—in their country's cause."[31]

Most cadets who remained at West Point absorbed at least part of the prevailing value system and were drawn into a distinctly military milieu. Even as they complained of the strict discipline, they grew accustomed to it and applied it enthusiastically to the classes below them. The superintendent, commandant of cadets, and other officers at the academy became their models for professional conduct. Ulysses S. Grant, who claimed in his memoirs that he disliked the academy and had little interest in a military career, also recalled that a visit by General Winfield Scott impressed him far more than one by President Van Buren. "In fact I regarded General Scott and Captain C. F. Smith, the Commandant of Cadets, as the two men most to be envied in the nation."[32] Senior cadets developed a military bearing—"that air of importance, that show of dignity and condecension to our inferiors which forms the great characteristic of First Class men"—and cultivated the manners of subalterns.[33] At dances and other social events during their last summer encampment, they mingled with fashionable guests and acquired a taste for the formal grace of army social life.

Although some cadets expressed cynicism about an army career and waited for the first opportunity to resign, many of them closely followed army news, eagerly anticipated their commissions, and longed for the chance to practice their profession. Even the technical curriculum failed to dampen ardent dreams of martial glory. "There is an undefinable something about the military profession," wrote Cadet George L. Welcker in 1836, "a something a little wild, a little glittering, and a little uncertain, but with all, so pleasing & fascinating, that when properly presented its temptations are seldom to be resisted." In a letter to a female relative, Cadet J. E. B. Stuart found the military profession to have "attractions which to one who has seen a little of the 'elephant' are overpowering. There is something in 'the pride and circumstance of glorious war,' which makes 'Othello's occupation' the most desirable of all. Now tell me candidly had you not rather see your Cousin or even your brother a bold Dragoon than a petty-fogger lawyer."[34]

West Pointers made much of the leveling and nationalizing influences of the academy. In their view, the broad recruitment base of the school, its emphasis on uniformity of dress and behavior, and the objectivity of the merit roll blurred social class and sectional distinctions and produced an egalitarian community among cadet classmates—a band of brothers. Hazing by upperclassmen taught new cadets "that no one here cares for their social positions, or their political friends, but that they must establish a position by their own qualities, and it makes men of them." Whatever their social standing, "all fare alike here and each must depend ultimately upon his own individual resources and not upon his family antecedents or paternal wealth for success." Indeed, the military academy was "a model republic in all things saving respect to constituted authority and obedience to orders, without which an army is impossible."³⁵ Some graduates saw the school as a dynamic force for national unity, molding a group of leaders whose sweeping vision would overcome the centrifugal impulse of sectionalism. Captain James Dalliba, an 1811 graduate, expressed this idea well.

> If there is a means stronger than any other of cementing the union of the States, and of perpetuating our government, it is the national Military Academy at West Point. To this institution young gentlemen are sent from all sections of the Union. They come together with all their sectional prejudices, habits, and knowledge. . . . Their former habits, manners, and prejudices soon become extinct. They form a new character, a national character, which is no where else formed in the country. . . . They are at an age when impressions are deep and will long continue. The attachments of personal friendship there made will be lasting. They become a band of brothers. . . . They separate and are scattered to every part of the country; but their feelings are not separated, and their interests are not divided, and generally never will be. . . . From this source an uniformity of political principles and opinions and national and personal attachments will be formed and disseminated, which will bind together our States, and perpetuate our union, when without this cord they might separate.

"If Mass. & S. C. get by the ears," wrote Lieutenant Henry L. Kendrick, an assistant professor at West Point, "we shall [need] something like the academy to sow the seeds of harmony—'t will do good that way if in no other."³⁶

Descriptions of West Point as the training ground of a nationally minded brotherhood of arms were overdone, which was demonstrated in 1861 when the majority of southern-born graduates left the service to join the Confederacy. Nevertheless, the shared experiences of four years in the unique environment of the military school did tend to weaken former identities and produce a web of new loyalties—less to the nation as an abstract ideal than to one's classmates, West Point, and the army. The personal correspondence of cadets and junior officers reveals little evidence of social class discrimination within the West Point contingent and, until the 1850s at least, surprisingly few signs of sectional tension. On the other hand, there are abundant references to strong and enduring friendships forged at the academy and to a steadfast loyalty to the school itself. Lieutenant Samuel Woods considered his classmates to be "almost without equals" and found "every trait, that dignifies human nature, most conspicuously adorning some of them"; mingling with such comrades formed "an oasis, that marks the trackless waste of my career." In the opinion of Lieutenant J. E. B. Stuart, the bond uniting West Point classmates "is unequalled by the strongest attachment and what is more remarkable, it becomes more and more intense as time continues. A thought which makes me fear that *out of the army* I will be miserably unhappy." Five years after graduation, Lieutenant Cyrus B. Comstock could still scarcely believe that his cadet days were over forever. "I doubt—if I shall ever find a place for which I shall have so much admiration & affection as for West Point."[37]

Not all West Point graduates recalled their cadet days fondly, of course, and the sentiments of those who did were not basically different from the loyalty civilian college graduates felt toward their classmates and alma maters. The special circumstances of the academy, however—its quasi-monastic isolation, its romantic mystique, the intensity of its program of indoctrination—gave it an exceptionally strong emotional hold on many of its graduates. Although difficult to trace, the West Point experience subtly encouraged an elitism among cadets—a pride in surviving the program's rigors and a patronizing attitude toward the civilian world. "If a man had nothing else to recommend him," wrote a cadet in 1859, "the mere fact of his being a graduate of West Point ought to entitle him to respect. It shows that he has done what hundreds have failed to accomplish, and what has tried the spirit and the strength of all the best officers of our army."[38] This tendency drew additional strength from the position of the academy in antebellum society: an island of discipline and authoritarian values in the midst of an expansive, individualistic nation touting democratic ideals. Indeed, the frequent attacks on the military school accentuated West Pointers' sense of uniqueness and their resentment of civilians and caused them to close ranks in defense of their institution. Elitist perspectives rooted in the academy experience intensified after graduation and formed the core of the "military mind" of the nineteenth-century officer corps.

It is impossible to measure precisely the total impact of West Point as an institution of professional socialization. Some youths were attracted strongly to military service before they entered West Point and the academy merely confirmed their earlier inclinations; others had little interest in an army career, having accepted their appointments because of parental pressure or economic need, and they simply endured West Point. It is probable, however, that the academy significantly affected the majority of cadets who fell between these extremes. First and fundamentally, it acquainted cadets with tactics, military discipline, and administrative routine, preparing them for their duties as company officers. Thus it assured the army of a uniform and dependable "product" in the junior commissioned grades—a level of technical competence that marked a significant improvement over the pre–War of 1812 officer corps. Second, exposure to the West Point environment drew cadets into a professional military ethos, causing them to internalize such military values as discipline and regularity, identify with the army as an institution, and, in many cases at least, make a strong personal commitment to military service. This influence, in combination with other factors, resulted in a dramatic lengthening of officers' careers after 1815, which was a crucial ingredient in the professional consolidation of the officer corps.

Moreover, the personal friendships and institutional loyalties begun at the military academy persisted long after graduation. In the modern army, where academy graduates constitute only a small minority of the officer corps, such identities are frequently criticized as divisive, the source of the "West Point Protective Association" that has allegedly promoted the interests of graduates at the expense of other officers and contributed to the cover-up of war crimes and other abuses. In the antebellum army, however, West Pointers composed well over half of the officer corps and the bulk of junior and middle-ranking officers. Although tensions existed between graduates and nongraduates, the principal outgrowth of academy ties was a cohesive element missing from the early army—a complex of shared values and experiences that united officers of diverse social and geographical origins. It also encouraged a sense of uniqueness, of standing apart from the civilian world, and thus helped forge a corporate identity among army officers.

11
MILITARY CAREERS IN THE ANTEBELLUM ERA

Closely related to the rising influence of West Point as an institution of professional socialization was the emergence of the long-term military career. Before the War of 1812, few officers were willing or able to make a permanent commitment to the army. After 1815, however, the changing circumstances of military life, especially the stabilization of the army's size and organization, encouraged regulars to view military service as a full-time endeavor and the focal point of their adult lives. Careers followed predictable patterns, and army society assumed a pace and flavor that it would retain well into the twentieth century. By the eve of the Civil War, the officer corps had developed into a distinct subculture that was partially isolated, both physically and intellectually, from the main currents of the civilian world.

Officers' growing attachment to military life may be easily demonstrated. Table 11.1 compares the careers of the men whose names appear on the army registers of 1797, 1830, and 1860. For officers of all ranks as well as for senior commanders, the median career length more than doubled between 1797 and 1830, increasing from ten to twenty-two years in the former case and from eighteen to thirty-nine years in the latter. While the average term of service of the 1860 regulars was roughly the same as that of the 1830 group, it would have been considerably longer if one-fourth of the officers had not left the service in 1861 to join the Confederacy, prematurely ending their regular army careers. The most striking evidence, however, is the jump in the percentage of regulars devoting most of their adult lives to the army. If twenty years of service is assumed to be the minimal definition of a career commitment, well over half of the officers in 1830 and 1860 would qualify as careerists, nearly five times the percentage in 1797. Moreover, two-fifths of the regulars in 1860 held their commissions for thirty years or longer; nearly a quarter had careers spanning at least four decades.

TABLE 11.1. Officers' Career Lengths, 1797, 1830, 1860*

	1797	1830	1860
Median career length (all officers)	10	22	23
Median career length (field officers)	18	39	41
Percentage of total serving 20 years	12.7	57.1	56.0
Percentage of total serving 30 years	2.6	37.7	41.5
Percentage of total serving 40 years	0.5	16.2	22.8

Source: Army registers of 1797, 1830, 1860; Francis B. Heitman, comp., *Historical Register and Dictionary of the United States Army, from Its Organization, September 29, 1789, to March 2, 1903* (Washington, D.C.: Government Printing Office, 1903).

*Revolutionary service as commissioned officer included for 1797 officers; cadet years excluded for 1830 and 1860.

Table 11.2 reveals the same trend from a somewhat different perspective. It compares the career lengths of the young men appointed to the lowest commissioned grades in four three-year periods: 1792–1794, 1821–1823, 1831–1833, and 1841–1843. The median service of entering junior officers doubled between the 1790s and the 1820s, rising from six to twelve years. Although it declined to five years for the West Point classes of 1831–1833, this dip reflects an aberrant event—an exceptionally high resignation rate among junior officers in the mid-1830s, which will be examined later in this chapter. By the early 1840s, the average second lieutenant could expect to spend fourteen years in uniform. Again, the most dramatic evidence is the growth in the percentage of officers qualifying as careerists. Only 3.5 percent of the entering officers of 1792–1794 would serve twenty or more years, but over a third of the West Point classes of 1841–1843 would spend at least two decades in the army and nearly one-fifth would serve at least thirty years. Although difficult to gauge precisely, the fact that a large proportion of the antebellum officer corps served together over a prolonged period of time, sharing common experiences and developing institutional loyalties, was certainly the most important ingredient in building a corporate identity.

THE SUBALTERN YEARS

The overwhelming majority of the officers received their first commissions in their early twenties and entered the service at the basic grade of second lieu-

TABLE 11.2. Career Length of Men Appointed to Lowest Commissioned Ranks in Selected Years*

	1792–1794	1821–1823	1831–1833	1841–1843
	N:86 (%)	N:99 (%)	N:120 (%)	N:147 (%)
Median career length (years)	6	12	5	14
Number serving 10 years	20 (23.3)	60 (60.6)	42 (35)	103 (70.1)
Number serving 20 years	3 (3.5)	31 (31.3)	27 (22.5)	52 (35.4)
Number serving 30 years	1 (1.2)	25 (25.3)	16 (13.3)	28 (19)
Number serving 40 years	1 (1.2)	10 (10.1)	10 (8.3)	15 (10.2)

Source: U.S. Senate, *Journal of the Executive Proceedings* (Washington, D.C., 1828–1948); George W. Cullum, comp., *Biographical Register of the Officers and Graduates of the U.S. Military Academy at West Point, N.Y., from . . . 1802 to 1890* (Boston: Houghton, Mifflin, 1891).

*In 1792–1794, ensign in infantry, lieutenant in artillerists and engineers, cornet in light dragoons; in 1820–1823, 1831–1833, and 1841–1843, brevet second lieutenant and second lieutenant (West Point classes).

tenant. Since the number of West Point graduates often exceeded the vacancies in the officer corps, many young men spent the initial months or even years of their careers as brevet second lieutenants, a supernumerary rank intended to keep them in uniform until permanent openings became available. For West Pointers, the transition to active duty was relatively smooth; they were familiar with military routine, had picked up patterns of conduct and expression from the junior officers attached to the academy, and joined units staffed largely by men with identical training, some of them friends from earlier graduating classes. The adjustment was more difficult for the minority of officers appointed directly from civil life, but they too entered a stable organization that operated by clearly defined regulations and procedures. Most of the citizen appointees had had at least some prior exposure to military life—as volunteers, West Point cadets who did not graduate, students at other military academies, War Department employees, or members of army families. In any case, West Pointers dominated the lower and middle levels of the officer corps, and they established the norms to which all junior officers conformed.

Some newly commissioned subalterns received advanced training before joining their regiments. For several years in the late 1820s and early 1830s, most West Point graduates destined for the artillery and infantry spent their first year or two of active duty at the Artillery School of Practice at Fortress Monroe, Virginia, or the Infantry School of Practice at Jefferson Barracks, Missouri. During the 1850s, brevet second lieutenants in the mounted regiments were first posted to the training depot for mounted troops, located at Jefferson Barracks until 1855 and then at Carlisle Barracks, Pennsylvania. The majority of junior officers reported directly to their companies, however, and they remained on company duty for the greater part of their careers.

Superficially at least, garrison life had not changed much since the early national period. The army's constabulary functions kept most garrisons small, limited to a handful of companies. In 1835, only two of the fifty-three army posts contained more than 500 officers and enlisted men, and nearly half the regulars served at garrisons of fewer than 200. The dispersion became even more extreme after the Mexican War, with the occupation of the Far West. By 1852, the army's 11,202 regulars garrisoned a total of eighty-four posts scattered from the Atlantic to the Pacific; the largest—Fort Hamilton, a recruit training depot in New York harbor—was manned by only 302 officers and men. In that year, the garrisons of forty-five posts did not exceed 100.[1]

Nevertheless, army procedure assumed a new regularity that contrasted sharply with the pre-1815 pattern. Garrison life followed a timeless rhythm, structured around the parade ground that formed the physical center of each military post. Using the now-standardized manuals, junior officers supervised the daily routine of the garrison, conducted tactical training (which was confined for the most part to small-unit drill), and kept the administrative records of their companies. The orderly book of one four-company post—Fort Winnebago in south-central Wisconsin Territory—that was kept during 1834–1836 reveals the pattern followed with slight variations at virtually all the garrisons.[2] In the spring, summer, and early fall, each day except Sunday began with reveille, sounded thirty minutes before sunrise, followed by the surgeon's call, breakfast, and formal guard mounting. The rest of the day was consumed by fatigue duties and two hour-long sessions of infantry drill, based on the Scott tactics. The troops were called to their main meal of the day at 2:30 P.M., and tattoo sounded at 10:00 P.M. Although the orderly book does not mention evening parade, this exercise was required by the General Regulations to begin thirty minutes before sunset, and it was so much a part of garrison ritual that it probably occurred without specific orders. A weekly inspection was held each Saturday morning—in a much debated and eventually rescinded move, the War Department had abolished Sunday inspections in 1833—and a formal muster and inspection by company took place at the end of each month. During the late fall and the long Wisconsin winter, the daily routine

Fort Winnebago in 1831. (Drawing by Mrs. Juliette A. Kinzie, wife of the resident Indian agent, in her memoir, *Wau-Bun: The "Early Day" in the North-West* [New York, 1856]; photo courtesy of the State Historical Society of Wisconsin)

began later but remained essentially the same, except that military training seems to have been suspended altogether.

Besides their regular company duties, junior officers served in rotation as officer of the day and officer of the guard. The former attended to the police and general discipline of the garrison and supervised the assemblies and roll calls that punctuated the military day. The latter commanded the post guard, and one of his duties was control of the enlisted prisoners, often a tense and difficult task. Subalterns also performed temporary staff functions—as post adjutant, for example, or acting assistant quartermaster. They served on recurrent boards of survey and inspection, organized to examine public property, and on the council of administration. The latter agency regulated the garrison's sutler, administered the post fund raised from taxes on the sutler's sales, and, in the case of the larger posts after 1838, appointed the chaplain. All company officers sat from time to time on garrison and regimental courts-martial; these tribunals, composed of three officers, were called frequently to try minor infractions by enlisted men, usually involving alcohol or unauthorized absences. The Fort Winnebago orderly book recorded thirty-seven such courts in slightly less than two years, a rather modest total. At Fort Gibson, a six-company post in the Indian Territory, fifty-five garrison courts convened in 1843 alone and heard 443 individual cases—a number that surpassed by a quarter the entire complement of enlisted soldiers.[3]

Throughout much of the antebellum period, the War Department required regulars to perform physical labor, constructing posts and military roads and cultivating crops for their own subsistence.[4] A large part of the Fort Winnebago garrison, for example, spent the summer of 1835 working on the military road that crossed Wisconsin from Fort Howard, at Green Bay, to Fort Crawford on the Mississippi. Inevitably, the supervision of these projects fell to junior officers, who found the work distasteful and detrimental to military training. Many would have agreed with Captain James J. Archer's assessment in 1859: "In fact the U. S. soldiers on the frontiers a little in advance of the settlements are rather hewers of wood and diggers of ground rather than soldiers—and it is very seldom that they are able to indulge in military exercises enough to enable them to preserve any of the appearance of a regular army."[5]

Not all garrison duty was confined to military routine and physical labor. On the Indian and international frontiers, young officers often participated in small-scale expeditions arising from the army's constabulary and exploratory roles. Wherever posts existed near Indian territory, enforcement of the trade and intercourse laws demanded regulars' attention; officers endeavored to halt unauthorized settlement on Indian lands and to suppress the liquor trade. For instance, the Fort Gibson orderly book mentions numerous details of troops making arrests and escorting prisoners. Beginning in the 1830s, the War Department encouraged periodic military expeditions onto the Great Plains, both to overawe the western tribes and to gather topographical information. Army exploratory parties crisscrossed the West after the Mexican War, mapping the new territories and surveying routes for roads and railroads. In particular, the military occupation of Oregon and the Mexican Cession generated almost continual police and counterinsurgency operations through the 1850s, mainly against the Indians but also against Mormons, filibusters, and bandits.

Many subalterns naturally welcomed such active duty as a break from garrison routine and an opportunity to exercise independent command. "There is an excitement in this adventurous life," wrote Lieutenant Alexander MacRae of his service on the Texas frontier in 1852, "in silently and cautiously following the trail with my wild looking half-indian guide, with my small party of picked men, armed to the teeth with Rifles, Revolvers and long knives;—or, returning from the scout, in shooting deer and wolves, and listening to the songs and stories of the men around the blazing campfire." Lieutenant George B. McClellan considered western exploration far preferable to engineering duty in the East: "These rides of a few thousand miles thro' a perfectly unsettled country are decidedly more interesting than laying pillages & building stone walls."[6]

Expeditions were the exception rather than the norm, for garrison life inevitably entailed a seemingly endless round of fixed duties combined with long periods of inactivity. Lieutenant Edmund Kirby Smith described life at Jefferson Barracks just after the Mexican War.

> We some time since regularly entered upon the routine of garrison life—drills, guard and dress parade, the billiard-room after breakfast and a visit to the ladies in the evening. Gracious! What a contrast to the excitement and incidents of the three past years. . . . [N]ow, automaton like we involuntarily glide through the same monotonous scene, needing only like the works of a watch to be wound up each twenty-four hours, when away we spin tickety tick till the stirring notes of reveille again winds up our rickety machinery for a repetition of the same revolutions.[7]

Junior officers relieved their boredom in a variety of ways, the most common of which was reading. Most garrisons maintained libraries for the use of both officers and men, supported by the post fund. Although the holdings could be a source of controversy, the emphasis was on military and general interest periodicals, works of history and biography, scientific texts, and fiction.[8] Many subalterns had their own collections as well, and their letters and diaries indicate a wide range of intellectual tastes. During the 1850s, Lieutenant Oliver Otis Howard's reading list included Shakespeare, Bacon, Paul's epistles, histories of the Napoleonic and Mexican wars, and biographies. The interests of Lieutenant Henry W. Halleck ran from professional works on military engineering to Carlyle's history of the French Revolution, biographies of Washington and Hamilton, and translations of ancient Greek poetry. Lieutenant George W. Hazzard's letters mentioned titles by Shakespeare, Plutarch, Longfellow, the historians George Bancroft and Thomas B. Macaulay, and the Hungarian patriot Kossuth, as well as *Tom Jones* and other novels.[9] Moreover, officers frequently wrote for publication; in particular, the service periodicals of the 1830s and early 1840s, the *Military and Naval Magazine of the United States* and the *Army and Navy Chronicle*, provided outlets for officers' authorial efforts.

Garrison officers also pursued less intellectual pastimes. Throughout the antebellum era, the quasi-aristocratic conception of officership continued to occupy an important place in the collective self-image of the officer corps. Among young line officers especially, the ideal remained the dashing, devil-may-care gentleman-soldier, quick to defend his honor and equally at home in the saddle, the tavern, or the ballroom. A colleague's description of Captain John R. Bell summarized the qualities widely admired in junior officers: "a gallant fellow, in the prime of early manhood, of a solid and strong constitution of body, a fearless rider, devoted to the sports of the field, as it were with him 'the day's reflection and the midnight dream'; . . . not only a lover of the chase, but an accomplished gentleman.''[10] Subalterns cultivated an independent, manly bearing, a bemused irreverence toward higher authority, and a talent for cutting a stylish figure in the social world. Occasionally defended as a means to increase military readiness, hunting was an obsession at virtually every frontier post. Henry Heth estimated that he had killed more than a thousand buffalo while stationed on the Plains during the 1850s; the hunting exploits of Martin Scott, the army's most famous marksman, made him a legend both inside and outside the service.[11]

Although the temperance movement won a few converts in the officer corps, whiskey remained the most widespread army vice. One army widow probably exaggerated but nevertheless captured the flavor of garrison life: "It would be said of a man, 'He is not a drinking man. He is never drunk before dinner.' It seemed that all that could be expected of a man was that he should be kept sober in the morning. Common descriptive terms were 'a one-bottle man,' 'a two-bottle man.' " According to Lieutenant George D. Bayard in 1856, the junior officers' quarters at Fort Leavenworth were "drenched with whiskey from morning till night. The temptation to a young officer to drink is hard to resist." "I am sorry to say that there is a great proclivity for spirit in the army in the field," Colonel Robert E. Lee warned his recently commissioned son. "It seems to be considered a substitute for every luxury."[12] Commanders tended to tolerate heavy drinking unless it threatened the unit's reputation or seriously impeded the conduct of duty. "Capt. Elzey got very drunk," an officer wrote from Fort Leavenworth in December 1857, "threw a glass of wine at Pemberton and even refused to lend a lantern to Gen. Harney, but every body knew Elzeys condition and the affair was overlooked."[13]

Predictably, bachelor officers devoted much of their leisure to chasing the opposite sex, although their opportunities varied with their branches and assignments. Staff officers and officers stationed at posts near large cities mingled in prestigious social circles. Despite the widespread distrust of the army as an institution, regulars as individuals usually enjoyed considerable status, because of their social backgrounds, education, and the glorification of military things so common in American culture. In the South in particular, the uniform gave access to the houses of leading families, and eligible subalterns were much in demand. Because of its proximity to St. Louis, Jefferson Barracks was widely regarded as the most desirable army post. As described by a lieutenant in 1860, an officer's life in St. Louis was "a constant round of festivity in the most charming society of ladies, excelled by those of no other city in the United States."[14] Artillery garrisons at the eastern ports boasted similar prospects. Officers at Fort Moultrie, South Carolina, were so deluged by invitations from Charleston that they formed a rotation system for attending social events. "These parties are very various," reported Lieutenant William T. Sherman in 1843, "from the highly aristocratic and fashionable, with sword and epaulettes, or horse-racing, picnicing, boating, fishing, swimming, and God knows what not." Although Lieutenant Thomas Williams expected to be lonely at tiny Fort Ontario in 1841, he was pleasantly surprised by the social life in nearby Oswego, New York: "I am permitted to lionize amongst scores of fair girls, who delight in a soldier, and long to have husbands."[15]

The social contacts of the majority of young line officers, stationed at frontier garrisons, were more circumscribed. Small, temporary, or newly established posts in unhealthy areas, such as those in the interior of Florida or the southwestern deserts, offered little female companionship of any kind. At larger and more settled garrisons, junior officers could socialize with the families of the older officers, with the limited number of white civilians in the area, and with Indian and Mexican women. As the most socially eligible young women available, officers' daughters were popular with bachelor subalterns, and parties, dances, picnics, and excursions relieved the garrison monotony. Indeed, the journals and letters of junior officers suggest an atmosphere of flirtatious eroticism suffusing garrison society. "The ladies are exceedingly importunate in their exactions of attention," wrote a lieutenant of the "contact & friction parties" at Fort Steilacoom, Washington Territory. "They are constantly getting up some plan by which they bring us all together. . . . These polka quadrilles find great favor with them, there is considerable hugging and rushing into each others arms that makes the dance unusually exciting."[16] Intra-army marriages, though not the rule, were frequent. Of the officers' marriages announced in the *Army and Navy Chronicle* between 1835 and 1840, at least 19 percent were to the daughters, sisters, or nieces of other regulars.[17] Veteran commanders such as Alexander Macomb, Zachary Taylor, John Clitz, and Joseph C. Plympton lost three or more daughters each to military suitors.

Although positive evidence is scarce, sexual relations between officers and Indian women seem to have been common. A missionary's wife claimed in 1837 that all but two officers at Fort Snelling, on the upper Mississippi River, kept Indian mistresses. Lieutenant Seth Eastman, later a noted artist of Indian life, had a daughter by a Sioux woman while stationed at Fort Snelling in 1830 and 1831. Apparently, sexual contacts were also common at Fort Gibson, Fort Wayne, and other garrisons on the edge of the Great Plains, where the eastern tribes were resettled in the 1830s and 1840s. While serving in Washington Territory in the late 1850s, Lieutenant August V. Kautz had at least two children by an Indian mistress.[18] During and after the Mexican War, regulars stationed in the Southwest intermingled with Mexican women. "The Senoras are pretty free and easy," wrote Lieutenant Jeremy F. Gilmer from Santa Fe in 1846, "and our dances are sometimes of the stagg order, which you may have seen in days of yore, when at the Academy." From the same place, Lieutenant William H. Warner reported that it was "the custom when you wait upon a lady home from a party (fandango) to go in & sleep with her"; he assured his correspondent, however, that he did not participate.[19] Of course, officers' relationships with Indian and Mexican women only occasionally resulted in formal marriages. Most regulars shared the racism of the larger society, and they faced social ostracism if they violated the prevailing norms.[20]

Some officers, reluctant to raise a family on a subaltern's pay or expose it to the physical rigors and constant separations of frontier army life, postponed marriage until their middle years or became confirmed bachelors. Lieutenant William M. Gardner wrote his brother that he "would not marry the Virgin Mary herself, if she was not backed by enough money to pay her *mess bill* at least." Lieutenant Robert H. Chilton favored a regulation prohibiting marriage "where an officer had not reached the rank of captain for the idea of one room and a kitchen with all the hardships & privations to which a man must subject a lady is sufficient in itself to destroy all inclination that way."[21] However, most officers who married did so as junior officers. For 113 officers whose nuptials were announced in the *Army and Navy Chronicle* between 1835 and 1840, the median tenure of active service at the time of marriage was six years; excluding the medical officers, 39 percent married as second lieutenants and 67 percent before their promotion to captain. The great majority of regulars were wed in their late twenties and early thirties, only slightly later than their counterparts in the other professions.[22] Although no comprehensive analysis has been attempted of the army wives, officers tended to marry women of their own social class: the daughters of "respectable" merchants, planters, landholding farmers, military or civil officeholders, and professional men.

Perhaps one factor in subalterns' decision to marry was a gradual though uneven increase in their compensation between 1815 and the 1850s. Throughout this period, base salaries remained fixed at $360 annually for first lieutenants and $300 for second lieutenants of infantry and artillery; by the Mexican War, moderate expansions of other allowances had raised their respective incomes to $834 and $774, increases of 25 percent and 27 percent over the War of 1812 levels. Officers of the mounted regiments received somewhat higher pay, presumably because of their need to maintain horses. A controversial act of 1838 extended mounted pay to the officers of the staff departments, and after that year, both first and second lieutenants in these branches drew $1,078 in salary and allowances.[23] Lieutenants of the line could supple-

Second Lieutenant Ulysses S. Grant, Fourth Infantry Regiment. (Courtesy of the State Historical Society of Wisconsin)

ment their income by serving as temporary staff officers, such as acting assistant quartermasters and commissaries of subsistence, regimental adjutants, and aides-de-camp to general officers.

Until the 1830s, the administration also permitted extra pay for other special duties. Officers working as clerks in the staff offices in Washington received a per diem allowance, for example, and officers disbursing public funds retained a small percentage of the money they handled. In addition, the War Department stretched the law to permit some regulars double-ration allowances even though they were not strictly eligible for that benefit. By taking advantage of all extra allowances, exceptionally fortunate second lieutenants were able to increase their compensation to over $1,200—about two-thirds above their basic income. In an economy effort, the Jackson administration cut back drastically on extra compensation during the early 1830s; Congress abolished most special duty allowances in 1835, and in 1842 it restricted the number of officers qualifying for double rations.[24]

As with the early national period, the scarcity of data on income in antebellum America makes it difficult to evaluate precisely the economic status of junior officers. When weighed against other federal employees, however, regulars seem to have improved their position significantly. If all benefits are considered, including publicly owned quarters and medical care, lieutenants' income compared fairly well with junior and mid-level clerks in the executive departments in Washington, most of whom made between $800 and $1,200 a year. Consumer prices declined through most of the antebellum period, so regulars experienced a significant improvement in their absolute standard of living.[25] Unmarried subalterns at least were able to live comfortably on their pay. Nevertheless, the question of pay aroused intense resentment in the army's junior grades. Whatever their absolute status, lieutenants contrasted themselves to civilians of their age in an expanding economy, whose prosperity they inevitably exaggerated. During the early and mid-1830s in particular, officers measured their own worsening plight, caused by the restrictions on extra allowances and a temporary rise in prices, against the opportunities available in the booming field of civil engineering. An anonymous "Subaltern" compared officers in 1836 with "those of our own age and class, who were not, in their boyhood, dazzled by the gilded trappings of some would-be Napoleon at a militia training" and thus were better able to maintain their families' respectability.[26] Certainly, junior officers' concerns about their relative economic standing contributed to the high resignation rate of the mid-1830s.

Officers' bitterness over their income eased during the long depression that began in 1837. Whatever the inadequacy of their compensation, it offered a modicum of security in hard times. After the Mexican War, however, regulars stationed in the Far West complained that inflated prices—according to one petition, 500 to 1,000 percent higher than in the East—drastically eroded their standard of living. A captain in California argued that privates on furlough made far more money than their officers; unless a change occurred, this situation would "compel officers to subsist on the *Same* and even to dress the Same as the soldier, with but the difference that the soldier is not charged with his clothing, but the officer must refund the cost price."[27] Congress responded with a $2-per-diem allowance for officers serving in the Far West, and an act of 1857 authorized a general increase of $20 a month in officers' salaries, the first raise in base pay since the 1790s. On the eve of the Civil War, first and second lieutenants in the infantry regiments averaged $1,573 and $1,305 respectively in salary and basic allowances, well over twice the War of 1812 levels.[28]

For the increasingly career-minded junior officers of the antebellum era, promotion was an all-absorbing fixation, certainly more so than for their counterparts of the early national period. The seniority rule established during the 1790s continued to dominate the army's promotion system. Subalterns' prospects varied considerably with the rates of attrition in their regiments or staff bureaus, but advancement for most was slow. Since there was no retirement or pension system before 1861, aging commanders were compelled to remain in uniform until they died. Moreover, the fact that far more middle-ranking officers were making careers out of the army obstructed the upward progress of their subordinates. Artillery subalterns confronted particular barriers. Until 1838, each artillery regiment included eighteen first lieutenants and eighteen second lieutenants but only ten captains; thus brevet second lieutenants faced the gloomy future of waiting for thirty-six or more officers above them to leave before they could command a company. The act expanding the army in 1838 corrected the situation only partially, reducing the second lieutenants' slots in each regiment to ten but raising to twenty the first lieutenants.[29] Only a relatively high resignation rate in the artillery—largely induced no doubt by the lack of opportunity—prevented total stagnation.

Table 11.3 lists the promotion rates to first lieutenant and captain for West Point graduates in nine rather typical classes: those of 1821–1823, 1831–1833, and 1841–1843. Throughout the period, an officer could expect to be in his late twenties before his first real promotion and in his mid-thirties before reaching the rank of captain. Combined with even slower promotion to the field grades, this situation kept the attainment of high rank a distant dream. In 1836, the adjutant general calculated that at the present rate of advancement, a second lieutenant receiving his initial commission at the age of twenty-one would first command a regiment at seventy-nine.[30]

Under these circumstances, junior officers closely followed their standings on the promotion list—and the health of their superiors.[31] Three channels existed outside the seniority system by which ambitious subalterns could speed their rise: promotion into the General Staff departments, promotion into new regiments, and brevet promotion. The act enlarging the army in 1838 created captaincies in several staff bureaus—adjutant general, quartermaster, and subsistence—that had no permanent lieutenants. By 1860, the number of such positions had grown to forty-six, 16 percent of the captaincies in the army. Not surprisingly, each anticipated opening brought a rush of applications from promotion-hungry line lieutenants, often with strong political backing. Although not a hard-and-fast rule, the War Department usually awarded

TABLE 11.3. Promotion Rates to Company Grades and Major, Selected West Point Classes

	1821–1823	1831–1833	1841–1843
	N:99	N:120	N:147
Number promoted to first lieutenant	68	60	123
Median service at promotion (years)	6	5	5
Range of service at promotion (years)	2–11	3–8	4–11
Number promoted to captain	42	43	79
Median service at promotion (years)	14	13	13
Range of service at promotion (years)	6–16	5–21	5–15
Number promoted to major	24	17	45
Median service at promotion (years)	26	28	20
Range of service at promotion (years)	19–36	13–30	14–23

Source: George W. Cullum, comp., *Biographical Register of the Officers and Graduates of the U.S. Military Academy at West Point, N.Y., from . . . 1802 to 1890* (Boston: Houghton, Mifflin, 1891).

these positions to men with experience as temporary staff officers at the regimental level—for example, acting assistant quartermasters or regimental adjutants. Likewise, the occasional expansions of the army brought bonanzas of irregular promotions that temporarily loosened the promotion logjam. In particular, the addition of the four new regiments in 1855 created forty captaincies which the administration filled by promotion, as well as seventeen new slots at the field and general grades that indirectly speeded junior officers' upward mobility.

The least satisfactory way to circumvent the seniority system was brevet promotion. An import from the British army, brevet rank was a type of supplementary rank, higher than the officer's regular grade. Congress introduced it in 1812 as a reward for "gallant actions, or meritorious conduct," or for ten years service in the same grade. An act of 1834 abolished the ten-year provision, much to the dismay of the officer corps, but the administration continued to grant brevets for merit through the nineteenth century.[32] Junior officers eagerly sought these promotions, both as public recognition of their ability and as consolation for the slowness of normal channels. Moreover, brevet rank allowed regulars to outrank militia and volunteer officers of higher basic grades and, under certain constantly debated conditions, to take precedence over regular officers who were otherwise their seniors. During the Mexican War especially, the pursuit of brevets became an obsession. Most subalterns returned from Mexico with at least one brevet, but many received two or three, and the result was intense jealousy and intraservice squabbling. Although Lieutenant Gustavus W. Smith was twice breveted for gallantry, he fumed for years over his failure to receive a major's brevet for his performance at the storming of Chapultepec: "G____d d____n the thing. I cant help thinking of it sometimes, a small touch of h____ll occasionally mingles with my feelings on this subject."[33] The quest for irregular promotion encouraged young officers to cultivate political sponsors, thus confirming a role for politics in the army's personnel system that had dated from the War of 1812.

The subalterns of the antebellum army remained an independent lot, jealous of their rights and sensitive on points of honor. One of the most striking trends within the officer corps, however, was the gradual decline of the rancorous feuds that had racked the junior grades during the early national period. Although impossible to measure precisely, lieutenants' private correspondence and diaries from the 1820s on contain relatively few references to intense controversies with other subalterns. Those that did occur arose more often from institutional tensions, such as disputes over rank or over the relative prerogatives of staff and line, than from personal animosity or differences in values or social background. In sharp contrast to the pre–War of 1812 army, few clashes between junior officers ended up in military courts. War Department general orders announced the results of ninety-six officers' courts-martial and courts of inquiry in the period 1828–1845; although lieutenants were the principals in fifty of these cases, personal friction between subalterns was clearly the cause of only two.[34]

In the immediate postwar years, dueling remained a common practice in the officer corps. Thirteen officers' duels are known to have occurred between 1815 and 1826, and the actual number was probably higher. Ethan Allen Hitchcock recalled his service with the First Infantry Regiment at Baton Rouge in the early 1820s: "The general talk was of duels—of what this one said and that one threatened."[35] Although officers continued to rattle their swords and occasionally challenged their rivals, actual encounters became extremely rare after the mid-1820s. Information has been found on only eleven duels or duel-like confrontations between 1827 and 1861 involving commissioned officers of the permanent establishment, and in only four of these affairs were both participants officers. Captain John C. Casey reacted strongly in

1843 to a report that the secretary of war favored legislation to prevent duels between officers and civilians: "Had he not better add a law to require officers to eat dinner or some other substantial meal every day unless prevented by poverty or sickness?" He considered American officers "the least pugnacious military men that ever graced a military established as we are." In his annual report of 1844, the commanding general stated that "it may be boasted, as it might have been at any time in a series of years, *not a duel has occurred between commissioned officers.*"[36]

The decline in subalterns' disputatiousness partly reflects a general effort by military authorities to reduce dissension in the officer corps. After 1821, general orders repeatedly denounced officers' quarrels. Although the record is somewhat ambiguous, officers and cadets were occasionally arrested for issuing challenges or otherwise participating in duels.[37] Yet official denunciations and arrests had not solved the problem of dissension in the army of the early national period. Surely more important than exhortations and sanctions was the growing homogeneity in the junior grades. By the late 1820s, most of the lieutenants were West Point graduates who had shared a remarkably uniform experience of professional socialization and had emerged with common styles of behavior and a sense of corporate identity. In the pre–War of 1812 army, the socialization of young officers had occurred after commissioning, and the process had generated a great deal of friction in the companies and regiments. In the antebellum army, undisciplined and aberrational conduct was suppressed at the cadet stage; young men who were unwilling or unable to accept the dominant norms left the military academy before receiving their commissions. Although it would be an overstatement to describe the army's junior officers as a "band of brothers," the increasing cohesiveness in the lower commissioned grades interacted with lengthening career commitments to form the social foundations of a nascent professional ethos.

MIDDLE AND LATE CAREERS

Promotion to captain, usually achieved in his midthirties, marked the beginning of the middle stage of an officer's career. For most regulars, the long-awaited preferment brought no dramatic expansion of duties or responsibilities. After years of garrison life, they were thoroughly familiar with the routine and internal administration of a company. Army regulations specifically required all officers of two years' standing to be prepared to assume a company command; failure to reach this proficiency was grounds for denial of promotion on the basis of seniority. In any case, most first lieutenants and many second lieutenants had already commanded their companies for considerable periods while their captains were absent on leave or detached service. A captain's bars meant higher status, but otherwise no abrupt change in the course of an officer's career.

Promotion did bring a significant increase in income. After 1838, for example, a captain of artillery or infantry drew $954 in salary and basic allowances, a raise of 14 percent over a first lieutenant's pay. In addition, captains benefited from an 1827 law that gave an extra $10 a month to officers in actual command of companies (intended as compensation for keeping the company's property records), and some were able to obtain the double-ration allowance granted to commanders of permanent posts.[38] With the general pay raise of 1857, the basic compensation of infantry captains averaged over $1,900 and that of staff and mounted captains, over $2,000. Despite their protests, the income of regular army captains compared quite favorably with that of senior clerks in the executive departments, inspectors of customs, and other midlevel federal employees. Coupled with "in kind" benefits such as quarters and medical care, it afforded a comfortable living even to married officers—no doubt a factor in the generally low resignation rate among captains. Robert E. Lee claimed that his promotion stirred mixed emotions, as he had hoped to resign and settle in Virginia: "I suppose the more comfortably I am fixed in the Army, the less likely I shall be to leave it."[39]

For most career regulars, promotion to captain was the start of a relatively long, frustrating wait for their next move up the seniority ladder. Advancement to the field grades (major, lieutenant colonel, and colonel) occurred by seniority in each branch or corps—for example, in the infantry, artillery, ordnance, and engineers. Before the Mexican War, each regiment included ten captains but only three field officers. As part of the wartime expansion, Congress added a second regimental major in 1847, but the promotion ratio remained unfavorable, especially since field officers were usually both long-lived and tenacious of their commissions.[40] The result was the tightest bottleneck in the army's promotion system. The adjutant general seems to have exaggerated when he estimated in 1836 that the average captain served twenty years in that grade.[41] Nevertheless, the median tenure as captain for West Point graduates in the classes of 1821–1823 and 1831–1833 was discouraging: twelve and thirteen years respectively (see Table 11.3). On the average, members of those classes were nearly fifty years old before they reached the rank of major, and some were considerably older. The upward mobility of the 1841–1843 graduates was faster, but this was mainly due to the exceptional conditions caused by the Civil War: a moderate enlargement of the regular army, the resignation of a number of high-ranking southerners, and the introduction of an officers' retirement system. Individual cases, especially in the staff departments, support the stereotype of the grandfatherly old army captain: George D. Ramsay was a captain in 1860, forty years after his West Point graduation, and James A. J. Bradford still wore his captain's bars when he resigned to join the Confederacy in 1861, thirty-four years after his graduation and twenty-nine years after his last promotion.[42]

Captains had fewer chances than lieutenants to circumvent the seniority system. Majors' slots in most staff bureaus were reserved for the captains of those departments, thus depriving line captains of opportunities for a staff "end run." Expansions of the army created occasional breakthroughs, and captains pursued brevet promotions as eagerly as did subalterns. A captain's best chance for speedy advancement, however, was a paymaster's appointment. Paymasters constituted 40 percent of the army's majors in 1830 and 30 percent in 1860. Though pay appointments were in most cases terminal promotions, many line captains, weary of frontier duty, coveted them and mobilized political support to acquire them. In his campaign for a paymastership in the 1850s, Captain Benjamin Alvord wrote personally to President Franklin Pierce and Attorney General Caleb Cushing, having served under both of them in the Mexican War. Although his wife and friends were concerned that he had abandoned the line promotion track, he thought his decision wise; he had stood twenty-ninth on the list of infantry captains, and the same man had been at the top of the list for fourteen months.[43]

Advancement in the field grades was generally more rapid, though much depended on one's branch and generation. For the West Point graduates in the classes of 1821–1823, 1831–1833, and 1841–1843 who ultimately reached full colonel, the median term of service was five years as major and five years as lieutenant colonel. Of course, those officers entering the army after 1830 were young enough to benefit in the field grades from the accelerated promotion rates of the Civil War. The colonels and lieutenant colonels on the eve of the Civil War present a clearer picture of the experience of field officers in the peacetime army. Officers of these ranks on the 1860 army register had served an average of 7.3 years as major, with a range of 1 to 22 years. The average tenure of the colonels in the grade of lieutenant colonel had been 7.7 years, with a range of less than 1 to 14 years. A few particularly fortunate officers were able to jump grades by obtaining appointments in new regiments or to high staff positions not covered by the seniority rule. The most striking cases were those of Captain Joseph K. F. Mansfield, appointed directly to full colonel and inspector general in 1853, and Captain Joseph E. Johnston, promoted to lieutenant colonel in the newly formed First Cavalry Regiment in 1855 and then to brigadier general and quartermaster general in 1860.[44] Usually, however, an officer was in his early or midfifties when he became lieutenant colonel and about sixty when he donned his colonel's eagles.

Field rank brought a gradual but significant expansion of an officer's responsibilities. If an entire regiment served together in the field—an uncommon occurrence in peacetime—the colonel exercised command of between 500 and 785 officers and men; the lieutenant colonel and major assisted the commander, and each had direct responsibility for a battalion of several companies. More commonly, field officers commanded large posts and, after 1837, administered geographical departments and divisions. Acting through their brevet rank as generals, some colonels conducted substantial military operations involving both regulars and militia. Colonels Duncan L. Clinch, Zachary Taylor, Walker K. Armistead, and William J. Worth each commanded the forces fighting the Second Seminole War, and Taylor was still a colonel when his small field army defeated the Mexicans on the Rio Grande at the start of the Mexican War. Colonel Albert Sidney Johnston led the multiregiment Utah expedition in the "Mormon War" of 1857–1860. As in the early national period, the administration sometimes charged commanders with important political and diplomatic responsibilities; several field officers served stints as territorial governors.

Promotion to major also brought the greatest step-up in an officer's financial situation. After 1838, majors of infantry and artillery drew $1,548 in pay and allowances, an increase of 62 percent over their basic compensation as captains. Lieutenant colonels made $1,740 and full colonels, $2,088.[45] As did captains, field officers commanding posts received a double-ration allowance, and some of them supplemented their pay by serving in their brevet rank. For example, a lieutenant colonel with the brevet rank of colonel could draw the compensation of the higher rank while commanding his regiment in the absence of the colonel. By 1860, infantry and artillery majors averaged $2,895 in basic compensation; lieutenant colonels, $3,393; and colonels, $3,713. When other benefits are considered, regular army field officers ranked near the top of the federal pay scale. Their income compared very favorably with that of the assistant secretaries of the executive departments, the commissioners of the Patent Office and Indian Affairs, the auditors of the Treasury Department, and federal district judges, all of whom earned about $3,000 annually in 1859.[46]

Only a handful of regulars in the antebellum era advanced to the highest rungs of the promotion ladder: brigadier and major general. After the reduction of 1821, army organization called for only one major general and three brigadiers: The major general served as the commanding general of the army, two of the brigadiers commanded geographical departments (called divisions after 1837), and the third was the quartermaster general. During the Mexican War, the command structure grew to four major generals and nine brigadiers, but this expansion was temporary, and five of the nine new slots were filled by citizen appointments. Congress did add a fourth brigadier general to the permanent establishment in 1855. Excluding the citizen-generals of the Mexican War, twelve regulars held general's rank in the forty years before the Civil War, and all but three of them were veterans of the War of 1812. For the few who succeeded, the reward was substantial. By 1860, the compensation of the brigadier generals averaged $5,474 annually, and Winfield Scott, who commanded the army in his brevet rank of lieutenant general, received $13,711 in pay and basic allowances.[47]

At the senior levels of the officer corps, the tradition of personal dissension remained strong throughout the antebellum period. One explanation was generational; most high-ranking commanders had entered the service during or soon after the War of 1812, and many continued to exhibit the cantankerous individualism that had characterized the early officer corps. Some had reached field or general's rank as young men, only to find their careers more or less stalled, so they manifested their frustrations in politically charged squabbles over precedence and in contention for the limited number of special command opportunities in the small peacetime army. Significantly, most of the courts-martial and courts of inquiry arising from senior officers' quarrels involved citizen appointees rather than officers who had undergone the socialization process at West Point.

A more tangible reason for the friction was the system of brevet rank, which scrambled the chain of command. Despite a long series of investigations, boards, and executive directives, the government never authoritatively defined the powers and privileges of brevet rank—in particular, the circumstances under which it would supersede regular rank and carry the power of command. The result was recurrent outbursts of controversy that at times threatened the stability of the army. The exceptionally bitter feud between generals Winfield Scott and Edmund P. Gaines, which ran from 1821 to Gaines's death in 1849, had its roots in the brevet question. Scott claimed that his promotion to brevet major general on 25 June 1814, twenty-two days before Gaines's, overrode his rival's eight-year advantage in length of service and entitled him to precedence. Scott wrote his views on the primacy of brevet rank into his edition of the General Regulations and tenaciously defended them through his long career, but he failed to win the consistent support of either the executive branch or the officer corps.[48] On the eve of the Mexican War, Zachary Taylor's army in Texas was riven by a dispute over the command powers of brevet rank between colonels David E. Twiggs and William J. Worth, culminating in impassioned appeals to the commanding general, the president, and Congress, and Worth's temporary resignation from the army.[49]

As their income expanded in midcareer, many regulars engaged in economic ventures outside the army. The antebellum era witnessed dramatic economic growth, and officers were by no means immune from the speculative spirit that imbued the larger society. Colonels Zachary Taylor, Mathew Arbuckle, Duncan L. Clinch, and William Lindsay, southern-born regimental commanders who were stationed for long periods on the Florida and southwestern frontiers, all owned plantations that greatly increased their income. Other officers gambled in land in developing regions of the West. "Land speculations is all the rage here," wrote Surgeon William Beaumont in 1835, "& though we have three paymasters in St. Louis . . . we have not money enough to satisfy the *insatiable* cravings of avarice."[50] Regulars also invested heavily in banking, transportation, and manufacturing companies, especially during the boom of the early and mid-1830s. Colonel John R. Fenwick owned $14,000 worth of stock in the West Point Foundry, for example, and Inspector General John E. Wool became wealthy through investments in real estate, banks, and railroads around his residence in Troy, New York. A number of officers bought shares in the Jefferson Woolen Company, a textile factory in northern New York founded by Paymaster Edmund Kirby.[51] Participation in internal improvements led engineering officers to sink funds into railroads and other transportation projects. Many officers were hurt in the depression of 1837, however, and the experience reinforced their attachment to their commissions. Colonel Abraham Eustis reported the failure of the Bank of the United States in 1841: "Vive—New York. Á bas Philadelphia. I lose only $13,000. . . . 'How happy the soldier, who lives on his pay.' " According to Captain Abner R. Hetzel, the poor performance of the Jefferson Woolen Company was "a lesson intended merely to show that officers of the Army do not make first rate speculators."[52]

Officers' economic involvements burgeoned during the 1850s. On the Pacific Coast in particular, commanders encouraged their subordinates to engage in business as a means to offset the extremely high cost of living. Colonel Ethan Allen Hitchcock, commander of the Department of the Pacific from 1851 to 1854, and many of his officers ventured into California real estate. Captain Joseph L. Folsom of the Quartermaster Department was reputed to be the largest landowner in California with an estate estimated at $2 million, though he was deeply in debt at the time of his death in 1855. Other officers took up farming or ranching, engaged in trade, or invested in western mining operations.[53] One of the most ambitious officer-capitalists, Major Samuel P. Heintzelman, plunged into a variety of projects while serving in the Southwest; during a two-year leave from 1857 to 1859, he organized and headed the Sonora Exploring & Mining Company, which attempted to exploit silver deposits in the Gila Valley of southern Arizona.[54] Inevitably, the economic machinations of some regulars interfered with their professional responsibilities and produced charges of conflict of interest. Major William R. Montgomery, a thirty-year veteran, was dismissed in 1855 for collusion in a land speculation scheme involving the government reserve at Fort Riley, Kansas Territory. Reports that officers in California, acting as private contractors, were selling supplies to the army prompted the secretary of war to issue a regulation banning such conduct under threat of dismissal.[55]

The investments of some regulars led them to quit the army; the wave of resignations in the mid-1830s was fueled in part by the economic boom, and the opportunities for wealth on the West Coast induced a number of regulars to leave the service during the 1850s. By midcareer, however, the majority of officers seem to have viewed their extracurricular ventures as a supplement to rather than a substitute for their military pay. Whatever the difficulties of military life, a military commission offered a sheet anchor of financial and emotional security that most regulars were reluctant to surrender.

Indeed, the army may have retained many men who, because of personality or family circumstances, placed an especially high value on the safety of a large bureaucratic organization. After nineteen years in the army, Captain John R. Vinton admitted that he had little of the "adventurer's spirit" and dreaded trusting his fortunes to chance. "The mere *certainty* of our small pittance of pay, is therefore a consideration more satisfactory to me than twice its amount would be if depending on the contingencies of luck or trade." Although Major William H. T. Walker was "tired of the glory of serving such an ungrateful old scoundrel as Uncle Sam," he considered himself "too poor and proud to resign. . . . To pull off my coat & commence at the bottom of the ladder without money or credit is rather too bitter a pill for a man of forty to swallow." Captain Jesse A. Gove wrote his wife from the West during the economic slump of 1858: "My dear Maria, is not our little salary, sure to us, better than the chances of business although it does occasionally separate us? . . . The pay of an officer in the army now amounts to something in this panic. . . . How many sleepless nights have been experienced by men of all classes! Our pay remains the same, and we go to bed and rise up in the morning and still it is the same." Captain Henry Whiting considered resigning and settling on his Michigan lands in 1833, but he decided "not to commence quite yet the conversion of my sword to a pruning hook. I might not succeed so well in wielding the latter."[56]

A MILITARY SUBCULTURE

Regulars' emphasis on financial security suggests the motivational pattern that military sociologists have termed the "occupational model" of military service: the orientation of military personnel toward individual self-interest and monetary rewards rather than toward the army as an institution or its larger goals.[57] While occupational concerns certainly figured prominently in the collective mindset of the officer corps, they represent only part of the picture. Another, more subtle development was the emergence by the 1830s and 1840s of a distinct military subculture—a complex of shared values, attitudes, loyalties, and patterns of behavior that overlapped with the broader civilian culture but contained its own unique emphases and configurations and provided the foundations for a corporate identity. This subculture evolved from the social trends discussed previously: the stabilization of army organization and procedure; the rise of West Point as an effective institution of professional socialization; and the lengthening of officers' career commitments. Although officers of all ranks were affected, midcareer officers and their families stood at the center of this subculture; the small service world had become the focal point of their lives.

Later chapters will consider aspects of the emerging mental world of the officer corps: regulars' conception of their professional role; their relationship to the political world; and their attitudes toward enlisted men, Indians, foreign relations, and war. This section will address the general contours of the subculture, whose most basic feature was the tendency of officers to identify with the army as an institution—or at least with their branch or regiment. Unquestionably, regulars constantly complained about the hardships of military life: family separations, inadequate pay and slow promotion, harsh living conditions at frontier posts, and no public appreciation for their services. Although such grievances convinced some regulars to resign, the dramatic increase in the proportion of the officer corps pursuing long-term careers suggests that these remarks mainly represented the inevitable grousing of members of an occupational group about their work. Officers' correspondence and journals actually reveal a deep absorption in the parochial concerns of the service world. They filled their personal letters with references to troop movements, transfers, promotions, congressional deliberations on army bills, the activities of army friends, and garrison events, often to the exclusion of political and social developments in the society at large. Clearly, the army had become their strongest identification, at least the one most central to their everyday lives.[58]

Although officers' private writings contain frequent references to economic security as a motivation for remaining in uniform, other recurring themes are a deep positive attachment to their profession and a sense of separateness from the civilian world. In explaining to an army friend why he did not resign in 1835, Captain Ethan Allen Hitchcock referred to his "insane attachment" to military life. "Whatever may be the errors of soldiers I verily believe our little army contains a better body of men than can be found in any other profession." Lieutenant William M. Gardner likewise rejected the idea of resignation. "You can not imagine how much one gets attached to his profession and Regiment by a few years service," he wrote his sister. "On leaving the 2nd [Infantry] I should feel as if I were breaking up family ties again." Lieutenant Lucius L. Rich described to a lady friend the camp of the Utah expedition: "To hear the hum of many voices, the sound of the drum & fife[,] the bugle and the Regimental Bands discoursing martial music is something that strikes every true soldier with admiration and [is] enough to make one proud that he belongs to a profession that brings him in contact with so many stirring scenes." "I never could be happy out of the army," Lieutenant Earl Van Dorn wrote from Mexico City in 1848. "I have no other home—could make none that would be genial with my feelings. The minds of civilians and ours run in different directions."[59]

Even when in cities and on leave, regulars frequently sought out military companionship. During a brief stay in St. Louis in 1843, for example, Lieutenant William T. Sherman twice visited nearby Jefferson Barracks, where he mingled with fellow officers and their families and observed with professional delight the garrison parades. On leave in New York City in May 1859, Lieutenant August V. Kautz encountered numerous army friends and spent the night at Fort Columbus in New York harbor. Moving on to West Point, he renewed more military acquaintances: "I visited many of the old haunts, and walked through the Buildings, every step calling up slumbering reminiscences." On reaching his hometown of Cincinnati two weeks later, he immediately crossed the Ohio River to Newport Barracks, Kentucky, where he caught up on army gossip and dined with the commander. When he toured Europe later that year, Kautz traveled and socialized mainly with other American officers whom he chanced to meet. During a stay at his family's Virginia home, Lieutenant Henry S. Turner longed to return to active duty: "The truth is, there is too much tameness about a life of this sort for me, after having passed so long a time on the frontier. I find the habits of the people altogether different, their notions on all subjects different from ours, on the frontier." The preoccupation of the civilians with money gave him "a disgust for the people country, and everything else."[60]

Service-oriented periodicals allowed regulars to follow army news. Between 1833 and 1844, three specialized service journals met this function: the *Mili-*

tary and Naval Magazine of the United States (1833–1836); the *Army and Navy Chronicle* (1835–1842); and the latter's short-lived successor, the *Army and Navy Chronicle and Scientific Repository* (1843–1844). The *Army and Navy Chronicle* in particular published a great deal of personal and unit news, informing the close-knit service world of promotions, transfers, unit movements, marriages, and deaths, as well as congressional debates on army bills. Indeed, the War Department gave this periodical semiofficial status by using it to circulate orders and advertise contracts. The specialized journals eventually failed because of circulation problems: Their clientele was small and dispersed, and officers at a particular post or aboard a particular ship tended to subscribe as a group. However, regulars and their families substituted more general periodicals to keep abreast of army events. In 1858, Captain Lafayette McLaws advised his wife to subscribe to the *Washington Star, Missouri Republican, Missouri Democrat*, and *New York Herald*, all of which had military correspondents and covered army news. In the opinion of Lieutenant George W. Hazzard, the *New York Daily Times* "is the best *news* paper in the U. S. and contains all the Army items."[61]

The army family had an important, though ambivalent, place in the military subculture. In many respects, officers' families resembled those of other middle-class Americans in the antebellum era. Officers tended to marry in their late twenties or early thirties, only slightly later than other professional men, and the size of their families probably did not differ significantly from the middle-class norm. The views of those who commented on the role of women were conservative and corresponded to the cult of domesticity emerging in the general culture, with its emphasis on separate gender spheres and its glorification of women's domestic functions.[62] Although the evidence is rather skimpy, no distinctive pattern can be discerned in officers' child-rearing methods. Some regulars followed an authoritarian approach toward their children that resembles the stereotype of the military patriarch, stressing strict discipline and the use of corporal punishment. On the other hand, the letters of many officers express intense interest in and deep affection for their children, suggesting that they shared in the contemporary trend toward the nurturing, child-centered middle-class family.[63]

Nevertheless, military families diverged in important ways from their civilian counterparts. Most notably, they were subjected to the exceptional pressures of extended separations, periodic movements, and the privations of frontier living. Recently, Edward M. Coffman has discussed these conditions in a sensitive study based on the surviving letters and accounts of army wives, most of which center on the 1850s when the army dispersed across the Great Plains and Far West.[64] These documents are filled with references to frequent, long, and exhausting journeys, cramped and primitive living quarters, recurrent partings from their husbands, boredom and loneliness at isolated posts, and nagging fear for the safety of their children. In 1851, the wife of Captain Lucien B. Webster epitomized the experiences of many officers' wives when she reproved her brother for his decision not to resign from the army and become a college professor.

> How is it possible that you can consent to throw away all these advantages willingly, and subject yourself to a life of exposure, in some out of the way half civilized region, compelled to associate with the many coarse minded, unrefined male and female specimens which are continually to be met with in garrisons— . . . being ordered from one extreme of the union to the other at every whim of the government—if you have a wife and family leaving them at some forlorn place, in anxiety and distress among unpitying strangers, or what would be almost as bad, dragging them about from pillar to post with you suffering all the various, discomforts, privations and *deteriorating* influences of campaigning and garrison life, and finally terminating this inglorious career, in some ignoble skirmish with the red skins—leaving a destitute wife and family to the short lived sympathies of your brother officers, and the cold charity of the world.[65]

Conditions such as these could exert considerable strains on army marriages. Some officers and their wives chose to live apart for long periods rather than endure the hardships of garrison family life, and for all military families, frequent and often sudden separations were a fact of life. In requesting a leave in 1854, Captain John C. Henshaw claimed that he had seen his family only twice in the past eight years; his wife was an invalid and would probably never be able to join him on the frontier. Mary Marcy, whose husband, Captain Randolph B. Marcy, was a prominent army explorer, complained in 1851 that she had lived at posts on the southern plains for two years and nine months but had been with her husband for only six months of that time, and she feared that it would be many more months before he joined her again. The wife of Surgeon Charles S. Tripler remained with her children in Detroit during Tripler's four-year tour of duty in California.[66] Through personal letters and journals runs a current of despair at the prolonged separations. "What shall I do if I don't get a letter soon from my husband," an army wife confided in her diary during the Mexican War. "I am nearly crazy to hear from him. I have to keep a strict watch to keep off the blues. My thoughts are always with him. I pray that we may soon meet. Time drags heavily away from him; with him hours are but minutes." Captain Joseph H. LaMotte wrote his wife from the Texas frontier in 1850: "I miss you, I need not say . . . but shall I tell you how bitterly I deplore the absence of the dear little children—my existence seems to be renewed—bound up in theirs and yet I cannot see—cannot embrace them. Their images are constantly before my mind, and altho' I might not be able to trace their lineaments, fancy will, and often does bring the little creatures before me." In some cases, living too long apart seems to have led to permanent estrangement.[67]

The circumstances of army life shaped the military family in less corrosive ways as well. The isolation and unavoidable intimacy of garrison living and the need for officers and their wives to rely on others in the absence of their spouses encouraged an interdependence among army families. When quarters were scarce, officers' families shared living accommodations and dining arrangements, sometimes for protracted periods. Although her husband was a regimental commander, Eliza Johnston and her family shared a two-room house at Fort Mason, Texas, with a lieutenant and his wife, their two children, and a soldier's child whom they were raising. "I had just as well have 6 children of my own for they are as much trouble," she noted in her diary; "the baby cries incessantly[;] it could not be avoided however." While she longed for a place of her own, Mariquitta Garesché stressed the kindness and attention extended by the captain's family with whom she and her husband, Lieutenant Julius P. Garesché, lived for several weeks at Fort Brown, Texas.[68] At small and remote posts, one or two officers' families often formed the hub of garrison society, constantly entertaining the single officers and those whose wives were elsewhere. The wife of Lieutenant Winfield Scott Hancock described how her house at Fort Myers, Florida, became an oasis for officers wearied from campaigning against the Seminoles in the 1850s, "who frequently said that without this trysting-place they would have been driven to extremities in their search for diversion."[69] The military community also offered support to members in distress; families of deceased regulars received temporary aid from the post fund, and officers' families often looked after the widows and orphans of their comrades in arms.[70]

At garrisons large and small, families organized intimate, mostly self-contained social circles, and interacted continually through visits, parties, and excursions. During the winter of 1831–1832, three officers' families constituted the "entire society" at Fort Independence in Boston harbor; they passed "every evening together playing cards, the piano, & talking." At remote Fort Vancouver in 1857, the seven officers' families made "a pleasant society within our selves"; diversions included listening to the post band and staging numerous cotillions. The wives and daughters of officers at Carlisle Barracks in 1856–1857 rendered that garrison "self-sustaining regarding the enjoyments

Fort Snelling, located on the upper Mississippi at the present site of Minneapolis–St. Paul. As one of the strongest permanent posts on the western frontier, Fort Snelling long remained a center of the military subculture. Painting by Seth Eastman, who served there as a young officer. (Painting in the United States Capitol Art Collection; photo by Architect of the Capitol)

of dinners and dancing." In her memoirs, an army wife recalled the courtesy that regulars invariably demonstrated toward officers' wives, regardless of the rank of their husbands. "I have seen gray-haired ladies at an army post dance at the hops with as much enjoyment as the younger ones, and they are always invited by the men, young and old, to do so as a matter of course. The hops are more like a family reunion than a gathering of strangers."[71] Whatever accuracy there is to the portrayal of the nineteenth-century middle-class family as an isolated, private world stripped of its broader social functions, it does not seem to describe the antebellum military family.

Another cohesive element of the military subculture was the existence of extensive kinship networks within the small service world. As discussed in previous chapters, many commanders sent their sons into the service; for example, of the 127 field-grade officers on the army register of 1860 (excluding pay officers), at least 41 (32.3 percent) had one or more sons who held commissioned rank in the regular army.[72] Some officers tried to dissuade their female relatives from enduring the trials of army marriages. "How in the world any girl of ordinary sense can think of marrying a line officer I cannot imagine, for they must make up their minds to spend a life of exile, deprivation and poverty," wrote a captain to his daughter, who was considering such a marriage.[73]

Many commanders seem not to have shared these concerns, however, since about one-fifth of officers' marriages were to the daughters, sisters, or nieces of fellow regulars. Although the dearth of biographical data on many officers makes a full count impossible, at least two-fifths of the officers on the 1830 army register had one or more close relatives who at one time or another held commissioned rank in the regular army.[74]

The extent of some army families was remarkable. One clan centered around army explorer William Clark, an officer in the 1790s and early 1800s and later a territorial governor and prominent citizen of St. Louis. Clark's nephew was Inspector General George Croghan; his stepdaughter married Stephen W. Kearny, later a brigadier general; and his grandniece became the wife of Kearny's nephew, Lieutenant Philip Kearny of the army. Croghan's sister married Quartermaster General Thomas S. Jesup; generals Kearny and Jesup each had a son in the army; and one of Jesup's daughters married an officer. Equally impressive was the family of Major General Alexander Macomb, whose army relatives included two half-brothers, one son, four sons-in-law, three nephews, and numerous cousins and cousins by marriage. Henry Whiting, a long-time quartermaster officer who married a first cousin of General Macomb's, was the son of a high-ranking revolutionary and regular army officer; his brother and first cousin were career regulars, and at least one of his sons served in the army. Among the army connections of Robert E. Lee were a half-brother, three sons, two nephews, and two cousins.[75]

Intraservice marriages and kinship ties certainly reinforced the army identities of many regulars, binding them ever more closely to the service world. In April 1847, Eliza Anderson received a letter from her husband, Captain Robert Anderson, who was serving in Mexico. Discouraged by his failure to gain recognition, Anderson proposed resigning after the war. Mrs. Anderson, whose father was former colonel Duncan L. Clinch, responded in a letter that merits extensive quotation.

> Gen'l. Scott might I think in consideration of his old friendship, etc., have said *something* about you—but "better luck next time" I hope—*I* am satisfied that you are *safe* but I should like the world to know that you acted as gallantly as any one there. I am very much in hopes that Genl. Worth, in his report, will speak of your services—I shall be *wofully* disappointed if he does not—You speak my dearest husband, of *resigning* after the war is over—*pray* do not think of such a thing—I have not breathed a word of your intention to *any* one as I sincerely hope it was only a passing thought—There will not, probably, be another war in a hundred years—and believe *me*, who knows you *well*, you would never be satisfied out of

the army—take *warning* by the many who have taken this step, and ever afterwards regretted it—You must, beyond a doubt, get more rank before the war is over, then you will return home, and we shall be *so* happy—Both you and I are very much attached to the army & have been from our very childhood, and during this war it has won itself so many *new* laurels—it has behaved so nobly, so gloriously!—how can you think of separating yourself from it—*Please* do not think of such a thing.

Her brother, recently commissioned in a Mexican War regiment, had visited, and her young daughter had observed his uniform. "She soon got down from her Uncle's lap and came to me—I asked her 'what do you want daughter?' She said 'little drummer boy bring my papa's sword and sash, Mother'—I do not think my own husband, that I ever loved her more than I did at that moment!!'"[76]

An additional factor defining and reinforcing the military subculture was the officer corps's relationship with the civilian sphere. As noted before, during the antebellum era, suspicion of the political and social dangers of an exclusive military elite coexisted with a widespread fascination for military history and an unrestrained adulation of martial heroes, expressed most dramatically during the Mexican War. Ignoring the ambivalence, regulars reacted against the expressions of popular antimilitarism and lamented the fate of the military profession in an egalitarian society. They portrayed themselves as devoted public servants, faithfully performing unpleasant though essential duties in the face of abuse by an uncaring and somewhat degenerate public.[77] As chapter 15 will demonstrate, officers developed a strong antipathy for politicians, whom they accused of currying popular favor to the neglect of the army and the broad national interest.

In particular, regulars took exception to citizen-soldiers—militiamen and volunteers. Beginning with the Black Hawk War of 1832 and continuing through Indian removal and the Mexican War, the government relied heavily on citizen-soldiers to supplement the thinly stretched regular army. In the period 1832–1838 alone, over 43,000 volunteers and militiamen saw active duty, and amateur soldiers made up a large part of the army's manpower in the invasion of Mexico.[78] Not only did regulars have an abundance of practical experience serving with and commanding citizen-soldiers, but the cadre plan—the officer corps's most common defense of its collective existence—in fact rested on the need to give structure and direction to the short-term soldiers called out in time of emergency.

Nevertheless, regulars were virtually unanimous in their contempt for citizen-soldiers. The traditional adulation of such troops as the bulwark of American democracy appeared an affront to the officer corps and a challenge to its claims to special expertise. Whenever amateur soldiers took the field, regulars denounced them as motivated by political ambition, undisciplined, ineffective in combat, extravagantly expensive, and brutal in their conduct of warfare. In a typical passage, an army surgeon described volunteers in the Creek War: "They presented a glorious display of dirks, pistols, and bowie-knives, with no scarcity of dirt. It seemed as if every ragamuffin in Georgia, deeming himself an invincible warrior, had enlisted under the standard of Mars, which many from their conduct must have mistaken for the standard of Bacchus, as they observed the articles of the latter god with much greater reverence." Lieutenant George B. McClellan compared volunteers in the Mexican War to "Falstaff's company" and disparaged their unkempt appearance and lack of discipline; they were "all hollowing, cursing, yelling like so many incarnate fiends—no attention or respect paid to the commands of their officers, whom they would curse as quickly as they would look at them." After commanding volunteers engaged in Cherokee removal, Colonel John E. Wool stated that he would prefer a force of 500 regulars to 2,000 citizen-soldiers: "The latter are little else than an unruly mob untill restrained and brought down by the force of discipline." Regular commanders frequently condemned the atrocities committed by volunteers, especially the mistreatment of Mexican civilians during the Mexican War. Major General Winfield Scott considered it "unchristian & cruel to let loose upon any people—even savages—such unbridled persons—free-booters."[79]

Some regulars were willing to acknowledge that citizen-soldiers were individually brave and might perform adequately under certain circumstances—for example, defending fortified positions as in the Battle of New Orleans. Overall, however, they were severely critical of the irregulars' reliability in battle. From the professionals' perspective, amateur soldiers did not possess the discipline, the training, and especially the leadership to fight effectively in the open field. Brigadier General Winfield Scott, Colonel Duncan L. Clinch, and Colonel Zachary Taylor all sparked civilian wrath when they censured the performance of volunteers in battles with the Seminoles. After his dramatic victory over the Mexicans at Buena Vista, Taylor publicly praised the volunteers, who had made up the great majority of his force. Privately, however, he attributed the triumph mainly to the three companies of regular artillery under his command, and he expressed concern that the battle would enhance the reputation of the volunteers to the detriment of the regulars.[80] According to Lieutenant Thomas Williams, volunteers lacked "*every thing* that constitutes the soldier. . . . They are useless, useless, useless—expensive, wasteful—good for nothing." In 1860, the commander in New Mexico Territory denounced volunteers raised to fight the Navajos as "an organized band of robbers" recruited from "the most despicable [class] on Earth;" he accused them of planning a war of plunder against the Indians and would not allow regulars to serve with them.[81]

The regulars' indictment of amateur soldiers contained a good deal of truth. Irregulars often were undisciplined, proved unreliable in combat, and treated their Indian and Mexican adversaries with extreme cruelty. Nevertheless, the unanimity and the hostility of the critique suggest that citizen-soldiers gave regulars a negative reference group—a foil against which they could further define their collective identity. The continued existence and popularity of the volunteers and militia, combined with recurrent civilian strictures of the army as elitist and unnecessary, sharpened regulars' awareness of their uniqueness, their sense of isolation from the mainstream of American society. From the viewpoint of the officer corps, the regular army represented all that citizen-soldiers—and citizens in general—did not: cohesion, expertise, devotion to duty, and professional neutrality and restraint. Increasingly, regulars perceived themselves as an embattled band of brothers, cultivating discipline and specialized knowledge for the defense of an ungrateful nation. However overblown this image might be, it formed an intellectual lowest common denominator for officers from diverse backgrounds and branches of the service, and it deepened their attachment to the military community.

LEAVING THE SERVICE

During the antebellum decades, attrition from the officer corps resulted from either death, resignation, dismissal, or retirement. In contrast to the earlier period, disbandment after reductions of the army played a very minor role. The reduction of 1821 was the last significant cutback of the basic establishment in the nineteeth century; only in 1842, as an economy move in the aftermath of the Second Seminole War and the Maine boundary crisis, did Congress order the discharge of a small number of staff officers.[82] The relative importance of the reasons for attrition of course varied according to year, branch, and rank. The regulars whose names appear on the 1830 army register were fairly representative, however, and attrition will be examined mainly through an analysis of their experiences. As Table 11.4 demonstrates, about one-half remained in the army until they died, just over one-third resigned their commissions, a smaller number retired from the service, and even fewer were dismissed by sentence of court-martial or summarily dropped from the rolls of the army for misconduct.

TABLE 11.4. Attrition among Officers on Army Register of 1830*

Type of Attrition	Number	Percentage
Death	281	47.3
Resignation	219	36.9
Dismissal/Dropped from rolls	21	3.5
Retired	71	12.0
Other	2**	0.3
Total	594	

Source: Army register of 1830; Francis B. Heitman, comp., *Historical Register and Dictionary of the United States Army, from Its Organization, September 29, 1789, to March 2, 1903* (Washington, D.C.: Government Printing Office, 1903).

*Attrition defined as final termination of service in basic establishment of the regular army (i.e., resignations and dismissals not included if officers were later reappointed to the peacetime army).
**One officer discharged in reduction of 1842; one transferred to U.S. Marine Corps.

Although information is missing on the precise conditions under which most regulars died in the service, the majority succumbed to disease or other "natural causes." As with the enlisted men, officers were at greatest risk at the southern posts. Not only was the mortality rate in the South generally higher than in the North, but the bulk of the army was usually stationed in that region until the Mexican War.[83] Of 169 natural deaths for which locations are known, 43 (25.4 percent) occurred in Florida, Louisiana, or elsewhere in the Lower South, 45 (26.5 percent) in the Upper South, including Missouri and the District of Columbia, and 14 (8.3 percent) in Texas or the Indian Territory. In 60 cases, the letters reporting officers' natural deaths or other sources indicate something about the cause. Twenty-one of these deaths were attributed to yellow fever or other types of fever, including "bilious," "intermittent," and "congestive"; probably this category covered such widespread infectious diseases as malaria, typhoid fever, typhus, and hepatitis. Five regulars are reported to have died in the outbreaks of cholera that periodically ravaged the South and West in the nineteenth century, and at least 6 succumbed to dysentery and other intestinal disorders. The remaining deaths resulted from strokes, heart attacks, respiratory ailments, and other miscellaneous or unidentifiable causes.

No fewer than thirty-six officers on the 1830 list died of other than "natural" causes. Accidents cost the lives of eight of these regulars; although most were due to boat or ship mishaps, one notable exception was Colonel Hugh Brady, the octogenarian commander of the Second Infantry Regiment. This doughty and highly respected veteran, who had first donned the uniform in

1792, was thrown from his carriage in Detroit in 1851 when his horses spooked at a telegraph cable, strung across the street by "some mischievous thoughtless boys."[84] Two regulars died in duels, one was killed by a soldier, and one appears to have committed suicide. The body of Colonel Trueman Cross, the third-ranking officer of the Quartermaster Department, was found in the scrub near the army's encampment on the Rio Grande in April 1846, just before the outbreak of the Mexican War; presumably he had been murdered by bandits.[85] Twenty-three officers, 3.9 percent of the total on the 1830 army list, were killed in action or died of combat wounds. Nine of these regulars perished in the Second Seminole War, twelve in the Mexican War, and two in the Civil War. Altogether, a total of ninety-seven officers in the basic establishment of the United States Army died of combat-related causes in the forty years preceding the Civil War.[86]

Most of the 219 regulars on the 1830 army register who resigned their commissions left no clear indication of their motives. In 1842, however, the adjutant general compiled a list of all the officers resigning in the period 1834–1842, which specified the reasons when they were known—probably derived from letters of resignation and other records in the War Department.[87] From this list and from scattered data found in other sources, it is possible to determine the likely grounds for the resignations of 86 officers on the 1830 register. No single motive predominated. Twenty-one regulars, the largest category, left to attend to family, personal, or financial matters. Thirteen resigned because of poor health, 9 because they were reluctant to perform the duty assigned them, and 10 because of dissatisfaction with aspects of army life—pay, promotion, or the tedium of garrison duty. Ten officers left the army to pursue more attractive employment prospects in civil life, and 12 resigned in 1861 to join the Confederacy. In 11 cases (12.8 percent), the officers surrendered their commissions under pressure—to avoid courts-martial or, in the case of 2 assistant surgeons, to avoid dismissal after failing the medical board examination required for promotion to the rank of surgeon.

Closely related to the forced resignations were the twenty-one regulars on the 1830 army register who were dismissed or dropped from the rolls, and information has been found concerning all of them. Seven regulars were summarily discharged by the president under an 1823 law that mandated the dismissal of any government officer who handled public funds and failed to render prompt quarterly returns to the Treasury Department.[88] This act claimed many victims in the antebellum army, mostly through negligence and error rather than fraud, and its violation brought relatively little stigma; indeed, at least two of the ejected officers were granted other government appointments soon after their dismissals. Five officers were dropped from the rolls, two for being absent from duty and one each for insanity, gambling away public funds, and failing the medical promotion examination. The government summarily dismissed Brigadier General David E. Twiggs in March 1861, after that Georgia-born commander surrendered the Department of Texas to the Confederates, then joined the Confederate army. In the remaining eight cases, the officers were expelled by sentence of court-martial for a variety of offenses, including embezzlement of public property, drunkenness on duty, and publicly denouncing a commanding officer in an apparent effort to provoke a duel. Interestingly, only one case involved an officer's performance in the field. In 1830, Captain Joseph Pentland was convicted on charges of cowardice and misconduct in the presence of hostile Indians; on a prairie expedition the previous year, he had ordered his small detachment to retreat rather than engage a party of warriors, resulting in the death and scalping of a private. If the dismissals and known forced resignations are combined, at least 5.6 percent of the officers on the 1830 list terminated their careers involuntarily, under less than honorable circumstances.[89]

The seventy-one officers on the 1830 register who retired from the service bear witness to a significant though belated reform in the army's personnel system. Before 1861, aging officers either remained in service until they died or resigned without pension benefits. As late as 1860, War of 1812 veterans occupied nineteen of the thirty-three positions at or above the rank of full colonel (57.6 percent), and nine had already held field rank in that distant conflict. Inevitably, the rolls of the army included the names of a number of veteran commanders who were too old and infirm to do any duty whatever. On his death in 1857, John de Barth Walbach was ninety-one years old, yet he was still the nominal commander of the Fourth Artillery Regiment; he had first been commissioned in the United States Army in 1799—after having already served twelve years as an officer in European armies.[90] For decades, regulars had lobbied for a retirement system, both to enhance military efficiency and to speed promotion for junior officers, but Congress had resisted the additional expense.

The Civil War accomplished what officers' petitions could not. Concerned about the deadwood at the top of the army roster, Congress approved a retired list in August 1861. Officers who had served forty consecutive years could be placed on the list at their own request. The act also empowered military boards to examine commanders suspected of being unfit for duty and to recommend them to the president for mandatory retirement. Retirement benefits were generous: Officers received the basic pay of their rank and an allowance of four rations a day, but no additional emoluments. A year later, Congress authorized the president to retire at his own discretion officers with

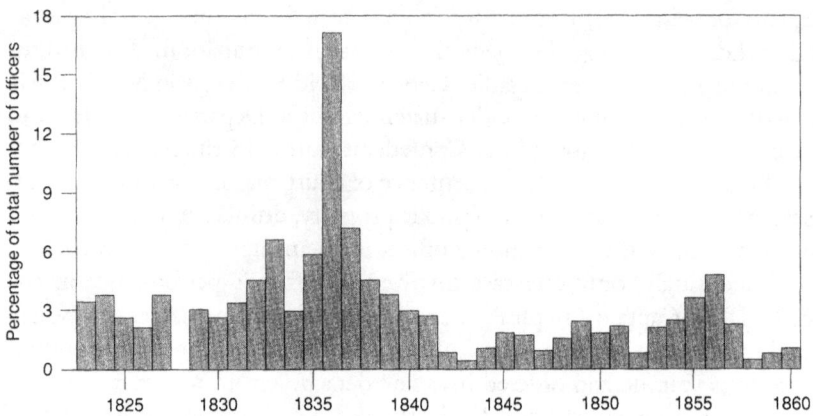

Figure 11.1. Annual Resignation Rate for Officers, 1823–1860 (data missing for 1828). *Source*: Annual army registers.

forty-five years of service or those who had reached age sixty-two and also to assign retired officers to special duties as he saw fit.[91] A number of retired veterans performed such duties during the Civil War, serving as recruiting and mustering officers, for example, or on military boards and courts-martial.[92]

One aspect of attrition from the antebellum officer corps deserves closer attention, since it functions as a rough measure of officers' commitment to their profession: the resignation rate. Figure 11.1 traces the annual rate between 1823 and 1859, defined as the percentage of resignees within the total complement of officers on the preceding year's army register. Throughout most of the period, the resignation rate remained consistently low—under 4 percent of the army's commissioned strength. Indeed, it virtually disappeared during several years in the early 1840s and again in the late 1850s, falling below 1 percent. No doubt these dips were related to the economic depressions after 1837 and 1857, which restricted employment opportunites outside the army. In any case, the bulk of the resignees were junior officers, and their departure was easily offset by the annual influx of West Point graduates. More than any other single fact, the overall infrequency of resignations demonstrates the growing cohesion within the military profession.

The major exception to this trend occurred during the 1830s. In all but one year between 1832 and 1838, the resignation rate exceeded 4 percent; in 1836, 117 regulars, over 17 percent of the total, surrendered their commissions. The dramatic increase in 1836 coincided with the opening stages of the Second Seminole War, and it aroused civilian claims that regulars had resigned to avoid the dangers and privations of Indian campaigning. As late as 1844, the House Committee on Military Affairs considered it necessary to counter the persistent argument that these resignations proved the unreliability of the officer corps and justified the abolition of the United States Military Academy.[93]

Certainly, the prospect of Florida service contributed to many of the 1836 departures, but the resignation rate had begun to rise before the Seminole war and returned to normal long before the close of that conflict. Most likely, the upswing reflected the coalescence of a number of factors in the mid-1830s that temporarily lessened the appeal of army life. One was a rapidly expanding economy, which offered regulars abundant opportunities for alternative employment; in particular, the transportation boom opened lucrative positions in civil engineering for which many officers were qualified. At the same time, the Jackson administration's attack on special allowances, discussed previously, tightened the economic squeeze on the officer corps and led to a decline in morale. Finally, the War Department, faced with a rising tide of complaints from line commanders that the absence of captains and lieutenants from their companies detracted from military efficiency, began in 1830 to restrict leaves of absence and the assignment of line officers to staff and other special duties. The demand for company officers became especially urgent in 1836, with the outbreak of fighting in Florida, the increasing demands of Indian removal in general, and threats of war with Mexico and France. On 28 June 1836, President Jackson ordered all captains and subalterns who "were not on duty with the army, nor engaged in military service *proper*" back to their regiments. He repeated this order in October, using even stronger language.[94] Although these directives were not universally enforced, many company officers no doubt considered them a threat to their leaves and preferable staff assignments. Of the ninety-eight line captains and lieutenants who resigned in 1836, seventy-nine (80.6 percent) did so in the second half of the year, after the promulgation of Jackson's original order; moreover, fifty-five of the officers (56.1 percent) were on staff or recruiting duty or on leave at the time of their resignations.[95]

Information on officers' postservice careers is fairly extensive, thanks largely to the superb biographical register of West Point graduates compiled by George W. Cullum of the Corps of Engineers.[96] Table 11.5 lists the principal postservice occupations pursued by 166 officers on the 1830 army register for whom data are available; though heavily weighted toward the West Pointers, these men represent nearly three-quarters of the total, exclusive of those dying in service or retiring. As might be expected, civil engineers composed the largest category by far—over one-quarter of all the former regulars—and many others were also engaged in that line of work during portions of their later careers.

TABLE 11.5. Principal Postservice Occuaptions of Officers on 1830 Army Register

Occupation	Number	Percentage
Agricultural	*31*	*18.7*
Farmer	20	12.1
Planter	11	6.6
Commercial/Manufacturing	*74*	*44.6*
Merchant/Transportation Entrepreneur	15	9.0
Banker	4	2.4
Manufacturer/Founder	3	1.8
Company employee	2	1.2
Civil engineer	47	28.3
Other	3	1.8
Professional	*32*	*19.3*
Lawyer/Judge	13	7.8
Medical doctor	4	2.4
Clergyman	3	1.8
College professor	11	6.6
Teacher	1	0.6
Government service	*29*	*17.5*
President/Congressman/ Senator	2	1.2
Federal officeholder	14	8.4
Local/State official	2	1.2
Officer Confederate Army	7	4.2
Officer U.S. Marine Corps	1	0.6
Officer Texan Army	1	0.6
Foreign official	2	1.2
Total known	166	
Total officer corps	594	

Source: Army register of 1830; George W. Cullum, comp., *Biographical Register of the Officers and Graduates of the U.S. Military Academy at West Point, N.Y., from* . . . *1802 to 1890* (Boston: Houghton, Mifflin, 1891); miscellaneous biographical sources.

The transportation revolution made civil engineering a booming field during most of the antebellum era, and West Point was the nation's chief source of trained engineers. Many former regulars used their technical skills as a means of occupational mobility, rising to chief engineer, president, and other top management positions in transportation and industrial companies. Even while in the army, Captain William H. Swift chaired the board of trustees of the Hannibal and St. Joseph Railroad; he resigned in 1849 to take the presidency of the Philadelphia, Wilmington, and Baltimore Railroad and later the

Massachusetts Western line. After his resignation in 1832, Walter Gwynn served as chief engineer of a variety of southern railroads and canals; during the 1840s, he was president of the Portsmouth and Roanoke Railroad and the Kanawha Canal Company. On leaving the army in 1834, Daniel Tyler launched a long and highly successful business career, during which he headed at least seven transportation and manufacturing firms.[97] According to a recent study, former regulars introduced techniques of military administration into the companies they served and thus pioneered in modern business management.[98]

Former officers prospered in other fields as well, at least partly because of their military education and experience. Several from the 1830 army register became prominent scientists and educators, and others pursued successful careers in law, commerce, and banking. A significant number of veterans obtained civil posts in the federal government, serving in such positions as customs officials, clerks, and military storekeepers. The proportion of officeholders was considerably smaller than among the officers on the army list of 1797, however, perhaps because West Point–trained veterans found more attractive employment options in the private sector. Few former regulars followed political careers. The 1830 list contained the name of a future president, of course, but Zachary Taylor was a career soldier who kept his commission until after his election in 1848. Although four of the 1830 regulars held seats in Congress, only former lieutenant Jefferson Davis served longer than two years. Several veterans had brief stints as state legislators or held local offices, but none became a state governor.[99] Perhaps the gradual dissociation of the military profession from the mainstream of partisan politics (a trend discussed in chapter 15) influenced regulars' postservice careers as well as their conduct while in uniform. Despite the penchant of parties to nominate famous generals for president, politics and military service increasingly diverged in the nineteenth century, each becoming a distinct career path.

Many officers did not terminate their military connections when they left the regular service but remained active in militia affairs or followed careers that allowed them to keep contact with the service world. Among the eleven college professors on the 1830 register were three members of the West Point faculty, and the lone teacher on that list, Zebina J. D. Kinsley, operated a preparatory school near West Point geared to the training of prospective cadets. At least two former ordnance officers occupied important niches in the government's ordnance-industrial complex. Robert P. Parrott broke new ground in the development of rifled artillery as superintendent of the West Point Foundry at Cold Spring, New York. After working at a Pittsburgh foundry, William Wade returned to government service in 1841 as "attending agent" or inspector of the private foundries involved in government contracting; in this capacity, he helped devise precise methods for testing weapons and munitions, which had broad implications for modern engineering procedures.[100] At least fourteen former regulars from the 1830 group served as volunteer or temporary regular officers in the Mexican War, and one fought as a sergeant. Excluding those resigning in 1861 to join the Confederacy, no fewer than twenty-eight aging veterans, evenly divided between North and South, took up arms again in the Civil War; sixteen held general rank, eleven in the Union volunteers and five in the Confederate forces. Of course, Civil War service was far more common among younger veterans who did their regular duty after 1830.

Perhaps the 1830 veteran who best exemplifies the continuing army identities of former regulars was George S. Greene, a West Point graduate of the class of 1823. Greene resigned in 1836 and pursued a distinguished career in civil engineering. During the Civil War, he commanded a brigade in the Army of the Potomac and was instrumental at Gettysburg, where his command held Culp's Hill on the critical second day of the battle. He resumed his engineering career after the war but remained interested in the affairs of West Point, from which a son graduated in 1870. Late in life, he took great pride in being known as the academy's oldest living graduate, and in 1894, Congress legislated him, at age ninety-three, back into the service as a first lieutenant of artillery, the rank he had held at the time of his resignation.[101]

12
THE EMERGENCE OF THE GENERAL STAFF OFFICER

Central to the self-image of the nineteenth-century officer corps was the line commander of infantry, artillery, or dragoons—the dashing, aggressive combat officer oriented toward active campaigning and the prospect of war. Nevertheless, the post–War of 1812 period marked the emergence of a large and very different category of officers who devoted their careers to logistical, support, and technical services. Staff officers were not entirely new; the staff-line distinction had become a fixture in European armies by the eighteenth century, and the Continental Army had developed a sizable staff component. Even the tiny army of the 1780s and 1790s had contained a group of medical officers, and the Corps of Engineers had engaged in highly specialized technical tasks since its formation in 1802.

Throughout the early national period, however, most logistical duties had been performed by civil agents of the War and Treasury departments or by line officers on temporary staff detail. Only during the War of 1812, and especially with the formation of a permanent General Staff structure in the postwar years, did full-time commissioned regulars assume responsibility for most support operations. The wide dispersion of the garrisons of the peacetime force and the multiplicity of the army's functions led to a gradual expansion of the staff bureaus, and by the 1840s and 1850s, the army had developed a lengthy logistical tail. The rise of the General Staff broadened and refined the traditional conception of military leadership, and it also introduced a source of intraservice rivalry that shaped the internal life of the officer corps through the nineteenth century.

PATTERNS OF STAFF DUTY

Between the reduction of the army in 1821 and its expansion in 1838, the officers permanently assigned to the General Staff bureaus composed about one-

TABLE 12.1. Permanent General Staff Officers, 1830 and 1860

	1830		1860	
Branch	N	% Officer Corps	N	% Officer Corps
Adjutant general	1	0.2	15	1.4
Inspectors general	2	0.3	2	0.2
Ordnance	0		41	3.8
Quartermaster	6	1.0	38	3.5
Subsistence	3	0.5	12	1.1
Engineers	26	4.4	48	4.4
Topographical engineers	10	1.7	43	4.0
Medical	52	8.8	116	10.7
Pay	15	2.5	29	2.7
Other	0		2	0.2
Total staff	115	19.4	346	31.9
Total officer corps	594		1,086	

Source: Army registers of 1830, 1860.

fifth of the total officer corps (see Table 12.1). The War Department supplemented them by appointing large numbers of line officers to temporary staff duty, a practice known as detached service. Although Congress had merged the Ordnance Department with the artillery regiments in 1821, several senior artillery officers remained continually on ordnance duty until the revival of the department in 1832, and artillery captains and subalterns had tours of duty in the ordnance service. Similarly, line officers served as regimental adjutants, aides-de-camp to generals, assistant quartermasters, and assistant commissaries of subsistence; others did temporary duty as engineers, particularly as the army expanded its role in civil works, and became instructors at the military academy. A report by the adjutant general in 1827 described 113 line officers as absent from their companies on various forms of staff duty, and this figure does not seem to have included officers who performed staff functions in addition to their regular company duties.[1] At any given time before the mid-1830s, about two-fifths of the officer corps were involved in full-time staff duty.

The 1830s brought a dramatic increase in the permanent personnel of the General Staff. Congress reestablished a separate ordnance department in 1832, and the act enlarging the army in 1838 expanded greatly the size of several bureaus. By 1860, permanent staff officers constituted nearly one-third of the officer corps (see Table 12.1). This expansion coincided with a reduction in the use of detached service, which was caused by the demand for company officers in Florida and on the western and Canadian frontiers. Nevertheless, some line officers continued to serve in staff capacities, and the overall proportion of regulars engaged in full-time staff duty probably remained at about two-fifths of the total officer corps. When part-time staff officers are considered, logistical, support, and technical functions consumed nearly as much of the officer corps's energy as did traditional military duties in the garrison and field.

Although the character of staff duty varied widely, staff officers may be divided into three broad categories based on their relationship to the line branches. The first category includes those regulars acting as administrative aides to commanders, a duty that kept them in close contact with the line army.[2] The largest contingent of this group was attached to the Adjutant General's Office. Stationed at Washington, D.C., the adjutant general served as the executive secretary and chief recordkeeper of the army. He worked closely with the secretary of war and, until Winfield Scott moved the Headquarters of the Army to New York City in 1849, the commanding general; he also directed the general recruiting service. The expansion of 1838 added other permanent members to this branch—assistant adjutants general—who worked at the central offices or functioned as chiefs of staff to commanders of geographical departments or major field commands. In addition, each regimental commander had the aid of a regimental adjutant, usually a first lieutenant on detached service from his company, and numerous subalterns served as part-time post adjutants. Performing roughly similar duties were a small number of aides-de-camp to general officers. Finally, the army's two inspectors general should be included in this category. Although they were largely independent of the chain of command, their regular tours of inspection involved them closely with the discipline, training, and internal administration of the line branches.

With the exception of the adjutant general and the inspectors general, whose rank and responsibilities allowed them to influence military policy, the work performed by staff officers of the first category consisted of administrative routine and paralleled the duties of midlevel and senior clerks in civil branches of the government or in commercial firms. They handled the official correspondence of the commanders they served, promulgated orders, and kept the personnel records of their commands. Much of their time was spent copying letters dictated by their superiors, recording orders and outgoing correspondence in orderly books and letterbooks, processing and filing incoming correspondence, and compiling muster rolls and returns for transmittal to higher headquarters. As compensation for the monotony of their duties, administrative officers enjoyed relatively stationary headquarters assignments and had the opportunity to gain the patronage of influential senior commanders. Although the pace of

Colonel Roger Jones. A member of the War of 1812 generation, Jones entered the army in 1812 after three years as a marine officer. He distinguished himself as an assistant adjutant general during the war and rose to adjutant general of the army in 1825, a position he held until his death in 1852. (Portrait from Lewis H. Jones, *Captain Roger Jones of London and Virginia; Some of His Antecedents and Descendants* [Albany, N.Y., 1891]; photo courtesy of the State Historical Society of Wisconsin)

work fluctuated considerably with the size and activity of the command, it could be demanding. Brevet Captain Julius P. Garesché captured the atmosphere at the Adjutant General's Office in Washington just before the start of a congressional session.

> We have worked unceasingly for the last three weeks, and especially this last week; not only to prepare and expedite our own Reports, but also to assist the Secretary of War in completing his. Each day was I unexpectedly interrupted to hunt up some information or prepare some memorandum for him. And the work one performs in this rushing manner, which is so important that not a single mistake must be made, I find, fatigues my mind more than any other kind. Thank God! I am in hopes that it is finished.[3]

The second category of General Staff officers encompasses those men performing duties that were strictly military in content but were specialized and largely independent of the line chain of command. Included were the officers of the Quartermaster, Subsistence, and Ordnance departments and those of the Corps of Engineers working on fortifications. In contrast to the adjutants, these regulars engaged in a wide and complex range of tasks and exercised a good deal of independent authority, being answerable in departmental matters only to their bureau chiefs. The permanent staff of the Quartermaster and Subsistence departments, called assistant quartermasters and assistant commissaries of subsistence, handled the procurement, transportation, and distribution of supplies and equipment, as well as the construction of army buildings and military roads. They were supported by a large number of temporary and part-time staff officers at the regimental and post level. Ordnance officers superintended the army's arsenals, enforced quality control at the two national armories and at the private manufacturing firms producing small arms and cannon, and experimented with new types of weapons and materiel. The majority of army engineers were occupied with the design and construction of the massive seacoast fortifications.

If the adjutants resembled clerks in the nature of their work, middle-ranking staff officers of the second category combined the skills of merchants, industrial managers, accountants, and, in the case of the ordnance and engineer officers, architects and technicians. They advertised and negotiated contracts with private businessmen for supplies, construction materials, and transportation. They hired and supervised civilian agents and workmen on construction projects and at ordnance installations, which at times embroiled them in civil-military and labor disputes. Because they handled large sums of money, staff officers were required to pay strict attention to financial accountability, enforced through the regular submission of numerous reports and returns. For example, engineers in charge of fortification projects regularly submitted sixteen separate forms to bureau headquarters, including monthly, quarterly, and annual estimates and returns. The quartermaster regulations of 1825 listed thirty-seven standardized forms. Indeed, the army's staff departments pioneered in the development of managerial control and accountability, refining procedures that would later be introduced into private corporations.[4]

The letterbooks of two staff officers fairly representative of the second category suggest the diversity of staff work in the antebellum army. Major Rufus L. Baker was a long-term ordnance veteran who commanded Watervliet Arsenal near Troy, New York, during the late 1830s and early 1840s.[5] Located at the eastern terminus of the Erie Canal, Watervliet was a key installation for manufacturing and repairing gun carriages and other types of materiel for posts in the eastern United States. Baker negotiated with private contractors to procure iron, timber, and various manufactured goods needed for the arsenal's operations. He corresponded frequently with his department head, Colonel George Bomford, and with other ordnance officers on the technical aspects of ordnance production and on shipments of weapons and equipment to the Indian war in Florida and to garrisons in the Northeast. The war scare with Great Britain over the Maine boundary brought a spurt of activity; Baker dispatched cannon and war materiel to Kennebec Arsenal in Maine, supplied arms to the New York militia, and worked to strengthen forts Ontario and Niagara, newly reactivated posts on the Great Lakes frontier. Baker was also engaged in his department's ongoing efforts to improve the quality of ordnance materiel. In the spring of 1839, for example, he supervised tests of the strength of iron transoms for artillery carriages, conducted at Watervliet and Governor's Island in New York harbor. During 1840, he suspended his arsenal duties to lead a board of officers on a seven-month tour of ordnance facilities in Europe.[6]

Although Baker's letterbooks are less informative about his management of internal arsenal affairs, a great deal of his time was certainly consumed in the functions of a factory manager, supervising a work force of about 35 enlisted men and 115 civilian armorers and other workmen.[7] He seems to have been a benevolent employer, recommending pay raises for his workers and defending his master artisans against charges of graft and political collusion, but he participated in a more general campaign by the Ordnance Department to institute time discipline and break artisan control of the production process. In March 1839, he issued instructions that forbade workers' children from entering the shops, prohibited books and newspapers in the workplace and the gathering of workers for private conversation, and required the master artisans to deduct absent time from their wages. During the following month, he requested permission to spend $450 for a clock "in consequence of the difficulty I have experienced in having the time for working hours accurately kept, and of some impositions that have been practiced in this respect."[8]

Baker took a strong interest in the arsenal's physical plant, personally designing architectural improvements and negotiating with the New York canal commissioners for clearance to add a basin to facilitate shipments to and from the arsenal. He also served as the arsenal's spokesman to the local community. Early in 1839, for example, he assured the mayor of Troy that the arsenal was on a higher elevation than the town and that "even should an explosion of it occur, it is believed that the force of it would not seriously affect your city."[9] Baker administered annual expenditures of more than $100,000, and accountability was a constant preoccupation; he punctually submitted monthly, quarterly, and annual packets of estimates and returns to the chief of ordnance for review by the Treasury Department.

The letterbook of Captain Justus McKinstry of the Quartermaster Department presents a somewhat different view of staff duty. McKinstry directed the quartermaster depot at San Diego, California, during the post–Mexican War period. He was responsible for supporting the garrison at San Diego, consisting of about two companies, and for several other small and temporary posts in southern California.[10] During the summer of 1849, McKinstry outfitted the government commission surveying the Mexican-American boundary and its two-company military escort; the late fall found him at remote Camp Far West, north of Sacramento, erecting quarters for the small garrison and feuding with the line commander over the progress of the work. After a protracted absence in 1850–1851, during which he may have been on leave, he returned to San Diego where he equipped sporadic operations by regulars and volunteers against the Yuma and Cocopa Indians. Especially troublesome were his efforts to supply Fort Yuma, an isolated post at the confluence of the Colorado and Gila rivers 150 miles east of San Diego. McKinstry dispatched wagon and pack trains across the desert, but contact remained tenuous and ultimately most provisions were brought up the Colorado River by boat. Probably because of the economically undeveloped nature of the region, McKinstry seems to have done little local contracting during his early years in California; he usually ordered supplies and draft animals through the chief quartermaster of the Department of the Pacific. As with so many staff officers, however, he was an employer of labor, supervising a shifting force of civilian agents, teamsters, and laborers.

As might be expected, much of McKinstry's correspondence related to financial matters and recordkeeping. During part of his tenure at San Diego, he handled subsistence as well as quartermaster duties, and thus he submitted returns to the headquarters of both departments. In response to government concerns about the high cost of maintaining troops in California, McKinstry struggled to cut expenses, which inevitably generated friction with line officers in the region. He also reported occasionally to the quartermaster general on the resources and inhabitants of the region, a practice that conformed to a departmental regulation requiring quartermaster officers to gather intelligence. In July 1849, he informed his chief of the commercial potential of San Diego and its vicinity; his lengthy assessment of Indian relations in southern California was published with the War Department's annual report of 1852.[11] No doubt McKinstry's position made him an important figure in San Diego, and he may have dabbled in local politics. A former regular once charged that McKinstry had tried to influence soldiers' votes in an election, and in response, the captain sent to department headquarters in San Francisco statements by other officers refuting the allegations.[12]

The third general category of staff officers includes regulars whose functions were furthest removed from traditional military duty: medical officers, paymasters, topographical engineers, and officers of the Corps of Engineers engaged in civil works. Of these, the medical officers had the most contact with the line army, since they were distributed among the garrisons. Indeed, Surgeon General Thomas Lawson, who headed the department between 1836 and 1861, and other senior surgeons stressed the military character of their branch and lobbied to have medical officers granted official rank and limited command powers.[13] Nevertheless, the highly specialized nature of the surgeons' work and their ties to the civilian medical profession made them a class apart from the other branches of the officer corps. In a recent study, Mary C. Gillett has so thoroughly described the duties and experiences of the medical officers and their relationship to the general context of nineteenth-century medicine that there is no need to elaborate further here.[14]

Paymasters were really military accountants; they operated individually and outside the chain of command, making bimonthly tours of payment to the posts within their districts and reporting through the paymaster general to the accounting officers of the Treasury. Although they carried rank and although many had prior experience in the line, they lived virtually as civilians. An officer recalled that the paymaster at Fort Snelling in the 1850s, "not doing military duty, seemed irresponsible and did about as he pleased. He allowed himself much latitude in dress, appearing in civilian dress, except at the pay table, when he appeared in uniform, or nearly so."[15]

The officers of the two engineering branches occupied with internal improvements constitute a final group of "civilianized" staff officers. As a rule, topographical officers had a small military role; they surveyed sites for fortifications and occasionally served on the staffs of line commanders, and a large portion of the Corps of Topographical Engineers saw combat in the Mexican War. However, most of these regulars spent by far the greater part of their careers working on civil projects.[16] Under the General Survey Act of 1824, they surveyed routes for roads, canals, and railroads deemed of national importance; they also supervised harbor and river improvements, conducted western explorations, built lighthouses and marine hospitals under the auspices of the Treasury Department, participated in various boundary surveys and the surveys of the Great Lakes and Atlantic Coast, and constructed wagon roads in the trans-Mississippi West. During the 1820s and early 1830s, some topographical officers were detailed to work on privately owned railroads and state transportation projects, though Congress banned this practice in 1838. Except during 1841–1852, when the topographical engineers held a virtual monopoly on civil works, many officers in the Corps of Engineers also engaged in internal improvements. This branch's primary responsibility remained the fortification program, however, and thus its officers tended to divide their careers between military and civil projects.

Engineers engaged in civil works had little contact with the line branches of the army, and their tasks closely resembled those of civil engineers and building contractors. Most commonly, they headed small survey parties or "brigades," composed mainly of civilian surveyors and laborers, which took to the field in the spring and remained active until the late fall. On larger projects, such as road building, major harbor improvements, and the clearing of obstacles from the western rivers, engineers engaged in extensive contracting and hiring of labor and handled substantial sums of money. As the work load increased after 1838, the topographical bureau established a number of field offices, headed by senior topographical officers. These men supervised several projects within a geographical district, most of which were under the immediate control of civilian agents. During the winter months, when most field work was suspended, the engineers settled their accounts, organized the data acquired in the field, repaired equipment and surveying instruments, and prepared estimates for the next year's work. Internal improvements continued to be a politically charged issue, and army engineers frequently found themselves enmeshed in political controversy.

The career of Stephen H. Long encapsulates the experience of the internal improvements engineers. Long entered the army in 1814 as a second lieutenant in the Corps of Engineers but was promoted to major and topographical engineer two years later, a rank that he held until 1861. As a young man, he won a place in western history by leading three highly publicized exploratory expeditions to the upper Mississippi and Rocky Mountains between 1817 and 1823. For the rest of his career, Long was almost totally absorbed in civil works. Beginning in the late 1820s, he surveyed numerous routes for roads and railroads,

Western exploration was an important function of the topographical engineers, especially after the Mexican War. This drawing, by Henrich B. Möllhausen, depicts the expedition commanded by Lieutenant Joseph C. Ives that explored the Colorado River and Grand Canyon in 1857–1858. (From Joseph C. Ives, *Report upon the Colorado River of the West, Explored in 1857 and 1858* [Washington, D.C., 1861])

planned harbor improvements, cleared river channels, and designed a system of inclined railroads for hauling canal boats over mountains on the Pennsylvania state canal. He earned a special reputation as a railroad designer, working on loan to the Baltimore & Ohio Railroad and the Georgia-owned Western and Atlantic line, and he published widely used manuals on railroad and bridge construction. During the early 1850s, he supervised the construction of marine hospitals for the care of merchant sailors employed on the western waterways. Much of his later career was devoted to the clearing of obstructions from the Mississippi and its tributaries—a difficult and frustrating task that required the supervision of dispersed work crews and at one point embroiled him in a dispute with Secretary of War Jefferson Davis over the use of patronage. He retired in 1863, after serving two years as chief of the topographical bureau in Washington, D.C. During a half-century of army service, the closest Long came to traditional military duty was a series of military surveys on the Mississippi River frontier in 1816–1818 and a two-year assignment during the Mexican War to build steamboats for the use of the Quartermaster Department.[17]

The General Staff might be expanded informally to cover one group of men who were not commissioned officers: chaplains. Before 1838, the government appointed very few chaplains to the regular army, and these men served mainly during the War of 1812.[18] After 1818, the only officially recognized chaplain was at West Point, where he doubled as professor of ethics. Some officers personally led religious exercises for their men, however, and the commanders or councils of administration at several posts unofficially employed clergymen to hold services. Influenced by the reform spirit of the age and concerned about low morale and disciplinary problems in the ranks, officers lobbied Congress during the 1830s to fund regular post chaplains. As part of the general expansion of the army in 1838, Congress authorized the councils of administration at no more than twenty posts to employ "from time to time" chaplains who would also act as schoolmasters; chaplains' salaries, determined by the councils, were not to exceed forty dollars a month, with allowances for rations, quarters, and fuel. In 1849, Congress increased the number of chaplains' posts to thirty. As might be expected, the denominations of the appointees resembled the religious preferences of the officer corps, not the rank and file. Of the forty-four post chaplains whose affiliations are known, thirty-one (70.5 percent) were Episcopalians and five (11.4 percent) were Presbyterians; only three Catholic priests held army chaplaincies in this period, though Catholics may well have composed a majority of the soldiers.[19]

Chaplains faced an uphill struggle in the antebellum army. Although the officer corps contained many devout Christians, the dominant mood was nonsectarian and rather contemptuous of open displays of religion. No doubt exceptional in his stringent philosophical consistency was Major Sylvester Churchill, who told a pious colleague that he was unable to reconcile the commandment not to kill with his obligation to order soldiers to shoot Indians—and so he had decided to renounce the Bible. However, Major William H. T. Walker reflected the attitudes of many officers when he instructed his wife to have their child christened in his absence: "I am a Christian who always according to scripture 'pray' in my 'closet' & dont say Lord Lord in the streets and on the highways."[20] Because of religious indifference or constitutional scruples, some officers refused to enforce the regulation requiring soldiers to attend divine services, and many viewed the chaplain's function with mild disdain. The War Department permitted chaplains to choose quarters before subalterns did, a provision bound to produce bad feeling. Lacking commissions, the military clerics were subject to dismissal whenever they ran afoul of the post council, and their plaintive letters suggest that such cases were not uncommon. In the opinion of the Fort Washita chaplain, control by the council of administration made chaplains into ciphers.

> It precludes them from the rights which belong to all other Grades in the Army. It is calculated to crush in them all manly independence and extin-

guish that spirit of religious freedom which becomes them as men and as preachers. It makes them liable to a tyranny more irksome and intolerable (because in a great measure irresponsible) than any that can be exercised by Ecclesiastical authority. It makes them, in short, both contemned and contemptible.[21]

Permanent staff officers typically selected their branches at the very start of their careers; medical officers and paymasters appointed from civil life are obvious examples. Only the highest members of West Point classes qualified for the engineers, topographical engineers, and ordnance, and most of the qualifying graduates chose to enter these prestigious corps as second lieutenants. Permanent appointment to the adjutant general, quartermaster, and subsistence branches came later in an officer's career, usually while a first lieutenant, although many appointees had already served stints as temporary officers in those branches. The choice of a staff assignment was not absolutely final; occasionally, staff officers transferred into the line, especially during expansions of the army.[22] Nevertheless, the great majority of staff officers remained in their branches for good and followed career paths that sharply separated them from their colleagues in the line. Rather than the traditional qualities of military command, they cultivated specialized technical and administrative skills that often resembled those of civilian businessmen, engineers, and technicians. As a result, the content of officership became increasingly subdivided into discrete categories of expertise, more so perhaps than in any civilian profession during the antebellum era.

STAFF VERSUS LINE

Accompanying the growth of the General Staff was constant line-staff friction, one of the most inveterate features of nineteenth-century army life. Such tension was by no means new. Since the Revolution, line officers had complained about the independence of the quartermaster service, and the quest of the Corps of Engineers for an elite position in the army had been a source of antagonism since the founding of that branch. However, the level of intraservice feuding rose dramatically with the formation of permanent staff departments during and after the War of 1812; expressed in myriad ways, it represented the deepest institutional cleavage within the antebellum officer corps.

The fundamental cause of staff-line tension was the autonomy of the bureaus. As they took shape under Calhoun, most were administratively independent of the line, responsible in their specialized functions directly to the secretary of war. The source of this arrangement is obscure; at least one line critic traced it to the British division of authority over the army between king and Parliament.[23] Originally, it may have reflected a Democratic Republican fear of concentrating excessive power in the hands of a single military chief. Whatever its cause, the existence of several parallel chains of command was sure to breed resentment among commanders, who saw it as a violation of the rules of military hierarchy. On several occasions after the War of 1812, Major General Andrew Jackson clashed with the president and secretary of war over his right to control staff officers within his division. Brigadier General Gaines considered the power of assistant quartermasters to withhold funds from their commanding officers "repugnant to the primary principles of subordination." In the opinion of Winfield Scott, the "absolute independence" of staff officers was "highly injurious to the general interests of the service, & the rights & duties of commanding officers."[24]

As commanding general between 1828 and 1841, Alexander Macomb strove to bring the staff departments under his authority. In 1830, he quarreled with Adjutant General Roger Jones over Jones's attempt to place his office directly under the secretary of war, bypassing the commanding general. In Macomb's opinion, the adjutant general should function as the commanding general's chief of staff, and a court-martial upheld his position by convicting Jones of insubordination. Macomb also worked to extend at least partial control over the other bureau chiefs. He employed the inspectors general to establish his right to oversee staff operations outside the capital, a move that sparked predictable resistance from the Corps of Engineers. In revising the General Regulations in 1834, he stretched the commanding general's powers to include the broad supervision of nearly all the functions of the General Staff. Asserting the right to control was easier than enforcing it, however, and high-ranking staff officers clung tenaciously to their autonomy and their special relationship with the secretary of war. Some developed ties to Congress that helped them parry the commanding general's incursions. In the long run, the esoteric nature of bureau administration, the want of disciplinary means at the disposal of the commanding general, and the weight of bureaucratic tradition combined to keep the staff departments, with one or two exceptions, virtually independent.[25]

At the post level, jurisdictional tension between staff and line was chronic. Almost invariably, the issues were minor, but they often generated impassioned petitions to higher authority and official charges. At Detroit in 1825, Captain John Garland of the infantry clashed with Major Henry Stanton of the Quartermaster Department over the right to occupy the post commander's quarters. Acting on the opinion of the adjutant general, Garland expelled Stanton from the quarters; Stanton in turn ordered Garland's arrest. After conflicting appeal from the adjutant general and the quartermaster general, the secretary of war decided that the senior officer, regardless of branch, should have precedence. Three years later, Captain William J. Worth, an artillery officer serving as commandant of cadets at West Point, ordered Assistant Quartermaster Aeneas Mackay to make repairs on his house. Mackay refused the order on the grounds that the building was part of the military academy and thus under the sole control of the Corps of Engineers. A court-martial convicted Mackay of insubordination, but the president overturned the decision.[26] When the commanding general ordered a company of artillery to Augusta Arsenal, Georgia, in March 1843, the Ordnance Department protested that the move violated its right to the exclusive control of arsenals. President Tyler eventually reviewed the case and decided in favor of the artillery. The controversy sputtered for another two and a half years, however, often embroiling the army's high leadership, until the removal of the artillery detachment at the start of the Mexican War.[27]

A persistent source of staff-line friction was the practice of detached service. Faced with a high desertion rate and other disciplinary problems, commanders opposed the separation of large numbers of line officers from their companies for temporary duty in the staff departments. In July 1835, for example, only 188 of the army's 421 company officers were present with their companies; of eighteen companies stationed in Florida the following year, only five were commanded by captains, and some had no officers at all.[28] In the opinion of Colonel James House, detached service was "calculated to discourage emulation among the officers & men of one Company with another; to destroy responsability & to extinguish all that pride & esprit du corps which is the soul of Discipline." Colonel Abraham Eustis considered the practice a prime cause of desertion: "When the Soldier sees his Captain & the senior Lieutenants of his company constantly on the watch for an opportunity to desert their proper station for detached service of any kind, can *he* be expected to attach any strong moral obligation to his bond of service?"[29] As noted in the previous chapter, the administration moved to restrict detached service in the mid-1830s, and the expansion of the staff bureaus in 1838 led to a significant decline in temporary details from the line. Nevertheless, line commanders long continued to grumble about the paltry number of company officers on duty with the troops.[30]

Institutional concerns, then, formed the foundation of staff-line antagonism: that is, line officers' belief that staff independence and detached service threatened discipline and the integrity of the chain of command. What magnified the intensity of intraservice discord was line resentment of the alleged advantages enjoyed by staff officers in rank, pay, stations, and prestige. Line officers objected to the system of dual rank, by which some staff officers continued to hold rank in their former regiments while performing no regimental duty, thereby blocking the promotion of their juniors. They denounced the granting of extra allowances to staff officers, including double rations, and especially the act of 1838 that gave mounted pay to the entire General Staff. They resented the political influence of the bureaus and the fact that many staff officers managed to avoid unpleasant frontier service. As they had since the era of Jonathan Williams, the officers of most branches opposed the elitist pretensions of the Corps of Engineers, particularly its monopoly of the top West Point graduates and its domination of the military academy.[31] Captain Robert C. Buchanan summed up the line indictment in a poetic appeal to his uncle, Congressman John Quincy Adams, urging him to support repeal of the act that allowed quartermaster and subsistence officers to retain their regimental rank.

> It broadly asserts that the Line is by far,
> Inferior in worth both in Peace and in War;
> Although 'tis well known that the Line do your fighting
> While the Staff in their Bureaus are busied in—writing!
> And what if 'tis said they have plenty to do?
> Sure that don't imply that the Line have not too!
> They've advantage enough, which we might deplore,
> In their pay and their stations without needing more.
> They're generally stationed in some pleasant city
> Where good things are plenty, and women are pretty!
> And then it is said to be one of their fashions
> *"To draw in the latch,"* while they eat *double rations!*
> 'Tis especially so, (which, we think, is a pity),
> With those who are stationed in Washington City![32]

Although usually on the defensive, staff officers energetically countered line criticism. In their view, the dispersion of the army and the multiplicity of its roles—including civil works, support for the militia, and the construction of weapons and permanent defenses for use in a future war—required proportionately large and independent staff services. The bureau system had proved its worth by the economy and efficiency of staff operations in comparison with the waste and confusion of the War of 1812. Differentials in pay were justified by staff officers' higher expenses—their need to maintain individual residences in expensive towns and cities, travel frequently, and buy professional books—and by the high degree of specialized knowledge demanded for their duties. Privately, they accused their critics of undermining army unity out of petty jealousy. An engineer lieutenant described a line officer opposed to staff pay as "an unadulterated defecated Hog—a miserable wretch who is bitterer than the bitterness of gall against the staff because his precious self could not get into it."[33]

The archrivals of staff-line feuding were the artillery regiments and the Ordnance Department. As part of the reduction of the army in 1821, the Ordnance Department had been merged with the artillery, but a number of former ordnance officers remained permanently on ordnance duty, and they lobbied incessantly to be restored to independent bureau status. Congress approved this step in 1832, and by the late 1830s, the Ordnance Department had grown into one of the largest of the military staff bureaus. Artillery commanders, frequently employed as infantry in Florida and the West, argued that the ordnance's tight control of the arsenals prevented them from working with cannon and thus achieving technical competence in their field. They also resented ordnance domination of the professional boards established to consider new weapons for adoption and especially the assignment of ordnance officers to command heavy artillery batteries in the Mexican War, thereby depriving the artillery of what it considered its share of the glory. Adding to the hostility was the artillerists' envy of the comfortable accommodations held by their rivals at the arsenals and armories. In the opinion of one artillerist, ordnance officers were "silk-stocking and boudoir gentlemen" who lived in "carpeted parlors within princely government edifices."[34] Through the 1840s and 1850s, the two branches engaged in an acrimonious pamphlet and petition war and importuned Congress—the artillery campaigning for remerger, the ordnance struggling to retain its independence.[35]

Line officers differed in their proposals for staff reform. Some favored "civilianizing" the staff—separating most of the bureaus completely from the rest of the army and even divesting staff officers of military rank. In the opinion of an artillery officer, the duties of the army engineers were so unmilitary that they "could not be deemed members of the army, on any principle which could not equally include the workmen whose labors they superintend!"[36] Others proposed an opposite tack—reducing or abolishing the bureaus and reintegrating staff services into the line. During the 1850s, Major General Winfield Scott promoted a movement to merge staff departments and cut drastically the number of lieutenants and captains on permanent staff duty, relying as before 1838 on temporary details from the line. To avoid a shortage of officers on duty with the troops, supernumerary officers would be added to each regiment. Although Congress considered bills to this effect, the bureau chiefs implacably resisted the plan, and the staff-line struggle remained a stalemate until the era of military reform at the start of the twentieth century.[37] Intraservice rivalries helped shape a distinctive pattern of political behavior within the officer corps, which focused on the pursuit of branch goals rather than a unified army interest, and thus they contributed indirectly to the tradition of civil control of the military.

13
PROFESSIONAL THOUGHT AND INSTITUTIONS

In a memoir of his service as an artillery lieutenant in the 1850s, Armistead L. Long related a story about Major Charles A. May, a gallant dragoon commander who had won national fame for a brave, though poorly executed, charge of the enemy guns at the Battle of Palo Alto in the Mexican War. Crossing the Plains on an expedition to Utah, May searched the wagons in an effort to reduce unnecessary baggage. When he reached the wagons of the light artillery battery, Captain Henry J. Hunt proudly pointed out the box containing the battery library. " 'Books!' " May exclaimed in astonishment. " 'You say books! Who ever heard of books being hauled over the plains? What in the H____ are you going to do with them?' At that moment Captain Campbell of the Dragoons came up and asked permission to carry a barrel of whiskey. 'Yes, anything in reason Captain, you can take along the whiskey, but D____nd if these books shall go.' "[1]

The anti-intellectualism described by Long was by no means unique in the antebellum officer corps. The quasi-aristocratic conception of officership, emphasizing an active, outdoors life centered around horses, hunting, and heavy drinking, remained an important component of the military subculture, especially in the infantry and mounted regiments. Even if commanders were not as openly hostile to books as Major May, the prevalence of such values at the frontier garrisons subtly discouraged intellectually oriented officers from pursuing their interests. Moreover, the dispersion of the army retarded professional study and improvement, as many regulars had no access to military books and periodicals. In a letter to the *Army and Navy Chronicle*, Philip St. George Cooke described the fate of a typical West Point graduate who arrives at a frontier post, full of ambition to continue his professional studies. Finding his military duty limited to fatigue details and his intellectual life stifled by the lack of books and stimulating companions, he eventually turns to cards and drink, and these habits shape his character. An infantry officer stated in 1860 that during eight years of service he had never known "a single instance of an officer studying theoretically his profession, (when away from West Point,) after graduating. They are usually scattered by single companies, and if concentrated are in the field on campaign in pursuit of Indians, and in consequence, cannot have recourse to books."[2]

While somewhat accurate, accounts of this type exaggerate the mental stagnation of the nineteenth-century officer corps. Actually, the army did develop an intellectual tradition during the antebellum era: A large number of regulars read military works, thought about problems related to military technology, tactics, strategy, and policy, and even contributed to the corpus of professional knowledge, broadly defined. Much of this activity was disparate and unorganized, carried on by individual officers rather than promoted by formal professional institutions. It also tended to be derivative, geared toward the adaptation of contemporary European thought to the American service. Nevertheless, a professional culture emerged that involved at least a significant minority of the officer corps. Indeed, if professional activity is viewed as the publication of books, reports, and articles on military subjects, almost certainly a larger proportion of antebellum army officers participated in the culture of their profession than do their late-twentieth-century counterparts.

THE TRANSATLANTIC MILITARY CONNECTION

Vital to the army's professional culture was ongoing contact with Europe. American reliance on European military expertise had dated from the Revolution, and this dependency persisted into the early national period, illustrated most clearly by the employment of foreigners in the early fortification program and as officer-instructors in the Corps of Artillerists and Engineers during the 1790s. European contacts expanded after 1815, as military reformers sought to draw upon the lessons of the Napoleonic Wars. At least a score of American officers visited Europe in the postwar years, and the administration recruited Napoleonic veterans to serve in instructional and advisory capacities. Among the most prominent were Simon Bernard, who helped design the seacoast fortification system; Claude Crozet, who revised and upgraded the engineering course at West Point; and Henri Lallemand, who wrote a three-volume treatise on artillery for use in the American service.[3]

Probably because of regulars' resentment of the implication of American inferiority, the administration gradually abandoned the hiring of foreign experts. The last of the Napoleonic veterans left the army and returned to France in the early 1830s after the July Revolution. Some American commanders resisted any reliance on European models. Brigadier General Gaines had little use for those officers "who have never seen the flash of an Enemy's Cannon—who have acquired distinction only in the mazes of French Books, with only that imperfect knowledge of the French Language which is better adapted to the Quackery of Charlatans, than the common-sense science of war."[4] Nevertheless, many officers continued to look to the European powers, France in particular, for guidance and inspiration. In common with Americans in other fields during the antebellum period—medicine, science, literature, reform—military men were part of a loosely knit transatlantic cultural community that grew stronger as communications improved. The result was a perennial infusion of European influence into the United States Army.

Beginning in the 1820s, the War Department frequently dispatched officers to Europe to examine installations, observe military operations, study in military schools, and procure books, plans, and equipment. A number of these missions arose from the continuing effort to improve artillery and ordnance materiel. On assignment in France in 1828–1829, Lieutenant Daniel Tyler translated and printed for American use the standard French system of artillery design and maneuvers. He also circumvented French security restrictions to obtain the details of a new, more advanced artillery system that the French were in the process of testing; it would eventually be adopted into the American service. A four-man ordnance task force toured Europe in 1840, examining foundries, arsenals, small-arms factories, and a variety of other installations. The board's lengthy report, published by Congress, contained a wealth of technical information on European arms production. During 1848–1849, Lieutenant Peter V. Hagner traveled extensively on the Continent, where he consulted with European officers, observed ordnance experiments, and gathered additional technical data.[5] Engineering and topographical officers often crossed the Atlantic for purposes related to their specialties. Lieutenant Colonel Sylvanus Thayer, who had first visited France after the War of 1812, traveled in Europe from January 1844 to June 1846 inspecting fortifications and military schools and buying professional books for the Corps of Engineers.[6]

Although less likely than staff officers to serve on official missions, many line officers sought professional improvement abroad. In an effort to upgrade the American mounted service, the War Department dispatched six dragoon subalterns to study at the French cavalry school at Saumur in 1839 and 1840. One of these officers, Lieutenant Philip Kearny, accompanied a French military expedition in Algeria and participated in combat with the Arabs.[7] Lieutenant Minor Knowlton of the artillery, another officer who studied in France, served as an aide-de-camp to Marshal Thomas-Robert Bugeaud, the ruthless conqueror of Algeria and founder of the French "colonial school" of warfare. The War Department sent Lieutenant Colonel Edwin V. Sumner to Europe in 1854 to gather information on the British and French cavalry.[8] Scores of other regulars went abroad on leave, combining the grand tour with professional interests. While Lieutenant August V. Kautz's main purpose for visiting Europe in 1859–1860 was to look up his German relatives, he spent two days observing the British training encampment at Aldershot, toured battlefields, fortifications, and military installations, discussed military matters with Austrian officers, and purchased military books for his own study.[9] In 1859, the outbreak of the War of Italian Unification inspired a rush of officers to head overseas in the hope of observing the action. A former regular reported that seven American officers had accompanied the Piedmontese army at the Battle of Solferino.[10]

The most ambitious military mission of the antebellum era occurred in 1855–1856, when Secretary of War Jefferson Davis ordered three officers—Major Richard Delafield of the Corps of Engineers, Major Alfred Mordecai of the Ordnance Department, and Captain George B. McClellan of the First Cavalry Regiment—to observe the Crimean War and report generally on the state of the military art in Europe. French and Russian security restrictions delayed the group's arrival in the Crimea until after the critical fighting had ended. The members carefully examined the battlefields with the aid of British officers, however, and they were able to reconstruct the progress of the campaign. They also visited a wide variety of military installations in Russia, Prussia, the Austrian Empire, France, Belgium, and Britain. On their return, the officers compiled separate reports on their specialties, which were published by Congress. These large and impressively illustrated volumes covered a vast array of subjects related to the "art of war," including the size and basic organization of the major European armies, the history of the Crimean campaign, the architecture of fortresses and arsenals, the technical dimensions of small arms, and the design of ambulances, knapsacks, and camp equipment.[11]

It is difficult to assess the overall impact of European connections on the professional culture of the officer corps. The frequent missions, supplemented by War Department purchases of European equipment and military books, allowed at least some officers to keep abreast of new developments in technology and tactics. Travel to Europe motivated a number of regulars to contribute to the professional literature. On his return from a trip to France in 1845, for example, Lieutenant Henry W. Halleck composed a sweeping survey of military strategy, tactics, and organization entitled *Elements of Military Art and Science*, a work that established his reputation as one of the army's leading intellectuals. A year at the cavalry school at Saumur seems to have sparked

Title page of Major (Brevet Colonel) Richard Delafield's report on the Crimean War mission, depicting a Russian artillery emplacement and the rope mantelet used to protect the gunners from rifle fire. (From Richard Delafield, *Report on the Art of War in Europe in 1854, 1855, and 1856* [Washington, D.C., 1861])

Lieutenant William J. Hardee's interest in tactical theory, and in the 1850s he headed a board that revised the army's infantry tactics to adapt to the introduction of the percussion rifle. After an extended leave in Europe in the late 1850s, Lieutenant Cadmus M. Wilcox published translations of Austrian manuals on rifle practice and infantry tactics.[12]

Perhaps of equal importance to the procurement of technical information was the inspiration officers drew from witnessing large military formations, touring famous battlefields, and mingling with their European counterparts. Indeed, some regulars appear to have taken from their contacts models of professional deportment and to have acquired a sense of membership in an international military fraternity. Lieutenant John C. Kelton considered the Austrian officer "the most perfect specimen of a modest, intelligent, well put up soldier I have seen. Their style and address can anywhere be imitated with advantage." Socializing with Prussian officers made Major Alfred Mordecai appreciate "the sort of freemasonry which exists among Mil[itar]y Men, and the easy and frank footing on which our intercourse with each other is immediately placed."[13]

FORTIFICATION, STRATEGY, AND ORDNANCE DESIGN

Most directly, exposure to Europe reinforced professional activity in the army's "scientific" branches, notably the Corps of Engineers and the Ordnance Department. The engineers in particular had a strong tradition of professional study, instilled by Colonel Jonathan Williams before the War of 1812. After 1815, the corps devoted most of its energy to designing and building seacoast fortifications. As described in chapter 6, the Board of Engineers had investigated the coastline and in the 1820s submitted to the government comprehensive plans of national defense that framed the debate on military planning through most of the remainder of the century. Although the board had mentioned the navy, the militia, and internal transportation as key elements in a sound defense system, it had focused on the need for permanent fortifications to defend the major ports and naval installations and provide refuges for merchant shipping. The original plan had called for 50 works, but the number inevitably expanded, in part because of territorial acquisitions and the increase in the number of ports deemed worthy of defending and in part because of the perceived need to construct multiple works at the more important sites. By 1851, the Corps of Engineers' list had grown to 186 proposed works.[14]

As the centerpiece of national defense, the fortification system generated considerable debate. On one level, engineer officers engaged in a great deal of discussion about the technical aspects of fortress construction, most of which was confined within the corps. They drafted countless reports concerning the architecture of particular works, the relative merits of various building materials and techniques, and the design of casemates, embrasures, and magazines.[15] On another, more important level, the fortification system prompted officers to address general questions of military policy and strategy, including the impact of changing technology on the nature of war. From the start of the program, the basic position of the Corps of Engineers had been firm: On the assumption that Great Britain and France were the most likely adversaries, large masonry fortifications were essential to prevent a superior fleet from closely blockading the American coastline, devastating the major seaports and naval bases, and establishing a foothold for an invasion. History had clearly shown the superiority of land fortifications over attacking ships, and this precept had been confirmed by the repulse of British assaults on Fort McHenry and other works during the War of 1812. While expensive, fixed fortifications would be far cheaper in the long run than the apparent alternative: maintenance of large naval and land forces at all the possible points of attack.[16]

Although frequently questioning the need for particular projects, Congress acceded to the engineers' basic argument and funded fortifications at a generous level throughout most of the antebellum era. By the 1830s, however, critics inside and outside the army were raising doubts about the viability of the program in light of new developments in military technology. One of the earliest and most tenacious of these critics was Brigadier General Edmund P. Gaines, who warned of an impending revolution in warfare wrought by steam power. In a series of increasingly strident reports, memorials, and circulars, Gaines proposed discarding the orthodox fortification program for a new system based on powerful steam-propelled floating batteries for harbor defense and a federally constructed railroad network that would radiate from the interior states to the seacoast and be capable of rapidly concentrating masses of militia to repel an invasion.[17] Less extreme but ultimately more influential was Andrew Jackson's secretary of war, Lewis Cass. Apparently impressed by the arguments of Gaines and of Captain John L. Smith of the Corps of Engineers, another advocate of floating batteries, Cass drafted a widely cited report to Congress in April 1836 during the diplomatic controversy with France over the repayment of French debts. He called for a reorientation of the defense program to take into account uniquely American conditions. Rather than the large works of the conventional system, Cass favored smaller, less expensive forts, augmented by steam batteries. He also predicted that railroads would soon make it possible to throw "almost any amount of physical force . . . , in

Fort Sumter, South Carolina, before the bombardment of 1861, as painted by Seth Eastman. Fort Sumter was typical of the large masonry works of the Corps of Engineers' system of seacoast fortification. (Painting in the United States Capitol Art Collection; photo by Architect of the Capitol)

a few hours, upon any point threatened by the enemy," and overall he stressed the need to adapt to innovations in technology.[18]

The points raised by Gaines and Cass during the 1830s became the crux of a heated debate on national defense that flared sporadically through the rest of the antebellum era, carried on in published congressional documents and articles in the general press.[19] Joining the opponents of the fortification program were several naval officers, who argued that fast and maneuverable steam warships, armed with rifled shell guns, would soon render fixed masonry forts obsolete. Not surprisingly, they urged the government to expand the navy.[20] A small clique of dissidents emerged within the Corps of Engineers itself who followed Cass in advocating smaller works and greater sensitivity to American circumstances and changing technology. In a much-discussed memoir addressed to the secretary of war, Lieutenant James St. Clair Morton warned of the increasing danger of a large-scale amphibious operation against New York City (and presumably other major seaports)—a threat not foreseen in the orthodox defense plan. He proposed deemphasizing new coastal works in favor of lines of earthen fortifications to ward off land attack.[21] Most of the engineers rallied in support of their beleaguered program and disparaged the revolutionary effects of the new technology. They buttressed their arguments with historical examples and cited the Crimean War, in which Russian batteries had fared well against the allied fleets. Assessing the Crimean campaign in his report of his European tour, Major Richard Delafield confidently concluded "that permanent sea-coast batteries are to be relied upon for the defense of our harbors; that they are superior to every known floating battery; and that the present experience of the best naval as well as military authorities in Europe, now confirms the supremacy of land batteries over those in the fleets of the present day."[22]

The preoccupation of military thinkers with the fortification program was perfectly logical in light of the prevailing view that the next major war would be with Great Britain—in effect, a replay of the War of 1812. However, engineers frequently broadened their commentary to embrace other aspects of military organization and strategy. The heart of Henry W. Halleck's eclectic treatise on military science was a discussion of strategic theory, drawn mainly from the writings of Antoine Henri Jomini, the most prominent European commentator on Napoleonic warfare; he also included sections on logistics, military education, the organization of armies, and a variety of other professional topics.[23] In 1846, Lieutenant Edward B. Hunt began an article defending the fortification program with an outspoken critique of American military policy, stressing the importance of military professionalism and the cadre system—a theme that Lieutenant Isaac Ingalls Stevens echoed in his book on the conduct of the Mexican War.[24]

During periods of crisis, the War Department assigned engineer and other officers to make reconnaissances of the proposed areas of operations, and their reports bore directly on questions of strategy. At the time of the Maine boundary controversy, Captain William G. Williams of the topographical engineers, Lieutenant Minor Knowlton of the artillery, and probably other officers made confidential trips into Canada to gather strategic intelligence, and Knowlton undertook a similar reconnaissance of Bermuda.[25] When the Oregon dispute flared in 1845, Chief Engineer Joseph E. Totten dispatched two officers on a secret mission to determine the best position for blocking British use of the St. Lawrence River and the feasibility of a coup de main to destroy the locks on the strategically vital Beauharnois Canal. At the same time, a board of senior engineers toured the Atlantic defenses and the Canadian frontier, reporting on potential points of attack.[26] Totten frequently advised the administration on policy and strategic matters. In March 1839, for example, he submitted a set of proposals for the raising of forces and the conduct of operations in case of a war with Britain; three years later, he reported at length on the strategic significance of the proposed settlement of the Maine boundary, arguing that the American concessions would not affect national security.[27]

With the exception of their defense of the fortification program, engineers' writings on strategic questions generally appeared in an ad hoc manner—the result of officers' individual interests or assignments arising from particular crises. At West Point, however, the corps made some effort to institutionalize the study of military theory. The central figure was Dennis Hart Mahan, a former engineer officer who served as professor of military and civil engineering from 1832 to 1871. Although firmly grounded in European theory, Mahan was an original thinker who sought to adapt strategy and tactics to American conditions, especially the inevitable reliance on poorly trained citizen-soldiers in a major war. Committed to offensive warfare, he nevertheless questioned the European emphasis on frontal assaults, which he considered too difficult for irregular troops to conduct and too costly in terms of lives for a democracy to tolerate; he developed instead an alternative system based on the extensive use of field fortifications. More generally, Mahan stressed professional education, the study of military history, and the flexible application of theory to the practical realities of warfare.[28]

Beginning in 1842, the chief engineer required the assistant professors in the Department of Engineering to take a postgraduate course in military engineering under the general supervision of Mahan, eventually fixed at two years in length. Each participant had to design a fortification for a given site and a plan for attacking it. The course also demanded extensive reading and recitation in military theory, ranging from technical works on fortification to histories of the Napoleonic Wars and strategic studies by such authors as Jomini, Jacques-Antoine de Guibert, and the archduke Charles of Austria.[29] During the 1850s, Mahan expanded the circle of officer-scholars by chairing the Napoleon Club, open to any of the officers at the academy. At weekly meetings, members presented papers on Napoleonic campaigns that were critiqued by Mahan and the other participants.[30] In the absence of formal schools of practice, Chief Engineer Totten considered the assignment of officers as assistant professors at West Point to be "a privilege of infinite value to the Army," and he favored a rotation system to allow as many regulars as possible to benefit.[31] Significantly, many of the officers who published works on strategy or tactics during the 1840s and 1850s had served stints as assistant professors.

Paralleling the endeavors of the army engineers were the ongoing efforts of the Ordnance Department to standardize and improve the army's weapons and materiel. Although the activity was technical, it forced regulars to confront directly the implications of changing military technology. The campaign originated during the period of reform after the War of 1812, when ordnance officers sought a uniform system of artillery design to replace the chaotic practices of the wartime years. It gathered momentum in the early 1830s with the reestablishment of the ordnance service as a separate department. Using materiel and information acquired through the European connection, a series of ordnance boards conducted experiments with artillery pieces of various designs and gradually worked out a detailed and comprehensive system of classification for the American artillery. Codified by Captain Alfred Mordecai and published in 1849 as *Artillery for the United States Land Service*, the system remained the foundation of the artillery service through the 1850s.[32]

Although standardization continued to be an important goal, ordnance reformers turned increasingly to the development and adoption of new forms of technology. In 1839, the War Department took an important step toward institutionalizing this function by creating a permanent ordnance board that consisted of several experienced ordnance officers. Meeting periodically and working with the arsenals, armories, and various ad hoc boards, the Ordnance Board became the hub of the army's first true program of research and development. During the two decades before the Civil War, the board carefully tested and reported on numerous innovations in weaponry and arms production, some devised by civilian inventors, some imported from Europe, and some generated within the Ordnance Department itself. The board oversaw the adoption of the percussion rifle in the mid-1850s; other important areas of research included breech-loading firearms, rockets, gunpowder and guncotton, wrought-iron carriages for heavy guns, rifled artillery, new techniques for casting cannon and conducting ballistics tests, fuses for shells, and the "Napoleon gun"—an artillery piece of French design that could be used as both a field gun and a howitzer and became the most popular artillery weapon of the Civil War. In the opinion of its principal historian, the Ordnance Board's most lasting contribution was its method—its careful, pragmatic, experimental tack to new technology. "With the natural conservatism of the scientist, the group approached each problem systematically, cautiously, doubting the easy solution, painstakingly testing and retesting every answer to remove all question of error, and, finally, accepting no solution as final or immutable."[33]

PRACTICAL PROFESSIONAL EDUCATION

Scattered at small garrisons and absorbed in labor and constabulary functions, the line branches faced more formidable obstacles than the staff bureaus in achieving professional proficiency. Beginning in the early 1820s, commanders and inspecting officers complained constantly that the dispersion eroded discipline and undermined the officer corps's ability to perform its newly defined core mission—to provide a cadre for a future mobilization. Reporting on a tour of infantry posts in 1823, Inspector General John E. Wool described how the strewn dispositions of the army and the troops' employment in roadbuilding and agriculture deprived officers of the opportunity to engage in any professional activity, even drill. "Incapacitated for acquiring practical they soon neglect theoretical knowledge, and indolence and pleasure fill the void anterior to the loss of every valuable qualification." The problem was most acute for artillery officers, because they often served as infantry and were deficient in the technical aspects of their branch. Visiting artillery companies stationed at small arsenals, Inspector General Samuel B. Archer found many examples "of intelligent, well educated, industrious, and to a certain degree zealous and active young men, becoming . . . indifferent officers, in these, and in other little separate commands for want of examples and emulation and opportunities to exalt themselves."[34]

As in so many areas of professional thought and reform, military authorities looked to France for solutions to this predicament. The French army maintained several "schools of practice" to give officers specialized education in their branches—most notably, an artillery school at Metz, a cavalry school at Saumur, and a school for staff officers at Paris.[35] American officers had visited Metz in the postwar period and studied its curriculum; Claude Crozet and probably other French advisers employed by the War Department had attended the school. In a report to Secretary of War Calhoun in 1818, Simon Bernard, the French fortification engineer, and Lieutenant Colonel William McRee of the Corps of Engineers argued that the West Point curriculum was too general to produce good artillery and engineer officers. They recommended the establishment of an American version of Metz, offering postgraduate training in mathematics, fortification, topography, and artillery.[36] Other officers echoed the call in the following years, though they suggested an additional purpose: concentrating several companies at one site to improve discipline and allow officers an opportunity to work with large bodies of troops.[37]

In order to give the artillery "that perfection which it is found impossible to obtain in the present dispersed condition of the corps," Calhoun instituted an artillery school of practice in April 1824. Eleven companies were drawn from the artillery garrisons and assembled at Fortress Monroe, a coastal fortification under construction at Old Point Comfort, Virginia. As soon as the original companies had reached "perfection," others would take their place, and all would eventually be rotated through the school.[38] Although the goal was to train the artillery as a whole—officers and enlisted men—Calhoun clearly intended the school to be an American Metz, providing specialized professional education to the artillery officers. As published in the Army Regulations of 1825, the curriculum included an ambitious range of subjects: the service, maneuvers, and firing of field, garrison, and seacoast artillery; the preparation of all types of ammunition; the construction of gun carriages and other materiel; fortification; bridge building; topographical surveys; and infantry and cavalry drill. The school was to be encamped two months a year for field training. As a permanent staff, the regulations designated a captain and first lieutenant of ordnance, a professor of chemistry, and instructors of applied mathematics, engineering, and military drawing.[39]

Military reformers continued to raise the problem of dispersion in the infantry. James Barbour, Calhoun's successor as secretary of war, responded in 1826 by authorizing an infantry school of practice at Jefferson Barracks, a post established especially for that purpose a few miles outside St. Louis.[40] Although the infantry school did not acquire a permanent staff or a formal curriculum, the commanding general hoped that it would impart "habits of uniformity and accuracy in the practical routine of service, fresh incitement to the cultivation of military knowledge, emulation and *esprit de corps* among the troops, and mutual conformity and general elevation of individual character among the officers." Significantly, the school's emphasis on discipline and military spirit rather than advanced academic study resembled the pattern at French schools for the infantry and cavalry at St. Cyr and Saumur.[41] The administration also intended that the Jefferson Barracks garrison serve as a reserve force for quelling Indian disturbances along the frontier, and by the end of 1827 it had grown to twenty-two companies.

The army's experiment in troop concentration and professional education continued into the early 1830s. Companies were rotated through the schools, and most West Point graduates destined for the line branches drew either Fortress Monroe or Jefferson Barracks as their initial assignment. The infantry school seems to have achieved both of its modest goals as a training institution and a frontier reserve. Inspecting officers reported favorably on the discipline and military spirit of the units stationed there, and troops from the school responded on several occasions to Indian outbreaks.[42] Although Fortress Monroe enjoyed similar success as a center for improving discipline, it made less progress as a school of advanced artillery practice. The post commanders strove to implement the expansive curriculum, including the field encampments, but they were hampered by the failure of Congress to appropriate funds for horses, textbooks, and equipment. The school never possessed the full staff prescribed by the regulations; only the two ordnance officers and the instructor of mathematics appear to have been appointed. Inspector General Wool, who visited the school on several occasions, was unimpressed. "It is true I found an excellent infantry Battalion," he reported in 1827, "but beyond that very little praise was due. It deserved not the name of a School of Artillery Practice." Officers had acquired some knowledge of pyrotechnics,

Jefferson Barracks, Missouri. Built in 1826 to house the Infantry School of Practice, Jefferson Barracks served off and on as a reserve garrison for the frontier and a training site for the infantry and dragoons. (From John C. Wild, *The Valley of the Mississippi; Illustrated in a Series of Views* [St. Louis, 1841]; photo courtesy of the State Historical Society of Wisconsin)

field maneuvers, and firing shells from a howitzer, but had received little or no training in the construction of batteries, the attack and defense of places, bridge construction, or the manufacture of gun carriages.[43]

Support for the schools of practice gradually faded. Alexander Macomb, who succeeded Jacob Brown as commander of the army in 1828, and Peter B. Porter, Adams's second secretary of war, were less committed to the program than their predecessors had been. Porter was concerned about the depletion of the posts on the Indian and Canadian frontiers, and Macomb feared that large assemblages of troops for instructional purposes might convince the public that the army was too big. By 1829, the War Department had reduced by half the garrisons at the two schools.[44] Jefferson Barracks lost its formal designation as a school of practice during this period, though it continued to serve as a training center and a sizable reserve force. Fortress Monroe—renamed Fort Monroe—experienced a brief revival in 1831; general orders declared the reestablishment of the artillery school, and its garrison returned to the pre-1828 level of eleven companies. The demand for troops during the Black Hawk War and nullification crisis interrupted the school's operations, however, and detached service depleted the commissioned staff. The end came on 19 April 1834, when Macomb announced that the "garrison of Fort Monroe will no longer be regarded as the exclusive School of Practice:—as at all Military Posts, the Commanding Officers will be responsible for the discipline and proper instruction of the troops in their duties."[45]

The demise of the ten-year experiment with schools of practice by no means ended efforts to improve the line army's discipline and professional knowledge. One area of activity involved the development of light or horse artillery batteries—fast-moving units of field artillery in which the cannoneers rode on the horses or caissons. Light artillery had played a prominent role in Napoleonic warfare, and the War Department had experimented briefly with it during the Jefferson administration. The act reducing the army in 1821 had specified that one company in each artillery regiment would be fitted out as a light battery, but because of the expense of maintaining mounted units, the War Department long postponed implementation of this provision.[46] In 1838, however, Secretary of War Joel R. Poinsett ordered the formation of a light battery in the Third Artillery Regiment, commanded by Captain Samuel Ringgold; three more companies were mounted the following year, one in each of the other regiments. In 1841, the War Department designated the stations of these four companies as regimental schools of practice and arranged for the rotation of artillery lieutenants through them.[47]

By 1844, the light artillery had grown to eight companies and had become something of an elite arm, attracting considerable public notice. When Lieutenant James Duncan's battery passed through New Haven, Connecticut, in September 1843, it put on a demonstration before a large crowd that included the governor and the mayor. "Every thing was done with admirable skill, rapidity and exactness," reported a New Haven paper. "The horses performed their parts with as much fidelity as the men; and when the whole company, powder carts, artillery pieces and officers mounted, went dashing across the field in full gallop, the scene was almost electrical."[48] During the Mexican War, the light batteries performed brilliantly on the battlefield and received the major credit for several victories, including Zachary Taylor's stunning triumph over a vastly superior Mexican army at Buena Vista. Although reduced and temporarily dismounted as a postwar economy measure, the light artillery remained a permanent feature of the army. One outcome was the emergence of a group of enthusiastic young artillery officers who took a strong professional interest in advancing their branch.[49]

From time to time, military authorities sanctioned concentrations that had the effect of enhancing discipline and esprit de corps. To offset the deteriorating impact of guerrilla warfare in Florida, the War Department gathered as many troops as could be spared from the frontiers at a "camp of instruction" at Trenton, New Jersey, during the summer of 1839. The entire Fourth Artillery attended, the soldiers wearing their dress uniforms for the first time in three years, as well as a detachment of dragoons, Ringgold's light battery, and several companies from other regiments. The climax of the camp was a formal review and demonstration of combined arms drill, executed before throngs of civilian spectators.[50] Although training was not their primary object, the concentration of troops for Zachary Taylor's "army of observation" in Texas in 1845–1846, the Utah expedition in the late 1850s, and the larger-scale Indian campaigns all rejuvenated the military spirit of segments of the army and gave officers a stimulating, though temporary, professional environment.

As a large and centrally located garrison, Jefferson Barracks continued to function off and on as an informal school of practice. During 1843–1844, for example, sixteen companies of the Third and Fourth Infantry regiments were organized as a "school for brigade drill" at that post, where they achieved a high degree of discipline and tactical proficiency; together with the light artillery batteries, they formed the core of Taylor's army in the opening stages of the Mexican War. Subalterns appointed to the mounted regiments in the 1850s attended a small cavalry school of practice, located at Jefferson Barracks until 1855 and afterwards at Carlisle Barracks, Pennsylvania.[51]

Proposals for advanced artillery training continued to circulate, many generated by the bitter artillery-ordnance dispute. In 1842, the War Department introduced a systematic program of practice firing at the seacoast garrisons; post commanders kept careful records of these exercises and forwarded them to army headquarters.[52] Responding to a rising number of complaints that artillery officers never had the opportunity for professional improvement, the Buchanan administration revived the artillery school of practice in the late 1850s. Orders of 18 May 1858 formalized the program, designating Fort Monroe as a school for "the theoretical and practical instruction of Artillery" and prescribing an elaborate curriculum that resembled the course of study at the first artillery school. Companies were to serve two-year tours at Fort Monroe on a rotation basis, two at a time from each regiment, and West Point graduates in the artillery were to attend the school for a year before joining their regiments.[53] During the following year, the War Department expanded the scope of the instructional program by shifting all artillery companies not stationed at the seacoast fortifications to several interior posts, with a company of light artillery assigned to each post. At all the artillery garrisons, seacoast and interior, commanders were directed to institute "a thorough system of instruction, theoretical and practical," involving recitations by company officers on artillery manuals, laboratory work, and drills. Senior officers were to make regular inspections of the posts and carefully examine the officers on professional subjects, transmitting detailed results to Washington.[54]

Artillery commanders sought to implement this ambitious plan in the brief interim before the Civil War. By September 1859, the school of practice had reached the authorized level of eight companies, and both officers and noncommissioned officers were attending regular classes and drills. Armistead L. Long, who served at the school as a lieutenant, recalled a rigorous and professionally stimulating program that covered the maneuvers of heavy guns, target practice with ordnance of every caliber, textbook recitations and lectures on the science of gunnery, and laboratory instruction in the manufacture of ammunition.[55] Inspectors reported progress at the post artillery schools as well, though the extent and quality of the instruction inevitably varied.[56] The sectional crisis interrupted the artillery's instructional program, however, and the artillery school did not reopen until 1867.

TACTICAL REFORM AND OTHER PROFESSIONAL ACTIVITY

Outside the scientific bureaus, the professional activities of regulars were extensive, though as disparate as the functions of the peacetime army. One area of persistent interest was related closely to the army's preparedness mandate: the revision of tactical manuals for the various arms. At one time or another, a great many regulars engaged in the translation and adaptation of European military works for use in the American service, acting as individual translators, contributors, and critics, or as members of professional boards. During 1824, Brigadier General Winfield Scott headed a board that revised the infantry tactics adopted at the end of the War of 1812, retranslating the original French system of 1791 and amending it in light of new developments in Europe.[57] Scott compiled a third edition in 1835, this one based on a somewhat modified French tactical system of 1831. Although approved by a panel of senior officers and officially adopted, Scott's manual sparked a debate that ran for a year in the *Army and Navy Chronicle*. Critics claimed that the translation was awkwardly done and that the chief changes from the 1825 edition—a three-rank system of firing to supplement the older two-rank system and the integration of the light infantry more closely with the infantry—were poorly suited to American conditions.[58] Regulars also developed manuals for the artillery, dragoons, and militia. In particular, the adoption of a tactical system for the artillery generated much heated discussion, which was closely related to the concurrent efforts to standardize ordnance materiel and introduce light artillery batteries. Several professional boards considered the problem during the

1830s and early 1840s; many artillery officers contributed their views, both officially and unofficially, before the War Department approved a manual in 1844.[59]

Officers' consideration of tactics and related professional issues intensified during the 1850s, in part as a result of the Mexican War and in part because of changing technology and tactical reform in Europe. The acceptance of the long-range percussion rifle as the standard infantry weapon prompted debate on the implications for infantry tactics. Captain William J. Hardee, who had studied French light infantry tactics as a young officer at Saumur, headed a board in 1854 that translated and adapted the basic French tactical system for American use. Although it retained the close-order line formations of earlier systems, it stressed rapid advances as a response to the impact of rifled weapons and encouraged greater individual and small group initiative, especially in skirmishing.[60] Other regulars suggested alternatives to the Hardee system or supplemented it by producing works on rifle practice and bayonet exercise and the manual of arms for the rifle.[61] Within the mounted regiments, debate on tactics and equipment continued through the 1850s, influenced late in the decade by George B. McClellan's extensive treatment of European cavalry in his report on the Crimean War mission and by a visit to Europe by Colonel Philip St. George Cooke of the dragoons. As a result, Cooke produced a revised system of cavalry tactics, Lieutenant Dabney H. Maury devised a set of tactics for the mounted riflemen, and others drafted manuals for the use of the Colt revolver and the Sharps breech-loading carbine.[62] Similarly, professional boards completed an instructional system for heavy artillery in 1851 and a revised field artillery system in 1859, the latter based in part on recommendations of battery commanders.[63]

As in most areas of professional thought, regulars' approach to tactics was conservative and derivative. Awed by the Napoleonic tradition, they focused on the translation of standard European works, mainly French, and were reluctant to contemplate major changes. For one type of warfare, however, officers lacked strong European precedents, yet it was the kind of conflict with which they had the greatest practical experience—Indian warfare. As later chapters will demonstrate, officers tended to disparage Indian fighting as frustrating, inglorious, morally disturbing, and an irritating distraction from the real business of their profession, and it was almost totally neglected by West Point, the schools of practice, and professional boards.

Nevertheless, the hard necessities of conducting Indian operations forced officers to confront the tactical and strategic questions of counter–guerrilla warfare. In particular, the seemingly interminable Second Seminole War generated many proposals either in the form of official correspondence or anony-

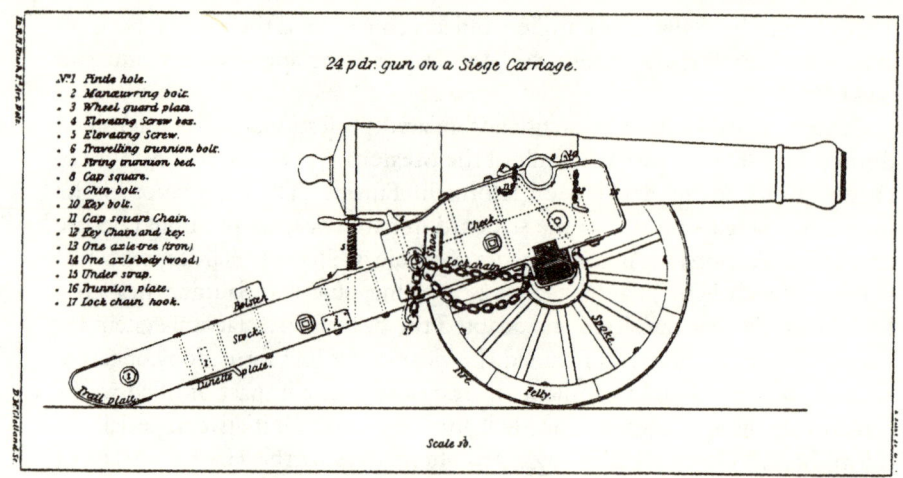

The compilation of military manuals required considerable technical skill. This drawing was made by Lieutenant Richard H. Rush of the Second Artillery Regiment for the heavy-artillery manual. (From U.S. War Department, *Instruction for Heavy Artillery; Prepared by a Board of Officers for the Use of the Army of the United States* [Washington, D.C., 1851])

mous letters published in the *Army and Navy Chronicle* and the general press. These recommendations ranged widely, from simply ceasing operations and permitting the Indians to remain in restricted parts of Florida to turning the war over to private bounty hunters or conducting an outright campaign of extermination. Those advocating continued operations usually suggested one or both of two approaches: first, instituting some form of armed occupation of the countryside, and second, employing small detachments of light troops to penetrate the Indians' sanctuaries, destroy their food supplies, and harass them relentlessly until they submitted. At one time or another in the seven-year conflict—and in the sporadic outbreaks of fighting that recurred in Florida into the late 1850s—the army employed nearly all of these schemes, none with decisive success.[64] Likewise, regulars involved in the campaigns against the tribes of the Plains, the Southwest, and the West Coast during the 1850s frequently speculated on the most effective methods to be used against their adversaries.[65] However, these proposals appeared mainly as random, stopgap responses to the exigencies of frontier campaigning. In general, officers' low estimation of Indian fighting as a field of professional endeavor prevented them from developing a systematic theory on counter–guerrilla warfare during the antebellum period.

The professional activities of regulars ranged far beyond the relatively narrow sphere of tactics. For instance, officer-inventors sought solutions to practical military problems. Captain Henry H. Sibley invented a highly efficient conical tent that was adopted by the War Department in the late 1850s; Assistant Surgeon Albert J. Myer designed a widely used system of military signaling based on semaphores and in 1860 became the army's first signal officer.[66] In military journals, newspapers, memoirs, and even literary magazines, regulars frequently expressed their views on operations, internal army problems, military policy and education, and the army's relationship with the civilian world.[67] While they lasted, the *Military and Naval Magazine of the United States* and the *Army and Navy Chronicle* served as rudimentary professional organs; most issues printed officers' letters, usually signed with pseudonyms, that commented on a wide variety of professional issues, such as pay, promotion, and the place of the military profession in American society. A few officers tried their hand at military history, a very popular field in nineteenth-century America. Especially noteworthy were Captain John T. Sprague of the infantry and Lieutenant Roswell S. Ripley of the artillery, whose respective histories of the Second Seminole and Mexican wars long remained the most thorough and reliable military studies of those conflicts.[68] By far the most important forum for officers' professional writings, however, was the vast array of military documents published by order of Congress, either as addenda to the annual reports of the War Department or in separate collections. These publications were widely circulated and often reprinted in the general press. In some respects, they were a substitute for a professional journal, disseminating officers' opinions through the service world and publicizing the army's activities to the larger society.

The topics covered in the congressional publications were myriad, and this study has drawn heavily on them in many areas. The annual reports of the secretary of war were actually based largely on officers' advice and were supported by reports of the commanding general and bureau chiefs, which summarized the army's activities during the year and recommended reforms in military organization, administration, and policy. Attached to these statements were reports and correspondence of officers in the field, and by the 1850s these compilations ran to many hundreds of pages. The War Department report for 1859, for example, was 1,134 pages long and included lengthy runs of officers' correspondence on the dispute with Great Britain over the San Juan Islands of Puget Sound, civil-military tensions resulting from the occupation of Utah, and ongoing Indian operations in New Mexico, Texas, and the Far West—much of this detailed information had general implications for the army's constabulary role. Also appended were accounts of army experiments with camels and artesian wells as possible solutions to logistical problems in the arid Southwest, a surgeon's proposal to revise the army ration, a long critique of the orthodox program of coastal defense by Lieutenant James St. Clair Morton, and a substantial amount of material on fortification construction, ordnance production, and internal improvements.[69]

The occasional reports responding to congressional inquiries likewise dealt with important professional issues. When Congress considered a reduction of the officer corps in 1830, for example, the secretary of war submitted statements from high-ranking regulars that opposed a cutback, several of which strongly defended military professionalism and the cadre plan.[70] During the late 1830s and early 1840s, officers' recommendations on frontier defense fueled a debate in Congress and the executive branch over military roadbuilding and the disposition of the army along the western Indian frontier.[71] As might be expected, seacoast fortification was a perennial topic of the congressional series. Published compilations of military correspondence allowed both officers and citizens to follow the course of military operations in Florida, Mexico, and the West, as well as the army's constabulary duties.[72] On several occasions, Congress sponsored statistical volumes assembled by the Medical Department that contained a wealth of data on sickness and mortality in the army; the climate, topography, and sanitation of army posts; the physical characteristics and national origins of American soldiers; and a variety of other subjects.[73] Regulars' reports on Indian relations were frequently printed, and the observations of army explorers filled whole volumes. In 1860, Congress published the findings of a Senate commission investigating West Point, which contained the views of many regulars on the army's system of professional education.[74]

In a recent study of French military thought in the post-Napoleonic period, Paddy Griffith has stressed the importance of looking beyond seminal works on strategy and the philosophy of war—obviously rarities in any age—and of instead interpreting military thought broadly, as the practical response of military men to the everyday problems of their profession. He has argued that the French officer corps supported a broad professional culture, much of it centered at the regimental level and oriented toward such unglamorous, mundane, but vital topics as small-unit tactics, training, and morale.[75] As in so many fields, the American officer corps resembled its French counterpart in this respect as well. The specific interests of American officers differed somewhat from the French—they gave relatively little attention to the morale of the enlisted men, for example, a fact that will be explored later—and the small size of the United States Army made it difficult to sustain professional schools and journals. With the possible exception of Dennis Hart Mahan, the antebellum army produced no major creative thinker on strategy or high policy. Nevertheless, American regulars gave considerable thought to the practical problems of their profession: tactics, administration, weapons and equipment, and ways to preserve unity and expertise in a dispersed frontier army. Although derivative and diffuse, officers' professional activity was extensive and a key element of the emerging military subculture.

14
OFFICERS AND ENLISTED MEN

William Tell Poussin, a Frenchman who served fifteen years as an officer in the United States Army before returning to France after the July Revolution, commented at length on the American military system in a Tocquevillean assessment of the American experiment entitled *The United States; Its Power and Progress*. He found much to praise: the program of seacoast fortifications; the military knowledge and moral character of the officer corps; and the general productivity of the American economy. However, he did note two defects, the first of which was the low morale of the enlisted men. Because civilian jobs paid more than military service, soldiers "must be infected with some moral infirmity, which renders them unfit for a useful and laborious life. Consequently, this lack of moral force in the composition of the army must be counterpoised by a very strict system of discipline." A second flaw was

> the complete isolation of the commissioned from the non-commissioned officers. This state of things, borrowed from English usage, is not recognized, it is true, by the laws which govern promotion in the American army; but opinion and custom, often more potent than laws, raise an insurmountable barrier between the two classes. The corps of non-commissioned officers occupies an inert position between the soldier and the commissioned officer.

The solution, Poussin suggested, was to adopt a system of conscription similar to that in France.[1]

Regardless of his low opinion of the American soldier, Poussin accurately described one of the dominant characteristics of the peacetime army: the officer–enlisted man dichotomy. The great majority of commissioned regulars spent the bulk of their careers as company officers, directly commanding privates and noncommissioned officers. At the scattered frontier posts and the artillery garrisons that dotted the Atlantic coastline, they lived in close proximity with the enlisted men and interacted with them continually—on the parade ground, in the barracks and guardhouse, and in the field. Despite this intimacy, a deep, nearly unbridgeable chasm separated officers from the rank and file. At best, officers viewed their men with a paternalistic condescension, but often their attitude was a mixture of suspicion, ethnic and social prejudice, and contempt. Rarely did officers question this social division or reconsider the inflexible system of command and discipline.

THE OFFICER-ENLISTED MAN DICHOTOMY

The pattern of officer-enlisted man relations that prevailed in the antebellum army had its roots in the practices of the Continental Army. A rigid barrier between officers and men had not characterized the militia system of the colonial era. It had begun to emerge in the later colonial wars, as provincial governments increasingly turned to volunteer forces to conduct operations outside their borders and found recruits largely among the economically deprived of the population. Congress had mitigated the division at the start of the Revolution by relying on short-term enlistments and adopting a code of military discipline considerably milder than that of the contemporary British service. Washington and other conservative commanders, however, insisted that stricter discipline was essential to sustain the revolutionary cause. After the disastrous 1776 campaign, Congress fixed a standard enlistment term of three years or the duration of the war. As popular enthusiasm waned, the Continental Army's ranks were increasingly filled with urban laborers, propertyless farm workers, and immigrants—men who were socially well below the majority of commissioned officers. Moreover, Congress revised the Articles of War in 1776, bringing them more into line with the British service. The limit on flogging, a punishment used exclusively on enlisted men, was raised from thirty-nine to one hundred lashes, and the number of capital offenses was considerably expanded. Orders and tradition forbade fraternization between officers and enlisted men. Although promotions from the ranks seem to have been common in some states' contingents, they were very rare in others; in the New Jersey brigade, rankers composed less than 2 percent of the officers.[2] The conservative revolutionary veterans who commanded the small regular force of the 1780s and 1790s incorporated the officer-soldier dichotomy into the peacetime service, and it became one of the basic features of nineteenth-century military life.

Recently, a clearer picture has begun to emerge of the early army's rank and file. The soldiers of the First Regiment of the Confederation era were overwhelmingly laborers and artisans who originally enlisted in the port towns. Their median age at enlistment was twenty-five, and 55 percent were foreign-born.³ As might be expected, the proportion of immigrants declined dramatically during the buildup for the War of 1812; foreign-born soldiers made up only 13 percent of the wartime rank and file. The foreign-born component rose to 27 percent in the early 1820s, however, and to about 40 percent in the early 1840s. In 1844, the government dropped a ban, never rigidly enforced, against the enlistment of aliens, and immigrants soon became a majority again; with the great wave of immigration in the 1850s, they totaled about two-thirds of the army's enlisted strength. Throughout the period, peacetime recruiters concentrated their efforts in the northeastern cities, and enlistees tended to be urban-dwelling artisans, laborers, and semiskilled workers.⁴ There were also soldiers from "respectable" circumstances, drawn to the army by a thirst for adventure or as an escape from personal problems. Nevertheless, a considerable social gap separated the enlisted regulars from their officers, most of whom derived from politically influential old-stock families engaged in the professions, commerce, government service, and agriculture.

Differences in social background, ethnicity, and education did not make antagonism inevitable. Army regulations consistently emphasized commanders' responsibility for the health and well-being of their men, and the ideal was a stern but compassionate paternalism. According to Baron von Steuben's "Blue Book," the official army regulations from the Revolution to the War of 1812, the first duty of a captain

> should be, to gain the love of his men, by treating them with every possible kindness and humanity, enquiring into their complaints, and when well founded, seeing them redressed. He should know every man of his company by name and character. He should often visit those who are sick, speak tenderly to them, see that the public provision, whether of medicine or diet, is duly administered, and procure them besides such comforts and conveniences as are in his power.⁵

The General Regulations adopted in 1821 and in force through most of the antebellum period began by elaborating on the "Base of Discipline."

> It is the intention of the Government that there be established in every regiment and corps, and throughout the army, as one corps, a gradual and universal subordination or authority, which without loss of force, shall be even, mild, and paternal, and which, founded in justice and firmness, shall maintain all subordinates in the strictest observance of duty. It

requires that enlisted soldiers shall be treated with particular kindness and humanity; that punishments, sometimes unavoidable, shall be strictly conformable to martial law; and that all in commission shall conduct, direct, and protect inferiors, of every rank, with the cares due to men from whose patriotism, valor, and obedience, they are to expect a part of their own reputation and glory.

While the regulations stressed the importance of "passive obedience" to higher orders, they enjoined the superior "not to injure those under him by abusive or unbecoming language, or by capricious or tyrannical conduct."[6]

Undoubtedly, the conduct of many officers approached the fatherly exemplar expressed in the regulations. A former soldier recalled Lieutenant Beverly H. Robertson, who instructed him in dragoon drill at Carlisle Barracks after the Mexican War: "He was, to my fancy, a splendid man; gentle, firm, persistent, never seeming to lose patience, yet never yielding to anything short of the most perfect performance of the movement undertaken." As a company officer in the 1850s, William W. Averell took a personal interest in his men, helping several with their alcohol problems; he proudly related in his memoirs the concern of his soldiers when an injury forced his departure from Fort Craig, New Mexico. Hospital Steward John Bemrose was deeply impressed by the attention shown by Colonel Duncan L. Clinch toward soldiers wounded in the Second Seminole War: "A stranger would have thought he was the chief surgeon so careful was he to see that his men were not neglected." More than once, Bemrose noticed the portly old commander seated on the dirt floor of the hospital at Fort Drane, consoling a dying private.[7]

Officers regularly interceded on behalf of enlisted men seeking benefits or special favors. In 1819, for example, Lieutenant Colonel John R. Fenwick wrote the secretary of war requesting bounty land for several soldiers in the Light Artillery Regiment; they had enlisted as substitutes and as such had been unable to obtain their warrants. When a sergeant's wife had her ration discontinued in 1855 after eighteen years as an army laundress, Major Oscar F. Winship appealed the case to the adjutant general. Similarly, Major Harvey Brown intervened in 1858 for the widow of an old soldier at Fort Monroe; she wished to have her fourteen-year-old son enlisted as a musician and stationed at that post, a petition readily granted by the commanding general.[8] Officers' recommendations were essential for the top rewards available to enlisted men: appointments as ordnance and quartermaster sergeants. These positions involved relatively light and stationary duties, and they were eagerly sought by aging soldiers. Under less happy circumstances, officers served as character witnesses during enlisted men's courts-martial; in fact, such testimony frequently amounted to the accused soldier's sole defense. Perhaps the most obvious example of officers' paternalism was the long, frustrating, but ultimately successful lobbying effort, led by Captain Robert Anderson of the artillery, to establish military asylums for elderly soldiers.[9]

Officers' benevolence was most often directed toward the "worthy" enlisted men—those who conformed to the stereotype of the deferential, courteous, faithful old soldier. There were other images more representative of officers' estimation of the rank and file. Relatively few officers made general remarks about enlisted men—indeed, the very rarity of such references in journals and private correspondence suggests the distance between the groups. Those commanders who did express opinions were overwhelmingly critical. Fairly typical was Lieutenant George G. Meade, who described enlisted men in 1846 as "the most heterogeneous mass of foreigners Irishmen, Germans & Poles principally—who have no feelings in common with us & who generally enter the service solely because they are unfit from bad habits or idleness to succeed in civil life." He acknowledged, however, that discipline and the "influence of blood & powder" had overcome their vices and caused them to perform gallantly in combat. Lieutenant Colonel George Bomford opposed using "common soldiers" as arsenal workers: "They are generally men of habits too dissolute, to be safely employed in Laboratories and magazines, where the carelessness of a workman may occasion so great a devastation of property and lives." In the opinion of Major William H. Chase, the army's immigrant soldiers "are ignorant & brutal & make no progress except in vice during their term of service"; he regretted that such "vicious materials" discouraged citizens from enlisting. Captain Thomas Claiborne commented sardonically on the enlisted men aboard a boat headed for Fort Snelling in 1848: "these interesting specimens of United States Chivalry, the most patriotic conceivable, as they bestow their precious time for the good of the public at the contemptible charge of $7 per month, noble, generous self sacrificing specimens of petit larceny in blue uniforms, very greasy & very dirty." In defending the tradition of Sunday inspections, a correspondent to a military periodical compared soldiers to "heedless and wayward urchins" who had to be scrubbed and decently dressed by their mother before going to church; without an inspection, the men would spend the day "in sleep or supine sloth, in plotting the means of procuring, or in using vicious indulgences, in drinking and gambling."[10]

Some officers took a more favorable view of the mounted regiments and the company of sappers and miners attached to the Corps of Engineers—relatively elite units that attracted mainly native-born recruits. In general, however, social class prejudice and nativism pervaded commanders' perception of the rank and file. Enlisted men appeared as an alien, menacing mass—ignorant, disorderly, hedonistic, childlike, too lazy or incompetent to function in civilian society and lacking the most elementary moral development. Such men could not be controlled by appeals to patriotism or duty; only strict discipline and the threat of physical punishment could overcome their vicious propensities and command their respect. This assessment was by no means unique to the American officer corps; it paralleled the more general attitudes of middle- and upper-class Americans toward immigrants and urban workers and even, in certain respects, southern slaveholders' perceptions of their slaves. It also matched the pattern of officer–enlisted man relations in the United States Navy and in most contemporary European armies. Even so, it was likely to produce tensions in the intensely egalitarian white male culture of antebellum America.

Although neither the Articles of War nor the General Regulations specifically prohibited fraternization between officers and men, the customs of the service did not tolerate it. Occasionally, officers who violated the caste line found themselves before courts-martial, facing such ambiguous charges as "conduct unbecoming an officer and a gentleman" or "conduct subversive of good order and discipline." Such was the case with lieutenants Platt R. Green and Benjamin Fitch, tried in 1815 for dancing at an enlisted men's ball "with soldiers, camp women, and with women of ill repute." In 1845, Lieutenant William A. Aisquith was dismissed after being convicted on a number of specifications, most of which stemmed from drinking with soldiers at Fort Kent, Maine, arguing with them about their services in the Second Seminole War, and otherwise fraternizing. Lieutenant Llewellyn Raguet was more fortunate in his trial on similar charges one year later; the president remitted the sentence of dismissal because of the "extreme youth, and the utter inexperience of the accused in military usages."[11] A former enlisted man recalled that there was "just as almighty a distance preserved between a *Sergeant-Major*, who is the highest noncommissioned officer in the service, and a *Brevet Second Lieutenant*, who is the lowest commissioned officer, . . . as though it were sacrilege in the former to approach the latter in a familiar way."[12]

CONTROLLING THE RANK AND FILE

Officers' unfavorable appraisal of the enlisted men led them to define leadership almost exclusively in terms of control, discipline, and punishment. In their mind, the American soldier's most serious character flaw was his unruly nature, a trait demonstrated most clearly in his predilection to desertion. The desertion rate in the American service was certainly high. During the Confederation era, the First Regiment lost about 26 percent of its strength to desertion, and the percentage remained approximately the same throughout the first half of the nineteenth century: Twenty-seven percent of the soldiers enlisting in nineteen selected years between 1821 and 1845 deserted at least once during their term of service.[13]

Of course, high rates of desertion were not confined to the peacetime army. The Continental Army had suffered heavily from desertion, and both the Union and Confederate armies would do so in the Civil War. The majority of desertions occurred during the first year—indeed, the first few months—of the soldier's enlistment. No doubt these new recruits had difficulty in adjusting to the discipline and physical rigors of army life. Major General Alexander Macomb suspected that many soldiers charged with desertion had not intended to leave the service permanently; he urged courts to screen cases carefully and to try the less serious offenses as absences without leave. In another sense, desertion may have been the military version of the geographical mobility and job turnover characteristic of nineteenth-century America.[14] The officer corps, however, thought of desertion as a threat to the very survival of the army and clear evidence of the American soldier's unreliable nature. According to the adjutant general, the "class from whence a majority of private soldiers are drawn scarcely regards the circumstance of desertion as an act of turpitude."[15]

Commanders considered desertion the most basic but by no means the only danger to the army's cohesion and internal order. The routines of garrison life generated almost continual tensions within the ranks and recurrent friction along the officer–enlisted man boundary, aggravated by both groups' heavy use of alcohol. As might be expected, the enlisted ranks did contain a minority of hard cases—men who plagued their commanders with chronic misbehavior—and the guardhouse was the locus of discord at virtually every post. Because of the paucity of recreational opportunities and the availability of whiskey, even normally well-disciplined soldiers occasionally engaged in drinking binges and disorderly conduct. On the other hand, many officers, subalterns in particular, seem to have been so insecure about their status that they were threatened by even small signs of disrespect. A sergeant's slowness to follow an order, a recruit's seemingly deliberate clumsiness on the drill field, a drunken soldier's surly remark—each could appear as a challenge to a young lieutenant's tenuous authority and thus require a stern response. Perhaps the central problem, however—and one rarely acknowledged by the officer corps—was the difficulty of maintaining an authoritarian, rigidly hierarchical system in the midst of an expansive, individualistic, self-consciously democratic culture. Many soldiers refused to accept higher authority unquestioningly, especially if an officer's actions appeared to violate their dignity or what they perceived as their rights as free Americans. Given their generally low opinion of enlisted men, officers inevitably regarded such behavior as mutinous—a challenge to the very survival of the army's rank structure.

From the start of the army's history, military authorities concentrated on physical punishment as the solution to problems of discipline and morale. The question was not the utility of such punishment but the form it should take. The commanders of the Confederation army faced a high desertion rate and the disorder inherent in organizing a new force, and they responded by reasserting the stringent disciplinary system of the Continental Army. Sergeant Joseph Buell described the arrival of newly enlisted troops at Fort McIntosh, on the Ohio River, in December 1785: "The troops are raw and unacquainted with duty; the officers strict and treatment excessively severe, flogging men with 120 lashes a daily occurence." As a deterrent to others, Major John P. Wyllys had three deserters summarily shot the following month. "The order and the shooting was the most inhuman act I ever saw," wrote Buell; "all three were young and the finest soldiers in the company."[16] Although a court of inquiry exonerated Wyllys, Congress took the occasion to revise the Articles of War. It lowered the number of officers required to form a general court-martial, thereby removing the grounds for summary punishments, and mandated a review by Congress (after 1796, the president) before the execution of a soldier in time of peace.[17]

Nevertheless, the strict disciplinary regime continued through the Confederation period. Incomplete regimental records indicate the sentences passed in 105 court-martial cases during 1785–1787: 57 called for flogging, 9 for running the gauntlet, and 3 for death, though in the last cases the offenders were pardoned. Of the flogging sentences, 1 called for three hundred lashes, three times the limit stated in the Articles of War; 37 sentences called for one hundred lashes; and the remainder, for between thirty-nine and eighty lashes. In about a quarter of the flogging cases, the offender was pardoned or his sentence partially remitted. Thirty-seven floggings seem to have been carried out in full, however, including two-thirds of the one-hundred-lash sentences and the lone three-hundred-lash sentence—which was inflicted on a private convicted of selling his shirt.[18]

The pattern established in the Confederation army became a fixture of the regular service. Certainly it meshed well with the hierarchical values of the Federalists who controlled the government and the army during the 1790s. As commander of the Legion, Anthony Wayne relied heavily on corporal punishments to stave off desertion and instill cohesion in the wake of defeat. A study of Wayne's orderly books in 1792 and 1793 found that flogging was by far the most common punishment, with one hundred lashes the standard; nineteen soldiers were sentenced to death and fifteen actually executed. Major General Alexander Hamilton wrestled with the discipline problem during the Quasi-war with France. While he feared that too frequent use of capital punishment might damage the army's public image, he did favor occasional executions as examples: "It is painful to urge a position of this Kind, especially where life is concerned, but a military institution must be worse than useless—it must be pernicious if a just Severity does not uphold and enforce discipline."[19]

The Jeffersonian era brought civilian pressures to moderate military punishment. In its revision of the Articles of War in 1806, Congress reduced the maximum flogging sentence to fifty lashes. Anticipating congressional action, the War Department suspended flogging in 1810, and an act of 1812 banned it altogether.[20] This step did not lead to a reevaluation of the army's disciplinary system, however; courts merely substituted a variety of other painful and increasingly exotic corporal punishments. Colonel Alexander Smyth disapproved a flogging sentence in 1810 but gave the court advice on alternatives: "Lash him to a tree. Splint all his limbs as if they were broken, and keep him there for days. Drench him with gallons of cold water pour'd down his sleeve. But let us not inflict 25 lashes on the naked back of an *american citizen* for being *some what groggy;* or 15 for being 'a little intoxicated.' " During the War of 1812, the administration permitted extensive use of the death penalty to discourage desertion; in the period 1812–1815, military courts sentenced 260 men to death, of whom 205 were executed.[21]

After the war, presidents adopted the practice of commuting virtually all sentences of death in peacetime. Nevertheless, military punishments became an increasingly controversial issue in the postwar years. Reports circulated that commanders regularly disregarded the ban on flogging. According to the surgeon general, the sentences of courts-martial were often "commuted for lashes," and company officers, "dictated often by caprice, without the sanction of a court, habitually inflict corporal punishment to such a degree of severity as frequently requires medical attendance," leaving the victim unfit for service.[22] In 1819, Congress ordered an inquiry into these allegations. The most notorious case involved Colonel William King; while commanding in occupied West Florida, King had sanctioned flogging and several other harsh punishments, both with and without the benefit of court-martial. He had ordered the immediate execution of all deserters captured in West Florida, and one nonresisting escapee had been shot. A court-martial, apparently instituted under congressional pressure, sentenced King to a five-year suspension from rank and command, and he was dropped from the army in the reduction of 1821.[23] The King case and other exposures of officers' brutality—some based on the complaints of the soldiers themselves—sensitized high commanders to the problem of illegal punishments. They reacted with denunciations of the practice in orders and occasional courts-martial of officers on charges of abusing enlisted men.[24]

While they disapproved of summary punishments, high-ranking commanders by no means lost faith in the utility of corporal punishment by sentence of court-martial. Through the 1820s, they lobbied for a variety of reforms to stem the desertion tide, most notably the reintroduction of flogging. In the opinion of Brigadier General Edmund P. Gaines, "*Stripes and lashes* stand . . . next to *Ball Cartridges* as a salutary means of extirpating from our army this most fearful and demoralizing crime." Gaines considered the uniform and systematic use of flogging far preferable to such exotic and degrading alternatives as branding, tattooing, mutilation, and wearing an iron collar and ball and chain in circumstances other than solitary confinement. Some such punishments "are repugnant to natural law, and at variance with the genius and spirit of our institutions. All of them tend rather to corrode and destroy the latent elements of moral feeling, and lead the miserable offender to irretrievable infamy, than to open to him the path of repentance and reformation." Commanders also pointed out the inconsistency of banning flogging in the army while allowing it in the navy.[25] In 1833, Congress approved most of the officer corps's agenda for curing desertion: shortening the enlistment term from five to three years; raising soldiers' pay while withholding part until the end of the second year of service; introducing a reenlistment bounty; and reestablishing flogging as a punishment for desertion if ordered by a general court-martial. Although flogging up to fifty lashes (the limit imposed by the Articles of War) soon became the most common sentence in desertion cases, the measure had no dramatic or long-term impact on the desertion rate.[26]

The legalization of flogging did not end courts' reliance on physical punishments for offenses other than desertion, including several of the penalties denounced by Gaines as cruel and degrading. Military punishments sometimes aroused public concern—as was the case in 1850 when a court-martial at Fort Constitution, New Hampshire, convicted four soldiers of mutiny for refusing to row an officer and a pair of ladies in Portsmouth harbor. Each soldier was sentenced to a year at hard labor, during which he would wear a ball and chain and an iron collar with seven-inch prongs attached, designed to produce intense discomfort. A Senate investigatory committee, headed by Jefferson Davis, approved the court's action as justified to preserve military discipline, but the commanding general remitted the part of the sentence that called for the spiked collar.[27] Probably as a result of this case, the commanding general issued an order the following year, prohibiting courts-martial from imposing "modes of inflicting pain" not condoned by the Articles of War or established military practice and clearly defining the permissible penalties. These consisted of death, presumably in wartime; flogging in cases of desertion; confinement; hard labor with or without a ball and chain; forfeiture of pay and allowances; discharges; reprimands; and requiring deserters to make up the time lost because of their desertion.[28]

Courts-martial were only the most visible instrument at the officer corps's disposal for enforcing order and maintaining the rank structure. Despite the effort to suppress them after the War of 1812, unofficial and summary punishments remained a central component of the army's disciplinary system—and the most explosive element in the officer–enlisted man relationship. In theory, officers' use of force against enlisted men was restricted by law and regulation. In a general order issued in 1842, Major General Winfield Scott summarized points made in earlier directives. Force was justified only to repel a personal attack or to secure an offender so that he might be brought to trial. In such cases, "any superior may strike and wound; but only to the extent clearly necessary to such lawful end. Any excess, wantonly committed beyond such measured violence, would, itself, be punishable in the superior." Scott added that force might occasionally be used "to iron prisoners for security, or to gag them for quiet," but his order made clear the necessity for restraint and legal procedure. Even the use of harsh and abusive words should be avoided.[29]

A wide gap existed between this policy and actual practice. Spontaneous and extralegal violence continued to permeate garrison life, especially when officers thought their authority challenged. At Fort Snelling in 1830, Private Charles Marigold created a disturbance at the sutler's store and refused to obey when Lieutenant Osborne Cross ordered him to the guardhouse. Furious, Cross hit him with his fist, then grabbed a whip from Marigold and beat him with the handle. In 1838, Private Charles Green was drunk when he returned from a pass to Madison Barracks, New York. He was disobedient and disrespectful to Lieutenant Thomas S. J. Johnson, who had him tied up and struck him across the temples, first with his hands and then with his sword. At Detroit the following year, an inebriated private, Patrick Clarke, refused Lieutenant Charles B. Daniels's order to "walk in charge of a sentinel." According to Daniels's own testimony, he then "struck [Clarke] several times, and beat him until he was insensible." During artillery drill at Fort Sumter, South Carolina, in 1852, Lieutenant Robert V. W. Howard ordered Sergeant Henry Clarke, a nine-year veteran, to his quarters after a disagreement on procedure. As Clarke passed Howard, the officer asked him if were in the habit of answering back. "God damn," responded Clarke, "as long as I am in the right I will reply." The officer seized Clarke by the throat and hit him in the jaw, threatening to "knock your Goddamned brains out." Clarke knocked Howard down, whereupon another sergeant intervened. As Clarke walked away, Howard repeatedly struck at him with his sword, wounding both Clarke and the other sergeant, who sought to shield him.[30]

Scores of similar instances of violence were recorded incidentally in the proceedings of general courts-martial of enlisted men; indeed, the four soldiers mentioned above were all convicted of mutinous conduct, willful disobedience, or assaulting an officer. These records give the strong impression that reflex punishments were widespread, perhaps routine, and tolerated by most junior and middle-ranking officers. The treatment of officers charged with inflicting illegal "correction" reinforces this impression: Though courts occasionally handed down verdicts of dismissal in such cases, they more frequently acquitted the defendant or issued only mild sentences.

In 1822, for example, Lieutenant Edward Harding was tried for "Illegal and unmilitary conduct" involving the severe flogging of several soldiers at Fort Niagara. The court found Harding guilty of the specifications but innocent of the charge; he had "received insolence which deserved chastisement," and exemplary measures were required to quell the garrison's insubordinate spirit. When the departmental commander ordered reconsideration, arguing that the punishment had occurred the day after the episode of insubordination and that the garrison as a whole had remained quiet, the court stuck by its original finding. On a march in northern Florida in 1839, Private James Jones lagged behind the column, complaining that he was sick. Captain Marshall S. Howe suspected him of malingering and flailed him repeatedly with his sword and with sticks he had cut especially for the purpose. As Jones lay dying in camp that night, he reached out to Howe and begged to be buried with military honors. Howe kicked his hand away and exclaimed, "I will have you buried. I have a grave already dug for you." A civilian court acquitted Howe of manslaughter on the basis of an army surgeon's testimony that the beatings had not caused Jones's death. On the commanding general's insistence, the captain was later court-martialed for cruelty and convicted, but was sentenced to only a twelve-month suspension.[31]

In 1841, a court tried Lieutenant James W. Penrose for the brutal beating of two drunken recruits on board a steamboat off St. Mary's, Florida. When one soldier, Private Stevens, stumbled past him, Penrose rushed at him, knocked him down, kicked him, then had him dragged onto the promenade deck. According to an officer witness, Penrose "stepped two or three paces backwards ran at the man as though he was a foot ball and kicked him in the face and stomach until Pat. Stevens was senseless." Thereupon, he gave a similar stomping to the other soldier, who had been tied hand and foot. The court acquitted Penrose, apparently accepting his claim that his actions were justified by the mutinous mood aboard the ship.[32]

During the early 1840s, military authorities made another effort to curb officers' mistreatment of enlisted men. Winfield Scott, an ardent opponent of illegal punishments, had taken command of the army in 1841. His attack on abuse was loosely analogous to contemporary reform movements to reduce or abolish corporal punishments in prisons, schools, and the United States Navy.[33] Scott issued his order denouncing illegal punishments in 1842, and at least eleven officers were brought before courts-martial or courts of inquiry for such actions in 1842 and 1843. The courts either acquitted or exonerated these officers or gave them reprimands or short suspensions from rank and command. In the most publicized case, Lieutenant Don Carlos Buell was tried for beating Private James P. Humphrey with his sword in his quarters at Jefferson Barracks; the soldier, under the charge of a sergeant at the time, had allegedly answered Buell back when asked why he had refused to do police duty. Buell admitted that he did not strike Humphrey in self-defense but "in defence of that service which is bleeding for the arrest of a spirit of insubordination which seems to be sweeping the army." The court found that Buell had committed the acts in question, but it attached no criminality to them and "honorably" acquitted him. On the other hand, the same court convicted Private Humphrey of willful disobedience and mutinous behavior and sentenced him to serve out his enlistment at hard labor with a ball and chain, then have his head shaven and be drummed out of the service. When ordered to reconsider their decisions in these cases, the members defied both Scott and the secretary of war by denying that a court-martial, once dissolved, could be legally reconvened.[34]

Whatever the short-term effects of Scott's campaign against extralegal abuse, it had little lasting impact. Commanders continued to resort to summary force when they considered it necessary to maintain order or preserve their authority, and their fellow officers steadfastly refused to punish them. On a march in New Mexico in February 1852, for example, Captain James H. Carleton ordered three drunken dragoons tied behind the wagons and made them follow the column on foot. When the horses broke into a trot, one of the soldiers fell and was dragged between a half-mile and a mile, passing at one point through a stream. Eventually Carleton had him placed in a wagon, but he died soon afterwards. Acting on the testimony of medical officers, a court of inquiry determined that the soldier had died of excessive drinking rather than ill treatment. In another incident six years later, Captain William R. Bradfute went to a grocery near his cavalry camp on the Brazos River of Texas, intending to warn the proprietors against selling liquor to his men. He ordered some soldiers he found there back to camp, then approached a group gathered around a box playing cards. He struck one man, calling him a "damned son-of-a-bitch," and sent him off. He then hit another soldier, Private Murray, who returned the blow. Bradfute staggered or stepped back, pulled out his revolver, and shot Murray dead. A court of inquiry accepted Bradfute's story that Murray had advanced toward him in a threatening manner—despite testimony by enlisted men that he had stood still after the initial exchange of blows—and declared that the officer had acted from "a proper regard for discipline and for his own safety."[35] Given the common attitude of the officer corps, soldiers who protested mistreatment stood little chance of redress. "I have had to whip Pvt. Drum severely," Captain Thomas Claiborne wrote his wife in 1860, "he made complaint officially, it was not noticed. I made him carry his saddle 'till he begged off & repented[;] he has been forgiven."[36]

SOLDIERS VERSUS OFFICERS

On 29 August 1838, Adjutant General Roger Jones forwarded to the secretary of war for presidential review the proceedings of a court-martial that had sentenced Private Bartholomew Rogers to death for an assault on Lieutenant Charles H. Larned. As in so many cases, the incident had begun with a remark considered insolent by the officer; Larned had reacted by striking Rogers across the head with a cane, and the soldier had responded with force of his own—thrusting at the lieutenant with his bayonet and wounding him slightly in the groin. Hoping for administration approval of the sentence, Jones described "the alarming degree of insubordination, which now prevails in the rank and file of the Army, as attested by the officers who serve with, and whose duties habitually bring them in contact with the soldiery." A regimental officer had assured him "that the personal dangers incident to the commanders of companies, from the lawless spirit of the men, exceed in his opinion the dangers of the field, and that he would prefer to meet with an open Enemy, than to be at the head of one of the Companies at the present time." Since the attorney general had decided earlier that year that a state of war existed between the United States and the Seminole tribe, the prohibition against military executions in time of peace did not apply. Apparently convinced of the seriousness of the situation, Martin Van Buren approved the sentence, and Private Rogers became one of possibly three soldiers to face the firing squad that year for attacks on commissioned officers.[37]

As Jones indicated, the late 1830s was in fact an exceptionally tense period in officer–enlisted man relations—stimulated perhaps by the rapid buildup of the army to carry out Indian removal and the pressures of guerrilla warfare in the debilitating climate of Florida. Nevertheless, soldier resistance to the army's disciplinary regime persisted throughout the antebellum era. Enlisted men were by no means willing to accept passively the sanctity of the rank structure, and many were quite prepared to use individual or collective force in their own defense. In some respects, the officer–enlisted man relationship resembled labor-management conflicts in nineteenth-century America, as soldiers, denied redress through established channels, resorted to protests, work stoppages, sabotage, and, occasionally, attempted assassinations.

Although there were exceptions, few soldiers seem to have questioned the technical competence or courage of their commanders, especially those with West Point training. Augustus Meyers, who served as a musician in the late 1850s, observed that enlisted men did not have much use for officers appointed from civil life, "but we respected the young officers from the military academy, who understood their business." Samuel E. Chamberlain recalled his experiences as a dragoon in the Mexican War: "Our officers were all graduates of West Point, and at the worst, were gentlemen of intelligence and education, often harsh and tyrannical, yet they took pride in having their men well clothed, and fed, in making them contented and reconciled to their lot."[38] Soldiers naturally responded well to officers who took a paternalistic interest in their welfare, and some admired certain senior commanders whose eccentric and colorful behavior seemed endearing—at least from a distance. According to a Mexican War veteran, Brigadier General David E. Twiggs was "a great favourite amongst the men who admired him principally, I believe, for his brusquerie and coarseness of manner, and a singular habit he had of swearing most vehemently and flying into a passion on the most trifling occasions."[39]

Enlisted men especially appreciated commanders who refrained from flaunting their rank and who demonstrated a willingness to share the hardships of their men. Although James Hildreth had little good to say about the officers he encountered as a dragoon in the 1830s, he did recall fondly Lieutenant John H. K. Burgwin, who consistently treated him more as a friend than an inferior. Similarly, a soldier serving on the Utah expedition praised Lieutenant Levi C. Bootes, an officer who had risen from the ranks; unlike other infantry officers who rode at the head of the column, Bootes marched on foot with his men to keep their spirits up. A minor episode of fraternization seems to have impressed Josiah M. Rice, who was stationed in the Southwest during the 1850s. A lieutenant joined his mess and was offered some of the stew that the men were eating. "At this, the Lieut. took a sip from the cup, giving a smack with his lips and saying, 'Shit, by God, shit.'" A German-born soldier informed his parents in 1857 that the distance between officers and men was far less in the American army than in those of his native land. "For example, I never hesitate to speak just as freely and frankly to our colonel as I might to one of our sergeants."[40]

The German soldier's comment notwithstanding, the testimony of enlisted men shows clearly that officers willing to forgo the prerogatives of rank were rare exceptions in the American service. Soldiers were offended by the rigid military rank structure and the officer–enlisted man dichotomy. To native-born and immigrant soldiers alike, the army's inflated hierarchy of power and privilege seemed to violate the egalitarian spirit that pervaded American culture in the antebellum decades—the assumption that all white male citizens, at least, possessed the same political and social rights. While soldiers realized that military service entailed a temporary limitation of their freedoms, they also considered their enlistment a contract involving obligations on the part of the government and their commanders. These terms included fulfillment of the conditions under which they had enlisted, concern for their physical well-being, and respect for their individual dignity and manhood—their status as free Americans. Inevitably, the arbitrary, authoritarian leadership style of the officer corps, which emphasized unquestioning obedience to higher rank and was suffused with nativism and social class prejudice, appeared to threaten soldiers' assessment of their rights.

Complaints about the demeaning aspects of the rank system run through soldiers' writings. The Mexican War narratives of Samuel Chamberlain and George Ballentine continually mentioned the haughty and tyrannical conduct of the company-grade officers. Indeed, Ballentine considered their abuse of authority the main cause of desertion in Mexico. An anonymous dragoon soldier bitterly denounced the inexperienced young officers who served in the Utah expedition: "Fellows are let loose from West Point, full of the idea that they are born to rule, and soon they let out their dignity in everything that affects their subordinates. Men, in many cases better men than themselves, are treated as brutes by these new fledged cadets, and they lord it over the veterans of the service with rods of iron." At the end of his memoir, James Hildreth warned his readers against enlisting, underscoring the tyranny of the officers and comparing a soldier's life to that of a slave. In a letter to the secretary of war, a former soldier criticized the employment of enlisted men "for the private convenience of the officer. This is a great reason why Americans will not stay in the Army, for they cannot be made to believe, that those in authority should have the power to compel them in a direct or indirect way to saw wood or do the chores."[41]

Although the gulf between officers and enlisted men bred resentment in the ranks, military punishments were by far the most corrosive element in the relationship. Nothing revealed more dramatically the differences in status and power separating the two groups or the discrepancy between the realities of the military system and the values professed by the larger society. Soldiers were appalled and disgusted by the sight of floggings and by the degrading ceremonies in which offenders were drummed out of the service at bayonet point after being tattooed and having their heads shaven. To Augustus Meyers, the latter punishment seemed like "a relic of barbarity"; he was "ashamed and indignant at being compelled to be an actor in this disgraceful scene."[42] Offensive as they were, such punishments were usually approved by courts-martial and thus were backed by the authority of law. Enlisted men resented even more the summary and extralegal violence visited on them by their officers, since such actions were clearly assaults on their personal integrity and violations of their contract with the government. In 1821, a private at Fort Howard described to the secretary of war how he had been "Stripped to the naked skin & severely flogged" and "ducked almost to strangulation with buckets of water" poured over his head. "If, Sir, personal malice and revenge, as I have been tempted to believe is the fact are allowed to pervert the Laws of the constitution, then is the Army (I speak boldly, for I have always thought freely) instead of being the bulwark of the national defence, *a nursery of traitors and incendiaries.*"[43]

The most common form of soldier resistance was spontaneous and individualized—a single soldier reacting against an officer's threats or blows or against a perceived affront to his dignity or manhood. At Fort Pike, Louisiana, in 1830, Captain John Mountfort accused Corporal Frederick Jordan of neglecting his duty. "By God I have not," responded Jordan. Mountfort advanced toward him, aiming to tear off his chevrons, but Jordan prepared to defend himself and declared, "I have attended to the police and I will be damned if I will be touched by any man." Only when the officer picked up a musket did Jordan go to the guardhouse. On a prairie march in 1839, Lieutenant Robert H. Chilton reprimanded Private Elbridge Gerry for allowing a horse to get loose; he ordered the soldier tied to his horse and said he would have him tied up that night "& let the mosquitos eat him up." "Will you," snapped Gerry. Chilton partially drew his sword and exclaimed, "I will cut you down you damn son of a bitch." Thereupon, the soldier called on his comrades for support, declaring that "before I will be tied up to a tree and eaten up by mosquitos I will loose my last drop of blood." When no one came to his aid, he sprang on his horse and rode away; Chilton pursued and subdued him by force. At Gerry's court-martial, enlisted witnesses stated their opinion that he had not intended to raise a mutiny or desert but had only wished to escape

Chilton's wrath. According to a sergeant, "the threats made by Lt. Chilton were enough to make a man try to get out of the way."⁴⁴

A more deliberate act of defiance occurred at Fort Columbus, New York, in 1842. Lieutenant James Duncan heard that Hospital Steward James Markiewicz was composing a letter to the president, defaming Duncan's character. Accompanied by his first sergeant, Stevens, Duncan went to Markiewicz's room, arrested the soldier, and confiscated the letter, which accused Duncan and Stevens of fraudulent use of public property and the brutal treatment of enlisted men. In particular, Markiewicz blamed Duncan for the death of Private Edward Shannon. Shannon, whose health had been weakened by venereal disease, had gotten drunk and been drenched at a pump on Duncan's orders, then confined for the night in a cold, damp cell where he had been found dead in the morning. Markiewicz also claimed that Stevens had beaten another soldier so badly that his face had been unrecognizable for weeks. A native of Poland, Markiewicz had "served in the army under the most despotic government in [the] whole globe that of Russia where we use to treat soldiers almost like slaves—and I take God to witness[,] never such treatment during my servitude met my eye—and can I look at it without indignation in a civilized free and happy United States." A court of inquiry investigated the Shannon affair and cleared Duncan of blame. Markiewicz was then called before a court-martial on charges of subversion of discipline and disobedience of orders. He defended himself ably, however, stressing his right to correspond personally with anyone he chose and citing the constitutional proscription against illegal seizures. Although convicted, he was sentenced only to dismissal from the service—a very light penalty in the general court-martial of an enlisted man.⁴⁵

Cases of collective resistance by enlisted men were less frequent than individual actions, but they were nevertheless fairly common. Most stemmed from the perennial grievances about punishment, and most involved little planning. On Christmas Day, 1829, fifteen or twenty soldiers formed on the Fort Mackinac parade ground to demand the release of a private who had been taken to the quarters of Lieutenant Ephraim Kirby Smith. Smith had flogged enlisted men in the past, and the soldiers wanted to prevent their comrade from suffering that fate. When Smith ordered them to disperse, Corporal Henry Goetzler answered "in broken english, I shant I have turned out to get my rights, and by God [I'll] have them." Goetzler brought his musket to the charge position, and the lieutenant struck at him with his sword until the blade separated from the hilt. Smith left to find another sword, and other officers convinced the soldiers to disperse. Nevertheless, Smith confirmed their fears by personally flogging Goetzler and several other men in his quarters—including the private whose plight had brought on the protest. Smith's actions backfired, however; testimony at the soldiers' mutiny trial revealed the extent of his use of illegal punishments, and he was court-martialed the following year and temporarily dismissed.[46] A similar though less justifiable "mutiny" occurred at Fort Snelling in 1831, when sixteen soldiers marched in arms to the guardhouse to demand the release of comrades imprisoned for rowdy behavior at an enlisted men's ball. On this occasion, other companies surrounded and disarmed the protesters.[47]

Three other cases suggest the variety of soldiers' joint action. In April 1838, a court-martial at West Point tried seven dragoon soldiers for disobeying an order to do guard duty. In their defense, the soldiers argued that the army had failed to fulfill the terms of their enlistments. They had been promised horses and special training for the duties of noncommissioned officers; instead, they had been required to serve as part of the regular West Point detachment. The court sentenced them to three months confinement but, in light of the ample evidence supporting their claim, recommended remission.[48]

Four years later, several soldiers were court-martialed for mutiny in connection with an incident at Volusia, Florida. The trouble began outside the stockade when Lieutenant Nathaniel Lyon, less than a year out of West Point, ordered Private Davis Osmond to be quiet. "I don't care a damn for you, you little puppy," snarled Osmond, who had been drinking; "green horn—You'll learn something by the time you have been in the service as long as I have." Furious at this assault on his fragile authority, Lyon tried to strike him with a pole, but other soldiers prevented him. He then had Osmond bound, fastened a rope around his shoulders, and threw him into the St. Johns River— merely to sober him, he later claimed. Corporal Horace Goodwin thereupon pushed Lyon into the water as well and ran to the fort for help. Returning with others, he attempted to release Osmond. "I'll be damned if I'll see a man drowned," Goodwin exclaimed. "You must be damned fools if you'll allow it." The garrison eventually quieted, but Osmond, Goodwin, and two other soldiers were sentenced to six months of solitary confinement or, if conditions did not permit it, hard labor with a ball and chain and then being drummed out of the service.[49]

An incident at Fort Davis, Texas, in 1856 apparently involved a type of collective sabotage. At a legal flogging supervised by Lieutenant Edward L. Hartz, five musicians and privates in succession struck the victim so lightly that the blows did not, in Hartz's opinion, constitute disciplinary action. Even when threatened with punishment themselves, the soldiers refused to strike harder. All were court-martialed, convicted of disobedience of orders, and sentenced to forfeiture of half their pay for ten months. "Humanity is a commendable virtue but must give way to the voice of law and the ends of justice," wrote Hartz to his father. "Much as the task before me was revolting to my feelings, the knowledge that this punishment was necessary, after it had been ordered for the good of the service, induced me to endeavor to have it inflicted according to the letter and the spirit of the law,—and I would have seen the blood start at every cut if I could have found one to use the whip."[50]

Obviously, direct attacks on officers were the most extreme form of soldier resistance. Although only three officers are known to have been killed by enlisted men in the period 1821–1861, army records reveal a significant number of attempted assassinations or other personal assaults. Some situations involved soldiers who were almost certainly deranged. Such was probably the case with Private John Reily, who fired a musket at the officers' quarters of Fort Heileman, Florida. His behavior was highly erratic during the confrontation, and there was no apparent motive for his action. Similarly, a sergeant may have been out of his mind with drink when he ran berserk on the parade ground of Fort Crawford in 1828 and shot and killed Lieutenant John Mackenzie.[51]

More often, the attacks reflected soldiers' intense reactions against military punishments. At Fort Howard in 1821, a soldier made "some impertinent remarks" on the capture of a deserter, and Captain Richard B. Mason ordered him to be quiet and boxed his ears. Soon afterwards, the soldier went to Mason's tent and fired at him with a load of pigeon shot. Mason was severely wounded but recovered; no record could be found of the soldier's fate. While in the commissary of the St. Augustine garrison in 1837, Lieutenant Charles A. May was warned by a soldier that Private John Murry was waiting in the cookhouse to shoot him as he walked by. May entered by the rear door and got the drop on Murry, who was seated facing the front window with a loaded carbine. At the subsequent court-martial, a witness testified that Murry, previously a good soldier, was drunk and angry at May for confining another soldier.[52]

At an encampment in Texas in 1849, Lieutenant Samuel H. Starr had a dragoon private tied up for grousing loudly about his duties. About twilight, seven or eight soldiers, led by a Private Foggerty, approached the officers' tents and asked to speak to Starr. If their comrade were not released, they stated, they all wished to be tied up. Starr was absent, and the other officers sent the men away. When Starr returned, he took a pistol and sword and called out to see the soldiers who had wished to speak to him. Foggerty advanced, cursing the others as "d_____d cowards" for not following. Starr reached forward as if to disarm Foggerty; according to a sergeant, he struck the soldier with his saber. Foggerty stepped back, drew his own pistol, and said, "Not so fast Mr.

Starr. Not so fast Sir." The two men leveled their pistols and fired simultaneously; Starr ducked and was not hit but his bullet killed Foggerty.[53]

The vast majority of enlisted men never resorted to assaults on their commanders, as fear of punishment and moral scruples restrained all but the most alienated and desperate. Desertion was always a ready option when pressures became intolerable.[54] In addition, noncommissioned officers acted as a buffer between the privates and the officers. While their role was complex, sergeants and corporals did serve as shock troops in the officer corps's struggle to maintain the rank structure; they confined soldiers for offenses and dispensed punishments—and they were more accessible targets than officers were for the frustrations of the rank and file. Indeed, the army's court-martial records include numerous cases involving soldiers' attacks on noncommissioned officers. Certainly they deflected much of the violence that might otherwise have been directed higher up the rank scale.

Although restrained from acting, many soldiers fantasized about taking revenge on their commanders, and sometimes when their tongues were loosened by anger or drink, these dreams poured out in the form of threats. As a drunken private, Peter Goodwin, was being tied up by his thumbs, he snarled at Lieutenant George W. Rains, "You are no Gentleman or you would not have me tied up this way like a dog. . . . You are no Gentleman nor Soldier, and the first Ball that goes into my Gun I will see you out with it." When Lieutenant Edgar Gaither ordered Private I. N. Livingston tied and gagged for unruly behavior, the soldier exclaimed, "Yes gag me! The time will come when I can gag those who gag me, and put a bullet through their hearts." "I'll shoot him," said Private Benjamin Arnold of Lieutenant Thomas W. Sherman, who had ordered his arrest. "I'll await my opportunity to have revenge on him. . . . A damned young Cow Boy just come from West Point is not fit to command men."[55]

Conflict and violence have figured prominently in this account of officer–enlisted man relations, and this reflects in part the records available to the historian; the court-martial files in particular, though by far the most extensive source of data, are unavoidably weighted toward confrontational events. Paternalism occupied an important place in the self-image of the officer corps, and most officers attempted to meet their responsibilities, as they saw them, to their inferiors in the military hierarchy. Nevertheless, a great deal of tension was inherent in the wide and tenaciously guarded gap in power, privilege, and opportunity that separated officers and enlisted men. While democratic values spread throughout the culture of nineteenth-century America, the officer corps remained committed to a rigidly stratified and authoritarian social system, resting on the imperative of unquestioning acceptance of higher authority. Rarely did commanders reconsider the traditional leadership style inherited from the standing armies of eighteenth-century Europe. Except for the gradual moderation of corporal punishment, the officer–enlisted man relationship was virtually the same in the 1850s as it had been in the 1780s.

15
OFFICERS, POLITICIANS, AND CITIZENS

In November 1840, Captain John R. Vinton wrote his mother from Florida, predicting the victory of William Henry Harrison in the presidential election. "What a grand channel the Army is to the Presidency!" he asserted. "Strange that in this enlightened age, mil[itar]y renown should still take such fast hold of the sentiments of the people." On further thought, however, Vinton decided that great military exploits would always stand out in the public mind.

> Politicians, as such, walk in a devious path. The people know they are self seeking, & naturally mistrust the sincerity of their professions. Belonging to party, they must necessarily have as many adversaries (nearly) as adherents,—enemies as friends. . . . The man with fewest enemies therefore, though of inferior parts, will often carry away the popular suffrage from another who shines as the brightest star of the political galaxy. Old generals are just of this kind. They stand forth for the country and not for a party, and the people take them up with confidence & even enthusiasm, whenever they are fain to look out a Candidate for their Chief Magistracy.[1]

Vinton's observations were certainly correct for the middle decades of the nineteenth century: Of twenty-seven individuals who were major candidates for the presidency between 1824 and 1880, eight were career officers or men whose reputations had been made through regular army service. Military men ran in eleven of the fifteen presidential races during that period, and four occupied the White House.[2] Clearly, the army was not isolated from the political arena. However, Vinton was also accurate in noting the nationally oriented, essentially nonpartisan character of the officer corps. Although they headed party tickets, most military candidates had not been active in party affairs before their nominations, and they usually stressed that they were running on national rather than strictly partisan platforms. Zachary Taylor, who claimed never to have mingled in politics as an officer, stated in 1847 that he would occupy the White House only if he could be "the president of a nation & not of a party."[3]

The conduct of the army candidates suggests a broader comment about the officer corps's relationship to politics—its tendency to be in the political world but not of that world. During the antebellum era, regulars developed for the first time a consistent pattern of political action. Professional ideology rejected partisanship and discouraged taking sides on purely civilian matters. The professed ideal was an apolitical officer corps and a rigid separation between the civilian and military spheres. On the other hand, regulars readily embraced political means to pursue goals defined as professional: individual career advancement, the interests of particular branches of the service, and the welfare of the army as a whole. By midcentury, the civil-military relationship in the United States had assumed the basic character it would retain into the late twentieth century—the most important aspect of which was the institutionalization of civil supremacy.

OFFICERS AND POLITICIANS

The civil-military relationship had been ill defined in the early national period, and no clear line had separated the army from political life.[4] Although officers had occasionally opined that the army should remain aloof from politics, commanders had regularly appealed to their political friends for redress and taken stands on contemporary political issues. The sudden expansions of the army had brought political activists and former officeholders directly into the highest rungs of the officer corps. Moreover, the executive branch had used military appointments for patronage purposes, and the political coloration of the officer corps had reflected the party in power: Federalist in the 1790s and early 1800s; Democratic Republican after 1808.

The years following the War of 1812 marked no sudden change in the traditionally tangled patterns of army politics. The euphoric nationalism of the postwar period briefly submerged popular antimilitarism; scores of veterans returned to heroes' welcomes and mingled in prestigious political circles. Most high-ranking commanders had entered the army during the expansions of 1808 and 1812–1814, and few were, in the strict sense, careerists. The senior generals, Jacob Brown and Andrew Jackson, established their headquarters at their personal residences, where they mixed military administration with agriculture and political interests. The complex political infighting of the Era of Good Feelings absorbed the attention of some regulars. The candidacy of Secretary of War John C. Calhoun was popular in the army; several officers supported him in the press, and General Brown and his aide-de-camp, Lieutenant John A. Dix, served as intermediaries when Calhoun agreed to run for vice-president under John Quincy Adams.[5]

Nevertheless, the changing circumstances of army life led officers to perceive politics in a different light. Most important was the post-1815 trend toward professional consolidation. The lengthening of career commitments, the rationalization of military procedures, the emergence of West Point as an institution of professional socialization—all encouraged regulars to adopt common modes of thought and behavior that were shaped more by their experiences as cadets and officers than by their preservice backgrounds or civilian contacts. By the 1820s and 1830s, officers had begun to distinguish consistently between the military and political worlds. As military professionals, their principal responsibility was to the nation as a whole rather than to a particular section, faction, or party. Their involvement in a centralized, restrictive bureaucratic institution led them to internalize hierarchical values—order, obedience, discipline—that set them apart from the rough-and-tumble egalitarian tenor of contemporary political life. Finally, Sylvanus Thayer and the West Point faculty emphasized the academy's national character and tried to isolate cadets from civilian politics.

Officers' perceptions of the political environment reinforced their inclination to separate the military from the civilian sphere. Although the army had enjoyed considerable prestige immediately after the War of 1812, antimilitary sentiment had resurfaced in Congress by the early 1820s, illustrated by a series of investigations into the War Department and the reduction of the army in 1821. Congressional hostility, or at least indifference, continued through the Adams administration. While specific military programs fared better under the Jacksonians, the regular army was frequently the target of Democratic congressmen, state legislators, and editors, who found its authoritarian structure and reliance on specialized expertise incompatible with egalitarian values. Antimilitary rhetoric peaked in the depression years of the early 1840s, as economy-minded congressmen considered reductions of the army and the abolition of West Point. However, the danger to the military was more apparent than real; the expanding frontier and threats of foreign war actually brought occasional increases in military strength. Nevertheless, regulars habitually exaggerated the extent of public hostility and came to see politicians as adversaries. Under these circumstances, officers' intervention in the world of civilian politics might provoke the wrath of Congress, threatening both the army as an institution and their careers along with it.

Though seldom expressed as a formal theory, officers developed a conception of the army as an apolitical instrument of public policy. As servants of the nation, they should stand aloof from party and sectional strife and avoid taking sides on civilian political issues. Colonel Henry Atkinson favored Andrew Jackson for the presidency in 1824 but felt himself "too delicately situated (being an officer of the army) to take an active part." Colonel Duncan L. Clinch stated in 1829 that he had "always deprecated the practice of officers of the Army interfering in elections, either of a general or local character, except so far as respects an honest and moderate expression of their opinions—and have never approached the polls, or given a vote, since I have been in the Army." Brigadier General Edmund P. Gaines repeatedly denounced partisan allegiances by officers: "In war we must serve our country with all our hearts, and with all our soul, and with all our strength; we are thus rendered incapable of serving a political party." Although Lieutenant William T. Sherman considered himself a Whig by family tradition, he asserted that as an officer it was his "intention and duty to abstain from any active part in political matters and discussions, and for that reason I never permit myself to become interested in the success of either party." According to a correspondent to the *Army and Navy Chronicle*, officers' political attachments might turn the army into "an armed mob, dangerous in its nature to the vital interests of the government, and subversive of the honor belonging to the profession of arms." By accepting a commission, an officer voluntarily surrendered his rights of political action.[6]

A corollary of officers' distinction between politics and military life was a negative view of politicians. In contrast to the patriotism and devotion to duty that allegedly characterized the military profession, politicians appeared shifty, factious, self-serving, and too willing to abandon principles. They placed sectional and party loyalties above the national interest, which was defined of course as a strong military establishment, and they failed to appreciate the sacrifices of the army. Few regulars went as far in print as Lieutenant Daniel H. Hill, who, in reference to the secretary of war, bemoaned the "melancholy fact, that the *soldier*, who has devoted himself to the science of war from his childhood, can never rise above an inferior grade, whilst the command of the Army is entrusted to a *politician*, who has gained distinction by courting the mob."[7] Such sentiments were common in private correspondence, however, and officers tended to use the word "demagogue" interchangably with "politician." In his memoirs, Colonel Philip St. George Cooke complained of Congress's reluctance to support the dragoons: "Oh! ye hypocrites,—demagogues—who swallow a million squandered on a fraudulent contract, or on an Eastern palace, and strain at a cent for the protection and peace of the simple border States!" Captain William H. T. Walker rejected the idea of applying to Washington, D.C., for promotion, as he refused to be "one of the fawning sychopants that crowd that rotten collection of demagogues." "Give my love to Congress & tell them to go to the place of which they are destined to become shining ornaments," wrote Captain George W. Cullum to a friend stationed at the nation's capital.[8]

Suggested in many officers' writings was an elitist disdain for the give-and-take nature of democratic politics. Politicians' reliance on compromise and their continual praise for the virtues of the common man offended the imperious values of these regulars. Although one correspondent to a military periodical professed respect for democracy in theory, he thought it endangered by the demagogue—"an individual who elevates himself in flattering the people, causing them to overrate themselves, and underrate their superiors." He regretted the trend toward breaking down "the natural barriers separating the different classes of society" and especially resented citizens' habit of considering army officers as their servants. In 1855, Captain Thomas Williams proposed that remote Mackinac Island be made into a military school:

> Here, there *can* be a *unity* of Government—no compromises between discipline on the one hand & rowdyism on the other. No collisions or collusions. Here, we can cultivate science, letters & art, manners & morals; & warm our patriotism in the society of men who live for their country. Mackinac would be confusion & a stumbling block, to traitors & demagogues, knaves & rowdies; & a sort of sheet anchor to lovers of law & order & government. And *order*, you know "is heaven's *first law.*"

Lieutenant John Van Deusen DuBois's faith in republicanism was shaken by the leniency of the Buchanan administration toward the Mormons, which he attributed to an unprincipled quest for Mormon votes. In contrast, officers and soldiers did not vote and thus were not fully citizens. "If ever the army is unfaithful it will be because they have no interest in the government," he confided in his diary.[9] Of course, officers were sensitive to the army's public image, and they usually confined such opinions to their journals or private letters.

It would be misleading to take at face value officers' professions of political neutrality. After both the War of 1812 and the Mexican War, senior commanders harbored political ambitions; Winfield Scott lusted for the presidency through much of his long career. The army contained a number of strongly partisan officers who continued to dabble in election politics. Nevertheless, the overwhelming weight of the evidence indicates that the dissociation of the military profession from politics was more than rhetorical. By the 1830s, most career officers were expressing little interest in political issues not directly pertinent to the army. Officers' personal correspondence and journals rarely mentioned such charged debates of the Jacksonian era as the tariff, the national bank, or even sectional controversies. National elections frequently passed without notice or were dismissed with comments similar to that of Colonel Abraham Eustis in 1840, who thought life "not long enough to devote any portion of it to reading long speeches, pro & con, on Log-cabins, & Hard Cider."[10] This attitude is especially striking when compared with the zealous popular interest in politics that marked the antebellum decades.

Officers were by no means indifferent to the political world, but they viewed it mainly from a professional perspective. If they ignored more general political developments, they closely followed congressional proceedings on army matters and filled countless letters with political news relevant to their profession. When they voiced a preference for a party or candidate, it was usually in the context of their individual career interests or the collective interests of their branch or of the army as a whole. Lieutenant Braxton Bragg found it difficult to understand why officers of his regiment supported the Whigs in 1844. "Independent of the democratic party being [the army's] main support and dependence in Congress, the policy of the party is such as to require a large increase of the army whenever they may be enabled to carry out their principles." On the other hand, Captain Benjamin Alvord rejoiced at the election of Zachary Taylor on the Whig ticket four years later, as the Democratic Polk administration's "studious neglect & odious discrimination against the army" made any change welcome. "I take but little interest in the debates in Congress farther than they relate to the army, & the foreign relations of the country," wrote Captain Thomas Williams in 1855—a statement borne out by the paucity of comments on domestic political subjects in his extensive and otherwise extremely opinionated private correspondence.[11]

PATTERNS OF ARMY POLITICS

Officers continued to be active in the political sphere, but they channeled their energies into the pursuit of professional goals, the most basic of which was the advancement of their personal careers. As discussed in chapter 11, promotion was an all-engrossing preoccupation among the increasingly career-minded officers of the antebellum army. Although seniority governed regular promotion through the grade of colonel, several types of preferment lay outside the seniority system and were therefore at least partially responsive to political influence: promotions from the line into the staff departments, promotions into new regiments, brevet promotions, and promotions to general's rank. Political support might advance an officer's interests in other ways as well, by allowing him to obtain or extend a leave of absence, for example, or procure a desirable station or assignment.

Angling for these advantages, officers suppressed their generalized disdain for politicians and cultivated influential sponsors. The nature of the political system facilitated their efforts. The army was a national bureaucracy existing in a decentralized, community-oriented social order. Virtually all officers had used their congressmen and prominent relatives and friends to obtain their original appointments, and most held on to these connections throughout their careers; many regulars extended their contacts through marriage or by fostering support in the regions where they were stationed. Although the War Department denied that political pressure affected its personnel decisions, each reorganization or expansion of the army and each death of a general officer brought a rush of claims from politically backed officers whom the government could ill afford to ignore. Politicians' intervention for other types of favors was a constant part of military administration. A veteran of War Department bureaucracy explained the facts of military life to a candidate for a staff appointment in 1857.

> You have enough of army recommendations, you want some *political* ones. Do not let this word deter you, from using in your own defence lawful weapons, which have been already turned against yourself. . . . Virginia influence is now in the ascendancy, and that, through your wife's relatives you can command. By all means, use it. . . . Request your friends, to watch for a vacancy, and, on the occurrence of one, to *lose no time*, in pressing your claim, in person, if they can, if not by letter.[12]

Examples of such activity abound. The reduction and reorganization of the army in 1821 created a maze of politically loaded officers' petitions that disrupted military administration for years. As in 1815, the administration established a board of generals to evaluate the relative merit of officers and recommend the best qualified for retention. Needless to say, the board's report sparked controversy, as commanders faced with discharge or demotion mobilized political sponsors and aired their cases in the press. Major Abraham Eustis refused to submit to an arrangement detrimental to his standing: "The matter must be decided in the Senate, & I have already found more than one member of that body, who is disposed to support my pretensions. . . . If the storm be once raised in Congress, it will, before it be allayed, sweep down some lofty heads." When President Monroe nominated colonels James Gadsden and Nathan Towson for the respective positions of adjutant general and commander of the Second Artillery Regiment, senatorial supporters of the unsuccessful candidates rejected the nominations on the grounds that they were violations of the seniority rule. The result was a constitutional debate over the president's appointment powers that kept the Adjutant General's Office without a permanent chief until 1825 and the Second Artillery without a colonel until 1832—and that appears never to have been settled on principle.[13]

Generals' promotions stirred similar controversy. When Major General Jacob Brown died in 1828, the struggle over succession to his position threatened to break up John Quincy Adams's cabinet. The political implications of choosing among the rival candidates led Adams to consider abolishing the office of commanding general altogether. When he selected a colonel, Chief Engineer Alexander Macomb, to fill the vacancy, Brigadier General Winfield Scott openly defied the administration. He refused to recognize Macomb as his superior, demanded his arrest as a usurper, and appealed to Congress for redress.[14] Although Scott failed on this occasion, he did rise to commanding general on Macomb's death in 1841. His promotion, however, touched off a scramble among the senior colonels for the vacant brigadier's spot. Inspector General John E. Wool emerged victorious, largely because he was in Washington, D.C., at the time and could lobby personally. After the confirmation battle, Wool wrote his chief Senate backer: "Thanks to you, [Senator George] Evans and others, that [senators Thomas Hart] Benton and [James] Buchanan failed in their unprincipled efforts to destroy me. I shall not forget them, and in due time I will pay them in their own coin."[15]

Lower-ranking regulars routinely resorted to political channels in search of promotions outside the seniority system, leaves, and desirable assignments. When Lieutenant Marcus C. M. Hammond sought a captaincy in the Quartermaster Department, for example, he urged a friend stationed at the capital to mobilize support: "My friends in Washington are [Attorney General Hugh S.] *Legaré*, [Senator William C.] Preston, [Congressman Francis W.] Pickens,— them especially. The first can do much with [President John] Tyler, the 2nd with [Major General Winfield] Scott & the 3d will promote my interest with Scott & [Secretary of War John C.] Spencer." In his quest for promotion in 1850, Captain Joseph E. Johnston contacted his brother-in-law in Congress: "I should be happy with a colonelcy[,] content with the next grade, dissatisfied to be sure with a 1st majority, but less so with a 2d than I now am—So you understand my case—I am hoping to see you named chairman of the Mil[itary] Com[mittee]."[16]

Political intervention reached something of a peak in 1854 and 1855, when Congress considered adding new regiments. Politicians deluged the War Department on behalf of promotion-starved regulars. The Georgia legislature passed a resolution backing Lieutenant James P. Flewellen for advancement. Lieutenant James Oakes bolstered his application with petitions signed by seventy-nine Pennsylvania legislators, fifteen congressmen, and the governor, as well as the top four executive officials of the Texas state government; Lieutenant Henry W. Benham had the support of the entire congressional delegations of all six New England states. Captain Thomas Williams's advocates included William Marcy, Robert McClelland, and Hamilton Fish: "Three *ex-governors*, two being of the Cabinet & one a Senator, ought surely, to be equal to a Colonelcy!" During a visit to Washington early in 1854, a subaltern counted over one hundred officers in the city, lobbying for advancement.[17]

It is difficult to measure how much politics actually influenced the army's personnel system. Throughout the antebellum era, military administrators tried to weaken patronage by placing personnel decisions on a more rational and equitable basis, but their success was limited. A general order of May 1833, for example, established clear guidelines for leaves and assignments to detached service and prohibited officers from visiting Washington without specific authorization from the commanding general. Almost immediately, the War Department began to permit exceptions to this regulation, and in September it dropped the visitation ban, presumably because of officers' claims that it violated their rights.[18] In an order of December 1837, Secretary of War Joel R. Poinsett specifically denounced officers' use of congressional sponsors to obtain favors or redress grievances and urged them to confine their applications to military avenues, where they would be considered strictly according to their merits. He also warned officers generally against involvement in party politics. Nevertheless, officers continued to shore up their requests with political muscle, and the War Department saw the need to reissue Poinsett's order in 1851. Although military authorities seem to have resisted the most flagrant types of political intervention, many regulars clung to the opinion expressed by an officer seeking a recruiting assignment in 1859: "Political and family influence determine everything." Perhaps the most important factor limiting the impact of political influence was its very ubiquity; officers' politically backed applications tended to cancel each other out.[19]

While the use of political influence for individual career advancement mainly continued and confirmed practices common before the War of 1812, a second category of officers' political action—promoting the interests of particular branches of the army—marked a significant new development. The origin of this trend was the period of army reform after the War of 1812, which resulted in permanent staff bureaus and a stable regimental structure. Because of the seniority system of promotion, most officers spent the greater part of their careers in a particular regiment or department, and they came to identify strongly with their branch—in some respects more so than with the army as a whole. One result was persistent intraservice rivalry, focusing on comparative prerogatives, jurisdictions, and resources and intensified recurrently by congressional budgetary pressures. The line branches and the staff bureaus sometimes quarreled among themselves; infantry officers, for example, envied the desirable seaboard posts of the artillery, and the Corps of Engineers clashed sporadically with the Corps of Topographical Engineers over control of politically popular internal improvements. As discussed in chapter 12, however, the deepest divisions ran between staff and line. Staff officers wished to perpetuate and expand their departmental prerogatives; line officers resented the size and independence of the bureaus and tried to curb the presumed privileges in pay, promotion, and stations hoarded by their staff colleagues.

Much intraservice friction was contained within the army, taking the form of angry exchanges of official correspondence and appeals to the War Department for redress. All sides turned to political channels whenever it seemed to their advantage, however. The staff departments had the upper hand in this bureaucratic warfare: Their headquarters were located in Washington and their chiefs had easy access to the president, the secretary of war, and Congress. Indeed, high-ranking staff officers frequently testified before congressional committees considering military legislation and even drafted bills supporting their departments' interests. Line officers, scattered at garrisons along the frontier and coastline, looked to the commanding general as their principal spokesman and made use of personal and local political connections.

Political action in pursuit of branch issues took many forms. Although appeals by individual officers to their congressmen or influential friends or relatives were most common, another important channel was the press. In their acrimonious feud of the 1840s and 1850s, for instance, the artillery regiments and the Ordnance Department made use of pamphlets and printed memorials to argue their cases.[20] Other intraservice concerns were aired in newspapers, military periodicals, and even literary magazines. Officers employed circular letters and petitions to attract congressional support and actively lobbied in Congress. The artillery mounted an especially systematic effort when an economy-minded Congress in 1844 considered reducing by half the number of first lieutenants in each of its regiments. The regiments responded by formally electing representatives to present their case in Washington, D.C. Although the commanding general disapproved of such quasi-official lobbying, the Third Artillery's delegate, Lieutenant Braxton Bragg, defied the order to return to his post and manipulated an invitation to testify before the House retrenchment committee. He also published a long series of unsigned articles in the *Southern Literary Messenger*, denouncing the perks and power of the General Staff. Whatever credit was due to the artillery lobby for this outcome, Congress took no action to reduce its officers.[21]

In some cases, regulars established ties with local and regional interests in a civil-military version of logrolling. Most prominent in this respect were the topographical engineers and the other officers engaged in internal improvements and exploration, whose duties brought them into frequent contact with businessmen and politicians. Acting in collusion with local leaders, civil works engineers often lobbied for the funding of particular projects. During the 1840s and 1850s, some aligned with powerful western and southern leaders in support of territorial expansion and a southern route for the proposed transcontinental railroad. Though frequently the center of controversy, the topographical engineers benefited from these connections. Collectively, the corps achieved separate bureau status, virtual autonomy within the military establishment, and nearly a quadrupling of its personnel. Individual engineers used their local and political contacts to obtain lucrative positions on leaving the service, and one topographical veteran, John C. Frémont, eventually ran for president of the United States.[22]

The most politically active branch of the army was the Corps of Engineers. Since its formation under Jonathan Williams in 1802, the corps had occupied a choice position within the army and wielded political influence to retain it. As with the topographical engineers, the army engineers supervised various civil works and thus were drawn into local political alliances.[23] However, the engineers had responsibility for two programs on which there was no public consensus. One was the military academy, perennially under attack during the "Age of the Common Man" as a seedbed of aristocratic privilege; the second was the seacoast fortification program. As noted before, skeptics in and out of Congress recurrently questioned the expense and utility of this operation, pointing to the absence of an immediate foreign threat and to advances in military technology that seemed to render large masonry works obsolete. In defending their vulnerable programs, the engineers could not expect the unified support of the army as a whole. Although the artillery and the Ordnance Department had a vested interest in the fortification program, all branches resented the corps's elite position, especially its exclusive control of West Point, and consequently often lobbied against it.

The Corps of Engineers countered their rivals by developing an arsenal of political weapons. Senior officers in Washington, D.C., kept in close contact with Congress, promoting and even drafting bills that might benefit the corps. Lower-ranking engineers looked after the corps's interests in the areas where they were stationed. When the Connecticut legislature passed resolutions in 1842 calling for the abolition of West Point, Captain George W. Cullum rushed to repair the damage: "I spent a day or two spouting to the loafers and trust I have put some right ideas in their heads."[24] The chief engineer attempted to stifle internal dissent potentially harmful to engineer projects and encouraged his subordinates to write articles for the civilian press, that would convince the public of the vital importance of coastal fortifications and formal military education.

The most elaborate political campaign waged by the Corps of Engineers before the Civil War occurred during the early 1850s. In 1851, the House of Representatives tabled the annual appropriations bill for fortifications, in part because of the unsettled state of military technology and in part because of western suspicions that the program was a worthless pork-barrel scheme to spend money in the coastal states. At the same time, junior staff officers favored legislation to speed promotion in their branches. An ambitious engineer officer stationed at the Coast Survey Office in Washington, D.C., Lieutenant Isaac Ingalls Stevens, coordinated a campaign to push the two causes simultaneously. Stevens and other officers at the capital personally solicited the support of scores of congressmen, raised funds from the corps to print memorials and reports bolstering their case, and distributed the materials to prominent men in the federal government and the states. On Stevens's advice, engineers lobbied in the districts where they were stationed, published articles in local newspapers, and mobilized their influential friends and relatives. The campaign succeeded; the army appropriation bill for 1853 restored the funds for fortifications and, much to the resentment of line officers, provided engineer, topographical, and ordnance lieutenants with automatic promotion to captain after fourteen years' service.[25] Stevens hoped that "our officers hereafter will realize their responsibilities as American Citizens, and will discharge, what I consider their bounden duty to enlighten the public mind."[26]

A third type of officers' political activity was very limited before the Civil War: the pursuit of general army interests. Military men were certainly aware that they were a group distinct from the rest of society, but this identity seldom found expression through political conduits. In contrast to the immediate, tangible demands of individual and branch interests, the army interest was poorly defined. Antimilitary rhetoric notwithstanding, a general consensus usually existed in the government that the regular army should be retained and even increased occasionally to meet the needs of national expansion.

Army-navy rivalry was not yet a significant incentive to internal service solidarity. The two services had relatively clear, mutually exclusive functions; service appropriations were determined by separate congressional committees and had little bearing on each other. The navy occasionally quarreled with the Corps of Engineers over coastal fortifications, but many line officers were indifferent to that program and viewed it as a branch rather than a service matter. Thus, few political issues compelled army officers as a group to close ranks.

Nevertheless, regulars sometimes did act on behalf of general service interests. The desire of commanders to enhance the army's public image subtly influenced decisions on troop distributions, the opening and closing of military posts, and army participation in transportation projects. In 1820, for example, Major General Jacob Brown suggested stationing additional troops in Maine in order to make that newly formed state's congressional delegation more receptive to the army. He also hoped that regulars would, through military road building, "achieve a victory over some of the prejudices of the country by their useful labours in peace if they could not by their deeds of arms in War."[27] Officers lobbied collectively for higher pay and other economic benefits, for expansions of the army, and for a retirement and pension system.[28] Military humanitarians promoted measures to improve the condition of the enlisted men. The most notable of these reformers was Captain Robert Anderson of the artillery; beginning in the late 1830s, he pressed tirelessly for the establishment of "military asylums" for old soldiers, a measure that Congress finally approved in 1851. A letter written during one of his lobbying trips to Washington suggests the extent of some officers' contacts.

> In the Senate Mil[itar]y Com[mitt]ee Room, I met yesterday [senators Lewis] Cass and [Thomas Hart] Benton—they condescended to be very gracious. I saw [senators William] Allen & [Charles G.] Atherton in the Senate Chamber, and sat some time with them, promising to call in the evening at their quarters. To day, I have been engaged getting information to shew [Senator] Jeff. Davis that his scheme for an Asylum is impracticable. . . . To morrow I dine with [Senator John J.] Crittenden.[29]

Service solidarity intensified briefly during the Mexican War. The officer corps greeted the outbreak of fighting in 1846 with an enthusiasm bordering on mania. Not only did the war offer an opportunity for glory and promotion, but it presented a chance to demonstrate the army's professional skills and thereby silence its political critics. Even so, the seemingly partisan direction of the war effort by the Polk administration soon produced dissatisfaction. Regulars resented the large-scale call-up of volunteers, the appointment of citizens to the temporary "regular" regiments created in 1847, and the commissioning of prominent Democrats as generals. No opinion was as widespread in the army as contempt for citizen-soldiers, and the administration's reliance on "mushroom generals" and its promotion of "partisans lawyers and quacks" over regulars and West Point graduates seemed a conscious plan to degrade the army. Captain William H. T. Walker predicted that every regular officer "with one spark of chivalry" who could make a living outside the army would resign after the war. "I would rather serve as a private in a foreign army than to be a captain in an army which is trodden upon as ours is by its government."[30]

The ultimate insult was Polk's recall of General Winfield Scott from Mexico early in 1848, after his spectacular conquest of the Mexican capital. Although it was caused by factional conflict that involved regular as well as volunteer officers, the "martyrdom" of Scott appeared to many regulars as the climax of the government's ingratitude. Lieutenant Francis Collins, who "was not ignorant of the foul workings of a contemptible scheme of political partyism," found Polk's action beyond belief. Lieutenant Colonel Ethan Allen Hitchcock considered the army in Mexico, aside from a small clique of dissidents, universally opposed to Scott's suspension. "We all see the enormity of the conduct of the President—deplore and abhor it."[31]

This upsurge of army unity was short-lived. Temporarily isolated in Mexico, officers could take little immediate action besides writing angry letters home. The brevity and overwhelming success of their campaign rapidly defused resentment. The budding militance of the officer corps dissipated as veterans returned to heroes' welcomes, saw their most popular commander elected president, and scrambled for individual rewards, especially brevets. The Mexican War left an important legacy for the regular army in the form of professional pride, but it did not create an alienated military class, prepared to use concerted political action on behalf of group goals.

One characteristic of officers' political behavior that worked against a cohesive army interest was the relatively bipartisan—or perhaps nonpartisan—nature of the officer corps. In contrast to the pre-1815 army, regulars appear to have favored neither major party consistently. Although it is risky to generalize from the incomplete evidence available, seventy-eight officers who expressed their preferences directly during the period of the second party system (approximately 1828–1852) were fairly evenly divided: forty-one Democrats (52.6 percent) and thirty-seven National Republicans or Whigs, or at least anti-Jacksonians (47.4 percent.)[32] In addition, officers' party identifications were remarkably soft when measured against the intense partisanship in the larger society. Even in private correspondence, they often expressed their allegiances obliquely, even apologetically, and they tended to view their choice as the lesser of two evils. Presidential candidates with military backgrounds inspired surprisingly little enthusiasm. Andrew Jackson and William Henry Harrison drew only mixed responses from the army. Although many regulars favored Zachary Taylor in 1848, mostly as a rejection of the Polk administration, the similar Whig candidacy of Winfield Scott four years later aroused minimal noticeable support within the officer corps and even some active opposition.[33]

Three factors help explain the absence of a strong partisan bias in the antebellum army. First, by the 1830s, Americans were moving toward an acceptance of parties and party conflict as legitimate and even beneficial—necessary to check the concentration of power, raise the political consciousness of the public, and structure political disagreements in a sprawling, heterogeneous society.[34] Meanwhile, the emerging professional ethic of the officer corps, with its emphasis on service to a unified nation, perpetuated the older view of partisanship as divisive and potentially disruptive. Officers might use party connections to pursue professional goals, but they saw such ties as a necessary evil—a compromise with an imperfect world—rather than as a virtue. Second, the military appointment process, especially congressional control of cadet nominations and the use of professional examining boards to determine medical appointees, splintered officers' political allegiances. The political identities that officers brought to the army—tempered in most cases by four years of West Point socialization—resembled the party composition of Congress and presumably of the nation as a whole.

A final factor weakening officers' partisanship was the relative insignificance of military policy as an issue in party conflict. From the 1790s to the reduction of 1821, military affairs had frequently prompted heated political debate, but after 1821, the size and organization of the army only occasionally aroused the attention of Congress. Although there has been no comprehensive analysis of congressional voting on military questions, neither Democrats nor Whigs seem to have consistently supported or opposed army interests. On six House of Representatives roll calls involving fairly well-defined army interests, for example, Whigs voted in favor of the army position by a 56.9 percent majority while Democrats did so by a 52.6 percent majority.[35] The expansionist foreign policy of national Democratic leaders, especially during the 1840s, appealed to officers' hopes for action and promotion; the usual Democratic domination of the federal government facilitated the passage of certain military bills. On the other hand, some regulars disliked the egalitarian flavor of Democratic political rhetoric, which they associated with opposition to West Point and the regular army, and felt more comfortable with the seemingly conservative Whigs. Divisions on some military questions tended to follow regional rather than party lines: The eastern seaboard usually supported coastal fortifications, while western states were likely to prefer expansions of the mounted service and the appointment of citizens directly to the army. In any case, military policy remained a secondary concern through the antebellum era, subordinated to debates over foreign policy and governmental expenditures. Thus, officers principally interested in professional objectives saw little uniform basis for choosing one party over the other.

By the 1850s, the pattern of army politics was becoming evident. Officers' professional ideology distinguished clearly between military and political life. While the army was dedicated to politically neutral national service, politicians and especially parties seemed divisive and self-serving. Officers continued to engage in political activity, but traditional notions of propriety and the quest for career security channeled their energies almost exclusively toward professional goals, individual and collective. In the process, the more politically oriented regulars became well versed in such common tactics of the second party system—and of interest group politics generally—as congressional lobbying, the manipulation of patronage, and the use of the press to gain public support. Although temporarily disrupted by the Civil War, the resulting template of political action, centering on nonpartisan pressure-group action in pursuit of professionally defined objectives, would become a lasting feature of civil-military relations in the United States.

OFFICERS AND CITIZENS

Important though it was for the future of the civil-military nexus in the United States, the army's political role was only a part of the complex involvement of the officer corps with the civilian world. Regulars interacted with citizens more or less continually, especially on the western and southern frontiers where the bulk of the army was stationed during the antebellum decades. As in the early national period, the routines of garrison life and the army's constabulary and administrative responsibilities generated considerable civil-military friction. Although a comprehensive treatment of this interaction is beyond the scope of this study, a survey of its broad patterns is necessary to understand the mental world of the officer corps, especially its shared sense of isolation and its self-image as an apolitical instrument of government policy.

The generalized distaste expressed by regulars for civilians took on special intensity when it came to the frontier population. While they were willing to accept the more "respectable" civilians they encountered—especially the handful of professional men, government officials, and established merchants found in frontier communities—officers felt only contempt for the disorderly conduct, unrefined manners, and self-conscious egalitarianism they associated with the majority of frontier whites. Captain John Stuart considered the frontier inhabitants of Arkansas Territory to be either lawless adventurers from abroad or those who "have been all their Lives moving along in Advance of Civilization and good order, And who have for their Governing Principles Self Interest alone, Without regard to Law or honesty." In the opinion of Major John Sedgwick, "there never was a viler set of men in the world" than the miners gathered near Fort Wise, Colorado Territory, in 1860; "no man's life is safe, and certainly not if he has fifty dollars to tempt one with."[36] Regulars often compared frontier whites unfavorably with the Indians in terms of order and civilization, and they usually attributed Indian-white conflicts to the greed and aggression of the frontiersmen. Moreover, most of the volunteers raised for Indian campaigning were frontier settlers, and thus they bore the brunt of the regulars' disdain for citizen-soldiers.

Compounding officers' resentments was their suspicion that civilians exploited the army for their own advantage, as a means to support the local economy through contracting, road building, and government employment. Major Enos Cutler thought that civilians in northern New York considered the army "a fatigue party" with no other function than to construct roads for them, much to the detriment of military efficiency. A great many regulars suspected citizens of provoking and perpetuating Indian wars so that they could profit from government expenditures. As commander in Florida, Colonel Zachary Taylor blamed the continuation of the Second Seminole War on the greed of the residents, who wished to prolong the struggle "as long as an Indian remains in the country, & Congress will make the necessary appropriation for carrying it on." Captain John T. Sprague was convinced that Florida residents were in secret contact with the Seminoles, abetting their resistance and undermining army efforts to terminate the war. In the opinion of Captain Thomas Williams, every civilian in Florida opposed negotiations with the Seminoles during the late 1850s: "Emigrate the Indians & what becomes of the million or so dollars a year income which Florida has derived from the war in the last 21 years!"[37] Officers also denounced the dogged lobbying efforts of citizens to retain unnecessary military posts in order to profit from government spending. According to a captain in 1840, Arkansas settlers hoped to provoke a crisis over the killing of a white so that the government would reopen Fort Wayne. "They want money—that's all—I have often d_____d the Indians, and now I include the frontier loafers with all my heart."[38]

Thus an indiscriminate antagonism, in part the outgrowth of officers' elitism, underlay relations between regulars and frontier civilians. The practical demands of the army's frontier role exacerbated this antagonism and sparked frequent civil-military disputes. At the most mundane level, the everyday interaction of military personnel and citizens in and around army garrisons produced continual friction. Commanders argued that civilian liquor dealers undermined discipline among the enlisted men and that unscrupulous lawyers and judges obtained discharges for soldiers on frivolous grounds. Access to the government reservation was a bitterly contested issue at many posts, and officers' efforts to expel squatters and assert public control aroused civilian wrath. "It would be a hard matter for any class of people to be more unpopular than Army officers are in this country," wrote Lieutenant Theodore Talbot from Oregon Territory in 1850; the source of hostility was the army's occupation of the most desirable places in the territory for government purposes.[39] Citizens objected to what they considered the oppressive and authoritarian conduct of regular commanders. Harsh and arbitrary military punishments frequently generated civilian concern and led to calls for the arrest of officers for mistreating their men. Occasionally, personal rivalries flared into violence. Clashes between soldiers and civilians were common at taverns and brothels near army posts. In an especially flagrant case in 1842, Lieutenant Charles Wickliffe killed a settler near Fort Gibson in a quarrel over a woman. He was supported by fellow officers, and, though he was dropped from the rolls of the army, he reentered the service five years later as a captain in a Mexican War regiment.[40]

An institutional source of civil-military tension was the army's constabulary function, especially its attempt to enforce the trade and intercourse laws. Officers' efforts to remove squatters from Indian lands and stop the illegal liquor trade invariably earned them the enmity of frontier whites. Moreover, the extent of commanders' legal authority was not entirely clear, and many officers found themselves enmeshed in expensive lawsuits in which the government offered little support. In 1817, for example, Lieutenant Colonel Talbot Chambers prohibited a party of the American Fur Company from trading with the Indians near Fort Crawford on the upper Mississippi. The company sued, and a federal court ordered him to pay $6,000 in damages. Although the verdict was overturned on appeal, the company renewed the suit in 1823, and Chambers asked the War Department to help defray his legal expenses. The secretary of war replied that the administration would compensate him only after the fact, that is, if it was determined that he acted strictly in the performance of his duty; otherwise he would have to appeal to Congress. In 1834, a captain engaged in enforcing the trade and intercourse laws expressed his anxiety about lawsuits and his "determination to make over to a Relative all of the little property which I possess, and to Stand Stripped, but Strongly nerved between my duty and the Populace."[41] As later chapters will demonstrate, officers also rankled civilians when they tried to protect the western Indians from white excesses and suppress filibustering on the Canadian and Mexican borders and sectional violence in Kansas.

Another arena of civil-military interaction was the army's participation in civil administration. Garrison government was far less extensive during the antebellum period than in the early republic, as an effective pattern of civilian territorial government gradually emerged. Nevertheless, commanders were occasionally called upon to exercise political as well as military authority in newly acquired territories. Although military men played a role in the administration of the Floridas in 1821, their most notable experience with territorial government came in New Mexico and California during and after the Mexican War. Brigadier General Stephen W. Kearny, who commanded the expedition that occupied New Mexico in 1846, oversaw the drafting of the "Kearny Code," the first Anglo-American code of law for New Mexico and the basis of its legal system to the present day. Two regular army majors, John M. Washington and John Munroe, served as military governors of the territory between 1848 and 1851, and Lieutenant Colonel Edwin V. Sumner exercised both military and civil powers during 1852–1853, when no civil governor was present.[42] In California, the interim of military government lasted from 1846 to 1849; although Commander Robert F. Stockton of the navy was the first military governor, four regulars held that office for varying lengths of time, and officers also filled lower positions in the territorial administration. As secretary of state, for example, Lieutenant Henry W. Halleck translated the Mexican law code and exercised substantial control over land matters in the territory.[43]

Regulars' involvement in territorial government was not always smooth. Wielding both military and civil powers over a conquered and potentially rebellious population, commanders emphasized internal order at the expense of local initiatives to restore civilian government. Moreover, they operated without clear guidelines from Washington, as the federal government, wrestling with the question of the extension of slavery, was slow to define the status of the territories. A civil-military crisis erupted in New Mexico during 1850, when Major Munroe sanctioned elections for a state constitutional convention, then suspended the resulting government when it tried to supplant his military regime. By that time, however, Congress had authorized a territorial government for New Mexico, and the administration directed Munroe to refrain from further intervention in political affairs.[44] Despite their professional inclinations toward authoritarian rule, most of the officer-administrators avoided entanglements in local politics and carried out their functions with fairness and objectivity. They usually saw themselves as reluctant care-

Major John Macrae Washington, chief of artillery of the army of occupation in northern Mexico and military governor of New Mexico in 1848–1849. (Courtesy of the Amon Carter Museum, Fort Worth, Texas)

takers performing a complex, troublesome, and unrewarding duty, and most welcomed relief. Of the military governors, only John C. Frémont, who nominally governed California for two months in early 1847, sought the position or continued to be active in regional politics after he left office.[45]

The army's constabulary role produced one other controversial episode in civil-military relations during the antebellum era—the Mormon War of the late 1850s. This curious affair grew out of a network of factors: widespread anti-Mormon prejudice in American society; Mormon refusal, after decades of persecution, to accede to the federally imposed Utah territorial government; and incompetent and belligerent conduct by federal officials in the territory that confirmed the Mormons in their defiance. By the summer of 1857,

President James Buchanan had come to believe that the Mormons were in a state of rebellion, and he ordered a military expedition to restore federal authority. Eventually commanded by Colonel Albert Sidney Johnston, the Utah expedition consisted of the better part of three regiments and may have been the largest force of regulars mobilized before the Civil War to subdue a domestic disorder. Logistical problems and Mormon resistance delayed its advance, and it was unable to reach Salt Lake City before the onset of the blizzard season. Encamped in tents and makeshift huts and suffering shortages of food, clothing, and draft animals, the little army spent the winter at remote Camp Scott, eighty miles east of the Mormon capital. Only in June 1858, after negotiations between federal commissioners and the Mormons cleared the way, did the expedition advance into the Utah settlements.[46]

The ensuing "occupation" lasted until 1861 and produced potentially explosive situations. Officers shared the anti-Mormon prejudice of American society, and their hostility was deepened by the hardships endured at Camp Scott and by rumors of Mormon involvement in murders and other atrocities. Indeed, many regulars longed for a chance to chastise the Latter-day Saints. "If the Mormons will only fight their days are numbered," a captain wrote to his wife. "We shall sweep them from the face of the earth and Mormonism in Utah will cease." Another regretted the decision to negotiate with the Mormon leadership: "The best commissioners for Brigham Young and his insolent following, would have been eighteen pounders, backed by plenty of good rifles."[47] Colonel Johnston tried to avoid problems by establishing his force at Camp Floyd, located in a valley south of Salt Lake City, out of close contact with the Mormon settlements. Although he despised the Mormons and considered force mandatory to bring them into line, the commander kept his troops under tight discipline and reluctantly worked to sustain the conciliatory policy of the territorial governor, Alfred Cumming.

The uneasy peace nearly collapsed in March 1859, when the territorial judges attempted to prosecute Mormons suspected of participation in the murder of apostates. Acting on the judges' request but without informing Governor Cumming, Johnston dispatched a company under Lieutenant Henry Heth to the town of Provo to guard the prisoners during the trials. As the arrests continued, Mormon anxieties grew, and Heth's detachment soon faced harassment and the threat of mob attack. Johnston ordered ten more companies to the Provo area to support Heth, whereupon the Mormon leadership began to mobilize for resistance and possible flight into the mountains. The immediate crisis passed. Pessimistic about the prospect of winning convictions, the judges temporarily abandoned their efforts to conduct trials; Governor Cumming worked to ease Mormon fears, and the troops returned

Colonel (Brevet Brigadier General) Albert Sidney Johnston, commander of the Utah expedition. (Courtesy of the State Historical Society of Wisconsin)

to Camp Floyd in early April.[48] Civil-military relations continued to fester, however, and the possibility of a bloody clash did not finally pass until the army withdrew from the region at the start of the Civil War. Captain William Chapman expressed the mood of the Utah army in November 1859 when he wrote that the Mormons were presently quiet, "but they look surly and require a sound thrashing more than any people I have ever seen, and they will get it whenever a collision takes place between them and the troops. We are all ready and only want the word to 'pitch in.' "⁴⁹

Perhaps the most significant aspect of the army's occupation of Utah, however, was the restraint demonstrated by Johnston and his subordinate officers. Despite their anti-Mormon rhetoric—more bloodcurdling than that expressed toward Indian or Mexican foes during this period—and despite the frustration of occupation duty in a remote region amid a sullen, resentful population, regulars maintained discipline and acted within the limits of their orders, which stressed their subordination in civil matters to the territorial officials. As with other elements of the army's constabulary and administrative functions, the conduct of the Utah expedition demonstrated the maturing service ethic of the officer corps—the internalization of its self-image as a dependable, politically neutral instrument of public policy. Together with the stabilization of the army's relationship with politics, it marked a major step toward the actualization of civil supremacy in the United States.

16
OFFICERS AND INDIANS

Between the Revolution and the Civil War, the officer corps of the United States Army was continually and intimately involved with the conduct of Indian affairs, more so by far than any other white leadership group with the exception of the officials of the Indian Department. Regulars enforced the trade and intercourse laws, the basic legislation regulating Indian-white contact; attempted to keep order along the extended Indian frontiers; served as the government's main instrument to carry out the controversial policy of Indian removal during the 1830s and 1840s; and later worked to extend government control over the vast array of native peoples inhabiting the Great Plains, the Pacific Northwest, and the Mexican Cession. Throughout most of the period, Indians were the army's principal adversary; officers confronted them in a long series of frustrating guerrilla operations, from the bloody northwestern Indian war of the 1790s to the campaigns against the Great Plains and far-western tribes of the 1850s. The officer was rare who did not spend part of his career in proximity to Indians, and a great many commanders, especially those of the infantry and mounted regiments, devoted the bulk of their service lives to Indian affairs.[1]

Despite this interaction, military authorities directed surprisingly little official attention to the army's role in Indian relations. Regulars viewed their professional mission mainly as preparation for a major war with a "civilized" European power—in others words, a replay of the War of 1812. Military doctrine followed European precedents and focused on conventional battlefield tactics and permanent fortification. Most commanders considered Indian affairs an unfortunate distraction from the real business of their profession—a messy, morally ambiguous, and unpleasant task that offered few chances for distinction. Although the secretary of war and the commanding general issued instructions on specific situations, there were few fixed guidelines to inform officers' conduct toward the native tribes. Aside from broad injunctions to enforce the trade and intercourse laws, the government's inclination was to leave decisions to the officers in the field, whose practical experience seemed to equip them to judge Indian character. Even the West Point curriculum neglected Indian affairs. For example, Dennis Hart Mahan gave only brief attention to Indian fighting in his course on military and civil engineering and the science of war. Although it is possible, though by no means certain, that the course in geography, history, and ethics touched on the moral implications of Indian-white relations, at no time in the four-year program did cadets receive in-depth instruction in the task that would likely occupy the greater part of their careers.[2]

Given the state of social thought in nineteenth-century America, it is unrealistic to expect that the government or the army itself would have provided officers with sophisticated training in human relations. Without clear guidance, however, officers' attitudes toward Native Americans evolved in an unsystematic, ad hoc manner, conditioned by contemporary ideas about race, by the pressures of the army's constabulary duties, and by the immediate observations and experiences of the men themselves.

OFFICERS' VIEWS OF INDIAN CHARACTER

Before 1815, few officers appear to have taken a serious interest in Indian life or character. During the 1780s and early 1790s and in the War of 1812 period, the army's relationship with Indians was intensely adversarial. Commanders usually perceived Native Americans in strictly military terms—as brave, tenacious, and wily enemies. Officers often commented on Indians' savage and bloodthirsty nature—an opinion that was commonplace in frontier society—but their tone also suggested considerable respect for the fighting prowess of the native peoples. Moreover, they usually attributed Indian-white conflicts to white influence, either British or Spanish machinations or the encroachments of white settlers and government agents into Indian lands, and they frequently tried to shield peaceful Indians from the attacks of frontier whites. Their most widely held opinion, however, was the necessity for strong military force to teach the tribes the superiority of the whites and command their respect. "The Indians are exceedingly troublesome," wrote Brevet Brigadier General Josiah Harmar in 1790. "I know of nothing that will cure the disorder, but government's raising an army to effectually chastise them—all treaties are in vain."[3]

After the War of 1812, officers' relationship with the Indians became more complex. East of the Mississippi at least, the tribes ceased to be a formidable military barrier, and the army was increasingly absorbed in the ongoing implementation of government policy. Officers encountered Native Americans in many capacities—as acting Indian officials, frontier policemen, and explorers as well as opponents in the field. Moreover, the growing uniformity in officers' education and careers encouraged common modes of thought on social questions. As a result, the officer corps developed during the antebellum period a set of ideas concerning Indians and the conduct of Indian relations that meshed with other aspects of the emerging military worldview and influenced officers' handling of the "Indian question" through the rest of the century.

In describing Indian character, a few officers, especially when writing for a general audience, adopted the stylized, sentimental image of the Indian that had long been a literary convention in Europe and the United States. Embedded in the cult of primitivism, this perception emphasized the guileless simplicity of the "red man," portraying him as a noble savage who compared favorably with the pretense, hypocrisy, and decadence of civilized society. Alexander Macomb, the commanding general of the army, took this approach in the prologue to a play based on the Pontiac uprising, published in 1835.

> When first we saw him in his pristine state,
> The native knew not what it was to hate.
> Free as the air he roamed the forests o'er,
> Rich in that freedom, otherwise quite poor.
> The stranger then might move through all the land,
> And meet the savage with a naked hand;
> A hearty welcome in his wigwam find,
> And every treatment of the generous kind.

Needless to say, the influx of whites and the introduction of liquor destroyed this idyllic picture and led the Indians, in desperation, to take the warpath. Colonel Philip St. George Cooke touched on a variation of this motif in his rambling, partially fictional memoirs. Relating a tale supposedly told him during a prairie expedition, Cooke described the warrior Sha-wah-now: "Untaught by man and his vain books, he had drank deep of the inspiration of Nature in her majestic solitudes." He then contrasted the naturalness of Indian life with Sha-wah-now's vision of a soulless industrial nightmare to come.[4]

The image of the noble savage did not represent mainstream military thinking about the Native American. As a literary device, borrowed directly from the general culture, it was primarily useful for criticizing contemporary society or lamenting the fate of the Indian. Most officers considered themselves realists in their assessments of Indian culture and drew their evidence from their own observations. Indeed, they often asserted that they were in a better position to judge Indian character than eastern reformers and politicians, who had no personal experience with the Indian tribes.

Although their attitudes naturally varied with the circumstances under which they encountered the Indian and the characteristics of the tribes concerned, distinct themes appeared in officers' writings. On the positive side, they credited Indians with certain virtues, notably physical strength and prowess, tenacity, dignity of bearing, and, sometimes, courage. In 1832, Lieutenant James Allen found the Chippewas near the headwaters of the Mississippi to be "strong, athletic, muscular men, of large stature, and fine appearance, looking proud, haughty, and unsubdued, and carrying an independence and fearlessness with their manner that indicates a full estimate of their own strength." Lieutenant John Van Deusen DuBois described an Apache warrior as "a noble specimen of humanity, tall and formed like an Apollo." The gravity of Indians in council frequently impressed military observers. "There was no foolish clap-trap or ridiculous intonation of voice, or unnecessary ranting about it," wrote Lieutenant James H. Carleton of a speech by a Pawnee chief. "It was spoken in a deliberate and dignified manner; and with an ease and self possession, which would be worthy of the imitation of ninety-nine men out of a hundred amongst us."[5]

The great body of officers' opinion, however, was unfavorable, especially when commenting on the more fundamental traits of Indian character. The evaluation offered by a young officer during the Creek campaign of 1836 was harsh but not atypical.

> I have seen more of the Indian character since I have been in Ala[bama] than I ever saw before. I take them to be naturally indolent, very revengeful, and far inferior to whites intellectually. I do not believe that they are capable of becoming civilized. They are destined to be crowded off their lands until they are driven into some barren mountainous region or into some desert, where a civilized community cannot exist.

Lieutenant Joseph C. Ives thought that the Mojaves of the Colorado Valley were, "perhaps, rather superior to the generality of their race, but, as far as we can judge, they have, with few exceptions, certain qualities common to the Indian character. They are lazy, cruel, selfish, disgusting in their habits, and inveterate beggars." "The pure native American population of our continent are least to be trusted of all its various peoples," Captain Thomas Williams informed his wife in 1858. "I hope it's no disparagement to excellence of climate, soil & institutions, that the native product should be so villainous." In

1857, an officer in Texas described the "treachery" of some Indians who ambushed a mail party. "That is Indian character as it is here. Philanthropists in their book moralizing make out an opposite case,—with me however seeing is believing."[6]

A common observation in officers' writings was the ferocity of Indian nature. Although frequently provoked by white mistreatment, bloodthirstiness seemed a universal trait of the Native American. Colonel Cooke's romantic style took on a sensationalist flavor when describing an Arikara attack on a fur trapper's boat. "They rioted in blood; with horrid grimaces and convulsive action they hewed into fragments the dumb, lifeless bodies; they returned to their camp a moving group of dusky demons, exulting in revenge, besmeared with blood, bearing aloft each a mangled portion of the dead—trophies of brutal success." A young officer expressed a similar image poetically in "The Seminole's Reply."

> Some strike for hope of booty,
> Some to defend their all.
> I battle for the joy I have,
> To see the white man fall:
> I love among the wounded
> To hear his dying moan,
> And catch while chanting at his side,
> The music of his groan.

"However strongly their condition would seem to appeal to philanthropy for relief," an officer wrote of the Texas and New Mexico Indians, "much sympathy is lost in the remembrance that their code of morals inculcates many of our vices as their cardinal virtues and regards our virtues as so many vices or traits of weakness, while their atrocious barbarities shock every sensibility of nature and humanity."[7]

Indolence, vengefulness, treachery, brutality—these were the qualities most often assigned to Indian character, and they recurred in broad references to Indian behavior as well as in descriptions of individual tribes. Despite the harshness of this judgment, officers did not generally embrace the concept of immutable, hereditary racial differences. Although few regulars gave analytical thought to the sources of racial distinctions, their writings suggest a vague environmental determinism, reflecting widespread assumptions about race in early nineteenth-century America. The flaws of the Indian's character stemmed from his harsh environment and cultural isolation rather than from inherent racial attributes. The more rigid biological theories of race that were making headway in scientific circles by midcentury and would carry the field after the Civil War had little apparent impact on the antebellum officer corps.[8]

While most officers wrote as if there were a basic Indian character, their assessment was by no means monolithic; instead, it was modified depending on the particular tribe under consideration. From officers' writings, it is possible to reconstruct a scale of Indian peoples ranging from the most "advanced"—and by implication virtuous—down to the most "primitive" and "degraded." As might be expected, the chief standard used to determine a tribe's ranking was an ethnocentric one: Indians merited respect to the extent that they resembled whites, either because of indigenous cultural features or because of their responsiveness to white civilization.

Although they did not entirely escape the opprobrium attached to Indian character in general, the southeastern peoples occupied the top of the scale, both before and after their removal. The settled, agricultural economies of these Indians, their complex social organizations, and their partial acceptance of white dress and living habits attracted much favorable comment from military observers, who saw them as potential yeoman farmers. In a typical evaluation, Major Ethan Allen Hitchcock considered the progress made by the western Cherokees a sign that all Native Americans might be assimilated into the dominant society. "They have among them many well informed, sensible, orderly industrious and pious people, regardful of everything that contributes to domestic peace, happiness and prosperity, and they exhibit fruits accordingly." Frequently, regulars extended this approbation to the sedentary, agrarian tribes of the Southwest. An officer described the Pimas and Maricopas of the Gila Valley as "a more civilized Indian than any we have seen—[they] seem wholly unlike savages except in their color & dress." Another found the Pueblo Indians to be "intelligent, moral, sober, and industrious; and, generally speaking, they are better off than the lower class of Mexicans."[9]

Military men usually ranked the Plains Indians and the warlike tribes of the Southwest near the middle of the scale of native peoples. Officers admired them for their martial skills and occasionally indulged in romantic analogies to the days of chivalry, but they thought their character marred by treachery, thievery, cruelty, and other unpleasant traits. Moreover, the migratory habits of many of these Indians and their resistance to acculturation appeared to make them poor candidates for assimilation. Lieutenant James H. Carleton followed his description of the "tall, erect, elegantly proportioned" Pawnees whom he encountered on a prairie expedition with a facetious account of a Pawnee village that dwelled on the filthiness and boorish behavior of the Indians. Although Captain Randolph B. Marcy praised the horsemanship and resourcefulness of the Plains Indians in a handbook written for prairie travelers, he referred to them as "inveterate beggars" and "merciless freebooters," and he considered them devoid of "any of those attributes which among civilized nations are regarded as virtues adorning the human character." Officers' admiration of Navajo craftsmanship did not offset their suspicion of that tribe's allegedly treacherous habits. As an army surgeon reported to the Smithsonian Institution in 1855, "In the whole nation one or two may be found who are reliable men, considering they are Navajo Indians, who would not falsify merely for the sake of falsifying, or steal for the love of stealing; but we would not advise any one to place confidence in even the best of these people, lest he should find himself leaning on a reed easily broken."[10] Although more difficult to pin down, the Seminoles inspired a similarly mixed reaction. Officers realized that they shared the culture of the other southeastern tribes, whom regulars regarded as advanced, but the bitter resistance of the Seminoles to removal earned them a reputation for duplicity, cunning, and cruelty.

By nearly universal agreement, the Indians at the bottom of the scale were the technologically primitive, loosely organized hunting and gathering peoples of California and the Rocky Mountains. One officer found the "Root-Diggers" of the Great Basin to be "the most degraded and lowest in the scale of being" of any Indians he had seen; another compared the same people to "the beasts that roam over these wilds, little removed from them in instincts and habits." In the opinion of a captain, the Indians at the mouth of the Eel River in California were "as low on the scale of humanity as possible to conceive, of brutish habits, hideous repulsive features, and loathsome from disease."[11] Of course, the reason for this obloquy was the fact that the cultures of these Indians appeared the very antithesis of technologically advanced white society. To most officers, progress seemed attainable only by following white society's example.

A few individuals were more tolerant and took an interest in Indian cultures as alternative ways of life, having their own integrity and value systems. Although none of these officers completely resisted the urge to judge, they strove to describe Indian appearance, dress, economy, and religion in objective terms. Henry Whiting, for example, a quartermaster officer long stationed at Detroit, composed two narrative poems on the tribes of the Old Northwest before the coming of the whites. Although his style was sentimental, Whiting attempted to be true to the details of Indian life and included scholarly footnotes by two of his associates, Governor Lewis Cass of the Michigan Territory and Henry R. Schoolcraft, the pioneer student of the Indian.[12] Another such figure was Seth Eastman, a West Point graduate who served most of his career on the frontier and devoted his leisure time to painting the Indians he encountered. While on detached service in Washington, D.C., during the early

"Dakota Encampment," by Seth Eastman. (From Henry R. Schoolcraft, *Historical and Statistical Information Respecting the History, Condition, and Prospects of the Indian Tribes of the United States*, 6 vols. [Philadelphia, 1851–1857], 2:190; photo courtesy of the State Historical Society of Wisconsin)

1850s, he illustrated Schoolcraft's massive study of the Indian tribes of the United States. Eastman differed from other artists of the Indian in his realism and objectivity, making him, in the opinion of his biographer, a "pictorial historian" of Indian life. The Whitings and Eastmans were rare, however; in the officer corps as in the larger society, ethnocentrism prevailed.[13]

INDIANS AS WARDS

Officers' generally negative view of Indian character might have supported a brutally repressive policy, but as long as Indians remained at peace, several factors mitigated military attitudes. One was the nascent professional ethic of the officer corps, by which regulars saw themselves as apolitical instruments of a government that, in theory at least, sought to strike a balance between the rights of the Indians and the interests of the whites. Second, regulars disliked most frontiersmen and citizen-soldiers, whom they considered disorderly, cruel, and greedy. As noted, this attitude arose from officers' reaction to the

"Medicine Dance of the Winnebagoes," by Seth Eastman. (From Henry R. Schoolcraft, *Historical and Statistical Information Respecting the History, Condition, and Prospects of the Indian Tribes of the United States*, 6 vols. [Philadelphia, 1851–1857], 3:286; photo courtesy of the State Historical Society of Wisconsin)

widespread criticism of their profession in American society, their tendency to define their collective role by using militia and volunteers as a foil, and their conservative disdain for the rough-and-tumble of frontier life. However, the result was often to place the Indian—the antagonist and victim of the frontiersman—in a comparatively favorable light. Finally, many commanders were deeply and sincerely troubled by the moral implications of suppressing and dispossessing the native peoples.

Consequently, paternalism dominated officers' peacetime interaction with Native Americans. Indians might be treacherous and bloodthirsty, but the army had an obligation to protect their rights as defined by the government and supply the guidance that a stern father would show his children. Through the 1830s at least, many commanders endorsed the civilization policy, by which the government tried to acculturate and eventually assimilate Indians into the mainstream of white society. By vigilant enforcement of the trade and intercourse laws, the army would shield the tribes from the encroachments and corrupting influences of frontier whites and provide a peaceful environment within which they might adopt white ways. In 1840, an officer called for a reform and revitalization of the civilization program, including the more careful selection of Indian agents, the more effective distribution of annuities, and employment of a strong military force to prevent all unauthorized Indian-white contact. "Who will say that it is not the *duty* of the American people to do all this, and more, for these helpless remnants of races which we have slaughtered, oppressed and driven off from all the best of land—the homes which they have loved and freely bled for?"[14]

Paternalism characterized the army's conduct of Indian relations on the trans-Mississippi frontier before the Mexican War, where white pressure on the tribes was relatively light and where Native Americans posed no major threat to the army. Veteran commanders such as Mathew Arbuckle, Henry Atkinson, Zachary Taylor, and John Stuart diligently labored to check the illegal liquor trade and expel trespassers from Indian lands. They interceded frequently with territorial officials and the government in support of the Indians within their districts. Brigadier General Edmund P. Gaines, long in command of the army's Western Department, consistently defended the Indians' rights, often pitting himself against administration policy. In his opinion, the government should observe treaties with Indian nations more scrupulously than those with foreign powers because the United States had usurped the Indians' land and thus owed them a special protection.[15] Almost invariably, officers found the root cause of Indian-white tensions to be the aggression and baneful influence of the frontier whites. In 1839, an officer wrote from Wisconsin Territory that the Menomonie Indians located in his area were "most barbarously treated" by their white neighbors. "Whiskey is introduced among them & all the furs & peltries cheatingly obtained for the veriest pittance, paid in liquor, & when under excitement they perpetrate mischief & commit thefts . . . they are whipt & otherwise punished by the whites, who take the law into their own hands." Remarking on a clash between whites and western Choctaws, Lieutenant Colonel Josiah H. Vose expressed the prevailing army view: "The white people were undoubtedly the aggressors, as is generally the case in all Indian difficulties."[16]

Indian removal presented the officer corps with an especially difficult and frustrating problem. The government relied heavily on the army to execute this policy. The Subsistence Department oversaw the logistics of removal, and many officers served under the Indian Department as temporary subagents or disbursing officers.[17] Moreover, the regular army acted as the government's main instrument to compel reluctant tribes to move, leading to the principal combat operations of the 1830s—the Black Hawk War of 1832, the Creek War of 1836, and the Second Seminole War of 1835–1842. Most commanders considered removal unavoidable in light of the vast discrepancy in power between the whites and the eastern tribes and the insatiable white demand for Indian lands. Embracing an opinion common in civilian circles, some officers justified the process as a humanitarian measure. Lieutenant Colonel John J. Abert believed that the separation of the Indians from the influence of corrupt whites was necessary for their successful acculturation and eventual assimilation. In the opinion of Brigadier General Thomas S. Jesup, the government owed the Indians "that protection which the parent owes to the child, or the guardian to the ward; and to secure them that protection, we must place them beyond the operation of state laws."[18]

Nevertheless, many regulars sympathized with the hard-pressed eastern tribes and questioned the morality of their role. In 1825 and 1826, General Gaines engaged in a heated controversy with the Georgia state government over the expropriation of Creek lands in that state. Indeed, Gaines opposed the entire policy of removal, declaring that he "would just as soon seek for fame by an attempt to remove the Shakers, or the Quakers, as to break up the Indians, take their lands & throw together twenty tribes speaking different languages where the most ferocious savage will cut the throat of the most civilized and orderly."[19] Participation in Cherokee removal caused one officer to regard himself as "a trespasser, as one of a gang of robbers." According to another, a planned movement against that tribe was intended "to enforce the treaty with them;—or, in other words, to take their country away from them." "If ever a curse could fall upon a people or nation for pure and unalloyed villainy towards a part of God's creatures," wrote Lieutenant William Tecumseh Sherman in 1844, "we deserve it for not protecting the Cherokees that lately lived and hunted in peace and plenty through the hills and valleys" of northwestern Georgia.[20] As discussed later, Seminole removal in particular pricked the consciences of commanders.

During the 1850s, officers almost universally denounced the exploitation and slaughter of the western Indians by miners and settlers. As commanders of the Department of the Pacific, Colonel Ethan Allen Hitchcock and Brigadier General John E. Wool repeatedly clashed with civil officials and militia leaders, whom they accused of conducting wars of extermination. In the opinion of a member of Hitchcock's staff, the true story of Indian relations in northern California "would exhibit a picture of cruelty, injustice and horror scarcely to be surpassed by that of the Peruvians in the time of Pizarro." Major Robert S. Garnett complained of the concentration of the northwestern Indians on reservations too small and unproductive for their survival. "We cant expect men to change their habits of life, the habits of their race," he wrote a cousin in the Senate, "or to starve to death quietly merely to satisfy the wild schemes of white men."[21] A number of officers urged forbearance in dealings with the Navajos during the late 1850s, as the claims against them were exaggerated and war would cause misery for the entire tribe. When white Texans harassed reservation Indians in 1859, regulars attempted to shield them and protested to the state governor. Major Hannibal Day summarized the sentiments of a great many officers in a report on the mistreatment of the Sioux.

> History teaches that we have gradually driven [the Indians] from the Rock of Plymouth west, and it has been my misfortune, or at least mortification, to have seen, within the last few years, the alternative presented them of standing and being shot down by the rifle of the western emigrant to California, or be literally driven into the Pacific Ocean—reluctantly yielding them a single acre, even there, on which to live by gathering *acorns* and *grasshoppers*, and where their friends may *burn their bodies*, when death shall luckily come to their relief.[22]

Compassion was one part of the officer corps's paternalistic relationship with Native Americans, but another was a readiness to use force. Like children, Indians were creatures of impulse; only the threat of immediate punishment would overcome their treacherous and unruly propensities and command their respect. According to an officer in Texas, the histories of Great Britain, Spain, and the United States all taught that the best way to handle Indians was to establish a strong garrison in their midst; "and the *surest*, and, in the end, the *most humane*, preventive is *retaliation*, not only on the offenders in person, but upon the *tribes to which they belong*."[23] Generally, officers favored centralized military control of Indian affairs, and they frequently denounced the Indian Department for its corruption and incompetence. Army officers alone had the experience to exercise the combination of discipline, support, and protection essential to the well-being of the Native American. Responding to Indian Department criticism that hasty army action had provoked bloodshed in 1854, the commanding general expressed the consensus of the officer corps: "The army whilst having to bear the brunt of the consequences of the mismanagement of others, in Indian affairs—has ever been the friend of the red man, and stood between him and the violence and extortion of the whites."[24]

Officers' willingness to guard Native Americans from white pressure did not indicate optimism about the Indian's future. In common with the majority of the general population, regulars assumed as inevitable the gradual spread of an agrarian-industrial society, republican political institutions, and Protestant

Christianity across the continent at the expense of seemingly primitive and backward cultures. Native Americans would have to conform to the advancing order or face extinction. Although the first alternative was preferable—and perhaps attainable for some tribes—the second seemed more likely, especially as time revealed the viability and persistence of Indian culture and the shortcomings of the acculturation programs. More often than not, Indians appeared to decline both physically and morally as they came into close contact with whites and succumbed to civilized vices, especially strong drink. Differences between the races, even if rooted in environment and culture rather than biology, seemed nearly unbridgeable. "I have seen most all of our Indians," wrote Captain Rufus Ingalls in a typical passage, "and the instances are rare where I have witnessed any permanent benefit resulting to the red man from contact with the white. Oil and water are more similar, and will mix on more easy terms."[25]

By the 1840s and especially after the Mexican War, a recurring theme of military writing was the inevitable passing of the Native American. Captain Robert C. Buchanan expressed it clearly in an analysis of the California Indians.

> I will . . . content myself with the remark, that, among these people, and all others of the Indian tribes of our country, the great laws of civilization and progress are surely developing themselves, and as a consequence, a few years more will number them with the things that *were*. From their difference of habits and interests, engendering hostility among themselves, *no general war* with *them* need ever be apprehended, and hence the steady encroachments of the white man, from every direction, will produce the certain, though perhaps gradual result of their utter annihilation.

The "improvidence" of the Indian convinced Brigadier General William S. Harney "that the red men of America will gradually disappear about the same time from the different sections of our country." From his experience with the Plains Indians during the 1850s, Colonel Randolph B. Marcy had no doubt that they were "destined ultimately to extinction," though he hoped "to make the pathway of their exit from the sphere of human existence as smooth and easy as possible" by teaching them to till the soil. "Wherever their race has come in contact with ours," wrote Lieutenant James H. Carleton in 1844, "it has begun to wither like those native plants which are overshadowed and blighted by the more vigorous growth of some hardy exotic—until drooping, they have perished, and passed away forever."[26]

INDIANS AS ADVERSARIES

During the antebellum period, the army increasingly confronted Native Americans as adversaries as well as wards. In the conflicts arising from removal in the 1830s and early 1840s and in the myriad campaigns against the Plains and western tribes in the 1850s, the army devoted the greater part of its manpower and energy to the suppression of hostile Indians. Inevitably, the pressures of guerrilla warfare eroded officers' sympathy and hardened their perceptions of the Native American. Out of this experience emerged a set of attitudes and practices that would characterize the army's conduct of Indian warfare long after the Civil War.

When they commented on the sources of Indian-white violence, regulars almost universally blamed frontier whites, whose dishonesty and greed for land subjected the Indians to intolerable stresses. On the other hand, officers' unfavorable assessment of Indian nature also led many to regard the bloodthirstiness of the Indian as a factor precipitating violence. These somewhat contradictory themes often appeared in the same writings. The accounts of the Second Seminole War by Assistant Surgeon Jacob Rhett Motte and Captain John T. Sprague, for example, seemed to attribute that conflict at times to white greed and at other times to the ferocity of the Seminoles.[27] One writer who tried to reconcile the contradiction was Rodney Glisan, a medical officer who served in the Pacific Northwest during the 1850s. He found the basic cause of strife to be the "diametrically antagonistic" cultures of the two races, which made it "simply impossible for them to live side by side for many years without contentions." More specifically, the attempts by whites to seize Indian land before extinguishing title provoked the red man's retaliation.

> It requires but a little cruel treatment under these circumstances to kindle in his savage breast a relentless thirst for blood. When once aroused he falls upon every white person he chances to meet; treating both friend and foe alike; thus often exhibiting one of the most inhuman of all traits—base ingratitude. Worse, if possible, than that other ignoble constituent of the Indian character—treachery.[28]

Whatever their opinions of the causes of Indian wars, regulars were called upon to fight them. To some officers—especially young men in the mounted regiments—frontier campaigning provided a welcome diversion from garrison duty, but the majority were of a different mind. They were trained for formal, "civilized" warfare; Indian fighting involved physical discomfort, frustration, civilian censure, and, for many at least, a feeling of guilt, with little opportunity for the ultimate professional reward—glory in battle. Brigadier General Thomas S. Jesup wrote of his experiences as commander in Florida: "This is a service which no man would seek with any other view than the mere performance of his duty; distinction, or increase of reputation, is out of the question; and the difficulties are such, that the best concerted plans may result in absolute failure, and the best established reputation be lost without a fault." Jesup's successor, Colonel Zachary Taylor, agreed, describing Florida duty as "a service where an officer who has any regard for honesty, truth or humanity, has but little to gain, & everything to lose"; the future president considered it "if possible worse than being a politician."[29]

Because of their distaste for Indian warfare and their views of Indian character, officers responded to Indian-white controversies with force. Once hostilities were unavoidable, a temporizing policy would appear as weakness to the tribes; consequently, the army should apply a sudden dose of overwhelming power to teach the Indians a lesson and deter them from future misbehavior. This belief received apparent confirmation from the army's experiences in the Black Hawk and Seminole wars. As many saw it, those conflicts had been precipitated by the refusal of the government to employ sufficient force at the outset, which had encouraged the Indians to rebel and, in the case of the Seminoles, led to the massacre of two companies of regulars. In his brief treatment of Indian fighting at West Point, Dennis Hart Mahan advised his students to use strong measures to overawe the Indians and, if hostilities should break out, "strike such a blow that it shall be handed down as memorable in the traditions of the Tribe."[30]

A punishment theme thus pervaded officers' thinking on Indian warfare. Captain George W. Hughes regarded war with the Comanches and Lipans to be inevitable in 1847 and expressed the opinion "that we shall never establish cordial relations with them until they have been severely punished." On completing a campaign in Washington Territory, Captain James J. Archer agreed with his fellow officers "that it was necessary to have fought and severely beaten the Indians, before negotiating, in order to render the peace durable." The commander in Navajo country considered that tribe ready to make peace in November 1858, but he hoped "to continue operations until they shall feel more sensibly the effect of their bad conduct." Captain Thomas Williams favored strong measures against the Cheyenne and Sioux.

> I'm not sure that good policy would not decide they should receive a sound thrashing first, & peace afterwards. The Indians of the Plains are all alike, in, that, they have to be flogged into decency, & flogged out of their predatory & murderous habits. . . . Their apprehensions are proba-

bly a better guarantee of good behavior, than professions of friendship. A periodical thrashing would be sure to keep alive their loyalty—rather their fears; the only sure guide to rely on.

Although he was sympathetic to the plight of the Comanches and favored increasing government aid, Captain William J. Hardee also believed that "one or two severe chastisements would intimidate the Indians & produce a most salutary effect on their future conduct."[31]

Faced with inconclusive, unpopular guerrilla combat and stung by civilian critics who questioned their competence as Indian fighters, officers made an informal distinction between "civilized" and Indian warfare. Since Native Americans were treacherous and savage, the usual standards of early nineteenth-century warfare—humane treatment of prisoners of war, protection of noncombatants and their property and provisions, and a general respect for one's opponents—did not always apply to them. The seven-year Second Seminole War offers the best example. At first, the army conducted the campaign along relatively conventional lines, marching large columns through Florida in a vain attempt to draw the Indians into a decisive battle. As the years passed and the frustration mounted, commanders gradually shifted to less orthodox methods, including the violation of flags of truce and promises of immunity. Resorting to a centuries-old frontier strategy—though one clearly contrary to the formal laws of war—regulars systematically destroyed Indian villages and food supplies in an effort to starve the Seminoles into surrender.[32]

By the middle stages of the war, ugly talk of extreme measures circulated through the Florida army. "We shall have no Indians here," wrote an officer of the Seminoles' failure to report for removal. "The war must be one of extermination." Correspondents of the *Army and Navy Chronicle* agreed. One denounced the "mawkish philanthropy" that had hitherto shaped government policy and recommended "nothing less than a war of extermination." He thought that a "few skeletons left to hang and bleach in the wild, would teach them too surely we were in earnest, and they would shortly be found sueing for peace on any terms." In the opinion of another correspondent, the Seminoles' surprise attack on an army detachment in 1839 had "sealed their fate—extermination. . . . They must be declared outlaws, and a price set upon their heads, in the same manner as other desperate criminals are dealt with." A medical officer likewise favored "*exterminating* an *ungrateful, treacherous,* and *bloodthirsty race of savages,*" though he made clear that he did not mean extermination in "the most *rigid sense.*" In his view, the army "should kill every male Indian over *fifteen years* of age, excepting the *old* men, and those who will deliver themselves into the hands of the white men," while transplanting the rest of the tribe.³³

To their credit, regulars never fully adopted a war of genocide, but the last years of the conflict brought a further toughening of army tactics. Officers found it difficult to understand the public outcry that erupted in 1840 when the army experimented with tracking the Indians with bloodhounds. Captain John R. Vinton, once sympathetic to the Seminoles, hoped that the government would not be deterred from using the dogs "by this sickly sympathy on the part of our northern dames & spinsters." In his mind, the Indians' "acts of bloody massacre & treachery" had settled "the question of humanity forever." Florida veterans praised Colonel William S. Harney when he hanged captured warriors in 1840, and Colonel Abraham Eustis wrote that Harney's action had considerably brightened the prospects of success: "I have long thought *that* was the only way of terminating the war, & he is the very man to enact Jack Ketch."³⁴ In 1841, Colonel William J. Worth assumed the Florida command and launched an aggressive strategy of year-round campaigning, employing small detachments of light troops to penetrate the Seminoles' hiding places. According to his aide-de-camp, he issued the "simple injunction, 'Find the enemy, capture, or exterminate,'" and removed most remaining restraints on the conduct of operations. Using a plan widely supported in the officer corps, he also introduced an unofficial bounty system, by which soldiers were paid $100 for every warrior captured or killed. Even these measures failed to break Seminole resistance completely, and in August 1842, the army simply declared the long struggle at an end.³⁵

No other Indian war approached the Seminole conflict in duration or subjected the officer corps to so much discomfiture. Nevertheless, the sporadic violence of the 1850s brought a similar hardening of officers' attitudes and a similar willingness to depart from the standards of "civilized" warfare. During a campaign in northern California in 1850, regulars led by Lieutenant Nathaniel Lyon twice trapped large groups of Indians on islands, then killed scores of men, women, and children. In his official report, Lyon described how the second island "soon became a perfect slaughter pen," as the troops hunted the Indians through the tangled thickets. In 1855, Colonel Harney pushed a band of Brulé Sioux into a fight, then smashed them mercilessly, killing women and children in the process and taking no warriors prisoner. While privately disturbed by the carnage, Lieutenant Gouverneur K. Warren reported that the defeat had been "a useful lesson, which they will not soon forget."³⁶ In case of war against the Mojaves, Captain Lewis A. Armistead recommended using a light draft boat on the Colorado River; troops could thus be landed "and the Indian's crops destroyed, if nothing more, which would result in death from starvation, of many." In a surprise attack on a Comanche village in 1858, regular cavalry killed fifty-six warriors, devastated the Indians' lodges and food supplies, and seized their pony herd, leaving the destitute survivors dispersed through the Wichita Mountains. Commanders in the Southwest struck at the flocks, herds, and crops of the elusive Navajo, despite explicit War Department instructions that such a strategy would impoverish the Indians, force them to become robbers, and so possibly require their extirpation.[37]

When Indian-white violence flared again in Florida during the mid-1850s, the army reinstituted the bounty system in a milder form, offering cash rewards for captured Seminoles. Inspector General Sylvester Churchill favored extending the bounty to include warriors killed while bearing arms, a step that he thought would have a "terrifying effect" on the Indians. He saw no moral difference between paying a bounty for killing a man and hiring a soldier for that purpose. In a circular to his subordinates, Colonel Gustavus Loomis stated the government's wish to remove the Seminoles without bloodshed if possible. "But as they have refused every overture for peace, they must be considered as outlaws & treated accordingly." During the same campaign, Colonel Harney reputedly interrogated Seminole women while threatening to hang their children.[38]

A surprisingly common practice, at least in the Pacific Northwest, was the execution of Indian captives, either summarily or after hasty military trials. Although the ostensible purpose was to punish specific crimes, officers intended the deaths to serve as warnings to terrify other tribesmen into submission. In July 1855, for example, a military commission found three Indians guilty of participating in a massacre of a party of whites on the Boise River and sentenced them to hang. The order announcing the decision stated "that the utmost decorum will prevail at the execution of these unfortunate warriors, who—although their people have shown the utmost barbarity towards their victims, and deserve death—are executed as an example, in hopes it will prevent other murders, and not from the instinct of revenge." Philip H. Sheridan recalled in his memoirs that the hanging of nine captives a year later had "a most salutary effect" on the northwestern Indian confederation, contributing to its eventual dissolution. Although sympathetic to Indians in time of peace, Major Robert S. Garnett and Colonel George Wright expected similar results from their 1858 operations, which included the execution of more than twenty Indian prisoners.[39] Needless to say, the army used capital punishment unilaterally—against Indian "criminals" but not against whites accused of crimes against Indians.

Not all regulars were calloused by Indian warfare. Even the most aggressive

Fort Deynaud, Florida, in 1855. Fort Deynaud was representative of the many small and temporary posts occupied by the army in its long campaigns against the Seminoles. (Drawn by Lieutenant Alexander S. Webb and published with his "Campaigning in Florida in 1855," *Journal of the Military Service Institution of the United States* 45 [November–December 1909])

Indian fighters had moments of compassion for their adversaries, and for many officers, combat accentuated vague feelings of guilt concerning their role in Indian affairs. The Second Seminole War in particular, with its abundant evidence of Indian resistance against overwhelming odds, caused some commanders to wrestle with their consciences. Surgeon General Thomas Lawson expressed misgivings about a forthcoming campaign in which he would command a battalion of volunteers.

> Should these brave & much injured people . . . , notwithstanding this great array of Forces against them, & our present knowledge of the Country, be able still to maintain their position, I am clear for acknowledging their independence, & yielding up to them the country for which they have so gallantly & so successfully fought, & so nobly won. It will be manifest then that the Almighty is in their favor, & God's will should be done.

"This service is harder on me than on most others," Major Ethan Allen Hitchcock wrote from Florida to a clerical friend, "for I know the cruel wrongs to which the enemy has been subjected, so I cannot help wishing that the right may prevail, which is, to use your own language, 'praying for the Indians.'" In a controversial published letter, an anonymous artillery officer—almost certainly Lieutenant John W. Phelps—denounced government policy, praised the heroism of the Seminoles, and recommended that opponents of the war urge their congressmen to withhold appropriations.[40]

No doubt many Florida officers felt emotions as mixed as those of Lieutenant Robert M. McLane, who thought that the Seminoles deserved a better fate

> than to be thus hunted like wolves over their own hunting grounds. . . . I feel a little curious too, with these strong sympathies in their favour, when I find myself panting to come up with them, but then its "our vocation Hal" besides duty—fame—glory—necessity and all that—God knows I will it over, and will fight hard to have it so. Yet I have the highest admiration for the Indians who remain hostile, with the fullest conviction that in the original quarrel, they had justice and right on their side, and only resisted knavery and fraud.[41]

Officers in the western campaigns of the 1850s frequently voiced similar moral doubts. A bloody surprise attack on an Apache village in 1857 disturbed Lieutenant John Van Deusen DuBois and made him question "why we had killed these poor harmless savages." He was particularly appalled by the shooting of an Indian prisoner, supposedly at the wish of the expedition commander. "May God grant that Indian fighting may never make me a brute or harden me so that I can act the coward in this way," he confided in his journal. "Humanity, honor, a soldier's pride, every feeling of good in me was & is shocked by this one act." Lieutenant August V. Kautz portrayed the ugliness of Indian warfare in the Pacific Northwest in a bitter satire apparently published in his hometown newspaper. "You must vow vengeance against every Indian you meet," he advised prospective Indian fighters, "but never molest any except peacable Indians, who are unarmed, and expect no danger; this is a very gallant thing, when done in the face of public opinion, law, and order." George Crook recalled in his autobiography the army's frustration at witnessing white harassment of the California Indians; "then when they were pushed beyond endurance and would go on the war path we had to fight when our sympathies were with the Indians."[42] Whenever regulars served with militia or volunteers, they carefully distinguished their conduct from the allegedly cruel and irresponsible behavior of the citizen-soldiers.

Whatever their private objections to their part in Indian warfare, few officers spoke out openly and fewer still followed their consciences to the point of resignation. With officers—as no doubt with other professional men—institutional loyalties and the quest for personal advancement usually proved stronger than moral reservations. Even the strongest critics of government policy could find balm for their consciences in the emerging professional ethic of the officer corps, with its emphasis on politically neutral, unquestioning service to the nation. In reply to a reprimand from his commander, for example, Captain John R. Vinton denied that his request for a leave was an attempt to avoid serving in an anticipated operation against the Cherokees, but he made clear that his willingness to fight should "not be understood to refer to my private sentiments as to the moral right or wrong of our [I]ndian policy." However, he assured his superior of his belief that an officer should "avoid any publication of such sentiments, especially when averse to the measures of the Government,—or to suffer them in any respect to impair his usefulness as a faithful and efficient public agent while he consents to remain in the public service."[43]

17
OFFICERS, FOREIGN AFFAIRS, AND WAR

Throughout most of the nineteenth century, regular army officers devoted the greater part of their careers to essentially domestic problems arising from Indian relations and the army's role as frontier police. Nevertheless, the officer corps itself considered preparation for a foreign war to be its primary mission—indeed, its very reason for existing. This conviction underlay such basic features of the military system as the scientific curriculum at West Point, the cadre plan for expanding the army, the program of seacoast fortification, and the efforts to incorporate European techniques into the American service. Nor was officers' orientation toward foreign conflict purely theoretical; the United States was a continental power in the nineteenth century, and officers were closely involved in the conduct of foreign policy in sensitive border regions. At times, commanders faced complex and potentially explosive crises and held in their hands the practical power to plunge the nation into war. The regular army also served as the nation's principal agent of territorial expansion—a task that gave the nascent military profession its first major combat trial in the 1840s. Officers' perceptions of foreign affairs and war thus formed an important element of their collective worldview.

NATIONAL SECURITY AND MANIFEST DESTINY

Few officers left extended statements of their outlook on foreign relations. In contrast to defense policy and Indian affairs, the administration rarely requested regulars' advice in formulating foreign policy, and commanders, perhaps reluctant to transgress their proper sphere, rarely volunteered their opinions. Nevertheless, officers did hold distinctive views on foreign affairs, and these may be reconstructed from their private correspondence and their reports and publications on other subjects, especially apologias for their profession and calls for strengthening the national defense.

Officers generally shared a conservative, pessimistic perception of the international scene, which might be expected considering their reading of history, their organizational loyalties, and their personal career ambitions. In their judgment, war and aggression were unavoidable aspects of the world order, deeply rooted in the human condition. A correspondent to a military journal stressed the anarchy of international relations, comparing independent nations to individuals in a state of nature: "Acknowledging no superior, the disputes arising from that interference with each other's pursuits, which ever characterizes the condition of independent communities, can find no other arbiter than physical force." Although Lieutenant Edward B. Hunt considered war "an immense evil" and expressed respect for the moral vision of unilateral disarmament, he did not believe "that mankind has yet so far progressed in cultivating the principles of gospel kindness, that nations in their dealings with each other shall be always controlled by a sense of justice, and never allow interest to lead to violations of right." In the opinion of a medical officer, "War is a grief imposed upon the world, from the very constitution of our nature, and hence under human institutions, no matter how governed, seems inevitable." "Ours, is a sad vocation, but a needful one," Captain Thomas Williams informed his wife, "& as it depends for its existence upon the passions of men, it is likely to last as long as man or his passions last. Soldiers, legislators, preachers, comprise a trinity as enduring as the evils they seek to redress."[1]

Naturally, officers held the contemporary peace movement in low esteem and discounted predictions that inevitable progress—the spread of education, science, and republican values—would eventually remove the foundations for war. Lieutenant Henry W. Halleck introduced his study of military science with a long refutation of the pacifist position as set forth in Francis Wayland's West Point ethics textbook. Winfield Scott's aide-de-camp described the general as in agreement with Hobbes "that war is the natural state of man. He had no faith in peace societies and congresses, and spoke of them with contempt as composed of fanatics and visionaries." In an article opening the first issue of the *Military and Naval Magazine of the United States*, an officer stated his "utter incredulity as to the immediate perfectability of the human race" and the purportedly widespread belief that the dissemination of secular knowledge would soon "convert all opinions into golden ones, and . . . metamorphose all our vile propensities into principles of purity. . . . We shall not look for those days of profound and uninterrupted peace that are promised, until our obstinate natures are radically changed, until the frame of our mind is differently constituted from what it is at present, or its elements are reorganized."[2]

More specifically, regulars highlighted the European threat to American liberties and interests. However secure Americans might feel behind their ocean barrier, they faced potential attack by European powers jealous of American prosperity or fearful that the republican spirit would spread to their own realms. During the decade after the War of 1812, commanders saw the reactionary Holy Alliance as the chief danger; they sympathized with the revolutions in Latin America and feared European intervention to suppress them. In opposing a reduction of the army in 1820, Major General Jacob Brown warned of the "pending struggle between free and despotic principles." If the reactionary governments of Europe succeeded in crushing the "infant structures of freedom" in their own countries, they might attempt "a further combination for the utter extinction of the flame of liberty throughout the circle of civilized man." Lieutenant Colonel Zachary Taylor had no doubt "that Europe, Asia, Africa, & a part of America, will be divided between Russia, England, Austria, & Prussia" and that the American people "will have to contend at no distant period on our own soil with them, for our very existence."[3] By the early 1830s, the threat had become more diffuse. Referring to the wave of European revolutions in 1830, Brigadier General Thomas S. Jesup argued that the moral power of the representative system was "gradually and certainly sapping the foundations of every absolute government in the civilized world." Should the forces of reaction prevail, however, they would have "all those motives of interest and of sympathy which so powerfully influence human action to unite against us." The same events made Inspector General John E. Wool fearful that a general war would result and that American neutral rights would again be tested: "Our peaceable relations with the nations of Europe are always endangered whenever those nations are belligerent and the United States neutral."[4]

Regulars repeatedly used diplomatic controversies with the continental powers to support their calls for preparedness—such as the quarrel with France in 1834–1836 over the repayment of debts owed American citizens and the one with Spain in the mid-1850s over Cuba. In the opinion of the officer corps, however, the British posed by far the greatest foreign menace. Britain's economic and naval power, her continued presence in North America, and her resentment of the United States as an emerging rival all pointed to eventual conflict. In planning and defending the seacoast fortification program, officers explicitly based their arguments on the prospect of war with Britain. War scares over filibustering on the Canadian border and the Maine boundary controversy in 1837–1842, over Oregon in 1845–1846, and over the disputed

San Juan Islands of Puget Sound in 1859–1860 reinforced their suspicions. Some regulars believed that Anglo-American antagonism was rooted in ideology rather than solely in territorial ambitions and economic self-interest. Writing during the Maine boundary dispute, a correspondent to the *Army and Navy Chronicle* predicted war, partly because of commercial tensions and Britain's desire to preserve her dominant world position, but also because of American democracy's challenge to monarchical principles. In his opinion, "the very next great martial strife in Christendom, whatever may be its origin, must ultimately settle into a contest between kings on the one hand and the people on the other. England has once taken the lead in fighting the battles of monarchy, and from her position, must do so again." According to Captain John R. Vinton, the rival claims to Oregon were only "moonshine": "Far higher & deeper considerations are involved in the issue—The spread of Republican institutions: the checking of England's inordinate ambition for territorial aggrandizement: the great principle that the earth belongs to the inhabitants there of, and not to certain families & Dynasties who happen to wear crowns and coronets."[5]

Although officers justified a strong military establishment mainly in terms of countering European enemies, their perception of the world was by no means purely defensive. Indeed, many commanders embraced an aggressively expansionist policy within North America. As they had since the early nineteenth century, officers stationed in the South after the War of 1812 panted to expel the Spanish from Florida and even from Cuba. Such a step would stabilize the southern frontier, give the United States control of the Gulf of Mexico, and open opportunities for military distinction. As commander at New Orleans in 1816, Lieutenant Colonel Thomas S. Jesup independently planned an attack on Cuba. He corresponded with other army and navy officers and with the administration, pointing out the strategic and economic importance of the island. In case of war, Jesup did not fear for the security of his department; "I only fear that the Dons will not have the courage to attack me."[6] Regulars hailed Andrew Jackson's attempted seizure of West Florida in 1818, and they vied for the honor of acquiring East Florida as well. In May 1818, Major James Bankhead requested permission to attack St. Augustine with the three hundred troops under his command: "It would add but little to the glory of our army if General Jackson, with 2 or 3,000 men were to take such a place, but if I, with an equal number of men with those in that fortified place; were to take it, it would tend to sustain the reputation of our army."[7]

Regulars were less united concerning the next great burst of expansionism—the drive for Texas, Oregon, and California in the late 1830s and 1840s. By that time, slavery had emerged as a political issue, and a significant minority within the officer corps, especially those with Whig inclinations, feared the political consequences of adding new territory. As with Indian relations, some commanders objected to expansionism on moral grounds as well. Lieutenant Colonel Ethan Allen Hitchcock considered the American insistence on the Rio Grande as the Texas-Mexican boundary to be "monstrous and abominable" and evidence of a decline in national character. In his opinion, the movement of Zachary Taylor's army to the Rio Grande was an act of patent aggression. "We have outraged the Mexican government and people by an arrogance and presumption that deserve to be punished." Indeed, Taylor himself expressed serious misgivings about the Polk administration's belligerent policies. "As regards the Callifornia affair," he wrote his son-in-law in August 1846, "I must entirely disapprove the course of the administration, & consider no act of the [British] govt as regards the acquirement of territory in the East, or any where else more outrageous than our attempt or intention of taking permanent possession of that country."[8]

Nevertheless, the great majority of the officer corps seems to have supported the expansionist surge. Many regulars responded enthusiastically to the spirit of Manifest Destiny that flourished in the mid-1840s—the belief in the inevitable extension of American power to the Pacific and even over all of North America. Along with large segments of civilian society, they had come to accept the idea of a distinct Anglo-Saxon race that was culturally, politically, and morally superior to the other peoples of the American continents.[9] Moreover, the drive for territory synchronized with the professional ambitions of military men; an aggressive foreign policy meant the prospect of war and the chance for glory and promotion. In 1845, Colonel William J. Worth expressed to the surgeon general his fear that the Mexican-American dispute would be settled peacefully, thereby depriving the army of the first opportunity "in the past, as it will probably be in the next[,] 30 years" to fight a major war.

> Why mince matters now? have not our Anglo Saxon race been land stealers from time immemorial and why shouldn't they? When their gaze is fixed upon others lands the best way is to make out the deeds: in this instance had our Eagles been perched upon the banks of the Rio Grande the Mexicans would have posted to Washington and solicited the honor of paying for recording the papers. . . . Oh what a glorious chance— . . . for the like of us it is the last throw; before another we shall be alike beyond the reach of praise or lampooning.[10]

For most officers, the Mexican War was their first extensive contact with Mexicans, and the experience strengthened their commitment to expansionism. Although some regulars commented favorably on the graciousness of the upper-class Mexicans they encountered, and although many were struck by the appearance and charm of the women, the overwhelming weight of army opinion was negative. Officers perceived Mexicans, as they had Indians, from an intensely ethnocentric standpoint, sharpened in this case by anti-Catholic prejudice and reinforced by the emerging ideology of Anglo-Saxon racial superiority. Mexicans appeared an indolent, cowardly, half-civilized people, dominated by a predatory ruling class and a corrupt priesthood. "It truly might be an earthly paradise were the inhabitants civilized," a captain wrote from northern Mexico in 1846. "They, alas, are lost in the most groveling superstition and ignorance and are under a government that tramples them into the dust." "Their religion is mockery, idolatry, priestcraft," commented another regular, "their liberty, an ever changing government of venal rulers,—extending to the people no security of life or property, but oppressing them with every species of taxation." While the larger towns contained a refined upper class, "the bulk of the population is so abject, ignorant, & depraved, that I can readily suppose it to be the will of God, as in the case of the people of India, that a great moral revolution should be brought about, through the agency of Anglo-Saxon civilization, and power." Officers frequently described the Mexicans as a degraded mongrel race, "a mixture of Indian, Negro, and Spanish blood, apparently a great deal below and more ignorant than either race."[11]

As the war progressed, the apparent inferiority of the Mexicans and their incapacity for self-government convinced many regulars that American institutions would permanently prevail in Mexico, and they embraced the movement to annex the entire country. Lieutenant William M. Gardner hoped that the war would continue until all of Mexico was conquered: "It is too good a country and too delightful a climate for so worthless a race." From the American blood shed in Mexico, predicted an army surgeon, "will spring up the principles of Republicanism, which proceeding slowly it may be but surely, will at last unite the Halls of the Montezumas and our Capital at Washington." American immigration would flow across the Rio Grande, and "the name of Mexico as a separate nation will soon be a thing extinct." Colonel William J. Worth considered it axiomatic that the United States would overrun the entire continent: "Put two distinct races in juxtaposition, one more powerful and superior in civilization, and it will absorb the inferior." In the opinion of Captain William S. Henry, northern Mexico was not intended to

remain in the hands of an ignorant and degenerate race. The finger of Fate points, if not to their eventual extinction, to the time when they will cease to be owners, and when the Anglo-American race will rule with republican simplicity and justice, a land literally "flowing with milk and honey;" who will, by their superior mental, if not physical abilities—by their energy and *go-a-head-a-tiveness*, . . . render available the surprising fertility of the soil, its immense mineral wealth, and populate the country with a race of men who will prove the infinite goodness of our Maker in creating nothing but what is for use and some good purpose.[12]

The Mexican War did not turn all regulars into ardent proponents of Manifest Destiny, and some remained concerned about the moral and political consequences of militant expansionism. Again, however, commanders could soothe their consciences by referring to their role as neutral instruments of public policy—and to the supposed obligation of all citizens to rally behind the government in time of war. Lieutenant George G. Meade considered the Mexican War unjust and the result of United States aggression; once begun, however, he thought that it should be waged in as vigorous and decisive a manner as possible. Seven months before his death in battle, Captain Ephraim Kirby Smith expressed dismay at the blood and treasure to be expended in "this war to extend the area of slavery, to increase the power of the southern aristocracy, under the name of Democracy. But enough of politics, we have got into the scrape for Mister Polk, and must fight it out for the credit of the United States." "As an individual, I condemn, I abominate this war," wrote Lieutenant Colonel Hitchcock from the American fleet preparing for the attack on Vera Cruz, "as a member of the government I must go with it until it shall be brought back to a sense of justice."[13]

OFFICERS AND THE CONDUCT OF FOREIGN RELATIONS

By the end of the War of 1812, the officer corps had accumulated much practical experience in the conduct of diplomatic relations in unstable borderland areas: the Mississippi, Sabine, and Florida frontiers through the 1790s and early 1800s, and the Canadian border during the embargo period. Yet the corps had still not achieved a stable pattern of civil-military interaction, or even a consensus on its precise role in foreign affairs. Because of problems of communication, the administration's failure to provide clear guidelines, and the individualism of the early officer corps, commanders had often acted on their own authority, making decisions of great potential importance. More than a few regulars had given their support to—indeed, participated in—filibustering and other interventionist movements that threatened to compromise American neutrality.

The custom of independent action continued into the postwar period, especially on the volatile Florida frontier. For years, the army had been enmeshed in various filibustering schemes along that border; as discussed previously, regulars in the region longed for an opportunity to depose the hated "Dons" and add the Floridas to the American empire, perhaps acquiring battlefield laurels in the process. In the spring of 1816, acting on the authority of Major General Andrew Jackson but apparently without the administration's prior knowledge or approval, Brigadier General Gaines ordered an expedition into West Florida to destroy a fort on the Apalachicola River that was occupied by escaped slaves—an act that, in the words of one historian, stood "in the grand American tradition of contemptuously disregarding Spanish sovereignty and territorial integrity." The American forces soon withdrew, but the border remained precarious through 1817 as white pressure provoked warfare with the Seminole Indians living in Spanish territory and American filibusters took Amelia Island off the northeastern Florida coast.[14]

This situation—a volatile, unstable frontier and an officer corps spoiling for a fight—formed the context for the most spectacular example of army freelancing: Andrew Jackson's attempted seizure of Florida. Jackson had long demonstrated the flamboyant individuality of the early officer corps, most notably during the martial law controversy in New Orleans at the end of the War of 1812. Jackson's ostensible purpose in crossing the Florida border was to chastise the Seminoles, and in this goal he had the clear approval of the Monroe administration. He intended from the start, however, to extend American dominion over the Spanish colony if offered the slightest opening. Indeed, President Monroe's personal instructions at least implied that this may also have been the administration's objective. In any case, Jackson entered West Florida in March 1818 at the head of an army of 3,000 regulars and volunteers and a force of Creek allies. He occupied the Spanish outpost of St. Marks, destroyed a large Seminole settlement on the Suwannee River, and hanged after hasty military trials two British subjects suspected of inciting the Indians. Jackson next marched on Pensacola, the capital of West Florida, bombarded the town, and forced its surrender. Thereupon, he proclaimed American possession of all parts of Florida that the Spanish could not effectively control, justifying his action by reference to the Indian menace and the "immutable laws of self defence." On his own authority, he appointed Colonel William King of the Fourth Infantry Regiment military and civil governor of Pensacola. He then proudly reported his actions to the administration, offering to take St. Augustine and even Cuba if reinforced.[15]

Jackson's impetuosity produced an international uproar and a major controversy in Congress. While the Monroe administration approved his trespass into Spanish territory in pursuit of the Indians, it disowned his attack on Pensacola and attempted seizure of Spanish lands. With some difficulty, Jackson's supporters managed to defeat a series of bills censuring his actions and restricting commanders' powers to engage in similar practices in the future.[16] The final acquisition of Florida awaited the negotiation and ratification of the Transcontinental Treaty, completed in 1821.

The tradition of officers' independent action in foreign affairs did not entirely end with Jackson. Occasionally in the decades that followed, regulars with expansionist inclinations stationed in sensitive border regions took steps that threatened to compromise United States neutrality or provoke international crises. During the Texan revolution of 1836, the commander on the southwestern frontier, Brigadier General Edmund P. Gaines, strongly sympathized with the Texan cause. He declared that if the Mexicans or their Indian allies menaced the United States border, he would advance into Mexican territory, "meeting the savage marauders wherever to be found in their approach to our frontier." Acting on his own authority, he called on state governors in the region to mobilize volunteer militia. As president, Andrew Jackson had lost much of his former enthusiasm for military freethinkers. Although he did permit Gaines to occupy temporarily a position in Mexican territory, he tried to rein in the willful brigadier by disapproving of his independent militia calls and repeatedly stating the administration's commitment to a strictly neutral posture. In the opinion of Jackson—ironically Gaines's commander in the Florida incursion—the general's intention had been to concentrate soldiers on the frontier who would have immediately joined the Texan army, thereby embarrassing the administration.[17] Another, more celebrated case of officers' freelancing was Captain John C. Frémont's "exploratory" expedition of 1845–1846, in which he entered the Mexican province of Upper California, defied Mexican authorities who ordered him to leave, and at least indirectly encouraged American settlers to rise in the "Bear Flag Rebellion." The outbreak of the Mexican War prevented Frémont's action from triggering an international incident.[18]

A final example of military recklessness might conceivably have led to war with Great Britain. The British-American treaty settling the northwestern boundary in 1846 had fixed the channel of Puget Sound as the westernmost section of the border. The exact location of the channel was unclear, however, and both nations claimed title to the San Juan Island chain. Tensions increased during the late 1850s, as small numbers of American and British settlers took up residence on San Juan Island, the largest of the group. In July

1859, Brigadier General William S. Harney, the commander of the Department of Oregon, ordered a company of regulars under Captain George E. Pickett to the island, ostensibly in response to a petition from settlers for protection against Indian raids but actually to establish American jurisdiction. Although Harney's motives are uncertain, his biographer ascribes the move to his erratic, belligerent personality—his forty-year career had been punctuated by outbursts of temper and violent behavior—his desire for popular attention and glory, and his expansionism. In any case, Pickett proclaimed that only American laws and courts would be recognized on the island; the British authorities in Victoria dispatched warships to the scene, Harney reinforced the American detachment, and violence loomed. Fortunately, the British demonstrated forbearance, and the two governments worked to defuse the situation. Ordered to the Northwest by the Buchanan administration, Major General Winfield Scott privately rebuked Harney and negotiated an informal arrangement for the joint occupancy of the island. Harney remained as department commander, however, and he revived the controversy briefly in the spring of 1860 by again asserting exclusive United States jurisdiction.[19]

Despite the publicity they received, free-lancing commanders such as Gaines, Frémont, and Harney were exceptions among the antebellum officer corps. In line with the general trend toward professional consolidation from the 1820s on, officers displayed a growing commitment to the army's function as a neutral tool of the government in the conduct of foreign affairs—an attitude that paralleled their approach to civil-military relations and Indian affairs. The clearest manifestation of this resolve was the role of the officer corps in the suppression of filibustering—the army's most important mission in peacetime foreign relations before the Civil War.

During the early national period, regulars' attitudes toward filibustering had been ambivalent at best, and they had sometimes supported bids at private expansionism, most notably the Burr-Wilkinson conspiracy and the various plots along the Florida frontier. Their conduct was dramatically different during the next major wave of border violence—the "patriot" troubles on the Canadian frontier between 1837 and 1842. The source of this unrest was the outbreak of rebellion in the provinces of Upper and Lower Canada in 1837. Many Americans living along the border sympathized with the uprisings, which they hoped would result in the expulsion of British rule and perhaps annexation by the United States; their hopes were encouraged by rebel "patriots" who sought to raise armies in American territory and launch attacks across the border. The situation became explosive at the end of 1837, when a British force burned the American steamboat *Caroline*, used to supply the filibusters on the Niagara frontier. This event put the entire border in turmoil and led to widespread demands for retaliation.[20]

Because civilian officials could not restrain the patriots, and indeed often supported them, the Van Buren administration ordered veteran regular officers to the scene. Since most of the army was deployed in Florida or on the western frontier, the officers were initially forced to depend on their own powers of persuasion and on volunteer militia of doubtful reliability. Dispatched to Buffalo, Brigadier General Scott nearly sparked a crisis when he chartered a steamboat to keep it out of rebel hands, then sent it up the Niagara River past British forces without announcing that it was under federal rather than patriot control. The British held their fire, however, and Scott's overall performance was impressive; during the early months of 1838, he opened communication with British authorities, cajoled filibuster leaders into abandoning their plans, and tirelessly met with political leaders and citizens' groups to calm the situation. Colonels Hugh Brady and John E. Wool performed similar services at Detroit and on the Lake Champlain–Vermont frontier, two other hotbeds of patriot activity.[21]

Although the unrest subsided in March, the filibusters organized themselves into secret societies and resumed their plotting during the summer of 1838. By that time, the army's position had been strengthened. On 10 March, Congress had passed a stronger neutrality act, giving federal officials the express power to prevent expeditions against foreign nations and specifically authorizing the president to employ the armed forces to counter filibustering. Also, the expansion of the army in July made possible the concentration of three regiments of regular troops along the Canadian border. The administration ordered Major General Alexander Macomb, the commanding general of the army, to the northern frontier, where he directly coordinated antifilibustering operations through October 1838. Cooperating with British authorities, the army gradually managed to suppress overt patriot activities along the thousand-mile border.[22] Plotting and agitation continued for several years, however, aggravated by the Maine boundary controversy, and a large portion of the army remained deployed along the Canadian frontier until the completion of the Webster-Ashburton Treaty in 1842. At Buffalo and probably elsewhere, regulars used paid informants to keep track of patriot plans—an early example of military surveillance of American citizens during peacetime.[23]

The officer corps responded similarly to the succession of filibustering plots in the 1850s, directed against Mexico, Cuba, and Central America. A minority of the officer corps sympathized with the filibusters, and a handful of regulars, their ambitions whetted by the Mexican War, resigned their commissions to join the expansionists. William L. Crittenden, an 1845 graduate of West

Point and a nephew of the attorney general of the United States, served as a "colonel" in Narciso Lopez's expedition to Cuba in 1851 and died before a Spanish firing squad.[24] However, most officers appear to have rejected such private operations. Many regulars—even those who were sympathetic—viewed filibusters as disorderly, brutal troublemakers whose professions of idealism were merely covers for their greed.[25] In the opinion of Captain Pierre G. T. Beauregard, the actions of William Walker in Nicaragua displayed "a ferocity, & vandalism, unworthy of the American Character & of the great object I had understood he had in view, the establishment of a Central American Republic, based on our system, & extending from the Isthmus of Panama to the Sierra Madre." Beauregard had been willing to join such a cause, "but for the mere pillage & burning of a neighboring Republic, more or less barbarous—I must decline my offer, however advantageous, to participate therein."[26] No doubt another factor discouraging officers from filibustering was their reluctance to abandon the security of their commissions for the risks and dubious respectability of private expansionism.

In their constabulary role, regulars confronted filibusters on the Mexican border and in California. During 1851–1853, a movement led by Mexican adventurer Jose Maria Jesus Carvajal that included a large number of Anglo-Americans kept the lower Rio Grande in an uproar, on several occasions launching attacks from American territory against Mexican border towns. The Fillmore administration announced American neutrality and used officers on the scene as pacifiers. The army twice arrested Carvajal, only to see him released by civilian courts. Nevertheless, military intervention did succeed at least temporarily in imposing order on the chronically turbulent Rio Grande frontier. According to Lieutenant Edmund Kirby Smith, "The only persons respected & feared on the Frontier (yet cordially hated) are the officers & soldiers of the army."[27]

Regulars faced a more frustrating situation in San Francisco, a seedbed of expansionist plotting in the 1850s. During the fall of 1853, the commander of the Department of the Pacific, Colonel Ethan Allen Hitchcock, tried to enforce the neutrality laws by seizing a brig that the celebrated filibuster William Walker intended to use in an expedition against the Mexican state of Sonora. The veteran officer was soon besieged by San Francisco politicians and officials, who sympathized with Walker and urged the release of the ship. Hitchcock defied his opponents, even when slapped with a $30,000 lawsuit, but the adventurers eluded him by sailing in another vessel.[28] Hitchcock's successor as department commander, Brigadier General John E. Wool, expended even greater energy in trying to suppress filibustering, arresting a number of men suspected of collusion in Walker's and other interventionist plots. Civil courts either released the accused filibusters, however, or issued only light sentences. Moreover, expansionist Secretary of War Jefferson Davis reprimanded Wool for overstepping his authority and moved his headquarters from San Francisco to the inland town of Benicia, making it even more difficult to enforce the neutrality laws. "Whatever may have been the policy which dictated the order," wrote one of Wool's staff officers, "one result has certainly been that filibusters now go and come as they choose, and no one cares a straw, except the poor citizens of another country who *happen* to be invaded by them."[29]

OFFICERS AND WAR

On the morning of 9 February 1837, a large body of Seminoles attacked a detachment of regulars encamped on the shore of Lake Monroe in central Florida. Though outnumbered, the soldiers repulsed the attackers during a firefight that lasted several hours. After twenty years on active duty, Captain John R. Vinton had passed his first combat test, and he triumphantly wrote home:

> I come out of the ordeal a firmer and a prouder man than I ever felt myself to be before. I have found myself cool and collected in danger, and firmly composed for the execution of my duties though on my right hand & on my left, my men were falling around me. . . . Thus, have I participated in fighting the battles of my country and by breasting the fire of her enemies, have repaid the debt I owe her.[30]

In common with Captain Vinton, most officers considered war the pinnacle of their professional lives. Although the antebellum era was supposedly a time of peace, the army engaged in some type of combat in well over half of the years between 1821 and 1861. A great many regulars experienced their first combat in the Indian campaigns or the war with Mexico, and almost one hundred officers of the basic establishment, Vinton among them, were killed in action or died of wounds in the four decades preceding the Civil War. Indeed, the Mexican War was one of the bloodiest conflicts in the history of the professional officer corps, nearly equalling the Civil War in the proportion of combat fatalities among the officers in service at the outbreak of fighting.[31] War also provided a collective trial for the proficiency of the regular army and for the professional skills of the officer corps. For all these reasons, war occupied a prominent place in the self-image of the officer corps.

Regulars' views of combat were generally positive, and their perceptions were strengthened by the widespread glorification of warfare and military heroes in contemporary American culture. Warfare was a key component of American nationalism in the nineteenth century; national heroes tended to be military heroes, and military themes pervaded historical writing, fiction, and art. Moreover, the Romantic movement contributed to an intense interest in the Middle Ages, best revealed in the enormous popularity of the novels of Sir Walter Scott, and encouraged Americans to draw parallels between the chivalric deeds of medieval knights and those of their own military leaders. The martial fever reached something of a peak during the Mexican War, because it captured the popular imagination and produced a host of military heroes, many of whom were members of the officer corps of the regular army.[32]

Whether influenced by the broader culture or by narrower professional concerns, officers eagerly sought opportunities to practice their trade. "War as such is to be deprecated," wrote Lieutenant William T. Sherman in 1844, "but if it is necessary for the interests or honor of the country of course I may with perfect propriety rejoice at the opportunity of being able to practice what in peace we can only profess."[33] Each rumor of war spawned hopes of active service, individual glory, and the advancement of the army as an institution. To shun combat was the most dishonorable act an officer could commit, an uneradicable stain on his courage and character.

As already noted, officers dreamed of a war with Spain over the Florida question, but during the early 1840s, the prospect of war with Great Britain and Mexico also sparked the ambition of many regulars. The officers at Fort Wood, Louisiana, were disappointed when the Texas question did not lead to hostilities in 1844: "Our swords are getting rusty in their scabbards, and we want something to brighten them, the Oregon question is for the present our only chance." Lieutenant Henry J. Hunt wished that the Oregon dispute would "lead to a war that will drive the d____d inveterate mercenaries from our continent." Colonel Stephen W. Kearny regretted the easing of tensions with Britain in 1842, "because I think War must ensue before our difficulties are settled, & therefore think the sooner it comes, the better! A War would tend to unite the feelings of our People & of our Public Men, who would then be willing to put the Country in a state of Defence, which they will not do, in these times of Peace."[34] The officer corps got its war in 1846, but by the 1850s regulars were again longing for action. Writing from remote Fort Davis, Texas, Lieutenant Edward L. Hartz hoped that a "war with England which our latest advices seem to warrant would open a field fraught with more scope for true military action than we can ever hope for in our police like expeditions after concealed and never-to-be-met-with Indians." Barring that prospect, to engage "any other civilized nation with systematized and recognized warfare" would be preferable to Indian war. Regulars eagerly anticipated a battle with the Mormons in the late 1850s; a former officer recalled in his memoirs that Brigham Young's submission to federal authority "disappointed many young officers, myself among them, anxious to see active service."[35]

A recurring theme of officers' writings was the potential advantage of war in the abstract, regardless of its causes or aims. A number of regulars argued that a foreign conflict would have beneficial side effects for the nation, both moral and political, and some came close to advocating war for its own sake. Writing in 1855, Captain Thomas Williams described the materialism of the age, contrasting it with the days of chivalry.

> There are greater calamities than war, such as those when men forget they have hearts or souls & prostrate themselves before the golden calf. And when war, arouses them to an activity which demands the sympathies of the heart as well as the use of the brains, it may be regarded as a blessing, restoring a healthful balance between the generous & more selfish sentiments. Man has both heart & soul, & war teaches it to him most impressively; commerce denies it.[36]

Other officers saw a clash with a foreign power as a means to enhance national unity. During the patriot troubles, Winfield Scott admitted to a concerned secretary of war that he had frequently referred to peace societies, nullification, antimasonry, Mormon troubles, and abolitionism as " 'cankers of a long peace & a calm world' " and had stated his opinion that "a good hot foreign war only could save the Union & our free institutions, by effectively curing the people of those moral distempers." He assured the secretary, however, that he opposed any war that was not declared by Congress or supported by a unified population. Lieutenant John J. Peck was not distressed by the possibility of war in 1845: "It would be an infinite benefit to the army and the country. Our national divisions and sections and strifes would be healed, and a common interest would bring us together."[37]

The army's response to the hostilities with Mexico offers the clearest picture of officers' attitudes toward the actual experience of war. The outbreak of fighting triggered a wave of enthusiasm within the officer corps, as subalterns and gray-haired veterans alike saw the best opportunity in a generation for glory and professional advancement. "Hip! Hip! Hurrah! War at last sure enough!" rhapsodized graduating Cadet George B. McClellan. "Ain't it glorious! . . . Well, it appears that our wishes have at last been gratified & we shall soon have the intense satisfaction of fighting the crowd—musquitoes & Mexicans &c." Officers' greatest fear was that they would miss out on the action. Stationed at St. Augustine in the summer of 1846, Captain Robert

Anderson longed to take the field: "To be hemmed up in garrison, when nominally belonging to a fighting army, whilst others were every day placed in positions where distinction and honor could be bought, would be more than my philosophy could stand." Although he strongly opposed the war as aggressive and immoral, Lieutenant Colonel Ethan Allen Hitchcock likewise dreaded that he would miss the golden chance for professional honors; he considered his illness-induced absence from his regiment to be "a species of death." Lieutenant Earl Van Dorn expressed the elation of a great many young officers in a letter to his sister from the Rio Grande.

> Don't you poor helpless female population wish you were *men* that you might snatch a sword and join in the game for glory? What does the gambler know of excitement who has millions staked on a card? He loses but millions, he can win but millions. But here *life* is to lose—glory to win. Who can know what the bosom feels, how the heart swells with burning emotions, hopes, proud longings for distinction.[38]

In addition to whetting individual ambition, the war offered a chance to prove the collective proficiency of the regular army. The early 1840s had been a demoralizing time for the officer corps, caused by intense civilian criticism of West Point and military professionalism and by congressional efforts at retrenchment. Whatever their opinions of the foreign policy that produced the war, regulars were virtually unanimous in hoping the army's performance would permanently silence its critics. A captain spoke for the entire officer corps when he expressed hope in April 1846 that Taylor's army would push the enemy back: "This *must* be done before the arrival of volunteers, or the army is *disgraced*." "We want a victory," wrote another; "the regular army is dead without one."[39] The ensuing victories at Palo Alto and Resaca de la Palma, achieved exclusively by regulars, realized officers' fondest wishes by generating a crop of national heroes and winning eulogistic praise for the army's combat abilities. Captain William S. Henry summarized the pride of the officer corps: "We were all aware of the undeserved remarks that had been made in reference to us by some portions of the press, and representatives in Congress, and we only asked for *an opportunity*, few as we were, to *prove* to our country she had a safe anchor in our *small* but gallant force."[40]

The experience of combat mainly confirmed regulars in their romantic notions about warfare. Officers were not unmoved by the carnage of battle, and many accounts contained passages similar to this captain's description of the battlefield of Resaca de la Palma: "Dead bodies of men and horses were piled up on each other exhibiting every expression of torture the most vivid imagi-

Bombardment of Vera Cruz, after a painting by Carl Nebel, depicting the naval battery that, in an uncommon episode of interservice cooperation, served under the army during the siege. (Courtesy the Amon Carter Museum, Fort Worth, Texas)

nation could picture, and so horribly mangled and torn, in many cases by cannon shot, that it was heart sickening to behold them."[41] In particular, the siege and bombardment of Vera Cruz in March 1847 impressed military observers, who were both awed and shocked by the impact of the American fire on the civilian inhabitants. Major Edmund Kirby described the "sublime spectacle" of the flight of the American shells, trailed by burning fuses, into the helpless city. "Falling upon the flat roofs which they crushed & exploding within[,] the effect was terrible. The crash of timber & the shrieks & moans of the poor victims within the town were heard distinctly in our trenches & filled even our rough soldiers with awe." An artillery officer found it difficult to perform his duty because of the knowledge "that every shot either injures or seriously distresses the poor inoffensive women and children, who have neither part nor lot in the War."[42] As the bloodshed dragged on into its second year, an undercurrent of disillusionment appeared in the private letters of some veterans. "'Twas an awful fight," wrote Captain Roger S. Dix of the Battle of Buena Vista. "Ten hours' fighting is *no trifle*. I came to Mexico to see the 'elephant.' I have seen him, and am perfectly willing never to see him again."[43]

Nevertheless, most regulars grew accustomed to scenes of slaughter, learning, as one subaltern put it, "to look upon the dead with as little emotion as I would regard a stone."⁴⁴ Instead, they punctuated their accounts with descriptions of battlefield heroics and glowing self-congratulations on the army's accomplishments. Many were enthralled by the grand spectacle of battle, which was enhanced by their romantic sensibilities and the exotic beauty of the Mexican landscape. Lieutenant John F. Reynolds compared the morning sun at Buena Vista with "Napoleon's sun at Austerlitz." "I never in my life beheld a more beautiful sight," he wrote of the Mexican line; "their gay uniforms, numberless pennants, standards and colors streaming in the sun shone out in all their 'pride and pomp.'" The Mexican advance at Contreras struck Lieutenant George W. Rains as "one of the most sublime sights that was ever seen. . . . 30 pieces of the enemy's artillery kept up a continual roar which joined to two batteries of our own and innumerable musketry fires lighted up the whole face of the earth, and the glistening of the bayonets & lances, and the endless files from the city as far as the eye could reach—formed together a scene which has few if any equals." To Lieutenant Charles S. Hamilton, the Mexican guns at Monterrey "sounded sublime beyond conception. . . . The thunder of the cannon and the majestic beauty of the scenery, all conspired to wrap the mind in intense excitement. The exhilaration was alone that of sublimity and it was long ere these feelings could be shaken off."⁴⁵

Officers waxed expansive on deeds of individual gallantry—at least when performed by fellow regulars. They eulogized heroic comrades, especially those who died dramatic combat deaths, and the war produced a pantheon of martyrs who lived on in the collective imagination of the officer corps. In a typical battle account, Lieutenant Isaac Ingalls Stevens described the assault of Captain Simon H. Drum's light artillery battery against the castle of Chapultepec.

> The iron men of Drum pushed [the battery] into the very teeth of the enemy's fire, and made it send forth an iron hail that drove the enemy from all his positions, even the garita itself. Drum paused not at the garita. With a sublime devotion, he marched boldly up to the very citadel itself, and fell mortally wounded with his gallant lieutenant, Benjamin, two thirds of his company being disabled.

Lieutenant Arthur T. Lee captured the sentimental haze through which the officer corps viewed the war in a poem written the day after the death of Captain Samuel Ringgold, commander of the army's first light battery, in the Battle of Palo Alto.

"Heights of Monterey, from the Saltillo Road Looking towards the City," as drawn by Lieutenant Daniel P. Whiting of the Seventh Infantry Regiment. Whiting's drawing depicts the division of Colonel William J. Worth advancing for an assault on the city's outer defenses and gives an idea of the spectacular Mexican scenery that so much impressed the regulars. (Courtesy the Amon Carter Museum, Fort Worth, Texas)

> When his death is told to-morrow
>   Where the shouts of battle swell,
> Many a tear will fall in sorrow
>   O'er the guns he loved so well.
> But their steeds will dash more proudly
>   O'er the field of smoke and fire;
> And those guns will ring more loudly,
>   Calling for a vengeance dire.[46]

The officer corps was by no means monolithic in its response to the Mexican War. Ambitious regulars competed among themselves for honors, and each publication of a general's battle report unleashed a backlash of recrimination by those who considered themselves slighted. The distribution of brevet promotions was an especially divisive issue. At the end of the war, the officer corps in Mexico City was riven by politically charged quarrels that resulted in the recall of Winfield Scott as commander of the occupation army and his appearance before a court of inquiry.[47] Even so, the war's bequest to the officer corps was institutional pride, since, as regulars interpreted its lessons, the key to victory had been the professional expertise of the officer corps, especially the West Point graduates who had come to dominate the middle and lower grades. The "science" of the regulars, long nurtured in the face of civilian hostility, had given structure and direction to the citizen-soldiers and had made possible an unbroken string of successes against heavy odds. In a dinner speech in Mexico City that became part of West Point lore, General Scott asserted that "but for the science of the Military Academy 'this army, multiplied by four, could not have entered the capital of Mexico.'" No officer followed the army's progress more proudly than an aging lieutenant colonel of engineers who spent most of the war working on harbor improvements in Boston. "The sons of West Point have covered themselves with glory," Sylvanus Thayer wrote a friend.[48]

However accurate this perception of West Point's contribution, the war gave rise to a body of tradition, exaggerated but nonetheless powerful, that fired regulars with professional self-esteem. Officers compared the army's exploits with the great military campaigns of history, and their claims were echoed by a hero-worshipping public. One lieutenant considered the construction and defense of Fort Brown on the Rio Grande to be "the most remarkable events in the American history." Another likened the victories of Palo Alto and Resaca de la Palma to Waterloo, and a third described the siege of Vera Cruz as "the most complete victory of science in modern warfare." Regulars rhapsodized about Winfield Scott's march to Mexico City, an event that predictably spawned analogies to Cortez's conquest of the Aztecs. Lieutenant William M. Gardner thought that Scott's campaign would "astound the world. As for myself I will be proud to my dying day to have participated in the success of the Army of Mexico." In the opinion of another subaltern, the clashes at Contreras and Churubusco constituted "the greatest battle that has ever been fought on this continent and the most brilliant." Lieutenant Thomas Williams flew the highest in hyperbole when he predicted that future generations would record the capture of the Mexican capital as "the great event—the epoch—of the 19th century; & as not surpassed by any military achievement in *all* previous history."[49]

The Mexican conflict represented the officers' ideal of war at its best—clean, dramatic victories in an exotic setting against a "civilized" opponent, albeit one of inferior racial stock. Such was far less the case with Indian warfare, the other major combat experience of the antebellum army. As discussed in the preceding chapter, Indian strife involved mainly messy, frustrating guerrilla campaigning with little opportunity for glory or distinction. On the rare occasions when the army engaged Indians in open battles, regulars indulged in romantic descriptions reminiscent of the Mexican War. The striking spectacle of aboriginal warfare impressed one lieutenant who witnessed an encounter with the Coeur d'Alene, Spokane, and Pelouze tribes in 1858.

> They were in all the bravery of their war array, gaudily painted and decorated with their wild trappings. Their plumes fluttered above them, while below skins and trinkets and all kinds of fantastic embellishments flaunted in the sunshine. . . . Beads and fringes of gaudy colors were hanging from their [horses'] bridles, while the plumes of eagles' feathers, interwoven with the mane and tail, fluttered as the breeze swept over them, and completed their wild and fantastic appearance.

He went on to describe how the troops decimated the unsuspecting warriors with their cannon and newly issued long-range rifles, then routed them with a dragoon charge.[50]

Most regulars did not approach Indian campaigns with the eager enthusiasm displayed toward formalized warfare. Although many officers sought active service against the Indians, they did so out of a sense of professional duty—or because Indian war, whatever its drawbacks, was the only action available. In a letter to his father late in 1836, Lieutenant William Gilpin revealed his desire to reach Florida before the end of the Seminole war. He thought that progress in his profession depended on seeking the "opportunity & trial" of active duty: "Where is a military man to find them but in Florida? bad I agree, but the only one." Although Lieutenant Robert M. McLane criticized the conduct of a battle with the Seminoles in January 1838, he was sorry to have missed it; "bad as this fight was," it had offered "a rare opportunity for a regular officer to distinguish himself." In 1855, an officer assessed the motives of Lieutenant John L. Grattan, whose rash and belligerent behavior had caused the Sioux to massacre his thirty-man detachment the previous year. "I think he was anxious to have an engagement, not with Indians particularly, but for want of a more noble foe, even with them, to gain credit for himself and his profession."[51]

Perhaps the most important effect of the Indian wars on the group mindset of the officer corps was to sharpen regulars' sense of isolation and martyrdom, their feelings of collective yet thankless sacrifice. Since little glory was to be won, they consoled themselves with the conviction that they were faithfully serving the public need. Captain John R. B. Gardenier illustrated this spirit perfectly in a poem commemorating the death of a fellow officer in Florida.

> But Mitchell fell not on the field of blood!
> His martial spirit, eager for the fight,
> That often urg'd him on through field and flood,
> Amid the din of arms took not its flight—
> But in the quiet camp, the fever blight
> Subdu'd the body toil could not o'erthrow.
> Yet, still his Country's good his sole delight,
> He gave his native land his heart's last throe—
> And whispered, as he died, "PRO BONO PUBLICO!"

Or, as Lieutenant William Wall put it more simply in 1836: "I feel that I cannot bear so much glory as is about to be obtained from this Florida concern. However as Uncle Sam wills it I shall try to bear up."[52]

18
THE OFFICER CORPS IN THE SECTIONAL CRISIS

On 25 March 1861, former major Edmund Kirby Smith wrote his mother that he had resigned to join the Confederacy. A native of Florida, Smith had earlier resolved to take this action if the South seceded, but he had hoped that the crisis might be averted. The abandonment of his career brought deep misgivings.

> Every tie that connects me with the Army has been broken, profession, kin, all the associations of my life have been given up—and not, suddenly, impulsively, but conscientiously—and after due deliberation—I was the senior major of my Regt at the time—and the youngest man in the army for my position, and am twenty years in advance of my contemporaries—what my future may be I cannot tell. I have no expectations, I only know, I sacrifice more to my principles, than any other officer in the Army can do.[1]

For a great many regulars of southern birth or connections, the events of 1860 and 1861 brought a similar crisis of loyalty, pitting identification with their nation and profession against ties to family, community, state, and section. In the end, a quarter of the officer corps decided that the latter ties were the stronger, and they either resigned their commissions to join the southern cause or were dismissed by the government for disloyalty or desertion to the enemy. A number of others, unable to make a choice, resigned and took no part in the conflict. The sectional crisis—covering the Civil War and Reconstruction periods—temporarily disrupted the normal pattern of army politics, eroding officers' inclination to remain aloof from the civilian political forum and forcing them to confront national issues. Only with the end of Reconstruction did the army again extricate itself from the political mainstream.

Throughout most of the antebellum era, sectional concerns caused barely a ripple within the officer corps. Regional cliques existed among West Point cadets, based on life-style and culture, and sectional animosity no doubt simmered beneath the surface. A Massachusetts cadet claimed in 1836 that southern cadets "have a great contempt for our yankee farmers and even tend to compare them with their slaves—they have the greatest contempt for all those who gain a subsistance by the sweat of their brows." Two years later, he described how a debate on lynch law by the cadet dialectical society had gotten "very warm indeed" and nearly turned into a discussion of abolitionism— "a very tender subject—and for our society a very improper one."[2] Nevertheless, academy authorities labored to dampen sectional loyalties; they banned the discussion of slavery, discouraged cadets generally from engaging in politics, and continually underscored the national character of the military school. They seem to have succeeded, as cadets' letters and accounts mention very few cases of overt sectional antagonism before the late 1850s and many examples of strong intersectional friendships. In 1851, Cadet J. E. B. Stuart noted the predominantly southern flavor of West Point society. "But we are far from entertaining towards each other as marked antipathy as the times would suggest were we 'cits,' but there seems to be a sentiment of mutual forbearance, in a word, with us all is harmony."[3]

After graduation, the conditions of army life further muted sectional friction. During and for several years after the War of 1812, regiments had carried strong regional identities, reflecting the state-oriented appointment policies of the wartime buildup. As late as 1823, all thirteen officers of the First Artillery Regiment above the rank of first lieutenant were from the Northeast, and only three officers of the Second Infantry had been born in slave states. Conversely, southern officers predominated in the First, Fourth, and Seventh Infantry regiments, units customarily stationed on the southern frontiers.[4] After the reduction of 1821, however, the War Department appears to have sought geographical balance in assigning newly commissioned subalterns to their units; in any case, the regionalism of the established regiments gradually faded and by the 1830s had largely disappeared. Regulars from North and South intermingled at virtually every army garrison, and the inescapable intimacy of social life imposed a high premium on the avoidance of contention. An observer whose father and two brothers served in the officer corps recalled that sectional topics were rarely discussed in the army: "not that these topics were avoided as painful by a tacit understanding, but for the same reason that, in social clubs and in well-ordered society, political and religious controversy is not considered to be in good taste."[5] Most officers were stationed outside their home region during long segments of their careers, and this experience tended to erode their parochialism.

The ideology and values of the officer corps reinforced the army's inclination to avoid sectional discord. As discussed previously, the conception of the army as an apolitical instrument of public policy, dedicated to serving a unified nation, emerged in the antebellum era as a central feature of the officer corps's collective worldview. Obviously, this image was incompatible with fervent expressions of sectional allegiance. Although the army contained a few avowed abolitionists, most regulars held conservative views on the slavery question and the rights of blacks—views that arose from their hierarchical social values and were strengthened in many cases by prolonged service in slaveholding regions. Although his leanings were sufficiently antislavery that he was offered the governorship of Liberia, Captain Ethan Allen Hitchcock of Vermont opposed abolitionism and considered "the great body of negros, especially on plantations . . . better situated than the lower orders as they are called of any other country." While stationed in Georgia in 1845, a Rhode Island–born captain sent his abolitionist mother a proslavery pamphlet: "Slavery in its social aspect appears to me, here, in no unfavorable light; for all the servants are as well treated here as at the north, and appear to be even more happy." Admitting slavery to be a curse, he nevertheless thought that it "must remain until means, not yet apparent, are devised for its abatement or removal." On a trip across Florida in 1856, Lieutenant Alexander S. Webb of New York witnessed the pursuit of an escaped slave with hounds and horses: "I never thought I could stand such a sight, but I have the evidence of the necessity for such action now."[6] Indeed, many regulars, northerners as well as southerners, owned slaves whom they used as personal servants. Dred Scott, whose master was Assistant Surgeon John Emerson of Pennsylvania, was only the most famous of a number of officers' slaves to reside at military posts in territory officially barred to slavery.[7]

One factor buttressing officers' conservativism about slavery was the use of the army for slave control. Regulars only rarely acted to suppress slave revolts, but military garrisons in the South served as a potential reserve for the local militia in policing the slave population and were of symbolic importance in relieving white anxieties. In fact, fear of slave revolts influenced the War Department's decisions on troop dispositions. In explaining the presence of an artillery company at the arsenal at Augusta, Georgia, for example, the commanding general wrote that he had "always denied the *moral* right of the U. States to pile up arms & ammunition, in a thick slave population, without placing a guard over such deposit."[8] Regulars from Fort Monroe marched to Southampton County, Virginia, when the Nat Turner rebellion erupted in

1831, and other detachments responded to calls from jittery local officials during the months that followed. The Second Seminole War could also be classified as a slave revolt, since it was partly an attempt to crush the population of former slaves and their descendants who had taken refuge with the Seminoles and who were determined to defend their freedom. Captain John T. Sprague, the Massachusetts-born chronicler of the war, described these blacks as "the most formidable foe, more blood-thirsty, active, and revengeful, than the Indian."[9]

Regulars' journals and private letters indicate few signs of strong sectional alignments within the officer corps. Instead, they reveal networks of friends and colleagues, sometimes centering on West Point classes or common branches of the service but usually crossing sectional lines. For example, lieutenants Braxton Bragg of North Carolina, Henry J. Hunt of Ohio, and James Duncan of New York were close comrades who collaborated in promoting artillery interests in the 1840s. When Lieutenant Isaac Ingalls Stevens of Massachusetts organized the engineer officers' lobby in the early 1850s, he communicated personally with regulars from both North and South. After his graduation in 1835, Lieutenant Abraham R. Johnston of Ohio corresponded frequently with other young officers, including lieutenants Philip Kearny of New York, Henry L. Kendrick of New Hampshire, and Robert H. Chilton and Henry S. Turner of Virginia. On a visit to Washington, D.C., in 1858, Lieutenant Dabney H. Maury of Virginia had a reunion with army friends from Pennsylvania, Maine, Indiana, and Virginia, where they "told the old stories about West Point &c &c."[10]

Only in times of crisis did sectional tensions appear in the officer corps, and until the late 1850s these were of very minor significance. During South Carolina's nullification of the federal tariff in 1832–1833, rumors of potential disaffection within the units in or ordered to Charleston led the administration to require all officers at that garrison to sign a loyalty statement. The principal suspect was Captain Francis S. Belton, a Maryland native, who at a Fourth of July dinner in 1830 had offered a toast to South Carolina's independence. Belton denied that he supported nullification, however, and insisted that his toast had referred to independence from Great Britain, not the United States—a claim that appears plausible from the context of his remarks.[11] The controversy over the expansion of slavery into the West during and after the Mexican War sharpened the sectional identities of some officers. Captain Braxton Bragg hoped that the South would take a firm stand in 1848; although he feared a confrontation, Lieutenant William M. Gardner affirmed his willingness to support the South. However, Lieutenant Colonel Gustavus Loomis probably came closer to expressing the views of the majority of the officer corps in a letter to Minnesota's territorial delegate in 1850: "What a spectacle would be presented by our country being in a state of civil war!! The most enlightened country in the world quarreling because one part say you shant take niggers *there* & the other saying I will, not only *there*, but where I please. I hope Old Zack will have firmness enough to bring up those who become obnoxious to the laws without regard to party."[12]

The army's first notable exposure to the developing impasse was the sectional violence in Kansas Territory that erupted in 1855. Early in 1856, the War Department ordered the commanders at forts Leavenworth and Riley to dispatch forces on the request of the territorial governor "for the suppression of insurrectionary combinations or armed resistance to the execution of the law." Through the year, regulars were embroiled in extremely complex constabulary operations, supporting the efforts of the territorial authorities to make arrests, hunting down and dispersing armed bands, and on occasion intervening physically between the rival groups to prevent bloodshed. As always in such situations, the haziness of the army's mandate generated civil-military tensions. In response to a request by the acting governor, Colonel Edwin V. Sumner broke up a meeting of the extralegal free-soil legislature at Topeka; for his action, the Massachusetts-born commander and cousin of antislavery senator Charles Sumner was sent on extended leave and reprimanded for overstepping his authority by Secretary of War Jefferson Davis. Although the major violence had subsided by the end of 1856, army detachments continued for some time to serve as a *posse comitatus* under the orders of the territorial governors.[13]

For some regulars, the Kansas troubles brought premonitions of impending disaster. Writing from Fort Leavenworth in September 1856, Lieutenant John P. Hatch predicted "a civil war ending in a dissolution of the Union" unless the government took immediate action. The aggressive conduct of the proslavery forces whetted Captain Nathaniel Lyon's free-soil sentiments; he opposed further northern concessions and foresaw "ultimate sectional strife which I do not care to delay." To most officers on the scene, however, the Kansas skirmishes appeared as a problem of law and order, brought on by incompetent or designing politicians and by greedy land speculators, and subjecting the army once again to public abuse. A New York–born lieutenant assessed the situation at the end of 1856.

> The army has been made the scapegoat throughout this whole *imbroglio*. The pro-slavery men denounce it, because it don't do all they require of it; and the Free-State men complain that it is merely here to help Kansas to become a Slave-State. I think neither party has any cause of complaint

against the army. The officers obey orders, and keep the people from murdering and violence—and in my opinion act with great prudence and discretion. If it were not for the interposition of the army here, there would be a civil war which would soon spread and involve the North and South in deadly conflict.[14]

Whatever their private views, commanders of both northern and southern backgrounds maintained a scrupulously neutral posture throughout the turmoil that reflected the maturing service ethic of the officer corps.

As politics polarized North against South during the late 1850s, officers found it increasingly difficult to remain detached from the general political milieu. The prospect of a sectional split threatened not only the survival of the army but their individual careers within it. Moreover, the dissolution of the Whig party and its replacement by the Republicans eroded the traditional bipartisanship of the officer corps. Although a former regular, John C. Frémont, headed the first Republican presidential ticket, the officer corps took on a decidedly Democratic flavor; whatever the flaws of that older party, it represented the best hope to placate the South and avoid a disruption of the Union. Of the officers whose party affiliations are positively known for the period 1856–1860, twenty-nine (72.5 percent) were Democrats, eight (20 percent) were Republicans, and three (7.5 percent) supported the Constitutional Union ticket in 1860. The Democratic advantage was probably greater than these figures indicate, since southern-born officers were sure to be almost unanimous in opposing the Republicans. Although a number of northern officers did not express their allegiances directly in their correspondence, their emphasis on moderation and compromise and their conservative opinions about slavery strongly imply "doughface" Democratic leanings. Captain Randolph B. Marcy of Massachusetts reported that all the officers at Fort Brown, Texas, rejoiced in the election of James Buchanan in 1856, as a Republican victory would have "ruined the army, if not the Union." Captain Abner Doubleday was the only one of the nine officers of the Charleston garrison to favor Lincoln in 1860.[15]

The election of 1860 and the five-month secession debate that ensued finally forced the officer corps into an inescapable crisis of loyalty. Some southern officers, most but by no means all from the Lower South, showed little hesitation in casting their lot with the Confederacy. Angry at what they considered northern aggression, pessimistic about the possibility of lasting compromise, perhaps ambitious to exercise high rank in a new army, these commanders submitted their resignations as soon as—and in some cases before—their home states seceded. In the judgment of Captain James J. Archer of Maryland, Lincoln's election meant that the "permanent sectional hostile majority" would soon trample on southern rights, and he saw no recourse but the "reserved right of secession." He was disgusted by his state's failure to secede and resigned in May 1861 to become a colonel and later brigadier general in the Confederate army. Similarly, Major James Longstreet of Alabama had few misgivings about his decision to resign in April. He saw no grounds for accommodation and thought the South "should be wanting in self respect" if it made another overture. As early as December 1860, Captain Lafayette McLaws had decided to go with his native Georgia, even if it meant breaking up his family. "Great will be the tribulation and many the heart breakings," he wrote his Kentucky-born wife, whom he thought would stand by the Union. "But be prepared for the struggle. I certainly will not be in the Northern Confederacy, and let me beg you not to prejudice the children beforehand." A Mississippian, Major Earl Van Dorn expressed his support "for secession at every cost."[16]

The weight of the evidence, however, indicates that most of the officer corps, northerners and southerners alike, approached the crisis with considerable trepidation. A civil war was one conflict they wished to avoid, and they tended to blame the state of affairs on politicians, whom they accused alternately of self-serving opportunism and blind fanaticism. "Most [congressmen] are more interested in making sensation speeches for their immediate constituents than in working for the good of the country," a Virginian officer wrote a comrade from Ohio. "I have heretofore thought them to be harmless; but they have finally succeeded in bringing the country to the verge of dissolution, if not to the fact." He was gratified that the national trauma "has not had the effect of dissolving the good feeling usually existing among officers of the Army for each other." Although he agreed to fight for the Union, a Pennsylvanian sympathized with the South's plight and reviled Republicans as "fanatics who regard the principles (?) of a political party as paramount to the interests of their country and the welfare of a few miserable negroes of more importance than the perpetuity of the American Union." An especially conservative Michigan captain believed that the root of the conflict lay in the linking of universal manhood suffrage with abolitionist fanaticism, which threatened the South's property rights. He favored "an hereditary Executive, an hereditary Senate, property qualification for voters; property qualification for Representatives, one Legislature for all the land,—no states."[17]

Although many southern-born regulars ultimately chose to support the Confederacy, they did so reluctantly, after wrestling with their consciences. The most famous such figure was Colonel Robert E. Lee, who was deeply saddened by the trend toward disunion but decided to follow his state, rejecting the administration's offer of the command of the army that would crush the rebellion. Stationed in New Mexico before his resignation, Captain Cadmus M. Wilcox of North Carolina wrote an old army friend that he could take no pride in calling himself "a citizen of the Southern Republic. I do not feel even now that I have a country[;] thus far in my profession, I have never known any difference between the North & South, have as many friends in the one section as the other." Captain George E. Pickett likewise opposed secession, but he decided in the end that his family ties were stronger than his national identity. "I could not be an infidel and lift my sword against my own kith and kin," he explained to his future wife, "even though I do believe, . . . that the measure of American greatness can be achieved only under one flag." Torn between clashing loyalties, Major Alfred Mordecai of North Carolina rejected an offer to head either the Confederate ordnance service or engineer department; instead, he resigned and withdrew from the conflict altogether. According to a northern officer, "a large majority of the officers who went South did not go until all hope of averting separation or war had fled."[18]

In the end, 269 regulars left the army to join the Confederacy between the election of 1860 and the summer of 1861, representing 24.7 percent of the total strength of the officer corps. Twenty-six others, mainly from the border states and the Upper South, resigned and declined to serve on either side.[19] A breakdown of those who resigned or were dismissed and later served in the Confederate army indicates that rank was a relatively minor factor; their distribution by rank resembled closely that of the officer corps as a whole on the eve of secession (see Table 18.1). The one exception to this generalization was the high-ranking officers in the line and military staff departments. Of the 30 general and field-grade officers born in the seceding states (excluding paymasters), only 12 (40 percent) joined the Confederacy, compared with 68 percent of all the officers born in those states. Understandably, senior commanders, some of whom had worn the uniform for four decades or more and were too old for active service, were more reluctant than their younger comrades to sever their institutional ties.

A more important factor than rank affecting the resignation pattern was the region of the South from which an officer came. As Table 18.2 reveals, four-fifths of the regulars born in the Lower South sided with the Confederacy, compared with under three-fifths of those from Arkansas, Tennessee, and Virginia, and just over one-quarter of those from the nonseceding slave states and the District of Columbia. Although officers most often referred to state loyalty as the cause of their resignations, these figures suggest that family and community ties were paramount.[20] Presumably, a principled desire to support one's state in secession would have exercised an equal pull on officers from all the se-

TABLE 18.1. Officers Leaving the U.S. Army to Join the Confederacy, by Rank

Rank	Officers Joining CSA N	Officers Joining CSA %	Rank as % of Total Officer Corps 1860
Second lieutenant	57	21.2	22.2
First lieutenant	77	28.6	25.9
Captain	80	29.7	26.7
Major	22	8.2	8.4
Lieutenant colonel	3	1.1	2.7
Colonel	5	1.9	2.9
General	2	0.7	0.5
Assistant surgeon	20	7.4	7.8
Surgeon	3	1.1	2.8
Total	269		

Source: Francis B. Heitman, comp., *Historical Register and Dictionary of the United States Army, from Its Organization, September 29, 1789, to March 2, 1903* (Washington, D.C.: Government Printing Office, 1903).

TABLE 18.2. Officers Staying in the U.S. Army or Joining the Confederacy, by Region of Birth*

Region	Joined CSA (%)	Stayed USA (%)	Resigned and Withdrew (%)	Total
Lower South (N.C., S.C., Ga., Fla., Ala., Miss., La., Texas)	100 (79.4)	20 (15.9)	6 (4.8)	126
Upper South (Va., Tenn., Ark.)	93 (58.9)	57 (36.1)	8 (5.1)	158
Border (Del., Md., Ky., Mo., D.C.)	48 (27.4)	118 (67.4)	9 (5.1)	175
North	28 (4.5)	597 (95.1)	3 (0.5)	628
Total	269 (24.7)	792 (72.9)	26 (2.4)	1,087

Source: Francis B. Heitman, comp., *Historical Register and Dictionary of the United States Army, from Its Organization, September 29, 1789, to March 2, 1903* (Washington, D.C.: Government Printing Office, 1903).

*Foreign-born officers and officers whose places of birth are unknown have been grouped by place of appointment.

ceding states. Yet regulars born in the Lower South, where public opinion strongly ratified the break, were far more likely to resign than those born in the Upper South, where the population was deeply divided on the secession issue and where regional pockets of dedicated unionism existed. Moreover, state loyalty cannot explain the resignations of the large group of officers born in the similarly divided slave states that did not secede.

A look at the officers who were most prominent in bucking their sectional trends gives further confirmation of the primacy of family as an influence on officers' decisions. Of the twenty regulars born in the Lower South who stayed with the Union, at least four and probably five had actually been appointed from northern states, suggesting that they and their families had long since shed their southern identities. The family ties of others encouraged them to support the federal government: At least three were the sons of postmasters, one was the son of a regular army officer from Pennsylvania who had been serving in Florida at the time of his son's birth, and another was the son-in-law of General Winfield Scott, who stayed with the Union. Similarly, seven of the twenty-eight northern-born regulars who fought for the Confederacy had been appointed from slave states. At least ten others were married to southern women, and an additional three had strong family connections to the South.

For most army officers, as no doubt for most nineteenth-century Americans, the constitutional question of states' rights versus federal supremacy was less central than traditional loyalties rooted in kinship and locality. When push finally came to shove during the secession winter and spring, relatively few regulars were sufficiently committed to their profession—or to the nation in the abstract—to pit themselves against their families and home communities. In his memoirs, Edward P. Alexander recalled his decision to resign as a young engineer lieutenant stationed at San Francisco early in 1861. His senior officer, Lieutenant James B. McPherson, had urged him to sit out the war on the West Coast, but Alexander had declined, saying that his people thought they were struggling for liberty. "If I don't come and bear my part, they will believe me to be a coward," Alexander had told McPherson. "And I shall not know whether I am or not. I have just *got* to go and stand my chances."[21]

With some exceptions—most notably Brigadier General David E. Twiggs, who surrendered the Department of Texas to Confederate officials, then became a Confederate major general—southern officers performed their duties faithfully until they relinquished their commissions and left for the war.[22] At military garrisons across the continent, the breakup was accompanied by surprisingly little animosity. Dabney H. Maury described his trip east, after his decision to join the southern cause: "At every Post upon our route the same kindly feeling met us, and at parting we were told: 'I hate to lose you, old fellow, but you are perfectly right. If I were in your place, I would do the same thing.'" The northern and southern officers in Washington at the time of Lincoln's inauguration commiserated with each other on the state of the nation. One recalled that "the chiefest and last lingering hope among us was that no gun would be fired and that some miraculous thing would come out of the Peace Congress or the Crittenden proposition or from some source by which the terrible strain of the situation might be relieved." At West Point in late April 1861, the cadets serenaded Captain Truman Seymour, who had served at Fort Sumter, and Lieutenant Fitzhugh Lee, who was leaving to join the Confederacy.[23]

CONCLUSION

On the eve of the Civil War, the army officer corps was an institution far removed from the cantankerous collection of individuals that had commanded the army of the early republic. A majority of regulars were now careerists who had experienced an intensive and remarkably uniform program of professional socialization. A military subculture had arisen, rooted in tightly knit garrison communities and strengthened by marriage and kinship ties, that reinforced the norms instilled at the military academy. Although garrison and constabulary duties continued to dominate the careers of most regulars, a significant proportion of the officer corps identified with the army's preparedness role and gave serious thought to such professional subjects as tactics, materiel, education, and policy. Through common training and service patterns, regulars had come to share a complex of ideas and values—in effect, a collective "military mind." Among its components were hierarchical and authoritarian social values, a positive identification with the service world, and a sense of isolation from the mainstream of civilian society. In the Mexican War, the emerging military profession had passed with flying colors its first major combat test and acquired a powerful legacy of group pride and heroic tradition. Of immense significance for the future of civil-military relations, the officer corps had quietly developed a professional ethic—a grudging acceptance of the primacy of civil authority and a commitment to politically neutral public service. Although regulars remained politically active, they focused on professional issues, especially individual and branch interests, and thus they posed no collective threat to the political order.

The consolidation of the military profession loosely paralleled developments in other American professions during the antebellum era. Although the egalitarian impulse of the Age of Jackson brought about the decline of formal licensing procedures and other corporate privileges, professional attitudes did not disappear. Reacting to widespread public distrust, lawyers used law magazines to develop a group image that distinguished law from politics and stressed the objectivity and social utility of their calling. The tension between regulars and citizen-soldiers had its analogue in the struggle of the orthodox medical profession against such irregular practices as Thomsonianism and homeopathy. Among physicians as well as officers, the emphasis was on professional education, internal standards, and a scientific approach to their field of responsibility as means to distinguish themselves from their rivals and justify their collective existence before a skeptical public. Likewise, civil engineers and scientists demonstrated growing corporate awareness.[1] Therefore, the rise of the military profession was not a unique event but part of a broader trend toward specialized education, group consciousness, and social responsibility that characterized the professions generally in the antebellum era. Where officers differed from their civilian counterparts was in their ability to retain and even extend their formal structure, including the practical control of licensing, in a time of institutional flux. In this respect at least, regulars served as a model for other professional men.

An interesting comparison may be made between the army officer corps and the professional group that resembled it most closely: the naval officer corps. During the 1790s and early 1800s, faced with almost continual war or quasi-war, naval officers reached a level of professional cohesion and competence far in advance of their army counterparts. This achievement resulted from sound civilian management in the Navy Department, and it also reflected the early emergence of a solid nucleus of exceptionally able, battle-proven leaders, many of whose backgrounds had been in the merchant marine. More important, the navy's performance was based on an effective system for the shipboard training and socialization of newly appointed midshipmen, geared to the recognition of merit, that weeded out incompetents and infused a high degree of proficiency into the junior and middle grades of the officer corps.[2]

Having early reached this plateau, the naval profession experienced stasis and even decline in the decades after the War of 1812. While army reformers, spurred by memories of failure in the early war years, renovated military management and education and sought to incorporate European standards, the navy's War of 1812 generation continued to rely on the formula that had brought wartime success. Entrenched in the Board of Navy Commissioners, senior captains resisted the introduction of steam power, ship armor, and other technological innovations. Moreover, the system of professional training fell into decay, as administrations appointed far more midshipmen than the navy required, many of whom remained permanently inactive. Through the 1830s, the naval officer corps was riven by personal dissension and factional rivalry that surely exceeded tensions in the army, and morale plummeted to a low ebb.

Late in the decade, a reform movement took shape, led by energetic younger officers who had come of rank since the War of 1812. In response to their proposals, the government replaced the ossified Board of Navy Commissioners in 1842 with a bureau system closely resembling the army General Staff, established a naval academy in 1845 that evolved along the general lines of West Point, and supported developments in steam warships and naval ordnance that paralleled the concurrent activities of the army's Corps of Engineers and Ordnance Department. Moreover, naval life coalesced into a distinct subculture, perhaps even more isolated and elitist than its army analogue.[3] By the outbreak of the Civil War, the two services had achieved roughly comparable levels of professional development.

The Civil War split the army officer corps, but it by no means destroyed the military profession. Mobilizing their political sponsors, active-duty regulars and former officers who had resigned scrambled for high commissions in the vast volunteer army raised in the North. During the war, men who had held commissioned rank in the peacetime regular service composed 43.9 percent of the general officers in the Union army and 36.7 percent of those in the Confederate army, including in both cases the great majority of army and corps commanders.[4] The procedures, traditions, and personal loyalties of the antebellum army suffused the high command levels of the rival forces and shaped in myriad ways the conduct of the war: strategy, tactics, logistics, staff operations, and civil-military relations.[5] After the war, the unprecedented problems of reconstructing the South and the constitutional turmoil leading to the impeachment of Andrew Johnson temporarily eroded the barrier separating the officer corps from civilian politics. Commanders exercised extensive political power in the defeated states, and they briefly allied with Radical Republican leaders to resist Johnson's policy of conciliation toward the former Confederate leadership, which appeared to endanger the hard-won victory.[6] As the war emergency receded, however, the army concentrated once more on its customary constabulary duties, and prewar patterns of thought and behavior reemerged.

With the waning of the Indian campaigns in the late nineteenth century, the officer corps embarked on a renewed effort at reform and professionalization. Responding to developments in Europe—and to internal concerns about the future of the army and their personal careers within it—regulars increasingly stressed the need to modernize their institution to keep pace with the dominant military powers. Military reformers revived and expanded the army's postgraduate school system, sponsored a lyceum project to encourage professional study at the post level, developed new institutions to gather and preserve military knowledge, modernized the program of seacoast fortification, and nurtured an expanding web of professional associations and journals. After the Spanish-American War revealed the need for greater coordination and planning within the army's command structure, the government replaced the office of commanding general with a new general staff system modelled on the German army, set up a war college as the capstone of the army's educational program, and took steps to harmonize the regular army and the militia, now formed as the national guard. By the early twentieth century, the army was gradually shedding its constabulary garb for a new mission as the military instrument of a modern world power.[7]

Rather than a radical departure from the past, however, these reforms represented an extension of the army's preparedness role, as originally defined by the War of 1812 generation of officers and nurtured by the officer corps through the antebellum era. In general, the "new" military professionalism of the late nineteenth century built on solid foundations laid in the old army: the West Point system of professional education and socialization; the long-term career patterns and the close-knit texture of the military subculture; the conception of the army as a specialized cadre oriented toward foreign war; the separation of the army from the civilian political forum; and the internalization of the officer corps's commitment to nonpartisan national service.

NOTES

Abbreviations

AGO:LR	Records of the Office of the Adjutant General. Letters Received by the Office of the Adjutant General, 1805–1821, 1822–1860
AGO:LS	Records of the Office of the Adjutant General. Letters Sent by the Office of the Adjutant General, 1800–1890
AGO: Orders and Circulars	Records of the Office of the Adjutant General. General Orders and Circulars of the War Department and General Headquarters of the Army, 1809–1860
ASP:MA	U.S. Congress. *American State Papers*. Class V: *Military Affairs*. 7 vols. Washington, D.C., 1832–1861
ASP:Misc.	U.S. Congress. *American State Papers*. Class X: *Miscellaneous*. 2 vols. Washington, D.C., 1834
BDC	U.S. Congress. *Biographical Directory of the American Congress, 1774–1961*. Washington, D.C., 1961
DAB	Johnson, Allen, and Dumas Malone, eds. *Dictionary of American Biography*. 21 vols. New York, 1928–1937
GCM Proceedings	Records of the Office of the Judge Advocate General (Army). Proceedings of U.S. Army General Courts-Martial, 1809–1890
HQA:LR	Records of the Headquarters of the Army. Letters Received by the Headquarters of the Army, 1828–1903
HQA:LS	Records of the Headquarters of the Army. Letters Sent by the Headquarters of the Army, 1828–1903
JEP	U.S. Congress. Senate. *Journal of the Executive Proceedings of the Senate of the United States of America*. 90 vols. Washington, D.C., 1828–1948

SW: Applications — Records of the Office of the Secretary of War. Applications

SW:LR-Reg. — Records of the Office of the Secretary of War. Letters Received by the Secretary of War, Registered Series, 1801–1870

SW:LR-Unreg. — Records of the Office of the Secretary of War. Letters Received by the Secretary of War, Unregistered Series, 1789–1861

SW:LS — Records of the Office of the Secretary of War. Letters Sent by the Secretary of War Relating to Military Affairs, 1800–1889

CHAPTER ONE. ARMY ORGANIZATION IN THE EARLY NATIONAL PERIOD

1. Douglas E. Leach, *Roots of Conflict: British Armed Forces and Colonial Americans, 1677–1783* (Chapel Hill: University of North Carolina Press, 1986), passim; John Shy, *Toward Lexington: The Role of the British Army in the Coming of the American Revolution* (Princeton, N.J.: Princeton University Press, 1965), passim; Lawrence D. Cress, *Citizens in Arms: The Army and the Militia in American Society to the War of 1812* (Chapel Hill: University of North Carolina Press, 1982), 1–50; Don Higginbotham, *The War of American Independence: Military Attitudes, Policies, and Practice, 1763–1789* (New York: Macmillan, 1971), 29–53.

2. Richard H. Kohn, *Eagle and Sword: The Federalists and the Creation of the Military Establishment in America, 1783–1802* (New York: Free Press, 1975), passim.

3. Ibid., 54–62.

4. Ibid., 62–72.

5. Worthington C. Ford, ed., *Journals of the Continental Congress, 1774–1789*, 34 vols. (Washington, D.C.: Government Printing Office, 1904–1937), 31:891–893, 33:719–722.

6. Joseph P. Warren, "The Confederation and the Shays Rebellion," *American Historical Review* 11 (October 1905): 42–67.

7. Harry M. Ward, *The Department of War, 1781–1795* (Pittsburgh: University of Pittsburgh Press, 1962), 7–125.

8. James R. Jacobs, *The Beginning of the U.S. Army, 1783–1812* (Princeton, N.J.: Princeton University Press, 1947), 40–65, 85–123; Wiley Sword, *President Washington's Indian War: The Struggle for the Old Northwest, 1790–1795* (Norman: University of Oklahoma Press, 1985), 79–200.

9. Acts of March 3, 1791, and March 5, 1792, Abner R. Hetzel, comp., *Military Laws of the United States* (Washington, D.C.: G. Templeman, 1846), 45, 48.

10. Jacobs, *Beginning of U.S. Army*, 124–175; Sword, *President Washington's Indian War*, 201–331.

11. Act of May 9, 1794, Hetzel, *Military Laws*, 54–55.

12. Ward, *Department of War*, 142–188; Erna Risch, *Quartermaster Support of the Army: A History of the Corps, 1775–1939* (Washington, D.C.: Office of the Quartermaster General, 1962), 81–113; statement of quarterly salaries paid War Department per-

sonnel, March 31, 1794, Henry Knox Papers, Massachusetts Historical Society, Boston; Acts of March 3, 1791, March 5, 1792, and May 8, 1792, Hetzel, *Military Laws,* 45–46, 49, 51.

13. Act of May 30, 1796, Hetzel, *Military Laws,* 62–63; Kohn, *Eagle and Sword,* 182–186.

14. Timothy Pickering, "Objects of the Military Establishment of the United States," February 3, 1796, and James McHenry to Abraham Baldwin, March 14, 1796, *ASP:MA,* 1:112–113, 114.

15. The principal acts expanding the regular army during the Quasi-war were those of April 27, 1798; July 16, 1798; March 2, 1799; and March 3, 1799—Hetzel, *Military Laws,* 69, 80–82, 83–85, 89–96.

16. Kohn, *Eagle and Sword,* 193–255.

17. Ibid., 256–273; Act of May 14, 1800, Hetzel, *Military Laws,* 98.

18. Act of March 16, 1802, Hetzel, *Military Laws,* 99–105; Theodore J. Crackel, *Mr. Jefferson's Army: Political and Social Reform of the Military Establishment, 1801–1809* (New York: New York University Press, 1987), 36–45. Crackel argues that the act of 1802 was intended mainly to "Republicanize" the army rather than to significantly reduce its strength.

19. Risch, *Quartermaster Support,* 99–105.

20. Crackel, *Mr. Jefferson's Army,* 98–157; Jacobs, *Beginning of U.S. Army,* 309–341.

21. Act of April 12, 1808, Hetzel, *Military Laws,* 125–127. For the debate in the House of Representatives in March and April 1808, see U.S. Congress, *Annals of the Congress of the United States, 1789–1824,* 42 vols. (Washington, D.C.: Gales and Seaton, 1834–1856), 10th Cong., 1st sess. (hereafter cited as *Annals of Congress*).

22. Jacobs, *Beginning of U.S. Army,* 345–352; Mary C. Gillett, *The Army Medical Department, 1775–1818* (Washington, D.C.: Government Printing Office, 1981), 140–143.

23. Act of January 11, 1812, Hetzel, *Military Laws,* 133–138; Henry Adams, *History of the United States during the Administrations of Thomas Jefferson and James Madison,* 9 vols. (New York: C. Scribner's Sons, 1909–1911), 6:154.

24. The military legislation of the War of 1812 years is printed in Hetzel, *Military Laws,* 138–182. For the organization of the army in 1814, see Francis B. Heitman, comp., *Historical Register and Dictionary of the United States Army, from Its Organization, September 29, 1789, to March 2, 1903,* 2 vols. (Washington, D.C.: Government Printing Office, 1903), 2:576–577. For the administration of the war effort, see generally J. C. A. Stagg, *Mr. Madison's War: Politics, Diplomacy, and Warfare in the Early American Republic, 1783–1830* (Princeton, N.J.: Princeton University Press, 1983).

25. In 1813, approximately 622 of the 3,260 officers (19.1 percent) performed staff functions; compiled from table of organization in Heitman, *Historical Register,* 2:574–575.

26. On supply problems in the War of 1812, see Risch, *Quartermaster Support,* 135–180.

CHAPTER TWO. RECRUITING AN OFFICER CORPS, 1784–1815

1. Christopher Duffy, *The Military Experience in the Age of Reason* (New York: Atheneum, 1988), 35–46.

2. T. H. Breen, "English Origins and New World Development: The Case of the Covenanted Militia in Seventeenth-Century Massachusetts," *Past & Present,* no. 56

(November 1972):74–96; Douglas E. Leach, *Arms for Empire: A Military History of the British Colonies in North America, 1607–1763* (New York: Macmillan, 1973), 16–17; Charles S. Sydnor, *American Revolutionaries in the Making: Political Practices in Washington's Virginia* (New York: Collier, 1962), 84–85; Richard L. Boucher, "The Colonial Militia as a Social Institution: Salem, Massachusetts 1764–1775," *Military Affairs* 38 (December 1973):126–127.

3. Don Higginbotham, *War and Society in Revolutionary America: The Wider Dimensions of Conflict* (Columbia: University of South Carolina Press, 1988), 19–38; Harold E. Selesky, *War and Society in Colonial Connecticut* (New Haven, Conn.: Yale University Press, 1990), 194–215 and passim; Fred Anderson, *A People's Army: Massachusetts Soldiers and Society in the Seven Years' War* (Chapel Hill: University of North Carolina Press, 1984), 48–62 and passim.

4. George Washington to Col. Elisha Sheldon, December 16, 1776, in George Washington, *The Writings of George Washington from the Original Manuscript Sources, 1745–1799*, ed. John C. Fitzpatrick, 39 vols. (Washington, D.C.: Government Printing Office, 1931–1944), 6:386.

5. Charles Royster, *A Revolutionary People at War: The Continental Army and American Character, 1775–1783* (Chapel Hill: University of North Carolina Press, 1979), 86–87.

6. Articles VII and IX of Articles of Confederation, James D. Richardson, comp., *A Compilation of the Messages and Papers of the Presidents*, 20 vols. (New York: Bureau of National Literature, 1917), 1:12, 14–15.

7. "Register of the Army of the United States," 1789, Thomas H. S. Hamersly, comp., *Complete Regular Army Register of the United States for One Hundred Years (1779–1879)* (Washington, D.C.: T. H. S. Hamersly, 1880), 44–47; Francis B. Heitman, comp., *Historical Register and Dictionary of the United States Army, from Its Organization, September 29, 1789, to March 2, 1903*, 2 vols. (Washington, D.C.: Government Printing Office, 1903), 1:passim.

8. List of commissioned officers [1786] in "Regimental Book, First Regiment," Ebenezer Denny and James O'Hara Papers, Historical Society of Western Pennsylvania, Pittsburgh. Information in this and the following four paragraphs has been drawn from biographies and biographical dictionaries, genealogies, local histories, and other published and manuscript sources. For an extended analysis of the officer corps of the Confederation era, see William B. Skelton, "Social Roots of the American Military Profession: The Officer Corps of America's First Peacetime Army, 1784–1789," *Journal of Military History* 54 (October 1990):435–452.

9. On Wyllys, see *DAB*, 20:581–582; Linda G. DePauw, ed., *Documentary History of the First Federal Congress of the United States of America, March 4, 1789–March 3, 1791*, 3 vols. (Baltimore: Johns Hopkins University Press, 1972–1979), 2:48. On Ford, see Elizabeth C. S. Eastwood, *The Descendants of Andrew Ford of Weymouth, Massachusetts* (Montpelier, Vt., 1968), 47. On Beatty, see Harry B. Weiss and Grace M. Ziegler, *Colonel Erkuries Beatty, 1759–1823: Pennsylvania Revolutionary Soldier; New Jersey Judge, Senator, Farmer, and Prominent Citizen of Princeton* (Trenton, N.J.: Past Times Press, 1958), passim; John B. Linn, "Erkuries Beatty: Paymaster of the Western Army 1786–1788," *Magazine of American History* 1 (June 1877):372–373. On Sumner, see William S. Appleton, *Record of the Descendants of William Sumner, in Dorchester, Mass., 1636* (Boston, 1879), 38.

10. George A. Katzenberger, "Major David Ziegler," *Ohio State Archeological and Historical Quarterly* 21 (April–July 1912):127–174; David Ziegler to Timothy Pickering, March 18, 1799, Timothy Pickering Papers, Massachusetts Historical Society,

Boston; Alfred Andrews, *Genealogical History of Deacon Stephen Hart, and His Descendants, 1632-1875* (Hartford, Conn.: Case, Lockwood and Brainard, 1875), 394-395; Jonathan Heart, *Journal of Capt. Jonathan Heart . . . to Which Is Added the Dickinson-Harmar Correspondence of 1784-5,* ed. Consul W. Butterfield (Albany, N.Y.: J. Munsell's Co., 1885), vii-viii; Franklin B. Dexter, *Biographical Sketches of the Graduates of Yale College with Annals of the College History, 1701-1815,* 6 vols. (New York: H. Holt, 1885-1912), 3:279-282; Major John Doughty to Henry Knox, March 12, 1785, Henry Knox Papers, Massachusetts Historical Society, Boston.

11. Henry Knox to George Washington, July 11, 1791; list of nominations for appointment and promotion, submitted by Knox to Washington, October 31, 1791; Tobias Lear to Knox, February 27, 1792, George Washington Papers, Library of Congress.

12. Based on lists of nominations submitted to the Senate, *JEP,* 1:passim.

13. John Doughty to Henry Knox, March 8, 1791; Henry Jackson to Knox, March 27, 1791; William Hull to Knox, May 21, 1791; John Brooks to Knox, June 14, 1791, Knox Papers.

14. Samuel Newman to Henry Knox, January 17, 1790, and Henry Jackson to Knox, July 11, 1790, ibid.; Heitman, *Historical Register,* 1:745, 787.

15. William Heth to Henry Knox, July 22, 1789, Knox Papers; Heitman, *Historical Register,* 1:527. For similar cases, see William Lee, "Record of the Services of Constant Freeman, Captain of Artillery in the Continental Army," *Magazine of American History* 2 (June 1878): 349-360; Constant Freeman to Alexander J. Dallas, June 2, 1815, file 8393, National Archives, AGO:LR; William Littlefield to George Washington, September 24, 1789; Catherine Greene to Washington, August 6, 1790, Washington Papers.

16. Capt. Thomas Lewis to Maj. Gen. Anthony Wayne, January 24, 1793, and Capt. Alexander Gibson to Wayne, February 28, 1794, Anthony Wayne Papers, Historical Society of Pennsylvania, Philadelphia; Wayne to James McHenry, October 8, 1796, Richard C. Knopf, ed., *Anthony Wayne, a Name in Arms: Soldier, Diplomat, Defender of Expansion Westward of a Nation. The Wayne-Knox-Pickering-McHenry Correspondence* (Pittsburgh: University of Pittsburgh Press, 1960), 534-535; Harry M. Ward, *The Department of War, 1781-1795* (Pittsburgh: University of Pittsburgh Press, 1962), 147; Henry Knox to George Washington, September 15, 1792, and Washington to Knox, September 24, 1792, Washington Papers.

17. Among others, the following junior officers were sons of high-ranking revolutionary officers: Joseph Campbell (Lt. Col. Richard Campbell); Richard Butler (Lt. Col. William Butler); Matthias Slough, Jr. (Col. Matthias Slough); Andrew and John McClary (militia Maj. Andrew McClary); Henry M. Muhlenberg (Bvt. Brig. Gen. Peter Muhlenberg); Nanning J. Visscher (Lt. Col. John Visscher); William G. Cobb (Bvt. Brig. Gen. David Cobb); Solomon Van Rensselaer (militia Col. Henry Kilian Van Rensselaer).

18. Carl E. Prince, *The Federalists and the Origins of the Civil Service* (New York: New York University Press, 1977), passim. Dayton was the brother of Representative Jonathan Dayton of New Jersey; the fathers of Izard and Mitchell were senators Ralph Izard of South Carolina and Samuel W. Mitchell of Connecticut.

19. Henry Jackson to Henry Knox, April 10, 1791, Joseph G. Andrews to Knox, April 5, 1792, Knox Papers.

20. Richard Dillon, *Meriwether Lewis: A Biography* (New York: Coward-McCann, 1965), 6-20; William Preston to George Washington, May 10, 1792, Washington Papers; James G. Wilson and John Fiske, comps., *Appleton's Cyclopaedia of American Biog-*

raphy, 6 vols. (New York: D. Appleton, 1894), 5:114; Jerome O. Steffen, *William Clark: Jeffersonian Man on the Frontier* (Norman: University of Oklahoma Press, 1977), 13-21.

21. This and the following six paragraphs are based on an analysis of the list of army officers in 1797, in Hamersly, *Regular Army Register,* 47-49. Biographical information has been drawn from Heitman, *Historical Register;* biographical dictionaries; genealogies; local histories; and other published and manuscript sources.

22. On Mitchell, see Timothy Pickering to Henry Knox, August 1, 1798, Knox Papers; *DAB,* 13:65-66. On Lovell, see Henry Jackson to Knox, November 7, 1787, Knox Papers; *BDC,* 1237. On Salmon, see George Salmon to James McHenry, June 9, 1797 (photocopy), James McHenry Papers, Library of Congress.

23. Based on a survey of alumni registers of the following colleges: Brown, Columbia, Dartmouth, Dickinson, Harvard, Princeton, Rutgers, University of North Carolina, University of Pennsylvania, William and Mary, Yale. The graduates of European military schools were: Lt. Col. Stephen Rochefontaine; Maj. Lewis Tousard; and Lt. Joseph Guimpe.

24. Horace P. McClary, *A Sketch Covering Four Generations of the McClary Family* (Windsor, Vt., 1896), 13-26. The case of Frederick Frye was virtually identical—Elizabeth F. Barker, comp., *Frye Genealogy; Adrian of Kittery, Me., John of Andover, Mass., Joshua of Virginia, Thomas of Rhode Island* (New York: T. A. Wright, 1920), 61-62, 78-80.

25. Richard H. Kohn, *Eagle and Sword: The Federalists and the Creation of the Military Establishment in America, 1783-1802* (New York: Free Press, 1975), 193-229; quotation is on p. 227.

26. The most thorough discussion of this complex controversy is in Alexander Hamilton, *The Papers of Alexander Hamilton,* ed. Harold C. Syrett, 26 vols. (New York: Columbia University Press, 1961-1979), 22:4-17. See also Kohn, *Eagle and Sword,* 230-238.

27. *DAB,* 13:563; *Appleton's Cyclopaedia,* 6:382; Lt. Gen. George Washington to James McHenry, September 30, 1798, and October 15, 1798, *Writings of Washington,* 36:474, 490-491.

28. Robert Gough, "Officering the American Army, 1798," *William and Mary Quarterly,* 3d ser. 43 (July 1986):460-471.

29. James McHenry to Maj. Gen. Alexander Hamilton, January 21, 1799; Hamilton to McHenry, February 6, 1799, *Papers of Hamilton,* 22:428-430, 467. Hamilton continued to recommend the use of military appointments to win converts to Federalism; Hamilton to McHenry, January 19, 1800, ibid., 24:202.

30. *JEP,* 1:377-379.

31. Henry Dearborn to William White, May 29, 1805, National Archives, SW:LS.

32. In a recent study, Theodore Crackel has asserted that the Jefferson administration used junior officers' appointments to break the Federalist hold on the army. Crackel, *Mr. Jefferson's Army: Political and Social Reform of the Military Establishment, 1801-1809* (New York: New York University Press, 1987), 71-73. However, there is little positive evidence to support this position. A careful study of the early naval profession has uncovered very little evidence of partisan influence on naval appointments in this period. Christopher McKee, *A Gentlemanly and Honorable Profession: The Creation of the U.S. Naval Officer Corps, 1794-1815* (Annapolis, Md.: Naval Institute Press, 1991), 104-108.

33. Peter Gansevoort to Henry Dearborn, August 23, 1805, file 9, AGO:LR.

34. In 1788, Henry Knox reportedly authorized the employment of up to six "vol-

unteers or Cadets with the appointments or allowances of Sergeants"; Thomas Mifflin to Bvt. Brig. Gen. Josiah Harmar, May 9, 1788, Josiah Harmar Papers, William L. Clements Library, Ann Arbor, Mich. Monthly returns of the First Regiment for April 1, 1789, describe four young men as cadets "doing privates duty"; "Regimental Book, First Regiment," Denny and O'Hara Papers. Acts of May 9, 1794, April 27, 1798, and March 3, 1799, Abner R. Hetzel, comp., *Military Laws of the United States* (Washington, D.C.: G. Templeman, 1846), 54–55, 69, 89.

35. Act of March 16, 1802, Hetzel, *Military Laws*, 105.

36. Henry Dearborn to Capt. Nehemiah Freeman, November 6, 1805, SW:LS. The academy's first official set of regulations were only slightly more specific, requiring that incoming cadets be between fifteen and twenty years of age, "well versed in the English language, in writing & Arithmetic; . . . of good moral character and of sound Constitution"; William Eustis, "Regulations Relative to the Military Academy at West Point," April 30, 1810, ibid. The age restrictions were not rigidly enforced, and early in 1815, the superintendent complained that fourteen cadets were under age fourteen. Jared Mansfield, Andrew Ellicott, and Christian E. Zoeller to Secretary of War, January 2, 1815, file M–1815, National Archives, SW:LR-Unreg.; Capt. Alden Partridge to James Monroe, January 31, 1815, file P–205(8), National Archives, SW:LR-Reg.

37. Samuel Dexter to Maj. Thomas H. Cushing, March 3, 1801, SW:LS.

38. Based on George W. Cullum, comp., *Biographical Register of the Officers and Graduates of the U.S. Military Academy at West Point, N.Y., from Its Establishment, in 1802, to 1890; with the Early History of the United States Military Academy*, 3 vols. (Boston: Houghton, Mifflin, 1891), 1:51–110, and various other biographical sources.

39. Five prewar West Point graduates were members of prominent French-speaking families of the Upper Louisiana (Missouri) Territory, appointed as a gesture of friendship to the leadership of that newly acquired region. These men were Pascal V. Bouis, Auguste Chouteau, Charles Gratiot, Louis Loramier, and Louis Vallé.

40. *DAB*, 7:127–128, 8:212–213; Alice P. Kenney, *The Gansevoorts of Albany: Dutch Patricians in the Upper Hudson Valley* (Syracuse, N.Y.: Syracuse University Press, 1969), passim.

41. Compiled from *DAB, BDC, Appleton's Cyclopaedia*, and other sources. The congressmen and senators were Dearborn, Chandler, Armstrong, Hampton, Leonard Covington, Benjamin Howard (also a territorial governor), Andrew Jackson, and David Rogerson Williams. The governors were Lewis, Joseph Bloomfield, William Hull, and William H. Harrison. The state legislators were Lewis Cass, Duncan McArthur, Eleazar W. Ripley, Alexander Smyth, and James Winchester. The administration's chief concession to bipartisanship was the appointment of Thomas Pinckney, previously a Federalist congressman, as major general in 1812.

42. These men, with dates of appointment to general's rank, were James Wilkinson (1792), Thomas H. Cushing (1812), Zebulon M. Pike (1813), George Izard (1813), Alexander Macomb (1814), Thomas A. Smith (1814), Daniel Bissell (1814), Edmund P. Gaines (1814), and Winfield Scott (1814). A tenth candidate for this category, John P. Boyd, had been an ensign in the Massachusetts regiment of 1786–1787 and later a soldier of fortune in India, where he accumulated much wealth commanding armies under native princes. He was appointed colonel in 1808 and brigadier general in 1812. John P. Boyd to Henry Knox, February 12, 1799, Knox Papers; *DAB*, 2:526–527.

43. Henry Dearborn to Nicholas Gilman et al., April 14, 1808; Dearborn to Alexander Wolcott, April 15, 1808; SW:LS. On the partisanship of the 1808 appointments, see also Crackel, *Mr. Jefferson's Army*, 170–173.

44. Joseph P. Varnum to Henry Dearborn, April 20, 1808, file V-4(4), SW:LR-Reg.; Dearborn to William Eustis, May 2, 1808, William Eustis Papers, Library of Congress. See also Dearborn to Eustis, May 11, 1808, ibid.; Dearborn to Varnum, June 12, 1808, Henry Dearborn Papers, Library of Congress.

45. John Culpeper to Henry Dearborn, June 13, 1808, file 199; Thomas Blount to Dearborn, July 1808, file 174; Buckner Thruston to Dearborn, April 16, 1808, file 332, AGO:LR.

46. William H. Crawford to William Eustis, February 13, 1812, file C-179(6), SW:LR-Reg. The appointment policy of 1812 is explained in Stephen R. Bradley to James Elliot, February 23, 1812, file 1088, AGO:LR. The administration made some effort to broaden support for the war effort by appointing Federalists in 1812, though the result was to cause resentment among the Republicans. J.C.A. Stagg, *Mr. Madison's War: Politics, Diplomacy, and Warfare in the Early American Republic, 1783–1830* (Princeton, N.J.: Princeton University Press, 1983), 166–167. For the government's reliance on field officers' recommendations, see adjutant general to Col. Joseph Goodwyn, March 6, 1813; adjutant general to cols. Daniel Dana, Elias Fasset, Joseph D. Learned, and Isaac Lane, June 29, 1813, National Archives, AGO:LS.

47. Winfield Scott, *Memoirs of Lieut.-General Winfield Scott, L.L.D., Written by Himself,* 2 vols. (New York: Sheldon, 1864), 1:34–35, 36n.

48. Compiled from Heitman, *Historical Register,* 1:50–138; correspondence on appointments in AGO:LR, SW:LR-Reg., and SW:LR-Unreg.; and various biographical sources. The other occupational categories were: Farmer/Planter 30 (24.4 percent); Merchant/Storekeeper 21 (17.1 percent); Artisan 9 (7.3 percent); Editor 4 (3.3 percent); Manufacturer, Medical Doctor, Civil Officeholder, and Navy/Marine Officer each 3 (2.4 percent); Clerk/Accountant 2 (1.6 percent); Educator 1 (.8 percent). Generals and staff officers were not included.

49. For Constant, see Daniel D. Tompkins to Henry Dearborn, July 19, 1808, file T-107(4), SW:LR-Reg. For Larned, see *BDC,* 1194; Simon Larned to Brig. Gen. Thomas H. Cushing, November 4, 1812, file 1478, AGO:LR. For Tod, see *DAB,* 18:568–569. For Drayton, see ibid., 5:448; *BDC,* 829. For Bogardus, see Maria S. Gray, *A Genealogical History of the Ancestors and Descendants of General Robert Bogardus* (Boston, 1927), 93–106.

50. On the Blounts, see John H. Wheeler, *Reminiscences and Memoirs of North Carolina and Eminent North Carolinians: Genealogy of the Blount, Haywood and Phifer Families* (Washington, D.C.: Henkle and Co., 1885), lix–lxi; John G. Blount, *The John Gray Blount Papers,* ed. Alice B. Keith et al., 4 vols. (Raleigh, N.C.: State Department of Archives and History, 1952–1982), 4:xiv–xv. On Desha, see *BDC,* 803. On Jackson, see file 8703, AGO:LR; *BDC,* 1112. On Grosvenor, see file 15138, AGO:LR; *BDC,* 980. On the Pierces, see George W. Browne, *The History of Hillsborough, New Hampshire, 1735–1921,* 2 vols. (Manchester, N.H.: John B. Clarke, 1921–1922), 2:454–456, 461. On Bowie, see Effie G. Bowie, *Across the Years in Prince George's County; A Genealogical and Biographical History of Prince George's County, Maryland, and Allied Families* (Richmond: Garrett and Massie, 1947), 677–681.

51. *JEP,* 2:475–479, 492–496.

52. Capt. Thomas Ramsey to Edward Tiffen, April 2, 1815, and Josiah Meigs to James Madison, July 18, 1815, file 9289, AGO:LR; Carolyn T. Foreman, "General Bennet Riley: Commandant of Fort Gibson and Governor of California," *Chronicles of Oklahoma* 19 (June 1941): 225; file 1734, AGO:LR.

53. Maj. James Miller to Catherine Flint, July 30, 1808, James Miller Papers, U.S. Military Academy Library, West Point, N.Y.

CHAPTER THREE. MILITARY CAREERS IN THE EARLY REPUBLIC

1. Morris Janowitz, *The Professional Soldier: A Social and Political Portrait* (New York: Free Press, 1960), 54.
2. Brig. Gen. James Wilkinson to Maj. Gen. Anthony Wayne, November 1, 1792, Anthony Wayne Papers, Historical Society of Pennsylvania. Statistics on attrition calculated from "Register of the Army of the United States," 1789, in Thomas H. S. Hamersly, comp., *Complete Regular Army Register of the United States for One Hundred Years (1779–1879)* (Washington, D.C.: T. H. S. Hamersly, 1881), 44–47; Francis B. Heitman, comp., *Historical Register and Dictionary of the United States Army, from Its Organization, September 29, 1789, to March 2, 1903*, 2 vols. (Washington, D.C.: Government Printing Office, 1903), 1:passim.
3. Calculated from lists of military appointments for 1791–1792 and 1803–1807, *JEP*, 1 and 2:passim; Heitman, *Historical Register*, 1:passim.
4. Samuel P. Huntington, *The Soldier and the State: The Theory and Politics of Civil-Military Relations* (Cambridge: Harvard University Press, 1957), 28–30.
5. Brig. Gen. Edmund P. Gaines to unknown, [1815], file 7687, AGO:LR; Maj. Gen. Charles C. Pinckney to Maj. Gen. Alexander Hamilton, April 3, 1800, in Alexander Hamilton, *The Papers of Alexander Hamilton*, ed. Harold C. Syrett, 26 vols. (New York: Columbia University Press, 1961–1979), 24:386; Lt. Col. Rufus Graves to Hamilton, July 26, 1799, Alexander Hamilton Papers, Library of Congress; Col. Alexander Smyth to Maj. Gen. Henry Dearborn, December 4, 1812, copy enclosed with Dearborn to William Eustis, December 11, 1812, file D–262(6), SW:LR-Reg.
6. Christopher McKee, *A Gentlemanly and Honorable Profession: The Creation of the U.S. Naval Officer Corps, 1794–1815* (Annapolis, Md.: Naval Institute Press, 1991), 153–215.
7. Frederich W. A. von Steuben, *Regulations for the Order and Discipline of the Troops of the United States* (Philadelphia: Styner and Cist, 1779).
8. The pre–War of 1812 versions of the Rules and Articles of War, approved by congressional acts of September 20, 1776, May 31, 1786, and April 10, 1806, are in Abner R. Hetzel, comp., *Military Laws of the United States* (Washington, D.C.: Tempelman, 1846), 13–30, 33–38, 107–123.
9. Ibid., 36. The 1806 edition merely prohibited "conduct unbecoming an officer and a gentleman"; ibid., 119.
10. General Orders, November 30, 1800, National Archives, Records of the Office of the Adjutant General (Record Group 94), General James Wilkinson's Order Book, December 31, 1796–March 8, 1808; General Orders, July 15, 1808, file W–1808, SW:LR-Unreg.
11. Return of the Army for 1803, *ASP:MA*, 1:175.
12. Lt. Col. John F. Hamtramck to Maj. Gen. Alexander Hamilton, October 5, 1799, *Papers of Hamilton*, 23: 502–505. See also Hamtramck to Hamilton, September 19, 1799, Hamilton Papers.
13. Lt. Col. William Duane to Henry Dearborn, July 27, 1809, in William Duane, "The Letters of William Duane," *Proceedings of the Massachusetts Historical Society*, 2d ser. 20 (1906–1907):322.
14. Joseph G. Andrews, *A Surgeon's Mate at Fort Defiance: The Journal of Joseph Gardner Andrews*, ed. Richard C. Knopf (Columbus: Ohio Historical Society, 1957).
15. Ibid., 26–27.
16. Ibid., 77.
17. Ibid., 22, 53.

18. Ibid., 33-34.
19. Ibid., 43, 69.
20. Ibid., 87.
21. Ibid., 57, 81-83.
22. *ASP:MA,* 1:5-6.
23. "Roll of the Officers, Civil, Military, and Naval, of the United States," *ASP: Misc.* 1:308-312.
24. *ASP:MA,* 1:5; Acts of March 3, 1797, and March 16, 1802, Hetzel, *Military Laws,* 67, 99-100.
25. Acts of March 3, 1791, March 5, 1792, and March 3, 1795, Hetzel, *Military Laws,* 47, 49, 58. This premium was intended in part to cover recruiting officers' expenses. James McHenry to Maj. Gen. Alexander Hamilton, August 29, 1799, Hamilton Papers.
26. Regulations on servants are included in James McHenry to Maj. Gen. Alexander Hamilton, March 12, 1800, *Papers of Hamilton,* 24:318-319.
27. "Roll of the Officers," *ASP:Misc.,* 1:261-319.
28. Lt. Col. William Duane to Thomas Jefferson, February 4, 1809, "Letters of Duane," 319-320.
29. Col. Thomas Hunt et al., memorial to U.S. Congress, November 8, 1805, Clarence E. Carter and John P. Bloom, eds., *The Territorial Papers of the United States,* 27 vols. (Washington, D.C.: Government Printing Office, 1934-1969), 13:267-268; Capt. Walker K. Armistead to Col. Jonathan Williams, October 14, 1807, Jonathan Williams Papers, Lilly Library, Indiana University, Bloomington. On army pay, see also Edward M. Coffman, *The Old Army: A Portrait of the American Army in Peacetime, 1784-1898* (New York: Oxford University Press, 1986), 30.
30. Maj. Gen. Alexander Hamilton to James McHenry, August 13, 1799, *Papers of Hamilton,* 23:313-314.
31. Lt. Col. William Duane to Thomas Jefferson, February 4, 1809, "Letters of Duane," 317-320. Duane's letters in this collection and in the files of the War Department indicate that his military service was spent entirely in Philadelphia, except for a trip to Washington, D.C., on a personal matter in 1814. In 1809, a visitor described him as writing six hours daily for the press. Maj. John Fuller to Patty Fuller, June 26, 1809 (typescript), John Fuller Papers, Ohio Historical Society, Columbus.
32. On St. Clair, Sargent, and Putnam, see *DAB,* 15:284, 16:294-295, 369. On Brent, see James D. Morgan, "Robert Brent, First Mayor of Washington City," *Records of the Columbia Historical Society* 2 (1899): 236-251. Joseph Bloomfield continued to perform the duties of governor of New Jersey for at least five months in 1812 while holding a major general's position. Bloomfield to William Eustis, July 15, 1812, file B-340(6), and August 6, 1812, file B-372(6), SW:LR-Reg.
33. There are many documents on the involvement of John Armstrong and other officers in land speculation in the John Armstrong Papers, Indiana Historical Society, Indianapolis. See, for example, Joseph F. Perrault and Benevist McCarty to John Armstrong, June 7, 1788; Armstrong to Francis Johnston, September 5, 1788, April 22, 1791, and November 8, 1792; Armstrong to William Johnston, September 5, 1788; Armstrong to Winthrop Sargent, July 30, 1791. For other examples of officers' land investments, see Capt. William Eaton to Timothy Pickering, September 13, 1796, Timothy Pickering Papers, Massachusetts Historical Society; Lt. William H. Harrison to Maj. Gen. Anthony Wayne, November 1, 1796, Anthony Wayne Papers, William L. Clements Library, Ann Arbor, Mich.; Maj. Jonathan Haskell to Wayne, November 8, 1794, Wayne Papers, Historical Society of Pennsylvania; John P. Huber, "General

Josiah Harmar's Command: Military Policy in the Old Northwest, 1784–1791" (Ph.D. diss., University of Michigan, 1968), 106–107, 166. For officers' economic activities, see also Coffman, *Old Army*, 30–31.

34. On Hamtramck, see James R. Jacobs, *The Beginning of the U.S. Army, 1783-1812* (Princeton, N.J.: Princeton University Press, 1947), 231; F. Clever Bald, "Colonel John Francis Hamtramck," *Indiana Magazine of History* 44 (December 1948):353; Daniel Mayo to Lt. Col. John F. Hamtramck, October 20, 1799, and John C. Wallace to Hamtramck, February 23, 1802, John F. Hamtramck Papers, Burton Collection, Detroit Public Library. On LeBarron, see Surg. Mate Francis LeBarron to Henry Dearborn, September 25, 1808, file L–150(4), SW:LR-Reg.; LeBarron to Col. Jacob Kingsbury, November 10, 1809, Jacob Kingsbury Papers, Burton Collection, Detroit Public Library.

35. General Orders, June 12, 1797, Wilkinson's Order Book. In 1810, the secretary of war stated that officers and men could raise livestock but should be restrained from "private emolument or speculation to the injury of the service." William Eustis to Col. Alexander Smyth, November 9, 1810, SW:LS.

36. Printed handbill, signed by Hosp. Surg. John M. Daniel, May 28, 1810, file D–76(5), SW:LR-Reg. The army regulations issued in December 1814 prohibited medical officers from engaging in private practice, but this regulation was not enforced. Harvey E. Brown, *The Medical Department of the United States Army from 1775 to 1873* (Washington, D.C.: Surgeon General's Office, 1873), 97, 120, 121–122.

37. Lt. Col. Josiah Harmar to Maj. John F. Hamtramck, August 27, 1790, Harmar to Capt. James Bradford, September 3, 1790, and Hamtramck to Harmar, January 25, 1791, in Gayle Thornbrough, ed., *Outpost on the Wabash, 1787–1791: Letters of Brigadier General Josiah Harmar and Major John Francis Hamtramck and Other Letters and Documents Selected from the Harmar Papers in the William L. Clements Library* (Indianapolis: Indiana Historical Society, 1957), 252–253, 257–258, 275; Harmar to Ens. John Jeffers, February 1, 1790, and Harmar to Joseph Howell, Jr., June 9, 1790, in Ebenezer Denny, "Military Journal of Major Ebenezer Denny, an Officer in the Revolutionary and Indian Wars," ed. William H. Denny, *Memoirs of the Historical Society of Pennsylvania* 7 (1860):450, 456–457.

38. General Orders, May 22, 1797, reissued July 15, 1808, file W-1808, SW:LR-Unreg.

39. William Eustis to Col. Thomas H. Cushing, May 16, 1810, SW:LS. The main controversy occurred at Fort Dearborn, where Capt. John Whistler granted the sutling rights to a partnership of his own son and the post medical officer. Citizens and at least one officer complained that Whistler and his friends restricted trade between the soldiers and other merchants, demanded personal discounts from civilian traders, sold corn raised by soldier labor for their own profit, and intimidated their critics by threatening violence. See the following files: C-150(5), C-257(5), C-258(5), I-55(5), I-144(5), J-95(5), W–112(5), SW:LR-Reg.

40. Lt. Henry Hopkins to Henry Dearborn, June 18, 1805, file H–316(1), and Lt. Heman A. Fay to William Eustis, April 13, 1812, file F–49(6), SW:LR-Reg. Hopkins's office is mentioned in *Territorial Papers*, 9:440. The War Department actually accepted Fay's offer and permitted him to stay at Baltimore.

41. Henry Dearborn to Maj. Daniel Jackson, April 19, 1803, and Dearborn to Lt. William Yates, May 20, 1803, SW:LS.

42. Calculated from lists of military appointments for 1791–1792 and 1803–1807, *JEP*, 1 and 2:passim; Heitman, *Historical Register*, 1:passim; George W. Cullum, comp., *Biographical Register of the Officers and Graduates of the U.S. Military Academy at West Point, N.Y., from Its*

Establishment, in 1802, to 1890; with the Early History of the United States Military Academy, 3 vols. (Boston: Houghton, Mifflin, 1891), 1:263–337.

43. Louis C. Hatch, *The Administration of the American Revolutionary Army* (New York: B. Franklin, 1971), 37–46; Charles Royster, *A Revolutionary People at War: The Continental Army and American Character, 1775–1783* (Chapel Hill: University of North Carolina Press, 1979), 197–200.

44. Henry Knox to Charles Thomson, August 18, 1785, National Archives, Records of the Continental and Confederation Congresses and the Constitutional Convention (Record Group 360), Papers of the Continental Congress, 1774–1789.

45. Henry Knox to George Washington, March 1, 1791, February 18, 1793, and July 19, 1793, George Washington Papers, Library of Congress; Knox to Washington, March 2, 1792, and Knox to Brig. Gen. John Brooks, May 3, 1792, Henry Knox Papers, Massachusetts Historical Society; General Orders, September 4, 1792, and February 26, 1793, Anthony Wayne's Orderly Books, Wayne Papers, Historical Society of Pennsylvania.

46. William E. Birkhimer, *The Law of Appointment and Promotion in the Regular Army of the United States* (New York: A. G. Sherwood, 1880), 50–51.

47. Rules relative to rank and promotion in the army, signed by James McHenry, September 3, 1799, Hamilton Papers; General Orders, June 9, 1801, Wilkinson's Order Book; Birkhimer, *Law of Appointment*, 52–57; Act of June 26, 1812, Hetzel, *Military Laws*, 153.

48. Birkhimer, *Law of Appointment*, 56; William Eustis to Brig. Gen. Peter Gansevoort, June 30, 1809, SW:LS; Theodore J. Crackel, *Mr. Jefferson's Army: Political and Social Reform of the Military Establishment, 1801–1809* (New York: New York University Press, 1987), 121–122.

49. George Washington to Alice DeLancey Izard, July 20, 1798; Washington to Jacob Read, August 19, 1798; Washington to Bushrod Washington, December 31, 1798, in George Washington, *The Writings of Washington from the Original Manuscript Sources, 1745–1799*, ed. John C. Fitzpatrick, 39 vols. (Washington, D.C.: Government Printing Office, 1931–1944), 36:353–355, 415–417, 37:80.

50. Lt. Col. John F. Hamtramck to Maj. Gen. Alexander Hamilton, February 2, 1799, *Papers of Hamilton*, 22:452. For similar concerns, see Brig. Gen. Thomas H. Cushing to William Eustis, July 10, 1812, file C–384(6), SW:LR-Reg.; Maj. James Bankhead to John Armstrong, March 8, 1813, James Madison Papers, Library of Congress; Lt. Col. James House to Col. Jacob Kingsbury, March 17, 1813, Kingsbury Papers, Detroit Public Library.

51. Act of January 20, 1813, Hetzel, *Military Laws*, 156–157.

52. For examples of officers' protests over these appointments, see the following files: 2560, 2981, 3634, 3969, AGO:LR; R–88(6), B–145(7), C–110(7), C–136(7), M–103(7), SW:LR-Reg.

53. See, for example, Col. Henry Atkinson to Bartlett Yancey, March 10, 1814, Bartlett Yancey Papers, Southern Historical Collection, University of North Carolina Library, Chapel Hill.

54. Lt. Thomas S. Jesup to James Findlay, January 19, 1812, "Torrence Family Papers V," *Quarterly Publication of the Historical and Philosophical Society of Ohio* 4 (July–September 1909):130–131.

55. Lt. Col. Josiah Snelling to Col. John DeBarth Walbach, March 20, 1814, and Snelling to Maj. John R. Bell, August 7, 1814, file 7079, AGO:LR; Lt. Patrick McDonogh to his parents, April 25, 1813, in Patrick McDonogh, "A Hero of Fort Erie: Letters Relating to the Military Service, Chiefly on the Niagara Frontier, of Lieutenant

Patrick McDonogh," *Publications of the Buffalo Historical Society* 5 (1902):83; Capt. William A. Blount to John G. Blount, [August 1814], in John G. Blount, *The John Gray Blount Papers,* ed. Alice B. Keith et al., 4 vols. (Raleigh, N.C.: State Department of Archives and History, 1952–1982), 4:243.

56. *JEP,* 3:39.

57. Richard H. Kohn, "General Wilkinson's Vendetta with General Wayne: Politics and Command in the American Army, 1791–1796," *Filson Club History Quarterly,* 45 (October 1971):361–372; Harry E. Wildes, *Anthony Wayne, Trouble Shooter of the American Revolution* (New York: Harcourt, Brace, 1941), 386–390, 400–407, 426–434, and passim. The quotation is from Maj. Gen. Anthony Wayne to James McHenry, July 28, 1796, in Richard C. Knopf, ed., *Anthony Wayne, a Name in Arms; Soldier, Diplomat, Defender of Expansion Westward of a Nation. The Wayne-Knox-Pickering-McHenry Correspondence* (Pittsburgh: University of Pittsburgh Press, 1960), 506.

58. Maj. John Fuller to Patty Fuller, July 28, 1809 (typescript), Fuller Papers.

59. Capt. Benjamin Forsyth to William Eustis, September 16, 1811, file F-112(5), SW:LR-Reg.

60. For a discussion of honor in the British army, see John Shy, *Toward Lexington: The Role of the British Army in the Coming of the American Revolution* (Princeton, N.J.: Princeton University Press, 1965), 344. For military honor generally in the eighteenth century, see Christopher Duffy, *The Military Experience in the Age of Reason* (New York: Atheneum, 1988), 74–80.

61. For a discussion of honor in the Continental Army, see Royster, *Revolutionary People at War,* 86–90, 206–210.

62. Staats Morris to James Monroe, November 17, 1814, file 6849, AGO:LR.

63. Capt. Lewis Howard to Col. Jacob Kingsbury, March 19, 1810, Kingsbury Papers, Detroit Public Library.

64. Surg. Fenn Deming to Maj. Gen. George Izard, January 3, 1815, file 8227, deposition of Capt. John McClelland, May 10, 1811, file 537, and Maj. Chester Lyman et al. to Brig. Gen. Winfield Scott, June 22, 1814, file 299, AGO:LR; Surg. Isaac Davis, Lt. William Nicholas, and Surg. William E. Lee to Brig. Gen. Peter Gansevoort, August 12, 1809, file D-299(4), SW:LR-Reg.

65. Steven J. Novak, *The Rights of Youth: American Colleges and Student Revolt, 1798–1815* (Cambridge: Harvard University Press, 1977), passim; Joseph F. Kett, *Rites of Passage: Adolescence in America, 1790 to the Present* (New York: Basic Books, 1977), 38–59 and passim.

66. McKee, *Gentlemanly and Honorable Profession,* 458–465.

67. Articles 25, 26, and 28 of Rules and Articles of War (1806 version), Hetzel, *Military Laws,* 111–112.

68. General Orders, June 6, 1793, and October 10, 1796, Wayne's Orderly Books, Wayne Papers, Historical Society of Pennsylvania; Thomas T. Underwood, *Journal, Thomas T. Underwood, March 26, 1792 to March 18, 1800: An Old Soldier in Wayne's Army,* ed. Lee Shepard (Cincinnati: Society of the Colonial Wars in the State of Ohio, 1945), 3, 5; John H. Buell, "A Fragment from the Diary of Major John Hutchinson Buell, U.S.A., Who Joined the American Army at the Beginning of the Revolutionary War and Remained in Service until 1803," *Journal of the Military Service Institution of the United States* 40 (January–March 1907):107–108; John Gassaway to Maj. Gen. Anthony Wayne, April 12, 1793, and April 19, 1793, Wayne to Henry Knox, April 29, 1793, Wayne Papers, Historical Society of Pennsylvania.

69. Brig. Gen. James Wilkinson to Maj. Moses Porter, April 19, 1806, Moses Porter Papers, Library of Congress. For references to Wilkinson's challenges, see James R.

Jacobs, *Tarnished Warrior: Major-General James Wilkinson* (New York: Macmillan, 1938), 240-242, 245-246; Wilkinson to Col. Jonathan Williams, October 27, 1807, and October 3, 1808, Jonathan Williams Papers; Wilkinson to Col. Jacob Kingsbury, January 11, 1808, Kingsbury Papers, Detroit Public Library.

70. Winfield Scott, *Memoirs of Lieut.-General Winfield Scott, L.L.D., Written by Himself*, 2 vols. (New York: Sheldon, 1864), 1:51-52; James A. Blake to Brig. Gen. James Wilkinson, July 12, 1812, James Wilkinson Papers, Library of Congress.

71. Officers fought civilians in seven of these duels, and only one participant could be identified in the remaining eleven.

72. Buell, "Diary," 107-108.

73. Decision in court-martial of which Lt. Col. William S. Smith was president, n.d. [1799 or 1800], Hamilton Papers; charges against Capt. Abraham A. Massias, brought by Lt. James Saunders, [1811], file 537, AGO:LR. See also Coffman, *Old Army*, 32.

74. Roger L. Nichols, *General Henry Atkinson: A Western Military Career* (Norman: University of Oklahoma Press, 1965), 41-43; General Orders, Third Military District, January 4, 1815, file 9046, Staats Morris to James Monroe, November 17, 1814, file 6849, Morris to Alexander J. Dallas, April 24, 1815, file 9341, AGO:LR; Lt. Col. William S. Hamilton to Brig. Gen. Daniel Parker, June 13, 1815, Daniel Parker Papers, Historical Society of Pennsylvania; Capt. Benjamin K. Pierce to Capt. Thomas Stockton, January 3, [1814], Thomas Stockton Papers, Library of Congress. For the antidueling regulation, see General Orders, May 22, 1814, National Archives, AGO: Orders and Circulars.

75. "Dr. William Beaumont and the Code of Honor," *Military Surgeon* 74 (1934):248-249.

76. Robert H. Berlin, "The Administration of Military Justice in the Continental Army during the American Revolution, 1775-1783" (Ph.D. diss., University of California, Santa Barbara, 1976), passim; Stuart L. Bernath, "George Washington and the Genesis of American Military Discipline," *Mid-America* 49 (April 1967):83-100; Edward F. Sherman, "Legal, Egalitarian, and Humanitarian Influences on American Military Justice from the Revolutionary War to the Mexican War" (Paper presented at the Biennial Conference of the Inter-University Seminar on Armed Forces and Society, Chicago, October 1977).

77. Rules and Articles of War (1806 version), Hetzel, *Military Laws*, 117-121.

78. Brig. Gen. James Wilkinson to Capt. James Bruff, June 18, 1797, *ASP:Misc.*, 1:586.

79. Calculated from Wayne's Orderly Books (1792-1796), Wayne Papers, Historical Society of Pennsylvania; and Wilkinson's Order Book (1796-1808).

80. Henry Knox to George Washington, July 11, 1791, July 21, 1792, and August 28, 1792, Washington Papers.

81. Capt. James House to William Eustis, February 16, 1809, enclosing charges against Lt. Joseph Kimball, file H-356(4), House to Eustis, May 28, 1809, file K-87(4), SW:LR-Reg. For similar cases, see the following files: 827, 2489, 7740, 8039, 8206, AGO:LR; W-413(3), R-196(4), P-172(5), B-454 1/2(6), SW:LR-Reg.

82. Compiled from court-martial decisions in Wayne's Orderly Books, Wayne Papers, Historical Society of Pennsylvania; Wilkinson's Order Book; and AGO: Orders and Circulars. Quotation is from General Orders, October 31, 1809, AGO: Orders and Circulars.

83. Brig. Gen. Wade Hampton to William Eustis, February 6, 1810, file H-56(5), SW:LR-Reg. In 1809, a major listed fifteen officers who had been recently court-mar-

tialed in his brigade alone. Maj. Ebenezer Beebe to Col. Jacob Kingsbury, November 7, 1809, Jacob Kingsbury Papers, Library of Congress.

84. General Orders, January 2, 1793, June 6, 1793, September 6, 1793, Wayne's Orderly Books, Wayne Papers, Historical Society of Pennsylvania; General Orders, November 29, 1801, June 20, 1804, July 5, 1804, Wilkinson's Order Book; William Eustis to Brig. Gen. Wade Hampton, December 1, 1809, March 9, 1810, SW:LS.

85. Calculated from list of army officers in 1797, Hamersly, *Regular Army Register*, 47–49; Heitman, *Historical Register*, 1:passim.

86. On disease and mortality in the army in general, see Mary C. Gillett, *The Army Medical Department, 1775–1818* (Washington, D.C.: Government Printing Office, 1981), 129–185.

87. Computed from Heitman, *Historical Register*, 2:13–42.

88. Col. Edward Pasteur to William Eustis, October 15, 1810, file P-163(5), Col. Alexander Parker to Eustis, December 1, 1809, file P-399(4), Capt. Isaac A. Coles to Eustis, January 16, 1810, file C-8(5), Capt. Jacob J. Faust to Eustis, June 20, 1810, file F-35(5), SW:LR-Reg.

89. Denny, "Journal," 381. Generalizations on causes of resignations are based on correspondence on resignations in: Knox Papers; Wayne Papers, Historical Society of Pennsylvania; SW:LR-Reg.; AGO:LR; and other manuscript collections.

90. Lt. Fayette Roane to John Armstrong, March 3, 1814, file 6843, AGO:LR.

91. War Office Register, July 24, 1801, Thomas Jefferson Papers, Library of Congress; Noble Cunningham, Jr., *The Jeffersonian Republicans in Power: Party Operations, 1801–1809* (Chapel Hill: University of North Carolina Press, 1963), 66–68. I have slightly recast Cunningham's statistics. Analyses by Edward M. Coffman and Donald Jackson also support the primacy of merit over political affiliation. Coffman, *Old Army*, 8–10; Donald Jackson, "Jefferson, Meriwether Lewis, and the Reduction of the United States Army," *Proceedings of the American Philosophical Society* 124 (April 1980): 95–96. In contrast, Theodore J. Crackel argues that the reduction as a whole was geared to weakening Federalist influence, and that meritorious officers designated as strong Federalists were far more likely to be discharged than meritorious Republicans. However, the total number of strong Federalists discharged (five of nine) is too small to represent much of a transformation. In general, Crackel's argument that the reduction marked a major reformation of the army is asserted rather than proven. Crackel, *Mr. Jefferson's Army*, 49–51. Donald Jackson argues that Capt. Meriwether Lewis made the notations on the list, but the evaluator's handwriting also resembles that of Brig. Gen. James Wilkinson. Neither of these officers is considered on the list.

92. Col. Nicholas Long, confidential report on officers of 43d Infantry Regiment, [1815], file L-1815, Lt. Col. William S. Hamilton to Alexander J. Dallas, April 26, 1815, file H-1815, SW:LR-Unreg. Most of the personnel reports are filed in this collection. The administration's handling of the reduction may be followed in George M. Dallas, *Life and Writings of Alexander James Dallas* (Philadelphia: J. B. Lippincott, 1871), 370–375, 397–446.

93. Calculated from Army Register for 1816, *ASP:MA*, 1:626–635; Heitman, *Historical Register*, 1:passim.

94. See officers' letters requesting retention or reinstatement in 1815, AGO:LR. Quotation is from Lt. George Getz to James Monroe, April 11, 1815, file 8436, ibid.

95. *JEP*, 3:23; Erastus Roberts to William H. Crawford, December 20, 1815, file 10658, Nathaniel Clarke to Maj. Gen. Andrew Jackson, November 10, 1815, file 8074, Capt. Aaron T. Crane to Brig. Gen. Daniel Parker, April 23, 1815, file 8136, AGO:LR; John C. Symmes to William H. Harrison, June 20, 1815, John C. Symmes

Papers, Lyman C. Draper Collection, State Historical Society of Wisconsin, Madison; Thomas R. Hay, "General James Wilkinson—The Last Phase," *Louisiana Historical Quarterly* 19 (April 1936):407-411; Jacobs, *Wilkinson*, 314-316. For the assassination rumor, see the anonymous letter from Carlisle Barracks to Brig. Gen. Daniel Parker, May 29, 1815, and Lt. Col. William S. Hamilton to Parker, June 9, 1815, June 15, 1815, and August 11, 1815, Parker Papers.

96. Brig. Gen. Thomas H. Cushing to Thomas T. Tucker, May 29, 1815, file 8166, AGO:LR. See also Jacob Kingsbury to William H. Crawford, April 16, 1816, quoted in Jacobs, *Wilkinson*, 315.

97. Acts of April 30, 1790, March 3, 1795, May 30, 1796, March 16, 1802, January 11, 1812, and January 29, 1813, Hetzel, *Military Laws*, 43-44, 60, 66, 102, 136, 159. For cases of debilitated officers kept on the army rolls, see Capt. Hugh McCall to Maj. Gen. Thomas Pinckney, April 9, 1815, file 8960, AGO:LR; James Dill to John C. Calhoun, April 1824, in John C. Calhoun, *The Papers of John C. Calhoun*, ed. Robert L. Meriwether and W. Edwin Hemphill, 18 vols. to date (Columbia: University of South Carolina Press, 1959-), 9:3-4.

98. Act of June 7, 1794, Hetzel, *Military Laws*, 56. This provision was reaffirmed in acts of March 14, 1798, March 16, 1802, January 11, 1812, January 29, 1813, and April 16, 1816, ibid., 68-69, 103, 136, 159-160, 184-185.

99. On North, see *DAB*, 13:563-564. On Denny, see Denny, "Journal," 224-229, 232-234. On Armstrong, see *DAB*, 1:355; Armstrong Papers, passim. On Sedam, see Emma Backus, "Cornelius Sedam and His Friends in Washington's Time," *Ohio State Archeological and Historical Society Publications* 41 (January 1932): 36-50. On Ziegler, see George A. Katzenberger, "Major David Ziegler," *Ohio State Archeological and Historical Quarterly* 21 (April-July 1912): 157-167. On the later careers of Confederation era officers, see also William B. Skelton, "Social Roots of the American Military Profession: The Officer Corps of America's First Peacetime Army, 1784-1789," *Journal of Military History* 54 (October 1990): 448-450.

100. Dorothy B. Goebel, *William Henry Harrison: A Political Biography* (Indianapolis: Indiana Library and Historical Department, 1926), 36-38; Lt. William H. Harrison to Maj. Gen. Anthony Wayne, November 1, 1796, Wayne Papers, Clements Library; Harrison to Robert G. Harper, May 26, 1798, Pickering Papers; Richard Dillon, *Meriwether Lewis: A Biography* (New York: Coward-McCann, 1965), 264-265; *DAB*, 9:523-524; *Territorial Papers*, 20:57n-58n.

101. On Cobb, see *BDC*, 711. On Van Renssalaer, see *DAB*, 19:210-211. McRee's appointment is listed in *JEP*, 1:267. For Eaton, see *DAB*, 5:613.

102. On Shaumburgh (or Schaumburgh), see Bartholomew Shaumburgh to Brig. Gen. James Wilkinson, October 28, [1809], James Wilkinson Papers, Chicago Historical Society; *Territorial Papers*, 9:600, 796, 838; Shaumburgh to William Eustis, August 9, 1812, file S-350(6), and Shaumburgh to John Armstrong, February 10, 1814, file S-403(7), SW:LR-Reg. On the Federalist veterans, see George Poindexter to Henry Dearborn, January 1808, *Territorial Papers*, 5:604-606. On Marschalk, see Isaiah Thomas, *The History of Printing in America, with a Biography of Printers, and an Account of Newspapers*, 2 vols. (Albany, N.Y.: J. Munsell, 1874), 2:304. On Claiborne, see Robert Williams to Thomas Jefferson, December 21, 1804, and Williams to Albert Gallatin, November 3, 1807, National Archives, Records of the Department of State (Record Group 59), Letters of Application and Recommendation during the Administration of Thomas Jefferson, 1801-1809.

103. William C. Beard to unknown, August 1, 1815, file 7769, AGO:LR.

104. See, for example, the cases of Lloyd Beall, Jacint Laval, Hugh McCall, Thomas

Martin, Alexander Thompson, and John Whistler, all of whom were released in the reductions of 1802 and 1815. Heitman, *Historical Register,* 1:passim.

105. The generalizations on federal employment of former officers are based primarily on *JEP,* 1–3:passim; "Roll of the Officers," *ASP:Misc.,* 1:260–319; and the annual registers of federal employees published by the Department of State, beginning with *A Register of the Officers and Agents, Civil, Military, and Naval, in the Service of the United States, on the Thirtieth Day of September, 1816* (Washington, D.C.: Jonathan Elliot, 1816). For Cushing and Freeman, see ibid., 10, 22.

106. List of officers appointed in Massachusetts regiment, 1786, Knox Papers; Heitman, *Historical Register,* 1:passim.

107. Heitman, *Historical Register,* 1:472, 982. Heitman lists two Thomas J. Van Dykes, one as a line officer and one as a medical officer, but these were almost certainly the same man. See Zella Armstrong, *Notable Southern Families,* 6 vols. (Chattanooga, Tenn.: Lookout Publishing Co., 1918–1933), 1:244–245.

108. The compilation was made by Christopher McKee and is based on personal correspondence with the author.

CHAPTER FOUR. A FRONTIER CONSTABULARY: CIVIL-MILITARY RELATIONS, 1784–1815

1. Charles Royster, *A Revolutionary People at War: The Continental Army and American Character, 1775–1783* (Chapel Hill: University of North Carolina Press, 1979), passim, esp. chapters 7 and 8.

2. Lt. Erkuries Beatty to Reading Beatty, December 12, 1786, in Joseph M. Beatty, Jr., ed., "Letters of the Four Beatty Brothers of the Continental Army, 1774–1794," *Pennsylvania Magazine of History and Biography* 44 (1920):258–259; Maj. John Doughty to Henry Knox, March 21, 1787, Henry Knox Papers, Massachusetts Historical Society.

3. Lt. Col. Josiah Harmar to William Irvine, May 25, 1787, Josiah Harmar Papers, William L. Clements Library, Ann Arbor, Mich.; Harmar to Henry Knox, June 14, 1788, in Ebenezer Denny, "Military Journal of Major Ebenezer Denny, an Officer in the Revolutionary and Indian Wars," ed. William H. Denny, *Memoirs of the Historical Society of Pennsylvania* 7 (1890):432–433; Harmar to Capt. John F. Hamtramck, October 13, 1788, in Gayle Thornbrough, ed., *Outpost on the Wabash, 1787–1791: Letters of Brigadier General Josiah Harmar and Major John Francis Hamtramck and Other Letters and Documents Selected from the Harmar Papers in the William L. Clements Library* (Indianapolis: Indiana Historical Society, 1957), 137; Lt. John Pratt to Harmar, May 4, 1788, Harmar Papers. See also Capt. Jonathan Heart to Harmar, July 7, 1788, and Maj. John P. Wyllys to Harmar, May 26, 1788, Harmar Papers.

4. For examples of officers' lobbying on pay, see Lt. Erkuries Beatty to Lt. Col. Josiah Harmar, October 26, 1786, December 18, 1786, February 3, 1788, February 1, 1789, and February 16, 1789, and Maj. John Doughty to Harmar, June 24, 1787, Harmar Papers; Erkuries Beatty's journal for April–June 1785, New York Historical Society, New York City. Harmar to Thomas Mifflin, March 19, 1787, Harmar Papers; Lt. Col. Henry Jackson to the Senate and House of Representatives of Massachusetts, March 4, 1787, copy enclosed with Jackson to Henry Knox, March 11, 1787, and Jackson to Knox, April 14, 1787, Knox Papers.

5. Stephen S. Webb, "Army and Empire: English Garrison Government in Britain and America, 1569–1763," *William and Mary Quarterly,* 3d ser. 34 (January 1977):1–

31. See also Stephen S. Webb, *The Governors-General: The English Army and the Definition of the Empire, 1569–1681* (Chapel Hill: University of North Carolina Press, 1979); Douglas E. Leach, *Roots of Conflict: British Armed Forces and Colonial Americans, 1677–1783* (Chapel Hill: University of North Carolina Press, 1986).

6. John Shy, *Toward Lexington: The Role of the British Army in the Coming of the American Revolution* (Princeton, N.J.: Princeton University Press, 1965).

7. Ensign John Armstrong to Lt. Col. Josiah Harmar, April 12, 1785, Ensign Ebenezer Denny to Harmar, August 23, 1785, and Maj. John Doughty to Harmar, November 30, 1785, Harmar Papers; John P. Huber, "General Josiah Harmar's Command: Military Policy in the Old Northwest, 1784–1791" (Ph.D. diss., University of Michigan, 1968), 54–59.

8. Maj. John F. Hamtramck to Lt. Col. Josiah Harmar, April 13, 1788, enclosing "Regulations for the Court of Post Vincennes," in Thornbrough, ed., *Outpost on the Wabash,* 67–75. Hamtramck later permitted the people of Kaskaskia to establish a similar government; Hamtramck to Father Jacobin Le Dru and John Edgar, October 14, 1789, ibid., 193.

9. Lt. Col. Josiah Harmar to Henry Knox, January 10, 1788, and Maj. John P. Wyllys to Harmar, April 15, 1789, Harmar Papers; Ensign John Armstrong to Wyllys, April 28, 1788, copy enclosed with Knox to the president of Congress, July 7, 1788, National Archives, Records of the Continental and Confederation Congresses and the Constitutional Convention (Record Group 360), Papers of the Continental Congress. See also Harmar to Knox, May 14, 1787, and December 15, 1788; Harmar to Wyllys, July 16, 1788, and December 9, 1788; Denny, "Journal," 421–422, 435, 437, 438.

10. Capt. Walter Finney to Lt. Col. Josiah Harmar, July 3, 1786, Harmar Papers.

11. Lt. Col. Josiah Harmar to Henry Knox, March 18, 1787, ibid.

12. Maj. John F. Hamtramck to Lt. Col. Josiah Harmar, August 31, 1788, and August 14, 1789, in Thornbrough, ed., *Outpost on the Wabash,* 114–117, 183.

13. Ibid., 208–209, 215; proceedings of a court of inquiry into the conduct of Capt. William McCurdy, November 29, 1789, Harmar Papers.

14. Maj. Gen. Anthony Wayne to Isaac Wayne, September 10, 1794, Wayne Papers, Historical Society of Pennsylvania; Maj. Jonathan Cass to Maj. Gen. Alexander Hamilton, November 11, 1799, in Alexander Hamilton, *The Papers of Alexander Hamilton,* ed. Harold C. Syrett, 26 vols. (New York: Columbia University Press, 1961–1979), 24:23.

15. Joseph G. Swift, *The Memoirs of Gen. Joseph Gardner Swift, L.L.D., U.S.A., First Grad. of the U.S.M.A., West Point* (Worcester, Mass.: F. S. Blanchard, 1890), 23; see also 42–43.

16. War Office Register, July 24, 1801, Thomas Jefferson Papers, Library of Congress; Noble E. Cunningham, Jr., *The Process of Government under Jefferson* (Princeton, N.J.: Princeton University Press, 1978), 175.

17. Maj. James Bruff to Henry Dearborn, March 17, 1807, file B-197(3), SW:LR-Reg.

18. Brig. Gen. James Wilkinson to Maj. Jonathan Williams, July 2, 1801, Jonathan Williams Papers, Lilly Library, Indiana University, Bloomington. See also Wilkinson to Williams, October 16, 1801, ibid.

19. Capt. Amos Stoddard to Edward Preble, August 25, 1801, Edward Preble Papers, Library of Congress.

20. Capt. Ebenezer Beebe to Col. Jacob Kingsbury, December 18, 1809, and December 6, 1810, Kingsbury to Dr. Mitchell, February 28, 1811, and Col. Daniel Bissell to Kingsbury, September 19, 1812, Jacob Kingsbury Papers, Burton Collection,

Detroit Public Library; Lt. Col. Alexander Macomb to Col. Jonathan Williams, April 29, 1812, and June 8, 1812, Jonathan Williams Papers.

21. Maj. John Fuller to Brig. Gen. Wade Hampton, February 7, 1811 (typescript), John Fuller Papers, Ohio Historical Society, Columbus; Lt. Col. William Duane to Thomas Jefferson, January 23, 1809, Duane to James Madison, December 1, 1809, December 5, 1809, December 8, 1809, February 22, 1814, and June 22, 1814, in William Duane, "The Letters of William Duane," *Proceedings of the Massachusetts Historical Society*, 2d ser. 20 (1906–1907): 312–316, 325–332, 365–368; Rowe and Harper to Brig. Gen. Daniel Parker, June 17, 1815, file 9705, AGO:LR.

22. For the interplay of politics and command in the conduct of the War of 1812, see J.C.A. Stagg, *Mr. Madison's War: Politics, Diplomacy, and Warfare in the Early American Republic, 1783–1830* (Princeton, N.J.: Princeton University Press, 1983).

23. Tommy R. Young II, "The United States Army in the South, 1789–1835" (Ph.D. diss., Louisiana State University, 1973), 27–52; Isaac Guion, "Military Journal of Captain Isaac Guion, 1797–1799," in *Seventh Annual Report of the Director of the Department of Archives and History of the State of Mississippi* (Nashville, Tenn., 1909), 27–108.

24. Capt. Isaac Guion to Brig. Gen. James Wilkinson, May 5, 1798, Guion, "Military Journal," 82.

25. Young, "Army in the South," 94–114; Clarence E. Carter and John P. Bloom, eds., *The Territorial Papers of the United States*, 27 vols. (Washington, D.C.: Government Printing Office, 1934–1969), 9:passim. The quotation is from Brig. Gen. James Wilkinson to Henry Dearborn, January 11, [1804], *Territorial Papers*, 9:159–160.

26. Henry Dearborn to Lt. Col. Constant Freeman, April 23, 1804, *Territorial Papers*, 9:230.

27. Young, "Army in the South," 123–128, 149–150; Henry Dearborn to Col. Constant Freeman, December 5, 1805, *Territorial Papers*, 9:541–542.

28. Young, "Army in the South," 107–115, 117–119. For the functions of civil commandants, see *Territorial Papers*, 9:38–39. For the activities of regulars as commandants, see ibid., 223–224, 238–239, 271–273, 292–293, 335–337, 384–385, 421–422, 440.

29. William C. C. Claiborne and Brig. Gen. James Wilkinson to Capt. Amos Stoddard, January 16, 1804, in Amos Stoddard, "Transfer of Upper Louisiana: Papers of Captain Amos Stoddard," *Glimpses of the Past* 2 (May–September 1935): 80–82.

30. William E. Foley, *A History of Missouri*, 3 vols. (Columbia: University of Missouri Press, 1971–1973), 1:70–78; Stoddard, "Transfer of Upper Louisiana," 69–122.

31. Foley, *History of Missouri*, 1:97–98.

32. Ibid., 97–119; *Territorial Papers*, 13:passim.

33. Brig. Gen. James Wilkinson to Henry Dearborn, December 31, 1805, and John B. C. Lucas to the secretary of the Treasury, February 13, 1806, *Territorial Papers*, 13:368–371, 444–447; General Orders, January 25, 1806, National Archives, Records of the Office of the Adjutant General (Record Group 94), General James Wilkinson's Order Book.

34. On Bissell, see Henry Dearborn to Capt. Daniel Bissell, March 24, 1803, SW:LS; Bissell's commissions as justice of the peace of St. Ferdinand Township, St. Louis County, Upper Louisiana Territory, February 14, 1810, and January 6, 1813, Daniel Bissell Papers, Missouri Historical Society, St. Louis. Dunham gave his title as "Chief Judge of the Court for the District of Michilimackinak" on a statement dated August 30, 1807, file D-199(3), SW:LR-Reg. For LeBarron, see Garrison Surg. Fran-

cis LeBarron to Henry Dearborn, March 20, 1809, file L-278(4), ibid. For Gaines, see James W. Silver, *Edmund Pendleton Gaines: Frontier General* (Baton Rouge: Louisiana State University Press, 1949), xi, 17–18, 20–21, 28. Carmichael's offices are mentioned in *Territorial Papers*, 5:191–192, 206–207. For officers as civil officials, see also Norman W. Caldwell, "The Frontier Army Officer, 1794–1814," *Mid-America* 37 (January 1955):105–108.

35. Francis Paul Prucha, *American Indian Policy in the Formative Years: The Indian Trade and Intercourse Acts, 1790–1834* (Lincoln: University of Nebraska Press, 1962), 45–50, 60–65, and passim; Maj. Gen. Alexander Hamilton to Lt. Col. John F. Hamtramck, May 23, 1799, *Papers of Hamilton*, 23:131–132; General Orders, March 1, 1800, Wilkinson's Order Book; Henry Dearborn to Maj. Moses Porter, August 14, 1802, SW:LS.

36. Lt. Thomas Swaine to Smith and Finley, April 11, 1798, excerpt in Isaac J. Cox, ed., "Documents Relating to Zachariah Cox," *Quarterly Publication of the Historical and Philosophical Society of Ohio* 8 (April–June 1913):113–114; Lt. George C. Allen to William Eustis, May 10, 1811, file A-136(5), SW:LR-Reg.; Lt. Col. John Bowyer to Maj. Abimael Y. Nicoll, August 5, 1812, file 793, AGO:LR.

37. See, for example, Maj. Gen. Anthony Wayne to Henry Knox, December 14, 1794, Anthony Wayne Papers, William L. Clements Library, Ann Arbor, Mich.; Lt. John Steele to Wayne, August 21, 1796, Capt. Zebulon Pike to Wayne, August 22, 1796, and Capt. Thomas Pasteur to Wayne, September 11, 1796, Wayne Papers, Historical Society of Pennsylvania; Capt. William H. Harrison to James McHenry, August 13, 1797 (photocopy), James McHenry Papers, Library of Congress.

38. Lt. Col. John P. Hamtramck to James McHenry, January 21, 1799, Alexander Hamilton Papers, Library of Congress.

39. For federal efforts to suppress Fries's Rebellion, see Robert W. Coakley, *The Role of Federal Military Forces in Domestic Disorders, 1789–1878* (Washington, D.C.: Government Printing Office, 1988), 69–77; Theodore J. Crackel, *Mr. Jefferson's Army: Political and Social Reform of the Military Establishment, 1801–1809* (New York: New York University Press, 1987), 21–27; *Papers of Hamilton*, 22:539–541, 548–554, 558–560, 584–585. Quotation is from Maj. Gen. Alexander Hamilton to James McHenry, March 18, 1799, ibid., 552–553.

40. *Annals of Congress*, 10th Cong., 1st sess., 1395.

41. Thomas P. Abernethy, *The Burr Conspiracy* (New York: Oxford University Press, 1954), 10–40 and passim.

42. Ibid., 24–26; Ens. Francis W. Small to Brig. Gen. James Wilkinson (deposition), January 10, 1807, and Lt. John R. N. Luckett to Wilkinson (deposition), January 11, 1807, file W-234(3), deposition of Joseph R. Henderson, March 18, 1807, file W-268(3), SW:LR-Reg.; excerpt of statement of Surg. Mate Richard Davidson, n.d., file D-1807, and deposition of Lt. William A. Murray, n.d., file M-1807, SW:LR-Unreg.

43. Abernethy, *Burr Conspiracy*, 104, 113–114, 115–117; Capt. Daniel Bissell to Henry Dearborn, July 10, 1807, enclosing deposition of Surg. Mate Trueman Tuttle, July 10, 1807, file B-275(3), and Bissell to Dearborn, December 28, 1807, enclosing deposition of Bissell, July 10, 1807, file B-363(3), SW:LR-Reg.; deposition of Post Surg. David Davis, January 1, 1807, file W-1807, SW:LR-Unreg.; deposition of Lt. Jacob Jackson, October 20, 1807, *ASP:Misc.*, 1:610–611.

44. W. Eugene Hollon, *The Lost Pathfinder: Zebulon Montgomery Pike* (Norman: University of Oklahoma Press, 1949), 158–170; Abernethy, *Burr Conspiracy*, 119–137.

45. Brig. Gen. James Wilkinson to Thomas Jefferson, October 21, 1806, quoted in

Abernethy, *Burr Conspiracy*, 150–151. A recent study argues that Wilkinson had decided to break with Burr as early as September 1805, after receiving a warning from the secretary of war; Crackel, *Mr. Jefferson's Army*, 113–116.

46. Abernethy, *Burr Conspiracy*, 181–182; Crackel, *Mr. Jefferson's Army*, 131–147; General Orders, January 5, 1807, Wilkinson's Order Book; Gen. James Wilkinson to Henry Dearborn, January 8, 1807, file W-1807, SW:LR-Unreg.

47. Abernethy, *Burr Conspiracy*, 222–223.

48. Ibid., 227–275; James R. Jacobs, *Tarnished Warrior: Major-General James Wilkinson* (New York: Macmillan, 1938), 240–244.

49. See the depositions and other documents cited in notes 42 and 43 above.

50. Henry Dearborn to Col. Henry Burbeck, March 30, 1807, SW:LS.

51. See, for example, Capt. Staats Morris to Maj. Gen. Alexander Hamilton, March 18, 1800, and Hamilton to Morris, March 22, 1800, *Papers of Hamilton*, 24:339, 353.

52. Henry Dearborn to commanding officers of seacoast garrisons, January 1, 1808, SW:LS.

53. Quoted in Frederick T. Wilson, "Federal Aid in Domestic Disturbances, 1787–1903," 57th Cong., 2d sess., Sen. Doc. no. 209, 52. On the army's role in enforcing the embargo, see generally Coakley, *Federal Military Forces*, 84–90.

54. Capt. Moses Swett to Henry Dearborn, July 26, 1808, file S-259(4), and August 9, 1808, file S-260(4); Capt. Jonathan Brooks to Dearborn, February 10, 1809, file B-405(4); Lt. Col. John Whiting to Dearborn, March 6, 1809, file W-484(4), Whiting to William Eustis, June 17, 1809, file W-584(4), SW:LR-Reg.

55. Capt. Joseph Cross to Henry Dearborn, October 21, 1808, file C-327(4), ibid. The former collector at Sackets Harbor considered Cross's provocative behavior to be largely to blame for his troubles. Augustus Sacket to Albert Gallatin, August 30, 1808, file S-247(4), ibid.

56. Maj. Moses Porter's correspondence for 1805–1806, Moses Porter Papers, Library of Congress; Abernethy, *Burr Conspiracy*, 138–157.

57. George W. Cullum, comp., *Biographical Register of the Officers and Graduates of the U.S. Military Academy at West Point, N.Y., from Its Establishment, in 1802, to 1890; with the Early History of the United States Military Academy*, 3 vols. (Boston: Houghton, Mifflin, 1891), 1:79–80.

58. Isaac J. Cox, *The West Florida Controversy, 1798–1813: A Study in American Diplomacy* (Baltimore: Johns Hopkins University Press, 1918), passim; Silver, *Gaines*, 8–19, 23–26; Lt. Col. Richard Sparks to William Eustis, July 12, 1810, file S-168(5), SW:LR-Reg.

59. Rembert W. Patrick, *Florida Fiasco: Rampant Rebels on the Georgia-Florida Border, 1810–1815* (Athens: University of Georgia Press, 1954), passim; T. Frederick Davis, ed., "United States Troops in Spanish East Florida, 1812–13," *Florida Historical Quarterly* 9 (July 1930):3–23, (October 1930):96–116, (January 1931):135–155, (April 1931):259–268; 10 (July 1931):24–34.

60. Capt. William Preston to Maj. Gen. Anthony Wayne, December 1793, Anthony Wayne Papers, Historical Society of Pennsylvania; Swift, *Memoirs*, 91–92. See also Young, "Army in the South," 205–206.

61. One especially divisive case occurred in Pittsburgh in 1809, where citizens petitioned for the removal of Lt. Francis W. Small, who allegedly treated his men "in a manner at which humanity shudders"—files C-633(4), D-315(4), P-356(4), P-361(4), R-256(4), S-692(4), S-699(4), S-700(4), S-711(4), S-737(4), SW:LR-Reg. For another such case, see file D-152(5), ibid.; file S-1811, SW:LR-Unreg.

62. Lt. Col. William Bentley to Maj. Gen. Alexander Hamilton, August 15, 1799,

Hamilton Papers; Capt. John T. Bentley to Henry Dearborn, October 1, 1808, file B-229(4), SW:LR-Reg. For examples of civil-military friction over recruiting in the War of 1812, see files 656, 1026, 2945, AGO:LR; Lt. Col. Joseph L. Smith to Maj. Thomas S. Jesup, December 26, 1814, and Jesup to secretary of war, January 21, 1815, Thomas S. Jesup Papers, Library of Congress; Stagg, *Mr. Madison's War,* 172–173, 264, 477, 483.

63. Deposition of Darius Orcutt, May 1794; John Ludlow to Maj. Gen. Anthony Wayne, June 17, 1794; Wayne to Capt. Isaac Guion, July 10, 1794; Wayne to Ludlow, July 10, 1794, Wayne Papers, Clements Library.

64. Proclamation issued by Brig. Gen. James Wilkinson, July 12, 1797, Wilkinson Papers; Lt. Col. David Strong to James McHenry, January 23, 1799, and March 22, 1799, Hamilton Papers; Maj. Gen. Alexander Hamilton to McHenry, April 23, 1799, and Hamilton to Strong, May 22, 1799, *Papers of Hamilton,* 23:64, 127–128.

65. This paragraph is based mainly on Robert V. Remini, *Andrew Jackson and the Course of American Empire, 1767–1821* (New York: Harper and Row, 1977), 308–315, and the documents in file C-226(8), SW:LR-Reg.

66. Remini, *Jackson,* 311, 312.

CHAPTER FIVE. SEEDS OF MILITARY PROFESSIONALISM

1. Allan R. Millett, *Military Professionalism and Officership in America* (Columbus: Mershon Center of the Ohio State University, 1977), 2.

2. This and the next paragraph have been based on the following sources: Christopher Duffy, *The Military Experience in the Age of Reason* (New York: Atheneum, 1988), 35–88; Russell F. Weigley, *The Age of Battles: The Quest for Decisive Warfare from Breitenfeld to Waterloo* (Bloomington: Indiana University Press, 1991), passim; Maury D. Feld, "Middle-Class Society and the Rise of Military Professionalism: The Dutch Army, 1589–1609," *Armed Forces and Society* 1 (Summer 1975):419–442; Lee Kennett, *The French Armies in the Seven Years' War: A Study in Military Organization and Administration* (Durham, N.C.: Duke University Press, 1967), 54–71 and passim; Samuel P. Huntington, *The Soldier and the State: The Theory and Politics of Civil-Military Relations* (Cambridge: Harvard University Press, 1957), 19–30.

3. Daniel J. Boorstin, *The Americans: The Colonial Experience* (New York: Random House, 1958), 191–265; Daniel H. Calhoun, *Professional Lives in America: Structure & Inspiration, 1750–1850* (Cambridge.: Harvard University Press, 1965), 1–19; Joseph F. Kett, *The Formation of the American Medical Profession: The Role of Institutions, 1780–1860* (New Haven, Conn.: Yale University Press, 1968), 1–31; Michael Kraus, *The Atlantic Civilization: Eighteenth-Century Origins* (Ithaca, N.Y.: Cornell University Press, 1949), 159–215 and passim.

4. For the investigations, see *ASP:MA,* 1:20–44.

5. Maj. Michael Rudolph to Maj. George M. Bedinger, November 18, 1792, Rudulph-Ney Papers, in Lyman C. Draper Collection, State Historical Society of Wisconsin, Madison.

6. Harry E. Wildes, *Anthony Wayne: Trouble Shooter of the American Revolution* (New York: Harcourt, Brace, 1941); Paul D. Nelson, *Anthony Wayne: Soldier of the Early Republic* (Bloomington: Indiana University Press, 1985).

7. Richard H. Kohn, *Eagle and Sword: The Federalists and the Creation of the Military Establishment in America, 1783–1802* (New York: Free Press, 1975), 124–126. See also Wildes, *Wayne,* 346–349; Nelson, *Wayne,* 224–226.

8. Based on Wayne's Order Books for 1792–1796, Anthony Wayne Papers, Historical Society of Pennsylvania.
9. Maj. Gen. Anthony Wayne to Henry Knox, September 13, 1792, in Richard C. Knopf, ed., *Anthony Wayne, a Name in Arms: Soldier, Diplomat, Defender of Expansion Westward of a Nation. The Wayne-Knox-Pickering-McHenry Correspondence* (Pittsburgh: University of Pittsburgh Press, 1960), 94. See also Wayne to Knox, December 6, 1792, ibid., 147; Wayne to Knox, March 22, 1793, Henry Knox Papers, Massachusetts Historical Society; Wayne to Brig. Gen. James Wilkinson, December 10, 1792, Wayne Papers, Historical Society of Pennsylvania.
10. Legion Orders, March 18, 1793, Wayne's Order Books, Wayne Papers, Historical Society of Pennsylvania.
11. Maj. Gen. Anthony Wayne to Henry Knox, November 15, 1793, Knox Papers; Wayne to Lt. Col. John F. Hamtramck, June 25, 1795, Anthony Wayne Papers, William L. Clements Library, Ann Arbor, Mich.
12. The theory of fortification and siege warfare is summarized in Christopher Duffy, *Fire and Stone: The Science of Fortress Warfare, 1660–1860* (New York: Hippocrene Books, 1975). For the French military school system, see Peter M. Molloy, "Technical Education and the Young Republic: West Point as America's École Polytechnique, 1802–1833" (Ph.D. diss., Brown University, 1975), 1–150.
13. Brooke Hindle, *The Pursuit of Science in Revolutionary America, 1735–1789* (Chapel Hill: University of North Carolina Press, 1956), 240–243.
14. Molloy, "Technical Education," 171–175.
15. Emanuel R. Lewis, *Seacoast Fortifications of the United States: An Introductory History* (Washington, D.C.: Smithsonian Institution, 1970), 21–25; Arthur P. Wade, "Artillerists and Engineers: The Beginnings of American Seacoast Fortification, 1794–1815" (Ph.D. diss., Kansas State University, 1977), 14–15; Robert S. Browning, *Two If by Sea: The Development of American Coastal Defense Policy* (Westport, Conn.: Greenwood Press, 1983), 7–10; Isidore Stouf to William Eustis, July 20, 1812, file 2087, and Joseph J. Mangin to secretary of war, November 12, 1812, file 1733, AGO:LR.
16. Act of May 9, 1794, in Abner R. Hetzel, comp., *Military Laws of the United States* (Washington, D.C.: G. Templeman, 1846), 55.
17. Wade, "Artillerists and Engineers," 33–35; Norman B. Wilkinson, "The Forgotten 'Founder' of West Point," *Military Affairs* 24 (Winter 1960–1961):177–188; Lt. Gen. George Washington to James McHenry, October 15, 1798, in George Washington, *The Writings of George Washington from the Original Manuscript Sources, 1745–1799*, ed. John C. Fitzpatrick, 39 vols. (Washington, D.C.: Government Printing Office, 1931–1944), 36:488–489. For the junior officers, see Lt. Joseph Guimpe to Maj. Gen. Alexander Hamilton, October 14, 1799, and Lt. Philip Landais to Hamilton, November 14, 1799, Alexander Hamilton Papers, Library of Congress.
18. Timothy Pickering, "Objects of the Military Establishment of the United States," February 3, 1796, *ASP:MA*, 1:113.
19. *Centennial of the United States Military Academy at West Point, New York, 1802–1902*, 2 vols. (Washington, D.C., 1904), 1:212–213.
20. Lt. Col. Stephen Rochefontaine to Timothy Pickering, February 19, 1796, and April 26, 1796; Maj. John J. U. Rivardi to Pickering, June 21, 1796, and August 6, 1796, Timothy Pickering Papers, Massachusetts Historical Society.
21. Capt. Donald G. Mitchell to Timothy Pickering, May 9, 1796, ibid.
22. Wade, "Artillerists and Engineers," 49–59; Lt. Col. Stephen Rochefontaine to Timothy Pickering, April 26, 1796, May 28, 1796, May 31, 1796, August 6, 1796,

and August 23, 1796, and Rochefontaine to Mr. Hopkins, August 5, 1796, Pickering Papers.

23. Wade, "Artillerists and Engineers," 74–77.

24. Timothy Pickering to Henry Knox, August 1, 1798, Knox Papers.

25. Hamilton's motives are assessed in Kohn, *Eagle and Sword,* 253–255.

26. Most of Hamilton's military correspondence is in the Hamilton Papers, Library of Congress. A large selection of it, ably edited under the supervision of Harold C. Syrett, is contained in volumes 22–24 of *The Papers of Alexander Hamilton,* 26 vols. (New York: Columbia University Press, 1961–1979). Perhaps daunted by the extent of this material, military historians and biographers have mostly ignored Hamilton's tenure as inspector general and the internal history of the army during the Quasi-war.

27. Maj. Gen. Alexander Hamilton to James McHenry, January 14, 1799, and James Gunn to Hamilton, January 23, 1799, *Papers of Hamilton,* 22: 416–417, 433–434; Act of March 3, 1799, Hetzel, *Military Laws,* 89–96.

28. Maj. Gen. Alexander Hamilton to James McHenry, January 21, 1799, *Papers of Hamilton,* 22:431–432; Act of March 2, 1799, Hetzel, *Military Laws,* 83–85.

29. General Orders, June 6, 1799; circulars to commandants of regiments, June 19, 1799, and August 27, 1799; General Orders, March 28, 1800, *Papers of Hamilton,* 23:169–170, 200–201, 351–352, 24:375–378.

30. Maj. Gen. Alexander Hamilton to Capt. Abraham R. Ellery, May 29, 1799; circular to commandants of regiments, August 9, 1799; Hamilton to Lt. Col. Aaron Ogden, April 15, 1800; General Orders, April–May 1800, ibid., 23:153–154, 308–309, 24:408–410, 436–438.

31. Maj. Gen. Alexander Hamilton to James McHenry, November 30, 1799; Hamilton to Maj. Gen. Charles C. Pinckney, December 2, 1799; Hamilton to Lt. Col. Aaron Ogden, December 3, 1799; Hamilton to Brig. Gen. William North, December 4, 1799; Hamilton to Maj. Lewis Tousard, December 22, 1799; Hamilton to Pinckney, Lt. Col. Nathan Rice, and Lt. Col. William S. Smith, March 18, 1800, ibid., 24:81–82, 83–84, 86, 117, 340–341. Correspondence on this project is scattered through vols. 23 and 24 of this series.

32. Maj. Gen. Alexander Hamilton to James McHenry, November 23, 1799, and March 9, 1800, ibid., 24:69–75, 306–311. McHenry submitted Hamilton's plan without substantial change to President Adams, who passed it on to Congress; *ASP:MA,* 1:133–139. A less ambitious version of this proposal was considered by the House of Representatives; printed bill, March 19, 1800, Hamilton Papers.

33. For the political debate over the additional army, see Kohn, *Eagle and Sword,* 256–273.

34. The supply and pay system was a major theme of Hamilton's correspondence through his tenure as inspector general. See, for example, *Papers of Hamilton,* 23:15–19, 25, 142–143, 186–187, 325–327, 370–372, 423–429, 24:50–54, 185–192, 456–458.

35. Molloy, "Technical Education," 183–187.

36. *Centennial of U.S.M.A.,* 1:218–219.

37. Act of March 16, 1802, Hetzel, *Military Laws,* 99, 105.

38. Theodore J. Crackel, *Mr. Jefferson's Army: Political and Social Reform of the Military Establishment, 1801–1809* (New York: New York University Press, 1987), 58–62, 71–73.

39. Jefferson's views on military education are examined in Molloy, "Technical Education," 171–175.

40. The best description of Williams's early career is ibid., 201–226. For his transla-

tion of military works, see Jonathan Williams to Maj. Gen. Alexander Hamilton, June 17, 1799, and McHenry to Hamilton, August 12, 1799, *Papers of Hamilton*, 23:195, 311; Williams to Henry Dexter, January 20, 1801, Jonathan Williams Papers, Lilly Library, Indiana University, Bloomington.

41. Lt. Col. Jonathan Williams to Maj. Decius Wadsworth, May 13, 1802, Jonathan Williams Papers. Loyalty to the Corps of Engineers is the dominant theme of the correspondence of Williams and other engineer officers in this collection.

42. For the early stages of the engineer-artillery dispute, see Williams's correspondence for 1802–1803, ibid.; George W. Cullum, *Campaigns of the War of 1812–15, against Great Britain, Sketched and Criticized; with Brief Biographies of the American Engineers* (New York: J. Miller, 1879), 25–33. Williams explained his resignation at length in Engineer Orders, June 20, 1803, Jonathan Williams Papers.

43. Lt. Col. Jonathan Williams to Samuel White, February 8, 1806, Williams to Uriah Tracy, February 10, 1806, Tracy to Williams, March 5, 1806, and White to Williams, April 21, 1806, Jonathan Williams Papers; Act of April 10, 1806, Hetzel, *Military Laws*, 116–117.

44. Cullum, *Campaigns*, 51–60; Col. Jonathan Williams to James Madison, July 10, 1812, enclosing copy of petition of Capt. George Armistead et al., July 8, 1812, file W-196(6), Brig. Gen. Joseph Bloomfield to William Eustis, July 6, 1812, file B-322(6), and July 9, 1812, file B-330(6), SW:LR-Reg.; Capt. Eleazar D. Wood to Capt. Alden Partridge, July 10, 1812, Alden Partridge Papers, Library of Congress.

45. See, for example, Col. Joseph G. Swift to Jonathan Williams, December 18, 1812, Jonathan Williams Papers.

46. Molloy, "Technical Education," 239–262. In 1810, the War Department adopted regulations for the administration of West Point. William Eustis, "Regulations Relative to the Military Academy at West Point," April 30, 1810, SW:LS; "Internal Regulations for the Military Academy," compiled by Capt. Alden Partridge, May 25, 1810, approved by Col. Jonathan Williams, file W-88(5), SW:LR-Reg.

47. Col. Jonathan Williams to Henry Dearborn, March 14, 1808, *ASP:MA*, 1: 229–230. The draft bill and supporting documents are filed with a copy of this report in file W-1809, SW:LR-Unreg. Williams expressed these views in other reports and letters. See, for example, Williams to Albert Gallatin, September 19, 1807, Jonathan Williams Papers; Williams to William Eustis, n.d. [postscript dated October 31, 1809], file W-1810, SW:LR-Unreg.; Williams to Eustis, November 12, 1810, file W-162(5), SW:LR-Reg. For the general drive to expand the military academy, see Molloy, "Technical Education," 309–345.

48. On engineers' lobbying, see Maj. Alexander Macomb to Col. Jonathan Williams, February 6, 1809, April 5, 1809, and June 15, 1809, Maj. Joseph G. Swift to Williams, October 8, 1809, Williams to Thomas Jefferson, September 15, 1810, and Williams to James Madison, June 1810, Jonathan Williams Papers; Williams to William Eustis, December 24, 1810, file W-187(5), and February 25, 1811, file W-221(5), SW:LR-Reg.

49. Molloy, "Technical Education," 334–336; Wade, "Artillerists and Engineers," 258–260.

50. Col. Jonathan Williams to William Eustis, November 17, 1811, file W-12(6), SW:LR-Reg.; Maj. Joseph G. Swift to Williams, January 1, 1812, Samuel L. Mitchill to Williams, January 12, 1812, and Capt. William McRee to Williams, January 16, 1812, Jonathan Williams Papers; Act of April 29, 1812, Hetzel, *Military Laws*, 145–146.

51. This discussion of the U.S. Military Philosophical Society has been based largely

on Sidney Forman, "The United States Military Philosophical Society, 1802-1815," *William and Mary Quarterly,* 3d ser. 2 (July 1945):273-285; Arthur P. Wade, "A Military Offspring of the American Philosophical Society," *Military Affairs* 38 (October 1974):103-107; Molloy, "Technical Education," 271-308.

52. U.S. Military Philosophical Society, "Constitution," printed copy, Jacob Kingsbury Papers, Missouri Historical Society, St. Louis.

53. "Extracts from the Minutes of the United States Military Philosophical Society, at an Occasional Meeting at New-York, December 28, 1809," printed pamphlet, 15-21, ibid.

54. For the society as a lobby, see Molloy, "Technical Education," 276-278, 284-285.

55. Ibid., 298; Alexander Macomb, *A Treatise on Martial Law and Courts-Martial; as Practiced in the United States of America* (Charleston, S.C., 1809); Forman, "U.S. Military Philosophical Society," 282-283.

56. Wade, "Artillerists and Engineers," 186-192; Lewis, *Seacoast Fortifications,* 31-32, 34; Browning, *Two If by Sea,* 17-18; Willard B. Robinson, *American Forts: Architectural Form and Function* (Urbana: University of Illinois Press, 1977), 70-84.

57. Lt. Col. Jonathan Williams to Albert Gallatin, September 19, 1807, Jonathan Williams Papers. See also "Extracts from Minutes . . . 1809," 3-13, Kingsbury Papers, Missouri Historical Society; Williams to William Eustis, November 12, 1810, and enclosed statement, file W-163(5), SW:LR-Reg. Many of Williams's reports on fortifications and other aspects of military policy are filed in SW:LR-Reg. for the pre-War of 1812 years.

58. Molloy, "Technical Education," 299-300.

59. Lt. Alexander Macomb to Lt. Col. Jonathan Williams, October 8, 1804, Jonathan Williams Papers.

60. Maj. Alexander Macomb to Col. Jonathan Williams, December 25, 1809, ibid.

61. Lt. Col. Alexander Macomb to Col. Jonathan Williams, April 29, 1812, and May 16, 1812; Williams to Macomb, May 20, 1812, ibid.

CHAPTER SIX. THE ERA OF ARMY REFORM, 1815-1821

1. *Niles' Weekly Register* 26 (March 27, 1824):50-51.

2. This and the following paragraph are taken mainly from biographical sketches in *DAB.* The youngest general was Brig. Gen. Thomas Flournoy, age thirty-seven.

3. The careers of Brown, Jackson, and Ripley are covered in *DAB,* 3:124-125, 9:526-534, 15:621-622. For Parker, see *General Catalogue of Dartmouth and the Associated Schools, 1769-1925* (Hanover, N.H.: Dartmouth College, 1925), 108; Daniel Parker Papers, Historical Society of Pennsylvania, passim.

4. This sketch is based primarily on George H. Richards, *Memoir of Alexander Macomb, the Major General Commanding the Army of the United States* (New York: M'Elrath, Bangs, 1833); and Macomb's letters in the Jonathan Williams Papers, Lilly Library, Indiana University, Bloomington.

5. Lt. Alexander Macomb to Jonathan Williams, May 2, 1804, Jonathan Williams Papers.

6. This sketch is based mainly on James W. Silver, *Edmund Pendleton Gaines: Frontier General* (Baton Rouge: Louisiana State University Press, 1949).

7. Brig. Gen. Edmund P. Gaines to Col. Roger Jones, May 29, 1830, file G-95, National Archives, AGO:LR.

8. For this sketch, see Charles W. Elliott, *Winfield Scott: The Soldier and the Man* (New York: Macmillan, 1937).

9. Capt. William J. Worth to his sister, August 30, 1814, in William J. Worth, "Never before Published Letters of Famous General Worth, Written during Mexican War," *New York Times Magazine*, July 16, 1916, 10.

10. Lt. Col. Edmund P. Gaines to Brig. Gen. Thomas H. Cushing, January 20, 1813, file 2961, AGO:LR.

11. Capt. Alexander Macomb to Henry Dearborn, July 1807, file M-225(3), SW:LR-Reg. See also Capt. Winfield Scott to the secretary of war, July 14, 1809, file S-622(4), ibid.; Lt. Col. Zebulon M. Pike to William Eustis, June 10, 1810, file 10 6/10, AGO:LR.

12. Elliott, *Scott*, 194–207.

13. R. Ernest Dupuy, *Where They Have Trod: The West Point Tradition in American Life* (New York: Frederick A. Stokes, 1940), 69–103; Alexander J. Dallas to Capt. Sylvanus Thayer, April 20, 1815, Thayer to Col. Joseph G. Swift, October 10, 1815, August 12, 1816, February 12, 1817, and March 30, 1817, Maj. William McRee to Swift, January 8, 1817 (typescripts), Sylvanus Thayer Papers, U.S. Military Academy Library, West Point, N.Y.

14. Harwood P. Hinton, "The Military Career of John Ellis Wool, 1812–1863" (Ph.D. diss., University of Wisconsin, 1960).

15. Chester L. Kieffer, *Maligned General: A Biography of Thomas S. Jesup* (San Rafael, Calif.: Presidio Press, 1979).

16. Ellen F. Vose, comp., *Robert Vose and His Descendants* (Boston: Fort Hill Press, 1932), 73–75, 143; Josiah H. Vose to William Eustis, February 26, 1811, file 620, Vose to Brig. Gen. Daniel Parker, March 8, 1815, file 9672, AGO:LR.

17. George Dangerfield, *The Awakening of American Nationalism, 1815–1828* (New York: Harper and Brothers, 1965), 1–35. The quotation is from p. 10.

18. James Monroe to the Military Committee of the Senate, February 22, 1815, in James Monroe, *The Writings of James Monroe, Including a Collection of His Public and Private Papers and Correspondence Now for the First Time Printed*, ed. Stanislaus M. Hamilton, 7 vols. (New York: G. P. Putnam's Sons, 1898–1903), 5:321–327.

19. Act of March 3, 1815, Abner R. Hetzel, comp., *Military Laws of the United States* (Washington, D.C.: G. Templeman, 1846), 183–184. This act set the level of the peacetime army at 10,000 men, but the administration interpreted this provision creatively—to refer to enlisted men only and not to include the enlisted personnel of the Corps of Engineers. Alexander J. Dallas to James Madison, April 11, 1815, and Madison to Dallas, April 14, 1815, George M. Dallas, *Life and Writings of Alexander James Dallas* (Philadelphia: J. B. Lippincott, 1871), 397–398; Francis B. Heitman, comp., *Historical Register and Dictionary of the United States Army, from Its Organization, September 29, 1789, to March 2, 1903*, 2 vols. (Washington, D.C.: Government Printing Office, 1903), 2:578–579.

20. James D. Richardson, comp., *A Compilation of the Messages and Papers of the Presidents*, 20 vols. (New York: Bureau of National Literature, 1917), 2:7–8.

21. For Calhoun's career as secretary of war, see Charles M. Wiltse, *John C. Calhoun*, 3 vols. (Indianapolis: Bobbs-Merrill, 1944–1951), 1:142–187, 198–264; John C. Calhoun, *The Papers of John C. Calhoun*, ed. Robert L. Meriwether and W. Edwin Hemphill, 18 vols. to date (Columbia: University of South Carolina Press, 1959–), vols. 2–9.

22. George R. Taylor, *The Transportation Revolution, 1815–1860* (New York: Holt, Rinehart, Winston, 1951).

23. For general descriptions of this period as one of mobility and social disorder, see Rowland Berthoff, *An Unsettled People: Social Order and Disorder in American History* (New York: Harper and Row, 1971), 127–232; David Donald, "An Excess of Democracy: The American Civil War and the Social Process," *Lincoln Reconsidered: Essays on the Civil War Era* (New York: Vintage, 1961), 209–235; Stanley M. Elkins, *Slavery: A Problem in American Institutional and Intellectual Life* (Chicago: University of Chicago Press, 1959), 27–37.

24. See, for example, Lynn L. Marshall, "The Strange Still-Birth of the Whig Party," *American Historical Review* 72 (January 1967):445–468; David J. Rothman, *The Discovery of the Asylum: Social Order and Disorder in the New Republic* (Boston: Little, Brown, 1971); Carl F. Kaestle, *The Evolution of an Urban School System: New York City, 1750–1850* (Cambridge: Harvard University Press, 1973); Taylor, *Transportation Revolution,* 229–249; Matthew A. Crenson, *The Federal Machine: The Beginnings of Bureaucracy in Jacksonian America* (Baltimore: Johns Hopkins University Press, 1975).

25. For the development of some important professions in the first half of the nineteenth century, see Daniel H. Calhoun, *The American Civil Engineer: Origins and Conflict* (Cambridge: Massachusetts Institute of Technology, 1960); Joseph F. Kett, *The Formation of the American Medical Profession: The Role of Institutions, 1780–1860* (New Haven, Conn.: Yale University Press, 1968); Maxwell Bloomfield, *American Lawyers in a Changing Society, 1776–1876* (Cambridge: Harvard University Press, 1976), esp. 136–190; George H. Daniels, *American Science in the Age of Jackson* (New York: Columbia University Press, 1968), esp. 6–62.

26. Joseph G. Swift, *The Memoirs of Gen. Joseph Gardner Swift, L.L.D., U.S.A., First Grad. of the U.S.M.A., West Point* (Worcester, Mass.: F. S. Blanchard, 1890), 124.

27. Act of March 3, 1815, Hetzel, *Military Laws,* 183–184.

28. Ibid., 187–190.

29. *Papers of Calhoun,* 2:lxi–lxix; Hetzel, *Military Laws,* 200–202.

30. Brig. Gen. Daniel Parker to Col. John E. Wool, August 1, 1816, AGO:LS. See also Parker to Lt. Col. William S. Hamilton, August 14, 1815, Parker to Wool, October 5, 1816, Parker to Col. Robert Butler, March 24, 1817, and Parker to Col. Thomas A. Smith, May 26, 1818, ibid.

31. Col. Decius Wadsworth to John C. Calhoun, July 22, 1818, *Papers of Calhoun,* 2:415.

32. William E. Birkhimer, *Historical Sketch of the Organization, Administration, Materiel and Tactics of the Artillery, United States Army* (Washington, D.C.: J. J. Chapman, 1884), 275–280; Stanley L. Falk, "Artillery for the Land Service: The Development of a System," *Military Affairs* 28 (1964):97–99.

33. Merritt Roe Smith, *Harper's Ferry Armory and the New Technology: The Challenge of Change* (Ithaca, N.Y.: Cornell University Press, 1977), 106–109, 324–326, and passim.

34. See, for example, Lt. Col. Zebulon M. Pike to William Eustis, June 10, 1810, file 10 6/10, AGO:LR; Brig. Gen. Peter Gansevoort to Eustis, October 25, 1811, file G-167(5), SW:LR-Reg.

35. Alexander Smyth, *Regulations for the Field Exercise, Manoeuvres, and Conduct of the Infantry of the United States; Drawn Up and Adapted to the Organization of the Militia and Regular Troops* (Philadelphia: T. G. Palmer, 1812). The War Department order of March 30, 1812, approving these regulations for official use, is printed at the front of this volume. For the origins of the French tactical system, see Robert S. Quimby, *The Background of Napoleonic Warfare: The Theory of Military Tactics in Eighteenth Century France* (New York: Columbia University Press, 1957).

36. William Duane, *A Hand Book for Infantry: Containing the First Principles of Military Discipline, Founded on Rational Method . . . for the Use of the Military Forces of the United States* (Philadelphia, 1812).

37. Henry Whiting, "Life of Zebulon Montgomery Pike," *The Library of American Biography*, ed. Jared Sparks, 2d ser., 25 vols. (Boston: Hillard, Gray, 1839–1848), 5:310–312; Col. William Duane to Brig. Gen. Daniel Parker, November 2, 1814, November 25, 1814, and December 22, 1814, Parker Papers; Maj. Gen. Thomas Pinckney to secretary of war, November 13, 1814, and December 2, 1814, file P-163(8), SW:LR-Reg.; Winfield Scott, *Memoirs of Lieut.-General Winfield Scott, L.L.D., Written by Himself*, 2 vols. (New York: Sheldon, 1864), 1:119–120; Col. Jacob Kingsbury to Maj. Horatio Stark, March 22, 1814, Jacob Kingsbury Papers, Burton Collection, Detroit Public Library.

38. U.S. War Department, *Rules and Regulations for the Field Exercise and Manoeuvres of Infantry, Compiled and Adapted to the Organization of the Army of the United States, Agreeably to a Resolve of Congress, Dated December, 1814* (New York: T. and W. Mercein, 1815). The general orders of December 27, 1814, and February 28, 1815, establishing the board and approving the new regulations, are printed in this manual.

39. "Rules and Regulations of the Army of the United States," *ASP:MA*, 1:425–437; S. Norman Lieber, *Remarks on the Army Regulations and Executive Regulations in General* (Washington, D.C., 1898), 52–53.

40. Brig. Gen. Winfield Scott to John C. Calhoun, September 2, 1818, *ASP:MA*, 2:199–200.

41. U.S. War Department, *General Regulations for the Army; or, Military Institutes* (Philadelphia: M. Carey and Sons, 1821); Act of March 2, 1821, Hetzel, *Military Laws*, 215.

42. For the controversy over the regulations, see William B. Skelton, "The United States Army, 1821–1837: An Institutional History" (Ph.D. diss., Northwestern University, 1968), 56–58.

43. Stephen E. Ambrose, *Duty, Honor, Country: A History of West Point* (Baltimore: Johns Hopkins University Press, 1966), 38–61; Peter M. Molloy, "Technical Education and the Young Republic: West Point as America's École Polytechnique, 1802–1833" (Ph.D. diss., Brown University, 1975), 347–366.

44. Dupuy, *Where They Have Trod*, 8–182; Molloy, "Technical Education," 384–394; James W. Kershner, "Sylvanus Thayer: A Biography" (Ph.D. diss., West Virginia University, 1976).

45. "Rules and Regulations for the Government of the Military Academy at West Point," *ASP:MA*, 2:77–79.

46. Ambrose, *Duty, Honor, Country*, 67–79; Molloy, "Technical Education," 425–440.

47. Orders, signed by Acting Secretary of War George Graham, November 16, 1816, National Archives, Records of the Office of the Chief of Engineers (Record Group 77), Letters Sent to Engineer Officers.

48. For Bernard's career, see Joseph H. Harrison, Jr., "Simon Bernard, the American System, and the Ghost of the French Alliance," in John B. Boles, ed., *America: The Middle Period. Essays in Honor of Bernard Mayo* (Charlottesville: University of Virginia Press, 1973), 145–167. For the controversy over Bernard, see Swift, *Memoirs*, 143–149, 179–180; *Papers of Calhoun*, 2:lxxi–lxxii.

49. Simon Bernard, Capt. Jesse D. Elliott, U.S.N., and Maj. Joseph G. Totten to John C. Calhoun, February 7, 1821, *ASP:MA*, 2:305–310.

50. Simon Bernard and Maj. Joseph G. Totten to Col. Alexander Macomb, March 24, 1826, ibid., 3:283-298.

51. John C. Calhoun to House of Representatives, December 11, 1818, ibid., 1:779-782.

52. Wiltse, *Calhoun*, 1:198-210; *Papers of Calhoun*, 5:xi-xiv, xx-xxi; Carlton B. Smith, "Congressional Attitudes toward Military Preparedness during the Monroe Administration," *Military Affairs* 40 (February 1976):22-25.

53. The generals' reports are: Brig. Gen. Henry Atkinson to John C. Calhoun, October 18, 1820, file A-28, Brig. Gen. Edmund P. Gaines to Calhoun, July 27, 1820, file G-144, Maj. Gen. Andrew Jackson to Calhoun, August 9, 1820, file J-60, Brig. Gen. Thomas S. Jesup, memorandum, [1820], file J-137, Brig. Gen. Alexander Macomb to Calhoun, September 30, 1820, file M-122, Brig. Gen. Winfield Scott to Calhoun, August 20, 1820, file S-37, SW:LR-Reg.; Maj. Gen. Jacob Brown to Calhoun, October 6, 1820, Jacob J. Brown Papers, Library of Congress. In addition, Calhoun seems to have consulted at least two earlier reports: Macomb to Calhoun, November 9, 1819, file M-121, SW:LR-Reg.; Jesup to Calhoun, March 31, 1820, *Papers of Calhoun*, 4:744-753.

54. Russell F. Weigley, *Towards an American Army: Military Thought from Washington to Marshall* (New York: Columbia University Press, 1962), 22-23; Roger J. Spiller, "Calhoun's Expansible Army: The History of a Military Idea," *South Atlantic Quarterly* 79 (Spring 1980):189-203; Lt. Col. Jonathan Williams to Albert Gallatin, September 19, 1807, Jonathan Williams Papers.

55. Maj. Gen. Jacob Brown to John C. Calhoun, October 6, 1820, Brown Papers, Library of Congress.

56. John C. Calhoun to John W. Taylor, December 12, 1820, *ASP:MA*, 2:188-191.

57. *Annals of Congress*, 16th Cong., 2d sess., 933-934. For the debate in the House, see ibid., 688-689, 758-794, 802-841, 901-907, 912-914, 928-934, 936-937.

58. Ibid., 238, 261, 364-365, 367-374, 379, 389; Hetzel, *Military Laws*, 213-215.

59. Richardson, comp., *Messages and Papers of the Presidents*, 3:168.

CHAPTER SEVEN. THE ORGANIZATIONAL SETTING, 1821-1861

1. *ASP:MA*, 2:452-456.

2. William B. Skelton, "The Commanding General and the Problem of Command in the United States Army, 1821-1841," *Military Affairs* 34 (December 1970): 117-122.

3. *Annals of Congress*, 17th Cong., 1st sess., 896; *Register of Debates in Congress*, 19 vols. (Washington, D.C.: Gales and Seaton, 1825-1837), 21st Cong., 1st sess., 774-776, 788-789, 791-795, 808-819.

4. William B. Skelton, "The United States Army, 1821-1837: An Institutional History" (Ph.D. diss., Northwestern University, 1968), 48-183; Francis Paul Prucha, *The Sword of the Republic: The United States Army on the Frontier, 1783-1846* (New York: Macmillan, 1969); Forest G. Hill, *Roads, Rails & Waterways: The Army Engineers and Early Transportation* (Norman: University of Oklahoma Press, 1957).

5. Skelton, "U.S. Army, 1821-1837," 202-404; Prucha, *Sword of the Republic*, 193-395 and passim.

6. Skelton, "U.S. Army, 1821-1837," 341-347; Prucha, *Sword of the Republic*, 235-248.
7. Acts of May 23, 1836, and July 5, 1838, Abner R. Hetzel, comp., *Military Laws of the United States* (Washington, D.C.: G. Templeton, 1846), 255, 261-262.
8. Skelton, "U.S. Army, 1821-1837," 254-256, 263-265; Acts of April 5, 1832, and June 28, 1832, Hetzel, *Military Laws*, 227, 229.
9. Act of July 5, 1838, Hetzel, *Military Laws*, 262-267.
10. Between 1822 and 1845, War Department expenditures (excluding veterans' pensions) amounted to 29.5 percent of total federal expenditures; Navy Department expenditures were 22.2 percent of federal expenditures. Computed from *Historical Statistics of the United States: Colonial Times to 1970*, 2 vols. (Washington, D.C.: Government Printing Office, 1975), 1:1115.
11. Act of August 23, 1842, Hetzel, *Military Laws*, 275-277.
12. Acts of April 4, 1844, and May 19, 1846, ibid., 277-278, 284-285.
13. Acts of May 13, 1846, May 13, 1846, and June 18, 1846, ibid., 280-282, 285; Francis B. Heitman, comp., *Historical Register and Dictionary of the United States Army, from Its Organization, September 29, 1789, to March 2, 1903*, 2 vols. (Washington, D.C.: Government Printing Office, 1903), 2:590-591. The actual strength fell far short of this figure: 10,690 in December 1846. Ibid., 626.
14. Acts of February 11, 1847, and March 3, 1847, in John F. Callan, comp., *Military Laws of the United States, Relating to the Army, Volunteers, Militia, and to Bounty Lands and Pensions, from the Foundation of the Government to the Year 1863* (Philadelphia: C. W. Childs, 1863), 379-387.
15. Acts of July 19, 1848, and August 14, 1848, ibid., 393-394, 397.
16. Robert M. Utley, *Frontiersmen in Blue: The United States Army and the Indian, 1848-1865* (New York: Macmillan, 1967), 1-210; Norman F. Furniss, *The Mormon Conflict, 1850-1859* (New Haven, Conn.: Yale University Press, 1960), passim; Marvin Ewy, "The United States Army in the Kansas Border Troubles, 1855-1856," *Kansas Historical Quarterly* 32 (Winter 1966):385-400.
17. Acts of June 17, 1850, and March 3, 1855, Callan, *Military Laws*, 408-409, 436.
18. Heitman, *Historical Register*, 2:596-597, 626; Raphael P. Thian, comp., *Notes Illustrating the Military Geography of the United States, 1813-1880* (Washington, D.C.: Government Printing Office, 1881), 8 and passim.

CHAPTER EIGHT. THE STABILIZATION OF OFFICER RECRUITMENT

1. John C. Calhoun to Orasmus C. Merrill, January 24, 1818, SW:LS.
2. Calculated from lists of nominations for army commissions, 1817-1820, *JEP*, 3:passim; Francis B. Heitman, comp., *Historical Register and Dictionary of the United States Army, from Its Organization, September 29, 1789, to March 2, 1903*, 2 vols. (Washington, D.C.: Government Printing Office, 1903), 1:passim.
3. "Rules and Regulations for the Government of the Military Academy at West Point," *ASP:MA*, 2:79; John C. Calhoun to Hugh Nelson, April 1, 1818, SW:LS.
4. Calculated from George W. Cullum, comp., *Biographical Register of the Officers and Graduates of the U.S. Military Academy at West Point, N.Y., from Its Establishment, in 1802, to 1890; with the Early History of the United States Military Academy*, 3 vols. (Boston: Houghton, Mifflin, 1891), 1:111-469.
5. Based on lists of nominations for army commissions, 1821-1831, *JEP*, 3-4:passim; Heitman, *Historical Register*, 1:passim.

6. Calculated from army register for 1817, *U.S. Army Registers*, 2 vols. (Washington, D.C., 1815–1839), 1:107–117; army register for 1830, *ASP:MA*, 4:251–261; army register for 1860, 36th Cong., 2d sess., House Exec. Doc. no. 54; Heitman, *Historical Register*, 1:passim.
7. Calculated from Cullum, *Biographical Register of U.S.M.A.*, 1:51–275.
8. James Barbour to Andrew Stevenson, February 28, 1828, *ASP:MA*, 3:794.
9. Joel R. Poinsett to L. G. Watson, July 14, 1838, SW:LS.
10. Act of March 1, 1843, U.S. Congress, *The Public Statutes at Large of the United States of America*, 100 vols. to date (Boston and Washington, D.C.: Government Printing Office, 1848–), 5:606.
11. John C. Calhoun to Jacob Bond I'On, July 28, 1823, Calhoun to Joseph G. Swift, September 10, 1823, in John C. Calhoun, *The Papers of John C. Calhoun*, ed. Robert L. Meriwether and W. Edwin Hemphill, 18 vols. to date (Columbia: University of South Carolina Press, 1959–), 8:181, 267; Lewis Cass to Capt. William Hoffman, February 9, 1836, SW:LS; Col. Charles Gratiot to Stephen Pleasonton, December 7, 1839, file 1840/223, National Archives, Records of the Office of the Adjutant General (Record Group 94), U.S. Military Academy Cadet Application Papers, 1805–1866 (hereafter cited as Cadet Application Papers).
12. West Point Board of Visitors to John H. Eaton, June 1830, *ASP:MA*, 4:608.
13. Gerrit Smith to Jefferson Davis, May 7, 1854, file 1854/196, Cadet Application Papers.
14. Col. Joseph G. Totten to Maj. Richard Delafield, January 19, 1842, National Archives, Records of the Office of the Chief of Engineers (Record Group 77), Letters and Reports of Col. Joseph G. Totten, 1803–1864; "Circumstances of Parents of Cadets, 1842–1879," U.S. Military Academy Library, West Point, N.Y.
15. For an anonymous cadet's description of this exercise, see *Cadet Life at West Point* (Boston, 1862), 128–131. Both the author and his friend described their economic circumstances as "indigent," though the author's father appears to have been a well-to-do farmer and his friend's father the owner of sawmills. This account has been attributed to George C. Strong, but the author's description of his background does not correspond to the information on Strong in his application file or the cadet register.
16. Report of the House Committee on Military Affairs, 1844, 28th Cong., 1st sess., House Rept. no. 476, 15–16.
17. Lt. Henry L. Scott to William B. Rose, September 5, 1845, National Archives, HQA:LS. General Scott claimed to have lobbied personally for inclusion of the ten at-large positions in the bill regulating the military academy, approved on March 1, 1843. Maj. Gen. Winfield Scott to George W. Crawford, February 14, 1850, ibid.
18. Based on Cullum, *Biographical Register of U.S.M.A.*, 2:passim; "Circumstances of Parents of Cadets;" and Cadet Application Papers. Polk's nephews were Lucius M. Walker and Marshall T. Polk.
19. Maj. Gen. Winfield Scott to George W. Crawford, February 14, 1850, Scott to Charles M. Conrad, February 25, 1851, March 12, 1852, and January 23, 1853, HQA:LS; Cullum, *Biographical Register of U.S.M.A.*, 2:passim. For the War Department's acceptance of Scott's position, see Jefferson Davis to W. I. Duane, August 10, 1855, SW:LS.
20. "Rules and Regulations for the Government of the Military Academy at West Point," *ASP:MA*, 2:78.
21. Cadet Edward L. Hartz to his father, June 24, 1851, Edward L. Hartz Papers, Library of Congress.

22. Between 1817 and 1829, the annual number of appointees who failed to report or were found unqualified averaged twenty-six. Calculated from a list in *ASP:MA,* 4:332–335. A historian has figured that 93.1 percent of the candidates examined between 1833 and 1861 were admitted as cadets; James L. Morrison, Jr., "Educating the Civil War Generals: West Point, 1833–1861," *Military Affairs* 38 (October 1974):108.

23. Rep. James Blair, January 21, 1830, *Register of Debates in Congress,* 19 vols. (Washington, D.C.: Gales and Seaton, 1825–1837), 21st Cong., 1st sess., 552–553. For general discussions of the attack on West Point in the 1830s and 1840s, see Marcus Cunliffe, *Soldiers & Civilians: The Martial Spirit in America, 1775–1865* (Boston: Little, Brown, 1968), 105–110; Stephen E. Ambrose, *Duty, Honor, Country: A History of West Point* (Baltimore: Johns Hopkins University Press, 1966), 106–120; Leonard D. White, *The Jacksonians: A Study in Administrative History, 1829–1861* (New York: Macmillan, 1954), 208–212; Arthur A. Ekirch, Jr., *The Civilian and the Military* (New York: Oxford University Press, 1956), 69–70.

24. Rep. Albert G. Hawes, April 26, 1836, *Register of Debates in Congress,* 24th Cong., 1st sess., 3371.

25. For the Democratic appointment ideology, see Sidney H. Aronson, *Status and Kinship in the Higher Civil Service: Standards of Selection in the Administrations of John Adams, Thomas Jefferson, and Andrew Jackson* (Cambridge: Harvard University Press, 1964), 14–21.

26. Cunliffe, *Soldiers & Civilians,* 153–155.

27. *JEP,* 4:283–284, 354–355. On Dodge, see *DAB,* 5:348–349.

28. Capt. Ethan Allen Hitchcock to Capt. John Garland, May 12, 1833, Ethan Allen Hitchcock Papers, Library of Congress. See also *Military and Naval Magazine of the United States* 1 (April 1833):118–121, (June 1833):252–253.

29. *JEP,* 4:554–555.

30. Ibid., 5:146–147.

31. Ibid., 150–151.

32. General Orders, August 17, 1837, AGO: Orders and Circulars; Joel R. Poinsett, "Regulations Respecting the Appointment in the Army of Persons from Civil Life," 1839, *Army and Navy Chronicle* 10 (May 14, 1840):313. For a candidate's description of the examination, see George C. Westcott to the Board of Examiners, September 5, 1838, George C. Westcott file, National Archives, SW: Applications, Subseries for 1820–1846.

33. *JEP,* 4:630, 5:37–40, 54, 147, 151, 156–161, 227–230.

34. John Bell to C. A. Belin, April 26, 1841, SW:LS.

35. U.S. Congress, *Congressional Globe,* 46 vols. (Washington, D.C., 1834–1873), 29th Cong., 1st sess., 655.

36. James K. Polk, *The Diary of James K. Polk during His Presidency, 1845 to 1849,* ed. Milo M. Quaife, 4 vols. (Chicago: A. C. McClurg, 1910), 1:404, 406–407, 412.

37. *JEP,* 7:74–75; Polk, *Diary,* 1:412–417, 478.

38. Polk, *Diary,* 1:417–418, 2:150–151, 236, 384–387, 3:26.

39. On the attempt to appoint Benton, see Justin H. Smith, *The War with Mexico,* 2 vols. (New York: Macmillan, 1919), 2:75. The other former congressmen were Maj. George A. Caldwell, Lt. Col. Thomas A. Moore, Maj. Thomas H. Seymour, and Col. John W. Tibbatts. For Cass and Ransom, see James G. Wilson and John Fiske, comps., *Appleton's Cyclopaedia of American Biography,* 6 vols. (New York: D. Appleton, 1894), 1:553, 5:181. For Pillow, see *DAB,* 13:603–604. For Savage, see *BDC,* 1564.

40. Based on lists of nominations for army commissions in *JEP,* 7:passim. The

number of citizen appointments was virtually the same as the number of officers of the basic establishment dying as a result of combat (sixty-two). Compiled from Heitman, *Historical Register,* 2:13–42.

41. *JEP,* 10:81–85, 105–106, 119, 201–202.

42. Based mainly on information in SW: Applications, Subseries for 1854–1861. On Drysdale, see John Dick to Augustus E. Maxwell, February 14, 1855, file Fla. 2, ibid.

43. For some reports of the examination boards, see the following files (1856): A-40, B-95, C-66, L-46, S-104, AGO:LR. A successful candidate thought that this examination was "only intended to give an opportunity to reject such persons as from their character as gentlemen (or rather the reverse) would be disgraceful to the service." Capt. James J. Archer to his mother, January 28, 1856, James J. Archer Papers, Maryland Historical Society, Baltimore.

44. Calculated from lists of nominations for military commissions, *JEP,* 3:passim.

45. See, for example, John H. Eaton to the president of the Senate, February 17, 1830, Maj. William S. Foster to Maj. Gen. Alexander Macomb, October 12, 1830, *ASP:MA,* 4:284–286, 651–652.

46. William Gill et al., petition dated January 16, 1837, 24th Cong., 2d sess., House Exec. Doc. no. 88. See also *Military and Naval Magazine of the United States,* 3 (April 1834):121–124.

47. Based on lists of nominations for army commissions, *JEP,* 5:passim. Joel R. Poinsett to Col. Zachary Taylor et al., March 15, 1838, SW:LS.

48. John F. Callan, comp., *Military Laws of the United States, Relating to the Army, Volunteers, Militia, and to Bounty Lands and Pensions, from the Foundation of the Government to the Year 1863* (Philadelphia: C. W. Childs, 1863), 386; General Orders No. 37, July 8, 1848, AGO: Orders and Circulars; Col. William Gates et al., petition to Senate and House of Representatives, n.d., copy enclosed with William Blaisdell to Maj. Gen. Winfield Scott, November 25, 1851, file B-2, National Archives, HQA:LR.

49. Serg. Samuel H. Starr to Eliza Starr, April 5, 1847, Samuel H. Starr Papers, Bixby Collection, Missouri Historical Society, St. Louis. More fortunate than most, Starr did receive a commission in 1848.

50. Act of August 4, 1854, Callan, *Military Laws,* 433; General Orders No. 17, October 4, 1854, AGO: Orders and Circulars.

51. Based on lists of nominations for officers' commissions, 1854–1860, *JEP,* 10:passim. For the case of the private, see Cornelius D. Hendren to H. Hendren, November 12, 1856, file Miss. 31, SW: Applications, Subseries for 1854–1861.

52. During the Restoration period, more than half of the officers of the French army were former enlisted men. Douglas Porch, *Army and Revolution: France, 1815–1848* (London: Routledge and Kegan Paul, 1974), 43–44. The Russian army drew approximately 5 percent to 7 percent of its infantry and cavalry officers from the enlisted ranks. John S. Curtiss, *The Russian Army under Nicholas I, 1825–1855* (Durham, N.C.: Duke University Press, 1965), 77. The military establishment most resembling the U.S. Army in its reluctance to promote enlisted men was the British army. Gwynn Harries-Jenkins, *The Army in Victorian Society* (London: Routledge and Kegan Paul, 1977), 65.

53. Polk, *Diary,* 3:30–33.

54. Rodney Glisan, *Journal of Army Life* (San Francisco: A. L. Bancroft, 1874), 453.

55. Cadet George B. McClellan to his sister, August 5, 1842, George B. McClellan Papers, Library of Congress.

56. National Archives, Records of the Office of the Adjutant General (Record Group 94), Registers of Enlistments in the United States Army, 1798–1914.
57. Application files for Caleb Smith and George L. Willard, SW: Applications, Subseries for 1846–1848; application files for Warren L. Lothrop (Army 105) and Alexander N. Shipley (Army 29), ibid., Subseries for 1854–1861. On Willard, see also Charles H. Page, ed., *Willard Genealogy* (Boston, 1915), 236. On Lothrop, see also Georgia D. Merrill, ed., *History of Androscoggin County, Maine* (Boston: W. A. Fergusson, 1891), 576.
58. Polk, *Diary,* 4:274–275.
59. Calculated from the army register for 1860, 36th Cong., 2d sess., House Exec. Doc. no. 54, 10–12; Heitman, *Historical Register,* 1:passim.
60. William Eustis to Hosp. Surg. John M. Daniel, August 5, 1809, SW:LS. Eustis was apparently following the advice of the faculty of the University of Pennsylvania medical school. Benjamin Rush et al. to James Madison, March 29, 1809, file R-200(4), SW:LR-Reg.
61. Hosp. Surg. David C. Ker to James Madison, June 1, 1812, file K-23(6), SW:LR-Reg.
62. Several men nominated as hospital surgeons' mates in 1813 were apparently selected by the physician and surgeon general on the basis of a medical examination; *JEP,* 2:477. Departmental regulations of 1814 required candidates for appointment who had not received a degree from a "respectable medical school or college" to be examined by a medical board. Harvey E. Brown, *The Medical Department of the United States Army from 1775 to 1873* (Washington, D.C.: Surgeon General's Office, 1873), 97. The War Department established several such boards during the last stages of the war. General Orders, November 15, 1814, November 27, 1814, December 9, 1814, and January 20, 1815, AGO: Orders and Circulars.
63. Brown, *Medical Department,* 128–129.
64. General Orders No. 58, July 7, 1832, AGO: Orders and Circulars; Act of June 30, 1834, Abner R. Hetzel, comp., *Military Laws of the United States* (Washington, D.C.: G. Templeman, 1846), 234; Mary C. Gillett, *The Army Medical Department, 1818–1865* (Washington, D.C.: Government Printing Office, 1987), 31–32.
65. Brown, *Medical Department,* 152–153, 199–201; "Army Medical Board of Examination," *Military and Naval Magazine of the United States* 4 (November 1834):186–191; National Archives, Records of the Office of the Surgeon General (Record Group 112), Records of the Army Medical Board, passim.
66. Surg. Thomas S. Mower to Surg. Gen. Thomas Lawson, June 14, 1839, filed with report of the Medical Board for 1839, Records of Army Medical Board. See also Surg. Henry L. Heiskell to Asst. Surg. Benjamin King, May 30, 1839, Benjamin King Papers, Library of Congress.
67. Brown, *Medical Department,* 152; reports of the Medical Board, 1839, 1846, 1858, Office of the Surgeon General, Records of Army Medical Board; Col. William Lindsay to Anna Lindsay, December 13, 1835, William Lindsay Papers, State Historical Society of Wisconsin, Madison.
68. Brown, *Medical Department,* 160–161.
69. Compiled from various sources, especially: National Archives, Records of the Office of the Surgeon General (Record Group 112), Military Service Cards of Retired or Deceased Medical Officers; National Archives, Records of the Office of the Adjutant General (Record Group 94), Medical Officers' Personal Files.
70. Joseph F. Kett, *The Formation of the American Medical Profession: The Role of Institutions, 1780–1860* (New Haven, Conn.: Yale University Press, 1968).

CHAPTER NINE. SOCIAL ORIGINS AND CAREER MOTIVATIONS

1. Based on the army register for 1830, *ASP:MA,* 4:251-261; army register for 1860, 36th Cong., 2d sess., House Exec. Doc. no. 54; Francis B. Heitman, comp., *Historical Register and Dictionary of the United States Army, from Its Organization, September 29, 1789, to March 2, 1903,* 2 vols. (Washington, D.C.: Government Printing Office, 1903), 1:passim.
2. Information on medical officers' education compiled from sources cited in chapter 8, note 69.
3. Although army organization in 1860 authorized only five generals, six are listed on the army register because Joseph E. Johnston succeeded to the post of quartermaster general on the death of Thomas S. Jesup in June.
4. Information on officers' backgrounds has been obtained from a variety of sources: Cadet Application Papers; SW: Applications; "Circumstances of Parents of Cadets, 1842-1879," U.S. Military Academy Library, West Point, N.Y.; biographies and biographical dictionaries; autobiographies and memoirs; genealogies; local histories; city directories; and manuscript collections.
5. For Fenwick, see Fairfax Harrison, *The John's Island Stud, 1750-1788* (Richmond: Old Dominion Press, 1931). For Delafield, see *DAB,* 5:208-210.
6. Marcus Cunliffe, *Soldiers & Civilians: The Martial Spirit in America, 1775-1865* (Boston: Little, Brown, 1968).
7. James S. Thompson to John C. Calhoun, January 30, 1821, file 1821/133, Cadet Application Papers; T. Harry Williams, *P. G. T. Beauregard: Napoleon in Gray* (Baton Rouge: Louisiana State University Press, 1954), 5-6; John W. DePeyster, *Personal and Military History of Philip Kearny, Major-General United States Volunteers* (New York: Rice and Gage, 1869), 27-47.
8. W. Ingraham Kip to Jefferson Davis, July 12, 1854, file California 25, SW: Applications, Subseries for 1854-1861. Kip's son Lawrence was appointed to the army in 1857.
9. Thomas L. Casey to William L. Marcy, February 21, 1848, file 1845/37, Cadet Application Papers; Bradford A. Whittemore, *Memorials of the Massachusetts Society of the Cincinnati* (Boston, 1964), 210-213.
10. Joseph H. Parks, *General Edmund Kirby Smith, C.S.A.* (Baton Rouge: Louisiana State University Press, 1954), passim: quotation on p. 77.
11. Application files for John F. Lee (1828/107), Richard C. Gatlin (1828/166), Frank S. Armistead (1851/10), Henry B. Clitz (1840/92), and George T. Balch (1847/10), Cadet Application Papers; John R. Cooke (Mo. 17), James J. Dana (Mass. 8), and Dunbar R. Ransom (Vt. 1), SW: Applications, Subseries for 1854-1861.
12. Quotations taken from the application files for Henry M. Judah (1838/113), Alexander Johnston, Jr. (1820/34), Joseph Cadle (1818/88), John M. Washington (1814/29), and Josiah Gorgas (1837/101), Cadet Application Papers.
13. Application file for Edward Dillon, Nebr. 5, SW: Applications, Subseries for 1854-1861. For examples of officers with civilian experience in the engineering services, see the files for Alexander E. Drake (Ky. 20), George P. Ihrie (Calif. 11), Edward Ingraham (Miss. 25), Joseph P. Minter (Washington Territory 1), and Edwin W. H. Read (Ind. 12), ibid.
14. Cornelius A. Ogden to John Armstrong, July 11, 1813, file 1813/Unregistered, Cadet Application Papers; Robert M. McLane, *Reminiscences, 1827-1897* (Wilmington, Del.: Scholarly Resources, 1972), 52-53.
15. John M. Schofield, *Forty-Six Years in the Army* (New York: Century, 1897), 1-2;

Lt. Abraham R. Johnston's journal, entry for March 3, 1841, Abraham R. Johnston Papers, U.S. Military Academy Library, West Point, N.Y.

CHAPTER TEN. THE WEST POINT EXPERIENCE

1. A number of studies examine the West Point curriculum in the antebellum era. See especially Stephen E. Ambrose, *Duty, Honor, Country: A History of West Point* (Baltimore: Johns Hopkins University Press, 1966), 87–105, 131–137; Peter M. Molloy, "Technical Education and the Young Republic: West Point as America's École Polytechnique, 1802–1833" (Ph.D. diss., Brown University, 1975), 440–453; James L. Morrison, Jr., *"The Best School in the World:" West Point, the Pre-Civil War Years, 1833–1866* (Kent, Ohio: Kent State University Press, 1986), 87–101; James L. Morrison, Jr., "Educating the Civil War Generals: West Point, 1833–1861," *Military Affairs* 38 (October 1974): 108–111.
2. Capt. Sylvanus Thayer to George Graham, August 28, 1817, file T-122(10), SW:LR-Reg.
3. Morrison, *"Best School in the World,"* 91.
4. Col. John E. Wool to John C. Calhoun, undated inspection report, approved by Maj. Gen. Jacob Brown, December 12, 1819, John E. Wool Papers, New York State Library, Albany; Col. Alexander Macomb to Capt. Sylvanus Thayer, August 22, 1822, Sylvanus Thayer Papers, U.S. Military Academy Library, West Point, N.Y.
5. Capt. Thomas Williams to Mary Williams, journal letter beginning February 16, [1857], entry for February 19, Williams Family Papers, Burton Collection, Detroit Public Library.
6. Col. Joseph G. Totten to William Wilkins, November 30, 1844, 28th Cong., 2d sess., Sen. Exec. Doc. no. 1, 199–200; Totten to Jefferson Davis, August 3, 1860, 36th Cong., 2d sess., Sen. Misc. Doc. no. 3, 233. The academic board regularly used the concept of mental discipline to defend the technical curriculum after 1843. Morrison, *"Best School in the World,"* 43–44.
7. Joseph Ellis and Robert Moore, *School for Soldiers: West Point and the Profession of Arms* (London: Oxford University Press, 1974), 39–41.
8. Morrison, *"Best School in the World,"* 114–125.
9. William Paley, *The Principles of Moral and Political Philosophy* (London: R. Faulder, 1785); Francis Wayland, *The Elements of Moral Science*, ed. Joseph L. Blau (Cambridge: Harvard University Press, 1963). For a list of textbooks used at the academy, see *Centennial of the United States Military Academy at West Point, New York, 1802–1902*, 2 vols. (Washington, D.C., 1904), 1:439–466.
10. Wayland, *Elements,* 188–198, 359–364; Col. Joseph G. Totten to Maj. Richard Delafield, February 28, 1842, National Archives, Records of the Office of the Chief of Engineers (Record Group 77), Letters and Reports of Col. Joseph G. Totten.
11. Wayland, *Elements,* 332–333.
12. Emmerich de Vattel, *The Law of Nations; or, Principles of the Law of Nature, Applied to the Conduct and Affairs of Nations and Sovereigns,* ed. Joseph Chitty and Edward D. Ingraham (Philadelphia: T. and J. W. Johnson, 1883).
13. James Kent, *Commentaries on American Law,* ed. Oliver Wendell Holmes, Jr., and John M. Gould, 2 vols. (Boston: Little, Brown, 1896), 1:passim.
14. Lt. John A. Tardy, testimony before commission investigating the military academy, July 27, 1860, 36th Cong., 2d sess., Sen. Misc. Doc. no. 3, 91. For similar remarks, see ibid., 89, 90, 93, 96, 108, 135.

15. Mahan's course is examined in Thomas E. Griess, "Dennis Hart Mahan: West Point Professor and Advocate of Military Professionalism, 1830–1871" (Ph.D. diss., Duke University, 1968), 209–248, and more critically in Morrison, "Educating Civil War Generals," 109. The comparison to veterinary science is made in Capt. George W. Cullum to Lt. Joseph C. Ives, August 18, 1860, 36th Cong., 2d sess., Sen. Misc. Doc. no. 3, 324–325.

16. Morrison, "Educating Civil War Generals," 109–110.

17. In the classes of 1841–1846 and 1851–1856, 12.1 percent of the graduates entered the three "scientific" corps. Compiled from George W. Cullum, comp., *Biographical Register of the Officers and Graduates of the U.S. Military Academy at West Point, N.Y., from Its Establishment, in 1802, to 1890; with the Early History of the United States Military Academy*, 3 vols. (Boston: Houghton, Mifflin, 1891), vol. 2.

18. Morrison, *"Best School in the World,"* passim; Ambrose, *Duty, Honor, Country*, 147–151; *Cadet Life at West Point* (Boston, 1862), 181–185; Tully McCrea, *Dear Belle: Letters from a Cadet & Officer to His Sweetheart, 1858–1865*, ed. Catherine S. Crary (Middletown, Conn.: Wesleyan University Press, 1965), 17–20; Cadet Edward L. Hartz to Samuel Hartz, July 29, 1851, and Hartz to Harriet Hartz, September 9, 1851, Edward L. Hartz Papers, Library of Congress.

19. "Regulations of the United States Military Academy at West Point," *ASP:MA*, 2:652–657.

20. Ibid., 655; *Cadet Life*, 185–186.

21. See, for example, Cadet Tully McCrea to Belle McCrea, April 27, 1861, quoted in McCrea, *Dear Belle*, 88–89; Morris Schaff, *The Spirit of Old West Point, 1858–1862* (Boston: Houghton, Mifflin, 1907), 102.

22. Morrison, *"Best School in the World,"* 91.

23. Ibid., 73–74.

24. Ibid., 101. Academic failure was considerably more common among southern cadets than among their northern colleagues. See tables in ibid., 180–182.

25. Cadet Edward L. Hartz to Jane E. Hartz, January 14, 1852, Hartz Papers.

26. This paragraph is based mainly on the list of officers of the military academy in Cullum, *Biographical Register of U.S.M.A.*, 1:21–25. On faculty recruitment and inbreeding, see also Molloy, "Technical Education," 400–415.

27. Ellis and Moore, *School for Soldiers*, passim, esp. chapters 2–4.

28. Cadet George D. Bayard to his father, July 18, 1853, in Samuel J. Bayard, *The Life of George Dashiell Bayard, Late Captain, U.S.A., and Brigadier-General of Volunteers, Killed in the Battle of Fredericksburg, December 1862* (New York: G. P. Putnam's Sons, 1874), 50.

29. Ulysses S. Grant, *Personal Memoirs of U. S. Grant*, 2 vols. (New York: C. L. Webster, 1885), 1:38–40; John M. Schofield, *Forty-Six Years in the Army* (New York: Century, 1897), 5; Henry Heth, *The Memoirs of Henry Heth*, ed. James L. Morrison, Jr. (Westport, Conn.: Greenwood Press, 1974), 14.

30. Cadet John C. Pemberton to his father, November 30, 1836, Pemberton Family Papers, Historical Society of Pennsylvania. See also: McCrea, *Dear Belle*, 39–46; Ambrose, *Duty, Honor, Country*, 159–166; Cadet Edward L. Hartz to Samuel Hartz, December 27, 1851, and Hartz to Jane E. Hartz, December 22, 1853, Hartz Papers; Morrison, *"Best School in the World,"* 84–85.

31. *Cadet Life*, 46–47; Cadet Thomas Rowland to his mother, August 9, 1859, in Thomas Rowland, "Letters of a Virginia Cadet at West Point, 1859–1861," *South Atlantic Quarterly* 14 (July and October 1915):214–215. See also Cadet Isaac Ingalls Stevens to William Stevens, June 13, 1835, Isaac Ingalls Stevens Papers, University of

Washington Library, Seattle; Cadet J. E. B. Stuart to George Hairston, March 6, 1851, in J.E.B. Stuart, "J. E. B. Stuart's Letters to His Hairston Kin, 1850–1855," ed. Peter W. Hairston, *North Carolina Historical Review* 51 (Summer 1974):269.

32. Grant, *Memoirs*, 1:41–42. On the cadets' admiration for Scott, see also Cadet James B. McPherson to R. B. McPherson, May 14, 1850, James B. McPherson Papers, Library of Congress.

33. Cadet Edward L. Hartz to Samuel Hartz, September 7, 1854, Hartz Papers.

34. Cadet George L. Welcker, valedictory address prepared for West Point graduation ceremony, June 1836, Lenoir Family Papers II, Southern Historical Collection, University of North Carolina Library, Chapel Hill; Cadet J. E. B. Stuart to Bettie Hairston, October 28, [1853], "Stuart's Letters," 304.

35. Cadet Nathaniel R. Chambliss, testimony before commission investigating the military academy, August 7, 1860, 36th Cong., 2d sess., Sen. Misc. Doc. no. 3, 112; Cadet Thomas Rowland to his mother, April 29, 1860, "Letters of a Virginia Cadet," 344; Erasmus D. Keyes, *Fifty Years' Observations of Men and Events, Civil and Military* (New York: C. Scribner's Sons, 1884), 190.

36. Capt. James Dalliba, *Improvements in the Military Establishment of the United States* (Troy, N.Y.: William S. Parker, 1822), 9; Lt. Henry L. Kendrick to Lt. Abraham R. Johnston, December 26, 1844, Abraham R. Johnston Papers, U.S. Military Academy Library, West Point, N.Y.

37. Lt. Samuel Woods to Jubal A. Early, April 22, 1839, Jubal A. Early Papers, Library of Congress; Lt. J. E. B. Stuart to Peter W. Hairston, August 3, 1854, "Stuart's Letters," 313–314; Lt. Cyrus B. Comstock to Lt. James B. McPherson, May 19, 1859, McPherson Papers.

38. Cadet Thomas Rowland to Kate M. Rowland, June 27, 1859, "Letters of a Virginia Cadet," 208.

CHAPTER ELEVEN. MILITARY CAREERS IN THE ANTEBELLUM ERA

1. *ASP:MA*, 5:638, 641; 32d Cong., 2d sess., House Exec. Doc. no. 1, 52–63.

2. Fort Winnebago Orderly Book, 1834–1836, State Historical Society of Wisconsin, Madison. This and the following paragraph have been based mainly on this source; the army general regulations of 1825, 1834, and 1847; and National Archives, Records of U.S. Army Continental Commands (Record Group 393), Orderly Books for Fort Conrad/Craig (1853–1856), Fort Gibson (1843), Fort Mackinac (1845), Fort Monroe (1852), and Fort Myers (1856–1857).

3. U.S. Army Continental Commands, Fort Gibson Orderly Book. In December 1842, the entire Fort Gibson command totalled 316 officers and men. Table stating dispositions of the army, 27th Cong., 3d sess., House Exec. Doc. no. 1.

4. Francis Paul Prucha, *Broadax and Bayonet: The Role of the United States Army in the Development of the Northwest, 1815–1860* (Madison: State Historical Society of Wisconsin, 1953), 104–148; Tommy R. Young II, "The United States Army in the South, 1789–1835"(Ph.D. diss., Louisiana State University Press, 1973), 248–252, 271–276, 290–292, and passim.

5. Capt. James J. Archer to his mother, January 13, 1859, James J. Archer Papers, Maryland Historical Society, Baltimore.

6. Lt. Alexander MacRae to his sister, October 9, 1852, John MacRae Papers, Southern Historical Collection, University of North Carolina Library, Chapel Hill; Lt.

George B. McClellan to his sister, October 9, 1852, George B. McClellan Papers, Library of Congress.

7. Lt. Edmund Kirby Smith to his mother, November 18, 1848, Edmund Kirby Smith Papers, Southern Historical Collection, University of North Carolina Library, Chapel Hill.

8. Richard D. Gamble, "Garrison Life at Frontier Military Posts, 1830–1860" (Ph.D. diss., University of Oklahoma, 1956), 199–205; Prucha, *Broadax and Bayonet*, 206–208.

9. Lt. Oliver Otis Howard to his mother, November 4, 1855, and Howard to his wife, February 11, 1857, Oliver Otis Howard Papers, Bowdoin College Library, Brunswick, Maine; Lt. Henry W. Halleck to Lt. Isaac Ingalls Stevens, February 9, 1840, April 8, 1840, and August 18, 1840, Isaac Ingalls Stevens Papers, University of Washington Library, Seattle; Lt. George W. Hazzard's correspondence for the 1850s, George W. Hazzard Papers, U.S. Military Academy Library, West Point, N.Y.

10. Lt. George A. McCall to H., December 1, 1822, in George A. McCall, *Letters from the Frontiers, Written during a Period of Thirty Years' Service in the Army of the United States* (Philadelphia: J. B. Lippincott, 1868), 31–32.

11. Henry Heth, *The Memoirs of Henry Heth*, ed. James L. Morrison, Jr. (Westport, Conn.: Greenwood Press, 1974), 82–84, 103–105; J. F. Williams, "Memoir of Capt. Martin Scott," *State Historical Society of Minnesota Collections* 3 (1904): 183–185; Randolph B. Marcy, *Thirty Years of Army Life on the Border* (New York: Harper and Brothers, 1866), 425. On officers' hunting, see also Gamble, "Garrison Life," 182–190; Rodney Glisan, *Journal of Army Life* (San Francisco: A. L. Bancroft, 1874), 54–64; Dabney H. Maury, *Recollections of a Virginian in the Mexican, Indian, and Civil Wars* (New York: C. Scribner's Sons, 1894), 96–102 and passim.

12. Eunice Tripler, *Eunice Tripler: Some Notes of Her Personal Recollections*, comp. Louis A. Arthur (New York: Grafton Press, 1910), 82; Lt. George D. Bayard to his father, September 24, 1856, in Samuel J. Bayard, *The Life of George Dashiell Bayard, Late Captain, U.S.A., and Brigadier-General of Volunteers, Killed in the Battle of Fredericksburg, December 1862* (New York: G. P. Putnam's Sons, 1874), 97–98; Col. Robert E. Lee to Lt. William H. F. Lee, May 30, 1858, in J. William Jones, *Life and Letters of Robert Edward Lee, Soldier and Man* (New York and Washington, D.C.: Neale Publishing Co., 1906), 93–94.

13. Lt. George W. Hazzard to his wife, December 20, 1857, Hazzard Papers.

14. Lt. George D. Bayard to his mother, April 28, 1860, Bayard, *Life of Bayard*, 169. For other descriptions of relations between the army and St. Louis, see Glisan, *Journal of Army Life*, 15; Thomas Wilhelm, *History of the Eighth U.S. Infantry, from Its Organization, in 1838*, 2 vols. (N.p., 1873), 1:128–129; William W. Averell, *Ten Years in the Saddle: The Memoir of William Woods Averell*, ed. Edward K. Eckert and Nicholas J. Amato (San Rafael, Calif.: Presidio Press, 1978), 58.

15. Lt. William T. Sherman to John Sherman, May 23, 1843, in William T. Sherman, *Home Letters of General Sherman*, ed. M. A. DeWolfe Howe (New York: C. Scribner's Sons, 1909), 23; Lt. Thomas Williams to John R. Williams, November 21, 1841, Williams Family Papers, Burton Collection, Detroit Public Library.

16. Lt. August V. Kautz's journal, entry for December 27, 1858, August V. Kautz Papers, Library of Congress. Generalizations on officers' social life in garrison are based on post histories; officers' published and unpublished letters and journals; Edward M. Coffman, *The Old Army: A Portrait of the American Army in Peacetime, 1784–1898* (New York: Oxford University Press, 1986), 105–112 and passim; and Gamble, "Garrison Life," 182–228.

17. Twenty-two of 113. The proportion of intra-army marriages among the officers on the 1830 army register for whom information is available is virtually the same: 33 of 177 (18.6 percent).

18. Coffman, *Old Army*, 107–108; Stephen R. Riggs, *Mary and I: Forty Years with the Sioux* (Minneapolis, Minn.: Ross and Haines, 1969), 46; John F. McDermott, *Seth Eastman: Pictorial Historian of the Indian* (Norman: University of Oklahoma Press, 1961), 18; Grant Foreman, *Advancing the Frontier, 1830–1860* (Norman: University of Oklahoma Press, 1933), 63–66; Lt. Richard S. Ewell to Benjamin S. Ewell, February 2, 1841, in Richard S. Ewell, *The Making of a Soldier: Letters of General R. S. Ewell*, ed. Percy G. Hamlin (Richmond: Whittet and Shepperson, 1935), 40; Lt. August V. Kautz's journal, entries for February 9, [1859], February 22, [1859], and passim, Kautz Papers.

19. Lt. Jeremy F. Gilmer to Lt. George L. Welcker, November 6, 1846, Lenoir Family Papers II, Southern Historical Collection, University of North Carolina, Chapel Hill; Lt. William H. Warner to Lt. John N. Macomb, September 22, 1846, Rodgers Family Papers, Library of Congress; Coffman, *Old Army*, 107–108; Grady McWhiney, *Southerners and Other Americans* (New York: Basic Books, 1973), 52; Heth, *Memoirs*, 57, 59–62; Lt. George A. H. Blake to Lt. Abraham R. Johnston, November 22, 1845, Abraham R. Johnston Papers, U.S. Military Academy Library, West Point, N.Y.

20. There were a few exceptions. At least two officers married Cherokee women while stationed at Ft. Gibson, at least one married a Sioux woman at Ft. Snelling, and at least one married an Indian girl at Ft. Washita. Foreman, *Advancing the Frontier*, 63–66; Nancy Huggan, "The Story of Nancy McClure," *Minnesota Historical Collections* 6 (1894):439; Lt. Nicholas B. Pearce to Lt. George B. McClellan, September 13, 1852, McClellan Papers. In 1860, an officer wrote that a fellow officer at Ft. Kearny had "a very fine Pawnee wife," though he may have meant a mistress. Lt. Thomas Berry to Lt. Edward P. Alexander, January 6, 1860, Edward P. Alexander Papers, Southern Historical Collection, University of North Carolina Library, Chapel Hill. In addition, at least two officers married Hispanic Californians and one a New Mexican. Langdon Sully, *No Tears for the General: The Life of Alfred Sully, 1821–1879* (Palo Alto, Calif.: American West, 1974), 60–64; John S. Griffin, "Dr. John S. Griffin's Mail, 1846–53," ed. Viola Lockhart Warren, *California Historical Society Quarterly* 33 (June 1954):109; McWhiney, *Southerners and Other Americans*, 51–52.

21. Lt. William M. Gardner to his brother, June 7, 1850, William M. Gardner Papers, Southern Historical Collection, University of North Carolina Library, Chapel Hill; Lt. Robert H. Chilton to Lt. Abraham R. Johnston, March 21, 1845, Johnston Papers.

22. The proportion of officers marrying as subalterns was probably greater, as some of the senior officers' announcements were probably of second marriages. For 177 officers born in the period 1800–1830 who married in the army and for whom data are available, the median age at first marriage was twenty-eight, and 84.2 percent were married by their thirty-fifth birthday. For 50 clergymen and 50 lawyers born in the same period, the median ages at first marriage were twenty-five and twenty-seven respectively. Data on lawyers and clergymen have been compiled from biographical sketches in the *DAB*.

23. Officers' pay levels in 1812, 1824, 1838, and 1846 are compared in 29th Cong., 1st sess., Sen. Exec. Doc. no. 246. Act of July 5, 1838, Abner R. Hetzel, comp., *Military Laws of the United States* (Washington, D.C.: G. Templeman, 1846), 262–264.

24. "Statement of Sums Paid to Officers of the Army on Account of Regular and Extra Pay in the Year 1829," *ASP:MA*, 4:694–699; William B. Skelton, "The United

States Army, 1821–1837: An Institutional History" (Ph.D. diss., Northwestern University, 1968), 278–281; Acts of March 3, 1835, and August 23, 1842, Hetzel, *Military Laws*, 251, 276–277.

25. Government clerks' salaries are listed in *Register of the Officers and Agents, Civil, Military, and Naval, in the Service of the United States, on the Thirtieth September, 1835* (Washington, D.C.: Blair and Rives, 1835); and *Register of the Officers and Agents, Civil, Military, and Naval, in the Service of the United States, from the Thirtieth September, 1841, to the Thirtieth September, 1843* (Washington, D.C., 1843). On consumer prices, see *Historical Statistics of the United States: Colonial Times to 1970*, 2 vols. (Washington, D.C.: Government Printing Office, 1975), 1:211. On officers' pay, see also Coffman, *Old Army*, 49–50.

26. *Army and Navy Chronicle* 2 (January 7, 1836):12–13. The pay issue is covered extensively in this periodical during the mid-1830s.

27. Printed memorial to the Senate and House of Representatives from officers in Oregon Territory [1849 or 1850], Theodore Talbot Papers, Library of Congress; Capt. Hannibal Day to Col. Roger Jones, January 1, 1850, file D-42, AGO:LR. See also Lt. John J. Peck to Jones, February 17, 1851, file P-18, printed circular signed by Maj. David H. Vinton et al., July 4, 1853, file V-43, petition of Capt. James V. Bomford et al. enclosed with Capt. Robert P. Maclay to Jefferson Davis, January 3, 1855, file M-46, Lt. Col. Silas Casey et al. to Jefferson Davis, June 9, 1855, file C-323, AGO:LR; Coffman, *Old Army*, 59–60.

28. Acts of September 28, 1850, August 31, 1852, and February 21, 1857, in John F. Callan, comp., *Military Laws of the United States, Relating to the Army, Volunteers, Militia, and to Bounty Lands and Pensions, from the Foundation of the Government to the Year 1863* (Philadelphia: C. W. Childs, 1863), 410, 423, 447–448. Infantry lieutenants' average compensation is based on salary and allowances for rations, servants, and forage as listed in army register for 1860, 36th Cong., 2d sess., House Exec. Doc. no. 54. Special allowances for fuel, baggage during moves, quarters when public quarters were not available, etc., increased many subalterns' income considerably.

29. Act of July 5, 1838, Hetzel, *Military Laws*, 261.

30. Col. Roger Jones to Lewis Cass, February 15, 1836, file A-109, SW:LR-Reg.

31. See, for example, Lt. Henry S. Turner to Lt. Abraham R. Johnston, September 2, 1844, Johnston Papers; Lt. John P. Hatch to his sister, October 26, 1858, John P. Hatch Papers, Library of Congress; Lt. Jacob E. Blake to Lt. David B. Harris, April 19, 1834, David B. Harris Papers, Duke University Library, Durham, N.C.

32. Acts of July 6, 1812, and June 30, 1834, Hetzel, *Military Laws*, 155, 250. On brevet rank in general, see James B. Fry, *The History and Legal Effects of Brevets in the Armies of Great Britain and the United States, from Their Origins in 1692 to the Present Time* (New York: D. Van Norstrand, 1877).

33. Lt. Gustavus W. Smith to Lt. Isaac Ingalls Stevens, October 14, 1850, Stevens Papers. For other examples of junior officers' concern about brevets, see Lt. George G. Meade to Margaret Meade, September 11, 1846, and October 5–8, 1846, George G. Meade Papers, Historical Society of Pennsylvania; T. Harry Williams, *P.G.T. Beauregard: Napoleon in Gray* (Baton Rouge: Louisiana State University Press, 1954), 34–35; J. S. Calhoun to George W. Crawford, January 25, 1850, and enclosures, file C-132, and T. Watkins Ligon to the president, March 9, 1857, file S-157, AGO:LR; Lt. Thomas Williams to John R. Williams, May 22, 1848, John R. Williams Papers, Burton Collection, Detroit Public Library.

34. Based on a survey of AGO: Orders and Circulars, 1828–1845; for the cases involving subalterns' disputes, see General Orders No. 30, June 18, 1828, and No. 26,

April 29, 1841. At least ten other cases arose from personal tension between lieutenants and their commanding officers.

35. Ethan Allen Hitchcock, *Fifty Years in Camp and Field: The Diary of Major-General Ethan Allen Hitchcock, U.S.A.*, ed. William A. Croffut (New York: G. P. Putnam's Sons, 1909), 47.

36. Capt. John C. Casey to Lt. George L. Welcker, December 7, 1843, Lenoir Family Papers II; Maj. Gen. Winfield Scott to William Wilkins, November 23, 1844, 28th Cong., 2d sess., Sen. Exec. Doc. no. 1, 133. Two of the eleven post-1827 encounters were shootouts rather than formal duels. In 1832, Asst. Surg. Philip Minis shot to death a Georgia state legislator who had called him a "damned Jew." In 1853, Asst. Surg. Josephus M. Steiner killed Capt. Ripley A. Arnold in a gunfight at Ft. Mason, Texas, apparently over repayment of a loan. Joseph L. Blau and Salo W. Baron, eds., *The Jews of the United States, 1790–1840: A Documentary History*, 3 vols. (New York: Columbia University Press, 1963), 1:176–181; Lt. Samuel H. Starr to Kate Starr, September 22, 1853, Samuel H. Starr Papers, Bixby Collection, Missouri Historical Society, St. Louis; file A-54 (1856), AGO:LR. See also Coffman, *Old Army*, 68–70.

37. General Orders, June 1, 1821, No. 11, February 24, 1824, No. 22, April 4, 1827, No. 64, December 29, 1827, No. 39, July 2, 1835, No. 41, July 6, 1835, AGO: Orders and Circulars; Charlotte O. Van Cleve, *"Three Score Years and Ten": Life-Long Memories of Fort Snelling, Minnesota, and Other Parts of the West* (Minneapolis, Minn.: Harrison and Smith, 1895), 151–152. The message transmitted by higher authorities seems to have been somewhat contradictory. President John Quincy Adams remitted the dismissal sentence of one lieutenant convicted of challenging his regimental commander because the commander had been "in the habitual practice of obtrusively declaring his readiness to waive his rank and meet in private combat any of his inferior Officers, who might be dissatisfied with his conduct." General Orders No. 64, December 29, 1827, AGO: Orders and Circulars.

38. 29th Cong., 1st sess., Sen. Exec. Doc. no. 246, 13; Act of March 2, 1827, Hetzel, *Military Laws*, 222.

39. Average income based on salaries and allowances for rations, servants, and forage as stated in the army register for 1860, 36th Cong., 2d sess., House Exec. Doc. no. 54. For salaries of government employees, see the registers listed in note 25 above and *Register of Officers and Agents, Civil, Military, and Naval, in the Service of the United States, on the Thirtieth September, 1855* (Washington, D.C.: A. O. P. Nicholson, 1855). In 1855, the chief clerks of the major executive departments earned $2,200 and customs inspectors $1,095. Capt. Robert E. Lee to Mrs. H. Hackley, August 7, 1838, quoted in Douglas Southall Freeman, *R. E. Lee: A Biography*, 4 vols. (New York: C. Scribner's Sons, 1934–1935), 1:156.

40. Act of February 11, 1847, Callan, *Military Laws*, 379.

41. Col. Roger Jones to Lewis Cass, February 15, 1836, file A-109, SW:LR-Reg.

42. Francis B. Heitman, comp., *Historical Register and Dictionary of the United States Army, from Its Organization, September 29, 1789, to March 2, 1903*, 2 vols. (Washington, D.C.: Government Printing Office, 1903), 1:237, 813.

43. Capt. Benjamin Alvord to Marcus C. M. Hammond, March 30, 1853, November 25, 1853, and July 24, 1854, James H. Hammond Papers, Library of Congress.

44. Heitman, *Historical Register*, 1:578, 688.

45. 29th Cong., 1st sess., Sen. Exec. Doc. no. 246, 13.

46. Officers' average income has been calculated from army register for 1860, 36th Cong., 2d sess., House Exec. Doc. no. 34. Special allowances raised field officers' overall income even higher.

47. Calculated from generals' salaries and basic allowances, ibid.

48. Charles W. Elliott, *Winfield Scott: The Soldier and the Man* (New York: Macmillan, 1937), 227–228, 238–239, 241–246, 294–303, 322–331; James W. Silver, *Edmund Pendleton Gaines: Frontier General* (Baton Rouge: Louisiana State University Press, 1949), 130–136, 167–190, 260–261.

49. Edward S. Wallace, *General William Jenkins Worth: Monterrey's Forgotten Hero* (Dallas: Southern Methodist University Press, 1953), 67–76.

50. Brainerd Dyer, *Zachary Taylor* (Baton Rouge: Louisiana State University Press, 1946), 55, 255–256; Rembert W. Patrick, *Aristocrat in Uniform: General Duncan L. Clinch* (Gainesville: University of Florida Press, 1963), 61; *Army and Navy Chronicle* 1 (May 28, 1835):173; Col. William Lindsay to Anna Lindsay, November 27, 1830, and August 31, 1834, William Lindsay Papers, State Historical Society of Wisconsin, Madison; Surg. William Beaumont to Major Edmund Kirby, September 16, 1835, Jacob J. Brown Papers, William L. Clements Library, Ann Arbor, Mich. For other examples of officers' land speculations see Silver, *Gaines*, 147, 270; Lt. Charles N. Hagner to Peter Hagner, April 10, 1839, and January 25, 1840, Peter Hagner Papers, Southern Historical Collection, University of North Carolina Library, Chapel Hill; Amos Binney to Brig. Gen. Daniel Parker, September 4, 1816, and Col. William King to Parker, May 31, 1819, Daniel Parker Papers, Historical Society of Pennsylvania; Capt. William Arnold to Lt. Col. William A. Trimble, November 26, 1817, December 3, 1817, and July 9, 1818, Allen Trimble Papers, Western Reserve Historical Society, Cleveland; Helen Dunlap Dick, "A Newly Discovered Diary of Colonel Josiah Snelling," *Minnesota History* 18 (1937):402; Capt. Henry Whiting to Henry R. Schoolcraft, May 9, 1833, July 8, 1837, and [May 24, 1839], Henry R. Schoolcraft Papers, Library of Congress.

51. *Army and Navy Chronicle* 9 (September 5, 1839): 153; Harwood P. Hinton, "The Military Career of John Ellis Wool, 1812–1863" (Ph.D. diss., University of Wisconsin, 1960), 77–79. On the Jefferson Woolen Company, see correspondence of Major Edmund Kirby for 1837, Brown Papers, Clements Library. On officers' economic activities in general, see also Coffman, *Old Army*, 84–87.

52. Col. Abraham Eustis to Lt. Robert Anderson, February 8, 1841, and Capt. Abner R. Hetzel to Anderson, June 14, 1843, Robert Anderson Papers, Library of Congress.

53. Coffman, *Old Army*, 86–87; Col. Ethan Allen Hitchcock's correspondence for the early 1850s in Ethan Allen Hitchcock Papers, Library of Congress; Glisan, *Journal*, 212–213, 408–411; William T. Sherman, *Memoirs of Gen. W. T. Sherman*, 2 vols. in 1 (New York: C. L. Webster, 1891), 1:61, 86–87, 101–105, 142–143; Lt. William M. Gardner to his brother, June 7, 1849, Gardner to Mrs. J. Gardner, January 31, 1853, Charles M. Hitchcock to Gardner, September 30, 1854, and William T. Sherman to Gardner, July 27, 1855, Gardner Papers; Erasmus D. Keyes, *Fifty Years' Observations of Men and Events, Civil and Military* (New York: C. Scribner's Sons, 1884), 228–230, 242, 290; Lt. Ulysses S. Grant to Julia D. Grant, October 7, 1852, October 26, 1852, December 3, 1852, March 19, 1853, and June 28, 1853, in Ulysses S. Grant, *The Papers of Ulysses S. Grant*, ed. John Y. Simon, 16 vols. to date (Carbondale: Southern Illinois University Press, 1967–), 1:268, 270, 275–276, 294–295, 304–305; Walter H. Hebert, *Fighting Joe Hooker* (Indianapolis: Bobbs-Merrill, 1944), 38–40.

54. Diane M. T. North, *Samuel Peter Heintzelman and the Sonora Exploring and Mining Company* (Tucson: University of Arizona Press, 1980). For a similar case, see Capt. John T. Sprague to John B. Floyd, April 27, 1860, file S-175, AGO:LR.

55. Proceedings of court-martial of Maj. William R. Montgomery, September 24,

1855, file HH-566, National Archives, Records of the Office of the Judge Advocate General (Record Group 153), Proceedings of U.S. Army General Courts-Martial, 1809–1890; B. Franklin Cooling, ed., *The New American State Papers, 1789–1860: Military Affairs*, 19 vols. (Wilmington, Del.: Scholarly Resources, 1979), 13:410–413.

56. Capt. John R. Vinton to Maj. Edmund Kirby, December 2, 1836, Brown Papers, Clements Library; Maj. William H. T. Walker to Molly Walker, [1858], William H. T. Walker Papers, Duke University Library, Durham, N.C.; Capt. Jesse A. Gove to Maria Gove, journal letter beginning December 16, 1857, entry for January 2, 1858, in Jesse A. Gove, *The Utah Expedition, 1857–1858: Letters of Capt. Jesse A. Gove, 10th Inf., U.S.A. of Concord, N.H., to Mrs. Gove, and Special Correspondence of the New York Herald*, ed. Otis G. Hammond (Concord: New Hampshire Historical Society, 1928), 110; Capt. Henry Whiting to Henry R. Schoolcraft, May 9, 1833, Schoolcraft Papers.

57. Charles C. Moskos, "From Institution to Occupation: Trends in Military Organization," *Armed Forces and Society* 4 (November 1977):41–50.

58. Almost every collection of officers' private correspondence contains "army news" letters. See, for example, Lt. Alfred Gibbs to Lt. George B. McClellan, July 3, 1853, McClellan Papers; Lt. Henry S. Turner to Lt. Abraham R. Johnston, February 8, 1844, Lt. Robert H. Chilton to Johnston, March 19, 1844, and April 23, 1846, Johnston Papers; Lt. George W. Hazzard to his wife, December 20, 1857, and September 4, 1858, Hazzard Papers; Lt. Roger Jones to Capt. Thomas Claiborne, March 3, 1858, Thomas Claiborne Papers, Southern Historical Collection, University of North Carolina Library, Chapel Hill; Col. Robert E. Lee's letters to Martha Custis Lee, in Francis R. Adams, Jr., ed., "An Annotated Edition of the Personal Letters of Robert E. Lee, April 1855–April 1861" (Ph.D. diss., University of Maryland, 1955), passim.

59. Capt. Ethan Allen Hitchcock to Capt. Richard Bache, December 13, 1835, Ethan Allen Hitchcock Papers, Missouri Historical Society, St. Louis; Lt. William M. Gardner to Margaret Wilson, July 20, 1850, Gardner Papers; Lt. Lucius L. Rich to Ellen Marcy, November 30, 1857, McClellan Papers; Lt. Earl Van Dorn to Octavia Sulivane, January 13, 1848, in Emily Van Dorn Miller, ed., *A Soldier's Honor, with Reminiscences of Major-General Earl Van Dorn* (New York: Abbey Press, 1902), 26.

60. Lt. William T. Sherman's diary entries for December 2–4, 1843, William T. Sherman Papers, University of Notre Dame Archives, South Bend, Ind.; Lt. August V. Kautz's journal, May 1859–March 1860, Kautz Papers; Lt. Henry S. Turner to Lt. Abraham R. Johnston, November 30, 1837, Johnston Papers.

61. Capt. Lafayette McLaws to his wife, August 8, 1858, Lafayette McLaws Papers, Southern Historical Collection, University of North Carolina Library, Chapel Hill; Lt. George W. Hazzard to his wife, April 4, [1858], Hazzard Papers.

62. For examples of officers' conservative views on women's role, see Maj. John J. Abert to Daniel Parker, May 30, 1828, Parker Papers; Philip St. George Cooke, *Scenes and Adventures in the Army: or, The Romance of Military Life* (Philadelphia: Lindsay and Blakiston, 1857), 323–326; Lt. Isaac Ingalls Stevens to Margaret Stevens, n.d., and Lt. Zealous B. Tower to Stevens, January 12, [year illegible], Stevens Papers; Capt. John R. Vinton to Mary Vinton, April 25, 1844, John R. Vinton Papers, Duke University Library, Durham, N.C.; McWhiney, *Southerners and Other Americans*, 52–55. On the "cult of domesticity" or "true womanhood," see Barbara Welter, "The Cult of True Womanhood, 1820–1860," *American Quarterly* 18 (Summer 1966):151–174; Nancy F. Cott, *The Bonds of Womanhood: "Woman's Sphere" in New England, 1780–1835* (New Haven, Conn.: Yale University Press, 1977), 63–100. On officers' ages at marriage, see note 22 above.

408 Notes to Pages 205-208

63. For examples of officers' authoritarian child-rearing methods, see Maj. George H. Crosman to Brig. Gen. Thomas S. Jesup, December 22, 1851, Thomas S. Jesup Papers, Library of Congress; Capt. John N. Macomb to his wife, November 17, 1857, Rodgers Family Papers; Capt. John R. Vinton to Mary Vinton, May 31, 1845, Vinton Papers; Capt. Thomas Williams to Mary Williams, journal letter beginning March 26, 1857, entry for March 27, Williams Family Papers. For examples of officers' nurturing approach to child-rearing and expressions of affection for their children, see Eliza Johnston, "The Diary of Eliza (Mrs. Albert Sidney) Johnston: The Second Cavalry in Texas," *Southwestern Historical Quarterly* 60 (April 1957):499–500; Sarah W. Wiggins, "Josiah Gorgas, A Victorian Father," *Civil War History* 32 (September 1986):229–246; Lt. Col. William Lindsay to Anna Lindsay, June 3, 1831, and Anna Lindsay to Martha Corprew, March 11, 1835, Lindsay Papers; Lt. George G. Meade to his wife, October 10, 1845, Meade Papers; Lt. John C. Pemberton to his mother, July 13, 1850, and October 25, 1850, Pemberton Family Papers, Historical Society of Pennsylvania. On the trend toward the child-centered family, see Carl N. Degler, *At Odds: Women and the Family in America from the Revolution to the Present* (Oxford and New York: Oxford University Press, 1980), 66–85.

64. Coffman, *Old Army*, 104–136.

65. Frances Webster to Lt. Edmund Kirby Smith, June 2, 1851, Kirby Smith Papers.

66. Capt. John C. Henshaw to Jefferson Davis, June 24, 1854, file H-275, AGO:LR; Mary Marcy to Ellen Marcy, November 30, [1851], McClellan Papers; Tripler, *Tripler*, passim.

67. Martha I. H. Barbour's diary entry for July 21, 1846, in Philip N. Barbour and Martha I. H. Barbour, *Journals of the Late Brevet Major Philip Norbourne Barbour, Captain in the 3rd Regiment, United States Infantry, and His Wife, Martha Isabella Hopkins Barbour; Written during the War with Mexico—1846*, ed. Rhoda van Bibber Tanner Doubleday (New York: G. P. Putnam's Sons, 1936), 123; Capt. Joseph H. LaMotte to Ellen LaMotte, February 27, 1850, LaMotte-Coppinger Papers, Missouri Historical Society, St. Louis. For examples of estranged marriages, see Thomas M. Settles, "The Military Career of John Bankhead Magruder" (Ph.D. diss., Texas Christian University, 1972), 20–22; George R. Adams, "General William Selby Harney: Frontier Soldier, 1800–1889" (Ph.D. diss., University of Arizona, 1983), 135, 178–180.

68. Eliza Johnston's diary entry for January 16, [1856], Johnston, "Diary," 490; Mariquitta Garesché to her parents, May 19, 1849, and June 20, 1849, in Louis A. Garesché, *Biography of Lieut. Col. Julius P. Garesché, Assistant Adjutant-General, U.S. Army* (Philadelphia: J. B. Lippincott, 1887), 87–89. See also Chris Emmett, *Fort Union and the Winning of the Southwest* (Norman: University of Oklahoma Press, 1965), 154–155.

69. Almira R. Hancock, *Reminiscences of Winfield Scott Hancock* (New York: C. L. Webster, 1887), 28.

70. Gamble, "Garrison Life," 172–173. For examples of officers and their families aiding the families of their deceased comrades, see Harvey E. Brown, *The Medical Department of the United States Army from 1775 to 1873* (Washington, D.C.: Surgeon General's Office, 1873), 201; Lt. John C. McFerran to Col. Roger Jones, May 28, 1852, file M-191, AGO:LR; Col. Robert E. Lee to Mary C. Lee, March 28, 1856, and March 13, 1857, Adams, ed., "Personal Letters of Lee," 106, 302–303.

71. Anna Lindsay to Martha Coprew, November 20, 1831, Lindsay Papers; Asst. Surg. William J. L'Engle to Edward L'Engle, July 18, 1857, Edward M. L'Engle Papers, Southern Historical Collection, University of North Carolina Library, Chapel

Hill; Averell, *Ten Years*, 73; Lydia S. Lane, *I Married a Soldier; or Old Days in the Old Army* (Albuquerque, N.Mex.: Horn and Wallace, 1964), 83–84.

72. Computed from army register for 1860, 36th Cong., 2d Session, House Exec. Doc. no. 54; War Department records; and various biographical and genealogical sources.

73. Capt. Randolph B. Marcy to Ellen Marcy, May 22, 1856, McClellan Papers.

74. Two hundred thirty-nine of a total of 594 (40.2 percent)—computed from army register of 1830, *ASP:MA*, 4:251–261; War Department records; and various biographical and genealogical sources. Close relatives defined as father, brother, son, father-in-law, brother-in-law, son-in-law, uncle, nephew, first cousin.

75. *DAB*, 4:557, 10:63, 272, 273; Henry A. Macomb, comp., *The Macomb Family Record* (Camden, N.J.: Sinnickson Chew and Sons, 1917); William Whiting, *Memoir of Rev. Samuel Whiting, D.D., and of His Wife, Elizabeth St. John, with References to Some of Their English Ancestors and American Descendants* (Boston: Rand, Avery, 1873); Bradford A. Whittemore, *Memorials of the Massachusetts Society of the Cincinnati* (Boston, 1964), 695–696; Frederick W. Alexander, comp., *Stratford Hall and the Lees Connected with Its History; Biographical, Genealogical, and Historical* (Oak Grove, Va.: F. W. Alexander, 1912).

76. Eliza Anderson to Capt. Robert Anderson, April 20, [1847], Anderson Papers.

77. See, for example, Lt. Peter V. Hagner to Peter Hagner, June 7, 1837, Hagner Papers.

78. Col. Roger Jones to Maj. Gen. Alexander Macomb, March 16, 1838, *Army and Navy Chronicle* 6 (April 26, 1838):263; 34th Cong., 1st sess., Sen. Exec. Doc. no. 96, 606–621.

79. Asst. Surg. Jacob Rhett Motte, *Journey into Wilderness: An Army Surgeon's Account of Life in Camp and Field during the Creek and Seminole Wars, 1836–1838*, ed. James F. Sunderman (Gainesville: University of Florida Press, 1953), 3; Lt. George B. McClellan's diary entry for January 1, 1847, in George B. McClellan, *The Mexican War Diary of George B. McClellan*, ed. William S. Myers (Princeton, N.J.: Princeton University Press, 1917), 38–39; Col. John E. Wool to Joel R. Poinsett, April 20, 1837, HQA:LR; Maj. Gen. Winfield Scott to William L. Marcy, January 16, 1847, quoted in Elliott, *Scott*, 448.

80. Elliott, *Scott*, 307–310; John K. Mahon, *History of the Second Seminole War, 1835–1842* (Gainesville: University of Florida Press, 1967), 106–111; Dyer, *Taylor*, 111–113; Maj. Gen. Zachary Taylor to Lt. Col. Joseph P. Taylor, April 25, 1847, Zachary Taylor Papers, Library of Congress.

81. Lt. Thomas Williams to John R. Williams, February 28, 1847, John R. Williams Papers; Col. Thomas T. Fauntleroy to Lewis Cass, May 7, 1860, file S-264, AGO:LR.

82. Act of August 23, 1842, Hetzel, *Military Laws*, 276; General Orders No. 57, August 27, 1842, AGO: Orders and Circulars.

83. Information on officers' mortality in this and the succeeding paragraph is drawn mainly from letters reporting officers' deaths in AGO:LR. On the general impact of disease on the army, see Mary C. Gillett, *The Army Medical Department, 1818–1865*, (Washington, D.C.: Government Printing Office, 1987), 3–149.

84. Bvt. Capt. Irvin McDowell to Col. Roger Jones, April 11, 1851, file B-167, AGO:LR.

85. K. Jack Bauer, *The Mexican War, 1846–1848* (New York: Macmillan, 1974), 46.

86. Heitman, *Historical Register*, 2:13–42. Of these fatalities, thirty-five occurred in the Seminole or other Indian wars and sixty-two in the Mexican War.

87. Twenty-seventh Cong., 3d sess., House Exec. Doc. no. 5, 3–14.
88. Act of January 31, 1823, Hetzel, *Military Laws,* 216.
89. Information on causes of dismissals has been obtained from George W. Cullum, comp., *Biographical Register of the Officers and Graduates of the U.S. Military Academy at West Point, N.Y., from Its Establishment, in 1802, to 1890; with the Early History of the United States Military Academy,* 3 vols. (Boston: Houghton, Mifflin, 1891), 1:passim; AGO: Orders and Circulars; and other War Department records. On Twiggs, see *DAB,* 19:83. On Pentland, see file AA-68, National Archives, Records of the Office of the Judge Advocate General (Record Group 153), Proceedings of U.S. Army General Courts-Martial, 1809–1890. Several other regulars, who were dismissed but subsequently reappointed to the army, have been excluded from this analysis.
90. James G. Wilson and John Fiske, comps., *Appleton's Cyclopaedia of American Biography,* 6 vols. (New York: D. Appleton, 1894), 6:319.
91. Act of August 3, 1861, Callan, *Military Laws,* 484–485; Act of July 17, 1862, U.S. Congress, *The Public Statutes at Large of the United States of America,* 100 vols. to date (Boston and Washington, D.C.: Government Printing Office, 1848–), 12:596.
92. Cullum, *Biographical Register of U.S.M.A.,* 1:passim.
93. Twenty-eighth Cong., 1st sess., House Rept. no. 476, 19–20.
94. Skelton, "U.S. Army, 1821–1837," 247–254, 282–285; General Orders No. 43, June 28, 1836, and No. 69, October 15, 1836, AGO: Orders and Circulars.
95. Calculated from statement drafted by Col. Roger Jones, February 28, 1837, *ASP:MA,* 7:111–113.
96. This and the following paragraphs have been based on Cullum, *Biographical Register of U.S.M.A.,* 1:passim; and data on officers' postservice lives in other biographical sources and War Department records. See also Dale E. Hruby, "The Civilian Careers of West Point Graduates: Classes of 1802–1833" (M.A. thesis, Columbia University, 1965).
97. Cullum, *Biographical Register of U.S.M.A.,* 1:222–232, 236–244, 280–281.
98. Charles F. O'Connell, Jr., "The United States Army and the Origins of Modern Management, 1818–1860" (Ph.D. diss., Ohio State University, 1982).
99. The officers on the 1830 army register who served in Congress were Duncan L. Clinch (House 1844–1845); Jefferson Davis (House 1845–1846, Senate 1847–1851, 1857–1861); Joseph E. Johnston (House 1879–1881); James Monroe (House 1839–1841)—*BDC,* passim. For lists of political offices held by West Point graduates in the classes of 1802–1833, see Hruby, "Civilian Careers," 139–152. He has counted six other congressmen and two governors in those classes whose names do not appear on the 1830 register.
100. Cullum, *Biographical Register of U.S.M.A.,* 1:211, 319–325, 326, 364–365, 404–406. The West Point professors were William H. C. Bartlett, Albert E. Church, and Dennis Hart Mahan. On Parrott, see also *DAB,* 14:260–261. On Wade, see Merritt Roe Smith, "Army Ordnance and the 'American System' of Manufacturing, 1815–1861," in Merritt Roe Smith, ed., *Military Enterprise and Technological Change: Perspectives on the American Experience* (Cambridge: Massachusetts Institute of Technology, 1985), 72–74.
101. *DAB,* 7:566–567.

CHAPTER TWELVE. THE EMERGENCE OF THE GENERAL STAFF OFFICER

1. *ASP:MA,* 3:622. Of these, twenty-eight were employed on ordnance duty; thirty-three on topographical duty; thirteen at the military academy; and thirty-nine

in other staff departments. In addition, eighteen company officers were on recruiting duty.

2. This and the following paragraph are based mainly on the author's general reading in AGO:LS and AGO:LR. For an excellent study of the career of an assistant adjutant general, see Matthew B. Veatch, "The Education of a Staff Officer: The Life and Career of Samuel Cooper, 1798–1852" (M.A. thesis, University of Missouri–Kansas City, 1989).

3. Bvt. Capt. Julius P. Garesché to Mariquitta Garesché, November 30, 1856, in Louis A. Garesché, *Biography of Lieut. Col. Julius P. Garesché, Assistant Adjutant-General, U.S. Army* (Philadelphia: J. B. Lippincott, 1887), 252.

4. Charles F. O'Connell, Jr., "The United States Army and the Origins of Modern Management, 1818–1860" (Ph.D. diss., Ohio State University, 1982); Merritt Roe Smith, "Army Ordnance and the 'American System' of Manufacturing, 1815–1861," and Charles F. O'Connell, Jr., "The Corps of Engineers and the Rise of Modern Management, 1827–1856," both in Merritt Roe Smith, ed., *Military Enterprise and Technological Change: Perspectives on the American Experience* (Cambridge: Massachusetts Institute of Technology, 1985), 39–116. For the quartermaster forms, see U.S. War Department, *General Regulations for the Army; or, Military Institutes* (Washington, D.C.: Davis and Force, 1825), 239–275.

5. This and the following paragraphs have been based on Maj. Rufus L. Baker's correspondence for 1839–1841, in National Archives, Records of the Office of the Chief of Ordnance (Record Group 156), Watervliet Arsenal, Letters Sent. For the activities of another arsenal commander, see Stanley L. Falk, "Soldier-Technologist: Major Alfred Mordecai and the Beginnings of Science in the United States Army" (Ph.D. diss., Georgetown University, 1959), 183–227 and passim.

6. For the board's trip, see Falk, "Soldier-Technologist," 254–275; 26th Cong., 2d sess., Sen. Exec. Doc. no. 229.

7. Table dated December 5, 1842, 27th Cong., 3d sess., House Exec. Doc. no. 3.

8. Maj. Rufus L. Baker to McAbeck, Ellis, Hitchcock, and Chapman, March 18, 1839, and Baker to Lt. Col. George Talcott, April 21, 1839, Watervliet Arsenal, Letters Sent. For the ordnance campaign see also Merritt Roe Smith, *Harper's Ferry Armory and the New Technology: The Challenge of Change* (Ithaca, N.Y.: Cornell University Press, 1977), 270–304, and passim.

9. Maj. Rufus L. Baker to J. C. Heartt, February 14, 1839, Watervliet Arsenal, Letters Sent.

10. This and the following paragraph are based on Capt. Justus McKinstry's correspondence for 1849–1853, National Archives, Records of the Office of the Quartermaster General (Record Group 92), Letters Sent by Justus McKinstry.

11. Capt. Justus McKinstry to Brig. Gen. Thomas S. Jesup, July 13, 1849, and McKinstry to Maj. Osborn Cross, June 28, 1852, ibid. For the published version of the second report, see 32d Cong., 2d sess., House Exec. Doc. no. 1, 94–103.

12. Capt. Justus McKinstry to Maj. Osborn Cross, January 6, 1852, Office of Quartermaster General, Letters Sent by McKinstry. McKinstry remained in the Quartermaster Department until the Civil War, when he was court-martialed for graft and had the distinction of being the only Civil War general to be cashiered from the service. Ezra J. Warner, *Generals in Blue: Lives of the Union Commanders* (Baton Rouge: Louisiana State University Press, 1964), 303–304.

13. Mary C. Gillett, *The Army Medical Department, 1818–1865* (Washington, D.C.: Government Printing Office, 1987), 79–80, 129; Harvey E. Brown, *The Medical De-*

partment of the United States Army from 1775 to 1873 (Washington, D.C.: Surgeon General's Office, 1873), 162–170, 173, 201–203.

14. Gillett, *Army Medical Department, 1818–1865*, 3–149.

15. Michael R. Morgan, "Memories of the Fifties," *Journal of the Military Service Institution of the United States* 37 (July–August 1905):155.

16. For officers' involvement in civil works, see Forest G. Hill, *Roads, Rails & Waterways: The Army Engineers and Early Transportation* (Norman: University of Oklahoma Press, 1957); William H. Goetzmann, *Army Exploration in the American West, 1803–1863* (New Haven, Conn.: Yale University Press, 1959); W. Turrentine Jackson, *Wagon Roads West: A Study of Federal Road Surveys and Construction in the Trans-Mississippi West, 1846–1869* (New Haven, Conn.: Yale University Press, 1965); Garry D. Ryan, "War Department Topographical Bureau, 1831–1863: An Administrative History" (Ph.D. diss., American University, 1968). See also the numerous official district histories of the Corps of Engineers—for example, Leland R. Johnson, *The Falls City Engineers: A History of the Louisville District Corps of Engineers, United States Army* (N.p., n.d.); Leland R. Johnson, *Men, Mountains and Rivers: An Illustrated History of the Huntington District, U.S. Army Corps of Engineers, 1754–1974* (N.p., 1977); John W. Larson, *Those Army Engineers: A History of the Chicago District U.S. Army Corps of Engineers* (N.p., n.d.).

17. Richard G. Wood, *Stephen Harriman Long, 1784–1864: Army Engineer, Explorer, Inventor* (Glendale, Calif.: Arthur H. Clark, 1966).

18. The chaplains are described in Herman A. Norton, *Struggling for Recognition: The United States Army Chaplaincy, 1791–1865* (Washington, D.C.: Office of the Chief of Chaplains, 1977), 1–81; and Richard D. Gamble, "Garrison Life at Frontier Military Posts, 1830–1860" (Ph.D. diss., University of Oklahoma, 1956), 229–267.

19. Acts of July 5, 1838, and July 7, 1838, in Abner R. Hetzel, comp., *Military Laws of the United States* (Washington, D.C.: G. Templeman, 1846), 265, 268; Act of March 2, 1849, John F. Callan, comp., *Military Laws of the United States, Relating to the Army, Volunteers, Militia, and to Bounty Lands and Pensions, from the Foundation of the Government to the Year 1863* (Philadelphia: C. W. Childs, 1863), 403; Col. Samuel Cooper to Lorenzo D. Johnson, March 26, 1856, transmitting statement of army chaplains, in Lorenzo D. Johnson, *Chaplains of the General Government, with Objections to Their Employment Considered* (New York: Sheldon, Blackman, 1856), 64–69.

20. Capt. John R. Vinton to Mary Vinton, March 28, 1840, John R. Vinton Papers, Duke University Library, Durham, N.C.; Maj. William H. T. Walker to Molly Walker, October 16, 1858, William H.T. Walker Papers, Duke University Library, Durham, N.C. On officers' religious views, see also Edward M. Coffman, *The Old Army: A Portrait of the American Army in Peacetime, 1784–1898* (New York: Oxford University Press, 1986), 78–81.

21. John Burke to Charles M. Conrad, June 7, 1852, file S-278, AGO:LR. For other examples of chaplains' troubles with councils of administration, see files R-246 (1854), P-119 (1860), S-170 (1860), ibid.; Norton, *Struggling for Recognition*, 58–60. A quartermaster officer predicted in 1842 that if the rule on chaplains' quarters stood, there would be very few chaplains appointed and those who were would be the object of constant jealousy and bickering on the part of the subalterns. "Religion and piety do not lessen a man's notions of his rights, or weaken his disposition to assert them." Capt. Charles O. Collins to Brig. Gen. Thomas S. Jesup, January 18, 1842, National Archives, Records of the Office of the Quartermaster General (Record Group 92), Letterbook of Charles O. Collins.

22. For example, Robert E. Lee, Joseph E. Johnston, William H. Emory, and

George B. McClellan were promoted from the engineering branches into the new cavalry regiments raised in 1855, and Albert S. Johnston was a paymaster before his appointment as colonel in one of these units. Francis B. Heitman, comp., *Historical Register and Dictionary of the United States Army, from Its Organization, September 29, 1789, to March 2, 1903,* 2 vols. (Washington, D.C.: Government Printing Office, 1903), 1:passim.

23. Capt. John L. Gardner, *Military Control, or Command and Government of the Army* (Washington, D.C.: A. B. Claxton, 1839), 16–41.

24. Leonard D. White, *The Jeffersonians: A Study in Administrative History, 1801–1829* (New York: Macmillan, 1951), 240–245; Charles M. Wiltse, *John C. Calhoun,* 3 vols. (Indianapolis: Bobbs-Merrill, 1944–1951), 1:150–151; John C. Calhoun, *The Papers of John C. Calhoun,* ed. Robert L. Meriwether and W. Edwin Hemphill, 18 vols. to date (Columbia: University of South Carolina Press, 1959–), 4:224–226, 304–305, 5:222–223; Brig. Gen. Edmund P. Gaines, inspection report, November 25, 1824, National Archives, Records of the Office of the Inspector General (Record Group 159), Inspection Reports, 1814–1842; Brig. Gen. Winfield Scott to Col. Roger Jones, September 8, 1827, AGO:LR.

25. William B. Skelton, "The United States Army, 1821–1837: An Institutional History" (Ph.D. diss., Northwestern University, 1968), 228–247; William B. Skelton, "The Commanding General and the Problem of Command in the United States Army, 1821–1841," *Military Affairs* 34 (December 1970)1:119–120.

26. Skelton, "U.S. Army, 1821–1837," 96–99.

27. Stephen V. Benét, comp., *A Collection of Annual Reports and Other Important Papers, Relating to the Ordnance Department, Taken from the Records of the Office of the Chief of Ordnance, from Public Documents, and from Other Sources,* 4 vols. (Washington, D.C., 1878–1890), 1:467–481; Maj. Gen. Winfield Scott to Capt. John R. Vinton, July 3, 1843, Vinton Papers.

28. Col. Roger Jones to Maj. Henry Stanton, July 9, 1835, AGO:LS; Jones to Lewis Cass, May 3, 1836, HQA:LR.

29. Col. James House to Brig. Gen. Edmund P. Gaines, December 1, 1824, National Archives, Records of the Office of the Adjutant General (Record Group 94), Confidential Inspection Reports, 1812–1826; Lt. Col. Abraham Eustis to Col. Roger Jones, April 21, 1832, file E-27, AGO:LR.

30. For the general debate over detached service in the period 1821–1836, see Skelton, "U.S. Army, 1821–1837," 247–254. For examples of commanders' continuing concern about the lack of officers with the troops, see Col. William S. Harney to Col. Roger Jones, January 11, 1851, file H-53, Col. James Bankhead to Lt. Col. Lorenzo Thomas, April 14, 1853, file B-208, Col. Albert S. Johnston to Col. Samuel Cooper, February 22, 1860, and enclosures, file S-125, AGO:LR.

31. Line officers' complaints about staff privileges and influence are a constant theme in the *Military and Naval Magazine of the United States* and the *Army and Navy Chronicle* in the 1830s and early 1840s. See also Lt. Braxton Bragg, "Notes on Our Army," *Southern Literary Messenger* 10–11 (February 1844–February 1845):passim; Col. Stephen W. Kearny to Maj. Ethan Allen Hitchcock, May 6, 1841, Ethan Allen Hitchcock Papers, Missouri Historical Society, St. Louis; Col. Zachary Taylor to Hitchcock, May 19, 1841, and November 3, 1841, Zachary Taylor Papers, Library of Congress; Lt. Col. Ichabod B. Crane to Daniel Parker, November 19, 1841, Daniel Parker Papers, Historical Society of Pennsylvania; Lt. Henry L. Kendrick to Lt. Abraham R. Johnston, January 19, 1840, and June 4, 1841, Abraham R. Johnston Papers, U.S. Military Academy Library, West Point, N.Y.; Capt. Erasmus D. Keyes to Lt.

Thomas Williams, November 22, 1848, Williams Family Papers, Burton Collection, Detroit Public Library.

32. Capt. Robert C. Buchanan to John Quincy Adams, March 27, 1842 (copy), Robert C. Buchanan Papers, Maryland Historical Society, Baltimore.

33. Lt. James L. Mason to Lt. George L. Welcker, June 30, 1842, Lenoir Family Papers II, Southern Historical Collection, University of North Carolina Library, Chapel Hill. For the staff side of the debate, see *Military and Naval Magazine of the United States* and *Army and Navy Chronicle,* passim; annual reports of the bureau chiefs published with the secretary of war's annual reports in *ASP:MA* and the congressional serial set; National Archives, Records of the Office of the Chief of Engineers (Record Group 77), Letters and Reports of Col. Joseph G. Totten, 1838-1860, passim; Benét, comp., *Annual Reports,* 1, 2:passim; Col. Joseph G. Totten, et al., memorial dated April 9, 1840, 26th Cong., 1st sess., Sen. Exec. Doc. no. 376; Capt. John C. Casey to Lt. Col. Ethan Allen Hitchcock, March 21, 1844, Ethan Allen Hitchcock Papers, Library of Congress.

34. Bragg, "Notes on Our Army," 10:286.

35. Benét, comp., *Annual Reports,* 2:417-488, 628-635. See also correspondence of Capt. Henry J. Hunt, 1851-1853, Henry J. Hunt Papers, Library of Congress; Capt. Thomas Williams to Col. Sylvester Churchill, July 21, 1853, file W-89, HQA:LR; Capt. William Maynadier to Capt. Robert Anderson, May 8, 1852, Lt. Thomas R. Tannatt to Anderson, March 2, 1860, and Capt. Edward O. C. Ord to Anderson, August 22, 1860, Robert Anderson Papers, Library of Congress; Maj. Harvey Brown to Lt. Col. Lorenzo Thomas, July 12, 1857, National Archives, Records of U.S. Army Continental Commands (Record Group 393), Ft. Monroe Artillery School Letterbook, 1855-1863.

36. Gardner, *Military Control,* 78-79.

37. 32d Cong., 1st sess., Sen. Rept. no. 217; 33d Cong., 2d sess., House Rept. no. 40; Maj. Gen. Winfield Scott to Jefferson Davis, December 8, 1854, HQA:LS.

CHAPTER THIRTEEN. PROFESSIONAL THOUGHT AND INSTITUTIONS

1. Armistead L. Long, "Recollections of a Lieutenant, U.S.A." (typewritten manuscript), 112, Armistead L. Long Papers, Southern Historical Collection, University of North Carolina Library, Chapel Hill.

2. Philip St. George Cooke, "Thoughts on the Army, and Suggestions for Its Improvement," *Army and Navy Chronicle* 10 (April 9, 1840):225-227; Lt. Alexander M. McCook, testimony before commission investigating U.S. Military Academy, July 26, 1860, 36th Cong., 2d sess., Senate Misc. Doc. no. 3, 86. See also Edward M. Coffman, *The Old Army: A Portrait of the American Army in Peacetime, 1784-1898* (New York: Oxford University Press, 1986), 98-102.

3. *DAB,* 2:223, 4:580-581; William E. Birkhimer, *Historical Sketch of the Organization, Administration, Materiel and Tactics of the Artillery, United States Army* (Washington, D.C.: J. J. Chapman, 1884), 302-303.

4. Brig. Gen. Edmund P. Gaines to Joel R. Poinsett, May 6, 1839, AGO:LR.

5. Daniel Tyler, *Daniel Tyler: A Memorial Volume Containing His Autobiography and War Record,* ed. Donald G. Mitchell (New Haven, Conn., 1883), 8-19; Birkhimer, *Historical Sketch of the Artillery,* 239-241, 304-305; Stanley L. Falk, "Soldier-Technologist: Major Alfred Mordecai and the Beginnings of Science in the United States Army" (Ph.D. diss., Georgetown University, 1959), 254-275; 26th Cong., 2d sess.,

Sen. Exec. Doc. no. 229; Stephen V. Bénet, comp., *A Collection of Annual Reports and Other Important Papers, Relating to the Ordnance Department, Taken from the Records of the Office of the Chief of Ordnance, from Public Documents, and from Other Sources*, 4 vols. (Washington, D.C., 1878-1890), 2:242-245, 290-336; Lt. Peter V. Hagner's correspondence for 1848-1849 in Peter Hagner Papers, Southern Historical Collection, University of North Carolina Lilbrary, Chapel Hill. For other such missions, see Falk, "Soldier-Technologist," 172-181; Harwood P. Hinton, "The Military Career of John Ellis Wool, 1812-1863" (Ph.D. diss., University of Wisconsin, 1960), 69-76.

6. Lt. Col. Sylvanus Thayer's correspondence for 1843-1846, Sylvanus Thayer Papers, U.S. Military Academy Library, West Point, N.Y. For other examples of engineering officers in Europe, see Thomas E. Griess, "Dennis Hart Mahan: West Point Professor and Advocate of Military Professionalism, 1830-1871" (Ph.D. diss., Duke University, 1968), 120-133; Robert M. McLane, *Reminiscences, 1827-1897* (Wilmington, Del.: Scholarly Resources, 1972), 74-81; Henry H. Humphreys, *Andrew Atkinson Humphreys: A Biography* (Philadelphia: John C. Winston, 1924), 60, 141-145; biographical sketches of George W. Hughes and William H. Swift, *DAB*, 9:348, 18:249.

7. Lt. Edmund Schriver to Lt. William Eustis, Lt. Henry S. Turner, and Lt. Philip Kearny, August 9, 1839, and Col. Roger Jones to Lt. Lloyd J. Beall, Lt. William J. Hardee, and Lt. Washington I. Newton, November 30, 1840, AGO:LS; John W. DePeyster, *Personal and Military History of Philip Kearny, Major-General United States Volunteers* (New York: Rice and Gage, 1869), 52-110; Lt. William Eustis to Lt. Abraham R. Johnston, October 27, 1839, Abraham R. Johnston Papers, U.S. Military Academy Library, West Point, N.Y.; Lt. Philip Kearny, "Service with the French Troops in Africa," *Magazine of History*, extra no. 22 (1913):1-54.

8. George W. Cullum, comp., *Biographical Register of the Officers and Graduates of the U.S. Military Academy at West Point, N.Y., from Its Establishment, in 1802, to 1890; with the Early History of the United States Military Academy*, 3 vols. (Boston: Houghton, Mifflin, 1891), 1:426; Douglas Porch, "Bugeaud, Gallieni, Lyautey: The Development of French Colonial Warfare," in Peter Paret, ed., *Makers of Modern Strategy from Machiavelli to the Nuclear Age* (Princeton, N.J.: Princeton University Press, 1986), 378-382; Col. Samuel Cooper to Lt. Col. Edwin V. Sumner, April 4, 1854, AGO:LS.

9. Lt. Albert V. Kautz's journal, June 1859-March 1860, Albert V. Kautz Papers, Library of Congress.

10. DePeyster, *Kearny*, 168. On officers in Europe in 1859, see also Lt. Ambrose P. Hill to George B. McClellan, June 18, [1859], George B. McClellan Papers, Library of Congress; Lt. Cyrus B. Comstock to Lt. James B. McPherson, May 19, 1859, James B. McPherson Papers, Library of Congress; Otis E. Young, *The West of Philip St. George Cooke, 1809-1895* (Glendale, Calif.: Arthur H. Clark, 1955), 318-319. One historian has counted 105 officers who travelled to Europe in the period 1815-1861. Dale E. Floyd, "U.S. Army Officers in Europe, 1815-1861," in David H. White and John W. Gordon, eds., *Proceedings of the Citadel Conference on War and Diplomacy, 1977* (N.p., 1979), 26-30. This figure is certainly conservative.

11. Falk, "Soldier-Technologist," 426-481; William S. Myers, *A Study in Personality: General George Brinton McClellan* (New York: D. Appleton-Century, 1934), 85-102; Lt. George B. McClellan's correspondence for 1855-1856, McClellan Papers. The reports of McClellan, Delafield, and Mordecai were published respectively as 35th Cong., Special Session, Sen. Exec. Doc. no. 1; 36th Cong., 1st sess., Sen. Exec. Doc. no. 59; 36th Cong., 1st sess., Sen. Exec. Doc. no. 60. An abridged version of McClellan's report was

adopted as a textbook at West Point. *Centennial of the United States Military Academy at West Point, New York, 1802-1902,* 2 vols. (Washington, D.C., 1904), 116.

12. *DAB,* 8:150-151; Lt. Henry W. Halleck, *Elements of Military Art and Science; or, Course of Instruction in Strategy, Fortification, Tactics of Battles, &c.* (Philadelphia: G. S. Appleton, 1846); Nathaniel C. Hughes, Jr., *General William J. Hardee: Old Reliable* (Baton Rouge: Louisiana State University Press, 1965), 20-21, 41-50; *DAB,* 20:201.

13. Lt. John C. Kelton to Lt. Edward P. Alexander, November 1, 1859, Edward P. Alexander Papers, Southern Historical Collection, University of North Carolina Library, Chapel Hill; Maj. Alfred Mordecai to Sara Mordecai, journal letter beginning July 26, 1855, entry for August 9, quoted in Falk, "Soldier-Technologist," 447.

14. Asst. Eng. Simon Bernard, Capt. J. D. Elliott, U.S.N., and Maj. Joseph G. Totten to John C. Calhoun, February 7, 1821, and Bernard and Totten to Col. Alexander Macomb, March 24, 1826, *ASP:MA,* 2:305-310, 3:283-298; Robert S. Browning, *Two If by Sea: The Development of American Coastal Defense Policy* (Westport, Conn.: Greenwood Press, 1983), 24-53.

15. On fortress design, see Browning, *Two If by Sea,* 59-75; Willard B. Robinson, *American Forts: Architectural Form and Function* (Urbana: University of Illinois Press, 1977), 85-132. Engineers' reports on fortification design are filed in National Archives, Records of the Office of the Chief of Engineers (Record Group 77), Letters Received by the Chief of Engineers.

16. Browning, *Two If by Sea,* 24-53 and passim.

17. James W. Silver, *Edmund Pendelton Gaines: Frontier General* (Baton Rouge: Louisiana State University Press, 1949), 223-257; memorial of Brig. Gen. Edmund P. Gaines to Senate and House of Representatives, December 31, 1839, 26th Cong., 1st sess., House Exec. Doc. no. 206, 118-143; Gaines, printed circular, January 14, 1846, Army Papers, Missouri Historical Society, St. Louis.

18. Lewis Cass to Andrew Jackson, April 7, 1836, *ASP:MA,* 6:366-376. For the context of Cass's report, see William B. Skelton, "The United States Army, 1821-1837: An Institutional History" (Ph.D. diss., Northwestern University, 1968), 389-404.

19. For an overview of the debate over alternatives to the orthodox system before the Civil War, see Browning, *Two If by Sea,* 78-115.

20. For naval officers' opinions, see report of Lt. L. M. Powell, U.S.N. (1841), 27th Cong., 2d sess., House Exec. Doc. no. 220, 2-34; 32d Cong., 1st sess., House Exec. Doc. no. 5, passim. Naval opinion was not monolithic, however, and some naval officers supported the fortification program.

21. Lt. James St. Clair Morton, "Memoir on the Dangers and Defences of New York City, Addressed to the Hon. John B. Floyd, Secretary of War," 35th Cong., 2d sess., Sen. Exec. Doc. no. 1, 494-581. Morton pointed to the American landing at Vera Cruz in the Mexican War and the allied invasion of the Crimea as examples of such a threat. See also Morton, paper submitted to Board of Visitors to U.S. Military Academy, June 1857, 35th Cong., 1st sess., Sen. Exec. Doc. no. 11, 204-218; Morton, "Memoir of American Fortification," 36th Cong., 1st sess., Sen. Exec. Doc. no. 2, 452-539. The central figure of the engineer dissidents was Maj. William H. Chase, a longtime gadfly of the corps. For his views on fortifications, see Chase to Charles M. Conrad, April 17, 1851, 32d Cong., 1st sess., House Exec. Doc. no. 5, 224-234.

22. Maj. Richard Delafield, *Report on the Art of War in Europe in 1854, 1855, and 1856* (Washington, D.C.: George W. Bowman, 1861), 49-50. For other examples of the engineers' defense of their program, see Capt. John G. Barnard, "Harbor Defence by Fortifications and Steam-Vessels," *Southern Literary Messenger* 11 (January

1845):25–30; Barnard, "The Dangers and Defences of New York," 36th Cong., 1st sess., Sen. Exec. Doc. no. 5, 2–50; Lt. Alexander J. Swift, "Fleets versus Forts," *United States Magazine and Democratic Review* 13 (December 1843):577–593; Lt. Edward Hunt, "Army Attack and National Defence," *American Review* 4 (August 1846):146–160; Lt. Henry W. Halleck, "Report on the Means of National Defence," transmitted to Col. Joseph G. Totten, October 20, 1843, 28th Cong., 2d sess., Sen. Exec. Doc. no. 85, 1–76; Totten, report on fortifications, transmitted to Col. Charles Gratiot, March 29, 1836, *ASP:MA,* 6:377–391; Totten, "Report on the Defence of the Atlantic Frontier from Passamaquoddy to the Sabine," 26th Cong., 1st sess., House Exec. Doc. no. 206, 5–70; Totten to Charles M. Conrad, November 1, 1851, 32d Cong., 1st sess., House Exec. Doc. no. 5, 42–130.

23. Halleck, *Elements.*

24. Hunt, "Army Attack," 146–154; Lt. Isaac Ingalls Stevens, *Campaigns of the Rio Grande and of Mexico; with Notices of the Recent Work of Major Ripley* (New York: D. Appleton, 1851), 10–16.

25. Capt. William G. Williams to Col. John J. Abert, March 18, 1842, National Archives, Records of the Office of the Chief of Engineers (Record Group 77), Records of the Topographical Bureau, 1818–1867; U.S. Lake Survey, Letters Sent. Knowlton's tours are mentioned in Col. Joseph G. Totten to Maj. Richard Delafield, March 31, 1843, Records of the Office of the Chief of Engineers (Record Group 77), Letters and Reports of Col. Joseph G. Totten. The chief engineer considered Knowlton's report on his Canadian tour a "precious document." Knowlton seems to have made another reconnaissance of Bermuda in 1849. Totten to Knowlton, January 10, 1849, ibid.

26. Col. Joseph G. Totten to Capt. William D. Fraser and Lt. John L. Mason, November 11, 1845, Office of the Chief of Engineers, Letters of Totten; Douglas Southell Freeman, *R. E. Lee: A Biography,* 4 vols. (New York: C. Scribner's Sons, 1934–1935), 1:195–196.

27. Col. Joseph G. Totten to Joel R. Poinsett, March 21, 1839, Totten to John C. Spencer, August 20, 1842, Office of the Chief of Engineers, Letters of Totten. During the late 1830s, Totten advised the secretary of war on the reform of the General Staff; in 1860, he submitted a confidential report on the defense of the Pacific Northwest. Totten to Poinsett, August 20, 1837, October 26, 1837, and November 7, 1837, Totten to John B. Floyd, March 26, 1860, ibid.

28. Mahan's originality is emphasized in Edward Hagerman, *The American Civil War and the Origins of Modern Warfare* (Bloomington: Indiana University Press, 1988), 6–27. See also Griess, "Mahan"; Russell F. Weigley, *Towards an American Army: Military Thought from Washington to Marshall* (New York: Columbia University Press, 1962), 38–53.

29. Griess, "Mahan," 162–164. For the origins and goals of the course, see Col. Joseph G. Totten to Maj. Richard Delafield, August 29, 1842, Office of the Chief of Engineers, Letters of Totten.

30. Griess, "Mahan," 236–237; Dabney H. Maury, *Recollections of a Virginian in the Mexican, Indian, and Civil Wars* (New York: C. Scribner's Sons, 1894), 50–51; Coffman, *Old Army,* 98.

31. Col. Joseph G. Totten to Charles Davies, January 4, [1855], Office of the Chief of Engineers, Letters of Totten.

32. Stanley L. Falk, "Artillery for the Land Service: The Development of a System," *Military Affairs* 28 (1964):97–110; Skelton, "U.S. Army, 1821–1837," 259–271.

33. Falk, "Soldier-Technologist," 286–545; the quotation is on p. 386. The Ord-

nance Department's impact on military technology is also stressed in Merritt Roe Smith, "Army Ordnance and the 'American System' of Manufacturing, 1815–1861," in Merritt Roe Smith, ed., *Military Enterprise and Technological Change: Perspectives on the American Experience* (Cambridge: Massachusetts Institute of Technology, 1985), 39–86.

34. Col. John E. Wool to Maj. Gen. Jacob Brown, November 9, 1823, John E. Wool Papers, New York State Library, Albany; Col. Samuel B. Archer, inspection report, October 30, 1823, National Archives, Records of the Office of the Inspector General (Record Group 159), Inspection Reports, 1814–1842. See also General Orders, June 1, 1821, AGO: Orders and Circulars.

35. Paddy Griffith, *Military Thought in the French Army, 1815–51* (Manchester, England: Manchester University Press, 1989), 143–148.

36. Asst. Eng. Simon Bernard and Lt. Col. William McRee to John C. Calhoun, [1818], *ASP:MA*, 1:834–836.

37. Maj. Gen. Jacob Brown to John C. Calhoun, March 21, 1823, and May 12, 1823, Brown Papers, Library of Congress; Brig. Gen. Thomas S. Jesup to Calhoun, November 5, 1823, *ASP:MA*, 3:604; Col. John E. Wool to Maj. Gen. Jacob Brown, November 9, 1823, Wool Papers.

38. General Orders No. 18, April 2, 1824, AGO: Orders and Circulars; John C. Calhoun to Col. John R. Fenwick, April 6, 1824, SW:LS; Calhoun to James Monroe, December 3, 1824, *ASP:MA*, 2:699. On the formation and history of the early schools of practice, see Skelton, "U.S. Army, 1821–1837," 169–183, 338–341.

39. U.S. War Department, *General Regulations for the Army; or, Military Institutes* (Washington, D.C.: Davis and Force, 1825), 398–402.

40. Skelton, "U.S. Army, 1821–1837," 173–175; Maj. Gen. Jacob Brown to James Barbour, December 8, 1825, Brown Papers, Library of Congress; General Orders No. 13, March 4, 1826, AGO: Orders and Circulars.

41. Maj. Gen. Jacob Brown to James Barbour, November 30, 1826, *ASP:MA*, 3:332–333; Griffith, *Military Thought*, 137–140, 146–148.

42. Brig. Gen. Edmund P. Gaines, inspection report, 1827, *ASP:MA*, 4:126; Lt. John R. Vinton to Col. Henry Atkinson, October 16, 1827, AGO:LS. Among other occasions, troops from Jefferson Barracks participated in the Winnebago campaign of 1827 and the Black Hawk War of 1832.

43. Skelton, "U.S. Army, 1821–1837," 177–181; Col. John E. Wool, inspection report, November 16, 1827, Office of the Inspector General, Inspection Reports, 1814–1842.

44. Peter B. Porter to John Quincy Adams, November 24, 1828, and Maj. Gen. Alexander Macomb to Porter, November 1828, *ASP:MA*, 4:1, 5–6; Macomb to Porter, August 20, 1828, HQA:LS.

45. Skelton, "U.S. Army, 1821–1837," 338–341; General Orders No. 31, April 19, 1834, AGO: Orders and Circulars.

46. Gunther E. Rothenberg, *The Art of Warfare in the Age of Napoleon* (Bloomington: Indiana University Press, 1978), 107–108 and passim; Act of March 2, 1821, Abner R. Hetzel, comp., *Military Laws of the United States* (Washington, D.C.: G. Templeman, 1846), 213. A regiment designated as light artillery existed from 1808 to 1821, but it does not seem to have served in this capacity. Francis B. Heitman, comp., *Historical Register and Dictionary of the United States Army, from Its Organization, September 29, 1789, to March 2, 1903*, 2 vols. (Washington, D.C.: Government Printing Office, 1903), 1:51.

47. Birkhimer, *Historical Sketch of the Artillery,* 54–61; General Orders No. 46, August 19, 1841, AGO: Orders and Circulars.
48. General Orders No. 42, October 17, 1844, AGO: Orders and Circulars; Maj. Gen. Winfield Scott to William Wilkins, November 23, 1844, 28th Cong., 2d sess., House Exec. Doc. no. 2, 130–131; New Haven *Courier,* September 8, 1843, reprinted in *Army and Navy Chronicle, and Scientific Repository* 2 (September 28, 1843):406–408.
49. Grady McWhiney, *Braxton Bragg and Confederate Defeat* (New York: Columbia University Press, 1969), 52–140; Edward G. Longacre, *The Man Behind the Guns: Biography of General Henry Jackson Hunt, Chief of Artillery, Army of the Potomac* (South Brunswick, N.J.: A. S. Barnes, 1977), 31–74; James Duncan Papers, U.S. Military Academy Library, West Point, N.Y., passim.
50. Col. Roger Jones to Maj. Gen. Alexander Macomb, April 27, 1839, AGO:LS; General Orders No. 28, May 20, 1839, AGO: Orders and Circulars; Col. Abraham Eustis to Col. Roger Jones, June 10, 1839, file E-34, AGO:LR; *Army and Navy Chronicle* 8 (June 20, 1839):390–391, 395; and 9 (July 18, 1839):37, (September 26, 1839):204–205.
51. On Jefferson Barracks as a sometime school of practice, see Theodore F. Rodenbough and William L. Haskin, eds., *The Army of the United States: Historical Sketches of Staff and Line with Portraits of Generals-in-Chief* (New York: Maynard, Merrill, 1896), 435; Maj. Gen. Winfield Scott to James M. Porter, November 24, 1843, 28th Cong., 1st sess., House Exec. Doc. no. 2, 64–65; Rodney Glisan, *Journal of Army Life* (San Francisco: A. L. Bancroft, 1874), 14. On the cavalry school, see William W. Averell, *Ten Years in the Saddle: The Memoir of William Woods Averell,* ed. Edward K. Eckert and Nicholas J. Amato (San Rafael, Calif.: Presidio Press, 1978), 53–80; Maury, *Recollections,* 103–104.
52. For examples of proposals for reviving the artillery school, see Lt. John W. Phelps to Col. Roger Jones, May 16, 1850, file P-103, AGO:LR; Maj. Harvey Brown to Lt. Col. Lorenzo Thomas, July 12, 1857, National Archives, Records of U.S. Army Continental Commands (Record Group 393), Fort Monroe Artillery School Letterbook, 1855–1863; "Memoir on the United States Artillery," in Benét, comp., *Annual Reports,* 2:428. For practice firing, see General Orders No. 21, April 1, 1842, and No. 10, March 25, 1844, AGO: Orders and Circulars.
53. General Orders No. 5, May 18, 1858, AGO: Orders and Circulars. Birkhimer, *Historical Sketch of the Artillery,* 125–126. Instruction at Ft. Monroe school appears to have begun in 1857.
54. General Orders No. 10, May 9, 1859, AGO: Orders and Circulars.
55. Long, "Recollections," 103–104, Long Papers. The operations of the artillery school may be followed closely in the semiannual and annual reports of the post commanders and other correspondence in AGO:LR for 1857–1860. See, for example, files B-210 (1858), T-22 (1858), B-111 (1859), B-342 (1859), B-331 (1860), D-53 (1860), D-162 (1860). As head of a board to determine a precise course of study at the school, Maj. Robert Anderson solicited recommendations from artillery officers, and their replies indicate strong interest in the program. See Anderson's correspondence for 1860 in Robert Anderson Papers, Library of Congress.
56. See, for example, files B-430 (1859), B-331 (1860), N-8 (1860), W-26 (1860), AGO:LR.
57. Skelton, "U.S. Army, 1821–1837," 159–162; General Orders No. 50, July 26, 1824, AGO: Orders and Circulars; files G-96 (1824), S-110 (1824), AGO:LR; files S-377 (1824), S-438 (1824), SW:LR-Reg.
58. Skelton, "U.S. Army, 1821–1837," 333–334; Perry D. Jamieson, "The Development of Civil War Tactics" (Ph.D. diss., Wayne State University, 1979), 7–10. For

the debate on tactics, see *Army and Navy Chronicle* 1–2 (March 1835–April 1836):passim.

59. Birkhimer, *Historical Sketch of the Artillery,* 303–306; Jamieson, "Civil War Tactics," 17–18; Maj. Gen. Winfield Scott to William Wilkins, October 17, 1844, HQA:LS. Capt. Robert Anderson was a central figure in compiling these tactics, and he corresponded extensively with other artillery officers concerning them; see his correspondence for 1839–1844 in the Anderson Papers. On tactics for the mounted service, see General Orders, July 23, 1832, No. 1, January 4, 1837, and No. 30, June 3, 1839, AGO: Orders and Circulars; Henry S. Turner, *The Original Journals of Henry Smith Turner: With Stephen Watts Kearny to New Mexico and California, 1846–1847,* ed. Dwight L. Clarke (Norman: University of Oklahoma Press, 1966), 11–12. On militia tactics, see Skelton, "U.S. Army, 1821–1837," 161–165; Matthew B. Veatch, "The Education of a Staff Officer: The Life and Career of Samuel Cooper, 1798–1852" (M.A. thesis, University of Missouri–Kansas City, 1989), 85–95.

60. Hughes, *Old Reliable,* 41–50; Jamieson, "Civil War Tactics," 36–45.

61. For alternatives to Hardee, see Hughes, *Old Reliable,* 44; Lt. Col. Silas Casey to Col. Samuel Cooper, May 27, 1859, file C-177, AGO:LR; Jamieson, "Civil War Tactics," 46–49; J. W. A. Whitehorne, "Inspector General Sylvester Churchill's Efforts to Produce a New Army Drill Manual, 1850–1862," *Civil War History* 32 (June 1986):159–168. For supplementary systems, see Jamieson, "Civil War Tactics," 29–30, 50; Myers, *McClellan,* 60; *DAB,* 20:201; Henry Heth, *The Memoirs of Henry Heth,* ed. James L. Morrison, Jr. (Westport, Conn.: Greenwood Press, 1974), 135, 138–142; file M-127 (1858), AGO:LR.

62. Jamieson, "Civil War Tactics," 60–66; Young, *Cooke,* 286–287, 317–321; Maury, *Recollections,* 95–96, 104; Lt. Dabney H. Maury to Capt. George B. McClellan, December 2, 1856, March 28, 1858, and December 8, 1860, McClellan Papers; files H-180 (1854), S-365 (1855), W-399 (1857), E-54 (1858), C-84 (1859), V-30 (1860), AGO:LR.

63. Birkhimer, *Historical Sketch of the Artillery,* 306–308; Jamieson, "Civil War Tactics," 57–60; Capt. Benjamin Huger et al. to Bvt. Maj. William G. Freeman, August 23, 1850, file H-35, HQA:LR; Capt. Charles F. Smith to Col. Roger Jones, May 7, 1851, and enclosures, file S-191, and Maj. Robert Anderson to John B. Floyd, October 27, 1859, and enclosures, file A-236, AGO:LR; Anderson's correspondence for 1859, Anderson Papers. For battery commanders' recommendations, see file G-5 (1855), AGO:LR.

64. Proposals for conducting the Second Seminole War commonly appeared in the *Army and Navy Chronicle* in the late 1830s and early 1840s. See, for example, 5 (August 3, 1837):72–74, 7 (October 18, 1838):249–250; 9 (August 29, 1839):132, 138–139, (November 7, 1839):289–291, (December 19, 1839):394–395; 11 (October 1, 1840):220–221. For the evolution of Florida strategy and tactics, see John K. Mahon, *History of the Second Seminole War, 1835–1842* (Gainesville: University of Florida Press, 1967); John T. Sprague, *The Origin, Progress, and Conclusion of the Florida War* (New York: D. Appleton, 1848).

65. In 1850, for example, officers in Texas recommended the use of mountain howitzers in operations against the Indians; in 1857, Capt. John G. Walker submitted to army headquarters a system of cavalry tactics designed for Indian warfare—files B-225 (1850), W-399 (1857), AGO:LR. For other examples of officers' proposals for conducting Indian warfare in the 1850s, see chapter 16. See also Robert M. Utley, *Frontiersmen in Blue: The United States Army and the Indian, 1848–1865* (New York: Macmillan, 1967), 53–58, 111–112, and passim; Averam B. Bender, *The March of Empire: Frontier Defense in the Southwest, 1848–1860* (Lawrence: University Press of Kansas, 1952).

66. Jerry D. Thompson, "Henry Hopkins Sibley: Military Inventor on the Texas Frontier," *Military History of Texas and the Southwest* 10 (1972):227-247; *DAB*, 13:374-375; Albert J. Myer Papers, Library of Congress, passim; reports on Myer's signaling experiments in file L-53 (1859), AGO:LR.

67. For references to officers' publishing in newspapers, see Col. Alexander Macomb to Joseph G. Swift, September 22, 1826, Joseph G. Swift Papers, U.S. Military Academy Library, West Point, N.Y.; Lt. Minor Knowlton to Capt. Robert Anderson, March 2, 1843, Anderson Papers; Capt. Randolph B. Marcy to Ellen Marcy, September 20, 1857, McClellan Papers; Maj. John G. Barnard to Lt. James B. McPherson, June 29, 1859, James B. McPherson Papers, Library of Congress. Many officers' letters in military journals were republished from newspapers. For examples of officers' articles in literary magazines, see [Capt. Henry Whiting], review article on military works, *North American Review* 23 (October 1826):245-274; [Capt. Philip St. George Cooke], "Scenes and Adventures in the Army," *Southern Literary Messenger* 9 (February 1843):109-124; [Lt. Braxton Bragg], "Notes on Our Army," ibid., 10-11 (February 1844-February 1845): passim; [Lt. Daniel H. Hill], "The Army in Texas," *Southern Quarterly Review* 9 (April 1846):434-457; and sources cited in note 22 above.

68. Sprague, *Florida War;* Lt. Roswell S. Ripley, *The War with Mexico*, 2 vols. (New York: Harper and Brothers, 1849).

69. 36th Cong., 1st sess., Sen. Exec. Doc. no. 2, passim. The War Department annual reports for 1821-1837 are in *ASP:MA;* those for 1838-1860 are in the congressional serial set.

70. *ASP:MA,* 4:632-661.

71. Ibid., 6:12-15, 149-153, and 7:777-785, 956-965; Francis Paul Prucha, *The Sword of the Republic: The United States Army on the Frontier, 1783-1846* (New York: Macmillan, 1969), 339-357.

72. For examples of congressional publications on coast defense, see notes 20-22 above. For examples of correspondence on army operations, see 27th Cong., 2d sess., House Exec. Doc. no. 262 (Florida); 29th Cong., 1st sess., House Exec. Doc. no. 209 (Mexican War); 35th Cong., 1st sess., House Exec. Doc. no. 71 (Utah).

73. Surg. Gen. Thomas Lawson, comp., *Statistical Report on the Sickness and Mortality in the Army of the United States, . . . from January 1819, to January 1839* (Washington, D.C., 1840); Asst. Surg. Richard H. Coolidge, comp., *Statistical Report on the Sickness and Mortality in the Army of the United States, . . . from January 1839, to January 1855* (Washington, D.C., 1856); Coolidge, comp., *Statistical Report on the Sickness and Mortality in the Army of the United States, . . . from January 1855, to January 1860* (Washington, D.C., 1860).

74. For examples of officers' reports on Indian affairs, see 34th Cong., 3d sess., House Exec. Doc. no. 76, and the congressional publications cited in the notes for chapter 16. For examples of exploration reports, see 28th Cong., 2d sess., Sen. Exec. Doc. no. 174; 30th Cong., 1st sess., Sen. Exec. Doc. no. 23; 33d Cong., 2d sess., Sen. Exec. Doc. no. 78. The West Point commission's report is 36th Cong., 2d sess., Sen. Misc. Doc. no. 3.

75. Griffith, *Military Thought,* 53-57 and passim.

CHAPTER FOURTEEN. OFFICERS AND ENLISTED MEN

1. William Tell Poussin, *The United States; Its Power and Progress,* trans. Edmund L. DuBarry (Philadelphia: Lippincott, Grambo, 1851), 390-395.

2. Stuart L. Bernath, "George Washington and the Genesis of American Military Discipline," *Mid-America* 49 (April 1967):83-100; Maurer Maurer, "Military Justice under General Washington," *Military Affairs* 28 (1964):8-16; James Kirby Martin and Mark E. Lender, *A Respectable Army: The Military Origins of the Republic, 1763-1789* (Arlington Heights, Ill.: Harlan Davidson, 1982), 87-97, 126-134, and passim; Robert H. Berlin, "The Administration of Military Justice in the Continental Army during the American Revolution, 1775-1783" (Ph.D. diss., University of California, Santa Barbara, 1976); Charles Royster, *A Revolutionary People at War: The Continental Army and American Character, 1775-1783* (Chapel Hill: University of North Carolina Press, 1979), 85-86; Mark E. Lender, "The Social Structure of the New Jersey Brigade: The Continental Line as an American Standing Army," in Peter Karsten, ed., *The Military in America from the Colonial Era to the Present* (New York: Free Press, 1980), 27-44.

3. William B. Skelton, "The Confederation's Regulars: A Social Profile of Enlisted Service in America's First Standing Army," *William and Mary Quarterly*, 3d ser. 46 (October 1986):770-785.

4. J. C. A. Stagg, "Enlisted Men in the United States Army, 1812-1815: A Preliminary Survey," *William and Mary Quarterly*, 3d ser. 43 (1986):615-645; Stanley S. Graham, "Life of the Enlisted Soldier on the Western Frontier, 1815-1845" (Ph.D. diss., North Texas State University, 1972), 44-45; Edward M. Coffman, *The Old Army: A Portrait of the American Army in Peacetime, 1784-1898* (New York: Oxford University Press, 1986), 138-141; Asst. Surg. Richard H. Coolidge, comp., *Statistical Report on the Sickness and Mortality in the Army of the United States . . . from January 1839 to January 1855* (Washington, D.C., 1856), 625-633.

5. Frederick W.A. von Steuben, *Regulations for the Order and Discipline of the Troops of the United States* (Philadelphia: Styner and Cist, 1779), 138-140.

6. "General Regulations of the Army" (1821), *ASP:MA*, 2:201. Commanders often made the same point. See, for example, Maj. Gen. Andrew Jackson to Division of the South, May 31, 1821, *Niles' Weekly Register* 9 (September 22, 1821):52-53.

7. Percival G. Lowe, *Five Years a Dragoon ('49 to '54)* (Norman: University of Oklahoma Press, 1965), 6; William W. Averell, *Ten Years in the Saddle: The Memoir of William Woods Averell*, ed. Edward K. Eckert and Nicholas J. Amato (San Rafael, Calif.: Presidio Press, 1978), 130-131, 226; John Bemrose, *Reminiscences of the Second Seminole War*, ed. John K. Mahon (Gainesville: University of Florida Press, 1966), 54, 58-59.

8. Lt. Col. John R. Fenwick to John C. Calhoun, January 19, 1819, file F-55(12), SW:LR-Reg.; Maj. Oscar F. Winship to Col. Samuel Cooper, January 31, 1855, file F-16, Maj. Harvey Brown to Bvt. Maj. Irvin I. McDowell, May 28, 1858, file B-178, AGO:LR.

9. The drive to found military asylums may be followed in the Robert Anderson Papers, Library of Congress.

10. Lt. George G. Meade to his wife, May 27, 1846, George G. Meade Papers, Historical Society of Pennsylvania; Lt. Col. George Bomford to John C. Calhoun, February 21, 1822, in John C. Calhoun, *The Papers of John C. Calhoun*, ed. Robert L. Meriwether and W. Edwin Hemphill, 18 vols. to date (Columbia: University of South Carolina Press, 1959-), 6:711; Maj. William H. Chase to Lt. George B. McClellan, October 24, 1850, George B. McClellan Papers, Library of Congress; Capt. Thomas Claiborne to his cousin, July 22, 1848, Thomas Claiborne Papers, Southern Historical

Collection, University of North Carolina Library, Chapel Hill; "Sunday Inspections," *Military and Naval Magazine of the United States* 3 (May 1834):183–187.

11. General Orders, June 19, 1815, No. 4, February 24, 1845, No. 1, January 2, 1847, AGO: Orders and Circulars.

12. *Recollections of the United States Army: A Series of Thrilling Tales and Sketches* (Boston, 1845), 43–44.

13. Skelton, "Confederation's Regulars," 781–782; Graham, "Enlisted Soldier," 194; Coffman, *Old Army*, 192–196. In 1831, the adjutant general compiled statistics indicating that total desertions represented 42.3 percent of total enlistments in the period 1823–1830. He does not seem to have accounted for the inflating effect of men deserting more than once, however. *ASP:MA*, 4:727.

14. James H. Edmonson, "Desertion in the American Army during the Revolutionary War" (Ph.D. diss., Louisiana State University, 1971), 217–261; Ella Lonn, *Desertion during the Civil War* (New York: Century, 1928), 21–37, 225–230, and passim; General Orders No. 19, April 15, 1829, AGO: Orders and Circulars. The connection between desertion and job turnover is suggested in Coffman, *Old Army*, 195–196. A recent study argues that harsh and inconsistent army punishments were a prime cause of desertion. Mark A. Vargas, "The Military Justice System and the Use of Illegal Punishments as Causes of Desertion in the U.S. Army, 1821–1835," *Journal of Military History* 55 (January 1991):1–19.

15. Col. Roger Jones to unknown, January 11, 1826, *ASP:MA*, 3:228.

16. Serg. Joseph Buell's diary, entries for December 26, 1785, and January 25, 1786, quoted in Laurence R. Guthrie, *American Guthrie and Allied Families* (Chambersburg, Pa.: Kerr Printing Co., 1933), 82. Pvt. Joel Guthrie was one of the soldiers executed.

17. Henry Knox to David Ramsay, March 15, 1786, and Knox to Congress, July 24, 1786, National Archives, Records of the Continental and Confederation Congress and the Constitutional Convention (Record Group 360), Papers of Continental Congress; Act of May 31, 1786, Abner R. Hetzel, comp., *Military Laws of the United States* (Washington, D.C.: G. Templeman, 1846), 33–38.

18. Compiled from list of courts-martial in Regimental Book of the First Regiment, Ebenezer Denny-James O'Hara Papers, Western Pennsylvania Historical Society, Pittsburgh. The remaining sentences imposed less severe penalties, such as stoppages of the whiskey ration and the demotion of noncommissioned officers.

19. Richard C. Knopf, "Crime and Punishment in the American Legion, 1792–1793," *Bulletin of the Historical and Philosophical Society of Ohio* 14 (July 1956):232–238; Maj. Gen. Alexander Hamilton to James McHenry, May 27, 1799, in Alexander Hamilton, *The Papers of Alexander Hamilton*, ed. Harold C. Syrett, 26 vols. (New York: Columbia University Press, 1961–1979), 23:151–152.

20. Acts of April 10, 1806, and May 16, 1812, Hetzel, *Military Laws*, 120, 151; William Eustis to Col. Thomas H. Cushing, May 16, 1810, SW:LS.

21. Col. Alexander Smyth to an unnamed lieutenant, October 29, 1810, copy enclosed with Smyth to William Eustis, October 27, 1810, file S-234(5), SW:LR-Reg.; John S. Hare, "Military Punishments in the War of 1812," *Journal of the American Military Institute* 4 (Winter, 1940):225–239.

22. Surg. Gen. Joseph Lovell, annual report for 1819, quoted in Charles W. Ayars, "Some Notes on the Medical Service of the Army, 1812–1839," *Military Surgeon* 50 (May 1922):515.

23. James Monroe to House of Representatives, January 8, 1820, with enclosures,

and John C. Calhoun to Speaker of House of Representatives, May 2, 1820, with enclosures, *ASP:MA*, 2:38-41, 139-187.

24. John C. Calhoun to Brig. Gen. James Miller, January 3, 1818, Lt. Col. Willoughby Morgan to Calhoun, September 8, 1820, Calhoun to Brig. Gen. Henry Atkinson, October 10, 1820, and December 4, 1820, Calhoun to Maj. Gen. Andrew Jackson, January 21, 1821, *Papers of Calhoun*, 2:56, 5:350-352, 387, 476, 568; Brig. Gen. Winfield Scott to Col. Ninian Pinkney, September 27, 1821, file 307, AGO:LR; General Orders No. 81, November 15, 1822, AGO: Orders and Circulars.

25. Brig. Gen. Edmund P. Gaines to adjutant general, January 14, 1824, file G-7, AGO:LR; Gaines, "General Courts-Martial, Crimes and Punishments," [1830], *ASP:MA*, 4:290-291. See generally the secretary of war's annual reports for the 1820s and early 1830s in *ASP:MA*.

26. Act of March 2, 1833, Hetzel, *Military Laws*, 231-232. On desertion rates, see Graham, "Enlisted Soldier," 194. In 1838, Congress again raised the enlistment period to five years. Act of July 5, 1838, Hetzel, *Military Laws*, 264.

27. Thirty-first Cong., 2d sess., Sen. Rept. no. 226; F. R. Backus to Millard Fillmore, November 11, 1850, and enclosures, file B-631, AGO:LR.

28. General Orders No. 21, April 3, 1851, AGO: Orders and Circulars. In 1853, Scott prohibited the use of "bucking," a common subjudicial punishment in which the victim's hands and feet were tied, his knees drawn up between his arms, and a pole inserted under his knees and above his arms. General Orders No. 3, January 27, 1853, ibid.

29. General Orders No. 53, August 20, 1842, ibid.

30. Files AA-117, CC-352, CC-405, HH-133, National Archives, GCM Proceedings.

31. General Orders No. 81, November 15, 1822, AGO: Orders and Circulars; file DD-125, GCM Proceedings.

32. File DD-33, GCM Proceedings. For officers' tendency to tolerate and cover up illegal punishments, see also Vargas, "Military Justice System," 12-16.

33. Myra C. Glenn, *Campaigns against Corporal Punishment: Prisoners, Sailors, Women, and Children in Antebellum America* (Albany: State University of New York, 1984); Harold D. Langley, *Social Reform in the United States Navy, 1798-1862* (Urbana: University of Illinois Press, 1967), 131-208.

34. For these cases, see the following general orders: No. 34, June 9, 1842, No. 63, September 27, 1842, No. 2, January 6, 1843, No. 4, January 17, 1843, No. 6, January 21, 1843, No. 13, February 20, 1843, No. 17, March 3, 1843, No. 68, December 18, 1843, No. 2, January 13, 1844, AGO: Orders and Circulars. For the Buell case, see also 28th Cong., 1st sess., Sen. Exec. Doc. no. 71; quotation is on p. 13.

35. Files HH-161, HH-962, GCM Proceedings. In his annual report for 1844, Scott noted an improvement of enlisted men's morale, which he attributed in part to the decline of illegal punishments. Maj. Gen. Winfield Scott to William Wilkins, November 23, 1844, 28th Cong., 2d sess., House Exec. Doc. no. 2, 131-132. However, the weight of evidence—in court-martial proceedings, soldiers' accounts, and officers' correspondence—makes clear that illegal punishments were widely used during and after the Mexican War.

36. Capt. Thomas Claiborne to his wife, November 10, 1860, Claiborne Papers. See also Claiborne to his wife, June 3, 1853, ibid.

37. Col. Roger Jones to Joel R. Poinsett, August 29, 1838, and proceedings of court-martial of Pvt. Bartholomew Rogers, file CC-328, GCM Proceedings. The other soldiers who may have been executed were privates James Byrne and John Reily,

though the final review of the Byrne case is uncertain. Files CC-305 and CC-312, ibid. For the attorney general's opinion, see Benjamin F. Butler to Joel R. Poinsett, March 9, 1838, in the latter file.

38. Augustus Meyers, *Ten Years in the Ranks, U.S. Army* (New York: Stirling Press, 1914), 44; Samuel E. Chamberlain, *My Confession,* ed. Roger Butterfield (New York: Harper, 1956), 68.

39. George Ballentine, *Autobiography of an English Soldier in the United States Army,* ed. William H. Goetzmann (Chicago: R. R. Donnelley and Sons, 1986), 150. See also Chamberlain, *My Confession,* 140–143.

40. James Hildreth, *Dragoon Campaigns to the Rocky Mountains, Being a History of the Enlistment, Organization and First Campaigns of the Regiment of United States Dragoons* (New York: Wiley and Long, 1836), 30; Harold D. Langley, ed., *To Utah with the Dragoons, and Glimpses of Life in Arizona and California, 1858–1859* (Salt Lake City: University of Utah Press, 1974), 34–35; Josiah M. Rice, *A Cannoneer in Navajo Country: Journal of Private Josiah M. Rice, 1851,* ed. Richard H. Dillon (Denver: Old West Publishing Co., 1970), 77; Eugene Bandel, *Frontier Life in the Army, 1854–1861,* ed. Ralph P. Bieber (Glendale, Calif.: Arthur H. Clark, 1932), 122–123.

41. Chamberlain, *My Confession,* 138–139, 187, 192–199, 200–206; Ballentine, *Autobiography,* 14, 128–129, 182–185, 235, 271–272, 285–286, 331–333; Langley, ed., *To Utah,* 121–123; Hildreth, *Dragoon Campaigns,* 284–288; William E. Boulger to John B. Floyd, January 7, 1858, file B-14, AGO:LR. See also *Recollections of U.S. Army,* passim.

42. Meyers, *Ten Years,* 42–43, 130–132; See also Ballentine, *Autobiography,* 31–32; Langley, ed., *To Utah,* 25; Hildreth, *Dragoon Campaigns,* 47–50; James A. Bennett, "James A. Bennett: A Dragoon in New Mexico, 1850–1856," ed. Clinton E. Brooks and Frank D. Reeve, *New Mexico Historical Review* 22 (January 1947):56.

43. Pvt. Joseph Baxter to John C. Calhoun, July 25, 1821, *Papers of Calhoun,* 6:279–280.

44. Files AA-104, CC-433, GCM Proceedings.

45. File DD-110, ibid. Two drafts of Markiewicz's letter are in this file. For the court of inquiry into Shannon's death, see file DD-100, ibid.

46. Files AA-116, AA-122, ibid. Smith was reappointed to the army at his former rank two years later.

47. File AA-184, ibid. A historian of naval discipline speculates that seamen's work stoppages and other collective actions may have been far more common than indicated by the court-martial record and that they were often tolerated by officers as a means to relieve tensions if they did not go too far. James E. Vallé, *Rocks & Shoals: Order and Discipline in the Old Navy 1800–1861* (Annapolis, Md.: Naval Institute Press, 1980), 102–127. This may also have been the case in the army. See Vallé's fascinating work generally for parallels with army discipline.

48. Files CC-293, CC-294, CC-295, CC-297, CC-298, CC-299, CC-300, GCM Proceedings. For a similar group protest over nonfulfillment of the enlistment "contract," see Pvt. Walker Black et al. to Capt. Thomas W. Sherman, May 2, 1851, file S-206, AGO:LR.

49. File DD-113, GCM Proceedings. This incident may help explain why Lyon developed an obsessive severity in his treatment of enlisted men. See Christopher Phillips, *Damned Yankee: The Life of General Nathaniel Lyon* (Columbia: University of Missouri Press, 1990), 87–91.

50. File HH-652, GCM Proceedings; Lt. Edward L. Hartz to Samuel Hartz, April 6, 1856, Edward L. Hartz Papers, Library of Congress. On other occasions, soldiers

refused altogether to administer punishments. See Meyers, *Ten Years*, 130–132; Chamberlain, *My Confession*, 192–199.

51. File CC-312, GCM Proceedings; Capt. Stephen W. Kearny to Col. Henry Atkinson, October 1, 1828, and enclosure, file M-214, AGO:LR; John H. Fonda, "Early Wisconsin," *Collections of the State Historical Society of Wisconsin* 5 (1907):238–239. The other officers known to have been killed by soldiers were Maj. Sanders Donoho and Lt. Amos Foster. Francis B. Heitman, comp., *Historical Register and Dictionary of the United States Army, from Its Organization, September 29, 1789, to March 2, 1903*, 2 vols. (Washington, D.C.: Government Printing Office, 1903), 1:378, 431. There may have been other instances as well, since murder cases were tried in civilian courts and thus do not always appear in the army records.

52. Col. Ninian Pinkney to Brig. Gen. Winfield Scott, September 3, 1821, copy enclosed with Capt. Charles J. Nourse to Col. James Gadsden, October 30, 1821, file 15330, AGO:LR; file CC-311, GCM Proceedings.

53. File GG-82, GCM Proceedings. For a similar case, in which Lt. Charles H. Ogle killed a soldier in a gunfight, see file HH-752, ibid.

54. In their defenses during desertion courts-martial, soldiers rarely mentioned officers' abuse as a motive for deserting. However, their statements may have been tailored to please the members of the courts, who were of course commissioned officers. Based on a survey of about 140 desertion courts-martial in GCM Proceedings.

55. Files AA-125, CC-479, CC-226, ibid.

CHAPTER FIFTEEN. OFFICERS, POLITICIANS, AND CITIZENS

1. Capt. John R. Vinton to his mother, November 13, 1840, John R. Vinton Papers, Duke University Library, Durham, N.C.

2. The military candidates and the years of their races were: Andrew Jackson (1824, 1828, 1832); William Henry Harrison (1836, 1840); Zachary Taylor (1848); Winfield Scott (1852); John C. Frémont (1856); George B. McClellan (1864); Ulysses S. Grant (1868, 1872); Winfield Scott Hancock (1880).

3. Maj. Gen. Zachary Taylor to Surg. Robert C. Wood, June 23, 1847, in Zachary Taylor, *Letters of Zachary Taylor, from the Battle-Fields of the Mexican War* (Rochester, N.Y.: Genessee Press, 1908), 110.

4. This and the following section are a revised version of the author's previously published article: "Officers and Politicians: The Origins of Army Politics in the United States before the Civil War," *Armed Forces and Society* 6 (Fall 1979):22–48.

5. Charles W. Elliott, *Winfield Scott: The Soldier and the Man* (New York: Macmillan, 1937), 232–235; Morgan Dix, *Memoirs of John Adams Dix*, 2 vols. (New York: Harper and Brothers, 1883), 1:66–67, 2:309–314; Jacob J. Brown Papers, Library of Congress, passim; Brown Papers, William L. Clements Library, Ann Arbor, Mich., passim. General Brown's first political loyalty, however, was to DeWitt Clinton. For other examples of officers' political loyalties in this period, see Maj. Timothy P. Andrews to Joseph G. Swift, October 10, 1823, Joseph G. Swift Papers, U.S. Military Academy Library, West Point, N.Y.; Andrews to Asst. Surg. Benjamin King, January 26, 1825, Benjamin King Papers, Library of Congress; John C. Calhoun, *The Papers of John Calhoun*, ed. Robert L. Meriwether and W. Edwin Hemphill, 18 vols. to date (Columbia: University of South Carolina Press, 1959–), 7:182, 454, 8:248; John M. O'Connor Papers, William L. Clements Library, Ann Arbor, Mich., passim.

6. Col. Henry Atkinson to Christopher Van Deventer, December 30, 1824, Chris-

topher Van Deventer Papers, William L. Clements Library, Ann Arbor, Mich.; Col. Duncan L. Clinch to John H. Eaton, August 29, 1829, quoted in Rembert W. Patrick, *Aristocrat in Uniform: General Duncan L. Clinch* (Gainesville: University of Florida Press, 1963), 62; Brig. Gen. Edmund P. Gaines to certain citizens of St. Louis, January 15, 1838, *Army and Navy Chronicle* 6 (February 15, 1838):97; James W. Silver, *Edmund Pendleton Gaines: Frontier General* (Baton Rouge: Louisiana State University Press, 1949), 138, 159–160; Lt. William T. Sherman to Ellen B. Ewing, September 17, 1844, in William T. Sherman, *Home Letters of General Sherman*, ed. M.A. DeWolfe Howe (New York: C. Scribner's Sons, 1909), 27; "Politics and Officers," *Army and Navy Chronicle* 2 (May 19, 1836):315–316.

7. Lt. Daniel H. Hill, "The Army in Texas," *Southern Quarterly Review* 9 (April 1846):448.

8. Philip St. George Cooke, *Scenes and Adventures in the Army: or, The Romance of Military Life* (Philadelphia: Lindsay and Blakiston, 1857), 230; Capt. William H. T. Walker to his wife, February 10, 1855, William H.T. Walker Papers, Duke University Library, Durham, N.C.; Capt. George W. Cullum to Lt. George L. Welcker, June 7, 1842, Lenoir Family Papers II, Southern Historical Collection, University of North Carolina Library, Chapel Hill.

9. "The Army and the People," *Army and Navy Chronicle* 9 (October 24, 1839):265–266; Capt. Thomas Williams to Mary Williams, January 21, 1855, Williams Family Papers, Burton Collection, Detroit Public Library; Lt. John Van Deusen DuBois, journal entries for June 23, 1858, and June 29, 1858, in John Van Deusen DuBois, *Campaigns in the West, 1856–1861: The Journal and Letters of Colonel John Van Deusen DuBois,* ed. George P. Hammond (Tucson: Arizona Pioneers Historical Society, 1949), 69, 71.

10. Col. Abraham Eustis to Bvt. Capt. Robert Anderson, June 5, 1840, Robert Anderson Papers, Library of Congress.

11. Lt. Braxton Bragg to Lt. James Duncan, December 6, 1844, James Duncan Papers, U.S. Military Academy Library, West Point, N.Y.; Capt. Benjamin Alvord to Marcus C. M. Hammond, March 20, 1849, James H. Hammond Papers, Library of Congress; Capt. Thomas Williams to Mary Williams, journal letter beginning February 2, 1855, entry for February 7, Williams Family Papers.

12. Bvt. Capt. Julius P. Garesché to Lt. James A. Hardie, July 24, 1857, James A. Hardie Papers, Library of Congress. The best source for officers' applications for favors is AGO:LR.

13. Maj. Abraham Eustis to Col. Daniel Parker, August 22, 1821, Daniel Parker Papers, Historical Society of Pennsylvania; William B. Skelton, "The United States Army, 1821–1837: An Institutional History" (Ph.D. diss., Northwestern University, 1968), 44, 54–56; *Papers of Calhoun,* 7: xi–xx.

14. Skelton, "U.S. Army, 1821–1837," 184–201; Elliott, *Scott,* 244–256.

15. Col. John E. Wool to Nathaniel P. Tallmadge, August 30, 1841, Nathaniel P. Tallmadge Papers, State Historical Society of Wisconsin, Madison; Capt. John R. Vinton to Mary Vinton, August 12, 1841, Vinton Papers; Col. Abraham Eustis to Lt. Robert Anderson, August 15, 1841, and Col. Henry Atkinson to Anderson, April 4, 1842, Anderson Papers; Maj. Ethan Allen Hitchcock, memorandum to Tallmadge, [Aug. 1841], Ethan Allen Hitchcock Papers, Library of Congress.

16. Lt. Marcus C. M. Hammond to Lt. George L. Welcker, May 7, 1842, Lenoir Family Papers II; Capt. Joseph E. Johnston to Robert M. McLane, January 14, 1850, Louis McLane Papers, Library of Congress.

17. Files Army 47, Army 123, Army 115, SW: Applications, Subseries for 1854–

1861; Capt. Thomas Williams to Mary Williams, February 2, 1855, Williams Family Papers; Lt. William B. Franklin to Capt. Robert Anderson, February 14, 1854, Anderson Papers.

18. General Orders No. 48, May 18, 1833, and No. 79, September 20, 1833, AGO: Orders and Circulars; Skelton, "U.S. Army, 1821–1837," 251–252, 281–285. In 1838, Senator Franklin Pierce attributed the repeal of the ban on visiting Washington, D.C., to public opinion that it had discriminated against the interests of line officers in favor of those of the staff, as the latter had branch representatives stationed permanently at the capital. U.S. Congress, *Congressional Globe,* 46 vols. (Washington, D.C., 1834–1873), 25th Cong., 2d sess., Appendix, 489.

19. General Orders No. 79, December 23, 1837, and No. 9, February 12, 1851, AGO: Orders and Circulars; Lt. George W. Hazzard to his wife, April 14, 1859, George W. Hazzard Papers, U.S. Military Academy Library, West Point, N.Y. For examples of authorities' resistance to political pressures, see Bvt. Maj. Samuel Cooper to George Evans, July 24, 1838, SW:LS; Maj. Gen. Winfield Scott to John Bell, August 12, 1841, and Scott to William L. Marcy, March 25, 1845, HQA:LS; Col. Roger Jones to Lt. George W. Hazzard, March 11, 1851, file H-64, AGO:LR. A sampling of officers' applications in AGO:LR during the 1850s suggests that, despite the opinion of most officers, political support was so common that it had little impact on War Department decisions in routine personnel matters.

20. Stephen V. Benét, comp., *A Collection of Annual Reports and Other Important Papers, Relating to the Ordnance Department, Taken from the Records of the Office of the Chief of Ordnance, from Public Documents, and from Other Sources,* 4 vols. (Washington, D.C., 1878–1890), 2:417–488, 628–635; Lt. Henry J. Hunt to Capt. Edward J. Steptoe, April 5, 1852, Williams Family Papers; Hunt to Lt. Isaac Ingalls Stevens, August 21, 1852, Isaac Ingalls Stevens Papers, University of Washington Library, Seattle.

21. Grady McWhiney, *Braxton Bragg and Confederate Defeat* (New York: Columbia University Press, 1969), 38–44; Lt. Braxton Bragg, "Notes on Our Army," *Southern Literary Messenger* 10–11 (February 1844–February 1845): passim; Lt. James Duncan's correspondence for 1844, Duncan Papers.

22. Topographical officers' political connections are discussed in William H. Goetzmann, *Army Exploration in the American West, 1803–1863* (New Haven, Conn.: Yale University Press, 1959), and Allan Nevins, *Frémont: Pathmarker of the West* (New York: D. Appleton-Century Co., 1939). The administration at times reprimanded officers for overly strong identification with local interests. See, for example, the case of Lt. John Pope, in file P-76 (1854), AGO:LR.

23. For an example of the extent to which civil works could enmesh engineer officers in politics, see Russell F. Weigley, *Quartermaster General of the Union Army: A Biography of M. C. Meigs* (New York: Columbia University Press, 1959), 57–112.

24. Lt. George W. Cullum to Lt. George L. Welcker, June 7, 1842, Lenoir Family Papers II. The best single source for the Corps of Engineers' pursuit of branch interests is the "private" and "confidential" letterbooks of Chief Engineer Joseph G. Totten, National Archives, Records of the Office of the Chief of Engineers (Record Group 77) Letters and Reports of Col. Joseph G. Totten.

25. *Congressional Globe* 31st Cong., 2d sess., 640–652; Lt. Isaac Ingalls Stevens's correspondence for 1851–1853, Stevens Papers; U.S. Congress, *The Public Statutes at Large of the United States of America,* 100 vols. to date (Boston and Washington, D.C.: Government Printing Office, 1848–), 10:214–219.

26. Lt. Isaac Ingalls Stevens to Lt. George B. McClellan, March 3, 1853, George B. McClellan Papers, Library of Congress.

27. Maj. Gen. Jacob Brown to John C. Calhoun, June 11, 1819, and November 14, 1820, *Papers of Calhoun*, 4:100, 5:436–437.

28. The pay question is discussed extensively in the *Army and Navy Chronicle*. See also *ASP:MA*, 3:230–231, 4:64–66, 849; memorial to Congress from officers in Oregon Territory [1849 or 1850], Theodore Talbot Papers, Library of Congress. Of course, pay was as often a source of intraservice feuding as of service solidarity. Examples of lobbying for a retirement system are Maj. Sylvanus Thayer to Gouverneur Kemble, December 15, 1837, and January 21, 1838, Sylvanus Thayer Papers, U.S. Military Academy Library, West Point, N.Y.; petition to Congress from army officers in Mexico, August 1, 1847, 30th Cong., 1st sess., Misc. Doc. no. 11; Maj. Theophilus H. Holmes to Capt. Thomas Claiborne, February 6, 1860, Thomas Claiborne Papers, Southern Historical Collection, University of North Carolina Library, Chapel Hill.

29. Capt. Robert Anderson to Eliza Anderson, May 5, 1848, Anderson Papers. For Anderson's lobbying efforts, see generally his correspondence in this collection.

30. Ethan Allen Hitchcock, *Fifty Years in Camp and Field: The Diary of Major-General Ethan Allen Hitchcock, U.S.A.*, ed. William A. Croffut (New York: G. P. Putnam's Sons, 1909), 321–322; Capt. Benjamin Alvord to Marcus C. M. Hammond, April 21, 1848, Hammond Papers; Capt. William H. T. Walker to Molly Walker, July 21, 1847, Walker Papers. For other typical remarks, see George Meade, *The Life and Letters of George Gordon Meade*, 2 vols. (New York: C. Scribner's Sons, 1913), 1:91, 102–103, 162–163; Capt. William S. Henry, *Campaign Sketches of the War with Mexico* (New York: Harper and Brothers, 1847), 128, 152, 159–160; George B. McClellan, *The Mexican War Diary of George B. McClellan*, ed. William S. Myers (Princeton, N.J.: Princeton University Press, 1917); Capt. Robert Anderson, *An Artillery Officer in the Mexican War, 1846–7: Letters of Robert Anderson, Captain 3rd Artillery, U.S.A.* (New York: G. P. Putnam's Sons, 1911), 83–84, 107–108, 276, 333; Lt. Daniel H. Hill, "The Army in Texas," *Southern Quarterly Review* 9 (April 1846):434–457, 14 (July 1848):183–197.

31. Lt. Francis Collins's journal entry for February 20, 1848, in Francis Collins, "Journal of Francis Collins, an Artillery Officer in the Mexican War," ed. Maria C. Collins, *Quarterly Publication of the Historical and Philosophical Society of Ohio* 10 (April–July 1915):97; Hitchcock, *Fifty Years*, 321. See also Capt. Benjamin Alvord to Marcus C. M. Hammond, February 24, 1848, Hammond Papers; Capt. Joseph H. LaMotte to his wife, March 25, 1848, LaMotte-Coppinger Papers, Missouri Historical Society, St. Louis; Lt. Abram B. Lincoln to Lt. Isaac Ingalls Stevens, February 25, 1848, Stevens Papers.

32. Compiled mainly from biographies and officers' published and unpublished correspondence and journals. This distribution closely resembles the distribution of popular voting for the presidency in 1828–1852: Democratic 51.2 percent; National Republican/Whig 48.8 percent.

33. Lt. Isaac Ingalls Stevens, organizer of the engineers' lobby of the early 1850s, and several other officers campaigned for Franklin Pierce in 1852, partly because they had known him as a temporary general in the Mexican War. Stevens was rewarded with the governorship of the Washington Territory. Hazard Stevens, *The Life of Isaac Ingalls Stevens*, 2 vols. (Boston: Houghton, Mifflin, 1900), 1:272–275; Stevens Papers, passim.

34. Richard Hofstadter, *The Idea of a Party System: The Rise of Legitimate Opposition in the United States, 1780–1840* (Berkeley and Los Angeles: University of California Press, 1970), 212–271.

35. The roll calls are: army expansion bill (June 28, 1838); amendment to army or-

ganization bill to abolish Second Dragoon Regiment (August 4, 1842); appropriation bill for military academy (March 15, 1844); amendment to bill to establish Regiment of Mounted Riflemen requiring selection of officers from regular army (April 10, 1846); motion to table appropriation bill for fortifications (February 22, 1851); amendment to army appropriation bill adding four new regiments and a brigadier general (March 2, 1855). These findings are substantiated by a general reading of debates on military issues in *Register of Debates in Congress* and the *Congressional Globe.* Party lines often held on specific roll calls: 84 percent of the Whigs opposed the expansion of the army in 1838, while 91.2 percent of them sustained the military academy in 1844. Such alignments followed no discernible long-term pattern, however, and probably reflected resistance to or support for administration measures as much as principled positions on the regular army question.

36. Capt. John Stuart to Lewis Cass, May 1, 1833, Clarence E. Carter and John P. Bloom, eds., *The Territorial Papers of the United States*, 27 vols. (Washington, D.C.: Government Printing Office, 1934–1969), 21:710; Maj. John Sedgwick to his sister, September 25, 1860, in John Sedgwick, *Correspondence of John Sedgwick, Major-General*, 2 vols. (New York: DeVinne Press, 1902–1903), 2:24. See also Jacob Rhett Motte, *Journal into Wilderness: An Army Surgeon's Account of Life in Camp and Field during the Creek and Seminole Wars, 1836–1838*, ed. James F. Sunderman (Gainesville: University of Florida Press, 1953), 53–54; Cooke, *Scenes and Adventures*, 37–38, 42, 113; Richard S. Ewell, *The Making of a Soldier: Letters of General R. S. Ewell*, ed. Percy G. Hamlin (Richmond: Whittet and Shepperson, 1935), 42–43; Randolph B. Marcy, *Thirty Years of Army Life on the Border* (New York: Harper and Brothers, 1866), 356–398.

37. Maj. Enos Cutler to Brig. Gen. Daniel Parker, June 24, 1820, Parker Papers; Col. Zachary Taylor to Brig. Gen. Thomas S. Jesup, [October 7, 1839], Zachary Taylor Papers, Library of Congress; John T. Sprague, *The Origin, Progress, and Conclusion of the Florida War*, (New York: D. Appleton, 1848), 267–270; Capt. Thomas Williams to Mary Williams, journal letter beginning January 6, [1857], entry for January 7, Williams Family Papers.

38. Bvt. Capt. James H. Prentiss to Lt. Abraham R. Johnston, February 4, 1840, Abraham R. Johnston Papers, U.S. Military Academy Library, West Point, N.Y. For an excellent example of successful civilian lobbying to maintain a post despite military opposition, see Ed Bearss and Arrell M. Gibson, *Fort Smith: Little Gibralter on the Arkansas* (Norman: University of Oklahoma Press, 1969), 137–152, 167–170, 185–188, 208–213.

39. Lt. Theodore Talbot to his sister, December 25, 1850, Theodore Talbot Papers, Library of Congress. Generalizations on civil-military tensions are based on histories of military posts and the army's broad frontier role and on officers' official and private correspondence. On tensions over liquor sales to soldiers, discharges of soldiers, and access to military land, see Brig. Gen. Edmund P. Gaines to John C. Calhoun, June 30, 1820, *Papers of Calhoun*, 5:233; Dwight L. Clarke, *Stephen Watts Kearny: Soldier of the West* (Norman: University of Oklahoma Press, 1961), 64; Tommy R. Young II, "The United States Army in the South, 1789–1835" (Ph.D. diss., Louisiana State University, 1973), 263–264; Erasmus D. Keyes, *Fifty Years' Observations of Men and Events, Civil and Military* (New York: C. Scribner's Sons, 1884), 292–296; files C-371 (1851), B-644 (1855), H-206 (1856), B-16 (1858), S-464 (1858), AGO:LR; Bruce E. Mahan, *Old Fort Crawford and the Frontier* (Iowa City: State Historical Society of Iowa, 1926), 73–74.

40. On tensions over military punishments, see Max L. Heyman, Jr., *Prudent Soldier: A Biography of Major General E. R. S. Canby, 1817–1873* (Glendale, Calif.: Arthur

H. Clark, 1959), 98–100; Chris Emmett, *Fort Union and the Winning of the Southwest* (Norman: University of Oklahoma Press, 1965), 141–145; Capt. Alexander S. Brooks to Brig. Gen. Daniel Parker, September 17, 1820, and enclosures, file 14198, AGO:LR. For examples of soldier-civilian violence, see Richard D. Gamble, "Garrison Life at Frontier Military Posts, 1830–1860" (Ph.D. diss., University of Oklahoma, 1956), 179–180; Nathan Willis et al. to John C. Calhoun, [1821], file 15512, file B-444 (1850), AGO:LR. For the Wickliffe affair, see Aurora Hunt, *Major General James Henry Carleton, 1814–1873: Western Frontier Dragoon* (Glendale, Calif.: Arthur H. Clark, 1958), 55–57, 59–65.

41. Col. Talbot Chambers to John C. Calhoun, September 19, 1823, and Calhoun to Chambers, December 16, 1823, *Papers of Calhoun*, 8:272–273, 409; Capt. John Stuart to Lewis Cass, February 7, 1834, *Territorial Papers*, 21:896–899. For other examples of civil-military tensions over enforcement of the trade and intercourse laws and the army's constabulary role, see Francis Paul Prucha, *Broadax and Bayonet: The Role of the United States Army in the Development of the Northwest, 1815–1860* (Madison: State Historical Society of Wisconsin, 1953), 55–103; Young, "Army in the South," 247–248, 281–283, 318–319, 332–339, and passim; *Territorial Papers*, 21:passim.

42. Clarke, *Kearny*, 135–160; Alvin R. Sunseri, "New Mexico in the Aftermath of the Anglo-American Conquest, 1846–1861" (Ph.D. diss., Louisiana State University, 1973), 123–156; Emmett, *Fort Union*, 80–153. On the army's role in the administration of Florida in 1821, see *Territorial Papers*, 22:passim.

43. Theodore Grivas, *Military Governments in California, 1846–1850, with a Chapter on Their Prior Use in Louisiana, Florida, and New Mexico* (Glendale, Calif.: Arthur H. Clark, 1963). The regulars who served as military governors were Lt. Col. John C. Frémont (1847); Brig. Gen. Stephen W. Kearny (1847); Col. Richard B. Mason (1847–1849); Lt. Col. Bennet Riley (1849).

44. Sunseri, "New Mexico," 146–148; 31st Cong., 2d sess., House Exec. Doc. no. 1, 91–108. On civil-military tensions in California, see Grivas, *Military Governments*, 100–148, 187–220.

45. See the assessment of the army's role in military government in Grivas, *Military Governments*, 221–224. Frémont, who resigned from the army in 1848, served as U.S. senator from California in 1850–1851. *DAB*, 7:22.

46. This and the succeeding paragraphs have been largely based on Norman F. Furniss, *The Mormon Conflict, 1850–1859* (New Haven, Conn.: Yale University Press, 1960); Charles P. Roland, *Albert Sidney Johnston: Soldier of Three Republics* (Austin: University of Texas Press, 1964), 185–237; Robert W. Coakley, *The Role of Federal Military Forces in Domestic Disorders, 1798–1878* (Washington, D.C.: Government Printing Office, 1988), 194–226.

47. Capt. Jesse A. Gove to Maria Gove, journal letter beginning September 14, 1857, entry for September 18, Jesse A. Gove, *The Utah Expedition, 1857–1858: Letters of Capt. Jesse A. Gove, 10th Inf., U.S.A. of Concord, N.H., to Mrs. Gove, and Special Correspondence of the New York Herald*, ed. Otis G. Hammond (Concord: New Hampshire Historical Society, 1928), 59; Capt. Albert Tracy, *The Utah War: The Journal of Albert Tracy, 1858–1860* (Salt Lake City: Utah State Historical Society, 1945), 23. See also W. Eugene Hollon, *Beyond the Cross Timbers: The Travels of Randolph B. Marcy, 1812–1887* (Norman: University of Oklahoma Press, 1955), 224; Bvt. Capt. Fitz John Porter to George B. McClellan, February 28, 1858, and Lt. Lucius L. Rich to Ellen Marcy, October 18, 1857, McClellan Papers.

48. Furniss, *Mormon Conflict*, 212–219; Roland, *Johnston*, 222–227; Henry Heth,

The Memoirs of Henry Heth, ed. James L. Morrison, Jr. (Westport, Conn.: Greenwood Press, 1974), 145-147.

49. Capt. William Chapman to his son, November 15, 1859, Chapman Family Papers, U.S. Military Academy Library, West Point, N.Y. See also Lt. Matthew R. Stevenson to Bowen, October 9, 1859, Kennerly Papers, Missouri Historical Society, St. Louis.

CHAPTER SIXTEEN. OFFICERS AND INDIANS

1. This chapter is a revised and expanded version of the author's previously published article: "Army Officers' Attitudes toward Indians, 1830-1860," *Pacific Northwest Quarterly* 67 (July 1976):113-124. The literature on the army's general relationship to Indians is vast. For an overview, see Francis Paul Prucha, *The Sword of the Republic: The United States Army on the Frontier, 1783-1846* (New York: Macmillan, 1969); John K. Mahon, *History of the Second Seminole War, 1835-1842* (Gainesville: University of Florida Press, 1967); Robert M. Utley, *Frontiersmen in Blue: The United States Army and the Indian, 1848-1865* (New York: Macmillan, 1967).

2. For the discretionary powers of local commanders, see Lt. Edmund Kirby to Brig. Gen. Edmund P. Gaines, August 3, 1821, AGO:LS; Roger L. Nichols, "The Army and the Indians 1800-1830—A Reappraisal: The Missouri Valley Example," *Pacific Historical Review* 41 (May 1972):165. In 1832, the War Department issued some regulations to guide officers engaged in Indian removal, but these focused on supply and administration. "Regulations concerning the Removing of the Indians," 23d Cong., 1st sess., Sen. Exec. Doc. no. 512, 1:343-349. For Mahan's course, see Thomas E. Griess, "Dennis Hart Mahan: West Point Professor and Advocate of Military Professionalism, 1830-1871" (Ph.D. diss., Duke University, 1968), 306-307.

3. Bvt. Brig. Gen. Josiah Harmar to Joseph Howell, Jr., June 9, 1790, Josiah Harmar Papers, William L. Clements Library, Ann Arbor, Mich.; see also chapter 4 above. One officer who did take an interest in Indian culture was Capt. Amos Stoddard. He included a lengthy and generally sympathetic discussion of the western tribes in a book on the Louisiana Territory. Amos Stoddard, *Sketches, Historical and Descriptive, of Louisiana* (Philadelphia: Mathew Carey, 1812), 409-463.

4. Maj. Gen. Alexander Macomb, *Pontiac; or, The Siege of Detroit: A Drama in Three Acts* (Boston: S. Colman, 1835), 9; Philip St George Cooke, *Scenes and Adventures in the Army: or, The Romance of Military Life* (Philadelphia: Lindsay and Blakiston, 1857), 62-65.

5. Lt. James Allen to Maj. Gen. Alexander Macomb, November 25, 1833, *ASP:MA*, 5:334; John Van Deusen DuBois, *Campaigns in the West, 1856-1861: The Journal and Letters of Colonel John Van Deusen DuBois*, ed. George P. Hammond (Tucson: Arizona Pioneers Historical Society, 1949), 31; Lt. James H. Carleton, *The Prairie Logbooks: Dragoon Campaigns to the Pawnee Villages in 1844, and to the Rocky Mountains in 1845*, ed. Louis Pelzer (Chicago: Caxton Club, 1943), 89.

6. Lt. William Wall to Lt. Robert Anderson, August 19, 1836, Robert Anderson Papers, Library of Congress; Lt. Joseph C. Ives, *Report upon the Colorado River of the West, Explored in 1857 and 1858* (Washington, D.C., 1861), 72; Capt. Thomas Williams to Mary Williams, journal letter beginning June 17, [1858], entry for June 19, Williams Family Papers, Burton Collection, Detroit Public Library; Lt. Edward L. Hartz to Samuel Hartz, February 10, 1857, Edward L. Hartz Papers, Library of Congress. See also *Army and Navy Chronicle* 10 (February 20, 1840):123.

7. Cooke, *Scenes and Adventures*, 145; Lt. George W. Patten, "The Seminole's Reply," *Army and Navy Chronicle* 4 (April 6, 1837):220; Capt. Samuel G. French to Brig. Gen. Thomas S. Jesup, November 2, 1851, 32d Cong., 1st sess., Sen. Exec. Doc. no. 1, 232.

8. For the environmentalist interpretation of Indian character, see Roy Harvey Pearce, *The Savages of America: A Study of the Indian and the Idea of Civilization* (Baltimore: Johns Hopkins University Press, 1965), 76–104; Bernard W. Sheehan, *Seeds of Extinction: Jeffersonian Philanthropy and the American Indian* (Chapel Hill: University of North Carolina Press, 1973), 15–44, 66–88, and passim. On the rise of biological racism, see William R. Stanton, *The Leopard's Spots: Scientific Attitudes toward Race in America, 1815–1859* (Chicago: University of Chicago, 1960); Reginald Horsman, *Race and Manifest Destiny: The Origins of American Racial Anglo-Saxonism* (Cambridge: Harvard University Press, 1981), 44–61, 116–157, and passim.

9. Ethan Allen Hitchcock, *A Traveler in Indian Territory: The Journal of Ethan Allen Hitchcock, Late Major-General in the United States Army*, ed. Grant Foreman (Cedar Rapids, Iowa: Torch Press, 1930), 238–244; Capt. Henry S. Turner, *The Original Journals of Henry Smith Turner: With Stephen Watts Kearny to New Mexico and California, 1846–1847*, ed. Dwight L. Clarke (Norman: University of Oklahoma Press, 1966), 107; Col. George A. McCall to the secretary of war, July 15, 1850, George A. McCall, *Letters from the Frontiers, Written during a Period of Thirty Years' Service in the Army of the United States* (Philadelphia: J. B. Lippincott, 1868), 498.

10. Carleton, *Prairie Logbooks*, 60, 62–104; Capt. Randolph B. Marcy, *The Prairie Traveler: A Hand-Book for Overland Expeditions* (New York: Harper and Brothers, 1859), 196–213; Asst. Surg. Jonathan Letherman, "Sketch of the Navajo Tribe of Indians, Territory of New Mexico," 34th Cong., 1st sess., Sen. Misc. Doc. no. 73, 295.

11. Capt. Howard Stansbury, *Exploration and Survey of the Valley of the Great Salt Lake of Utah . . . Including a Reconnoissance of a New Route through the Rocky Mountains* (Philadelphia, 1852), 148; Capt. Rufus Ingalls to Brig. Gen. Thomas S. Jesup, August 25, 1855, 34th Cong., 1st sess., House Exec. Doc. no. 1, 163; Capt. Henry W. Wessells to Bvt. Capt. Joseph Hooker, November 14, 1851, enclosed with Col. Ethan Allen Hitchcock to Lt. Col. Lorenzo Thomas, October 15, 1853, file H-478 (1853), AGO:LR.

12. Henry Whiting, *Ontwa, the Son of the Forest: A Poem* (New York: Wiley and Halsted, 1822); Henry Whiting, *Sannillac: A Poem* (Boston: Carter and Babcock, 1831).

13. John F. McDermott, *Seth Eastman: Pictorial Historian of the Indian* (Norman: University of Oklahoma Press, 1961).

14. On the trade and intercourse laws and the army's enforcement of them, see Francis Paul Prucha, *American Indian Policy in the Formative Years: The Indian Trade and Intercourse Acts, 1790–1834* (Lincoln: University of Nebraska Press, 1962); Francis Paul Prucha, *Broadax and Bayonet: The Role of the United States Army in the Development of the Northwest, 1815–1860* (Madison: State Historical Society of Wisconsin, 1953), 55–103; Francis Paul Prucha, *The Sword of the Republic: The United States Army on the Frontier, 1783–1846* (New York: Macmillan, 1969), 193–209. [Capt. Philip St. George Cooke?], "An Appeal for the Indian," *Army and Navy Chronicle* 10 (April 16, 1840):250–252.

15. Clarence E. Carter and John P. Bloom, eds., *The Territorial Papers of the United States*, 27 vols. (Washington, D.C.: Government Printing Office, 1934–1969), 21:245–246, 804, 1170–1171, and passim; Col. Mathew Arbuckle to John H. Eaton, May 21, 1831, 23d Cong., 1st sess., Sen. Exec. Doc. no. 512, 4:458; Roger L. Nich-

ols, *General Henry Atkinson: A Western Military Career* (Norman: University of Oklahoma Press, 1965), 76–77, 145, 184, 201–203; Brainerd Dyer, *Zachary Taylor* (Baton Rouge: Louisiana State University Press, 1946), 138–139, 142–143; Brad Agnew, *Fort Gibson: Terminal on the Trail of Tears* (Norman: University of Oklahoma Press, 1980), 89–113, and passim; James W. Silver, *Edmund Pendleton Gaines: Frontier General* (Baton Rouge: Louisiana State University Press, 1949), 217–218 and passim.

16. Lt. Charles N. Hagner to Peter Hagner, January 13, 1839, Peter Hagner Papers, Southern Historical Collection, University of North Carolina Library, Chapel Hill; Lt. Col. Josiah H. Vose to Col. Roger Jones, April 13, 1838, 25th Cong., 2d sess., House Exec. Doc. no. 434, 3.

17. The best overview of Indian removal is Ronald N. Satz, *American Indian Policy in the Jacksonian Era* (Lincoln: University of Nebraska Press, 1975). For the army's role, see Prucha, *Sword of the Republic,* 249–268. For a vast amount of documentation on the army's involvement in the logistics of removal, see 23d Cong., 1st sess., Sen. Exec. Doc. no. 512, 5 vols.

18. Lt. Col. John J. Abert to Lewis Cass, August 15, 1833, Sen. Exec. Doc. no. 512, 4:511–512; Brig. Gen. Thomas S. Jesup to Joel R. Poinsett, February 11, 1838, in John T. Sprague, *The Origin, Progress, and Conclusion of the Florida War,* (New York: D. Appleton, 1848), 199–200.

19. Silver, *Gaines,* 109–129, 137. See also Lt. Edward G. W. Butler to Frances Parke Lewis, July 1, 1825, July 11, 1825, August 6, 1825, August 20, 1825, and August 31, 1825, Edward G. W. Butler Papers, Duke University Library, Durham, N.C.

20. Erasmus D. Keyes, *Fifty Years' Observations of Men and Events, Civil and Military* (New York: C. Scribner's Sons, 1884), 133; Lt. Joseph R. Smith to his wife, March 5, 1838, in Joseph R. Smith, "Letters from the Second Seminole War," ed. John K. Mahon, *Florida Historical Quarterly* 36 (April 1958):338; Lt. William T. Sherman to Hugh B. Ewing, March 10, 1844, William T. Sherman Papers, Ohio Historical Society, Columbus.

21. Ethan Allen Hitchcock, *Fifty Years in Camp and Field: The Diary of Major-General Ethan Allen Hitchcock, U.S.A.*, ed. William A. Croffut (New York: G. P. Putnam's Sons, 1909), 396; Col. Ethan Allen Hitchcock to unknown, August 31, 1852, 32d Cong., 2nd sess., House Exec. Doc. no. 1, 30; Hitchcock to Col. Samuel Cooper, March 31, 1853, 34th Cong., 3d sess., House Exec. Doc. no. 76, 78–79; Hitchcock to Cooper, February 11, 1854, file H-94, AGO:LR; Brig. Gen. John E. Wool's correspondence in 34th Cong., 1st sess., House Exec. Doc. nos. 93 and 118; Bvt. Maj. Edward D. Townsend, *The California Diary of General E. D. Townsend,* ed. Malcolm Edwards (Los Angeles: W. Ritchie, 1970), 55–57, 67–68; Maj. Robert S. Garnett to Robert M. T. Hunter, April 20, 1856, in *Correspondence of Robert M. T. Hunter, 1826–1876,* ed. Charles H. Ambler (Washington, D.C.: Government Printing Office, 1918), 188–189.

22. For the Navajos, see Capt. John G. Walker to Lt. John H. Edson, August 3, 1859, and Maj. John S. Simonson to Lt. John D. Wilkins, September 28, 1859, 36th Cong., 1st sess., Sen. Exec. Doc. no. 2, 323, 341–345; Maj. Charles F. Ruff to Capt. Thomas Claiborne, October 26, 1859, Thomas Claiborne Papers, Southern Historical Collection, University of North Carolina Library, Chapel Hill. For the Texas incident, see 36th Cong., 1st sess., Sen. Exec. Doc. no. 2, 362–374. Maj. Hannibal Day to assistant adjutant general, Department of the West, January 26, 1855, file H-88, AGO:LR.

23. Lt. William H. C. Whiting to Bvt. Capt. George Deas, March 14, 1850, 31st Cong., 1st sess., Sen. Exec. Doc. no. 64, 248.

24. Bvt. Capt. Irvin McDowell to Col. Samuel Cooper, December 15, 1854, HQA:LS. For examples of officers' criticism of the Indian Department and desire for army control of Indian affairs, see Brig. Gen. Alexander Macomb to Maj. John McNeil, September 23, 1816, and Macomb to Maj. Gen. Jacob Brown, September 7, 1818, Macomb Family Papers, Burton Collection, Detroit Public Library; Brig. Gen. Persifor F. Smith to Lt. Col. Lorenzo Thomas, April 8, 1854, file A-54 (1856), and Brig. Gen. David E. Twiggs to Thomas, November 20, 1858, file T-216, AGO:LR; Lt. George D. Bayard to his father, February 14, 1857, in Samuel J. Bayard, *The Life of George Dashiell Bayard, Late Captain, U.S.A., and Brigadier-General of Volunteers, Killed in the Battle of Fredericksburg, December 1862* (New York: G. P. Putnam's Sons, 1874), 116–117; Lt. John Van Deusen DuBois to his father, May 18, 1859, DuBois, *Campaigns*, 120.

25. Capt. Rufus Ingalls to Brig. Gen. Thomas S. Jesup, August 25, 1855, 34th Cong., 1st sess., House Exec. Doc. no. 1, 163.

26. Capt. Robert C. Buchanan to Bvt. Maj. Edward D. Townsend, August 1, 1853, Robert C. Buchanan Papers, Maryland Historical Society, Baltimore; Brig. Gen. William S. Harney to assistant adjutant general, Headquarters of the Army, November 5, 1858, 36th Cong., 1st sess., Sen. Exec. Doc. no. 2, 92; Capt. Randolph B. Marcy, *Thirty Years of Army Life on the Border* (New York: Harper and Brothers, 1866), 62; Carleton, *Prairie Logbooks*, 131.

27. Jacob Rhett Motte, *Journey into Wilderness: An Army Surgeon's Account of Life in Camp and Field during the Creek and Seminole Wars, 1836–1838*, ed. James F. Sunderman (Gainesville: University of Florida Press, 1953), 103, 175, 199–200; Sprague, *Florida War*, 24–25, 43, 46–48, 73, 88–89, 93.

28. Rodney Glisan, *Journal of Army Life* (San Francisco: A. L. Bancroft, 1874), 316–318.

29. Brig. Gen. Thomas S. Jesup to Col. Roger Jones, February 7, 1837, Sprague, *Florida War*, 173; Col. Zachary Taylor to Maj. Ethan Allen Hitchcock, May 19, 1841, and July 28, 1841, Zachary Taylor Papers, Library of Congress. For similar remarks on Indian war, see Sprague, *Florida War*, 274, 285; Cooke, *Scenes and Adventures*, 175–176; Lt. Thomas W. Sweeny, *Journal of Lt. Thomas W. Sweeny, 1849–1853*, ed. Arthur Woodward (Los Angeles: Westernlore Press, 1956), 56–58.

30. Dennis Hart Mahan's lithographed notes, quoted in Griess, "Mahan," 306–307.

31. Capt. George W. Hughes to Col. John J. Abert, February 1, 1847, 31st Cong., 1st sess., Sen. Exec. Doc. no. 32, 35; Capt. James J. Archer to his mother, August 16, 1856, James J. Archer Papers, Maryland Historical Society, Baltimore; Col. Benjamin L. E. Bonneville to Lt. Col. Lorenzo Thomas, November 14, 1858, 36th Cong., 1st sess., Sen. Exec. Doc. no. 2, 268; Capt. Thomas Williams to Mary Williams, July 11, [1858], Williams Family Papers; Capt. William J. Hardee to Lt. Isaac Ingalls Stevens, September 9, 1851, Isaac Ingalls Stevens Papers, University of Washington Library, Seattle.

32. Mahon, *Second Seminole War;* Sprague, *Florida War*. It is possible that some officers thought themselves justified in distinguishing between civilized and Indian war by Emmerich de Vattel's work on international law, used as a textbook at West Point for several years during the 1820s. Vattel urged restraint toward unresisting enemies but condoned harsh measures—the execution of prisoners, the devastation of the countryside—in order to force a "savage nation, who observe no rules" to conform to the "laws of humanity." Vattel, *The Law of Nations; or, Principles of the Law of Nature, Applied to the Conduct and Affairs of Nations and Sovereigns*, ed. Joseph Chitty and Edward

O. Ingraham (Philadelphia: T. and J.W. Johnson, 1883), 348, 366. Officers' writings include no reference to Vattel or any other legal authority, however. More likely, they drew any support they considered necessary from the tradition of "total war" against Indians, dating from the colonial era.

33. Lt. William G. Grandin to Capt. Samuel P. Heintzelman, May 5, 1839, Samuel P. Heintzelman Papers, Library of Congress; *Army and Navy Chronicle* 9 (August 29, 1839):132, 138–139, (October 2, 1839):289–291. See also ibid., 10 (April 23, 1840):267–268; 11 (October 1, 1840):220–221, (December 3, 1840):361–362.

34. Capt. John R. Vinton to his mother, March 28, 1840, John R. Vinton Papers, Duke University Library, Durham, N.C.; Mahon, *Second Seminole War*, 282–284; Col. Abraham Eustis to Lt. Robert Anderson, February 8, 1841, Capt. William L. McClintock to Anderson, December 31, 1840, and Capt. George H. Pegram to Anderson, February 3, 1841, Anderson Papers; Asst. Surg. John S. Griffin to Capt. Robert C. Buchanan, January 19, 1841, Buchanan Papers.

35. Sprague, *Florida War*, 274–280 and passim; Mahon, *Second Seminole War*, 294–320; Francis F. McKinney, *Education in Violence: The Life of George H. Thomas and the History of the Army of the Cumberland* (Detroit: Wayne State University Press, 1961), 26. The commanding general of the army supported the bounty system. Endorsement by Maj. Gen. Winfield Scott, February 25, 1842, on Col. William J. Worth to Scott, February 14, 1842, *Territorial Papers*, 26:438–439.

36. Christopher Phillips, *Damned Yankee: The Life of General Nathaniel Lyon* (Columbia: University of Missouri Press, 1990), 66–70; Lt. Nathaniel Lyon to Bvt. Capt. Edward R. S. Canby, May 22, 1850, file L–105, AGO:LR; Utley, *Frontiersmen in Blue*, 116–117; Emerson G. Taylor, *Gouverneur Kemble Warren: The Life and Letters of an American Soldier, 1830–1882* (Boston: Houghton, Mifflin, 1932), 24–29; Lt. Gouverneur Kemble Warren to Colonel William S. Harney, March 15, 1856, 34th Cong., 1st sess., Sen. Exec. Doc. no. 76, 19.

37. Capt. Lewis A. Armistead to Bvt. Maj. William W. Mackall, July 3, 1859, 36th Cong., 1st sess., Sen. Exec. Doc. no. 2, 414–415; Department of Texas, Orders No. 25, October 19, 1858, 35th Cong., 2d sess., House Exec. Doc. no. 2, 277–278; Utley, *Frontiersmen in Blue*, 165–173; Col. Samuel Cooper to Col. Thomas T. Fauntleroy, October 29, 1860, AGO:LS.

38. Col. Sylvester Churchill, report of inspection tour, March 29–May 22, 1856, file C–217, and Capt. John C. Casey to Jefferson Davis, August 17, 1856, file C–379, AGO:LR; Col. Gustavus Loomis, circular dated January 12, 1857, National Archives, Records of U.S. Army Continental Commands (Record Group 393), Ft. Myers Orderly Book; Almira R. Hancock, *Reminiscences of Winfield Scott Hancock* (New York: C. L. Webster, 1887), 32–34.

39. Expedition orders, issued by Capt. Granville O. Haller, July 18, 1855, 34th Cong., 1st sess., Sen. Exec. Doc. no. 26, 12–19; Philip H. Sheridan, *Personal Memoirs of P. H. Sheridan*, 2 vols. (New York: C. L. Webster, 1888), 1:81–84, 89; Maj. Robert S. Garnett to Bvt. Maj. William W. Mackall, August 30, 1858, and Col. George Wright to Mackall, September 15, 1858, 35th Cong., 2d sess., House Exec. Doc. no. 2, 379, 396; Lt. Lawrence Kip, *Army Life on the Pacific: A Journal of the Expedition against the Northern Indians, the Tribes of the Coeur d'Alenes, Spokans, and Pelouzes, in the Summer of 1858* (New York: Redfield, 1859), 99–106, 110–111, 116–117, 124; George Crook, *General George Crook: His Autobiography*, ed. Martin F. Schmitt (Norman: University of Oklahoma Press, 1946), 61–64.

40. Surg. Gen. Thomas Lawson to Asst. Surg. Benjamin King, August 18, 1837, Benjamin King Papers, Library of Congress; Maj. Ethan Allen Hitchcock to W. G.

Eliot [1841 or 1842], quoted in Hitchcock, *Fifty Years*, 125; letter signed "An Officer of 4th Artillery," *Army and Navy Chronicle* 6 (January 25, 1838):55–56. For evidence that Phelps was the author of the anonymous letter, see Asst. Surg. Samuel Forry to Lt. John W. Phelps, March 25, 1838, in Samuel Forry, "Letters of Samuel Forry, Surgeon U.S. Army, 1837–1838," *Florida Historical Quarterly* 7 (July 1928): 101.

41. Lt. Robert M. McLane to Mrs. Louis McLane, December 24, 1837, Louis McLane Papers, Library of Congress. For a remarkable example of an officer wrestling with his conscience during the Seminole War, see Reynold M. Wik, "Captain Nathaniel Wyche Hunter and the Florida Indian Campaigns, 1837–1841," *Florida Historical Quarterly* 39 (July 1960):73–74.

42. DuBois, *Campaigns*, 29–33; [Lt. August V. Kautz?], "Indian Hunting in Washington Territory," May 28, 1856, newspaper clipping [n.d.], probably from *Cincinnati Enquirer*, August V. Kautz Papers, Library of Congress; George Crook, *General George Crook: His Autobiography*, ed. Martin F. Schmitt (Norman: University of Oklahoma Press, 1946), 15–16.

43. Capt. John R. Vinton to Brig. Gen. Winfield Scott, July 3, 1838, Vinton Papers. The author has found only one possible example of an officer resigning over an objection to Indian policy. Col. Ethan Allen Hitchcock claimed that he resigned in 1855 rather than serve under Col. William S. Harney, whom he considered ignorant and brutal, on the Sioux campaign of that year. Hitchcock, *Fifty Years*, 418. Other considerations seem to have influenced Hitchcock's decision, however.

CHAPTER SEVENTEEN. OFFICERS, FOREIGN AFFAIRS, AND WAR

1. "On the Necessity and the Advantages of an Army and the Utility of War," *Military and Naval Magazine of the United States*, 2 (December, 1833):210–211; Lt. Edward L. Hunt, "Army Attack and National Defence," *American Review*, 4 (August, 1846):149; "Army Medical Board of Examination," *Military and Naval Magazine of the United States* 4 (November 1835):186; Capt. Thomas Williams to Mary Williams, July 31, [1859], Williams Family Papers, Burton Collection, Detroit Public Library.

2. Henry W. Halleck, *Elements of Military Art and Science; or, Course of Instruction in Strategy, Fortification, Tactics of Battles, &c.* (Philadelphia: G. S. Appleton, 1846), 7–34; Erasmus D. Keyes, *Fifty Years' Observations of Men and Events, Civil and Military* (New York: C. Scribner's Sons, 1884), 40–41; *Military and Naval Magazine of the United States* 1 (March 1833):3–4.

3. Maj. Gen. Jacob Brown to John C. Calhoun, October 6, 1820, in John C. Calhoun, *The Papers of John C. Calhoun*, ed. Robert L. Meriwether and W. Edwin Hemphill, 18 vols. to date (Columbia: University of South Carolina Press, 1959–), 5:377–378; Lt. Col. Zachary Taylor to Brig. Gen. Thomas S. Jesup, June 18, 1821, Zachary Taylor Papers, Library of Congress.

4. Brig. Gen. Thomas S. Jesup to John H. Eaton, October 20, 1830, and Col. John E. Wool to Maj. Gen. Alexander Macomb, October 23, 1830, *ASP:MA*, 4:634, 642.

5. "National Defence: Probabilities of a War with England," *Army and Navy Chronicle* 13 (April 2, 1842):163 (follows p. 168 because of error in pagination); Capt. John R. Vinton to Mary Vinton, November 13, 1845, John R. Vinton Papers, Duke University Library, Durham, N.C.

6. Lt. Col. Thomas S. Jesup's correspondence for August–September 1816, Thomas S. Jesup Papers, Duke University Library, Durham, N.C. Quotation is from Jesup to Maj. Gen. Andrew Jackson, August 21, 1816. By 1819, Jesup favored annexing not only Flor-

ida and Cuba but Mexico and the Spanish port of Cueta in North Africa. Jesup to "Dear General," November 7, 1819 (draft), Thomas S. Jesup Papers, Library of Congress.

7. Maj. James Bankhead to Brig. Gen. Daniel Parker, May 25, 1818, Daniel Parker Papers, Historical Society of Pennsylvania. See also Col. William King to Parker, January 25, 1817, and Col. Duncan L. Clinch to Parker, October 2, 1819, ibid.; Lt. Col. William A. Trimble to Allen Trimble, March 19, 1817, Allen Trimble Papers, Western Reserve Historical Society, Cleveland; James W. Silver, *Edmund Pendleton Gaines: Frontier General* (Baton Rouge: Louisiana State University Press, 1949), 83–84. For Jackson's incursion into Florida, see Robert V. Remini, *Andrew Jackson and the Course of American Empire, 1767–1821* (New York: Harper and Row, 1977), 341–377.

8. Ethan Allen Hitchcock, *Fifty Years in Camp and Field: The Diary of Major-General Ethan Allen Hitchcock, U.S.A.*, ed. William A. Croffut (New York: G. P. Putnam's Sons, 1909), 203, 212; Maj. Gen. Zachary Taylor to Surg. Robert C. Wood, August 23, 1846, in Zachary Taylor, *Letters of Zachary Taylor, from the Battle-Fields of the Mexican War* (Rochester, N.Y.: Genessee Press, 1908), 49. See also Erasmus D. Keyes, *Fifty Years' Observations of Men and Events, Civil and Military* (New York: C. Scribner's Sons, 1884), 202–203; Lt. Benjamin Alvord to Marcus C. M. Hammond, October 8, 1844, James H. Hammond Papers, Library of Congress; Christopher Phillips, *Damned Yankee: The Life of General Nathaniel Lyon* (Columbia: University of Missouri Press, 1990), 40–41.

9. On the ideology of Manifest Destiny, see Reginald Horsman, *Race and Manifest Destiny: The Origins of American Racial Anglo-Saxonism* (Cambridge: Harvard University Press, 1981); Albert K. Weinberg, *Manifest Destiny: A Study of Nationalist Expansion in American History* (Baltimore: Johns Hopkins University Press, 1935).

10. Col. William J. Worth to Surg. Gen. Thomas Lawson, November 1, 1845, Thomas Lawson Papers, Library of Congress. For other examples of officers' support for territorial expansion before the Mexican War, see Col. Henry Stanton to Brig. Gen. Thomas S. Jesup, July 18, 1845, Jesup Papers, Library of Congress; Capt. John R. Vinton to Mrs. Mary Vinton, March 29, 1844, and January 11, 1845, Vinton Papers; Capt. Thomas Swords to Lt. Abraham R. Johnston, August 10, [1845], Abraham R. Johnston Papers, U.S. Military Academy, West Point, N.Y.; Lt. Henry J. Hunt to Lt. James Duncan, March 17, 1844, James Duncan Papers, U.S. Military Academy Library; Lt. Ulysses S. Grant to Julia Dent, October 10, 1845, in Ulysses S. Grant, *The Papers of Ulysses S. Grant*, ed. John Y. Simon, 16 vols. to date (Carbondale: Southern Illinois University Press, 1967–), 1:56–57; Philip St. George Cooke, *Scenes and Adventures in the Army: or, The Romance of Military Life* (Philadelphia: Lindsay and Blakiston, 1857), 370–371.

11. Capt. Ephraim Kirby Smith to his wife, November 2, 1846, Ephraim Kirby Smith, *To Mexico with Scott: Letters of Captain E. Kirby Smith to His Wife*, ed. Emma J. Blackwood (Cambridge: Harvard University Press, 1917), 69; Capt. John R. Vinton to Mary Vinton, November 19, 1846, Vinton Papers; Lt. Edmund Kirby Smith to Frances K. Smith, May 20, 1846, Edmund Kirby Smith Papers, Southern Historical Collection, University of North Carolina Library, Chapel Hill. For other examples of officers' opinions of Mexicans, see Capt. Joseph H. LaMotte to his wife, May 24, 1848, LaMotte-Coppinger Papers, Missouri Historical Society, St. Louis; John Sedgwick, *Correspondence of John Sedgwick, Major-General*, 2 vols. (New York, 1902–1903), 1:9, 30, 37, 135–136; Capt. William H. T. Walker to his wife, March 27, 1847, and May 26, 1847, William H.T. Walker Papers, Duke University Library, Durham, N.C.; Lt. Francis Collins, "Journal of Francis Collins, an Artillery Officer in Mexico," ed. Maria C. Collins, *Quarterly Publication of the Historical and Philosophical Society of Ohio* 10 (April–July 1915):67–68, 87–89; Lt. Jeremy F. Gilmer to Capt.

George L. Welcker, September 23, 1846, and November 6, 1846, Lenoir Family Papers II, Southern Historical Collection, University of North Carolina Library, Chapel Hill; Ashbel Woodward, *Life of General Nathaniel Lyon* (Hartford, Conn.: Case, Lockwood, 1862), 92–93, 134–136. Officers' impressions of Mexicans resembled those of other soldiers campaigning in Mexico—and of large segments of the general public. See Robert W. Johannsen, *To the Halls of the Montezumas: The Mexican War in the American Imagination* (New York: Oxford University Press, 1985), 164–174; Horsman, *Race and Manifest Destiny*, 208–248.

12. Lt. William M. Gardner to his brother, November 23, 1847, William M. Gardner Papers, Southern Historical Collection, University of North Carolina Library, Chapel Hill; Asst. Surg. George E. Cooper to Asst. Surg. Benjamin King, November 17, 1847, King Papers; Col. William J. Worth to William L. Marcy, October 30, 1847, in William J. Worth, "Never before Published Letters of Famous General Worth, Written during Mexican War," *New York Times Magazine*, July 16, 1916, 11; Capt. William S. Henry, *Campaign Sketches of the War with Mexico* (New York: Harper and Brothers, 1847), 120–121.

13. Lt. George G. Meade to his wife, November 10, 1846, in George Meade, *The Life and Letters of George Gordon Meade*, 2 vols. (New York: C. Scribner's Sons, 1913), 1:154; Capt. Ephraim Kirby Smith to Alpheus S. Williams, February 12, 1847, Alpheus S. Williams Papers, Burton Collection, Detroit Public Library; Lt. Col. Ethan Allen Hitchcock to Theodore Parker, February 27, 1847, in George W. Smith and Charles Judah, eds., *Chronicles of the Gringos: The U.S. Army in the Mexican War, 1846–1848. Accounts of Eyewitnesses and Combatants* (Albuquerque: University of New Mexico Press, 1968), 27.

14. Silver, *Gaines*, 59–74; Remini, *Jackson and the Course of American Empire*, 341–346.

15. Remini, *Jackson and the Course of American Empire*, 346–365; Andrew Jackson, *Correspondence of Andrew Jackson*, ed. John S. Bassett, 7 vols. (Washington, D.C.: Carnegie Institution, 1926–1935), 2:341–381.

16. Remini, *Jackson and the Course of American Empire*, 366–377.

17. Silver, *Gaines*, 191–215; William B. Skelton, "The United States Army, 1821–1837: An Institutional History" (Ph.D. diss., Northwestern University, 1968), 365–372.

18. Allan Nevins, *Frémont: Pathmarker of the West* (New York: D. Appleton-Century Co., 1939), 190–286.

19. George R. Adams, "General William Selby Harney: Frontier Soldier, 1800–1889" (Ph.D. diss., University of Arizona, 1983), 304–325, 329–334; Charles W. Elliott, *Winfield Scott: The Soldier and the Man* (New York: Macmillan, 1937), 664–671; James O. McCabe, *The San Juan Island Water Question* (Toronto: University of Toronto Press, 1965); 36th Cong., 1st sess., Sen. Exec. Doc. no. 2, 39–90.

20. Albert B. Corey, *The Crisis of 1830–42 in Canadian-American Relations* (New Haven, Conn.: Yale University Press, 1941), 7–69.

21. Elliott, *Scott*, 335–344; Col. Hugh Brady, "Reports of General Brady on the Patriot War," ed. Francis Paul Prucha, *Canadian Historical Review* 31 (March 1950):56–68; Harwood P. Hinton, "The Military Career of John Ellis Wool, 1812–1863" (Ph.D. diss., University of Wisconsin, 1960), 136–161.

22. Act of March 10, 1838, U.S. Congress, *The Public Statutes at Large of the United States of America*, 100 vols. to date (Boston and Washington, D.C.: Government Printing Office, 1848–), 3:212–214; Act of July 5, 1838, Abner R. Hetzel, comp., *Military Laws of the United States* (Washington, D.C.: G. Templeman, 1846), 261–267; Albert B. Corey, *The Crisis of 1830–42 in Canadian-American Relations* (New Haven, Conn.: Yale University Press, 1941), 70–145; Maj. Gen. Alexander Macomb to Joel R. Poinsett,

November 29, 1838, 25th Cong., 3d sess., Sen. Exec. Doc. no. 1, 117–120. For the army's general role in the patriot troubles, see also Francis Paul Prucha, *The Sword of the Republic: The United States Army on the Frontier, 1783–1846* (New York: Macmillan, 1969), 311–318; Robert W. Coakley, *The Role of Federal Military Forces in Domestic Disorders, 1789–1878* (Washington, D.C.: Government Printing Office, 1988), 110–119.

23. Lt. Col. Ichabod B. Crane to Maj. Gen. Winfield Scott, January 4, 1842, January 11, 1842, February 3, 1842, March 4, 1842, March 17, 1842, and June 25, 1842, HQA:LR. See generally Scott's correspondence, 1841–1842, in HQA:LS.

24. The best general study of filibustering in the 1850s is Charles H. Brown, *Agents of Manifest Destiny: The Lives and Times of the Filibusters* (Chapel Hill: University of North Carolina Press, 1980). For Crittenden, see ibid., 80, 87–88. Former lieutenants Mansfield Lovell and Gustavus W. Smith were reportedly involved in the stillborn Quitman plot of 1854–1855 to invade Cuba. Maj. Samuel P. Heintzelman journal, entry for February 3, 1855, Samuel P. Heintzelman Papers, Library of Congress. Capt. Robert E. Lee considered an offer to lead an expedition against Cuba in 1849, but declined. Douglas Southall Freeman, *R. E. Lee: A Biography*, 4 vols. (New York: C. Scribner's Sons, 1934–1935), 1:306–308.

25. For examples of officers' hostility to filibustering, see Lt. Francis T. Bryan to William S. Bryan, May 12, 1854, William S. Bryan Papers, Southern Historical Collection, University of North Carolina Library, Chapel Hill; Maj. John R. Hagner to Capt. Peter V. Hagner, August 20, 1855, Peter Hagner Papers, ibid.; Lt. Edward L. Hartz to Samuel Hartz, May 2, 1859, Edward L. Hartz Papers, Library of Congress; Lt. John C. Pemberton to Israel Pemberton, June 1, 1850, Pemberton Family Papers, Historical Society of Pennsylvania; Edward D. Townsend, *The California Diary of General E. D. Townsend*, ed. Malcolm Edwards (Los Angeles: W. Ritchie, 1970), 91–96; Brig. Gen. John E. Wool to Lt. James A. Hardie, May 4, 1857, and June 17, 1857, James A. Hardie Papers, Library of Congress.

26. Capt. P. G. T. Beauregard to Col. Persifor F. Smith, January 24, 1856 [probably 1857], Persifor F. Smith Papers, Historical Society of Pennsylvania. See also Lt. Col. Joseph E. Johnston to George B. McClellan, [December 6, 1857], George B. McClellan Papers, Library of Congress.

27. Ernest C. Shearer, "The Carvajal Disturbances," *Southwestern Historical Quarterly* 55 (October 1951):201–230; Col. Persifor F. Smith to assistant adjutant general, Eastern Division, July 18, 1852, 32d Cong., 2nd sess., Sen. Exec. Doc. no. 1, 15–20; Adams, "Harney," 175–178; Lt. Edmund Kirby Smith to his mother, March 16, 1853, Kirby Smith Papers.

28. Hitchcock, *Fifty Years*, 400–403; Brown, *Agents of Manifest Destiny*, 192–193.

29. Brown, *Agents of Manifest Destiny*, 209–218; Hinton, "Wool," 232–282; Townsend, *California Diary*, 95; 33d Cong., 2nd sess., Sen. Exec. Doc. no. 16.

30. Capt. John R. Vinton to Mary Vinton, February 9, 1837, Vinton Papers; John T. Sprague, *The Origin, Progress, and Conclusion of the Florida War* (New York: D. Appleton, 1848), 168–170.

31. Of 826 officers in service in November 1845, 57 (6.9 percent) were killed in action or died of combat wounds in the Mexican War. Computed from Francis B. Heitman, comp., *Historical Register and Dictionary of the United States Army, from Its Organization, September 29, 1789, to March 2, 1903*, 2 vols. (Washington, D.C.: Government Printing Office, 1903), 2:13–42; 626. Of 1,086 officers on the 1860 army register, at least 83 (7.6 percent) died as a result of combat in the Civil War, including those joining the Confederacy. The actual percentage of Civil War deaths may be slightly higher, be-

cause available sources do not describe the fates of a small number of non–West Point graduates who joined the Confederate forces and failed to reach the rank of general.

32. Marcus Cunliffe, *Soldiers & Civilians: The Martial Spirit in America, 1775–1865* (Boston: Little, Brown, 1968), 65–98, 387–423, and passim; Johannsen, *To the Halls of the Montezumas*.

33. Lt. William T. Sherman to Ellen S. Ewing, September 17, 1844, in William T. Sherman, *Home Letters of General Sherman*, ed. M.A. DeWolfe Howe (New York: C. Scribner's Sons, 1909), 26.

34. Lt. James W. Schureman to Mary E. Schureman, April 10, 1844, James W. Schureman Papers, Library of Congress; Lt. Henry J. Hunt to Lt. James Duncan, March 17, 1844, Duncan Papers; Col. Stephen W. Kearny to Ravaud Kearny, Jr., February 24, 1842 (typescript), Stephen W. Kearny Papers, Missouri Historical Society, St. Louis.

35. Lt. Edward L. Hartz to Samuel Hartz, June 24, 1856, Hartz Papers; Edward P. Alexander, *Military Memoirs of a Confederate* (New York: Scribner, 1912), 2.

36. Capt. Thomas Williams to Mary Williams, February 21, 1855, Williams Family Papers. See also "On the Necessity and the Advantages of an Army and the Utility of War," *Military and Naval Magazine of the United States* 2 (December 1833):213.

37. Brig. Gen. Winfield Scott to Joel R. Poinsett, January 12, 1839, in C. P. Stacey, ed., "A Private Report of General Winfield Scott on the Border Situation in 1839," *Canadian Historical Review* 21 (December 1940):412; Lt. John J. Peck, letter of October 31, 1845, in John J. Peck, *The Sign of the Eagle: A View of Mexico—1830 to 1855*, ed. Richard F. Pourade (San Diego: Union-Tribune Publishing Co., 1970), 7–9. See also Capt. John R. Vinton to Mary Vinton, April 9, 1838, Vinton Papers.

38. Cadet George B. McClellan to his sister, May 3–13, 1846, McClellan Papers; Capt. Robert Anderson to Maj. Gen. Winfield Scott, July 3, 1846, Robert Anderson Papers, Library of Congress; Lt. Col. Ethan Allen Hitchcock's diary entry for May 24, 1846, Hitchcock, *Fifty Years*, 225; Lt. Earl Van Dorn to Octavia Sulivane, July 20, 1846, Emily Van Dorn Miller, ed., *A Soldier's Honor with Reminiscences of Major-General Earl Van Dorn* (New York: Abbey Press, 1902), 22–23.

39. Capt. Philip N. Barbour's journal entry for April 27, 1846, in Philip N. Barbour and Martha I. H. Barbour, *Journals of the Late Brevet Major Philip Norbourne Barbour, Captain in the 3rd Regiment, United States Infantry, and His Wife, Martha Isabella Hopkins Barbour; Written during the War with Mexico—1846*, ed. Rhoda van Bibber Tanner Doubleday (New York: G. P. Putnam's Sons, 1936), 47; Capt. John Sanders to Capt. James Duncan, April 27, 1846, Duncan Papers.

40. Capt. William S. Henry, *Campaign Sketches*, 112. See also Lt. Benjamin Alvord to Marcus C. M. Hammond, May 22, 1846, Hammond Papers; Lt. Jencks Beaman to Mrs. C. R. Mallory, May 29, 1846, Smith and Judah, eds., *Chronicles of the Gringos*, 73; Lt. Leslie Chase to Capt. James Duncan, November 21, 1846, Duncan Papers; Capt. Ephraim Kirby Smith to his wife, May 13, 1846, Smith, *To Mexico*, 53.

41. Capt. Philip N. Barbour to Martha I. H. Barbour, May 12–13, 1846, *Journals of Barbour and Barbour*, 174.

42. Maj. Edmund Kirby to Frances K. Smith, April 7, 1847, Kirby Smith Papers; Capt. Robert Anderson to his wife, March 23, 1847, in Robert Anderson, *An Artillery Officer in the Mexican War, 1846-7: Letters of Robert Anderson, Captain 3rd Artillery, U.S.A.* (New York: G. P. Putnam's Sons, 1911), 91. See also Lt. Francis Collins, journal entry for March 19, 1847, Collins, "Journal," 54; Freeman, *Lee*, 1:231; Bvt. Maj. George A. McCall to M., March 28, 1847, George A. McCall, *Letters from the Frontiers, Written during a Period of Thirty Years' Service in the Army of the United States* (Phila-

delphia: J. B. Lippincott, 1868), 483–484; Parmenas T. Turnley, *Reminiscences of Parmenas Taylor Turnley* (Chicago, 1892), 85–86.

43. Capt. Roger S. Dix to John A. Dix, February 25, 1847, Morgan Dix, *Memoirs of John Adams Dix,* 2 vols. (New York: Harper and Brothers, 1883), 1:210–212.

44. Lt. Charles S. Hamilton to Mrs. F., Mary, and Louise, October 6, 1846, Charles S. Hamilton, "The Letters of General Charles Hamilton Written from the Seat of War in Mexico," *Macfadden Fiction Lover's Magazine* 27 (December 1907):318. For similar remarks, see Lt. Ulysses S. Grant to John W. Lowe, June 26, 1846, *Papers of Grant,* 1:97; Bvt. Maj. George A. McCall to Peter McCall, June 14, 1846, McCall, *Letters,* 453–454.

45. Lt. John F. Reynolds to his sister, March 1, 1847, quoted in Edward J. Nichols, *Toward Gettysburg: A Biography of General John F. Reynolds* (University Park: Pennsylvania State University Press, 1958), 39–40; Lt. George W. Rains to his brother, August 28, 1847, George W. Rains Papers, Southern Historical Collection, University of North Carolina Library, Chapel Hill; Lt. Charles S. Hamilton to Mrs. F., Mary, and Louise, October 6, 1846, Hamilton, "Letters," 317.

46. Lt. Isaac Ingalls Stevens's journal entry for September 1847, quoted in Hazard Stevens, *The Life of Isaac Ingalls Stevens,* 2 vols. (Boston: Houghton, Mifflin, 1900), 1:211; Arthur T. Lee, "The Burial of Ringgold," *Army Ballads and Other Poems* (New York, 1871), 107–108.

47. K. Jack Bauer, *The Mexican War, 1846–1848* (New York: Macmillan, 1974), 371–374; Elliott, *Scott,* 565–590.

48. Hitchcock, *Fifty Years,* 310; Lt. Col. Sylvanus Thayer to Ichabod Chadbourne, June 28, 1846 (typescript), Sylvanus Thayer Papers, U.S. Military Academy Library, West Point, N.Y.

49. Daniel H. Hill, "The Army in Texas," *Southern Quarterly Review* 14 (July 1848):193; Lt. John F. Peck, letter of May 12, 1846, Peck, *Sign of the Eagle,* 26; Lt. John Sedgwick to his father, April 2, 1847, Sedgwick, *Correspondence,* 1:78; Lt. William M. Gardner to his brother, October 24, 1847, Gardner Papers; Lt. George W. Rains to his brother, August 28, 1847, Rains Papers; Lt. Thomas Williams to John R. Williams, December 27, 1847, Smith and Judah, eds., *Chronicles of the Gringos,* 418.

50. Lawrence Kip, *Army Life on the Pacific: A Journal of the Expedition against the Northern Indians, the Tribes of the Coeur d'Alenes, Spokans, and Pelouzes, in the Summer of 1858* (New York: Redfield, 1859), 56–58. See also Capt. John B. S. Todd, "The Harney Expedition against the Sioux: The Journal of Capt. John B. S. Todd," ed. Ray H. Mattison, *Nebraska History* 43 (1962):113.

51. Lt. William Gilpin to Joshua Gilpin, December 4, 1836, William Gilpin Papers, Missouri Historical Society, St. Louis; Lt. Robert M. McLane to Louis McLane, January 29, 1838, Louis McLane Papers, Library of Congress; Asst. Surg. Charles Page to Maj. William Hoffman, May 28, 1855, 34th Cong., 1st sess., Sen. Exec. Doc. no. 91, 12.

52. Capt. John R. B. Gardenier, "To the Memory of the Late Capt. E. G. Mitchell, U.S.A.," *Army and Navy Chronicle* 9 (October 31, 1839):278–279; Lt. William Wall to Lt. Robert Anderson, August 19, 1836, Anderson Papers.

CHAPTER EIGHTEEN. THE OFFICER CORPS IN THE SECTIONAL CRISIS

1. Maj. Edmund Kirby Smith to his mother, March 25, [1861], Edmund Kirby Smith Papers, Southern Historical Collection, University of North Carolina Library, Chapel Hill.

2. Cadet Isaac Ingalls Stevens to William Stevens, July 6, 1836, and Isaac Ingalls Stevens to Isaac Stevens, November 17, 1838, Isaac Ingalls Stevens Papers, University of Washington Library, Seattle. On sectional cliques, see also John C. Tidball, "Getting through West Point: The Cadet Memoirs of John C. Tidball, Class of 1848," ed. James L. Morrison, Jr., *Civil War History* 26 (December 1980):311–312.

3. Cadet J. E. B. Stuart to George Hairston, March 6, 1851, in J.E.B. Stuart, "J. E. B. Stuart's Letters to His Hairston Kin, 1850–1855," ed. Peter W. Hairston, *North Carolina Historical Review* 51 (Summer 1974):269–270. The most thorough study of West Point in the antebellum era finds little evidence of overt sectional tensions before the mid-1850s. James L. Morrison, Jr., *"The Best School in the World": West Point, the Pre–Civil War Years, 1833–1866* (Kent, Ohio: Kent State University Press, 1986), 126–131.

4. Based on the army register for 1823, *ASP:MA*, 2:515–523, and Francis B. Heitman, comp., *Historical Register and Dictionary of the United States Army, from Its Organization, September 29, 1789, to March 2, 1903*, 2 vols. (Washington, D.C.: Government Printing Office, 1903), 1:passim.

5. Franklin H. Churchill, *Sketch of the Life of Bvt. Brig. Gen. Sylvester Churchill, Inspector General U.S. Army* (New York: W. McDonald, 1888), 183.

6. Capt. Ethan Allen Hitchcock to Capt. Richard Bache, December 13, 1835, Ethan Allen Hitchcock Papers, Missouri Historical Society, St. Louis; Capt. John R. Vinton to Mary Vinton, November 6, 1845, John R. Vinton Papers, Duke University Library, Durham, N.C.; Lt. Alexander S. Webb to unknown, January 1856, quoted in Alexander S. Webb, "Campaigning in Florida in 1855," *Journal of the Military Service Institution of the United States* 45 (November–December 1909):399–400.

7. Edward M. Coffman, *The Old Army: A Portrait of the American Army in Peacetime, 1784–1898* (New York: Oxford University Press, 1986), 94–95; Richard D. Gamble, "Garrison Life at Frontier Military Posts, 1830–1860" (Ph.D. diss., University of Oklahoma, 1956), 160–161; Evan Jones, *Citadel in the Wilderness: The Story of Fort Snelling and the Old Northwest Frontier* (New York: Coward-McCann, 1966), 163–165; Aurora Hunt, *Major General James Henry Carleton, 1814–1873: Western Frontier Dragoon* (Glendale, Calif.: Arthur H. Clark, 1958), 120–122; Augustus Meyers, *Ten Years in the Ranks, U.S. Army* (New York: Stirling Press, 1914), 129; Dwight L. Clarke, *Stephen Watts Kearny: Soldier of the West* (Norman: University of Oklahoma Press, 1961), 49, 51; Erasmus D. Keyes, *Fifty Years' Observations of Men and Events, Civil and Military* (New York: C. Scribner's Sons, 1884), 174; W. Eugene Hollon, *Beyond the Cross Timbers: The Travels of Randolph B. Marcy, 1812–1887* (Norman: University of Oklahoma Press, 1955), 54; Lt. Robert H. Chilton to Lt. Abraham R. Johnston, November 6, 1842, Abraham R. Johnston Papers, U.S. Military Academy Library, West Point, N.Y. Until 1828, officers were permitted to hire out their slaves to the government for work on public projects. Lt. Col. Zachary Taylor to Surg. Thomas Lawson, August 28, 1828, Zachary Taylor Papers, Library of Congress.

8. Tommy R. Young II, "The United States Army in the South, 1789–1835," (Ph.D. diss., Louisiana State University, 1973), 444–522; Maj. Gen. Winfield Scott to Capt. John R. Vinton, July 3, 1843, Vinton Papers. For other examples of the link between slave control and army dispositions, see John C. Calhoun, *The Papers of John C. Calhoun*, ed. Robert L. Meriwether and E. Edwin Hemphill, 18 vols. to date (Columbia: University of South Carolina Press, 1959–), 7:210, 219–221, 433–434, 461; James W. Silver, *Edmund Pendleton Gaines: Frontier General* (Baton Rouge: Louisiana State University Press, 1949), 139–140.

9. Young, "Army in the South," 508–519; Robert W. Coakley, *The Role of Federal*

Military Forces in Domestic Disorders, 1789-1878 (Washington, D.C.: Government Printing Office, 1988), 92-94; John T. Sprague, *The Origin, Progress, and Conclusion of the Florida War* (New York: D. Appleton, 1848), 309-310.

10. James Duncan Papers; U.S. Military Academy Library, West Point, N.Y.; Stevens Papers; Johnston Papers; Lt. Dabney H. Maury to George B. McClellan, March 28, 1858, George B. McClellan Papers, Library of Congress.

11. William B. Skelton, "The United States Army, 1821-1837: An Institutional History" (Ph.D. diss., Northwestern University, 1968), 286, 303-309; Brig. Gen. Winfield Scott to Lt. Col. James Bankhead, January 12, 1833, HQA:LR; Col. Roger Jones to Bankhead, January 26, 1833, *ASP:MA*, 5:160; Capt. Francis S. Belton to Lewis Cass, March 31, 1833, file B-431 (1832), SW:LR-Reg.; Cass to Belton, May 1, 1833, SW:LS. Belton's toast is quoted in *Niles' Weekly Register*, July 24, 1830, 387.

12. Capt. Braxton Bragg to Marcus C. M. Hammond, August 15, 1848, James H., Hammond Papers, Library of Congress; Lt. William M. Gardner to Mrs. James Gardner, April 26, 1850, William M. Gardner Papers, Southern Historical Collection, University of North Carolina Library, Chapel Hill; Lt. Col. Gustavus Loomis to Henry H. Sibley, January 9, 1850, Henry H. Sibley Papers, Minnesota Historical Society, St. Paul. For other examples of officers' conservatism, see Capt. Benjamin Alvord to Marcus M. C. Hammond, August 21, 1848, Hammond Papers; Lt. George W. Hazzard to "My dear friend," May 16, 1852, George W. Hazzard Papers, U.S. Military Academy Library, West Point, N.Y.; Ethan Allen Hitchcock, *Fifty Years in Camp and Field: The Diary of Major-General Ethan Allen Hitchcock, U.S.A.*, ed. William A. Croffut (New York: G. P. Putnam's Sons, 1909), 377, 389-390, 397; Lt. George B. McClellan to his sister, March 1850, McClellan Papers.

13. Marvin Ewy, "The United States Army in the Kansas Border Troubles, 1855-1856," *Kansas Historical Quarterly* 32 (Winter 1966):385-400; Coakley, *Federal Military Forces*, 145-188; Otis E. Young, *The West of Philip St. George Cooke, 1809-1895* (Glendale, Calif.: Arthur H. Clark, 1955), 273-290; George R. Adams, "General William Selby Harney: Frontier Soldier, 1800-1889" (Ph.D. diss., University of Arizona, 1983), 251-256, 269-272.

14. Lt. John P. Hatch to M.P. Hatch, September 1, 1856, John P. Hatch Papers, Library of Congress; Ashbel Woodward, *Life of General Nathaniel Lyon* (Hartford, Conn.: Case, Lockwood, 1862), 209-210, 213-214; Lt. George D. Bayard to his sister, December 7, 1856, in Samuel J. Bayard, *The Life of George Dashiell Bayard, Late Captain, U.S.A., and Brigadier-General of Volunteers, Killed in the Battle of Fredericksburg, December 1862* (New York: G. P. Putnam's Sons, 1874), 100-101. See also Capt. Thomas Williams to Mary Williams, October 22, 1857, Williams Family Papers, Burton Collection, Detroit Public Library.

15. W. Eugene Hollon, *Beyond the Cross Timbers: The Travels of Randolph B. Marcy, 1812-1887* (Norman: University of Oklahoma Press, 1955), 202-203; Abner Doubleday, *Reminiscences of Forts Sumter and Moultrie in 1860-'61* (New York: Harper and Brothers, 1876), 32.

16. Capt. James J. Archer to H. W. Archer and R. H. Archer, January 27, 1861, and Archer to his mother, April 14, 1861, James J. Archer Papers, Maryland Historical Society, Baltimore; Maj. James Longstreet to Capt. Thomas Claiborne, April 24, 1861, Thomas Claiborne Papers, Southern Historical Collection, University of North Carolina Library, Chapel Hill; Capt. Lafayette McLaws to Emily McLaws, December 17, 1860, Lafayette McLaws Papers, ibid.; Maj. Earl Van Dorn to his wife, December 14, 1860, quoted in Robert G. Hartje, *Van Dorn: The Life and Times of a Confederate General* (Nashville, Tenn.: Vanderbilt University Press, 1967), 75-76.

17. Lt. George W. Custis Lee to Lt. James B. McPherson, November 19, 1860, James B. McPherson Papers, Library of Congress; Lt. Edward L. Hartz to Samuel Hartz, February 25, 1861, Edward L. Hartz Papers, Library of Congress; Capt. Thomas Williams to Asst. Surg. Joseph H. Bailey, January 16, 1861, Williams Family Papers.

18. Douglas Southall Freeman, *R. E. Lee: A Biography*, 4 vols. (New York: C. Scribner's Sons, 1934–1935), 1:412–442; Capt. Cadmus M. Wilcox to George B. McClellan, March 24, 1861, McClellan Papers; George Pickett to LaSalle Corbell, September 17, 1861, in George E. Pickett, *Soldier of the South: General Pickett's War Letters to His Wife*, ed. Arthur C. Inman (Boston: Houghton, Mifflin, 1928), 1–6; Stanley L. Falk, "Soldier-Technologist: Major Alfred Mordecai and the Beginnings of Science in the United States Army" (Ph.D. diss., Georgetown University, 1959), 546–588; William W. Averell, *Ten Years in the Saddle: The Memoir of William Woods Averell*, ed. Edward K. Eckert and Nicholas J. Amato (San Rafael, Calif.: Presidio Press, 1978), 239–240.

19. Other compilations of officers leaving to join the Confederacy vary somewhat. This figure represents officers in service between November 1, 1860, and February 1, 1861, and has been calculated from the army register for 1860 and the West Point graduating class of 1860. Excluded are military storekeepers, who were really civilian employees of the War Department rather than army officers, and West Point graduates of the class of 1861, who were commissioned after the outbreak of hostilities. For a fairly comprehensive list of officers joining the Confederacy, see Heitman, *Historical Register*, 2:180–184.

20. In 1863, the Adjutant General's Office compiled a list of officers who left the army to join the Confederacy that summarized reasons given for their resignations. Of thirty-six officers whose reasons are listed, twenty-one (58.3 percent) referred to state loyalty, six (16.7 percent) to sectional loyalty, four (11.1 percent) to conscience, and five (13.8 percent) to miscellaneous factors; see 36th Cong., 1st sess., Sen. Exec. Doc. no. 7, passim. In their private letters also, officers usually referred to the secession of their states as the basis of their decision.

21. Edward P. Alexander, *Military Memoirs of a Confederate* (New York: Scribner, 1912), 5–7. For officers' disinterest in the abstract constitutional question, see also Edward M. Coffman, "The Army Officer and the Constitution," *Parameters* 17 (September 1987):2–12.

22. Charles Anderson, *Texas, before, and on the Eve of the Rebellion* (Cincinnati: Peter G. Thomson, 1884), 21–51; Russell K. Brown, "An Old Woman with a Broomstick: General David E. Twiggs and the U.S. Surrender of Texas, 1861," *Military Affairs* 48 (April 1984):57–61.

23. Dabney H. Maury, *Recollections of a Virginian in the Mexican, Indian, and Civil Wars* (New York: C. Scribner's Sons, 1894), 133; Averell, *Ten Years*, 241; Cadet Tully McCrea to Belle McCrea, April 27, 1861, in Tully McCrea, *Dear Belle: Letters from a Cadet & Officer to His Sweetheart, 1858–1865*, ed. Catherine S. Crary (Middletown, Conn.: Wesleyan University Press, 1965), 88–89. See also Coffman, *Old Army*, 95–96.

CONCLUSION

1. Maxwell Bloomfield, *American Lawyers in a Changing Society, 1776–1876* (Cambridge: Harvard University Press, 1976), 136–190; Joseph F. Kett, *The Formation of the American Medical Profession: The Role of Institutions, 1780–1860* (New Haven, Conn.:

Yale University Press, 1968); Daniel H. Calhoun, *The American Civil Engineer: Origins and Conflict* (Cambridge: Massachusetts Institute of Technology, 1960); George H. Daniels, *American Science in the Age of Jackson* (New York: Columbia University Press, 1968), 6–62.

2. Christopher McKee, *A Gentlemanly and Honorable Profession: The Creation of the U.S. Naval Officer Corps, 1794–1815* (Annapolis, Md.: Naval Institute Press, 1991).

3. Leonard D. White, *The Jacksonians: A Study in Administrative History, 1829–1861* (New York: Macmillan, 1954), 213–250; Geoffrey S. Smith, "An Uncertain Passage: The Bureaus Run the Navy, 1842–1861," in Kenneth J. Hagan, ed., *In Peace and War: Interpretations of American Naval History, 1775–1978* (Westport, Conn.: Greenwood Press, 1978), 79–104; Charles O. Paullin, *Paullin's History of Naval Administration, 1775–1911* (Annapolis, Md.: Naval Institute Press, 1968), 159–247; Peter Karsten, *The Naval Aristocracy: The Golden Age of Annapolis and the Emergence of Modern Navalism* (New York: Free Press, 1972). Karsten's treatment of the naval subculture focuses on the late nineteenth century, but the subculture certainly had its roots in the antebellum era.

4. Calculated from lists of generals in James Spencer, comp., *Civil War Generals: Categorical Listings and a Biographical Directory* (New York and Westport, Conn.: Greenwood Press, 1986). Of the Union generals at or above the rank of major general, 65.5 percent had at least some regular army experience. In the Confederate army, the proportion of former regulars at these ranks was virtually identical: 66 percent.

5. Virtually all studies of the Civil War acknowledge the influence of the antebellum army on the conduct of the war, though they differ as to its effects. See, for example, Russell F. Weigley, *The American Way of War: A History of United States Military Strategy and Policy* (New York: Macmillan, 1973), 77–152; Russell F. Weigley, *History of the United States Army* (New York: Macmillan, 1967), 197–253; David Donald, "Refighting the Civil War," *Lincoln Reconsidered: Essays on the Civil War Era* (New York: Vintage, 1961), 82–102; Edward Hagerman, *The American Civil War and the Origins of Modern Warfare: Ideas, Organization, and Field Command* (Bloomington: Indiana University Press, 1988); Perry D. Jamieson, "The Development of Civil War Tactics" (Ph.D. diss., Wayne State University, 1979); June I. Gow, "The Old Army and the Confederacy, 1861–1865," in Kenneth J. Hagan and William R. Roberts, eds., *Against All Enemies: Interpretations of American Military History from Colonial Times to the Present* (New York and Westport, Conn.: Greenwood Press, 1986), 133–154.

6. James E. Sefton, *The United States Army and Reconstruction, 1865–1877* (Baton Rouge: Louisiana State University Press, 1967); Harold M. Hyman, "Johnson, Stanton, and Grant: A Reconsideration of the Army's Role in the Events Leading to Impeachment," *American Historical Review* 66 (October 1960):85–96; Weigley, *History of the Army*, 257–264.

7. Weigley, *History of the Army*, 270–292; Edward M. Coffman, *The Old Army: A Portrait of the American Army in Peacetime, 1784–1898* (New York: Oxford University Press, 1986), 269–284; Hagan and Roberts, eds., *Against All Enemies*, 183–234; Peter Karsten, "Armed Progressives: The Military Reorganizes for the Twentieth Century," in Peter Karsten, ed., *The Military in America from the Colonial Era to the Present* (New York: Free Press, 1980), 246–259; James L. Abrahamson, *America Arms for a New Century: The Making of a Great Military Power* (New York: Free Press, 1981).

SELECTED BIBLIOGRAPHY

This bibliography is not a complete listing of all books and sources consulted for this study or even of all those cited in the notes. The emphasis is on primary sources cited in the notes or of significant use in formulating my generalizations on the careers and views of regular army officers. For obvious reasons, I have excluded the many hundreds of genealogies, local histories, biographical dictionaries, and college alumni registers consulted for the collective biographical sections of the study. Moreover, I have not listed individual documents and reports in the Congressional Serial Set, and I have been very selective in including articles, professional books, and military manuals written by the regulars themselves. Finally, I have restricted secondary sources to biographies and other works of most direct relevance to the social, political, and intellectual history of the early military profession.

REGISTERS, BIOGRAPHICAL DICTIONARIES, AND OTHER REFERENCE WORKS

Allen, Jeremiah C., comp. *Subject Index of the General Orders of the War Department from January 1, 1809, to December 31, 1860.* Washington, D.C.: Government Printing Office, 1886.

Cullum, George W., comp. *Biographical Register of the Officers and Graduates of the U.S. Military Academy at West Point, N.Y., from Its Establishment, in 1802, to 1890; with the Early History of the United States Military Academy.* 3 vols. Boston: Houghton, Mifflin, 1891.

Hamersly, Thomas H. S., comp. *Complete Regular Army Register of the United States for One Hundred Years (1779-1879).* Washington, D.C.: T. H. S. Hamersly, 1880.

Heitman, Francis B., comp. *Historical Register and Dictionary of the United States Army, from Its Organization, September 29, 1789, to March 2, 1903.* 2 vols. Washington, D.C.: Government Printing Office, 1903.

———. *Historical Register of Officers of the Continental Army during the Revolution, April, 1775, to December, 1783.* Washington, D.C.: Rare Book Shop, 1914.

Johnson, Allen, and Dumas Malone, eds. *Dictionary of American Biography.* 21 vols. New York: Charles Scribner's Sons, 1928-1937.

Prucha, Francis Paul. *A Guide to the Military Posts of the United States, 1789-1895*. Madison, Wis.: State Historical Society of Wisconsin, 1964.
Spencer, James, comp. *Civil War Generals: Categorical Listings and a Biographical Directory*. New York and Westport, Conn.: Greenwood Press, 1986.
Thian, Raphael P., comp. *Notes Illustrating the Military Geography of the United States, 1813-1880*. Washington, D.C. Government Printing Office, 1881.
U.S. Congress. *Biographical Directory of the American Congress, 1774-1961*. Washington, D.C.: Government Printing Office, 1961.
Warner, Ezra J. *Generals in Blue: Lives of the Union Commanders*. Baton Rouge: Louisiana State University Press, 1964.
―――. *Generals in Gray: Lives of the Confederate Commanders*. Baton Rouge: Louisiana State University Press, 1959.
Wilson, James G., and John Fiske, comps. *Appleton's Cyclopaedia of American Biography*. 6 vols. New York: D. Appleton, 1894.

PRIMARY SOURCES

Manuscript Records in National Archives, Washington, D.C.

Records of the Department of State (Record Group 59)
    Letters of Application and Recommendation during the Administration of Thomas Jefferson, 1801-1809.
Records of the Office of the Chief of Engineers (Record Group 77)
    Letters Received by the Chief of Engineers, 1826-1866.
    Letters and Reports of Col. Joseph G. Totten, 1803-1864.
    Records of the Topographical Bureau, 1818-1867: U.S. Lake Survey, Letters Sent.
Records of the Office of the Quartermaster General (Record Group 92)
    Letterbook of Charles O. Collins, April 16, 1840-November 20, 1842.
    Letters Sent by Justus McKinstry, June 1849-December 1854.
Records of the Office of the Adjutant General (Record Group 94)
    Letters Sent by the Office of the Adjutant General, 1800-1890.
    Letters Received by the Office of the Adjutant General, 1805-1821.
    Letters Received by the Office of the Adjutant General, 1822-1860.
    Confidential Inspection Reports, 1812-1826.
    General James Wilkinson's Order Book, December 31, 1796-March 8, 1808.
    General Orders and Circulars of the War Department and General Headquarters of the Army, 1809-1860.
    Medical Officers' Personal Files.
    Registers of Enlistments in the United States Army, 1798-1914.
    U.S. Military Academy Cadet Application Papers, 1805-1866.
Records of the Office of the Secretary of War (Record Group 107)
    Letters Sent by the Secretary of War Relating to Military Affairs, 1800-1889.
    Letters Received by the Secretary of War, Registered Series, 1801-1870.
    Letters Received by the Secretary of War, Unregistered Series, 1789-1861.
    Applications: Subseries for 1820-1846, 1846-1848, 1854-1861.
Records of the Headquarters of the Army (Record Group 108)
    Letters Sent by the Headquarters of the Army, 1828-1903.
    Letters Received by the Headquarters of the Army, 1828-1903.
Records of the Office of the Surgeon General (Record Group 112)

Military Service Cards of Retired or Deceased Medical Officers.
Records of the Army Medical Board.
Records of the Office of the Judge Advocate General (Army) (Record Group 153)
Proceedings of U.S. Army General Courts-Martial, 1809–1890.
Records of the Office of the Chief of Ordnance (Record Group 156)
Watervliet Arsenal, Letters Sent.
Records of the Office of the Inspector General (Record Group 159)
Inspection Reports, 1814–1842.
Records of the Continental and Confederation Congresses and the Constitutional Convention (Record Group 360)
Papers of the Continental Congress, 1774–1789.
Records of U.S. Army Continental Commands, 1821–1920 (Record Group 393)
Fort Conrad/Craig Orderly Book, 1853–1863.
Fort Gibson Orderly Books, 1842–1843; 1843–1845.
Fort Mackinac Orderly Book, 1844–1860.
Fort Monroe Artillery School Letterbook, 1855–1863.
Fort Monroe Orderly Book, 1849–1854.
Fort Myers Orderly Book, 1856–1857.

Other Manuscript Collections

Beinecke Rare Book and Manuscript Library, Yale University, New Haven, Conn.
  Bradford, Edmund. Papers.
  Emory, William H. Papers.
Bowdoin College Library, Brunswick, Maine
  Howard, Oliver Otis. Papers.
Chicago Historical Society
  Wilkinson, James. Papers.
Detroit Public Library
  Backus, Electus. Papers. Burton Collection.
  Hamtramck, John F. Papers. Burton Collection.
  Kingsbury, Jacob. Papers. Burton Collection.
  Macomb Family Papers. Burton Collection.
  Williams, Alpheus S. Papers. Burton Collection.
  Williams, John R. Papers. Burton Collection.
  Williams Family Papers. Burton Collection.
Duke University Library, Durham, N.C.
  Butler, Edward G. W. Papers.
  Harris, David B. Papers.
  Jesup, Thomas S. Papers.
  Vinton, John R. Papers.
  Walker, William H. T. Papers.
Historical Society of Pennsylvania, Philadelphia
  Meade, George G. Papers.
  Parker, Daniel. Papers.
  Pemberton Family Papers.
  Smith, Persifor F. Papers.
  Wayne, Anthony. Papers.
Historical Society of Western Pennsylvania, Pittsburgh
  Denny, Ebenezer, and James O'Hara. Papers.

Indiana Historical Society, Indianapolis
  Armstrong, John. Papers.
Library of Congress, Washington D.C.
  Anderson, Robert. Papers.
  Brown, Jacob J. Papers.
  Clinch, Duncan L. Papers.
  Croghan, George. Papers.
  Dearborn, Henry. Papers.
  Early, Jubal A. Papers.
  Eustis, William. Papers.
  Force, Peter. Papers.
  Halleck, Henry W. Papers.
  Hamilton, Alexander. Papers.
  Hammond, James H. Papers.
  Hardie, James A. Papers.
  Hartz, Edward L. Papers.
  Hatch, John P. Papers.
  Heintzelman, Samuel P. Papers.
  Hitchcock, Ethan Allen. Papers.
  Hunt, Henry J. Papers.
  Jackson, Thomas J. Papers.
  Jefferson, Thomas. Papers.
  Jesup, Thomas S. Papers.
  Kautz, August V. Papers.
  King, Benjamin. Papers.
  Kingsbury, Jacob. Papers.
  Lawson, Thomas. Papers.
  McClellan, George B. Papers.
  McHenry, James. Papers.
  McLane, Louis. Papers.
  McPherson, James B. Papers.
  Madison, James. Papers.
  Myer, Albert J. Papers.
  Partridge, Alden. Papers.
  Porter, Moses. Papers.
  Rodgers Family Papers.
  Schoolcraft, Henry R. Papers.
  Schureman, James W. Papers.
  Stockton, Thomas. Papers.
  Talbot, Theodore. Papers.
  Taylor, Zachary. Papers.
  Washington, George. Papers.
  Wilcox, Cadmus M. Papers.
  Wilkinson, James. Papers.
Lilly Library, Indiana University, Bloomington
  Williams, Jonathan. Papers.
Maryland Historical Society, Baltimore
  Archer, James J. Papers.
  Buchanan, Robert C. Papers.

Massachusetts Historical Society, Boston
　Knox, Henry. Papers.
　Pickering, Timothy. Papers.
Minnesota Historical Society, St. Paul
　Sibley, Henry Hastings. Papers.
Missouri Historical Society, St. Louis
　Army Papers.
　Bissell, Daniel. Papers.
　Gilpin, William. Papers.
　Hitchcock, Ethan Allen. Papers.
　Kennerly Papers.
　Kingsbury, Jacob. Papers.
　LaMotte-Coppinger Papers.
　Ruff, Charles F. Papers.
　Starr, Samuel H. Papers. Bixby Collection.
New York Historical Society, New York City
　Beatty, Erkuries. Journals.
New York State Library, Albany
　Wool, John E. Papers.
Ohio Historical Society, Columbus
　Fuller, John. Papers.
　Sherman, William T. Papers.
State Historical Society of Wisconsin, Madison
　Armstrong, William. Papers.
　Fort Winnebago Orderly Book, 1834–1836.
　Gibbs Family Papers.
　Lindsay, William. Papers.
　Rudulph-Ney Papers. Lyman C. Draper Collection.
　Symmes, John C. Papers. Lyman C. Draper Collection.
　Tallmadge, Nathaniel P. Papers.
State Historical Society of Wisconsin, Area Research Center, Lacrosse
　Comstock, Elizabeth. Papers.
United States Military Academy Library, West Point, N.Y.
　Chapman Family Papers.
　"Circumstances of Parents of Cadets, 1842–1879"
　Duncan, James. Papers.
　Hazzard, George W. Papers.
　Johnston, Abraham R. Papers.
　Miller, James. Papers.
　Swift, Joseph G. Papers.
　Thayer, Sylvanus. Papers.
University of North Carolina Library, Chapel Hill (Southern Historical Collection)
　Alexander, Edward P. Papers.
　Bryan, William S. Papers.
　Claiborne, Thomas. Papers.
　Gardner, William M. Papers.
　Hagner, Peter. Papers.
　Kirby Smith, Edmund. Papers.
　L'Engle, Edward M. Papers.

Lenoir Family Papers II.
Long, Armistead L. Papers.
McLaws, Lafayette. Papers.
MacRae, John. Papers.
Rains, George W. Papers.
Yancey, Bartlett. Papers.
University of Notre Dame Archives, South Bend, Ind.
Sherman, William T. Papers.
University of Washington Library, Seattle
Stevens, Isaac Ingalls. Papers.
Western Reserve Historical Society, Cleveland, Ohio
Pike, Zebulon M. Papers.
Trimble, Allen. Papers.
William L. Clements Library, University of Michigan, Ann Arbor
Brown, Jacob J. Papers.
Fish, Nicholas. Papers.
Harmar, Josiah. Papers.
McHenry, James. Papers.
O'Connor, John M. Papers.
Van Deventer, Christopher. Papers.
Wayne, Anthony. Papers.

Published Primary Sources

Alexander, Edward P. *Military Memoirs of a Confederate.* New York: Scribner, 1912.
Anderson, Robert. *An Artillery Officer in the Mexican War, 1846-7: Letters of Robert Anderson, Captain 3rd Artillery, U.S.A.* New York: G. P. Putnam's Sons, 1911.
Andrews, Joseph G. *A Surgeon's Mate at Fort Defiance: The Journal of Joseph Gardner Andrews.* Edited by Richard C. Knopf. Columbus: Ohio Historical Society, 1957.
Army and Navy Chronicle. 1-13 (January 3, 1835-May 21, 1842).
Army and Navy Chronicle and Scientific Repository. 1-3 (January 12, 1842-June 27, 1844).
Averell, William W. *Ten Years in the Saddle: The Memoir of William Woods Averell.* Edited by Edward K. Eckert and Nicholas J. Amato. San Rafael, Calif.: Presidio Press, 1978.
Ballentine, George. *Autobiography of an English Soldier in the United States Army.* Edited by William H. Goetzmann. Chicago: R. R. Donnelley and Sons, 1986.
Bandel, Eugene. *Frontier Life in the Army, 1854-1861.* Edited by Ralph P. Bieber. Glendale, Calif.: Arthur H. Clark, 1932.
Barbour, Philip N., and Martha I. H. Barbour. *Journals of the Late Brevet Major Philip Norbourne Barbour, Captain in the 3rd Regiment, United States Infantry, and His Wife, Martha Isabella Hopkins Barbour; Written during the War with Mexico—1846.* Edited by Rhoda van Bibber Tanner Doubleday. New York: G. P. Putnam's Sons, 1936.
Beatty, Erkuries. "Diary of Major Erkuries Beatty, Paymaster of the Western Army, May 15, 1786, to June 5, 1787." *Magazine of American History* 1 (March-July 1877):175-179, 235-243, 309-315, 380-384, 432-438.
Beatty, Joseph M., Jr., ed. "Letters of the Four Beatty Brothers of the Continental Army, 1774-1794." *Pennsylvania Magazine of History and Biography* 44 (1920):193-263.
Bemrose, John. *Reminiscences of the Second Seminole War.* Edited by John K. Mahon. Gainesville: University of Florida Press, 1966.

Benét, Stephen V., comp. *A Collection of Annual Reports and Other Important Papers, Relating to the Ordnance Department, Taken from the Records of the Office of the Chief of Ordnance, from Public Documents, and from Other Sources.* 4 vols. Washington, D.C., 1878–1890.
Blount, John G. *The John Gray Blount Papers.* Edited by Alice B. Keith et al. 4 vols. Raleigh, N.C.: State Department of Archives and History, 1952–1982.
Brady, Hugh. "Reports of General Brady on the Patriot War." Edited by Francis Paul Prucha. *Canadian Historical Review* 31 (March 1950):56–68.
Bragg, Braxton. "Notes on Our Army." *Southern Literary Messenger* 10–11 (February 1844–February 1845); 10:86-87, 155-157, 246-251, 283-287, 372-377, 750-753; 11:39-47, 104-105.
Buell, John H. "A Fragment from the Diary of Major John Hutchinson Buell, U.S.A., Who Joined the American Army at the Beginning of the Revolutionary War and Remained in Service until 1803." *Journal of the Military Service Institution of the United States* 40 (January-March 1907):102–113, 260–268.
Cadet Life at West Point. Boston, 1862.
Calhoun, John C. *The Papers of John C. Calhoun.* Edited by Robert L. Meriwether and W. Edwin Hemphill. 18 vols. to date. Columbia: University of South Carolina Press, 1959–.
Callan, John F., comp. *Military Laws of the United States, Relating to the Army, Volunteers, Militia, and to Bounty Lands and Pensions, from the Foundation of the Government to the Year 1863.* Philadelphia: C. W. Childs, 1863.
Carleton, James H. *The Prairie Logbooks: Dragoon Campaigns to the Pawnee Villages in 1844, and to the Rocky Mountains in 1845.* Edited by Louis Pelzer. Chicago: Caxton Club, 1943.
Carter, Clarence E., and John P. Bloom, eds. *The Territorial Papers of the United States.* 27 vols. Washington, D.C.: Government Printing Office, 1934–1969.
Chamberlain, Samuel E. *My Confession.* Edited by Roger Butterfield. New York: Harper, 1956.
Chapman, William. "Letters from the Seat of War—Mexico (1846–47)." *Green Bay Historical Bulletin* 4 (July–August 1928):1–23.
Chapman, William W. "A West Point Graduate in the Second Seminole War: William Warren Chapman and the View from Fort Foster." Edited by Edward C. Coker and Daniel L. Schafer. *Florida Historical Quarterly* 68 (April 1990):447–475.
Collins, Francis. "Journal of Francis Collins, an Artillery Officer in the Mexican War." Edited by Maria C. Collins. *Quarterly Publication of the Historical and Philosophical Society of Ohio* 10 (April–July 1915):37–109.
Cooke, Philip St. George. *Scenes and Adventures in the Army: or, The Romance of Military Life.* Philadelphia: Lindsay and Blakiston, 1857.
Cooling, B. Franklin, ed. *The New American State Papers, 1789–1860: Military Affairs.* 19 vols. Wilmington, Del.: Scholarly Resources, 1979.
Croghan, George. *Army Life on the Western Frontier: Selections from the Official Reports Made between 1826 and 1845 by Colonel George Croghan.* Edited by Francis Paul Prucha. Norman: University of Oklahoma Press, 1958.
Crook, George. *General George Crook: His Autobiography.* Edited by Martin F. Schmitt. Norman: University of Oklahoma Press, 1946.
Dalliba, James. *Improvements in the Military Establishment of the United States.* Troy, N.Y.: William S. Parker, 1822.
Dana, Napoleon J. T. *Monterrey Is Ours!: The Mexican War Letters of Lieutenant Dana,*

1845–1847. Edited by Robert H. Ferrell. Lexington: University of Kentucky Press, 1990.
Davis, T. Frederick, ed. "United States Troops in Spanish East Florida, 1812–13." *Florida Historical Quarterly* 9–10 (July 1930–July 1931); 9:3–23, 96–116, 135–155, 259–278; 10:24–34.
Denny, Ebenezer. "Military Journal of Major Ebenezer Denny, an Officer in the Revolutionary and Indian Wars." Edited by William H. Denny. *Memoirs of the Historical Society of Pennsylvania* 7 (1860):205–492.
DePauw, Linda G., ed. *Documentary History of the First Federal Congress of the United States of America, March 4, 1789–March 3, 1791.* 3 vols. Baltimore: Johns Hopkins University Press, 1972–1979.
Duane, William. "The Letters of William Duane." *Proceedings of the Massachusetts Historical Society*, 2d ser. 20 (1906–1907):257–394.
DuBois, John Van Deusen. *Campaigns in the West, 1856–1861: The Journal and Letters of Colonel John Van Deusen DuBois.* Edited by George P. Hammond. Tucson: Arizona Pioneers Historical Society, 1949.
Ewell, Richard S. *The Making of a Soldier: Letters of General R. S. Ewell.* Edited by Percy G. Hamlin. Richmond: Whittet and Shepperson, 1935.
Fonda, John H. "Early Wisconsin." *Collections of the State Historical Society of Wisconsin* 5 (1907):205–284.
Ford, Worthington C., ed. *Journals of the Continental Congress, 1774–1789.* 34 vols. Washington, D.C.: Government Printing Office, 1904–1937.
Forry, Samuel. "Letters of Samuel Forry, Surgeon, U.S. Army, 1837–1838." *Florida Historical Quarterly* 6 (January 1928):133–148; (April 1928):206–219; 7 (July 1928):88–105.
French, Samuel G. *Two Wars: An Autobiography of Gen. Samuel G. French, an Officer in the Armies of the United States and the Confederate States, a Graduate from the U.S. Military Academy, West Point, 1843.* Nashville, Tenn.: Confederate Veteran, 1901.
Gardner, John L. *Military Control, or Command and Government of the Army.* Washington, D.C.: A. B. Claxton, 1839.
Glisan, Rodney. *Journal of Army Life.* San Francisco: A. L. Bancroft, 1874.
Gove, Jesse A. *The Utah Expedition, 1857–1858: Letters of Capt. Jesse A. Gove, 10th Inf., U.S.A. of Concord, N.H., to Mrs. Gove, and Special Correspondence of the New York Herald.* Edited by Otis G. Hammond. Concord: New Hampshire Historical Society, 1928.
Grant, Ulysses S. *The Papers of Ulysses S. Grant.* Edited by John Y. Simon. 16 vols. to date. Carbondale: Southern Illinois University Press, 1967–.
_____. *Personal Memoirs of U. S. Grant.* 2 vols. New York: C. L. Webster, 1885.
Guion, Isaac. "Military Journal of Isaac Guion, 1797–1799." In *Seventh Annual Report of the Director of the Department of Archives and History of the State of Mississippi*, 25–112. Nashville, Tenn., 1909.
Halleck, Henry W. *Elements of Military Art and Science; or, Course of Instruction in Strategy, Fortification, Tactics of Battles, &c.* Philadelphia: G. S. Appleton, 1846.
Hamilton, Alexander. *The Papers of Alexander Hamilton.* Edited by Harold C. Syrett. 26 vols. New York: Columbia University Press, 1961–1979.
Hamilton, Charles S. "The Letters of General Charles Hamilton, Written from the Seat of War in Mexico." *Macfadden Fiction Lover's Magazine* 27 (December 1907):313–321.
Hancock, Almira R. *Reminiscences of Winfield Scott Hancock.* New York: C. L. Webster, 1887.

Heart, Jonathan. *Journal of Capt. Jonathan Heart . . . to Which Is Added the Dickinson-Harmar Correspondence of 1784-5.* Edited by Consul W. Butterfield. Albany, N.Y.: J. Munsell's Co., 1885.
Henry, William S. *Campaign Sketches of the War with Mexico.* New York: Harper and Brothers, 1847.
Heth, Henry. *The Memoirs of Henry Heth.* Edited by James L. Morrison, Jr. Westport, Conn.: Greenwood Press, 1974.
Hetzel, Abner R., comp. *Military Laws of the United States.* Washington, D.C.: G. Templeman, 1846.
Hildreth, James. *Dragoon Campaigns to the Rocky Mountains, Being a History of the Enlistment, Organization and First Campaigns of the Regiment of United States Dragoons.* New York: Wiley and Long, 1836.
Hill, Daniel H. "The Army in Texas." *Southern Quarterly Review* 9 (April 1846):434–457; 14 (July 1848):183–197.
Hitchcock, Ethan Allen. *Fifty Years in Camp and Field: The Diary of Major-General Ethan Allen Hitchcock, U.S.A.* Edited by William A. Croffut. New York: G. P. Putnam's Sons, 1909.
———. *A Traveler in Indian Territory: The Journal of Ethan Allen Hitchcock, Late Major-General in the United States Army.* Edited by Grant Foreman. Cedar Rapids, Iowa: Torch Press, 1930.
Hunt, Edward L. "Army Attack and National Defence." *American Review* 4 (August 1846):146–160.
Jackson, Andrew. *Correspondence of Andrew Jackson.* Edited by John S. Bassett. 7 vols. Washington, D.C.: Carnegie Institution, 1926–1935.
Johnston, Eliza. "The Diary of Eliza (Mrs. Albert Sidney) Johnston: The Second Cavalry in Texas." *Southwestern Historical Quarterly* 60 (April 1957):463–500.
Keyes, Erasmus D. *Fifty Years' Observations of Men and Events, Civil and Military.* New York: C. Scribner's Sons, 1884.
Kip, Lawrence. *Army Life on the Pacific: A Journal of the Expedition against the Northern Indians, the Tribes of the Coeur d'Alenes, Spokans, and Pelouzes, in the Summer of 1858.* New York: Redfield, 1859.
Knopf, Richard C., ed. *Anthony Wayne, a Name in Arms: Soldier, Diplomat, Defender of Expansion Westward of a Nation. The Wayne-Knox-Pickering-McHenry Correspondence.* Pittsburgh: University of Pittsburgh Press, 1960.
Lane, Lydia S. *I Married a Soldier; or Old Days in the Old Army.* Albuquerque, N.Mex.: Horn and Wallace, 1964.
Langley, Harold D., ed. *To Utah with the Dragoons, and Glimpses of Life in Arizona and California, 1858–1859.* Salt Lake City: University of Utah Press, 1974.
Lazelle, Henry M. "Puritan and Apache: A Diary." Edited by Frank D. Reeve. *New Mexico Historical Review* 23 (1948):269–301; 24 (1949):12–53.
Lee, Arthur T. *Army Ballads and Other Poems.* New York, 1871.
Lee, Robert E. *"To Markie:" The Letters of Robert E. Lee to Martha Custis Williams.* Edited by Avery Craven. Cambridge: Harvard University Press, 1933.
McCall, George A. *Letters from the Frontiers, Written during a Period of Thirty Years' Service in the Army of the United States.* Philadelphia: J. B. Lippincott, 1868.
McClellan, George B. *The Mexican War Diary of George B. McClellan.* Edited by William S. Myers. Princeton, N.J.: Princeton University Press, 1917.
McCrea, Tully. *Dear Belle: Letters from a Cadet & Officer to His Sweetheart, 1858–1865.* Edited by Catherine S. Crary. Middletown, Conn.: Wesleyan University Press, 1965.

McDonogh, Patrick. "A Hero of Fort Erie: Letters Relating to the Military Service, Chiefly on the Niagara Frontier, of Lieutenant Patrick McDonogh." *Publications of the Buffalo Historical Society* 5 (1902):63–93.
McLane, Robert M. *Reminiscences, 1827–1897*. Wilmington, Del.: Scholarly Resources, 1972.
Macomb, Alexander. *Pontiac; or, The Siege of Detroit: A Drama in Three Acts*. Boston: S. Colman, 1835.
Marcy, Randolph B. *The Prairie Traveler: A Hand-Book for Overland Expeditions*. New York: Harper and Brothers, 1859.
———. *Thirty Years of Army Life on the Border*. New York: Harper and Brothers, 1866.
Maury, Dabney H. *Recollections of a Virginian in the Mexican, Indian, and Civil Wars*. New York: C. Scribner's Sons, 1894.
Meyers, Augustus. *Ten Years in the Ranks, U.S. Army*. New York: Stirling Press, 1914.
Military and Naval Magazine of the United States. 1–6 (March 1833–February 1836).
Monroe, James. *The Writings of James Monroe, Including a Collection of His Public and Private Papers and Correspondence Now for the First Time Printed*. Edited by Stanislaus M. Hamilton. 7 vols. New York: G. P. Putnam's Sons, 1898–1903.
Morgan, Michael R. "Memories of the Fifties." *Journal of the Military Service Institution of the United States* 37 (July–August 1905):147–167.
Motte, Jacob Rhett. *Journey into Wilderness: An Army Surgeon's Account of Life in Camp and Field during the Creek and Seminole Wars, 1836–1838*. Edited by James F. Sunderman. Gainesville: University of Florida Press, 1953.
Patten, George W. *Voices of the Border*. New York: Hurd and Houghton, 1867.
Peck, John J. *The Sign of the Eagle: A View of Mexico—1830 to 1855*. Edited by Richard F. Pourade. San Diego: Union-Tribune Publishing Co., 1970.
Pickett, George E. *Soldier of the South: General Pickett's War Letters to His Wife*. Edited by Arthur C. Inman. Boston: Houghton, Mifflin, 1928.
Polk, James K. *The Diary of James K. Polk during His Presidency, 1845 to 1849*. Edited by Milo M. Quaife. 4 vols. Chicago: A. C. McClurg, 1910.
Poussin, William Tell. *The United States; Its Power and Progress*. Translated by Edmund L. DuBarry. Philadelphia: Lippincott, Grambo, 1851.
Recollections of the United States Army: A Series of Thrilling Tales and Sketches. Boston, 1845.
Rice, Josiah M. *A Cannoneer in Navajo Country: Journal of Private Josiah M. Rice, 1851*. Edited by Richard H. Dillon. Denver: Old West Publishing Co., 1970.
Richardson, James D., comp. *A Compilation of the Messages and Papers of the Presidents*. 20 vols. New York: Bureau of National Literature, 1917.
Ripley, Roswell S. *The War with Mexico*. 2 vols. New York: Harper and Brothers, 1849.
Rowland, Thomas. "Letters of a Virginia Cadet at West Point, 1859–1861." *South Atlantic Quarterly* 14–15 (July 1915–July 1916); 14:201–219, 330–347; 15:1–17, 142–156, 201–215.
Schofield, John M. *Forty-Six Years in the Army*. New York: Century, 1897.
Scott, Winfield. *Memoirs of Lieut.-General Winfield Scott, L.L.D., Written by Himself*. 2 vols. New York: Sheldon, 1864.
Sedgwick, John. *Correspondence of John Sedgwick, Major-General*. 2 vols. New York: DeVinne Press, 1902–1903.
Sheridan, Philip H. *Personal Memoirs of P. H. Sheridan*. 2 vols. New York: C. L. Webster, 1888.

Sherman, William T. *Home Letters of General Sherman*. Edited by M. A. DeWolfe Howe. New York: C. Scribner's Sons, 1909.
_____. *Memoirs of Gen. W. T. Sherman*. 2 vols. in 1. New York: C. L. Webster, 1891.
Smith, Ephraim Kirby. *To Mexico with Scott: Letters of Captain E. Kirby Smith to His Wife*. Edited by Emma J. Blackwood. Cambridge: Harvard University Press, 1917.
Smith, George W., and Charles Judah, eds. *Chronicles of the Gringos: The U.S. Army in the Mexican War, 1846-1848. Accounts of Eyewitnesses and Combatants*. Albuquerque: University of New Mexico Press, 1968.
Smith, Joseph R. "Letters from the Second Seminole War." Edited by John K. Mahon. *Florida Historical Quarterly* 36 (April 1958):331-352.
Sprague, John T. *The Origin, Progress, and Conclusion of the Florida War*. New York: D. Appleton, 1848.
Stacey, C. P., ed. "A Private Report of General Winfield Scott on the Border Situation in 1839." *Canadian Historical Review* 21 (December 1940):407-414.
Steuben, Frederick W. A., von. *Regulations for the Order and Discipline of the Troops of the United States*. Philadelphia: Styner and Cist, 1779.
Stevens, Isaac Ingalls. *Campaigns of the Rio Grande and of Mexico; with Notices of the Recent Work of Major Ripley*. New York: D. Appleton, 1851.
Stoddard, Amos. *Sketches, Historical and Descriptive, of Louisiana*. Philadelphia: Mathew Carey, 1812.
_____. "Transfer of Upper Louisiana: Papers of Captain Amos Stoddard." *Glimpses of the Past* 2 (May-September 1935):78-122.
Stuart, J. E. B. "J. E. B. Stuart's Letters to His Hairston Kin, 1850-1855." Edited by Peter W. Hairston. *North Carolina Historical Review* 51 (Summer 1974):261-333.
Sweeny, Thomas W. *Journal of Lt. Thomas W. Sweeny, 1849-1853*. Edited by Arthur Woodward. Los Angeles: Westernlore Press, 1956.
Swift, Joseph G. *The Memoirs of Gen. Joseph Gardner Swift, L.L.D., U.S.A., First Grad. of the U.S.M.A., West Point*. Worcester, Mass.: F. S. Blanchard, 1890.
Talbot, Theodore. *Soldier in the West: Letters of Theodore Talbot during His Service in California, Mexico, and Oregon, 1845-53*. Edited by Robert V. Hine and Savoie Lottinville. Norman: University of Oklahoma Press, 1972.
Taylor, Zachary. *Letters of Zachary Taylor, from the Battle-Fields of the Mexican War*. Rochester, N.Y.: Genessee Press, 1908.
Thian, Raphael P., comp. *Legislative History of the General Staff of the Army of the United States (Its Organization, Duties, Pay, and Allowances), from 1775 to 1901*. Washington, D.C.: Government Printing Office, 1901.
Thornbrough, Gayle, ed. *Outpost on the Wabash, 1787-1791: Letters of Brigadier General Josiah Harmar and Major John Francis Hamtramck and Other Letters and Documents Selected from the Harmar Papers in the William L. Clements Library*. Indianapolis: Indiana Historical Society, 1957.
Thorndike, Rachel S., ed. *The Sherman Letters: Correspondence between General and Senator Sherman from 1837 to 1891*. New York: C. Scribner's Sons, 1894.
Tidball, John C. "Getting through West Point: The Cadet Memoirs of John C. Tidball, Class of 1848." Edited by James L. Morrison, Jr. *Civil War History* 26 (December 1980):304-325.
Todd, John B. S. "The Harney Expedition against the Sioux: The Journal of Capt. John B. S. Todd." Edited by Ray H. Mattison. *Nebraska History* 43 (1962):89-130.
Townsend, Edward D. *The California Diary of General E. D. Townsend*. Edited by Malcolm Edwards. Los Angeles: W. Ritchie, 1970.

Tracy, Albert. *The Utah War: The Journal of Albert Tracy, 1858–1860*. Salt Lake City: Utah State Historical Society, 1945.
Tripler, Eunice. *Eunice Tripler: Some Notes of Her Personal Recollections*. Compiled by Louis A. Arthur. New York: Grafton Press, 1910.
Turner, Henry S. *The Original Journals of Henry Smith Turner: With Stephen Watts Kearny to New Mexico and California, 1846–1847*. Edited by Dwight L. Clarke. Norman: University of Oklahoma Press, 1966.
Turnley, Parmenas T. *Reminiscences of Parmenas Taylor Turnley*. Chicago, 1892.
Tyler, Daniel. *Daniel Tyler: A Memorial Volume Containing His Autobiography and War Record*. Edited by Donald G. Mitchell. New Haven, Conn., 1883.
U.S. Congress. *American State Papers*. Class V: *Military Affairs*. 7 vols. Washington, D.C.: Gales and Seaton, 1832–1861.
———. *American State Papers*. Class X: *Miscellaneous*. 2 vols. Washington, D.C.: Gales and Seaton, 1834.
———. *Annals of the Congress of the United States, 1789–1824*. 42 vols. Washington, D.C.: Gales and Seaton, 1834–1856.
———. *Congressional Globe*. 46 vols. Washington, D.C., 1834–1873.
———. *The Public Statutes at Large of the United States of America*. 100 vols. to date. Boston and Washington, D.C.: Government Printing Office, 1848–.
———. Serial set of congressional publications.
———. Senate. *Journal of the Executive Proceedings of the Senate of the United States of America*. 90 vols. Washington, D.C.: Government Printing Office, 1828–1948.
U.S. War Department. *General Regulations for the Army of the United States, 1847*. Washington, D.C., 1847.
———. *General Regulations for the Army of the United States; also, The Rules and Articles of War, and Extracts from Laws Relating to Them*. Washington, D.C., 1835.
———. *General Regulations for the Army; or, Military Institutes*. Philadelphia: M. Carey and Sons, 1821.
———. *General Regulations for the Army; or, Military Institutes*. Washington, D.C.: Davis and Force, 1825.
Washington, George. *The Writings of George Washington from the Original Manuscript Sources, 1745–1799*. Edited by John C. Fitzpatrick. 39 vols. Washington, D.C.: Government Printing Office, 1931–1944.
Webb, Alexander S. "Campaigning in Florida in 1855." *Journal of the Military Service Institution of the United States* 45 (November–December 1909):398–429.
Wilkinson, James. *Memoirs of My Own Times*. 3 vols. Philadelphia: Abraham Small, 1816.
Willcox, Orlando B. *Faca: A Military Memoir*. Boston: James French, 1857.
Worth, William J. "Never before Published Letters of Famous General Worth, Written during Mexican War." *New York Times Magazine*. July 16, 1916, 10–11.

SECONDARY SOURCES

Biographies

Alexander, Charles B. *Major William Ferguson: Member of the American Philosophical Society, Officer in the Army of the Revolution and in the Army of the United States*. New York: Trow Press, 1908.
Bayard, Samuel J. *The Life of George Dashiell Bayard, Late Captain, U.S.A., and Briga-*

dier-General of Volunteers, Killed in the Battle of Fredericksburg, December 1862. New York: G. P. Putnam's Sons, 1874.
Churchill, Franklin H. *Sketch of the Life of Bvt. Brig. Gen. Sylvester Churchill, Inspector General U.S. Army.* New York: W. McDonald, 1888.
Clarke, Dwight L. *Stephen Watts Kearny: Soldier of the West.* Norman: University of Oklahoma Press, 1961.
Dallas, George M. *Life and Writings of Alexander James Dallas.* Philadelphia: J. B. Lippincott, 1871.
DePeyster, John W. *Personal and Military History of Philip Kearny, Major-General United States Volunteers.* New York: Rice and Gage, 1869.
Dillon, Richard. *Meriwether Lewis: A Biography.* New York: Coward-McCann, 1965.
Dix, Morgan. *Memoirs of John Adams Dix.* 2 vols. New York: Harper and Brothers, 1883.
Dyer, Brainerd. *Zachary Taylor.* Baton Rouge: Louisiana State University Press, 1946.
Elliott, Charles W. *Winfield Scott: The Soldier and the Man.* New York: Macmillan, 1937.
Freeman, Douglas Southall. *R. E. Lee: A Biography.* 4 vols. New York: C. Scribner's Sons, 1934–1935.
Garesché, Louis A. *Biography of Lieut. Col. Julius P. Garesché, Assistant Adjutant-General, U.S. Army.* Philadelphia: J. B. Lippincott, 1887.
Goebel, Dorothy B. *William Henry Harrison: A Political Biography.* Indianapolis: Indiana Library and Historical Department, 1926.
Hartje, Robert G. *Van Dorn: The Life and Times of a Confederate General.* Nashville, Tenn.: Vanderbilt University Press, 1967.
Hebert, Walter H. *Fighting Joe Hooker.* Indianapolis: Bobbs-Merrill, 1944.
Heyman, Max L., Jr. *Prudent Soldier: A Biography of Major General E. R. S. Canby, 1817–1873.* Glendale, Calif.: Arthur H. Clark, 1959.
Hollon, W. Eugene. *Beyond the Cross Timbers: The Travels of Randolph B. Marcy, 1812–1887.* Norman: University of Oklahoma Press, 1955.
——. *The Lost Pathfinder: Zebulon Montgomery Pike.* Norman: University of Oklahoma Press, 1949.
Hughes, Nathaniel C., Jr. *General William J. Hardee: Old Reliable.* Baton Rouge: Louisiana State University Press, 1965.
Hunt, Aurora. *Major General James Henry Carleton, 1814–1873: Western Frontier Dragoon.* Glendale, Calif.: Arthur H. Clark, 1958.
Jacobs, James R. *Tarnished Warrior: Major-General James Wilkinson.* New York: Macmillan, 1938.
Jones, J. William. *Life and Letters of Robert Edward Lee, Soldier and Man.* New York and Washington, D.C.: Neale Publishing Co., 1906.
Kieffer, Chester L. *Maligned General: A Biography of Thomas S. Jesup.* San Rafael, Calif.: Presidio Press, 1979.
Lamers, William M. *The Edge of Glory: A Biography of General William S. Rosecrans, U.S.A.* New York: Harcourt, Brace, 1961.
Longacre, Edward G. *The Man behind the Guns: Biography of General Henry Jackson Hunt, Chief of Artillery, Army of the Potomac.* South Brunswick, N.J.: A. S. Barnes, 1977.
McDermott, John F. *Seth Eastman: Pictorial Historian of the Indian.* Norman: University of Oklahoma Press, 1961.
McKinney, Francis F. *Education in Violence: The Life of George H. Thomas and the History of the Army of the Cumberland.* Detroit: Wayne State University Press, 1961.

McWhiney, Grady. *Braxton Bragg and Confederate Defeat*. New York: Columbia University Press, 1969.
Meade, George. *The Life and Letters of George Gordon Meade*. 2 vols. New York: C. Scribner's Sons, 1913.
Myer, Jesse S. *Life and Letters of Dr. William Beaumont; Including Hitherto Unpublished Data concerning the Case of Alexis St. Martin*. St. Louis: C. V. Mosby, 1912.
Myers, William S. *A Study in Personality: General George Brinton McClellan*. New York: D. Appleton-Century, 1934.
Nelson, Paul D. *Anthony Wayne: Soldier of the Early Republic*. Bloomington: Indiana University Press, 1985.
Nevins, Allan. *Frémont: Pathmarker of the West*. New York: D. Appleton-Century Co., 1939.
Nichols, Edward J. *Toward Gettysburg: A Biography of General John F. Reynolds*. University Park: Pennsylvania State University Press, 1958.
Nichols, Roger L. *General Henry Atkinson: A Western Military Career*. Norman: University of Oklahoma Press, 1965.
Parks, Joseph H. *General Edmund Kirby Smith, C.S.A.* Baton Rouge: Louisiana State University Press, 1954.
Patrick, Rembert W. *Aristocrat in Uniform: General Duncan L. Clinch*. Gainesville: University of Florida Press, 1963.
Phillips, Christopher. *Damned Yankee: The Life of General Nathaniel Lyon*. Columbia: University of Missouri Press, 1990.
Remini, Robert V. *Andrew Jackson and the Course of American Empire, 1767-1821*. New York: Harper and Row, 1977.
Richards, George H. *Memoir of Alexander Macomb, the Major General Commanding the Army of the United States*. New York: M'Elrath, Bangs, 1833.
Roland, Charles P. *Albert Sidney Johnston: Soldier of Three Republics*. Austin: University of Texas Press, 1964.
Silver, James W. *Edmund Pendleton Gaines: Frontier General*. Baton Rouge: Louisiana State University Press, 1949.
Steffen, Jerome O. *William Clark: Jeffersonian Man on the Frontier*. Norman: University of Oklahoma Press, 1977.
Stevens, Hazard. *The Life of Isaac Ingalls Stevens*. 2 vols. Boston: Houghton, Mifflin, 1900.
Stewart, George R. *John Phoenix, Esq., the Veritable Squibob: A Life of Captain George H. Derby, U.S.A.* New York: H. Holt, 1937.
Sully, Langdon. *No Tears for the General: The Life of Alfred Sully, 1821-1879*. Palo Alto, Calif.: American West, 1974.
Taylor, Emerson G. *Gouverneur Kemble Warren: The Life and Letters of an American Soldier, 1830-1882*. Boston: Houghton, Mifflin, 1932.
Vandiver, Frank E. *Ploughshares into Swords: Josiah Gorgas and Confederate Ordnance*. Austin: University of Texas Press, 1952.
Wallace, Edward S. *General William Jenkins Worth: Monterrey's Forgotten Hero*. Dallas: Southern Methodist University Press, 1953.
Weigley, Russell F. *Quartermaster General of the Union Army: A Biography of M. C. Meigs*. New York: Columbia University Press, 1959.
Weiss, Harry B., and Grace M. Ziegler. *Colonel Erkuries Beatty, 1759-1823: Pennsylvania Revolutionary Soldier; New Jersey Judge, Senator, Farmer, and Prominent Citizen of Princeton*. Trenton, N.J.: Past Times Press, 1958.

Whaley, Elizabeth J. *Forgotten Hero: General James B. McPherson: The Biography of a Civil War General.* New York: Exposition Press, 1955.
Wildes, Harry E. *Anthony Wayne: Trouble Shooter of the American Revolution.* New York: Harcourt, Brace, 1941.
Williams, T. Harry. *P. G. T. Beauregard: Napoleon in Gray.* Baton Rouge: Louisiana State University Press, 1954.
Wiltse, Charles M. *John C. Calhoun.* 3 vols. Indianapolis: Bobbs-Merrill, 1944-1951.
Wood, Richard G. *Stephen Harriman Long, 1784-1864: Army Engineer, Explorer, Inventor.* Glendale, Calif.: Arthur H. Clark, 1966.
Woodward, Ashbel. *Life of General Nathaniel Lyon.* Hartford, Conn.: Case, Lockwood, 1862.
Young, Otis E. *The West of Philip St. George Cooke, 1809-1895.* Glendale, Calif.: Arthur H. Clark, 1955.

General Books

Abernethy, Thomas P. *The Burr Conspiracy.* New York: Oxford University Press, 1954.
Adams, Henry. *History of the United States during the Administrations of Thomas Jefferson and James Madison.* 9 vols. New York: C. Scribner's Sons, 1909-1911.
Ambrose, Stephen E. *Duty, Honor, Country: A History of West Point.* Baltimore: Johns Hopkins University Press, 1966.
Bauer, K. Jack. *The Mexican War, 1846-1848.* New York: Macmillan, 1974.
Bearss, Ed, and Arrell M. Gibson. *Fort Smith: Little Gibralter on the Arkansas.* Norman: University of Oklahoma Press, 1969.
Birkhimer, William E. *Historical Sketch of the Organization, Administration, Materiel and Tactics of the Artillery, United States Army.* Washington, D.C.: J. J. Chapman, 1884.
_____. *The Law of Appointment and Promotion in the Regular Army of the United States.* New York: A. G. Sherwood, 1880.
Brown, Charles H. *Agents of Manifest Destiny: The Lives and Times of the Filibusters.* Chapel Hill: University of North Carolina Press, 1980.
Brown, Harvey E. *The Medical Department of the United States Army from 1775 to 1873.* Washington, D.C.: Surgeon General's Office, 1873.
Browning, Robert S. *Two If by Sea: The Development of American Coastal Defense Policy.* Westport, Conn.: Greenwood Press, 1983.
Centennial of the United States Military Academy at West Point, New York, 1802-1902. 2 vols. Washington, D.C., 1904.
Coakley, Robert W. *The Role of Federal Military Forces in Domestic Disorders, 1789-1878.* Washington, D.C.: Government Printing Office, 1988.
Coffman, Edward M. *The Old Army: A Portrait of the American Army in Peacetime, 1784-1898.* New York: Oxford University Press, 1986.
Corey, Albert B. *The Crisis of 1830-42 in Canadian-American Relations.* New Haven, Conn.: Yale University Press, 1941.
Cox, Isaac J. *The West Florida Controversy, 1798-1813: A Study in American Diplomacy.* Baltimore: Johns Hopkins University Press, 1918.
Crackel, Theodore J. *Mr. Jefferson's Army: Political and Social Reform of the Military Establishment, 1801-1809.* New York: New York University Press, 1987.
Cullum, George W. *Campaigns of the War of 1812-15, against Great Britain, Sketched and Criticised; with Brief Biographies of the American Engineers.* New York: J. Miller, 1879.
Cunliffe, Marcus. *Soldiers & Civilians: The Martial Spirit in America, 1775-1865.* Boston: Little, Brown, 1968.

Duffy, Christopher. *The Military Experience in the Age of Reason.* New York: Atheneum, 1988.
Ekirch, Arthur A., Jr. *The Civilian and the Military.* New York: Oxford University Press, 1956.
Emmett, Chris. *Fort Union and the Winning of the Southwest.* Norman: University of Oklahoma Press, 1965.
Foley, William E. *A History of Missouri.* 3 vols. Columbia: University of Missouri Press, 1971–1973.
Foreman, Grant. *Advancing the Frontier, 1830–1860.* Norman: University of Oklahoma Press, 1933.
Forman, Sidney. *West Point: A History of the United States Military Academy.* New York: Columbia University Press, 1950.
Furniss, Norman F. *The Mormon Conflict, 1850–1859.* New Haven, Conn.: Yale University Press, 1960.
Gillett, Mary C. *The Army Medical Department, 1775–1818.* Washington, D.C.: Government Printing Office, 1981.
———. *The Army Medical Department, 1818–1865.* Washington, D.C.: Government Printing Office, 1987.
Goetzmann, William H. *Army Exploration in the American West, 1803–1863.* New Haven, Conn.: Yale University Press, 1959.
Griffith, Paddy. *Military Thought in the French Army, 1815–51.* Manchester, England: Manchester University Press, 1989.
Grivas, Theodore. *Military Governments in California, 1846–1850; with a Chapter on Their Prior Use in Louisiana, Florida, and New Mexico.* Glendale, Calif.: Arthur H. Clark, 1963.
Hagan, Kenneth J., and William R. Roberts, eds. *Against All Enemies: Interpretations of American Military History from Colonial Times to the Present.* New York and Westport, Conn.: Greenwood Press, 1986.
Hagerman, Edward. *The American Civil War and the Origins of Modern Warfare: Ideas, Organization, and Field Command.* Bloomington: Indiana University Press, 1988.
Hill, Forest G. *Roads, Rails & Waterways: The Army Engineers and Early Transportation.* Norman: University of Oklahoma Press, 1957.
Huntington, Samuel P. *The Soldier and the State: The Theory and Politics of Civil-Military Relations.* Cambridge: Harvard University Press, 1957.
Jackson, W. Turrentine. *Wagon Roads West: A Study of Federal Road Surveys and Construction in the Trans-Mississippi West, 1846–1869.* New Haven, Conn.: Yale University Press, 1965.
Jacobs, James R. *The Beginning of the U.S. Army, 1783–1812.* Princeton, N.J.: Princeton University Press, 1947.
Janowitz, Morris. *The Professional Soldier: A Social and Political Portrait.* New York: Free Press, 1960.
Johannsen, Robert W. *To the Halls of the Montezumas: The Mexican War in the American Imagination.* New York: Oxford University Press, 1985.
Jones, Evan. *Citadel in the Wilderness: The Story of Fort Snelling and the Old Northwest Frontier.* New York: Coward-McCann, 1966.
Karsten, Peter. *The Naval Aristocracy: The Golden Age of Annapolis and the Emergence of Modern Navalism.* New York: Free Press, 1972.
Kett, Joseph F. *The Formation of the American Medical Profession: The Role of Institutions, 1780–1860.* New Haven, Conn.: Yale University Press, 1968.

Kohn, Richard H. *Eagle and Sword: The Federalists and the Creation of the Military Establishment in America, 1783-1802.* New York: Free Press, 1975.
McCabe, James O. *The San Juan Island Water Question.* Toronto: University of Toronto Press, 1965.
McKee, Christopher. *A Gentlemanly and Honorable Profession: The Creation of the U.S. Naval Officer Corps, 1794-1815.* Annapolis, Md.: Naval Institute Press, 1991.
McWhiney, Grady. *Southerners and Other Americans.* New York: Basic Books, 1973.
Mahan, Bruce E. *Old Fort Crawford and the Frontier.* Iowa City: State Historical Society of Iowa, 1926.
Mahon, John K. *History of the Second Seminole War, 1835-1842.* Gainesville: University of Florida Press, 1967.
_____. *The War of 1812.* Gainesville: University of Florida Press, 1972.
Millett, Allan R. *The American Political System and Civilian Control of the Military: A Historical Perspective.* Columbus: Mershon Center of the Ohio State University, 1979.
_____. *Military Professionalism and Officership in America.* Columbus: Mershon Center of the Ohio State University, 1977.
Morrison, James L., Jr. *"The Best School in the World:" West Point, the Pre-Civil War Years, 1833-1866.* Kent, Ohio: Kent State University Press, 1986.
North, Diane M. T. *Samuel Peter Heintzelman and the Sonora Exploring and Mining Company.* Tucson: University of Arizona Press, 1980.
Norton, Herman A. *Struggling for Recognition: The United States Army Chaplaincy, 1791-1865.* Washington, D.C.: Office of the Chief of Chaplains, 1977.
Patrick, Rembert W. *Florida Fiasco: Rampant Rebels on the Georgia-Florida Border, 1810-1815.* Athens: University of Georgia Press, 1954.
Prucha, Francis Paul. *Broadax and Bayonet: The Role of the United States Army in the Development of the Northwest, 1815-1860.* Madison: State Historical Society of Wisconsin, 1953.
_____. *The Sword of the Republic: The United States Army on the Frontier, 1783-1846.* New York: Macmillan, 1969.
Risch, Erna. *Quartermaster Support of the Army: A History of the Corps, 1775-1939.* Washington, D.C.: Office of the Quartermaster General, 1962.
Robinson, Willard B. *American Forts: Architectural Form and Function.* Urbana: University of Illinois Press, 1977.
Royster, Charles. *A Revolutionary People at War: The Continental Army and American Character, 1775-1783.* Chapel Hill: University of North Carolina Presss, 1979.
Shy, John. *Toward Lexington: The Role of the British Army in the Coming of the American Revolution.* Princeton, N.J.: Princeton University Press, 1965.
Smith, Justin H. *The War with Mexico.* 2 vols. New York: Macmillan, 1919.
Smith, Merritt Roe, ed. *Military Enterprise and Technological Change: Perspectives on the American Experience.* Cambridge: Massachusetts Institute of Technology, 1985.
Stagg, J. C. A. *Mr. Madison's War: Politics, Diplomacy, and Warfare in the Early American Republic, 1783-1830.* Princeton, N.J.: Princeton University Press, 1983.
Sword, Wiley. *President Washington's Indian War: The Struggle for the Old Northwest, 1790-1795.* Norman: University of Oklahoma Press, 1985.
Utley, Robert M. *Frontiersmen in Blue: The United States Army and the Indian, 1848-1865.* New York: Macmillan, 1967.
Ward, Harry M. *The Department of War, 1781-1795.* Pittsburgh: University of Pittsburgh Press, 1962.

Weigley, Russell F. *The American Way of War: A History of United States Military Strategy and Policy.* New York: Macmillan, 1973.
———. *History of the United States Army.* New York: Macmillan, 1967.
———. *Towards an American Army: Military Thought from Washington to Marshall.* New York: Columbia University Press, 1962.
White, Leonard D. *The Jacksonians: A Study in Administrative History, 1829-1861.* New York: Macmillan, 1954.
———. *The Jeffersonians: A Study in Administrative History, 1801-1829.* New York: Macmillan, 1951.

Articles

Backus, Emma. "Cornelius Sedam and His Friends in Washington's Time." *Ohio State Archeological and Historical Society Publications* 41 (January 1932):28-50.
Bald, F. Clever. "Colonel John Francis Hamtramck." *Indiana Magazine of History* 44 (December 1948):335-354.
Bernath, Stuart L. "George Washington and the Genesis of American Military Discipline." *Mid-America* 49 (April 1967):83-100.
Caldwell, Norman W. "The Frontier Army Officer, 1794-1814." *Mid-America* 37 (January 1955):101-128.
Coffman, Edward M. "The Army Officer and the Constitution." *Parameters* 17 (September 1987):2-12.
Ewy, Marvin. "The United States Army in the Kansas Border Troubles, 1855-1856." *Kansas Historical Quarterly* 32 (Winter 1966):385-400.
Falk, Stanley L. "Artillery for the Land Service: The Development of a System." *Military Affairs* 28 (1964):97-110.
Floyd, Dale E. "U.S. Army Officers in Europe, 1815-1861." David H. White and John W. Gordon, eds., *Proceedings of the Citadel Conference on War and Diplomacy, 1977,* 26-30. N.p., 1979.
Foreman, Carolyn T. "General Bennet Riley: Commandant of Fort Gibson and Governor of California." *Chronicles of Oklahoma* 19 (June 1941):225-244.
Forman, Sidney. "The United States Military Philosophical Society, 1802-1813." *William and Mary Quarterly,* 3d ser. 2 (July 1945):273-285.
Gardner, Asa B. "Henry Burbeck, Brevet Brigadier-General United States Army—Founder of the United States Military Academy." *Magazine of American History* 9 (1883):251-265.
Gough, Robert. "Officering the American Army, 1798." *William and Mary Quarterly,* 3d ser. 43 (July 1986):460-471.
Hall, Virginius C. "Richard Allison, Surgeon to the Legion." *Bulletin of the Historical and Philosophical Society of Ohio* 9 (1951):283-298.
Hare, John S. "Military Punishments in the War of 1812." *Journal of the American Military Institute* 4 (Winter 1940):225-239.
Hay, Thomas R. "General James Wilkinson—The Last Phase." *Louisiana Historical Quarterly* 19 (April 1936):407-435.
Jordan, Philip D. "George W. Patten: Poet Laureate of the Army." *Journal of the American Military Institute* 4 (Fall 1940):162-167.
Katzenberger, George A. "Major David Ziegler." *Ohio State Archeological and Historical Quarterly* 21 (April-July 1912):127-174.
Knopf, Richard C. "Crime and Punishment in the American Legion, 1792-1793." *Bulletin of the Historical and Philosophical Society of Ohio* 14 (July 1956):232-238.

Kohn, Richard H. "General Wilkinson's Vendetta with General Wayne: Politics and Command in the American Army, 1791–1796." *Filson Club History Quarterly* 45 (October 1971):361–372.

Lee, William. "Record of the Services of Constant Freeman, Captain of Artillery in the Continental Army." *Magazine of American History* 2 (June 1878):349–360.

Maurer, Maurer. "Military Justice under General Washington." *Military Affairs* 28 (1964):8–16.

Morgan, James D. "Robert Brent, First Mayor of Washington City." *Records of the Columbia Historical Society* 2(1899):236–251.

Morrison, James L., Jr. "Educating the Civil War Generals: West Point, 1833–1861." *Military Affairs* 38 (October 1974):108–111.

Nelson, Harold L. "Military Roads for War and Peace, 1791–1836." *Military Affairs* 19 (Spring 1955):1–14.

Nichols, Roger L. "The Army and the Indians 1800–1830—A Reappraisal: The Missouri Valley Example." *Pacific Historical Review* 41 (May 1972):151–168.

Prucha, Francis Paul. "The United States Army as Viewed by British Travelers, 1825–1860." *Military Affairs* 17 (Fall 1953):113–124.

Shearer, Ernest C. "The Carvajal Disturbances." *Southwestern Historical Quarterly* 55 (October 1951):201–230.

Skelton, William B. "Army Officers' Attitudes towards Indians, 1830–1860." *Pacific Northwest Quarterly* 67 (July 1976):113–124.

———. "The Commanding General and the Problem of Command in the United States Army, 1821–1841." *Military Affairs* 34 (December 1970):117–122.

———. "Officers and Politicians: The Origins of Army Politics in the United States before the Civil War." *Armed Forces and Society* 6 (Fall 1979):22–48.

———. "Professionalization in the U.S. Army Officer Corps during the Age of Jackson." *Armed Forces and Society* 1 (Summer 1975): 443–471.

———. "Social Roots of the American Military Profession: The Officer Corps of America's First Peacetime Army, 1784–1789." *Journal of Military History* 54 (October 1990):435–452.

Spiller, Roger J. "Calhoun's Expansible Army: The History of a Military Idea." *South Atlantic Quarterly* 79 (Spring 1980):189–203.

Thomas, Samuel W. "George Croghan (1791–1849): A Study of the Non-Military Life of the Inspector General of the United States Army." *Filson Club History Quarterly* 41 (October 1967):304–322.

Thompson, Jerry D. "Henry Hopkins Sibley: Military Inventor on the Texas Frontier." *Military History of Texas and the Southwest* 10 (1972):227–247.

Vargas, Mark A. "The Military Justice System and the Use of Illegal Punishments as Causes of Desertion in the U.S. Army, 1821–1835." *Journal of Military History* 55 (January 1991):1–19.

Wade, Arthur P. "A Military Offspring of the American Philosophical Society." *Military Affairs* 38 (October 1974):103–107.

Warren, Joseph P. "The Confederation and the Shays Rebellion." *American Historical Review* 11 (October 1905):42–67.

Webb, Stephen S. "Army and Empire: English Garrison Government in Britain and America, 1569–1763." *William and Mary Quarterly* 3d ser. 34 (January 1977):1–31.

Wiggins, Sarah W. "Josiah Gorgas, a Victorian Father." *Civil War History* 32 (September 1986):229–246.

Wik, Reynold M. "Captain Nathaniel Wyche Hunter and the Florida Indian Campaigns, 1837–1841." *Florida Historical Quarterly* 39 (July 1960):62–75.

Wilkinson, Norman B. "The Forgotten 'Founder' of West Point." *Military Affairs* 24 (Winter 1960–1961):177–188.

Young, Tommy R., II. "The United States Army and the Institution of Slavery in Louisiana, 1803–1835." *Louisiana Studies* 13 (Fall 1974):201–222.

Dissertations and Theses

Adams, Francis R., Jr., ed. "An Annotated Edition of the Personal Letters of Robert E. Lee, April 1855–April 1861." Ph.D. diss., University of Maryland, 1955.

Adams, George R. "General William Selby Harney: Frontier Soldier, 1800–1889." Ph.D. diss., University of Arizona, 1983.

Berlin, Robert H. "The Administration of Military Justice in the Continental Army during the American Revolution, 1775–1783." Ph.D. diss., University of California, Santa Barbara, 1976.

Falk, Stanley L. "Soldier-Technologist: Major Alfred Mordecai and the Beginnings of Science in the United States Army." Ph.D. diss., Georgetown University, 1959.

Gamble, Richard D. "Garrison Life at Frontier Military Posts, 1830–1860." Ph.D. diss., University of Oklahoma, 1956.

Graham, Stanley S. "Life of the Enlisted Soldier on the Western Frontier, 1815–1845." Ph.D. diss., North Texas State University, 1972.

Griess, Thomas E. "Dennis Hart Mahan: West Point Professor and Advocate of Military Professionalism, 1830–1871." Ph.D. diss., Duke University, 1968.

Hinton, Harwood P. "The Military Career of John Ellis Wool, 1812–1863." Ph.D. diss., University of Wisconsin, 1960.

Hruby, Dale E. "The Civilian Careers of West Point Graduates: Classes of 1802–1833." M.A. thesis, Columbia University, 1965.

Huber, John P. "General Josiah Harmar's Command: Military Policy in the Old Northwest, 1784–1791." Ph.D. diss., University of Michigan, 1968.

Jamieson, Perry D. "The Development of Civil War Tactics." Ph.D. diss., Wayne State University, 1979.

Kershner, James W. "Sylvanus Thayer: A Biography." Ph.D. diss., West Virginia University, 1976.

Molloy, Peter M. "Technical Education and the Young Republic: West Point as America's École Polytechnique, 1802–1833." Ph.D. diss., Brown University, 1975.

O'Connell, Charles F., Jr. "The United States Army and the Origins of Modern Management, 1818–1860." Ph.D. diss., Ohio State University, 1982.

Ryan, Garry D. "War Department Topographical Bureau, 1831–1863: An Administrative History." Ph.D. diss., American University, 1968.

Settles, Thomas M. "The Military Career of John Bankhead Magruder." Ph.D. diss., Texas Christian University, 1972.

Skelton, William B. "The United States Army, 1821–1837: An Institutional History." Ph.D. diss., Northwestern University, 1968.

Sunseri, Alvin R. "New Mexico in the Aftermath of the Anglo-American Conquest, 1846–1861." Ph.D. diss., Louisiana State University, 1973.

Veatch, Matthew B. "The Education of a Staff Officer: The Life and Career of Samuel Cooper, 1798–1852." M.A. thesis, University of Missouri–Kansas City, 1989.

Wade, Arthur P. "Artillerists and Engineers: The Beginnings of American Seacoast Fortification, 1794–1815." Ph.D. diss., Kansas State University, 1977.

Young, Tommy R., II. "The United States Army in the South, 1789–1835." Ph.D. diss., Louisiana State University, 1973.

INDEX

Abert, John J., 315
Adams, Henry, 9
Adams, John, 7, 95, 96, 98; and officers' appointments, 23–25, 26
Adams, John Quincy, 132, 235, 284, 289
Adjutant and inspector general, 6, 8, 9, 120–121
Adjutant General's Office, 120, 131–132, 193, 232, 289; duties of officers of, 223–225
Aisquith, William A., 265
Alexander, Edward P., 357
Alien and Sedition Acts, 23, 80
Allen, James, 308
Alvord, Benjamin, 198, 287
American Fur Company, 299
American Legion, 5–6, 16, 17, 19, 35, 39, 51–52, 54, 55–56, 61, 62, 94, 267–268; Anthony Wayne's reform of, 90–93
American Philosophical Society, 99, 103
Anderson, Eliza, 209–210
Anderson, Robert, 209–210, 340–341; and military asylums, 264, 294
Andrews, Joseph G., 18, 41–42
Appointments, officers'. *See* Officers: appointment of, to army
Arbuckle, Mathew, 201, 314
Archer, James J., 186, 319, 353–354
Archer, Samuel B., 249
Armistead, Frank S., 165
Armistead, Lewis A., 321–322
Armistead, Walker K., 44, 199
Armstrong, Francis W., 37
Armstrong, John (Confederation era officer), 45, 64, 71
Armstrong, John (War of 1812 general and secretary of war), 27, 122
Army: dispersion of, 39–41, 184, 248–249; as frontier constabulary, 68–72, 76–86, 186, 297–304, 313–325, 332–338, 352–353; functions of, 3–11, 127–129, 131–136; military justice system of, 57–59, 195, 261, 265–281 (*see also* Rules and Articles of War); organization and strength of, 4–11, 131–136, 184; origins of, 4; reductions of, 4–11, 61–63, 126–128, 131, 134, 135, 212, 288–289; reform of, after War of 1812, 109–130; role of, in civil works, 132, 222, 228–230. *See also* American Legion; Artillery; Enlisted men; General Staff; Infantry; Military posts; Mounted troops; Officers
Army, geographical departments of, 131, 135; Department of Oregon, 335; Department of the Pacific, 201, 227, 315, 337; Department of Texas, 215, 357; Western Department, 314
Army and Navy Chronicle, 187, 189, 190, 205, 238, 254, 256, 285, 320, 329; as a professional military journal, 257
Army and Navy Chronicle and Scientific Repository, 205
Arnold, Benjamin, 280
Articles of Confederation, 3, 13, 48
Articles of War. *See* Rules and Articles of War
Artillerists and Engineers, Corps of, 6, 7, 10–11, 16, 19, 37, 52, 54, 98, 239; and early professional education, 93–95
Artillerists and Engineers, Second Regiment of, 7, 23
Artillery, 26, 40, 101, 137, 222, 240, 291, 292; conflict of, with Ordnance Department, 234, 236, 291–292; formation of light batteries of, 252; geographical distribution of officers in, 156–157; political action by, 291–292; promotion in, 193
Artillery, units of: First Regiment, 349; Second Regiment, 289; Third Regiment, 156, 252, 292; Fourth Regiment, 215, 253; Corps of Artillery, 128; Regiment of Artillerists, 26, 77, 98; Regiment of Light Artil-

469

Artillery, units of, *continued*
  lery, 128, 263. *See also* Artillerists and Engineers, Corps of; Artillerists and Engineers, Second Regiment of
Artillery School of Practice. *See* Schools of practice: artillery school
Association of the United States Army, 103
Atherton, Charles G., 294
Atkinson, Henry, 285, 314
Aurora, 45
Averell, William W., 263

Baker, Rufus L., 226–227
Balch, George T., 165
Ballentine, George, 275
Bankhead, James, 329
Barbour, James, 139, 250
Battles: Buena Vista, 176, 211, 252, 342, 343; Chapultepec, 145, 343; Chippewa, 114; Churubusco, 345; Contreras, 343, 345; Fallen Timbers, 5–6, 41, 51, 79, 92; Fort Brown, 345; Fort Erie, 111, 114; Fort McHenry, 244; Gettysburg, 220; Harmar's defeat, 5; Lundy's Lane, 113, 114; Monterrey, 176, 343; New Orleans, 85, 114, 211; Palo Alto, 176, 238, 341, 343, 345; Plattsburgh, 114, 115; Queenstown, 112; Resaca de la Palma, 341, 342, 345; St. Clair's defeat, 5, 17, 32, 35, 90; Solferino, 241; Tippecanoe, 60, 63; Vera Cruz, 342, 345; Waterloo, 115, 345
Bayard, George D., 175, 188
Beall, William D., 37
Beall family, 164
Beard, William C., 66
Beatty, Erkuries, 15, 69, 70
Beaumont, William, 57, 201
Beauregard, Pierre G. T., 163, 337
Beebe, Ebenezer, 74
Bell, John, 144
Bell, John R., 187–188
Belton, Francis S., 351
Bemrose, John, 263
Benham, Henry W., 290
Benjamin, Calvin, 343
Benton, Thomas Hart, 145, 289, 294
Bernard, Simon, 125, 239, 249
Beverlee, Catherine, 85
Bissell, Daniel, 35, 74, 78, 81, 82
Black Hawk War (1832), 132, 133, 143, 210, 251, 314, 319
Blount, John G., 31, 50
Blount, William A., 31
Board of Engineers, 125, 243
Board of Navy Commissioners, 360–361
Bogardus, Robert, 31

Bomford, George, 226, 264
Bootes, Levi C., 274
Boston Massacre, 70
Bowie, James J., 31
Bowyer, John, 62, 79
Bradford, James A. J., 198
Bradfute, William R., 272–273
Brady, Hugh, 213–214, 336
Bragg, Braxton, 287, 291–292, 351
Brent, Robert, 45
Brevet rank, 194–195, 200–201, 344–345
British army. *See* Great Britain, army of
Brooks, John, 17
Brown, Harvey, 263
Brown, Jacob J., 39, 61, 110, 251, 283–284, 289, 294; on foreign threat, 328; reports on reduction of army, 126
Bruff, James, 73
Buchanan, James, 286, 289, 302, 335, 353
Buchanan, Robert C., 235, 317
Buell, Don Carlos, 272
Buell, John H., 56
Buell, Joseph, 267
Bugeaud, Thomas-Robert, 240–241
Burbeck, Henry, 35, 62
Burgwin, John H. K., 274
Burr, Aaron, 8, 78, 80–82, 111
Burr conspiracy, 8, 80–82, 83, 335

Cadets: appointment of, 25–26, 137–142; origins of rank of, 25–26. *See also* United States Military Academy
Cadre plan (for expanding the army), 104, 126–129, 134, 135, 210, 246, 326
Calhoun, John C., 131, 169, 232, 249, 284; appointed secretary of war, 117; cadre plan of, 126–129; and military reform after the War of 1812, 109, 117, 120–128; and officers' appointments, 138–139
Campbell, Reuben P., 238
Camp of instruction (1839), 252–253
Carleton, James H., 272, 308, 310, 317
Carmichael, John F., 79
Caroline (steamboat), 335–336
Carvajal, Jose Maria Jesus, 337
Casey, John C., 195–196
Casey, Thomas L., 164
Cass, Lewis, 294, 311; on national defense, 244–245
Cass, Lewis, Jr., 146
Cavalry. *See* Mounted troops
Chamberlain, Samuel E., 274, 275
Chambers, Talbot, 299
Chandler, John, 27
Chaplains, 185, 230–232
Chapman, William, 303–304

Charles, archduke of Austria, 247
Chase, William H., 264
Chesapeake, U.S.S., 9, 26, 60, 82, 87, 111
Chilton, Robert H., 190, 276–277, 351
Churchill, Sylvester, 231, 322
Civil commandants, 77–78
Civil-military tensions. *See* Officers: and civil-military tensions
Civil War, 170, 172, 248, 254, 266, 297, 303, 318, 348, 359; army officer corps in, 361; former officers' service in, 220, 361; impact of, on promotion rates, 197–198; officers' deaths in, 214, 338; and officers' retirements, 215–216. *See also* Officers: and sectional controversy
Civil works, army role in, 132, 222, 228–230, 292, 294
Claiborne, Ferdinand L., 66
Claiborne, Thomas, 264, 273
Claiborne, William C. C., 77
Clark, George Rogers, 19
Clark, Jonathan, 19
Clark, William, 19, 209
Clarke, Henry, 270–271
Clarke, Patrick, 270
Clinch, Duncan L., 199, 201, 209, 211, 263, 285
Clitz, Henry B., 165
Clitz, John, 189
Coast Survey Office, 293
Cobb, Howell, 65
Coffman, Edward M., xii, 205
Coles, Isaac A., 60
Collins, Francis, 295
Commanding general, 257, 289, 290, 291, 305; attacks staff independence, 233; functions of, 131; origins of office of, 131. *See also* Brown, Jacob J.; Macomb, Alexander; Scott, Winfield
Comstock, Cyrus B., 179
Confederate army, 181, 214, 215, 220, 266, 354–358, 361
Confederation Congress, 4, 13, 69, 70, 71, 94. *See also* Continental Congress
Congress, U.S., 291, 292, 293; and army legislation, 6–10, 48, 61, 63, 82, 90, 98, 101, 102, 117, 122, 128, 131–135, 139, 148, 192, 194, 231, 244, 268, 269, 293, 296–297; former officers serve in, 219; influence of, on officers' appointments, 27–29, 50, 139–140, 143, 154–158, 296; officers' opinion of, 285–286, 341, 354. *See also* Confederation Congress; Continental Congress; Officers: and politics
Constant, Joseph, 30
Constitution, U.S., 5, 6, 16, 71, 87, 144, 148, 171, 289, 361; officers support ratification of, 69; three-fifths clause of, as factor in officers' appointments, 154–155
Constitutional Union party, 353
Continental Army, 4, 5, 7, 13, 14, 15–16, 17, 20, 22, 24, 38, 39, 62, 93, 161, 221, 266, 267; alienation of, from civil society, 69; honor in, 53; as model for the American Legion, 90, 92; officer–enlisted man relations in, 261; promotion in, 47–48, 50
Continental Congress, 4, 13, 22, 31, 261. *See also* Confederation Congress
Cooke, John R., 165
Cooke, Philip St. George, 238–239, 255, 285, 307, 309
Cooper, William L., 80
Corps du Genie (French military engineers). *See* France, army of: Corps du Genie of
Corps of Artillerists and Engineers. *See* Artillerists and Engineers, Corps of
Corps of Engineers. *See* Engineers, Corps of
Corps of Topographical Engineers. *See* Topographical Engineers, Corps of
Courts-martial. *See* Army: military justice system of; Enlisted men: courts-martial of *and* punishment of; Officers: courts-martial of; Rules and Articles of War
Crackel, Theodore J., 99
Crawford, William H., 29, 126, 128
Creek War (1836), 132, 211, 308, 314
Crimean War, 241, 245–246
Crittenden, John J., 145, 294, 358
Crittenden, William L., 336–337
Croghan, George, 209
Crook, George, 324
Cross, Joseph, 82–83
Cross, Osborne, 270
Cross, Trueman, 214
Crozet, Claude, 239, 249
Cullum, George W., 217, 286, 293
Cumming, Alfred, 302
Cunliffe, Marcus, xii, 163
Cunningham, Noble, Jr., 61
Cushing, Caleb, 198
Cushing, Thomas H., 35, 42, 62–63, 67, 110
Cutler, Enos, 298

Dalliba, James, 178
Dana, James J., 165
Daniel, John M., 45
Daniels, Charles B., 270
Davis, Jefferson, 219, 230, 241, 269, 294, 338, 352; and officers' appointments, 146, 157
Day, Hannibal, 316
Dayton, Horatio R., 18

Dearborn, Henry, 27, 46, 73, 77, 98, 101; and officers' appointments, 25–29, 151
Delafield, Richard, 162, 241, 246
Deming, Fenn, 54
Democratic party, 134, 284, 287, 295; officers' allegiances to, 295–297, 353; and officers' appointments, 142–150; support of, for army legislation, 296
Democratic Republican party, 6–9, 18, 23, 66, 73, 87, 99, 102, 110, 115, 116, 233, 283; officers' allegiances to, 74–76; and officers' appointments, 25–33
Denny, Ebenezer, 60, 64
Department of War. *See* War Department
Desertion, 41, 265–269, 280
Desha, Robert, 31
Detached service, 222–223, 234, 290
Dillon, Edward, 166
Dix, John Adams, 284
Dix, Roger S., 342
Dodge, Henry, 143
Doubleday, Abner, 353
Doughty, John, 16, 69
Dragoons. *See* Mounted troops
Drayton, William, 30–31
Drum, Simon H., 343
Drysdale, John, 146
Duane, William, 41, 44, 45, 76, 121
DuBois, John Van Deusen, 286, 308, 324
Dueling. *See* Officers: dueling by
Duncan, James, 252, 277, 351
Dunham, Josiah, 37, 78
Dutch army, 88–89

Eastman, Seth, 189, 311–312; paintings by, 176, 208, 245, 312, 313
Eaton, William, 65
École du Genie. *See* France, army of: military school system of
École Polytechnique. *See* France, army of: military school system of
Ellis, Joseph, 175
Elzey, Arnold, 188
Embargo Act, army enforcement of, 8, 27, 82–83, 332
Emerson, John, 350
Engineers, Corps of, 8, 26, 42–43, 74, 93, 111, 120, 132, 133, 134, 137, 172, 232, 240, 264, 291, 294, 361; duties of, 101, 225–226, 228–229; and formation of U.S. Military Academy, 98–105; geographical distribution of officers of, 158; political activities of, 102–103, 292–293; and seacoast fortification system, 103–104, 125–126, 225–226, 243–246, 292–293; and strategic thought, 243–247; tensions of, with other branches, 101, 104–105, 232, 233, 234, 235, 236, 292–293; and West Point curriculum, 168–170, 172. *See also* Artillerists and Engineers, Corps of
Enlisted men: appointment of, to officer corps, 14, 17, 20, 25, 31–32, 33, 147–150, 160–161, 261; conflict of, with officers, 273–281; courts-martial of, 263–264, 269–271, 273, 275–279; exploitation of, by officers, 46; on officers, 274–276; punishment of, 84, 261, 267–281, 299; social backgrounds of, 150, 261–262; social gap between officers and, 149–150, 260–265, 273–276, 280–281
Eustis, Abraham, 201, 234, 287, 288–289, 321
Eustis, William, 56, 59, 151; and officers' appointments, 26, 29, 151–152
Evans, George, 289
Expansible army plan. *See* Cadre plan

Faust, Jacob J., 60
Fay, Heman A., 46
Federalist party, 6, 7, 9, 25, 26, 27, 29, 50, 66, 76, 80, 83, 85, 87, 92, 94, 95, 96, 99, 104, 140, 267, 283; collapse of, 116; officers' allegiances to, 72–74; and officers' appointments, 16–25
Fenwick, John R., 162, 201, 263
Filibustering, army involvement with, 80–82, 83–84, 135, 333–338
Fillmore, Millard, 337
Finney, Walter, 72
Fish, Hamilton, 290
Fitch, Benjamin, 265
Flewellen, James P., 290
Flogging. *See* Enlisted men: punishment of
Floridas, Spanish, army involvement in, 83–84, 329, 333–334
Foggerty, Private, 279–280
Folard, Jean-Charles, Chevalier de, 92
Folsom, Joseph L., 201
Ford, Mahlon, 15
Forsyth, Benjamin, 52–53
Forts. *See* Military posts; Seacoast fortifications
France, army of, 89; Corps du Genie (military engineers) of, 100, 102, 105; military school system of, 93, 97, 102, 115, 123, 168, 240–241, 249–250; as model for U.S. Army, 97, 100–101, 115, 121, 123, 168, 239–243, 249–250, 254–255, 258–259
Franklin, Benjamin, 99
Frederick the Great, 121
Freeman, Constant, 35, 62, 67, 77
Frémont, John C., 292, 301, 334, 335, 353
French army. *See* France, army of

Fries's Rebellion (1799), 80
Frothingham, Peter, 42
Frye, Frederick, 56
Fuller, John, 76
Fulton, Robert, 103

Gadsden, James, 289
Gaines, Edmund P., 37, 79, 81, 110, 114, 233, 333, 335; career of, 111; on defense policy, 126, 144, 244–245; on European influence on U.S. Army, 240; and Indians, 314, 315; on military punishments, 269; on officers and politics, 285; portrait of, 112; quarrel of, with Winfield Scott, 200; and Texan Revolution, 334
Gaither, Edgar, 280
Gansevoort, Peter, 27
Gardenier, John R. B., 347
Gardner, William M., 190, 204, 331, 345, 351
Garesché, Julius P., 207, 225
Garesché, Mariquitta, 207
Garland, John, 233–234
Garnett, Robert S., 315–316, 322
Garrison life. *See* Officers: garrison life of
Gatlin, Richard C., 165
General Regulations, 38–39, 90, 92, 97, 184, 200, 233, 249, 265; define officer–enlisted man relationship, 262–263; reform of, after War of 1812, 122
General Staff, 6–10, 42–43, 122, 131–132, 135, 212, 361, 362; attempted reform of, by Alexander Hamilton, 95–98; conflict of, with line branches, 101, 104–105, 232–237, 291–292; and duties of officers, 223–232; expansion of, during 1830s, 133–134; geographical distribution of officers of, 156–158; promotion into, 193–194, 198, 288; reform of, after War of 1812, 119–121; strength of, 221–223. *See also* Adjutant and inspector general; Adjutant General's Office; Engineers, Corps of; Inspectors general; Medical Department; Ordnance Department; Pay Department; Purchasing Department; Quartermaster Department; Topographical Engineers, Corps of
General Survey Act (1824), 229
Germany, army of, 362
Gerry, Elbridge, 276–277
Ghent, Peace of, 10, 61, 86, 115
Gillett, Mary C., 228
Gilmer, Jeremy F., 189–190
Gilpin, William, 346
Glisan, Rodney, 149–150, 318
Goetzler, Henry, 277
Goodwin, Horace, 278

Goodwin, Peter, 280
Gove, Jesse A., 202
Grant, Ulysses S., 175, 177; portrait of, 191
Grattan, John L., 346
Graves, Rufus, 37
Gray, Robert, 67
Great Britain, army of, 3, 39, 49, 57, 70, 87, 194, 233, 241, 261
Green, Charles, 270
Green, Platt R., 265
Greene, George S., 220
Griffith, Paddy, 258
Grosvenor, George H., 31
Guadalupe Hidalgo, Treaty of, 135, 146
Guibert, Jacques-Antoine de, 247
Guion, Isaac, 66, 85; as military governor of Natchez, 76–77
Gwynn, Walter, 219

Hagner, Peter V., 240
Hall, Dominick A., 86
Halleck, Henry W., 187, 300, 327; author of treatise on military science, 241, 246
Hamilton, Alexander, 7, 44, 85, 98, 99, 117, 121, 129; appointment of, to army, 23; and army reform during Quasi-war, 95–98, 121; and military punishments, 268; and officers' appointments, 24; proposes a military academy, 97, 98, 102; and suppression of Fries's Rebellion, 80
Hamilton, Charles S., 343
Hamilton, William S., 62
Hammond, Marcus C. M., 289
Hampton, Wade, 27, 56; portrait of, 28
Hamtramck, John F., 45, 49, 80; as civil administrator, 71; on dispersion of army, 40; and Indian relations, 72
Hancock, Almira, 207
Hancock, Winfield Scott, 207
Hardee, William J., 243, 255, 320
Harding, Edward, 271
Harmar, Josiah, 5, 46, 69, 70, 71, 72, 90, 306
Harney, William S., 188; and Indians, 317, 321, 322; and San Juan Island dispute, 334–335
Harrison, William Henry, 65, 282, 296
Hartford Convention, 116
Hartz, Edward L., 278–279, 339; cadet experience of, 142, 174
Hatch, John P., 352
Hazzard, George W., 187, 205
Heart, Jonathan, 15–16; drawing by, 40
Heintzelman, Samuel P., 201–202
Henry, William S., 331–332, 341
Henshaw, John C., 206

474 Index

Heth, Henry, 175, 188, 302
Heth, John, 17
Hetzel, Abner R., 201
Hildreth, James, 274, 275
Hill, Daniel H., 285
Hitchcock, Ethan Allen, 195, 201, 204, 295; on Indians, 310, 315, 323; on Mexican War, 330, 332, 341; on slavery, 350; and suppression of filibustering, 337
Holy Alliance, 126, 328
Hoops, Adam, 56
Hopkins, Henry, 46
House, James, 58, 234
Howard, Lewis, 54
Howard, Oliver Otis, 187
Howard, Robert V. W., 270-271
Howe, Marshall S., 271
Hughes, George W., 319
Humphrey, James P., 272
Hunt, Edward B., 246, 327
Hunt, Henry J., 238, 339, 351
Hunt, Thomas, 42
Hunt family, 164
Huntington, Samuel P., xii, 36

Indian Department, 79, 305, 314, 316
Indian removal, army role in, 132, 134, 210, 274, 314-315. *See also* Second Seminole War
Indian Trade and Intercourse Laws, 79, 186, 299-300, 305, 306, 313-314
Indian Tribes: Apache, 308, 324; Arikara, 309; California tribes, 311, 315, 317, 321, 324; Cherokee, 211, 310, 315, 325; Cheyenne, 319; Chippewa, 308; Choctaw, 314; Cocopa, 227; Coeur d'Alene, 346; Comanche, 319, 320, 322; Creek, 79, 315, 333 (*see also* Creek War); Delaware, 42; Lipan, 319; Maricopa, 310; Menomonie, 314; Mojave, 308, 321; Navajo, 212, 311, 316, 319, 322; Pawnee, 308, 310; Pelouze, 346; Pima, 310; Pueblo, 310; "Root-Digger," 311; Seminole, 273, 298, 309, 315, 322, 333 (*see also* Second Seminole War); Shawnee, 41; Sioux, 316, 319, 321, 346; Spokane, 346; Yuma, 227
Indian warfare: officers' views of, 255-256, 318-325, 339, 345-347; teaching of at West Point, 172, 306
Infantry, 26, 138, 291; geographical distribution of officers in, 156-157
Infantry, units of: First Regiment, 4, 13-16, 19, 34, 48, 51, 69, 70, 71, 156, 195, 261-262, 349; Second Regiment, 5, 16, 17, 19, 90, 204, 213, 349; Third Regiment, 20, 253; Fourth Regiment, 20, 253, 333, 349; Sixth Regiment, 57; Seventh Regiment, 349; Eighth Regiment, 133, 144; Ninth Regiment, 54; Tenth Regiment, 62; Forty-third Regiment, 62. *See also* Tactical manuals: infantry
Infantry School of Practice. *See* Schools of practice: infantry
Ingalls, Rufus, 317
Inspectors general, 97-98, 131, 132, 223, 233
Ives, Joseph C., 308
Izard, George, 18, 65

Jackson, Andrew, 110, 132, 133, 143, 166, 192, 217, 233, 244, 283, 285, 296, 334; attempted seizure of Florida by, 329, 333-334; and civil-military clash at New Orleans, 85-86; praises cadre plan, 129; restricts detached service, 217
Jackson, George W., 31
Janowitz, Morris, 34
Jay Treaty, 6
Jefferson, Thomas, 7, 9, 44, 73, 76, 81, 83, 98, 102, 103, 252, 268; and officers' appointments, 25-29, 50, 74; on professional military education, 94, 98-99
Jefferson Woolen Company, 201
Jesup, Thomas S., 50, 209; career of, 116; on foreign relations, 328, 329; and Indians, 315, 319; reports on reduction of army, 126
Johnson, Andrew, 361
Johnson, Thomas S. J., 270
Johnston, Abraham R., 166, 351
Johnston, Albert Sidney, 199, 302-304; portrait of, 303
Johnston, Eliza, 207
Johnston, Joseph E., 198, 289-290
Jomini, Henri, 246, 247
Jones, James, 271
Jones, Roger, 149, 233, 273; portrait of, 224
Jordan, Frederick, 276

Kansas troubles, army role in, 135, 352-353
Kautz, August V., 189, 204, 241, 324
Kearny, Philip, 164, 209, 240, 351
Kearny, Stephen W., 164, 209, 339; as military governor of New Mexico, 300
Kelton, John C., 243
Kendrick, Henry L., 178, 351
Kent, James, 171
Kimball, James, 58
King, William, 37, 268, 333
Kingsbury, Jacob, 35, 62, 74; portrait of, 75
Kinsley, Zebina J. D., 219
Kirby, Edmund, 201, 342

Kirby family, 164
Kirby Smith, Edmund. *See* Smith, Edmund Kirby
Knowlton, Minor, 240–241, 246
Knox, Henry, 5, 6, 23, 58, 90, 95; and officers' appointments, 16–18, 19; and officers' promotion, 48

Lallemand, Henri, 239
LaMotte, Joseph H., 206–207
Larned, Charles H., 273
Larned, Simon, 30
Lawson, Thomas, 228, 323
LeBarron, Francis, 45, 78
Lee, Arthur T., 343
Lee, Fitzhugh, 358
Lee, Henry, 23
Lee, John F., 165
Lee, Robert E., 188, 197, 209, 354–355
Lee family, 164, 209
Legare, Hugh S., 289
Legion. *See* American Legion
Leopard, H.M.S., 9
Lewis, Meriwether, 18, 65
Lewis, Morgan, 27
Lincoln, Abraham, 353, 354, 358
Lindsay, William, 201
Livingston, I. N., 280
Long, Armistead L., 238, 254
Long, Nicholas, 62
Long, Stephen H., 229–230
Longstreet, James, 354
Loomis, Gustavus, 322, 351–352
Lopez, Narciso, 337
Lothrop, Warren L., 150
Louisiana Purchase, army role in administering, 8, 77–79
Lovell, John M., 21
Lucas, John B. C., 78
Lyon, Nathaniel, 278, 321, 352

McClary, Andrew, 22
McClary, John, 22
McClellan, George B., 150, 186, 255; on Mexican War, 340; mission of, to Europe, 241; opinion of, of citizen-soldiers, 211
McClelland, John, 54
McClelland, Robert, 290
McCurdy, William, 58
McDonogh, Patrick, 50
McHenry, James, 19, 22, 23, 96, 98, 151
Mackay, Aeneas, 234
McKee, Christopher, 55
MacKenzie, John, 279
McKinstry, Justus, 227–228
McLane, Robert M., 166, 324, 346

McLaws, Lafayette, 205, 354
Macomb, Alexander, 74, 103, 105, 115, 156, 189, 266; and army schools of practice, 251–252; attacks staff independence, 233; career of, 110–111; on Indians, 307; military relatives of, 209; promotion of, to commanding general, 289; role of, in suppressing patriot troubles, 336
Macomb family, 164, 209
McPherson, James B., 357
McPherson, Mark, 58
MacRae, Alexander, 186
McRee, Griffith J., 65
McRee, William, 115, 125, 249
Madison, James, 9, 61, 76, 83, 102, 103, 117, 120, 137; and officers' appointments, 27–32, 50, 74, 147
Magee, Augustus W., 83
Mahan, Dennis Hart, 258; and Indian fighting, 306, 319; and postgraduate military education at West Point, 247; West Point course of, 168, 172
Maine boundary dispute, army role in, 133, 212, 226, 246, 328, 329, 336
Mansfield, Joseph K. F., 198
Marcy, Mary, 206
Marcy, Randolph B., 206, 310–311, 317, 353
Marcy, William, 290
Marigold, Charles, 270
Marine Corps, 7, 67, 141, 161
Markiewicz, James, 277
Marschalk, Andrew, 66
Mason, Richard B., 279
Massias, Abraham, 54
Maury, Dabney H., 255, 351, 357–358
May, Charles A., 238, 279
Mead, William C., 81
Meade, George G., 264, 332
Medical Board, U.S. Army, 152–153, 157, 214
Medical Department, U.S. Army, 9, 45, 97, 98, 120, 132, 133, 138, 144, 228, 232, 258; appointments of officers to, 151–153; education of officers of, 153, 157; geographical distribution of officers in, 157
Metz (French school of application). *See* France, army of: military school system of
"Mexican Association," 80
Mexican War, 146, 172, 187, 189–190, 198, 199, 209–210, 229, 234, 236, 238, 246, 253, 255, 257, 274, 275, 300, 336, 338, 339, 346, 351; expansion of army for, 134–135, 200, 210; former officers' service in, 220; officers' appointments during, 143, 145–146, 148, 161; officers' deaths in, 214, 338; officers' opinions of, 330–331,

Mexican War, *continued*
340–345; promotion during, 195; service of light artillery in, 252; as source of civil-military tension, 294–295; as source of professional pride, 295, 341, 344–345, 359; and West Point mystique, 176

Meyers, Augustus, 274, 276

Military and Naval Magazine of the United States, 187, 204–205, 257, 327

Military asylums, 264, 294

Military posts: Augusta Arsenal, 234, 350; Baton Rouge, 195; Benicia Barracks, 338; Camp Far West, 227; Camp Floyd, 302–303; Camp Scott, 302; Cantonment Washington, 45; Carlisle Barracks, 184, 207–208, 253, 263; Charleston, S.C., 351, 353; Detroit, 39, 85, 233–234, 270; Fort Adams, 59, 79; Fort Brown, 207, 353; Fort Claiborne, 59; Fort Columbus, 204, 277; Fort Constitution, 269; Fort Craig, 263; Fort Crawford, 186, 279, 299; Fort Davis, 278, 339; Fort Defiance, 41–42; Fort Deynaud, picture of, 323; Fort Drane, 263; Fort Gibson, 185, 186, 189, 299; Fort Hamilton, 184; Fort Heileman, 279; Fort Howard, 186, 276, 279; Fort Independence, 207; Fort Kent, 265; Fort Leavenworth, 188, 352; Fort McHenry, 244; Fort McIntosh, 267; Fort Mackinac, 277, 286 (*see also* Michilimackinac); Fort Mason, 207; Fort Massac, 78, 81, 82; Fort Mifflin, 41; Fort (Fortress) Monroe, 184, 249–252, 253–254, 263, 350; Fort Moultrie, 188–189; Fort Myers, 207; Fort Niagara, 226, 271; Fort Norfolk, 53; Fort Ontario, 189, 226; Fort Pickering, 79; Fort Pike, 276; Fort Riley, 202, 352; Fort Snelling, 189, 228, 264, 270, 278; Fort Snelling, picture of, 208; Fort Steilacoom, 189; Fort Stoddert, 78–79, 81, 83; Fort Sumter, 270, 358; Fort Sumter, picture of, 245; Fort Vancouver, 207; Fort Washington, picture of, 40; Fort Washita, 231; Fort Wayne (Indian Territory), 189, 298; Fort Wayne (Indiana Territory), 45; Fort Wilkinson, 39; Fort Winnebago, 184–186; Fort Winnebago, picture of, 185; Fort Wise, 298; Fort Wood, 339; Fort Yuma, 227; Jefferson Barracks, 184, 187, 188, 204, 250–251, 253, 272; Jefferson Barracks, picture of, 251; Kennebec Arsenal, 226; Madison Barracks, 270; Michilimackinac, 45, 78 (*see also* Fort Mackinac); Natchitoches, La., 83; New Orleans, 39, 62, 77, 80–81, 85–86, 329; Newport Barracks, 204; Plattsburgh, N.Y., 56, 62; Post Vincennes, 71, 72; St. Augustine, 279; St. Louis, 44; San Diego, 227–228; San Francisco, 337–338, 357; Santa Fe, 190; Volusia, Fla., 278; Watervliet Arsenal, 226–227; West Point, 8, 26, 94–95, 98–105 (*see also* United States Military Academy)

Military professionalism: in early modern Europe, 86, 88–89, 93; in U.S. Army (*see* Officers: professional thought and activities of)

Military punishments. *See* Army: military justice system of; Enlisted men: punishment of

Militia, colonial, 3–4, 12–13, 261

Militia, state, 7, 9, 87, 89, 125, 362. *See also* Officers: on militia and volunteers

Miller, James, 32

Millett, Allan R., 88

Missouri Democrat, 205

Missouri Republican, 205

Mitchell, Donald G., 18, 21

Mitchell, Enos G., 347

Monroe, James, 122, 123, 126, 131, 132, 137, 289, 333–334; on military policy, 117

Montalembert, Marc René de, 99–100, 103–104

Montgomery, William R., 202

Moore, Robert, 175

Mordecai, Alfred, 241, 243, 248, 355

Mormon War, army's role in, 135, 199, 253, 301–304, 339–340

Morton, James St. Clair, 245, 258

Motte, Jacob Rhett, 318

Mounted troops, 297; formation of units of, 5, 7, 133–135; geographical distribution of officers of, 157; officers of, visit Europe, 240–241, 255

Mounted troops, units of: First Regiment of Dragoons, 133, 143; Second Regiment of Dragoons, 133, 134, 144; First Cavalry Regiment, 157, 198; Second Cavalry Regiment, 157; Battalion of Mounted Rangers, 133, 143; Regiment of Mounted Riflemen, 134, 145

Mountfort, John, 276

Munn, John G., 32

Munroe, John, 300

Murray, Private, 273

Murry, John, 279

Myer, Albert J., 257

Napoleon I, 74, 163

Napoleon Club, 247

Napoleonic influence, on U.S. Army. *See* France, Army of: as model for U.S. Army

National Republican party, 295

Nat Turner Revolt (1831), 350–351

Navy, 7, 125, 161, 265, 269, 272, 360–361;

Index   477

army officers with service in, 67; criticizes seacoast fortification system, 245, 294; officer training in, 38, 55, 360
Navy Department, 43, 360
Navy League of the United States, 103
Netherlands, the, army of, 88–89
Newburgh conspiracy, 69
Newman, Samuel, 17
New York Daily News, 205
New York Herald, 205
Niles, Hezekiah, 109
Niles' Weekly Register, 109
North, William, 23–24, 64, 97
Northwestern Indian war (1790-1794), 5–6, 16–17, 34–35, 63, 67, 90–93; officers' combat deaths in, 60
Nullification crisis (1832-1833), 132, 251, 351

Oakes, James, 290
Officers: and administration of new territories, 70–72, 76–79, 300–301; age of, 14, 110; appointment of, to army, 12–33, 137–153, 296; attrition of, from service, 59–63, 212–217; and Burr conspiracy, 80–82; career motivations of, 15–16, 18–19, 30, 32, 115–116, 163–166, 202, 203–204; career patterns of, 34–67, 181–220; and civil-military tensions, 68–72, 76–86, 210–212, 284–285, 294–295, 297–304; college education of, 14, 22; conceptions of, of honor, 53, 55–56; conceptions of, of military leadership, 36–37, 187–188, 232, 265–267; contacts of, with Europe, 115, 125, 204, 226, 239–243; courts-martial of, 57–59, 195 (*see also* Army: military justice system of); deaths of, 59–60, 213–214; discharges of (in reductions of army), 61–63, 212, 288–289; dismissals of, 57–58, 59, 202, 214–215, 265, 278; dissension among, 51–59, 92–93, 94–95, 122–123, 195–196, 200–201, 288–289; drinking habits of, 42, 57–58, 62, 188; dueling by, 55–57, 195–196; economic activities of, 44–46, 201–202; enlisted experience of, 14, 20, 161; experience of, as captains, 196–199, 201–202; experience of, as field and general officers, 198–202; experience of, as lieutenants, 182–196; and filibustering, 80–82, 83–84, 333–338; and foreign relations, 74, 83–84, 326–338; on frontiersmen, 297–298, 312–313; garrison life of, 41–42, 184–190, 205–208, 260–281; geographical origins of, 13–14, 19–20, 26, 143–144, 147, 154–158; on Great Britain, 74, 328–329, 339; kinship ties among, 141, 208–210; length of service of, 34–35, 181–183; and Manifest Destiny, 316–317, 330–332; marriage and family life of, 189, 190, 205–210; on Mexican War, 330–332, 340–345; military subculture of, 203–212; on militia and volunteers, 90, 114, 210–212, 294–295, 298, 324; on Mormons, 302–304, 339–340; pay and allowances of, 43–44, 69–70, 190–193, 197, 199–200, 235; and politics, 50–51, 68–70, 72–76, 79–82, 84, 102–103, 219, 228, 237, 282–297, 351–358; postservice benefits of, 63, 215–216; postservice careers of, 63–67, 217–220; professional thought and activities of, 87–105, 119–130, 238–259, 361–362; professional training and socialization of, 37–39, 92, 93–95, 98–105, 122–125, 153, 167–180, 240–241, 247, 249–254; promotion of, 47–51, 193–195, 196–200, 235, 287–290; reading preferences of, 187; and reform of army after War of 1812, 110–116, 119–130; relationship of, to enlisted men, 45–46, 149–150, 260–281; relationship of, to Indians, 41–42, 71–72, 79, 189–190, 255–256, 258, 299–300, 305–325, 345–347; relationship of, to Mexicans, 189–190, 330–332; religious preferences and views of, 162–163, 231; resignations of, 58, 60–61, 214, 216–217, 353–357; retirement of, 197–198, 215–216; revolutionary experience of, 14, 20, 27, 110; and sectional controversy, 348–358; and slavery, 171, 329, 332, 350–351; social origins of, 14–16, 20–23, 30–32, 141, 150, 154–163, 165–166; on war, 74–76, 327–328, 330, 332, 338–347; and women, 42, 188–190, 205 (*see also* Officers: marriage and family life of)
Ogden, Aaron, 97
Ogden, Cornelius, 166
Ordnance Board, 248
Ordnance Department, 9, 120, 125–126, 128, 132, 134, 137, 172, 222, 232, 243, 292, 361; conflict of, with artillery, 234, 236, 291–292; contacts of, with Europe, 226, 240, 241; duties of officers of, 225–227; geographical distribution of officers of, 157; and standardization and development of army ordnance, 121, 226, 240, 247–248
Oregon dispute, 246, 328, 339
Osmond, Davis, 278
Ostrander, Philip, 25

Paley, William, 170, 175
Paris, Peace of (1783), 4
Parker, Alexander, 60

Parker, Daniel, 110, 120–121
Parott, Robert P., 219
Partridge, Alden, 122–123, 143
Pasteur, Edward, 60
Patriot troubles, army role in, 328, 335–336, 340
Pay and allowances, of officers. *See* Officers: pay and allowances of
Pay Department, army, 8, 9, 97, 120, 132, 138, 144, 232; appointments to, 151, 198; duties of officers of, 228; geographical distribution of officers of, 156
Peck, John J., 340
Pemberton, John C., 175, 188
Penrose, James W., 271–272
Pentland, Joseph, 215
Phelon, Patrick, 17
Phelps, John W., 324
Pickens, Francis W., 289
Pickering, Timothy, 19, 94–95
Pickett, George E., 335, 355
Pierce, Benjamin K., 31
Pierce, Franklin, 145, 150, 198; and officers' appointments, 146
Pierce, John S., 31
Pike, Zebulon M., 81, 103
Pillow, Gideon J., 146
Pinckney, Charles Cotesworth, 23, 24, 37, 96, 97
Pinckney Treaty (1795), 76
Plympton, Joseph C., 189
Poinsett, Joel R., 252, 290; and officers' appointments, 139, 144, 148
Polk, James K., 287, 294–295, 330, 332; and officers' appointments, 141, 145–146, 149, 151
Pope, Piercy S., 42
Porter, Moses, 35
Porter, Peter B., 251
Posey, Thomas, 17
Post Office Department, 118
Poussin, William Tell, 260
Pratt, John, 69
Preston, William, 18–19, 84
Preston, William C., 289
Professionalism, definition of, 34, 87–88
Professions, civilian, 89, 119, 153, 359–360
Promotion. *See* Officers: promotion of
Prussia, army of, 168, 243
Public Land Office, 118
Purchasing Department, army, 9, 132, 134
Purdy, Robert, 62
Putnam, Rufus, 17, 45

Quartermaster Department, 6, 8, 9, 96–97, 98, 120, 132, 193, 198, 222, 230, 232, 233–234, 289; duties of officers of, 225–226, 227–228
Quasi-war (1798–1800), 7–8, 9, 18, 25, 27, 44, 48, 49, 61, 64, 72, 73, 80, 98, 99, 121, 131, 134, 137, 268; army reform during, 95–98, 121; officers' appointments during, 23–24

Raguet, Llewellyn, 265
Rains, George W., 280, 343
Ramsay, George D., 198
Ramsey, Thomas, 32
Randolph, John, 80
Randolph, Thomas Mann, Jr., 50
Ransom, Dunbar R., 165
Ransom, Trueman B., 146
Reconstruction era, 348, 361
Recruiting, civil-military tension over, 84–85
Reily, John, 279
Republican party, 354, 361; officers' allegiances to, 353
Revolutionary War, 3–4, 5, 13, 14, 15, 17, 18, 19, 20, 22, 34, 47–48, 62, 69, 70, 87, 110, 176, 232, 239. *See also* Continental Army
Reynolds, John F., 343
Rice, Josiah M., 274
Rich, Lucius L., 204
Richards, George H., 56
Riley, Bennet, 32
Ringgold, Samuel, 252, 253, 343–344
Ripley, Eleazar W., 110
Ripley, Roswell S., 257
Rivardi, John J. U., 94–95
Robertson, Beverly H., 263
Rochefontaine, Stephen, 52, 94–95
Rogers, Bartholomew, 273
Royster, Charles, 13, 69
Rules and Articles of War, 38, 55, 57, 59, 73, 90, 92, 101, 122, 261, 265, 267, 268, 270. *See also* Army: military justice system of

St. Clair, Arthur, 5, 17, 35, 45, 90
Salmon, George, Jr., 21
San Juan Island dispute (1859–1860), 257, 329, 334–335
Sargent, Winthrop, 45
Saumur (French cavalry school). *See* France, army of: military school system of
Savage, John H., 146
Schofield, John M., 166, 175
Schoolcraft, Henry R., 311, 312
Schools of practice, 132, 183–184, 249–252, 253–254, 255; artillery post schools, 253–254; artillery school (Fort Monroe), 184, 249–252, 253–254; cavalry school (Jeffer-

son Barracks, Carlisle Barracks), 184, 253; infantry school (Jefferson Barracks), 184, 250–252; light artillery regimental schools, 252
Schuyler, Dirck, 58
Scott, Dred, 350
Scott, Martin, 188
Scott, Sir Walter, 339
Scott, Winfield, 39, 110, 126, 135, 141, 145, 158, 177, 196, 200, 223, 233, 236, 286, 289, 296, 335, 345, 357; career of, 111–114; on citizen-soldiers, 211; on military punishments, 269–270, 272; portrait of, 113; quarrel of, with Edmund P. Gaines, 200; recalled as commander in Mexico, 295, 345; revises army general regulations, 122; revises army infantry tactics, 121–122, 254; role of, in suppressing patriot troubles, 336; visits Europe, 115; on war, 327, 340; on War of 1812 officers, 29–30
Seacoast fortifications, 6, 7, 8, 94, 99, 103–104, 225–226, 239, 243–246, 258, 292–293, 294, 297, 326, 362; origin of post–War of 1812 system of, 125–126
Second Seminole War (1835–1842), 132, 133, 134, 199, 211, 212, 226, 252, 257, 263, 265, 273–274, 314, 318, 319, 338, 346–347, 351; army tactics in, 255–256, 320–321; civil-military tensions during, 298; officers' deaths in, 214; officers' opposition to, 323–324; officers' resignations during, 216–217
Sedam, Cornelius R., 64
Sedgwick, John, 298
Seymour, Truman, 358
Shannon, Edward, 277
Shaumburgh, Bartholomew, 65
Shays's Rebellion, 4, 7, 14, 17, 61, 67, 69, 70, 71
Sheridan, Philip H., 322
Sherman, Thomas W., 280
Sherman, William T., 189, 204, 285, 315, 339
Shipley, Alexander N., 150
Sibley, Henry H., 257
Slavery, army and. *See* Officers: and slavery
Smith, Caleb, 150
Smith, Charles F., 177
Smith, Edmund Kirby, 164, 187, 337, 348
Smith, Ephraim Kirby, 277–278, 332
Smith, Gerrit, 140
Smith, Gustavus W., 195
Smith, John L., 244
Smith family, 164
Smithsonian Institution, 311
Smyth, Alexander, 37, 121, 268

Snelling, Josiah, 50
Society of the Cincinnati, 4, 14, 69
Sonora Exploring & Mining Company, 202
Southern Literary Messenger, 292
Spanish-American War, 362
Sparks, Richard, 84
Spencer, John C., 289
Sprague, John T., 257, 298, 318, 351
Staff-line conflict. *See* General Staff: conflict of, with line branches
Stanton, Henry, 233–234
Starr, Samuel H., 148, 279–280
Steuben, Frederich W. A. von, 38, 42, 90, 94, 97, 121, 122, 262
Stevens, Isaac Ingalls, 240, 246, 293, 343, 351
Stockton, Robert F., 300
Stoddard, Amos, 74; as military governor of Upper Louisiana, 77–78
Strategy: army officers' ideas on, 243–247; taught at West Point, 172, 247. *See also* Seacoast fortifications
Strother, George, 42
Stuart, James E. B., 177, 179, 349
Stuart, John, 298, 314
Subsistence Department, 120, 132, 193, 222, 225, 227, 232, 314
Sumner, Charles, 352
Sumner, Edwin V., 241, 300, 352
Sumner, Joshua, 15
Swaine, Thomas, 79
Swett, Moses, 82
Swift, Joseph G., 73, 84, 119–120, 125
Swift, William H., 218–219

Tactical manuals: artillery, 254–255; cavalry, 254–255; infantry, 38, 42, 97, 121–122, 254–255; mounted riflemen, 255; revision of, during Quasi-war, 97–98
Tactics: army officers' views on, 254–256; teaching of at U.S. Military Academy, 172. *See also* Tactical manuals
Talbot, Theodore, 299
Taylor, Josiah, 80
Taylor, Zachary, 134, 145, 189, 199, 200, 201, 219, 252, 253, 283, 287, 296, 298, 330, 341; on citizen-soldiers, 211; on foreign relations, 328, 330; and Indians, 314, 319
Taylor family, 164
Thayer, Sylvanus, 172–173, 174–175, 284, 345; career of, 123; portrait of, 124; and U.S. Military Academy, 123–125, 138, 167–169, 172–174; visit of to Europe, 115, 240
Thompson, James S., 163

Tod, George, 30
Topographical Engineers, Corps of, 133, 134, 172, 232, 240, 291; appointment of citizens to, 144; duties of officers of, 228–230; geographical distribution of officers in, 158; political activities of, 292
Totten, Joseph G., 140, 169–170, 246, 247
Tousard, Lewis, 94–95, 97
Towson, Nathan, 289
Transcontinental Treaty, 334
Treasury Department, 6, 43, 96, 117, 199, 214, 221, 227, 229
Tripler, Charles S., 206
Tripler, Eunice, 206
Turner, Henry S., 204, 351
Twiggs, David E., 144, 200, 215, 274, 357
Tyler, Daniel, 219, 240
Tyler, John, 141, 234, 289

United States Military Academy, 8, 26, 37, 47, 74, 147, 153, 158–162, 164–166, 182, 183, 204, 219, 220, 222, 232, 234, 235, 255, 258, 274, 275, 278, 284, 292–293, 296, 358; appointment of cadets to, 26, 139–142, 154–155, 164; cadet register kept at, 140–141, 158–160; civilian criticism of, 134, 138, 142–143, 284, 293, 341; as cohesive force in officer corps, 179–180, 196, 200, 351; curriculum of, 102, 123, 167–172, 306, 326; faculty recruitment at, 174–175; five-year program at, 170; founding and early history of, 98–105; geographical distribution of graduates of, 26, 139; graduates of, as proportion of officer corps, 137–139; merit roll of, 173–174; and Mexican War, 345; and officers' professional socialization, 172–180; postgraduate military education at, 247; reform of, after War of 1812, 122–125; register of graduates of, 217; regulations of, 123–124, 138, 142, 173; sectional tensions at, 349; social backgrounds of cadets and graduates of, 140–141, 158–160
United States Military Philosophical Society, 102–104
United States Naval Academy, 361
Utah expedition. *See* Mormon War

Van Buren, Martin, 132, 134, 143, 177, 273, 336; and officers' appointments, 144
Van Dorn, Earl, 204, 341, 354
Van Dyke, Thomas J., 67
Van Rensselaer, Solomon, 65
Vattel, Emmerich de, 171
Vauban system of fortification, 104

Vinton, John R., 202, 282, 321, 325, 329, 338
Vose, Josiah H., 116, 314

Wade, William, 219–220
Wadsworth, Decius, 95, 121
Walbach, John de Barth, 215
Walker, William, 337
Walker, William H. T., 202, 231, 286, 295
Wall, William, 347
War Department, 5, 6, 10, 17, 18, 39, 43, 48, 50, 55, 56, 61, 63, 76, 82, 100, 101, 102, 103, 131, 133, 170, 184, 185–186, 191, 193, 195, 191–192, 221, 222, 228, 231, 246, 248, 255, 268, 284, 291, 299, 349, 350, 352; annual reports of, 257–258; and army-Indian relations, 305–306, 322; and army reform after the War of 1812, 119–128; former officers employed by, 66–67; and incorporation of European influence into army, 125, 239–243; and officers' appointments, 16–33, 137–153; opposes political intervention in army administration, 288–290; promotes practical military education, 249–254; restricts detached service, 217. *See also entries for individual secretaries of war*
Warner, William H., 190
War of 1812, 9–10, 26, 30, 31, 38, 48, 51, 66, 67, 85–86, 101, 104, 138, 195, 200, 215, 221, 232, 235, 244, 246, 262, 283, 305, 306, 332, 349, 360, 362; civil-military tensions over recruiting during, 85; efforts to quell dueling during, 56–57; military executions during, 268; officers' appointments during, 27–33; officers' combat deaths in, 60; officers' discharges after, 61–63; officers' opinions of, 74–76, 114–115; officers' resignations during, 60–61; promotion during, 49–51; as source of army reform, 110–116, 121–122
Warren, Gouverneur K., 321
Warren, Winslow, 18
Washington, George, 6, 23, 44, 48, 49, 53, 58, 73, 90, 96, 127, 131, 261; and officers' appointments, 13, 16–18, 19, 24, 94
Washington, John Macrae, 300; photo of, 301
Washington, William, 24
Washington Star, 205
Waterhouse, Benjamin, 76
Wayland, Francis, 170–171, 327
Wayne, Anthony, 5, 17, 39, 58, 79, 85, 129, 267; and army reform, 90–93; career of, 90; condones officers' dueling, 55–56; portrait of, 91; quarrel of, with James Wilkin-

son, 51–52, 73, 92. *See also* American Legion
Webb, Alexander S., 350; drawing by, 323
Webster, Frances, 206
Webster, Lucien B., 206
Webster-Ashburton Treaty (1842), 134, 336
Welcker, George L., 177
West Point. *See* United States Military Academy
West Point Foundry, 201, 219
Whig party, 285, 287, 330, 353; officers' allegiances to, 295–297; and officers' appointments, 144–146; support of, for army legislation, 296
Whiskey Rebellion, 18, 99
Whistler family, 164
Whiting, Daniel P., drawing by, 344
Whiting, Henry, 202, 209, 311–312
Whiting, John, 82
Whiting family, 164, 209
Whitney, Eli, 103
Wickliffe, Charles, 299
Wilcox, Cadmus M., 243, 355
Wilkinson, James, 17, 43, 57, 58, 96, 110; command of, on Sabine frontier, 81, 83; condones officers' dueling, 56; on Confederation era officers, 34–35; criticizes officers' economic activities, 45, 46; personal quarrels of, 51–52, 73, 92; political attachments of, 73; portrait of, 52; role of, in administration of Louisiana Purchase, 77–78; role of, in Burr conspiracy, 80–82
Willard, George L., 150
Williams, Jonathan, 111, 123, 125, 127, 129, 167, 168, 235, 243, 292; career of, 99–100; and early history of U.S. Military Academy, 99–105; founds U.S. Military Philosophical Society, 102–103; on military policy, 103–104; portrait of, 100; promotes U.S. Army Corps of Engineers, 99–105
Williams, Thomas, 189, 290, 298; on army in Mexican War, 345; on citizen-soldiers, 211; on Indians, 308, 319–320; on politics, 286, 287; on war, 327, 340
Williams, William G., 246
Winship, Oscar F., 263
Woods, Samuel, 178–179
Wool, John E., 201, 248–249, 250–251; career of, 115–116; on citizen-soldiers, 211; on foreign relations, 328; and Indians, 315; promotion of, to brigadier general, 289; and suppression of filibustering, 336, 337–338; on West Point curriculum, 169
Worth, William J., 114, 199, 200–201, 234; favors expansionism, 330, 331; in Second Seminole War, 321
Wright, George, 322
Wyllys, John P., 15, 71, 267

Young, Brigham, 302, 340

Ziegler, David, 15, 64

www.ingramcontent.com/pod-product-compliance
Lightning Source LLC
Chambersburg PA
CBHW030814210126
38551CB00012B/62